Administering Instructional Media Programs

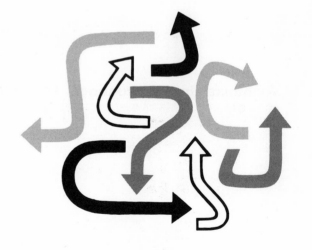

Administering Instructional Media Programs

Carlton W. H. Erickson *Director of the Audiovisual Center and Professor of Education, University of Connecticut*

The Macmillan Company, New York / Collier-Macmillan Limited, London

Sixth Printing, 1971

Library of Congress catalog card number: 68–12281

THE MACMILLAN COMPANY
866 THIRD AVENUE, NEW YORK, NEW YORK 10022
Collier-Macmillan Canada, Ltd., Toronto, Ontario

Printed in the United States of America

This book has its roots in thirty-five years of direct and indirect experience in the field of instructional media. In the roles of science teacher, city director of audiovisual services, school principal, U.S. Navy training aids officer, and finally university professor and audiovisual center director, I have had many opportunities to define problems of administering instructional media programs and to seek their solutions at different levels of action.

First and foremost the contents of this textbook are directed toward graduate students who are undertaking their preparation for leadership in the instructional media field, but the very nature of the purpose and arrangement of the content enhances its value as a handbook for school-building media-program coordinators and as a guide for planning by school superintendents, principals, and curriculum specialists.

Years of experience have led me to the belief that there are no pat answers, no single solutions, to what appear to be the common problems of media-service administrators. Observation of the variety of local environments and the unique points of view held within city-wide as well as university service centers in the United States cautions against setting up inflexible patterns of professional effort. Therefore, instead of prescribing a recipe for action, this book includes guidelines and principles, case studies of common practice, and examples of advanced media programs that should aid the prospective media director in his preparation for creativity.

Although the title of this book, *Administering Instructional Media Programs*, properly implies that the content is broad and comprehensive in scope, dealing with all media in their application to instructional problems in the schools, it would be incorrect to say that this book treats all media with equal emphasis and in equal space. The content has been arranged to deal primarily with technological media (or, as they have been referred to for so long, *audiovisual media*), because of the complexity that has developed in the field.

This arrangement is not intended to detract in any way from a realization of the great need that exists today to expand print-medium services throughout the land. Quite to the contrary, as the reader will discover when he delves into Chapter 12, which treats the school

Preface

v

library—or, more particularly, the print-medium services—as a part of the school's instructional media program development. The purpose of the book is rather to open up and deal comprehensively with audiovisual media service problems, while also focusing attention in a useful and clarifying manner on print-medium needs as a vital part of the media activity spectrum. Concentration of attention on both of the major aspects of media services, separately, facilitates the delineation and analysis of problems and thus should assist school leaders to make wiser decisions regarding organization and support of service programs now and in the future. It is also obvious that many discussions of vital processes in connection with some audiovisual media programs are equally applicable to all media activities, including school library or print-medium services.

It is hoped that the unique way of organizing the content in this book will be of benefit to both print-medium and audiovisual or techno-logical media specialists as they work toward the fulfillment of self-improvement programs. Only when such understanding and skill is developed in both aspects of media service, at least at the irreducible minimum level, will specialists in one aspect be able to implement change effectively in the other.

When using this book as a basic reference in formal teaching situations, instructors should note the questions, problems, and references for further study at the end of each chapter. Under the heading "Problem-Solving Activities" are some suggested learning experiences that students may undertake voluntarily or on a required assignment basis as a part of their creative course activity, working as individuals or in groups. Other questions and problems also may and should serve as a basis for class discus-sions and presentations; such additional exercises should of course be suggested by both students and instructors according to special needs. Actually the "Problem-Solving Activities" sections constitute a study guide for the course or courses for which this book is intended as a basic text. Students should be aware that many of the problems presented demand sustained, creative behavior indicative of future professional activity.

The writer has drawn heavily upon the widespread periodical literature and upon textbooks, yearbooks, manuals, and pamphlets that have appeared during the past ten years. The permission of such publishers and authors to use their materials as needed is gratefully acknowledged, and due credit is given in the footnotes. Also gratefully acknowledged are the illustrations contributed by individuals, schools, and business organizations. The source appears with each illustration.

Special thanks are due members of the author's secretarial and technical staff for valuable assistance, and he is most grateful to many instructional media specialists around the country for taking time out of busy schedules to answer questions and supply helpful materials about problems, procedures, services, and trends in their respective programs.

The author is also indebted to Dr. James L. Page, Director of the Instructional Materials Center and Instructional Development Consultant, College of Education, Michigan State University, for the many valuable suggestions made in connection with his critical reading of the manuscript.

Finally, the author wishes to express his gratitude to his wife, Ernestine B. Erickson, who has so generously contributed to the completion of this undertaking.

The University of Connecticut   C. W. H. E.

Contents

One day as school closed for the summer season in San Diego in 1965, a caravan of motor vans and trucks moved onto the loading ramp of the city's instructional media service division in its pink stucco Education Center to begin a giant project. Some three hundred tons of instructional material and equipment were about to be moved into a newly constructed 70,000-square-foot Instructional Materials Center, citywide headquarters for an effective, comprehensive media program serving 2,208 elementary and 1,945 secondary school classrooms.

Another much larger moving project had been carried out three years earlier when Los Angeles had reorganized its Instructional Services Branch, and shifted its gigantic media program to a new 150,000-square-foot building. Now more comprehensive than ever, this instructional materials headquarters for teachers encompasses, under unitary leadership, citywide library, audiovisual, radio-television, science center, and conservation services. The scope of these services is vast, having direct lines to 430 elementary schools and 125 secondary schools, as well as the city's junior colleges. The pupil enrollment is in excess of 800,000. A conservative estimate places budgetary support for this branch at approximately $7,500,000. Growth of the services has been so rapid that not all of the service sections can even now be housed in the new structure, hence a new and more adequate building is presently being planned. In 1957 the Audio-Visual Section was housed with other services, in the city education headquarters known as the Sentus Center, and at that time the annual budget for the single section amounted to $1,000,000.

It was in 1957 that the author first visited the West Coast city media-service centers and, for example, at the Education Center in San Diego saw and heard canvas bags come sliding down a chute to the basement from the two floors above, where teachers' orders for publications, library books, textbooks, study prints, exhibits, films, and filmstrips had been filled and were now to be whisked away in walk-in trucks to classrooms throughout the city. Or as another example, the author also stood in the study-print assembly room at the Los Angeles City Schools' Audio-Visual Center and took a picture of 1,000 sets of study prints on a single topic, *Conservation*, produced, assembled, and

The Nature of the Media Program Director's Job

1

packaged on the spot. The author also studied on that visit the massive service programs carried on by the California counties, as well as the media programs in a number of other western cities, both large and small.

Little wonder then that in 1966, almost a decade later, it was a thrilling experience to visit these same centers again and especially to note what can only be described as phenomenal progress on almost every hand. Yet such vitality is not confined to western cities and villages. Let us take note of instructional media services in a small eastern city, Penfield, New York, where schools enroll 5,300 pupils in five elementary schools and two junior high schools. The schools of Penfield have a centralized media-service program that includes large school-owned collections of media, and a well-developed material preparation center for teachers that uses the talents of an artist who works with teachers as a consultant and a producer.

According to the author's estimates, in 1965 some 2,300 school districts of the 27,000 in the

United States had designated media programs in operation with centralized leadership at one stage or another of development. We shall discuss a number of these programs, some in detail, as we move through the chapters in this book. But before we proceed to our various presentations and discussions, let us raise a few questions about the three specific examples of city media programs just referred to.

1. What services do these media program directors give? What is the true nature of their work?

2. What kinds of facilities do they have to be able to prescribe and design?

3. Who are these people and what is the nature of their educational backgrounds?

To obtain some introductory answers to these questions, and to take a pictorial tour, though an admittedly superficial one, of the centers mentioned, the reader is referred to Figures 1-1 through 1-10 and their captions.

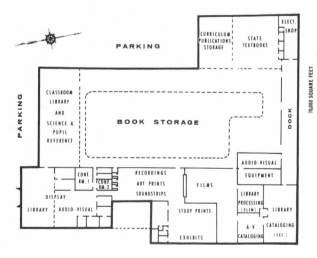

Figure 1-1. San Diego. This building is the media distribution center for the City Schools. The floor shows the nature of the functions carried on at this 70,000 square-foot building occupied in 1965. Dr. Robert Burgert, Director of the Center and its services, was responsible for the initiation and planning of the building, a phase of his work that took two years to complete. Major administrative functions, the professional library, graphic production services, recording and duplication of tapes, and conference facilities remain at the Education Center. Dr. Burgert was a teacher, elementary school principal, and Audiovisual Education supervisor, prior to becoming the Director in 1948. *Courtesy San Diego City Schools.*

Figure 1-2. San Diego. The three views show some of the major media services of the Center. According to a 1965 press report, the inventory included 13,000 motion pictures, almost a million books purchased by the district and an additional 500,000 state texts, 30,000 filmstrips, 20,000 recordings, 13,000 study prints, 1,600 art prints, and many dioramas, slides, tapes, and transparencies. What is the nature of the work that underlies the effectiveness of such immense collections? Evaluation of media? Analysis of curriculum needs? Selection, purchasing, cataloging, storing, distributing, and on time? *Courtesy San Diego City Schools.*

Figure 1-3. San Diego. One of the time-saving features in the Center is a Towveyor system operating on a recessed 500-foot conveyor chain in the floor for book dispersal and collection in the stock area. Motion pictures are inspected on electronic machines arranged in pairs for more efficient use of the operator's working time. There are six miles of shelving. What insight and ability are required to design and implement work patterns for people? Need for technological know-how? Deployment of workers? Adequate supervision of assistants? Specifying supplies and equipment? *Courtesy San Diego City Schools.*

Figure 1-4. San Diego. This classroom in the Keiller elementary school, and over 2,200 others in the city system, are the only reasons why media service centers like the one depicted must be organized and operated effectively. The total impact of media on the learning process is activated through both teachers and pupils. *Courtesy San Diego City Schools.*

Figure 1-5. Los Angeles. In the lower right-hand corner of this aerial view is shown the Instructional Materials Center for the city school districts. In downtown Los Angeles, close to interconnecting highways and near new structures in the city's redevelopment program, this all-media center houses six major sections in the Instructional Services Branch. Approximately 35,000 motion picture prints are on the Center's distribution inventory and some 1,400 prints are delivered daily to the schools. The film inspection unit shown is being used for special purposes. The main film inspection operation uses 22 machines arranged in pairs. In 1966 there were ninety staff members in the Audio-Visual Section alone, with 255 as the total for the Instructional Materials Center. *Courtesy Los Angeles City Schools.*

Figure 1-6. Los Angeles. The three illustrations show the main storage and distribution area for media other than motion pictures, the main instructional television studio, and the book-processing space in the Library Services Section. What vital roles does the director of this metropolitan media service center play? How would you describe the main duty of each sectional specialist? *Courtesy Los Angeles City Schools.*

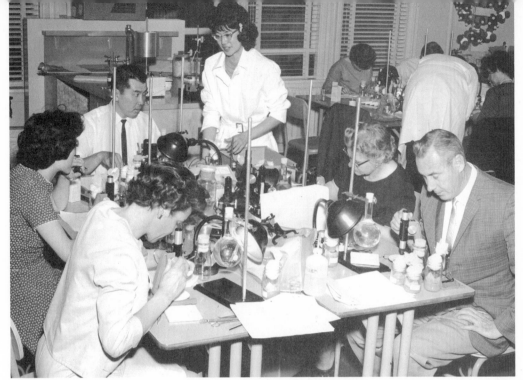

Figure 1-7. Los Angeles. A group of life-science teachers in an in-service education situation organized at the Science Center, one of the major sections. This center provides, among other services, refrigerated animal tissues and skeletal structures for study in senior high schools. One of the chief planners, designers, and implementors of this Instructional Services Branch of the Instructional Planning and Services Division through the years was Margaret W. Divizia, who retired from her public school position during the school year 1966–67. Mrs. Divisia became the Administrator of the Branch in 1962 after serving since 1947 as Supervisor of the Audio-Visual Section. The new chief administrative officer for the Instructional Services Branch holds the rank of Assistant Superintendent. Eugene H. White is the director of the Audio-Visual Section. *Courtesy Los Angeles City Schools.*

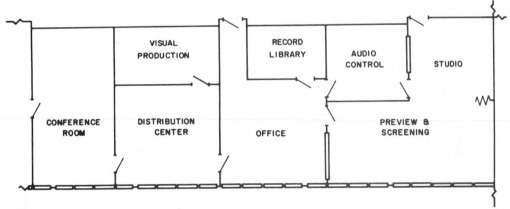

Figure 1-8. Penfield, N.Y. In sharp contrast to the gigantic programs just depicted, we turn to views of a school system with only eight school plants. The audio-visual media center serves the district as well as the senior high school in which it is located. The floor area measures approximately 30 feet by 79 feet for a total of 2,370 square feet. The school's library occupies an equal adjacent area. The floor plan was developed in 1956. New plans have been made that include a new resource-center structure with functional areas that may exceed 30,000 square feet. The organization under which the Center developed is shown later in Chapter 8. In the other Penfield illustrations, we present both central and decentralized activities to show the nature of leadership and technological duties by implication. *Courtesy Penfield, New York, Schools.*

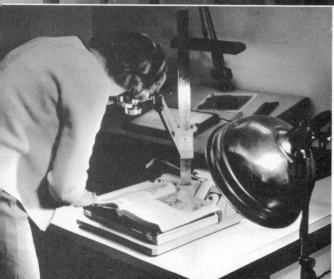

Figure 1-9. Penfield, N.Y. In the top picture is a centralized filmstrip library, which, in addition to tape and phonograph records, is the largest collection of media owned. Except for a small collection, motion pictures are rented for use in the eight schools. Media for special purposes are produced in large quantities as implied by the full-time graphic technician who assists teachers in media preparation. Rapid expansion in the recognition of media-use values can be seen in the array of media equipment purchased for the Bay Trail Junior High School, just before it was occupied in 1966. James M. Meagher, who has his Master's degree, and who has had an extensive background of teaching experience, taught secondary school English before becoming the Coordinator of the district program. *Courtesy Penfield, New York, Schools.*

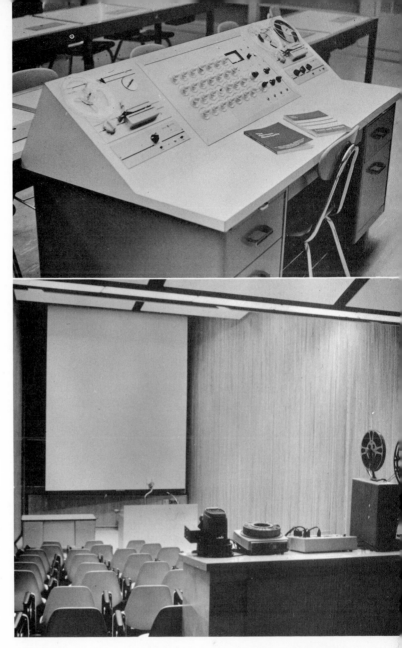

Figure 1-10. Penfield, N.Y.
Showing the concern for modern technological methods, the Bay Trail JHS has a number of fixed media installations. Shown at the right is one of four electronic classrooms to be used for language and other subjects. Below, is one of the four teaching auditoriums, each with a fully equipped projection platform, and a front-projection screen with special lectern. An overhead projector, a tape recorder, and a public address system are installed in the lectern together with the control devices for the lights and the projectors at the rear platform. The four teaching auditoriums can be opened up by means of movable walls for larger combinations of students. The reader will without doubt observe, even though the school system is a small one by comparison, the similar nature of duties that are required in connection with media services. *Courtesy Penfield, New York, Schools.*

Before we examine the nature of the media specialist's job in greater detail, we ought first to note the relationship of leadership to the success of media-service programs in general. We shall then identify and describe the so-called audiovisual media program director as an educator, an executive, a supervisor, a technological expert, and as an equipment technician.

Leadership, a Characteristic of Successful School Media Services

An effective audiovisual media service program doesn't just happen for a city school department, a county, a church, or for an industrial company. It is most likely to happen, however complex the environment, in locales where leadership for it exists on at least two levels. The first of these is the leadership in facilitating the inauguration of an operational plan of service, arising at the top administrative level of any organization. Such leaders must take overt action regarding the use and support of instructional media, and they must exercise skillfully the executive function of selecting a qualified person to implement the plan of action envisioned or the plan legislated by school boards or other law- or policy-making groups. At the second level is the indispensable leadership of an individual who is charged with responsibility for developing and maintaining the media-service program itself.

Too often the writer has observed a tottering service program existing in peril and at great odds because, for example, a school superintendent has for one reason or another adopted a "laissez-faire" attitude. The same results may be observed when the leadership at the second —the service organization level—resides in an unqualified person, an insecure committee, a too busy curriculum director, or in a group of individual school-building coordinators without adequate direction, however deeply dedicated each is to his own program. The conclusion is obvious. Adequate leadership is one of the first essentials for the effective use of media and for the development of desirable media service programs. In a Michigan audiovisual association publication, now unfortunately out of print, Lemler[1] generalized from reports of fourteen Michigan city and county programs, as follows:

It is not surprising that such a broad program should have overlapping and interlocking problems which cannot be solved except through the united efforts of all school staff members. The audio-visual program is in a real sense an effort to mobilize for this united effort. Mobilization for anything implies centralization of responsibility. "Audio-Visual" mobilization is no exception. . . . The Audio-Visual program requires order, direction, and leadership. . . . It is clear that the best way to provide these essentials is to centralize responsibility in an audio-visual director or coordinator with the necessary competencies of leadership and administration.

The Media Program Director As an Educator

As an educator, the media specialist must see himself as an expert in curriculum and curriculum change, being fully able to make sound judgments about the many aspects of the teaching process. Unless the instructional media leader can pull the teaching process apart and divide it into some of its many, often sharply defined components, it is doubtful that he can

operate in the other essential roles of a specialist in technological matters. He must therefore excel in his ability to discuss the problems of teachers and curriculum planners in accomplishing their specific objectives. He must excel in his ability to formulate educational objectives and to predict which responses of learners are likely to be desirable en route to their attainment. He needs to be able to suggest rearrangements in learning conditions and to evaluate results in pupils and effects upon teachers. The media specialist must make his judgments in the light of how learning takes place and what pupils actually learn. There is little doubt that this leader of teachers must not fall short in his role of being an innovator in the field of educational method. Such a role ties the media specialist to the entire range of the curriculum, hopefully bringing to his problems a breadth of insight into philosophical and cultural values. See Figure 1-11.

The Media Program Director As an Executive

In whatever job situation the media director wishes to work—large or small, public school or private, city school or university, state or county—he must function effectively as an executive. As such he must lead in the formulation of policy and see to its execution; he must mobilize service personnel and train and deploy them for agreed-upon undertakings; he must develop understanding and support of the organization, its purposes and activities; he must prepare and administer the budget; he must develop close cooperative effort of all concerned; he must procure, distribute, and maintain necessary materials and equipment for use in an environment of appropriate facilities; and he must promote needed innovations.

The Media Program Director As a Supervisor and Consultant

Inasmuch as the director is a curriculum worker, he must pursue vigorously his role of supervisor of instruction and consultant for both teachers and other school leaders. As a supervisor and consultant, the director of media services needs to see his mission broadly in terms of guiding teachers in specialized methods to greater valid accomplishment. Such a role

[1] Ford L. Lemler (ed.), "Audio-Visual Programs in Action" (reports from fourteen Michigan school systems), prepared by members of Michigan Audio-Visual Association, Ann Arbor, Michigan, 1951, pp. 1–2. (Out of print.)

Figure 1-11. Do you perceive in the situations portrayed the nature of the teaching objectives that may be achieved? What may the little girl who is reading a thermometer be actually learning? What may the boys in the school library be learning besides how to find a book in the card catalog? What is the predicted value in providing media facilities such as those shown in the bottom picture? Is there any magic in just looking at a film? What guidance may need to be given beforehand? What responses that youngsters make to film content, with or without the headsets, may be truly important to personal growth in any specific learning environment? Does it really matter when assisting teachers, if the major aspects of the teaching process are understood, at least to a desirable degree of insight? (*Left picture*, courtesy Science Curriculum Improvement Study, University of California, Berkeley; photograph by Herbert D. Thier. *Right picture*, courtesy American Library Association, Knapp Project. *Bottom picture*, courtesy Encyclopaedia Britannica Educational Corp., Project Discovery.)

will demand complex and effective action on his part as a planner and organizer working for the betterment of teaching–learning processes. It will also demand that he be bigger than the technological hardware, operating in a spirit of real service to teachers. He must not avoid, however, the work of identifying and correcting weaknesses in his sphere of responsibility. Such a role ties the instructional media specialist irrevocably to the job of implementing changes in people.

The Media Program Director As a Technological Expert

In the role of a technological expert the director must be able to prescribe and advise with authority, growing out of wide knowledge and experience in matters relating to the selection and use of a wide range of instructional media. He must be able to appraise and specify required media equipment and facilities. In this role also the director is an implementor of change, and he must not shrink from the effort to develop personal communicative skills. He

can hardly escape in this role the necessity of becoming a skilled designer and producer of audiovisual media for unique instructional uses. When he has neither the time nor the staff for local media preparation, he must be prepared to serve as a consultant in terms of purposes, plans, scripting, and specifications for procuring laboratory services, whether the resulting material is to be a motion picture, tape, television program, or an overlay transparency. See Figure 1-12.

The Media Program Director As an Equipment Technician

In his role as equipment technician it is essential that the media director be familiar

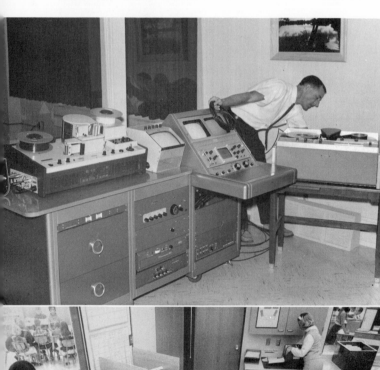

Figure 1-12. In many of the modern changes in the classroom, media play indispensable roles. New technical services are demanded in order to maintain flow of media into both large and small groups. New and complex equipment installations call for technological insight and ability that are balanced by adequate curriculum planning and implementation. *Top picture*, courtesy Public Schools, Los Alamos, New Mexico. *Bottom picture*, courtesy Fountain Valley School District, Huntington Beach, California.

with the output standards of various types of audiovisual media equipment. He must devise appropriate ways to have it inspected, cleaned, and maintained in satisfactory operating condition. Adequate understanding of mechanical and electronic operations is not required for the purpose of becoming a repairman, but rather to facilitate correct decisions regarding planning, budgeting, training of operators, local servicing contracts, and employment of technical personnel, to mention just a few.

Certainly any media director who endeavors to supply the leadership implicit in the closely interwoven roles just described will find himself challenged during a lifetime of professional effort. How did such an educational job evolve?

The Media Program Director's Job in Historical Perspective

Some Connections with Early Educational Thinkers

The roots of the media director's job are deep in the history of education, deep in the forces that led to the rise of such thinkers as Francis Bacon, Ratke, Comenius, Rousseau, Basedow, Pestalozzi, and Froebel. Cubberley[2] in a succinct introduction to his discussion of the rise of realism in education wrote:

. . . during the sixteenth century, and as a further expression of the new critical spirit awakened by the Revival of Learning, a demand for a type of education which would make truth rather than beauty, and the realities of the life of the time rather than the beauties of a life of Roman days, the aim and purpose of education. This new spirit became known as Realism, was contemporaneous with the rise of scientific inquiry, and was an expression of a similar dissatisfaction with the learning of the time. As applied to education this new spirit may be said to have manifested itself in three different stages, as follows: 1. Humanistic realism, 2. Social realism, 3. Sense realism.

However complex the environment, and however difficult to designate who got the idea first, it is sufficient here to indicate that the concept of the picture, object, and field study, as

having value in the teaching process, spread to America.

Some Early Inventions and Proposed Applications

Significant technological events reported by Quigley[3] need to be mentioned because of their bearing on the American audiovisual media job perspective as follows. In 1645 Athanasius Kircher invented the magic lantern at Rome and used drawings for his first screen show; in 1671 he published the second edition of *Ars Magna Lucis et Umbrae*, with an expanded treatment of the magic lantern and specific instructions on how it could be used for entertainment and instruction; in 1870 Bourbouze used posed motion pictures at Sorbonne University to show the actions of pistons, vapor, and air machines; in 1889 George Eastman applied for a patent on flexible photographic film; in 1887 H. W. Goodwin, an Episcopalian minister, conducted a magic lantern entertainment for his congregation; in 1891 Thomas A. Edison completed his kinetograph camera and kinetoscope viewing apparatus; in 1894 Edison opened his peep-show in New York; in 1895 successful screen projections were conducted by Louis and Auguste Lumiere with the Cinematographe in France, by R. W. Paul with the Bioscope in England, and by Armat, Jenkins, Lathams, and others in the United States; and in 1896 screen projection became a commercial reality on April 23 at Kosten and Bial's Music Hall in New York City, which showed a series of short films on an Edison-made, Armat-designed Vitascope.

Krows[4] pointed out another interesting fact as follows: In August, 1910, Frank Woods wrote in the *Dramatic Mirror* of New York City, ". . . out of 140 releases in that one month, thirteen percent were scenic and industrial subjects." Elliott[5] emphasized this also by revealing that, "American movie programs of 1910 included, along with entertainment reels, such films as *The Taos Indians of*

---

2 By permission. From (Helen Cubberley) Ellwood P. Cubberley, *The History of Education* (Boston: Houghton Mifflin Company, 1948), p. 397.

3 By permission. From Martin Quigley, Jr., *Magic Shadows: The Story of the Origin of Motion Pictures* (Washington, D.C.: Georgetown University Press, 1948), pp. 163–176.

4 Arthur Edwin Krows, "Motion Pictures Not for Theatres," *Educational Screen*, Vol. 17, No. 7, September 1938, p. 211.

5 Godfrey M. Elliott (ed.), *The Film and Education* (New York: The Philosophical Library, 1948), p. 13.

Figure 1-13. The St. Louis citywide service program, the nation's first, featured the delivery of objects and models to teachers. *Courtesy St. Louis Public Schools.*

New Mexico at Home, The Tea Industry of the United States, The Story of Coal, . . . and *The Story of Pottery . . .*" Lyceum lecturers also taught useful lessons in the value of the film as an educative medium, and students have but to look up a certain 1925 issue of *Colliers* magazine to read Edison's own words:

In short our system of education is leaving a good deal of its work to an untrained imagination. . . . Develop the imagination by all means, but develop it from actualities . . . we must substitute for mental pictures of how the world might look and act physical pictures of how it really does look and act. . . . And so we get back to the big hope I had in the beginning for the motion picture camera.[6]

In a later issue of the same magazine Edison made another significant statement that seems to have an air of disappointment about it:

It may seem curious, but the money end of the movies never hit me the hardest. The feature that did appeal to me about the whole thing was the educational possibilities . . . when the educators failed to respond, I lost interest . . . maybe I'm wrong, but I should say that in ten years textbooks as the principal medium of teaching will be as obsolete as the horses and carriages are now. . . .

[6] H. Weir, "Thomas A. Edison Goes to School," *Colliers,* Vol. 75, No. 1, January 3, 1925, pp. 14, 40.

Visual education—the imparting of exact information through the motion picture camera—will be a matter of course in all our schools.[7]

Early Citywide Systematic Media Services

A man of Edison's fame must have hastened the day of acceptance by schoolmen of the time. However, many forces[8] contributed to the development of a more favorable climate in which school jobs in the then-called Visual Education field were to open up. One condition

[7] H. Weir, "What Edison Would Like to Do with the Movies," *Colliers,* Vol. 75, No. 8, February 28, 1925, pp. 20–21.

[8] The following influences leading to the use of motion pictures in the schools are easily recognizable: (1) the magic lantern; (2) film projection by pioneer teachers; (3) pronouncements of motion picture inventors; (4) film salesmen and distributors; (5) popularizing forces such as the 9,000 theaters in the year 1910 and Hale's Tours at the 1913 St. Louis Exposition, not to mention World Wars I and II; (6) educational-film producers; (7) the commercial enterprise system; (8) teacher-preparation programs and state and national promotional organizations; and (9) experimentation by educators and other research agencies. Many other forces, interlocked with each other, led to the development of advanced concepts regarding a broad range of audiovisual media and their relationship to teaching and to communication in general. Most recent of these forces is national legislation for financial support of media development, the vast technological changes in society, and the growing awareness in people of the need for universal and continuous education.

that became increasingly clear to almost everyone was that *teachers needed help* from somebody in getting and using the early visual materials in the teaching process and, of course, this is still the case today. To provide this help, both formal and informal service organizations, known as "visual education departments," came into being with the head of such organizations being given the title of director or supervisor.

Fortunately, information about these early departments is available. McClusky[9] in an unpublished report to the National Education Association revealed that the St. Louis Educational Museum, established in 1905, was the first administrative unit for visual education to be organized in a public school system, and that "By 1923, sixteen city school systems had organized departments of visual education..."[10] Saettler[11] in an article based on his doctoral dissertation, contributed significantly to the understanding of early developments in this field. He writes:

The organization of audio-visual education in city school systems proceeded along four distinctive paths: (a) the emergence of school museums, (b) the founding of slide libraries, (c) the establishment of film libraries, and (d) the nondepartmentalized systematization of audio-visual education ... however these growth patterns may overlap or supplement each other, it is indisputably clear that the school museum movement gave the first vital impetus to the organization of audio-visual education in city school systems.

Saettler[12] also pointed out that "Perhaps the most notable example of a cooperative educational undertaking of a museum is that offered by the Philadelphia Commercial Museum, which, about 1900, prepared and presented free of cost a total of 250 collections to the Pennsylvania schools."

Table 1-1 is also the result of Saettler's exploration of available sources. In this table a date of 1904 is given for the founding of the St. Louis School Museum, and in a previous quotation, a date of 1905 was reported. Probably the later date is the beginning of active service to schools via a horse-drawn delivery wagon. The first curator, Amelia Meissner, is reported to have worked on the organization of the materials during 1904.

It is important to note that formal organizations for visual education soon expanded their services to include field trips and slides, and eventually silent motion pictures. The following quotation from Saettler[13] tells the interesting Chicago slide library story.

A second developmental stream in the organization of audio-visual education departments was the establishment of slide libraries in the cities of Philadelphia, Detroit, and Chicago. Undoubtedly, the most intriguing historical narrative of an individual slide library is the Chicago story.

In 1895 a group of ten enthusiastic principals in the Chicago schools organized a projection club entirely independent of the Chicago Board of Education. This group of principals, with their own funds, contributed $25 each to a "slide fund" which was used to purchase slides and projection equipment. As a consequence, this small group of educators not only distributed slide sets among their respective schools and the community, but they also purchased additional slide sets and kept their collection in good repair.

The Chicago Projection Club eventually gained such wide appeal that it began to assume proportions which made it impossible for this group of volunteers to operate it effectively. Therefore, in 1917, the complete collection of some 8,000 slides was given to the Chicago Board of Education with the proviso that it be built up, its use fostered, and its advantages extended to all the schools in the system. The Board accepted this responsibility and began to administer it as part of an organized audio-visual department.

Expansion of the Audiovisual Media in Education Movement

By 1946 the Research Division of the National Education Association[14] was able to report that for the school year 1945–46:

[9] F. Dean McClusky, *The Administration of Visual Education: A National Survey*, an unpublished report made to the National Education Association in 1923.

[10] F. Dean McClusky in *Audio-Visual Administration*, Fred Harcleroad and William Allen (eds.) (Dubuque, Iowa: Wm. C. Brown Company, 1951), p. 7.

[11] By permission. From L. Paul Saettler, "History of A-V Education in City School Systems," *Audio-Visual Communication Review*, Vol. 3, No. 2, 1955, pp. 109–118.

[12] *Ibid.*, p. 110.

[13] *Ibid.*, p. 115.

[14] National Education Association, "Audio-Visual Education in City School Systems," *Research Bulletin*, Vol. 24, No. 4, December 1946, p. 136.

Table 1-1. Early Audiovisual Departments [15]

City	Date Established	Director	Title of Director
St. Louis	1904	A. Meissner	Curator, Educational Museum
Reading, Pa.	1907	L. W. Mengel	Director, Reading Public Museum and Art Gallery
Cleveland	1909	W. M. Gregory	Director, Educational Museum
Philadelphia	1915	A. F. Liveright	Librarian, Pedagogical Library
Chicago	1917	Dudley C. Hays	Director, Bureau of Visual Instruction
Newark	1918	A. S. Balcom	Ass't Supt. of Schools in Charge of Visual Instruction
Detroit	1919	B. A. Barnes*	Supervisor of Visual Instruction
Detroit	1919	Julia Gilmore†	Curator, Children's Museum
Kansas City	1919	Rupert Peters	Director, Division of Visual Instruction
Los Angeles	1920	A. Loretto Clark‡	Acting Director, Visual Education
New York	1920	E. L. Crandall	Director of Public Lectures and Visual Instruction
Atlanta	1922	E. R. Enlow	Supervisor of Visual Education
Pittsburgh	1922	John A. Hollinger	Director of Department of Visual Education and Nature Study
Berkeley	1922	Anna V. Dorris	Director of Visual Instruction
Sacramento	1922	(unknown)	Director of Visual Instruction
Buffalo	1923	Orrin L. Pease	Supervisor of Visual Instruction
Buffalo	1920	Carlos Cummings§	Director of Visual Instruction
Oakland	1923	H. O. Welty‖	Director, Department of Visual Instruction

* Appointed for 1923–24.
† Children's Museum under general direction of the Supervisor of Visual Instruction.
‡ Organized as a separate department in 1923.
§ Buffalo Society of Natural Sciences, Department of Visual Instruction, subsidized in part by city for service to public schools.
‖ Chairman of committee that organized department in September, 1923.
SOURCE: F. Dean McClusky, *The Administration of Visual Education, A National Survey*, 1923, p. 11.

... More than three-fourths of the cities over 100,000 in population have created special agencies of some type to take general oversight of audio-visual instruction. More than a third of the cities, 30,000 to 100,000 also have special audio-visual centers. For smaller cities the percents drop rapidly to 5 percent for cities below 25,000 in population ... for cities of all sizes, the school systems without special audio-visual departments are, by and large, the ones making minimum use of audio-visual materials.

This same report [16] reveals that there were as of that date a total of 164 directors. In a later survey report [17] by the same agency for the school year 1953–54, the following summary should be noted as a general trend, "On the

single item of departmental status, figures for 1946 are available for comparison ... the per cent of districts with formal departments increased from 16 in 1946 to 27 in 1954." In connection with this report [18] it is important to note also that, "Fifty-one per cent of the 1310 school districts replying to the question reported central coordination of the program but no formal departmentalization."

In 1963 Finn, Perrin, and Campion reported comprehensive surveys and estimates of technological development, and made the following interpretation of the growth pattern of over-all audiovisual equipment investment by the public schools:

After a slow start, the rise was fairly consistent after 1948 until the fateful 1957–58 period (Sputnik —NDEA). Since that time the rise has been explo-

[15] *Ibid.*, p. 111.
[16] *Ibid.*, p. 137
[17] National Education Association, "Audio-Visual Education in Urban School Districts, 1953–54," *Research Bulletin*, Vol. 33, No. 3, October 1955, p. 94.

[18] *Ibid.*

sive. Expenditures have almost doubled since 1958. ... In 1958, the investment in nine basic items of audio-visual equipment was $18.3 million.[19]

In one of his earlier articles Finn had the following to say about the degree to which technology had penetrated the educational system of our times:

Turning now to education, it becomes apparent under this national and international drive for technological superiority that: (1) those concerned professionally with education have not developed a well-conceived point of view and a position and/or positions concerning technology and education, (2) because of this lack of a point of view and because of certain cultural lag factors naturally associated with education, the acceleration of technological development has tended to bypass the entire educational enterprise until very recently, (3) professionals in education are not prepared now to deal with the tremendous impact that technology is beginning to have on the instructional process itself as, by the technological process of extension, technology begins to invade education with full force.[20]

The technological developments that formed the base for this national educational movement began around the turn of the century. In a rush of invention came Edison's phonograph, Marconi's "wireless," then radio broadcasting, magnetic wire and tape recording, television, FM radio, stereophonic sound, multiple sound tracks for films, videotape, the computer, programed instruction, teaching machines and other automated devices, together with some unique ways of combining such media for new instructional roles. This electronic and communications revolution placed in the hands of educators an array of technological instruments of vast potential. We may say, in the face of burgeoning developments in the use of media in schools, that the sweep of technology in our

society has at last spawned a revolution in education.

We ought to take special note of the fact that with the passage of the NDEA legislation in 1958, the amendments to this act in October 1964, and the Elementary and Secondary Education Act of 1965, the preparation of media specialists became in actuality a matter of public policy. Relative to the new legislation concerning institute programs, in two summers (1965 and 1966) 72 institutes for educational media specialists involving approximately 2,700 participants were conducted at a cost in excess of $4,000,000. These acts plus the passage of the 1965 Elementary and Secondary Education Act have had tremendous influence on the rate of public school expenditures for audiovisual media. Tanzman[21] reported the following situation for 1965–66: "... a whopping $189 million was spent on AV materials, supplies, and salaries in U.S. elementary and secondary schools. This was 54% more than the previous year and almost double the year 1962–63."

In fact, based on its 1964 market review, the Society of Motion Picture and Television Engineers, has estimated that the total nontheatrical film and audiovisual media-use expenditure in the United States has already exceeded $660 million for equipment, materials, and services. Because of the pyramiding impact of increased expenditures and other influences, it appears that an annual half-billion-dollar audiovisual media market for schools alone is likely. Therefore with the expected continuation of federal support under the previously mentioned federal laws, as well as under many other support programs that are stimulating media use in the schools, the major breakthrough in educational media development in schools may actually be at hand.

Including, then, the present observable march of technology, the present interest in and emphasis on instructional media and learning resources centers in colleges and universities throughout the country, and the observable growth of organized educational media programs in school systems, industry, and churches, we see that the job of the media program director appears to be growing steadily in importance and complexity.

[19] James D. Finn, Donald G. Perrin, and Lee E. Campion. *Studies in the Growth of Instructional Technology, I: Audio-Visual Instrumentation for Instruction in the Public Schools, 1930–1960, a Basis for Take-Off* (Occasional Paper No. 6, a Report Prepared for the Technological Development Project of the NEA in cooperation with the U.S. Office of Education) (Washington, D.C.: The Department of Audiovisual Instruction of the NEA, 1962), pp. 61, 63.
[20] James D. Finn, "Automation and Education: III. Technology and the Instructional Process," *Audio-Visual Communication Review*, Vol. 8, No. 1, Winter 1960, p. 8.

[21] Jack Tanzman, "ESEA: Three Ways to Make Your AV Know-How Count," *Audiovisual Instruction*, Vol. 11, No. 10, December 1966, pp. 797–799.

Not only has the nature and scope of the media specialist's job changed, but the shortage of qualified personnel to fill current vacancies has become acute. It is conservatively estimated that by 1972 a work force of 20,000 or more professional educational media specialists will be needed to fill the vacancies and new positions likely to be open in elementary and secondary schools at that time. If this estimate seems high, we have but to remember that according to U.S. Office of Education statistics for 1963–64 there were 26,431 secondary and 67,700 elementary public schools (not including the 9,895 one-teacher elementary schools still in existence). The report for 1966[22] estimates the number of teachers in regular public elementary and secondary schools to be 1,014,000 and 779,000 respectively. In view of these numbers, and in the face of expanding media-use development, we assert that the estimate of the need for media personnel is indeed a conservative one.

The fact is that we ought to speculate in making some predictions as to what the total need for media personnel will be a decade from now. Before stating some estimates, we should take note of the fact that school districts are decreasing in number—with beneficial effects on the development of media-use programs because of the increase in the optimum size of school-building units. If we adjust the number of elementary schools to 50,000 of considerable size and the secondary schools to 25,000 and school districts to 20,000, we can, on this basis and on the basis of personnel services recommended in this book, anticipate that a desirable minimum need for media personnel will be:

1. One-hundred-thousand program directors and school-building coordinators.
2. Two-hundred-thousand technicians and secretaries.

The plateau of need will exist and we shall have to work upward toward it, knowing that it will increase with new school buildings and the requirements of more complex media services. In this connection we must not fail to point out that we have been considering elementary and secondary schools and school-district headquarters only, without including in our specula-

[22] Kenneth A. Simon and W. Vance Grant, *Digest of Educational Statistics*, 1966. (U.S. Office of Education.) (Washington, D.C.: Superintendent of Documents, U.S. Government Printing Office, 1966.)

tion the accelerating growth and development at higher levels of education. This aspect of media services with its emphasis on research, teaching, and technological services adds a new dimension to the personnel problem.

In providing a view of the media program director's job as it now opens up at various levels of instruction, it is important to differentiate between its immediate and long-range aspects. Without this understanding on the part of the director, an intelligent balance of his many efforts seems unlikely. It is certain that he will be continually besieged by the pressure of everyday problems relating to personnel, budgets, materials, equipment facilities, and routine management. This is the immediate aspect. The long-range aspect of the director's work is the improvement of instruction through innovation with the needs of the learner in sharp focus. This is the director's ultimate purpose. With both of these major aspects of the director's work in mind, let us turn to an analysis of his duties in greater detail.

Duties of the Media Program Director

Any statement of duties should be considered in the light of a special set of circumstances under which a given director must work. Specific assignments and the emphasis placed upon them will necessarily vary. A number of listings are to be found in the literature, and it will be helpful to quote a few of them to show differences in points of view, changes in points of emphasis, and to assist the present or prospective audiovisual media director in laying out his own plans for action. Great similarity in the listings is to be noted, since there is marked agreement among specialists as to their general functions. Experience shows, however, that agreement is not evident (and this is to be expected) as to the means used to accomplish the ends, and the degree to which emphasis is given to the various duties.

National Education Association Survey, 1953–54

In the questionnaire used in the 1953–54 survey conducted by the National Education Association, school district respondents were called on to check the types of services provided for audiovisual education. This part of the survey report therefore offers a list of duties, which at least one of the responding school districts with formal departments checked off as being already provided. The following list of duties is excerpted from tabulated data presented in the research report:[23]

Obtaining free and rental materials for teachers upon request
Consulting with individual classroom teachers on use of audiovisual materials
Keeping classroom teachers informed of available materials and new acquisitions
Selecting and purchasing audiovisual materials
Providing operators and equipment for school use
Keeping equipment and materials in repair
Classifying and storing materials
Training operators of audiovisual equipment
Selecting and purchasing audiovisual equipment
Arranging previews of audiovisual materials
Assisting curriculum committees on appropriate audiovisual materials for instruction
Providing delivery and pickup service to schools
Providing operators and equipment for community use
Assisting in workshops for classroom teachers in demonstrating how to use audiovisual materials and equipment
Helping classroom teachers and students with the production of simple teaching materials
Photographing significant school activities
Assisting classroom teachers in planning field trips
Producing audiovisual materials for the classroom
Assisting in producing radio programs (commercial stations)
Assisting in producing television programs (commercial stations)
Directing school-operated radio station
Directing school-operated television station

Others:
Assistance in planning and equipping school buildings for audiovisual use
Research work
Training of building coordinators
Audiovisual public relations work

NSSE Yearbook, Part I, 1949

In addition to developing a lengthy analysis of the functions of an audiovisual department, Noel[24] stated the following generalized duties:

... the director and his professional assistants ... should be responsible for or share leadership in the following areas:

1. Evaluation and selection of materials and equipment
2. Supervision of all aspects of utilization within the schools
3. Consultation services to teachers, principals, supervisors, audiovisual co-ordinators, architects, and outside agencies on problems and activities in audiovisual education
4. In-service education programs for school personnel
5. Experimentation and research on evaluation, uses of materials, and needs for future production
6. Interpretation of the school's program, including audiovisual education, to the school personnel and to the public
7. Production of special curriculum materials.

Oregon Audio-Visual Association, 1952

Another helpful analysis of duties for directors of instructional materials centers was developed by members of the Oregon Audio-Visual Association.[25] This listing, which follows, is classified according to administrative, supervisory, advisory, and technical.

1. *Administrative*
   a. Organize and maintain a central "Instructional Materials Center," serving all the schools within the district
   b. Supervise the organization and operation of the materials program within the separate schools
   c. Administer this program, with the assistance of the coordinator
   d. Determine the equipment and materials needs of the schools and determine what it will cost to fill these needs
   e. Keeps reports and records of materials, equipment, and their use
   f. Select and purchase new materials, with the help of teacher committees
   g. Select and purchase new equipment, with teacher and technical assistance
   h. Organize and administer an efficient circulation service
   i. Promote public relations leading to an understanding of and support of the program
   j. Make reports to the school administration

23 National Education Association, *op. cit.*, p. 100.

24 By permission. From Francis W. Noel, "Principles of Administering Audio-Visual Programs," *Audio-Visual Materials of Instruction*, 48th Yearbook of the National Society for the Study of Education, Part I (Chicago: University of Chicago Press, 1949), p. 194.

25 Oregon Audio-Visual Association, *Recommended Minimum Standards for Instructional Materials Programs in Oregon Public Schools*; prepared by members of the Oregon Audio-Visual Association, May 1952, pp. 2–3. (Mimeographed.)

concerning the operation and the needs of the program

2. *Supervisory*
   a. Supervise, through the coordinators, the operation of the program in the individual school
   b. Plan and carry on an in-service teacher training program through
      (1) Conferences
      (2) Staff meetings
      (3) Noncredit classes and training sessions
      (4) Extension (credit) classes
      (5) Demonstrations, previews, auditions
      (6) Inter- and intra-school visitations
   c. Confer with teachers regarding utilization of materials
   d. Visit classrooms
   e. Issue bulletins giving information on availability and use of materials and equipment
   f. Organize and make available a handbook giving information on the "Community Resources" available for educational use
   g. Train teachers to produce certain teaching aids

3. *Advisory*
   a. Confer with administrators in the planning of new buildings and the remodeling of old structures
   b. Assist in curriculum planning
   c. Advise administrators, supervisors, and curriculum specialists in the selection and use of equipment and materials for their work

4. *Technical*
   a. Organize and maintain a library of materials (books, records, pictures, motion pictures, filmstrips, slides, exhibit materials, etc.)
   b. Repair and maintain equipment and materials
   c. Produce or supervise production of certain materials (slides, exhibits, recordings, photographs, motion pictures, radio programs, etc.)
   d. Train teachers and students in the operation of equipment.

Okoboji Leadership Conference List

As a result of the work done by participants at the 1961 Okoboji Audiovisual Leadership Conference the following list of duties and responsibilities was prepared and later reported by Lewis:[26]

1. Be directly involved in curriculum planning.
2. Promote among teachers, administrators,

[26] Philip Lewis, "The Role of the Education Communications Specialist," *American School Board Journal*, Vol. 142, No. 143, December 1961, pp. 16–17.

school governing bodies, and school patrons the concept that the use of resource materials is integral to instruction and not an adjunct to be used when time permits.

3. Establish an educational climate suitable for the optimum use of instructional media and materials.

4. Develop new measures for determining the effectiveness of instructional materials in specific applications.

5. Be responsible for evaluating emerging innovations for possible introduction into the learning process and for interpreting and promoting those innovations which can make a significant contribution.

6. Become involved in the development of central classification systems that will permit rapid location of related instructional materials for specific learning situations.

7. Arrange for the production of instructional materials which are not readily available but are necessary for the instructional program, and provide the incentive, training, and materials for production by teachers and others.

8. Provide consultation opportunities for all teachers, including teachers-in-training, to secure assistance in the use of new media and materials in their lesson planning.

9. Contribute to the improvement of methods of communication within the profession on matters relative to the emerging practices and innovations, the exchanging of ideas, and the establishing of liaison with outside agencies—the "clearinghouse" idea.

10. Be involved in decision-making activities on such matters as building-planning, classroom design, etc., as they affect the instructional materials program.

11. Assume the leadership responsibility for initiating programs or activities that will bring about needed improvements and innovations.

12. Develop and implement instructional systems involving automation approaches to expedite free flow of information and ideas (communications center, learning laboratories, random access devices, etc.).

13. Make use of research results.

14. Provide a variety of well-selected instructional materials and equipment, easily accessible for use by teachers and pupils and give encouragement and/or administrative support for the effective use of these materials.

Superior Media Program List

In a highly informative doctoral study conducted by Jones, thirty-two practices common to media directors in 112 superior programs throughout the country, as nominated by a jury, were identified in seeking data for comparison with a sample of school programs in the North Central Association.[27] The practices constitute a listing of implicit or explicit duties and responsibilities and are as follows:

1. Is clerical or technical help provided for: Keeping all equipment and materials readily accessible to all teachers?
2. Periodic inventories of equipment and materials?
3. Do you prepare reports for the administration on the status and needs of audio-visual services?
4. Do you involve teachers in the actual selection of materials and equipment?
5. Is clerical or technical help provided for: Keeping teachers informed of new acquisitions, materials, film confirmations, and pending equipment purchases?
6. Regular checking of equipment and materials to determine that all items are serviceable and in working order?
7. Maintaining records on equipment usage and costs?
8. Do you serve your superintendent or principal as an audio-visual consultant or advisor on matters of: Specifications of materials and equipment?
9. If you provide facilities and/or opportunities for in-service training for teachers, do you: Lend assistance in locating source materials? (e.g., film catalogs, index of free films, etc.?)
10. Is clerical or technical help provided for: Classifying and cataloging a wide variety of materials for teachers?
11. Making minor repairs, servicing or replacement of parts?
12. Do you utilize any of the following? Training opportunities for teachers, pupils, and technica personnel in the operation and care of equipment?
13. Do you provide facilities and consultative services to teachers and/or pupils in: Arranging preview sessions for films, film-strips, etc.?
14. Do you provide for the acquisition of free and rental materials for teachers?
15. Do you serve your superintendent or principal as an audio-visual consultant or advisor on matters of: Improving physical facilities of classrooms in terms of: Acoustics, light control, room darkening or ventilation?
16. Repairing and/or servicing of equipment?
17. Do you involve teachers in establishing criteria for the selection of audio-visual materials and equipment?
18. Is clerical or technical help provided for: Preparing handbooks for teachers which describe the services of the Center?
19. Do you provide equipment and materials for special classes such as: Foreign language departments?
20. Do you serve your superintendent or principal as an audio-visual consultant or advisor on matters of: Providing information about equipment ratios and/or standards?
21. Do you provide equipment and materials for special classes such as: Special education classes? (e.g., Retarded or slow learners?)
22. Do you make available an extensive selection of audio-visual books and magazines as a professional library for teachers and other personnel?
23. Do you provide facilities and consultative assistance to teachers and/or pupils in: Planning the utilization of materials and equipment?
24. Is clerical or technical help provided for: Regular checking of sources of indexes of enrichment materials?
25. Do you provide student operators for equipment operation in the classrooms?
26. Do you serve your superintendent or principal as an audio-visual consultant or advisor on matters of: Curriculum revision and development?
27. If you provide facilities and opportunities for the audio-visual in-service training for teachers, do you utilize any of the following: Demonstrations on preparation and uses of materials?
28. Do you provide facilities and consultative assistance to teachers and/or pupils in: Arranging demonstrations and/or doing demonstration teaching *when invited*?
29. Do you devote a major portion of your time encouraging and stimulating teachers to develop a high degree of audio-visual competencies?
30. If you provide facilities and opportunities for the audio-visual in-service training for teachers, do you utilize any of the following: Individual conferences with teachers on audio-visual problems?
31. Do you provide publicity through appropriate media about the activities and services of the audio-visual center?
32. Do you provide facilities and consultative assistance to teachers and/or pupils in: Preparation and production of audio-visual materials?

Utah State Board of Education Survey List [28]

LeRoy R. Lindeman conducted a survey of selected public school and university media

[27] Wilbur C. Jones, *The Practices, Duties and Responsibilities of the Audio-Visual Director in Selected School Systems of the North Central Association*, Doctoral Dissertation, The University of Oklahoma, Norman, Oklahoma, 1963. (Available in microfilm from University Microfilms, Inc., Ann Arbor, Mich.)

[28] LeRoy R. Lindeman, Administrator, Instructional Media Division, Utah State Board of Education, Salt Lake City, Utah, 1965.

experts as jury members obtaining their judgments as to the importance of identified responsibilities of citywide media program directors. Using a system of raw scores, he constructed a rank-order listing of nineteen items. This list is presented here to direct attention to the nature of basic duties, without emphasizing the rank-order nature of the list. For example, the author would disagree with those jury members who placed the *Production of Materials*, *Promoting Public Relations*, and *Repairing Materials and Equipment* so low in importance. This position may indicate the fact that jury members may have felt that the particular activity was not carried out personally by the media director. In this case repairing of equipment certainly should be at the bottom of the list, with others performing this duty under the director's administrative jurisdiction. It is also a fact that attention to any one of the specified activities of any given director may have to be assigned a new top *priority* for perhaps a week, a month, or a year under a particular set of circumstances. The list, without further comment, is as follows:

1. Promoting in-service teacher education.
2. Supervising and coordinating district A-V committee and supervising school A-V personnel.
3. Supervising the selection of A-V materials and equipment.
4. Co-operating with school architects on the functional planning of new buildings and remodeling of old.
5. Serving as a specialist in his field.
6. Organizing a department or center of audio-visual materials.
7. Keeping in touch with sources of new materials.
8. Preparing and supervising the expenditure of a budget.
9. Maintaining the district A-V library.
10. Consulting with teachers regarding utilization of materials.
11. Consulting with teachers regarding specific needs.
12. Issuing bulletins, newsletters, and information on A-V materials, etc.
13. Establishing minimum standards for equipment.
14. Classifying and cataloging materials.
15. Circulating materials and equipment.

16. Visiting schools.
17. Producing materials such as slides, filmstrips, charts, models, etc.
18. Promoting public relations.
19. Repairing and maintaining materials and equipment.

Duties Based on Broad Principles of Service

In any statement of duties, broad principles of service ought to be evident. Thus it is profitable for the prospective media service director to consider duties grouped into appropriate categories. As an aid to this process, and at the risk of oversimplification, we shall state six broad generalizations for organizing media-service programs and then list under each of them several representative duties that we predict would lead to fulfilment of the basic condition proposed. They are listed in the following paragraphs:

Principle 1. *The work of organizing and developing instructional media services will proceed most effectively under specialized, centralized leadership, working coordinately with other curriculum personnel and under adequate system-wide financial support for auxiliary staff, equipment, materials, and facilities.* This principle demands that school system officials commit themselves publicly to a plan for positive action, and that the media program director fulfil his role as executive. After his appointment the chief media program director would

1. Formulate and recommend policy for adoption.
2. Execute adopted policies.
3. Prepare and administer the budget.
4. Employ and deploy personnel.
5. Serve as a consultant for school officials.
6. Prepare reports and plans for action.
7. Plan and conduct research and implement evaluative activities.
8. Plan and carry out a public relations program.
9. Provide leadership for educational innovation.

Principle 2. *Media materials and equipment should be easily accessible to teachers at the time they are needed in an appropriate environment.* This principle demands that generous help be available to teachers in selecting media from local sources as well as from sources outside the school system; that catalogs and subject- or unit-correlated lists of materials be made up for teacher use; that simple, convenient systems for ordering, delivery, and pickup be devised; and that materials used frequently by a number of teachers be purchased and made a part of the media service center. This principle also demands that teachers be able to select their own materials; hence, help must be given in facilitating pre-use or prepurchase examination. Duties would be to

1. Provide an efficient ordering, delivery and pickup system for materials.
2. Formulate and carry on an efficient catalog process.
3. Prepare or organize the preparation of special subject listings of materials (select and purchase sourcebooks).
4. Arrange for optimum centralization and decentralization of media close to teachers.
5. Establish channels for consultative assistance for teachers.
6. Establish efficient rental and purchase procedures for media materials.
7. Determine ratio of new titles or subjects to multiple copies on the basis of curriculum needs (basal or supplementary).

Principle 3. *Instructional media equipment should be made available to teachers with a minimum of inconvenience and distraction.* This principle demands that each school building be equipped with the necessary media equipment units to meet the needs of curriculum; that eventually all classrooms be provided with necessary light-control systems and suitably located electrical outlets for picture-projection systems. This principle seems also to demand that sources of assistance for equipment ordering, handling, and use be located as close as is feasible to the teacher. Duties would be to

1. Plan, schedule and carry out adequate procedures for the decentralization of equipment units.
2. Organize school-building media service centers.
3. Provide a technical and clerical staff in each school and a unit director as a coordinator to assist teachers as needed.

4. Provide each school with adequate classroom facilities for teacher convenience.
5. Prepare specifications for the purchase of high quality equipment.
6. Set up efficient equipment repair and inspection programs.
7. Organize and maintain a stock of spare parts and supplies.
8. Plan and carry out an adequate equipment replacement program.

Principle 4. *The instructional media-service program should include a variety of materials for teachers.* This principle demands that many kinds of instructional materials be made available to teachers, including materials for production, maps and globes, library books, and textbooks; that assistance be given in coordinating school-community relationships of all kinds, thus making possible field trips, resource persons, interviews, a library of community documents, and cooperation between schools and local radio and television stations. Duties would be to

1. Organize efficient teacher panels for selection and purchase of materials.
2. Set up effective rental and purchasing systems.
3. Plan and carry out adequate production of materials programs.
4. Plan and carry out modern media programs: Listening–response laboratories, ITV, automation.
5. Organize and coordinate school use of community resources.

Principle 5. *The instructional media-service program should provide for the continuous, effective in-service growth of teachers in accordance with their needs.* This principle demands that teachers be given ample opportunity to develop competence in the use of a wide variety of teaching tools and that the participation of teachers in planning for their significant growth-building activities be sought. This implies creative supervision—the work of friendly, understanding, capable, democratic leadership. Such a program has tremendous implications on many fronts for the betterment of the teaching staff, in addition to the upgrading of specific competencies with media. Duties would be to

1. Establish utilization standards.

2. Determine teacher-competence needs.

3. Organize and carry on effective growth programs for teachers.

4. Conduct demonstrations and assist school leaders with their use of media.

5. Work co-operatively with curriculum leaders in establishing plans and priorities for in-service programs.

6. Set up and maintain professional library services.

7. Make plans for the deliberate implementation of needed changes in media-use programs.

Principle 6. *Provisions for citywide instructional media services need to be based on continuous long-term planning.* This principle demands that any plan of action must be conceived as a long-term project; that continuing financial support be provided to meet curriculum needs; that the process of providing building facilities must be carried on as part of a master plan for all the schools. This principle applies to the in-service growth of teachers as well. Duties would be to

1. Make surveys of present facilities and inventories.

2. Develop equipment and competence standards in terms of school-system needs.

3. Prepare reports as to how goals should be achieved.

4. Prepare long-term financial support programs.

5. Prepare long-term plans for reaching the standards established.

6. Select and organize colleagues for assistance in programs to achieve long-range goals.

7. Prepare formal proposals and requests for state and national grants for pilot program and research as covered by legislation.

The main objective of the media program is to bring the full impact of technological development to bear upon the improvement in the quality and quantity of instruction needed by society. It is obvious that this objective can be met in many creative ways. It is also obvious that the host of duties in the complex educational media field is so vast and interwoven with the work of so many people that the prospective media director of a citywide school system must quite properly be apprehensive to the point of reversing his decision to enter the

field at all. However, we hasten to make clear that it is not likely that all of the abilities and understanding implied will reside in one individual. Further, as the media program increases in scope, or as the area to be served widens, the staff must increase along lines of specialized skills and experience. It is at this point that the media director makes use of his own broad knowledge of technology and becomes a full-time leader and manager.

Basis for Action

The Value of an Operational Plan

The author discovered long ago that many media-service programs were set up in haphazard fashion, growing into being without benefit of adequate operational planning and without solid legislative support. A far healthier condition would exist in many school systems if the audiovisual media services were operated according to a well-formulated, written, administrative plan voted into action by Boards of Education. An example of such a plan, which is in generalized form ready for modification and application to a specific locality, appears on pages 28 and 29.

The Media Program Director in the Administrative Organization

In the Operational Plan for Instructional Services, the line of responsibility is spelled out to cover any future expansion of the top decision-making staff. Just how should the media director be oriented to the total action of an administrative organization? What are some of the recommended patterns?

A media specialist who is moving into a new position in a school system may have nothing whatever to say about his status in the local administrative hierarchy. He may of course decline to accept any position that doesn't suit his beliefs and convictions, but he may also accept an unsatisfactory arrangement with the intention of influencing change at the opportune time. Many are the unique local arrangements, both formal and informal.

The main issues are whether or not the media administrator operates on a system-wide basis, whether or not he is close to policy-forming levels of action, whether or not he is close to curriculum leaders and other key personnel such as school principals and business managers in promoting needed changes, and whether or not the media program leader may concentrate his time and energy on media-development problems. In view of these issues the conviction has become well established that leadership for developing media-service programs should be specialized and at an optimum level in any given sphere of operation.

At this point we are not concerned with staffing problems and auxiliary personnel as a particular organization is being developed. We are instead concentrating our attention on the media program director of a city school system or district, a county school administrative and service organization, a large regional school with a separate board of education and chief administrative officer that operates as an independent unit, and a university. In such cases we can say that the media director should be placed at the highest possible point in the administrative and instructional hierarchy that permits him to work coordinately with other leaders, but under direct authority of the chief decision maker. He should be in a position to focus all of his energy and effort on the media development program.

A few examples of media director placement in the administrative-instructional staff organization will be helpful for both present and future planning and discussion. See Figure 1-14 on pages 26 and 27.

There is a wide variety of instructional situations at different levels and in different kinds of school organizations. We may state with considerable assurance of being correct that the teaching staff in every school building needs technological assistance at both professional and technical-clerical levels. Every school district, every countywide or regional, comprehensive school-service organization requires media-program leadership. Every junior college, college and university, and state department of education also needs full professional and technical-clerical support to provide the help in various ways and through various channels that teachers need to master technological innovations. It is just as necessary to develop the capability to retool and retrain workers in schools as it is in industry. We know also that as media-service organizations grow

larger and more comprehensive in scope, the media generalist must have the concentrated effort of media specialists who can concentrate their efforts and total energies along specific lines of activity, such as television programing or the design and preparation of slides and transparencies for teachers.

All of these media program directors, wherever they may be employed, have many duties in common and, in fact, many have common preparation for the positions they hold. However, these media program directors operate under different circumstances, which may preclude agreement on the importance of any single duty in a list common to all. Many city-wide media program directors are moving toward new emphases. For example, large city media program directors are moving into research activity, a primary concern of university media center directors. This situation may have come about because of the inauguration and expansion of federal financial support. It seems quite obvious that media program directors at the university level are, in addition to many common duties, greatly concerned with teaching graduate media courses, publishing, counseling advanced degree students, and research activities.

As we observe media programs around the country or receive reports from their directors, it becomes clear that as the program increases in size and scope, the director becomes less involved with specific media activities in depth. He is not likely to spend much of his time selecting films and writing descriptions of them, writing scripts for telecasts, or teaching teachers how to operate equipment. This is to say that as special talents become available among new staff members, the media program director can devote more of his time to creative executive functions. See the operational plan given on pages 28–29.

The Media Program Director Launches His Career

The newly appointed director of an instructional-media-service program may report for his or her first day of work as a stranger, or as frequently is the case, he may already have been a well-known local staff member. He may, of course, begin to operate according to an administrative operational plan that represents the careful cooperative effort of a local

SCHOOL BUILDING SITUATION

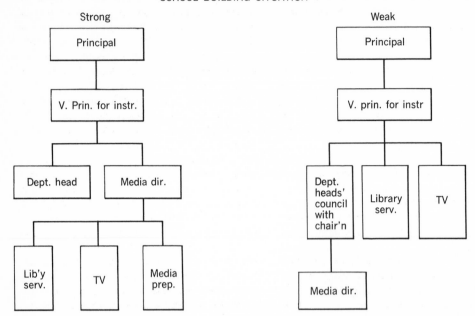

Figure 1-14. These four sketches should be viewed as a set of generalized predictions without the benefit of a specific set of local circumstances. The observer should be aware that in any given sketch, only a few of the possibilities are indicated. Further, we must not conclude that the *weak* patterns will not work. Cases could be cited where they have worked with reasonable effectiveness. Placement of the media program director in an administrative organization is, however, a vital matter. Leadership, decision-making, design and planning activity, responsibility, all a part of the total capacity for change, are some of the vital factors involved. The viewer should test his insights into administrative processes by postulating some for and against judgments regarding the strengths and weakness in the diagrams.

SCHOOL DISTRICT SITUATION

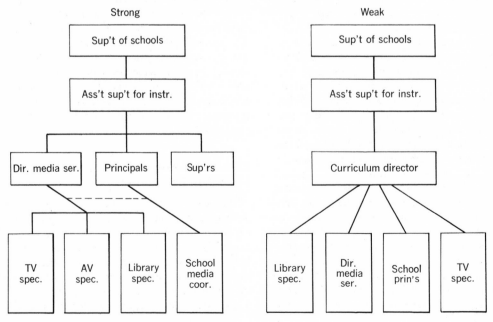

COUNTY SCHOOLS SITUATION

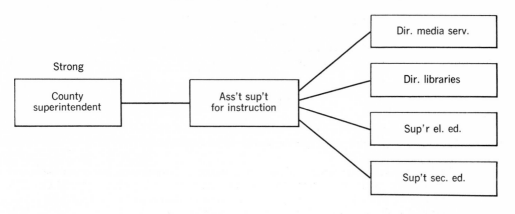

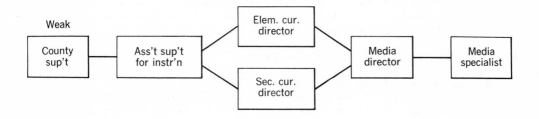

MEDIA CENTER
UNIVERSITY SITUATION

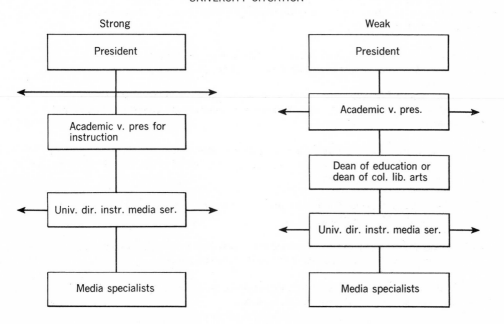

OPERATIONAL PLAN
FOR
INSTRUCTIONAL MEDIA SERVICES

_____

(School Department)

_____

(Date)

I.   Establishment of Organized Instructional Media Services

    A.   To facilitate the economical use of a variety of instructional materials and equipment by teachers who are seeking to provide significant learning experiences for their pupils, the superintendent shall establish an organized service program for the schools of _____ .

    B.   The necessary services to principals, teachers, and pupils shall be made available through a centralized agency to be known as the <u>Instructional Media Center</u>.

II.   Leadership for Instructional Media Services

    A.   The superintendent shall be responsible for staffing the center with a full-time director, subject to the approval of the Board of Education, who is qualified to direct and supervise this city-wide service at all levels of instruction.

    B.   The full title of the director shall be "Director of Instructional Media Services". The salary range for this position shall be_____ .

III.   Duties of the Director of Instructional Media Services

    The superintendent, or the assistant superintendent in charge of instruction, shall be responsible for the supervision of the director. The director's major duties shall be as follows:

    A.   With the advice of those who are concerned, formulate over-all policies for city-wide instructional media services.

    B.   Formulate and carry through long-term plans for the acquisition of equipment, materials, and facilities necessary to satisfy educational needs.

    C.   Formulate and carry through adequate plans and procedures to assist teachers in the selection of appropriate materials and the convenient operation of equipment.

    D.   Organize and conduct an adequate in-service education program for teachers and principals.

    E.   Establish and maintain cooperative consultative relationships with supervisors, principals, and all curriculum committees.

    F.   Make detailed budgetary recommendations to the superintendent of schools in terms of long-term needs.

G. Establish and maintain an adequate public relations program.

H. Evaluate continuously the results of the service.

I. Prepare proposals and plans for state and national financial support in the light of unique local needs.

J. Formulate and carry out a program for his own professional growth.

K. Conduct research and experimentation concerning the application of new media as well as of existing, commonly used media.

L. Work cooperatively with other school systems concerning utilization plans, acquisitions and consultative services.

M. Coordinate the school system use of community resources such as museums, art galleries, and industrial and commercial organizations.

IV. Financial Support

A. Expenditures for the media program shall be considered an integral part of the over-all instructional program.

B. The superintendent shall be responsible for the preparation of detailed plans for expenditures in terms of well-defined needs and goals.

C. The Board of Education, in recognizing its obligation to meet the costs of an instructional media service program, should recommend the following financial support:

   (1) A first year financial outlay amounting to $_____ per pupil to bring _____ required facilities up to a "desir-
   (school department)
   able minimum" operating basis.

   (2) A minimum average annual expenditure for a ten-year period amounting to $_____ per pupil.

Such a basis for action gives a new director a great potential for success.

study committee. He may be fortunate enough to have immediate access to a local school-system survey of equipment, classroom facilities, professional status of teachers, and well-worked-out cataloging and distribution procedures. He may even find an advisory council and a school-building coordinator group waiting for his first bulletin or the resumption of a series of meetings. If he is lucky, he may walk into a well-equipped media center with secretarial and technical staff at work on routine business. On the other hand, he may have to start from scratch. Is there a safe and sure formula? The answer is no.

It is no simple matter to start out on any new job, let alone one that cuts across the entire range of academic instruction. The primary purpose of this book is to contribute to the preparation of the prospective media director for just such a task. To be able to define problems in this field and to discover sound solutions for them in terms of a unique environment is what this book will emphasize. However, as to initiating a program, the following good advice merits careful consideration.

1. Find out what positive and negative influences are at work.

2. Be friendly, sincere, modest, objective, and industrious.

3. Get the facts about school materials, equipment, and facilities at once. Study existing procedures.

4. Make personal commitments only for services that can be met on time.

5. Enlist the cooperation of colleagues to get the work of the organization done.

6. Give attention to the proper pacing of activities and work loads.

7. Define problems and assign priorities for their solution.

8. Get to know your colleagues at all levels.

9. Make an *operational plan* for the superintendent if one doesn't already exist.

10. Find some objective nearby sources of advice.

Such a list could be stretched out interminably but it would be of no value at this point. The reader will soon turn, however, to the next chapter for discussions on topics having to do with growth toward administrative competence that will hopefully lead the prospective media director to undertake the jobs of self-scrutiny and, under proper guidance, his own development in terms of personal needs. Then the reader will be urged to consider in depth several sets of problems associated with decisions in the field of media services. But first, we should clarify the terms used in this book to refer to the director's title and his organization.

The reader has already been subjected to a number of terms, some of which may have been confusing to him. However, even though the individual who turns to this book may be inexperienced, he is not likely to be unsophisticated. In basic courses and in his study of the literature, he has already been subjected to similar communication difficulties. It is likely that media terminology will eventually become standardized.

Terminology

On the following pages are some of the terms and their semantic reference bases—at least as conceived by the writer and found in the literature—used in this book.

Audiovisual Materials. *Audiovisual* is the second oldest term in our field of technology, having started out as *visual* in the early centralized service departments of *visual education*, dating back, it is believed, to Chicago in 1917.

This term was the most commonly used until the terms *media, new media,* and *educational media* gained popularity because of their use in the National Defense Education Act of 1958 and its amendment of 1964. The term *audiovisual* refers semantically to sound and visual stimuli as used in educational processes, but in common practice it includes all materials generally used in classroom instruction except those that use verbal symbols (printed) only.

Media. We use this term in set expressions such as *educational media* and *new educational media*. Definitions of these two terms appear in two official publications of the Department of Audiovisual Instruction of the NEA. The first of these terms, *educational media*, is defined as follows:

Educational media are defined here as those things which are manipulated, seen, heard, read or talked about, plus the instruments which facilitate such activity. Educational media are both tools for teaching and avenues for learning . . .[29]

The second, *new educational media*, is defined as follows:

Terms used in various titles of the National Defense Education Act of 1958 to describe pertinent materials and technological devices: TV, teaching machines, programed learning material, electronic learning laboratories; it also includes many well-established audiovisual media such as motion pictures, filmstrips, slides and recorders.[30]

Instructional media is a similar expression that is widely used in the field, and also in this book. It is a somewhat more specific expression than *educational media*, connoting formal and systematic application to pedagogy. The term *instructional television*, rather than *educational television*, is generally used throughout this book.

Since the terms *audiovisual* and *new educational media* or *new instructional media*, refer generally to the same kinds of media, namely all instructional media exclusive of the print medium, we shall use them interchangeably.

[29] Barry Morris (ed.), "The Function of Media in the Public Schools" (A Task Force Position Paper), *Audiovisual Instruction*, Vol. 8, No. 1, January 1963, p. 11.

[30] Donald P. Ely (ed.) (prepared by the Commission), "Alphabetical Listing of Terminology," *Audiovisual Communication Review*, Vol. 11, No. 1, Supp. 6, January 1963, p. 78.

Educational media and *instructional media* are both broad terms that include the medium of print. When we use the term *media* we may *in context* be using a shortened expression to refer to either *audiovisual* or *new educational* media. For example, we have used and will use often throughout this book the expression *media director*. Such an individual may in a present or future position be involved with all media or, in a restricted way, with new instructional media.

Audiovisual Media. This expression refers to materials of instruction with the exception of printed ones. We have selected, however, the expression *instructional media* to be used in the title of this book. If we attempt to categorize *media* broadly for discussion or for analytical purposes, we are forced to use such terms as *print* and *nonprint*, or *audiovisual media*. We shall therefore in this book deal specifically and comprehensively with audiovisual media, and also, though not as comprehensively, with print-medium services. (Dealing with print-medium services in a major way would require a book twice the size of the present volume.) Media are generally assumed to include both materials and equipment, but for purposes of discussion in this book we may on occasion use each separately, especially when discussing hardware and instruments as separate from the body of content that is to be used in them or with them.

Instructional Materials. This is a broad and all-inclusive term that is serviceable when referring to all kinds of materials for instructional purposes. Many schools have named their audiovisual organizations *Instructional Materials Centers*, and these centers—either central or functioning as separate centers in school buildings—either include or should include all kinds of instructional media. We shall explain and illustrate the work of such centers thoroughly. Some schools use this expression incorrectly to describe the organization and its director when reference and textbook materials are excluded from the director's purvue. However, misuse of the term is understandable in the light of local developments.

Curriculum Materials. Like *instructional materials*, *curriculum materials* is broad and inclusive in scope. The two terms seem to be synonymous, both referring to all media, including print. Curriculum materials center directors should—by virtue of administering

the entire spectrum of media—be in charge of the school's textbook selection and distribution operations. Both terms seem to be synonymous with *instructional media*. Both would include *new educational media*.

Instructional Technology. This expression lays the greatest emphasis of any on the sweep of technological development and pinpoints the technological expertise that professionals in this field must possess. The use of *instruction* with the term *technology* pins down the area of technology yet broadens its base of application to all instructional, technological media. The use of the expression *technology* tends to have mechanical and electronic connotations and therefore appears to emphasize the new instructional media rather than the old. We may because of this connotation use the term as a synonym for *audiovisual media* or *audiovisual technology*, thus referring to both materials and instruments.

Instruments. Readers should not be alarmed over the use of the expression *instruments*, which is a technological term used whenever audiovisual technology is emphasized. It is also a synonym for *hardware*. We shall, however, use the terms *instruments*, *hardware*, and *equipment* interchangeably in this book.

Learning Resources. We use this expression to refer to the entire spectrum of educational media. In this sense all of the media from print to computer may be linked in a system, or used individually, in optimum combinations to achieve educational objectives. As a name for a center of services, it is beginning to appear in universities. It has been and is more commonly associated with the new educational media. In the 1965 deliberations over a possible name change for the DAVI of the NEA, this expression was one of three new proposals, the others being *Instructional Technology* and *Educational Communications*, but not ruling out the possibility that the name *Audiovisual Instruction* might well be continued in the interests of stability. Actually, there are also many additional possibilities that could be eventually proposed and accepted.

Educational Communications. We shall refer many times to a number of expressions based on the implied concept of communication in a teaching-learning situation. The expressions *audiovisual communications center* and *instructional communications center* are found both in city school systems and in universities. *Educational communications* is another broad and inclusive expression, and *audiovisual communications* refers mainly to all instructional media except print. In 1963, the DAVI Commission on Terminology defined *audiovisual communications* in an unrestricted sense as follows:

That branch of educational theory and practice concerned primarily with the design and use of messages which control the learning process. . . . Its practical goal is the efficient utilization of every method and medium of communication which can contribute toward developing the full potential of the learner.[31]

This definition also fits most admirably the term *educational communications*. Both expressions emphasize communications theory.

Multimedia and Cross Media. These terms are similar semantically. The Commission on Terminology has also defined these terms—considering them to have the same meaning—as follows:

Methodology based on the principle that a variety of audiovisual media and experiences correlated with other instructional materials overlap and reinforce the value of each other. Some of the material may be used to motivate interest; others, to communicate basic facts; still others to clear up misconceptions and deepen understanding.[32]

This concluding section of the chapter was not intended to serve as a glossary of terms in the entire book, nor was it intended to augment confusion. All of us should strive for clarity in the use of our terminology especially with those who are not in a position to have developed insight into our unique field problems.

In the next chapter we will move into a deeper involvement with the entire sweep of media-program development in order to orient ourselves to the need for growth toward administrative competence.

Problem-Solving Activities

1. Explore several references that tell the story of early use of audiovisual media in this country. State some of the major forces that contributed to the growth of the audiovisual-media movement.

2. List a few of the earliest citywide systems of audiovisual education with their inauguration dates. Give a few details relative to the city in your own state that was first with a citywide system. How many centralized school-system media programs are now operating with full-time directors in your state?

3. Do you believe that the general public is more or less ready than ever before to support an instructional media-service program? Why?

4. Skim through the listings of duties in the text and note the following: (a) Changes in terminology; (b) Differences in the lists in the degree to which duties have been generalized; (c) Several items common to all lists; (d) A few important areas in which you believe you ought to develop competence.

5. Consider the duties stated in the Operational Plan. Note that they are broad in character. Study the list and write down two additional duties (stated at the same level of breadth) not already included or implied.

6. Study the six broad principles for instructional media services and commit them to memory, change them into your own language, or mark your book to facilitate repeated reference to them in connection with other exercises and readings. Study the duties under each principle and in the light of new media developments or unique situations in your own locality add two or three new duties to those listed with each principle.

7. If your school superintendent called you for advice on the problem, what name for the director and the organization that was to serve as the centralized service headquarters would you advise him and his Board of Education to formally adopt? List three or four of the most popular choices in order of preference. What factors would enter into your decision? Do you know of any labels for the media field that differ from the terminology presented in this text?

8. Find out if an *Operational Plan for Instructional Media Services* has been written out and formally adopted in the city where you teach or would like to work in the future.

9. In the model of an operational plan formulated in this chapter, was the position of the media program director spelled out specifi-

---

[31] Donald P. Ely (ed.), *op. cit.*, p. 36.
[32] *Ibid.*, p. 44.

cally? What difference would it make if a new director of media services were employed and given the status of a full-time teacher to give system-wide media development leadership? What difference would it make if he were paid a salary equal to that of a school principal? Without a formal operational plan, is anyone's position, except by the implications of salary scale designation, made clear? Study the diagrams relating to administrative patterns in Figure 1-14 and draw up a set of conclusions that may prove to be invaluable to you in your personal administrative career.

References

"Audio-Visual Education in City School Systems," NEA *Research Bulletin*, Vol. 24, No. 4, 1946, pp. 131–170.

"Audio-Visual Education in Urban School Districts, 1953–54," NEA *Research Bulletin*, Vol. 33, No. 3, 1955, pp. 91–123.

Audio-Visual Materials of Instruction, 48th Yearbook of the National Society for the Study of Education, Part I (Chicago: University of Chicago Press, 1949).

Brown, James W. and John A. Moldstad, "Administration of Instructional Materials," *Review of Educational Research*, Vol. 32, April 1962, pp. 194–209.

Brown, James W. and Kenneth D. Norberg, *Administering Educational Media* (New York: McGraw-Hill, 1965).

Cohen, Samuel. "Audiovisual Instruction," *Audiovisual Instruction*, Vol. 10, No. 3, March 1965, pp. 196–99.

———. "The Import of the Wantagh Interviews and a Modest Proposal for Next Steps," *Audiovisual Instruction*, Vol. 9, No. 1, January 1964, pp. 61–63.

Dale, Edgar, Fannie W. Dunn, Charles F. Hoban, Jr., and Etta Schneider. *Motion Pictures in Education: A Summary of the Literature*, prepared under the auspices of the Committee on Motion Pictures in Education of the American Council on Education (New York: The H. W. Wilson Company, 1937). (Out of print.)

Elliott, Godfrey M. (ed.). *The Film and Educa-tion* (New York: The Philosophical Library, 1948).

Finn, James D. "Instructional Technology," *Audiovisual Instruction*, Vol. 10, No. 3, March 1965, pp. 192–194.

———. "Professionalizing the Audiovisual Field." *AV Communication Review*, Vol. 1, No. 1, Winter 1953, pp. 6–17.

Harcleroad, Fred and William Allen (eds.) *Audio-Visual Administration* (Dubuque, Iowa: Wm. C. Brown Company, 1951).

Kinder, James S. and F. Dean McClusky (eds.) *The Audiovisual Reader* (Dubuque, Iowa: Wm. C. Brown Company, 1954).

Lehman, Frederick M. "A Study of a Small Audiovisual Community." *Audiovisual Instruction*, Vol. 9, No. 1, January 1964, pp. 37–39.

Lindeman, LeRoy R. Administrator, Instructional Media Division, Utah State Board of Education, Salt Lake City, Utah. 1965.

Quigley, Martin, Jr. *Magic Shadows; The Story of the Origin of Motion Pictures* (Washington, D.C.: Georgetown University Press, 1948). (Out of print.)

Ramsaye, Terry. *A Million and One Nights* (New York: Simon and Schuster, 1926). (Out of print.)

Saettler, L. Paul. "Historical Overview of Audio-Visual Communications," *Audio-Visual Communication Review*, Vol. 2, No. 2, 1954, pp. 109–117.

———. "History of A-V Education in City School Systems," *Audio-Visual Communication Review*, Vol. 3, No. 2, 1955, pp. 109–118.

———. "Technological Legacy of Audio-Visual Communications," *Audio-Visual Communication Review*, Vol. 4, No. 4, 1956, pp. 279–290.

Schuller, Charles F. (ed.). *The School Administrator and His Audio-Visual Program* (Yearbook of the DAVI), Department of Audio-Visual Instruction (Washington, D.C.: National Education Association, 1954).

Torkelson, Gerald M. "Learning Resources," *Audiovisual Instruction*, Vol. 10, No. 3, March 1965, pp. 199–200.

Twyford, Loran C. "Educational Communications," *Audiovisual Instruction*, Vol. 10, No. 3, March 1965, pp. 194–195.

2

Growth Toward Administrative Competence

What are the differences between a highly competent media director and one who is of only mediocre caliber? Why do some people perform with outstanding effectiveness, seeming almost always to make correct decisions even in complex situations? Why do some individuals seem to be able to ask the right questions at the right time in their respective fields? Why can some be so confident in their own powers for action while others feel unsure of the outcomes of their efforts?

Such questions can be answered as the reader works through this book, but they are raised here to focus attention upon some dependable principles and insights that, as a part of his own personal complex of capacities, drives, and technical skills, will enable the media specialist to work toward effective service in the day-to-day problem-solving process. Therefore, in this chapter we suggest that the prospective media specialist examine as objectively as possible some of his weaknesses and strengths in his orientation to the broader aspects of activity in the area of administration. As prospective media specialists grow toward administrative competence we believe that they will have to keep pace with technological developments and also put forth a solid effort to deepen their insights about the process of education. One of the basic assumptions in this book is that the need for experience as a classroom organizer of learning experiences on a sustained professional basis has been fulfilled. We urge those who lack these insights and skills to seek the necessary experience at once. The reader ought to be sure to comprehend the nature of the administrative function, for he will then realize why this process is a crucial ingredient in the success of any large-scale media program, regardless of the level of operation—city, county, school building, university, or state department of education.

In this chapter, then, we hope to open up some avenues to or sources of administrative knowledge and skill. In the remaining chapters we shall deal with the basic technological problems of planning, organizing, and developing media services in the schools.

The Nature of the Administrative Process

The administrative function is concerned with two main aspects of a director's action, namely, leadership and management. We discussed earlier the media director's role as an executive and how being an executive is the same as carrying out the administrative functions—hence these terms are similar. *Leadership* is the creative activity that is concerned with assisting an organization to discover, identify, and define its basic and specific purposes, or to redefine and change its old ones. *Management*, on the other hand, is the process of implementing or carrying out plans, procedures, and purposes that have been predetermined. Hence, the execution of policy is management, but modifying or establishing policy is the leadership process in action.

Is it likely that a media program director will be successful as an administrator if he is not an expert in media technology? Should he be an educator also? Does it really matter one way or the other so long as he is a good administrator? We maintain that it does matter because without technological knowledge and skill in teaching, his action will be slowed down disastrously, he will be unable to evaluate plans and proposals in terms of educational impact, and his ability to anticipate difficulties and make a host of other judgments about such matters as cost and needed facilities for group and individual responses, is likely to be so undeveloped that serious errors are almost certain to be made. Thus we believe that the success of the school-system media program director will be maximum when administrative expertise is combined with technological and teaching skills and insights. But at this point we shall, for the purposes of discussion, deal with the administrative process as a separate system of activities.

Some Views of Administrative Activity

For some analytical views of administrative activity we would be well advised to refer to published statements of recognized theorists in the field. For it seems that these leaders themselves have no simple answers to such questions as: What are the characteristics of a good administrator? What kinds of activities are common to all administrators? How are good administrators produced? We ourselves continue to seek answers to these important questions. The reason for the difficulties generally met by leaders who discuss the subject of administra-

tion is best indicated by a statement appearing in the preface of one of the leading books[1] on the subject of preparing educational administrators. This statement is as follows:

There is, at this point in time, no clearly defined concept accepted by all administrators or preparatory institutions as one which describes accurately all administrative functions, nor which precisely predicts outcomes of specific administrative behavior; in short there is no commonly accepted, cohesive theory of administration.[2]

But in the same volume, as the writers analyze various problems in identifying common elements, there appears this quotation in a chapter by Norman J. Boynan:

James D. Thompson . . . has identified three major executive functions common to all organizations: organization-directing; organization-managing; supervision. The first concerns itself primarily with setting the lines of responsibility; the second primarily with setting the "climate" of the organization . . .

The supervisory function of the executive deals primarily with the governing and coordinating of human resources and includes the activities of (a) dealing with people, practices, motivation and performance; (b) establishing and coordinating work priorities, and (c) linking technical processes with the managerial functions.[3]

It is a fact that scanning the three preceding executive functions and the lists of duties in Chapter 1 we can make direct comparisons with the activities of a media program director as follows:

1. He sets lines of responsibility between himself and his central office staff, his media specialists, his clerical and technological staff, defining his more tenuous connections with other curriculum leaders and more remotely in a sensitive way to his publics at large. He elicits cooperation of all concerned in the group to define and agree on the purposes to be achieved.

[1] Donald J. Leu and Herbert C. Rudman (eds.), *Preparation Programs for School Administrators*, prepared for the Seventh UCEA Career Development Seminar at Michigan State University (East Lansing, Michigan: Office of Research and Publications, College of Education, MSU, 1963), p. 154.

[2] *Ibid.*, p. ix.

[3] *Ibid.*, pp. 13–14, Chapter 1, "Common and Specialized Learnings for Administrators and Supervisors: Some Problems and Issues," by Norman J. Boynan.

2. As an organization-manager, our media program director carries out pre-determined policy and is concerned with the establishment of "climate" in which people work effectively with a feeling of satisfaction. Chester I. Barnard[4] of business philosophy fame distinguished between *effective* and *efficient*. *Effective*, he said, meant reaching a specified objective, and *efficient* meant reaching an objective in such a way as to leave along the trail of action a net surplus of satisfaction for all concerned.

3. As a supervisor the media program director utilizes technological knowledge and skill in a major way in setting up and eliciting recommended practices from film distribution to self-instruction systems. He motivates his own staff and all other school personnel involved, encourages adequate quality control of input and output of human resources, and sets up control arrangements for all media equipment in all learning situations, for both staff and students. As a supervisor he must also set up, with the advice of his staff consultants and/or representatives, the necessary work priorities and then check the quality of workmanship. Without technical understanding, judgments of staff workmanship are practically impossible to make.

Thus we see in the functions previously quoted a general applicability to the media director's activity. But these activities are misleading in their oversimplification. To paint a more realistic picture we shall turn to some of the difficult problems faced by school-system media program directors everywhere.

Some Administrative Problems. This list of problems is presented in reference to the duties stated in Chapter 1, and to the views of administration just expressed. The list is not meant to be inclusive. Instead, it is representative of the kinds of problems that call for creative administrative action. A general commentary follows the list.

1. Persuade the superintendent of schools to inaugurate a system-wide teacher-preparation of media program with teacher workrooms and supplies located in each school building.

Some likely subsidiary problems: (a) Elicit

---

[4] C. I. Barnard, *Functions of the Executive* (Cambridge, Mass.: Harvard University Press, 1950), pp. 19–20.

support by teachers and school principals. (b) Prepare proposals and plans. (c) Design and prepare a media supported presentation before the Board of Education. (d) Figure the annual and long-range costs. (e) Identify needs for and contributions of the program. (f) Persuade the superintendent to exert his decision-making power through the Board of Education.

2. Develop and put into operation a new arrangement of equipment and materials storage as a part of a new shipping and receiving system at the instructional materials center.

3. Inaugurate a plan for the selection and purchase of media for the entire school system, based on panels of cooperating teachers within subject-matter areas who will serve as evaluators.

4. Write the job specifications for a new technical position for each of five large elementary schools, employ the men, assign them to schools, having established the lines of responsibility between the school-building media co-ordinators and the school principals and teachers.

5. Plan and formulate policies for recommendation to superintendent for the loan of media equipment to local community organizations for their own programing purposes.

6. Plan and carry out a series of meetings with school-building media coordinators to train them to conduct workshop meetings for all teachers in their respective schools for the preparation of overlay transparencies and 2×2 inch color slides.

7. Plan and write a series of monthly bulletins regarding teacher participation in listening-response pilot programs just inaugurated.

8. Carry out a citywide school survey among teachers, through the various school principals, to ascertain status of teacher interests and skills with media utilization.

9. Appoint a series of committees and their chairmen through the superintendent of schools to undertake the planning of operations research programs in testing a new teaching system for science laboratories.

10. Serve as a member of a team of curriculum planners for implementing a change in the school program for teaching mathematics.

11. Prepare with the advice of staff assistants and school-building personnel, a five-year budget for upgrading the school system media program, and get the superintendent to propose this plan for schoolboard action.

12. Design, as a member of a three-city, proposal-writing task force, a cooperative plan for inaugurating an instructional CCTV program to be financed by state and federal grants.

13. Devise and inaugurate with the help of a teacher-principal, citywide steering committee, a plan for all teachers of twelfth grade social studies to make use of the basal list of motion pictures procured for the purpose.

14. Analyze the work assignment schedule for all central-staff media workers and sketch out for duplication purposes the lines of responsibility and assignments for each individual.

Commentary on Administrative Duties. The list of problems involving administration may seem to the reader to be needlessly long, but actually it may be too short. The list points up the almost obvious fact that not a single problem mentioned is purely administrative in nature. Without technological insight, not one of these problems could have been solved without bungling. This conclusion is likely to be abundantly clear as each of the problems in succeeding chapters is opened up for analysis. In fact the media program director's administrative tasks are complicated by not one but two technologies, namely, audiovisual media and teaching. Both of these technologies are enmeshed in leadership and management problem-solving activity. We therefore are ready to state several postulates regarding our view of administrative competence.

1. The more a media program director knows about media and teaching technologies the greater will be his success as a media program administrator.

2. The more a technologically oriented media–program director knows about and is sensitive to the administrative process, the more successful he will be in his basic mission.

3. The administrative process is a system of problem-solving activities that facilitates control and achievement of an organization's purposes through any given combination of technologies.

The would-be media program administrator must work toward competence in this aspect of his total activity principally by learning how to work with and through people. He will be continually faced with problem situations in which he works as a coordinate member of a team. Along other lines of responsibility he must analyze thoroughly what specific actions have to be carried out and on what time schedules. In these cases he has to make assignments personally and must check on the way these assignments are being carried out. It is surprising to realize how many individuals, professional and otherwise, believe that all there is to the business of administration is laying out the jobs, getting every possible job handed out to someone else to be done on schedule. The writer has actually been praised for being a good administrator simply because he has made certain job assignments or has remembered, for example, to pay a guest speaker on time. This is a matter of scheduling specific work to be completed and then checking to see that the work was done in accordance with the stated specifications.

In the media field, however, and in other fields as well, even simple duty assignments may not be purely administrative at all. For example, where does technological judgment apply in the simple following request: "Harry, will you handle the projection assignment for the superintendent this afternoon at the board meeting?" Do technology judgments enter in to complicate administrative activity in regard to Harry's personality problems? No. In regard to Harry's wearing the right clothes? No. In regard to Harry's politeness to board members? No. In regard to checking on Harry's decisions about choice of equipment, whether or not it needs adjustment, where it should be located, what basic room conditions have to be changed? Yes!

Broad experience with people and technology, being able to make observations, possessing detailed information about personnel assignments within the organization, and being able to use such information to do one critical job, namely, anticipate difficulties likely to be met under a host of special circumstances, point the way in part to improved administrative decisions. Much more may be needed.

If we assume that we are going to develop the required competence in technological and teaching skills, or have them already, then where else do we turn for growth toward administrative competence? Will it come with job experience? Is it compounded by a happy combination of courses, lectures, degrees, and good wishes?

Formal Preparation of Educational Administrators

Shall we send the prospective educational media director off to school again to take courses in a number of related fields, to study intensively the theory of administration, and then cap the program by explaining how to organize and administer the various technological phases of media services? This just may have to be done.

A vast amount of consideration has been given to the problem of preparing educational administrators, and it may be that planners and researchers in this field will develop programs of a formal nature that will provide the core of needed content as a basis for competence. As a means of checking into such plans let us turn to two quotations. One of these is specifically in relation to the preparation of supervisors, and, as we have seen in the preceding pages, the process of supervision is included as one of the phases of the administrative process. The other maps out the guidelines of a formal two-year professional program. Both of the quotations are of value at this point as a means of focusing attention on those elements which leaders in the field of educational administration believe are significant.

Competence of Supervisors. In the volume we have frequently referred to in our discussion of administrative competence, John A. Ramseyer made this succinct summary statement relative to the competence of supervisory personnel:

If supervisors are to help teachers teach, administrators make arrangements which best facilitate teaching and learning, and communities provide a climate in which learning is enhanced, they should have learned how to learn and how to help others learn. Both scholars and master teachers, administrators derive their competence from their understanding of the disciplines they experienced in mastering a field of knowledge; the rigor of obtaining a broad and liberal education in the context of a changing culture; an understanding of processes of human growth, development and learning; an understanding of the role of the school in the social order; an understanding of the organizational structure of the school, an understanding of, and skill in, the use of processes of curriculum change; skill in communication and human relationships; an under-

standing of, and skill in, methods of analysis, evaluation, and research.[5]

Because we have already postulated the great need for teaching experience, we see in the knowledge and skill areas identified so much of value for the instructional media program administrator. In the list presented, we see not a single entry that would not have a strong bearing on the day-to-day problems of a competent media administrator and supervisor.

But we shall turn next to a more comprehensive plan to highlight other broad preparational areas of rich potential.

Two-Year Plan for Preparing School Administrators

Jack Culbertson in a comprehensive plan for the preparation of school administrators suggested the following two-year program of which excerpts are quoted here:

The thesis is advanced here that from one-fourth to one-third of the content in a two-year preparatory program should be devoted to developing competence in the process aspects of administration.
. . . Examples of content pertinent to these processes follow:

Decision-making. Included would be concepts and theories pertinent to group, individual and organizational decision-making; the relationships of basic research, operations research and computer technology to decision-making would be examined, as would value dilemmas which administrators face.

Communication. Theories of one-way, small group, and organizational communication would be studied. Special consideration would be given to such matters as opinion change, mass communication, informal networks, and communication in large bureaucracies. Value issues faced by administrators would also be examined.

Change. The dynamics of change would be examined with reference to individuals, groups, organizations, and communities. Specific attention would be given to such matters as barriers to change, factors facilitating change, conflict in change, and the role of leadership in change.

Morale. Bases of personnel satisfaction in the context of organizations would be examined. Special consideration would be given to motivation, perception, interpersonal relations, value infusion, organizational loyalty and related matters.
. . . from one-third to one-half of the content in programs would be organized to help administra-

[5] Leu and Rudman, *op. cit.*, p. 162, Chapter IX, "Supervisory Personnel," by John A. Ramseyer.

tors be more competent in purpose setting and policy making. This would mean that blocks of content distributed in such classifications as those that follow would be appropriate:

Philosophical concepts. Concepts which illuminate educational opportunity and excellence would be assessed. Literary and philosophical works would be selected to provide administrators-to-be opportunities to clarify their own definitions of the "good" life, the "good" society, and the "good" education.

Economic trends. Such subjects as those that follow would be assessed in order to discover important implications for defining and attaining educational excellence and opportunity: (1) the economics of education both in this country and in developing countries, (2) trends in automation and technology and their effect upon the vocations and the professions, (3) human and natural resources in relation to future societal needs, and (4) the long-range economic implications of the arms and space race.

Political trends. The following matters, among others, would be carefully examined to discover significant implications for defining and attaining educational excellence and opportunity: (a) changing relationships of state, local and federal government, (b) governmental structures of metropolitan communities and their relationship to rural governments, (c) church and state relationships, (d) governmental responsibilities for health and welfare, (e) the impact of the industrial-military complex upon government, and (f) the political struggle between Russia and Western countries.

Sociological trends. A mastery of basic sociological concepts would be sought and such matters as the following would be given careful consideration in order to develop explicit implications for defining and attaining educational excellence and opportunity: (a) population trends with special consideration for (1) the mobility of minority groups, (2) the mobility of those in different social classes, and (3) distribution of people in rural, suburban and urban areas as well as distribution in different age groups; (b) health, housing, vocational, and educational opportunities for members of different ages, races, and social classes; (c) the impact of science and specialization on society, and (d) trends in leisure and recreation patterns.

. . . Finally, the thesis as advanced from one-fourth to one-third of the content in two-year preparatory programs should be of a technical nature. All school administrators should have a basic grounding in all of the major technical concepts . . .[6]

[6] Leu and Rudman, *op. cit.*, pp. 54–57, Chapter III, "Common and Specialized Content in the Preparation of Administrators," by Jack Culberton. (By major technical concepts, Dr. Culberton refers to such areas as business management, finance, housing, law, and so on.)

Such a program has great apparent value for the would-be media program director especially at the large school district level and higher in the sense of county, university, and state organization structures. We pose the serious question, "Just where would the technical aspects of administration be dealt with in sufficient depth in present-day preparation programs for media program directors?" We are presently utilizing specific courses in many instances in School Finance, School Law, School Plant, and School Personnel Policies, and giving increasing emphasis to need for work in behavioral science departments of Psychology, Sociology, Anthropology, and Political Science. We are almost universally studying the technical phases of administering media-service programs as a separate and concentrated course.

Until more appropriate programs are developed it would seem reasonable to encourage those who are preparing for administrative positions in the media program field to move toward such broad program experiences or even selected aspects of them where they are offered as valid means of broadening their understanding and skill. As we have mentioned, the problem of preparation is being studied, but at this time we have only suggested guidelines. It remains for us to push deeper into the study of our own needs and propose effective and workable plans in our own field of endeavor.

We have, however, been keenly aware of the need to study the process of change, knowing well that in order to make changes at an optimum tempo in the face of urgent needs, we ought to study the process itself as a source of guidance. We therefore present at this point a brief treatment of this important aspect of the media program director's work as another important avenue to administrative competence.

The Media Program Director and Change

Process of Implementing Change

This book can do little more than indicate to the would-be media program director and to the media specialist working in any specific medium, be it transparency or television, the nature of the problem of making educational changes. In general, media professionals work only with people who have changed or are in the process of changing over to new patterns of action. We say we are working on in-service education processes, which is to say that if we are successful, we then harvest a new crop of media users. Getting people to learn new ideas, getting people to put old ideas to work with new tools, getting people to use commonly available devices and instruments in entirely new ways and in new configurations is the process of change in action. Fortunately there is such a thing as an innovating personality. Some people change easily, but others resist change solidly. It would seem that teachers themselves would be the very ones to understand this process better than others, since to learn means to make a new response, and hopefully to want to make good use of a given valuable response again and again in the future. But human nature being what it is, we know that some teachers undergo change slowly indeed. Teachers, however, are not by any means unique in this respect. School superintendents and members of boards of education seem also to be slow at the process, and media program directors like ourselves seem to be traveling along paths of change at a snail's pace. So the conclusion is we ought to agree to devote a part of our energies to the study of change, making good use of the growing body of literature. Researchers in this field have pointed out some promising routes to insight.

In providing help to media program personnel working at the professional level we ought to consider answers to the following questions regarding the process of change as it is likely to be carried on in our schools and by school people: Who makes changes in the schools? What kinds of changes do the various categories of people make? What kinds of forces are likely to accelerate change? What kinds of action can and should the instructional media program director take in implementing change? We shall now answer these questions in sufficient detail to make it clear that the continuing study of the change process is a vital necessity.

People Who Make Educational Changes

Who Makes Changes in the Schools? As we answer this question we ought to keep in mind

the administrative relationship of the media program director to other administrators, specifically the superintendent of schools and the school principal. These administrators are the so-called decision makers. Now let us move the classroom teacher into full view as the one who has a unique responsibility for the activities that go on in most classrooms, both as to the quality and quantity. These are the people who ultimately make the changes. The superintendent of schools is the decision maker for the school district, ordering, in effect, changes to be carried out, through the various school principals, and down in category and level to the classroom teacher who has a unique kind of autonomy, as we have said before. Can any one of the ten school principals, for example, make a decision to inaugurate a new method for teaching spelling by the use of taped instructions and headsets in 100-pupil learning spaces in his own school? Of course, if he can get his teachers to do it. Can the same principal order the other nine principals to try it out? Of course not. Can the superintendent in effect order the changeover for the entire school system? Of course. (Hoping that good *change processes* have been utilized.) Apart from the principal and superintendent, can an innovating teacher decide to change from the lecture method to a rotating-activity schedule involving taped instruction and work sheets for guiding pupil responses? Yes. But can this teacher demand that other teachers in her building carry out the same innovation? Of course not. We thus readily see that the superintendent of schools, the school principals, and teachers are cast in vastly different roles for change, and because of his usual position in the administrative hierarchy, the media program leader cannot initiate change, but instead acts to influence others to make such changes as are within their areas of jurisdiction.

In reporting on his study of the dynamics of instructional change in the elementary and secondary schools of New York State, conducted in 1961 for the Department of Education, Henry M. Brickell stated a number of conclusions that have been widely quoted and discussed. We now turn to his statements as a link between the two questions we are answering about what people make changes, and what changes these various categories of people make. Brickell put it this way:

New types of instructional programs are introduced by administrators. Contrary to general
opinion, teachers are not change agents for instructional innovations of major scope. *Implication:*
To disseminate new types of instructional programs,
it will be necessary to convince administrators of their
value. . . .

Instructional changes which call for significant
new ways of using professional talent, drawing upon
instructional resources, allocating physical facilities,
scheduling instructional time or altering physical
space—*rearrangements of the structural elements of*
the institution—depend almost exclusively upon
administrative initiative. Even in the best of circumstances for the expression of new ideas—in schools
where administrative authority is exercised with a
light hand and faculty prerogative is strong—
teachers seldom suggest distinctly new types of
working patterns for themselves. . . .

Classroom teachers can make only three types of
instructional change in the absence of administrative initiative: (1) change in classroom practice,
(2) relocation of existing curriculum content, and
(3) introduction of single special courses at the high
school level. *Implications:* (1) *Classroom teachers*
cannot be expected to introduce new types of in-
structional programs without administrative attention
and (2) *In-service courses designed for individual*
teachers rather than for entire departments or faculties
(that is, courses designed to improve the teacher
rather than to change the program) should be limited
to matters which can be accomplished in one of the
three ways indicated above.[7]

These statements by Brickell not only point
out clearly the categories of people that make
changes, but they indicate the nature and scope
of the changes that these innovators create and
implement. We now turn to a discussion of the
nature of the changes that can be made.

Kinds of Educational Changes
People Make

What Changes do the Various Categories of
People Make? In the examples cited in the
preceding discussion we have indicated that
the changes made by a superintendent and a
school principal are different in scope, and
these changes differ widely from the changes
that can be introduced by the teacher. Changes

[7] Henry M. Brickell, *Organizing New York State for*
Educational Change (Albany, New York: University of
the State of New York, State Education Department,
1961), pp. 22–24.

made by all three categories of individuals are
related to their administrative lines of responsibility. The teacher is responsible to his or her
principal and can, as has been pointed out, make
procedural modifications, relocate content in
the curriculum, and even undertake to teach
a new course, assuming a permissive climate.
The principal would, as an administrator
responsible to his superintendent, make changes
in his own school along the lines of procedural
changes, new courses, new presentational
methods, and pilot programs of wide diversity,
again assuming a permissive climate at the
administrative level above him. Even without
such permissiveness, the principal being a key
person in the educational structure, may undertake so far as his school is concerned, drastic
changes, provided that he does not incur
serious opposition from his own public—the
parents of his pupils. The superintendent on the
other hand, may undertake broad and sweeping
changes of major proportions, provided that
the board of education will legislate operational
plans, or simply approve his recommendations
even in broad outline form. By the same token,
no major changes can be carried out without
his decision to give the "go ahead" sign.

We raise again the questions: "Where does
the media program administrator fit into this
change process? What changes can he make?"
He can order no changes for the principal to
carry out, no major system-wide procedural
changes not approved by the superintendent or
other chief executive officer. However, he can
create changes in his own procedure as would
a teacher in her own classroom; also, as a
principal within his own staff organization
where individuals responsible to him are carrying out services and duties already assigned;
and, he can influence other coordinate as well
as higher-level administrators to support and
implement his proposals. He cannot, therefore,
undertake changes that require new policy
formulations, new appropriations, formulate
new objectives and means for achieving them.
He cannot order changes to be made outside of
established policy. How obvious it is then that
the media director recognize that he is truly an
agent of change, an implementor of ideas that
he creates and surrenders to others for final
disposition.

Thus innovators work at different levels of

action in accomplishing change. Knowing this we can stress the importance of knowing what the nature is of forces that have a strong impact on the direction and tempo of change. This question is next in line for discussion.

Forces That Facilitate Change in Schools

What Kinds of Forces are Likely to Accelerate Change in the Schools? The forces that tend to facilitate change are many and complex, and no claim is put forth that this discussion is erudite and comprehensive. Fortunately we have a growing body of literature, and conclusions by mature thinkers in the field are available for guidance. There seems of course to be agreement on the conclusion that schools and their public boards of education and the people employed by them tend to remain stable. We shall identify a few of the major forces that facilitate change and then describe and support them briefly.

FORCE 1. Special events of major importance of national scope and impact, such as massive legislated financial support, outbreak of war, major discoveries, impending disaster, threats, or serious accidents and the like, tend to shock people into innovative action. Such events are generally external to the school system.

In cases like these, boards of education may turn their attention to the need for more and improved educational programs, triggering action by key administrators. Brickell startled many by his revelation that:

The rate of instructional innovation in New York State public elementary and secondary schools *more than doubled within 15 months* after the firing of the Soviet Sputnik I on October 4, 1957. Changes swept not only foreign languages, mathematics and science—which led the field by tripling their rate of change—but all other subjects, *non-academic as well as academic.*[8]

With reference to action by boards of education it is important to take note of Brickell's additional comment:

The board of education in most communities is not a strong agent in determining the pace of educational innovation, but its influence is decisive when exerted.

[8] *Ibid.*, p. 18.

Implication: New programs must be disseminated in a manner which will not arouse the opposition of boards of education.[9]

Obviously if boards make demands for changes, key administrators had better act accordingly, and if key administrators desire to innovate, boards had better not be in a mood to oppose.

FORCE 2. People with innovating personalities facilitate change. We will discuss the influence of an innovating personality in relation to administrative competence in the next main section of this chapter. For the present we ought to point out the fact that it is responsive people, for one reason or another, who influence change. People are also stable in this regard, hence it takes people with inquiring minds at work in problem-solving capacities who are striving for betterment, who are alert, imaginative, and critical, to suggest new patterns of procedure.

In the book *Innovation in Education*, of which he was the editor, Matthew B. Miles had this to say in his statement of generalizations:

Official authority aside for the moment, it has been asserted that strong, benevolent persons often find themselves in an important and central role in utopian change efforts. . . . In addition, intelligence and verbal ability seem important . . . the innovator also appears to be less bound by local group norms, more individualistic and creative. . . . Intelligence and creativity have been suggested not to be enough, however. When the innovator must persuade or enlist the support of others, and overcome resistance, authenticity . . . and enthusiasm for the innovative enterprise . . . also seem to be important.[10]

FORCE 3. General favorable features of society may be instrumental in speeding up change. On the one hand, we find again and again in the literature the emphasis on stability as a characteristic of the public and of the schools; and on the other, we know the nature of technological development and the tempo of change as a characteristic of twentieth-century society in general. There is in fact a plexus of forces that exerts stress on an organization to change, and stress at the same time to remain stable. This plexus is a system of

[9] *Ibid.*, p. 21.
[10] Reprinted with the permission of the publisher from Matthew B. Miles (ed.), *Innovation in Education* (New York: Teachers College Press, 1964), p. 642.

forces external to any given school system or other educational agency. In addition, as will be discussed a little later, a plexus of forces also exerting stress for change is located inside the organization. We shall therefore deal here with some of the forces at work in an organization's external environment.

Again, when reporting his study of educational change in New York State schools, Brickell explains the role of the public as follows:

Most parents do not know enough about educational methodology to favor or to oppose specific innovations. Parents and the public seem to exert their influence by creating a general climate of interest—or the lack of it—in school affairs rather than by singling out and endorsing particular approaches used in other school systems. However, if for some reason the public develops a lively interest in a new type of program—foreign languages in the elementary school, for example—that program is likely to appear in the local classrooms. In the same way, if parents decide to oppose a new program for any reason, it is difficult if not impossible to make it succeed.[11]

We see in this quotation the reference to a favorable general climate on the part of the public, and this is the aspect of change facilitation that we are holding in focus for the time being. Miles refers to several of the features of American society in connection with acceleration of change rates as follows:

Some present features of American society are said to be accelerating educational change rates. These include widespread social change; affluence and the resultant need for intellectually sophisticated manpower; the growth of cultural and aesthetic activities; growth in the rate of production of knowledge; and increases in information-handling and information retrieval capacity. . . . In addition, it seems very likely that the mass media influence the processes and rate of educational innovation by stimulating the desire for change, aiding communication between educational decision-makers and the larger society, and serving occasionally as a kind of feedback device on the public's attitudes toward particular innovative efforts.[12]

As laymen generally come to understand and develop strong commitments to universal and continuous educational programs, and as they come to associate the use of modern, effective, technological devices and processes in carrying on their own work and even in their own leisure-time activities, they will then be a part of a developing climate favorable to change.

FORCE 4. Situations inside an organization often precipitate change. Earlier discussions are appropriate for the description of this particular and major force for educational change. We can obviously include both administrative and classroom teacher personnel within the framework of situations within the organization to promote change, some of minor nature, others major, sweeping, and system-wide in scope. However, we shall emphasize the major force for change identified as administrative initiative in the next item. We may therefore include for brief description here a few other conditions within an organization that have a likely bearing on the tempo of change. In his discussion of internal pressures for change, Miles states the following generalizations based on reported case studies:

Though, as we have seen, most change initiations come from external sources, there are also sources internal to the target system. Sheer size and growth of a system tend to force adaptive changes and increased concern for innovation. . . . Discrepancies between ideals and existing practice . . . and conflict among subsystems . . . over the allocation of scarce personnel, money, or time . . . are also likely precursors of change.

Most organizational analysis has stressed the "return to equilibrium" following a disturbing stimulus. However, it is also entirely possible that there may be organizational analogues of the wish for change, growth, and development in the individual. . . . Organizations, like individuals, may actively seek the excitement and drive of change for its own sake, rather than solely wishing to return to a familiar equilibrium.[13]

FORCE 5. Administrative initiative is the key to an increased tempo of change. We have already shown the importance of this force in previous discussions. In adding to his earlier statement relative to the importance of the administrator in initiating changes of major scope, Brickell[14] pointed out that, "An administrator is powerful because he can marshall the

---

[11] Brickell, *op. cit.*, pp. 20–21.
[12] Miles, *op. cit.*, p. 645.

[13] *Ibid.*, pp. 645–646. (Refer to the Miles volume for reference to specific studies.)
[14] Brickell, *op. cit.*, p. 23.

necessary authority—if not the necessary leadership—to precipitate a decision."

It is obvious that such forces for change as have been here discussed operate in balance as interlinked systems. The forces cut across each other in complex ways, and the stresses exerted inside or outside the organization, in which changes are being or need to be implemented, will have a net positive or negative influence. It is in this framework of reference that we turn for the answer to the question regarding the kinds of action that the educational media program administrator may and ought to take.

Media Program Directors As Change Agents

What Kinds of Action Can and Should Media Program Directors Take in Implementing Change in Their Schools? In the previous sections we have made statements describing school-system situations and presented succinct excerpts from authoritative writers. These statements certainly provide valuable guidelines on which to predict the value of well-defined action toward change by media specialists. The meaning of several terms, found in the quotations, particularly *target system* and *change agent* may need some clarification, and consequently we turn to Lippitt, Watson, and Wesley for a few helpful explanations:

. . . the *planned change* . . . originates in a decision to make a deliberate effort to improve the system and to obtain the help of an outside agent in making this improvement. We call this outside agent a *change agent*. The decision to make a change may be made by the system itself, after experiencing pain (malfunctioning) or discovering the possibility of improvement, or by an outside change agent who observes the need for change in a particular system and takes the initiative in establishing a helping relationship with that system. . . .

We call all of these helpers, no matter what kind of system they normally work with, change agents. Even when assistance is given by a team of helpers, each contributing a different skill, we shall call the team a change agent.

We shall call the specific system—person or group—that is being helped the *client system*.[15]

We need but point out that the term *target system* is a synonym for *client system*, and as was indicated we need to take special note of the fact that *client system* refers to a group or community. If we note that the change agent is our media program administrator, and that the client or target system is generally in our case the school and its public or publics, we can then proceed to a discussion of kinds of action that can or should be taken by the media program directors and specialists. Perhaps also we should note that these people are not outside professionals, but generally inside the organization and hence are in a good position to understand the special internal and external forces at work in the situation. Naturally, the preceding quotation refers to generalized situations in which the change agents are employed for specific accomplishments from sources of supply outside of the client system.

The reader will at this point need to review the answers to preceding questions with reference to: What people make changes? What changes can they make? What forces speed up change? We shall ourselves draw upon the meanings presented in them. We shall proceed first to list two levels of action that seem to be demanded of the media program director:

1. Discover educational needs, problems, that teachers face in day-to-day teaching activity, by means of surveys, observations, and reports. Bring research findings, technical knowledge, and teaching skill to focus on evaluation, need, and scope of change.

Write up an announcement for all coordinate and chief administrators and for all teachers involved, obtain approval for action from the school principal or principals, and through meetings and bulletins prepare teachers to try the new techniques. Check personally on progress or have other staff members help on a special, continuing fashion.

2. Identify special needs of larger scope, map out a proposed plan of action in broad outline form and after conferences with the chief administrator, prepare a proposal in considerable detail, for presentation to the board of education. (From this point the board assigns topics to study groups for contacts with staff, receives continuing reports, finally refers the proposal to the school administrative and curriculum

15 Ronald Lippitt, Jeanne Watson, and Bruce Westley, *The Dynamics of Planned Change* (New York: Harcourt, Brace and World, 1958), pp. 10–12. The authors of this noteworthy work report the following about the term *change agent*. "The term was adopted by the National Training Laboratory staff in 1947 to facilitate discussions among heterogeneous groups of professional helpers. It is a term which has since proved very useful."

council for study and possible acceptance or rejection.) Throughout the processing and adoption procedures, advise committee and council, and later if the innovation is adopted, participate in in-service education procedures and set up assistance programs on a pilot or system-wide basis.

It can be readily seen that in these two patterns for implementing change we see action to discover needs that can be met by innovation on the part of specific teachers, very possibly without administrator decisions, or with only an enabling climate of permissiveness. Such changes would be largely confined to the area of using old media in new ways, or along the lines of using new equipment units to present established content, both areas of action being under the full and unique control of volunteering teachers. In the other case, the superintendent and the board must be consulted during the early planning stages. Hence the media program director acts as a change agent to point out technology's role in meeting educational objectives in a new and more effective way, but this time on a system-wide basis. Such an example may be the reorganization of pupils in all fifth-grade social studies classes into larger groups for instruction by closed-circuit television. The work of the original planning and proposal writing by the media director in consideration of new staff, equipment, facilities, in-service education, is of course extensive.

Before we move to another listing of more specific practices of change agents, specifically the media program change agent (as an administrator), we should take note of the more general phases of change as classified by the authors previously quoted:

Phase 1: The client system discovers the need for help, sometimes with stimulation by the change agent.

Phase 2: The helping relationship is established and defined.

Phase 3: The change is identified and clarified.

Phase 4: Alternative possibilities for change are examined; change goals or intentions are established.

Phase 5: Change efforts in the "reality situation" are attempted.

Phase 6: Change is generalized and stabilized.

Phase 7: The helping relationship ends or a different type of continuing relationship is defined.[16]

16 *Ibid.*, p. 123.

These phases of change are indicative of the variety of action that change agents have to take as generally conceived. We see readily how the phases listed apply to specific situations such as school systems, and more specifically to system-wide innovations where unconventional media play important roles, such as in teaching by closed-circuit television, providing new preparation of media services in each school building, or the use of a combination of media in a self-instruction, teaching system for laboratory work in all biology classes, to mention just a few.

We should not miss one of the main points in this presentation, namely, that once key administrators have, either alone or at the suggestion of a media program director, decided upon any given change in the field of instructional technology, the media director then becomes the principal change agent, or shall we say has the opportunity to play this important role. In fact, he and his whole staff of specialists may become a team, still referred to in this discussion as the *change agent*. Looking at the key change agent as a person let us consider the importance of the image that the organization has of this change agent. We turn again to Lippitt, Watson, and Wesley for another general statement that has obvious application to our specific discussion:

... in cases where the potential change agent has himself taken the initiative to stimulate a need for help, the client system must try to assess the validity of the change agent's diagnoses and the expedience of his recommendations.

One of the most crucial features ... is the way in which the client system ... forms its early conceptions of the change agent, particularly in respect to estimates of his ability to give help, his inferred motives, and his attributed friendliness or unfriendliness. When a change agent offers to help in solving a problem which involves labor-management relations, he may be sure that the president of the company and the president of the union are both very much concerned to discover and evaluate his personal attitudes toward labor and management....

Often the client system seems to be seeking assurance that the potential change agent is different enough from the client system to be a real expert and yet enough like it to be thoroughly understandable and approachable. What the client system really wants is two change agents in one. It wants an agent who will identify himself with the client system's problems and sympathize with the system's needs and values, but who will at the same time be neutral enough to take a genuinely objective and different view of the system's predicament.[17]

We insist that both as an administrator and educator in general, and as an instructional technology specialist, our media program director needs to be radiating a favorable image. We of course do not pour this man from a mold and mass-produce him. We recognize the need for unique and diverse capacities and for individualistic tendencies, but we suggest the great need for adequate insights and skills in working with individuals and groups. We shall deal with this aspect of his work again under the major topic of in-service education in a later chapter.

It has been pointed out that the media program director becomes a change agent after initiating decisions have been made and that he may have suggested some of these innovations for initiation, while other decisions may have been initiated by others who now need his help in significant ways. A curriculum director, for example, because of a decision to make a major change, may himself become a change agent requiring technological assistance of the media specialist as a part of the team of people who are implementing the change. An example may be the inauguration of a new mathematics program in the entire school system that requires the use of taped instruction and overhead projection in both large- and small-group situations. Bearing these situations in mind we now turn to a brief description of some specific kinds of action that the instructional technology change agent may need to take.

Enabling Action

1. Write reports for key decision-making personnel describing need for staff and increased budget allotments in the light of the proposed innovation and, as needed, compete vigorously with other departments for existing resources at the decision-making level.

2. Organize and deploy existing personnel into situations where help can be given to teachers who are implementing changes.

3. Conduct meetings and issue bulletins establishing a permissive climate for innovation.

Evaluative Action

1. Through reading and discussion, keep

abreast of environmental climates for change, paying particular attention to technological applications in home, industrial, health, and recreational situations.

2. Prepare in written form, priority time schedules for introduction of change efforts.

3. Collect data based on accurate observations of the need for educational changes.

Energizing Change

1. Organize and conduct special meetings to stimulate teachers to make changes within their own areas of jurisdiction.

2. Prepare and distribute stimulating bulletins to school principals to facilitate their decisions concerning technological changes under their jurisdiction.

3. Write proposals and operational plans for chief administrative officers for submission to governing boards, or for their own decision-making processes.

4. Identify people who seem to exhibit innovating personalities or who have a history of innovations behind them.

5. Formulate new practices for meeting educational needs and objectives.

Readiness for Change Action

1. Prepare public-relations programs in all forms to develop readiness for change action in accordance with need.

2. Identify successful instructional programs operating in situations similar to those in the local organization.

3. Plan and carry out local demonstrations of the use of recommended innovations under close-to-normal circumstances.[18]

4. Arrange visits for key administrators and others to observe innovations being considered as they are underway in other schools.

Implementing Change

1. Prepare step-by-step implementation procedures for staff including the purchase of new equipment, production of materials and teaching guides, in-service meetings for teaching new practices, employment of additional staff as needed, initial starting dates, and the assignment of staff assistants to aid day-by-day operation of the innovation.

2. Execute the detailed plans previously

[17] *Ibid.*, p. 134.

[18] See Brickell, *op. cit.*, pp. 26–29, for details on items 3 and 4.

made, approved, and agreed to by staff study committees, advisory council, and steering committee.

3. Provide—and arrange for other key personnel to do likewise—praise for participation, full recognition for creative effort, and suitable attention from sources outside the local organization.[19]

4. Conduct and/or assist others to do it, evaluation activities making comparisons that are based on optimum control of variables operating in new as well as conventional situations.[20]

5. Plan and/or prepare, or organize this activity by others, adequate public-relations releases giving adequate coverage to innovation progress.

6. Adjust services to optimum levels to stabilize the innovation, that is by staff, periodically checking on progress, and maintaining sources of supply.

The listing of possible and probable activities to be carried on by a change agent is by no means exhaustive, nor is it meant to serve as a model. The change agent is a creative problem solver, and as such he works out in the light of, to borrow the term, his client or target system, an optimum plan for carrying on the process of change. It can be readily seen that each innovation may demand a different set or system of activities. It can also be observed that administrative activity is to be seen in every aspect of the change agent's work.

In the next section the reader will find another avenue toward growth in administrative competence because there we present a description of several personal values that will hopefully provide focus and enrichment for the entire administrative process.

Personal Values and Administrative Focus

The development of a comprehensive index of personal values to give direction and focus to the entire process of administration is beyond the scope of this book, but it seems obvious

that the unique experiences of different administrators with varying degrees of responsibility are, or could be, a significant source of guidance for the neophyte. We hope the reader will be persuaded to consider our selection of values for administrative focus and to bring his own beliefs and value systems under scrutiny as well. The list could be almost endless and the one presented seems unusually brief. We believe, however, that leadership and management will be inestimably enriched if these values are developed and applied.

Fortunate indeed is the media director, and also the organization that has him for its leader, when he brings a democratic conscience to the meeting room where policy is formulated and crucial decisions arrived at, who brings a sturdy desire to seek the facts, who brings an attitude of criticalness, who brings the power to channel his energy toward well-marked-out objectives, and who brings to his everyday work the love of learning, who brings a genuine liking for people as a basis for interpersonal relationships, who brings to his administrative tasks an innovating personality and who brings to his many day-to-day problems a staunch and benevolent character.

These valuable assets for administrative performance must be the subjects for exhaustive study as the prospective director plans his program of preparation, and certainly they should be the targets for self-improvement on the part of practitioners. We now treat each of the selected personal values in sufficient depth to indicate their relationship to good administration of the media program.

The Democratic Conscience

In a memorable book for school administrators, Mort[21] undertook the formulation of a basic set of principles expressing the common sense of the culture. He pointed out that:

Attitudes toward educational policy are influenced by considerations that are a heritage of the culture. . . . Some of these considerations are humanitarian. The public are concerned not only with ends to be achieved, but with democratic, just and egalitarian treatment of persons affected by the process of

[19] See Brickell, *op. cit.*, pp. 35–36, for details on this item.
[20] See Brickell, *op. cit.*, pp. 35–36, for details on this item.

[21] By permission. From Paul R. Mort, *Principles of School Administration* (New York: McGraw-Hill, 1946), pp. 2–3.

achieving them. . . . Other considerations are prudential: The public are concerned that the ends be achieved without outraging the sense of the practical that they have built up in their business relationships, at work, or in the operation of their homes. They are concerned with economy: they believe that the really important things are simple; they are suspicious of cleverness; they want schools to achieve their ends in ways that appeal to their sense of the practical, of the common sense . . . closely related are the three principles . . . of change: adaptability, flexibility, and stability.

According to Mort,[22] the humanitarian considerations include the principles of democracy and equality of opportunity. He says that in seeking to avoid bad public reaction and to help him achieve the best the culture expects, the administrator should remind himself of the following, "When I set any operation into play to achieve an objective, I involve action of human beings: teachers, other staff members, pupils, parents, citizens in general. I require them to change their behavior. I affect their lives."

Briefly, then, by what principle does our culture expect that administrators will be guided? Mort[23] states it this way, "Democracy demands that each human being be dealt with by his fellows as a living, growing, potentially flowering organism that has a right to be a participant in decisions that stand to affect him."

Such a principle is the only reference point for the building of a democratic conscience, which Burton and Brueckner[24] define as follows: ". . . a firm belief in the principles of democracy, a sincere and persistent attitude of desiring to conduct oneself democratically, and an unshakable faith in the ability of human beings to achieve the difficult levels of democratic life."

It is this well-developed, personal sensitivity to this aspect of human relations that is essential for outstanding administrative performance. Without a democratic conscience the director of media services is bound to impede his own progress, not only in small matters handled within the confines of his own operating staff but in matters of broader scope involving fellow administrators, teaching staff, parents, and citizens.

[22] *Ibid.*, p. 94.
[23] *Ibid.*, p. 99.
[24] William H. Burton and Leo J. Brueckner, *Supervision a Social Process*, 3rd ed. (New York: Appleton-Century-Crofts, 1955), p. 76.

Focusing on the Facts

Throughout this book as aspect after aspect comes under analysis, the point of view advanced is that the media director needs to make unique decisions. When the director makes a recommendation, when he has opposition and is challenged, when he sets out to solve a problem, there is no better plan of action than one that is backed up by the facts. Facts, not intuition, fancy, whim, or guesswork, if the director will but realize it, are the starting points for successful action. But knowing how to mobilize information is an ability that is all too rare. The media program leader needs to work at it diligently. If he possesses the priceless attribute of willingness to inquire with an open mind, he will have the best chance to influence people who have closed theirs despite what they say.

Today as never before the media specialist has a body of literature, a number of organized research agencies, and professional organizations at local, state, and national levels, all of which are sources of facts for his own situation. He must have facts about professional workers and laymen, facts on the history of school operations and what key principals and supervisors have tried to accomplish, and facts about what is going on in every school plant falling within his sphere of operations. The ability to mobilize information for action is a fulcrum upon which success and failure may well turn.

An Attitude of Criticalness

Not everyone is right and not everyone is competent. Some materials and equipment are poor and some are good. There are high standards and low standards for conduct and achievement. If the director has the tendency to put on rose-colored glasses whenever he is called upon to make a judgment, evaluate a situation, or formulate an objective, he will be ineffective indeed. He needs to be critical of what he hears, what he is told, what he sees, and what he reads. The critical approach recommended here does not imply meanness, unfriendliness, impatience, lack of sensitivity to the feelings of others, vocal criticism or letters of censure, brashness, or rudeness. On the other hand, it does imply power to discriminate, accuracy in observation, skill in judgment, and willingness to recognize weakness in oneself as well as in others. The media director will certainly enhance his powers of appraisal and diagnosis and his over-all usefulness if he develops such an attitude of criticalness.

Defining Problems and Goals

It is true that there will never be enough time or staff in any one locality to carry out adequately all the proposed duties of a director of instructional media services. In fact the selection of targets for energy and action in terms of outstanding needs is a very significant problem in itself. It is urgent, therefore, in the economy of time and effort, to define specific local problems and to mark out as clearly as possible the goals that are to be achieved. It isn't sufficient to make a listing of general duties. The director must define in terms of his own situation what level of competence in teachers he will seek to develop and how comprehensive his program of service must be, and then plan for a five- or ten-year effort. A list of conditions won't suffice. The media director will also have to set foot in every classroom, or organize others to do it, to map out a facilities and equipment program, and then set up a long-range plan to achieve it.

The director's attitude of criticalness and his desire to mobilize the facts go hand in hand with his drive to define problems and set up objectives, and of course not the least of his problems will be to get his colleagues to set up their own objectives for improved action in the area of his concern. Evidence may lead to the definition of a need, and then how to meet it becomes the problem, and this of course may call for another set of data. It is the purpose of this book to open up clusters of problems likely to confront the school-system media specialist and to point out fruitful lines of attack on these problems, but it will be the degree to which the director of the media program can identify his local problems in terms of clear-cut needs and the degree to which he can set up his own purposes for action that will determine his effectiveness.

To Be a Life-Long Learner

Most individuals have reserves of energy, stamina, and creative capacity that have never been tapped. These reserves of power have been called forth in thousands of individuals by the free enterprise system of America in a gigantic how-to-do-it sales campaign. From making a Polaroid camera transparency to building your own home seems for some to be but a short step.

All of us say that our schools must give prime consideration to the need for life-long learning as one of its major objectives. Many times, however, we do not act as though we mean it. Perhaps in this regard if the schools fail in their attempts, the advertisers will succeed, at least in the area of technical skills.

Technical Skills. Outstanding administrative performance by directors of media service programs demands the self-teaching of new skills, and a love of learning will make this process both enjoyable and successful. It will take drive to overcome the inertia that is often the principal barrier to change, and of course stamina, but fortunately these are in our heritage. Furthermore, if he doesn't know it already, the director should learn that not all the needed professional skills have to be acquired in formal courses for university credit. The director will quite naturally identify needed operational skills as problems arise in his day-to-day work, and instead of delaying action until time is available and the right course may be found, he should try to locate appropriate reference material and direction sheets, obtain needed equipment, and then engage in some serious study and practice. To speed up the process, he should obtain help from friends, specialists, tradesmen, manufacturers, salesmen, and hobbyists. Out of such effort can come a storyboard for the production of a new automated tape-slide presentation for public-relations purposes, a scaled drawing for a school-building media preparation facility, a script for a TV program, a plan for an illustrated handbook on taped instruction, or a schematic plan for a programed teaching system for in-service education.

However, in addition to the love of learning that shows up in the continual development of new technical skills, there are a number of other dimensions. One of these we shall emphasize more than the others and deal with it here because of its significance. This trait is intellectual curiosity.

Intellectual Curiosity. The values we mention, as we have seen, are pervasive in character, affecting the entire range of administrative activity in the educational media field. Intellectual curiosity is also pervasive and is valuable as an asset for administrative work in the area of personal relations. None of us can hope to be a subject-matter specialist in a number of fields, but to the degree that each of us has prepared for and has been active in a teaching career we have been conditioned to keep abreast of developments in our field. But what we urge in the sense of intellectual curiosity is a habitual interest in intellectual matters in general, and in our own intellectual development specifically. What this means in action is putting forth deliberate effort to keep abreast of the work being done and the ideas being developed by other people. Such action involves reading, discussions, and conversations with colleagues about their own areas of knowledge, inevitably and importantly in areas beyond the confines of our own interests arising as a result of college teacher-preparation days. Don Ely [25] has his own way of expressing the results of intellectual curiosity when he says about his students and degree candidates, "I want them to be *at home* with ideas." We are quite certain that intellectual curiosity is basic to success in carrying out the administrative function, and that it has implications for the development of other personal values as well.

An Innovating Personality

In any social climate that is conducive to change, a high premium is placed on creativity. The very nature of the instructional media program, functioning as it does in the field of education which is quite generally recognized as running many years behind new instructional ideas insofar as universal adoption is concerned, provides such a climate.

Hagen [26] uses the term, *innovating personality*, when discussing creativity, and he has identified and described the qualities of personality associated with creative activity. Before we introduce his characteristics we should note one of the main points he makes about the quality of creativity.

When it is stated that innovation requires creativity, the reader should not assume that the term

"creativity" refers to genius. Creativity exists in varying degrees; the man who conceives of an improvement in a can opener as well as the man who conceives of the theory of relativity is creative. Technological progress results from the actions of men characterized by varying degrees of creativity. The discussion of creativity refers, therefore, not merely to the limiting case of genius but to the quality of creativity in general, in whatever degree it may be found in a given individual. [27]

With this clarification of the terms in mind, we present Hagen's analysis of the major qualities underlying creative action.

The major qualities that constitute creativity are easy to list imprecisely: openness to experience, and, underlying this, a tendency to perceive phenomena, especially in an area of life that is of interest to the individual, as forming systems of interacting forces whose action is explainable; creative imagination, of which the central component is the ability to let one's unconscious processes work on one's behalf; confidence and content in one's own evaluations; satisfaction in facing and attacking problems and in resolving confusion or inconsistency; a sense that one has a duty or responsibility to achieve; intelligence; energy; and, often, related to several of these, a perception that the world is somewhat threatening and that one must strive perpetually if one is to be able to cope with it. [28]

We are quick to perceive in this statement of characteristics our own peculiar needs. But we also see as we examine the list, those characteristics without which innovations are not likely to be made. Hagen [29] emphasizes that, "creativity requires only somewhat more of these qualities than characterizes the average person." It is hardly necessary to discuss the need for such qualities as *intelligence* and unusual *energy* in any highly intellectual endeavor, and for admission specifically to any of the instructional-media-director training programs, or for professional assignments in a school system.

We suggest that the would-be school media director ought to be bold enough to take an introspective look at the dimensions of his performance in the light of the need for an innovating personality. None of us, especially if he possesses an innovating personality, should abhor the thought of observing his own patterns of action in comparison with a set of qualities

[25] Director, Center for Instructional Communications, Syracuse University. From a 1965 DAVI Convention general session presentation, Milwaukee, Wisconsin.

[26] Everett E. Hagen, *On the Theory of Change* (Homewood, Ill.: The Dorsey Press, 1962), p. 88.

[27] *Ibid.*, p. 88.

[28] *Ibid.*, p. 88.

[29] *Ibid.*, p. 95.

being viewed as a system. We may well go a step further and proceed to the task of improving ourselves along these lines by sustained effort. Using Hagen's list of qualities expressed in terms of personal performance demands from each of us action something like the following:

1. Open ourselves up to new experiences, be ready for new understanding, and view in a detached way interacting forces as systems.

2. Develop our creative imagination through more sensitive responses to stimuli from the field of media, emphasizing the substance of problems, not frustrations.

3. Develop accuracy in our own evaluation of situations and thus come to have justifiable trust in our capacity to make judgments.

4. Find new satisfaction in attacking and solving problems, and resolve confusion and inconsistency at every opportunity.

5. Develop a sense of responsibility to achieve.

6. Use our intelligence, whatever we have, as fully as we can.

7. Tap our energy resources more completely.

8. Develop a desirable type of anxiety, tied to problem-solving action, being more deeply concerned in a wholesome, perpetual way with a world that needs a lot of fixing.

We believe that it is reasonable to suggest that possessing, or trying to develop, an innovating personality is one of the great assets of a person who is growing toward competence in administration. We may well say, *creative* administration, because this is the main point we are making in presenting this analysis. One may ask: is a person who solves a problem creative? Was an administrator who worked with a group of teachers in developing a set of objectives for a new course of study creative? Was an administrator who read about a way to use television and audio programs on tape for self-instruction in high school, and then implemented such a program in his own schools, creative? The answers must be in the affirmative. Let us return to Hagen for the following explanation:

Innovation consists of organizing reality into relationships embodying new mental or aesthetic concepts, the new relationships serving the purpose of the innovator better than the old. Analytically, and also in time sequence, innovation involves two steps: arriving at a new mental conception, and converting it into material form.

In technological innovation the second step may involve only design or rearrangement of some items of physical equipment or it may involve the organization of a group of human beings into a going concern that carries out a new concept.[30]

The truth is that each of us can accomplish more if we redirect our efforts into higher levels of thinking and planning. To do this we have to find out if the work on which we spend our time and energy is truly productive. Should the energy and time available to each of us and to administrators in general be stratified at more productive levels? The big question is, can we discover changes that we ought to make in ourselves? At this point we discover whether or not each of us possesses an innovating personality, and if not, whether we want to try to develop one?

A Staunch and Benevolent Character

Dishonest, unscrupulous, and imprudent men should have no opportunity to enter positions of leadership in any organization that has beneficent goals, and they wouldn't if would-be employers had adequate information about such perversion. Perhaps the career-seeking reader will quickly ask, "Is it being suggested that the media specialist and the clergyman are in comparable professions?" Of course not, but what we hasten to point out is that high ideals are to be commended anywhere and at any time and that the administrator who brings them to his job possesses a basis for many value judgments and an enviable foundation for his dealings with his professional and lay colleagues. The kind of character we have referred to is simply good for anyone in any job, but for the implementor, the agent of change, the professional educator, the man who spends public money and works with people and their ideas, it seems indispensable as one of the conditions for eliciting respect.

The personal value of character is also pervasive in influence upon the nature of an administrator's operations and plans, and we feel certain that it has a bearing on the next personal value to be discussed.

[30] *Ibid.*, pp. 86–87.

A Genuine Liking for People

We have already dealt with the subject of *the innovating personality* in an effort to persuade the would-be media director to take an objective look at his own pattern of reacting to problem situations, and now we look at another facet of personality development. We insist again that even though this value may not be polar in nature, a deeply ingrained liking for people is probably associated with an adequate sensitivity to the feelings and rights of all with whom we come into contact, an open-mindedness to suggestions and contributions of others, a basic sincerity in dealing with individuals and groups, and the faith that a leader must develop that people can and will change along lines of improvement. This is not to suggest that the administrator who has a sincere liking for people will be uncritical in his judgment or that he will shrink from making evaluations that may call for censure. Perhaps in these cases the administrator may exhibit a capacity to understand actions and a degree of patience that perhaps will at least tend to prevent action based on inadequate information.

We should cautiously suggest also that an individual who has developed a wholesome liking for people has the best chance of being liked in return, making good progress toward social competence and facilitating the building of a climate of mutual respect.

The personal values that we have perhaps all too rashly selected are not discrete and quantitative, and not polar in the sense of possessing them or not. They are complex and interlocked in a unique balance. They are interwoven with unique strengths and weaknesses in technical capabilities, and with what we know and what we are able to do with the knowledge we possess or are able to get. The reader knows well that complex forces are at work in the organism, and some of these forces and conditions are or have been and may continue to be beyond our control. Therefore we would not by any means imply that we can cast the would-be media director into a common mold, or that we have crystallized the characteristics we claim are potentially influential on success into a firm and dependable system. We are fully aware that even though all of us are very much alike in many ways, each of us is also vastly different and we shall remain that way.

If the reader happens to be an on-the-job worker in the media field, or if he is a full-time graduate student, he ought to ask himself, "Why was I selected for this job?" Or, "How did it happen that *I* was selected among several for admission to this educational media specialist program?" He should also ask himself, "How much did those who selected me really know about me? What are my beliefs, commitments, prized values?"

It is a matter of vital concern, or it ought to be, to all prospective media professionals how they are chosen for new positions or admitted to the profession. For learners, like patients, may be maimed, mentally, by incompetents. The selection process is crucial. Many times people who are chosen because of one quality, fail because of another. Some people simply cannot get a job even after completing a course of advanced study. Sometimes a man cannot seem to get himself hired because he is obese, even though he is honest, jolly, and likes people. The writer once admitted a student to a media program with high hopes that certain changes would take place under some gentle prodding. As it turned out this applicant simply could not sell himself to his would-be employers and consequently was turned down again and again. The reason came to light finally. This man *talked* himself right out of one job after the other. (Perhaps we should have written a paragraph or two on loquaciousness and its possible effects on employers.) Yet other individuals could, even with defective and deficient value systems, to say nothing about the lack of technological understanding, talk themselves into as many jobs as placement agencies can offer. How long they remain in these positions is another story.

As the would-be media administrator seeks higher levels of skill, service, and responsibility, we urge him to consider making changes in himself, based on critical judgments of his own successes and failures, of an image he would like to create. There may be no definitive formula, but there are dependable guidelines aplenty. The person who would seek to lead others to change must be willing first to undertake needed changes in himself. As we have said earlier, some of the changes leading to growth in administrative competence may well be carried out on a self-instructional basis, others may call for assistance through formal preparation programs. It is almost certain that the administrator at any level at which he works never really reaches his goal of excellence. If he is to be worth his salt, he must keep on learning through his day-by-day experiences.

Now we turn to the remaining chapters to focus our attention on technical problems in administering an instructional media program. We envision our media director at work in a school system organization, but in a number of chapters we deal with technical problems of media personnel working in a single school building. However, suggested solutions to problems, or guidelines for such solutions, are likely to be applicable to the operation of instructional media programs at all levels: building, city, county, university, state, and national educational and research agencies, and even in religious education and industrial training programs. Of course in these various programs and at various levels, points of emphasis and concentration on special objectives will demand a new balance in application of skills and knowledge. The remainder of this book, then, is devoted to the task of preparing the professional educator to identify problems and find creative solutions for them in his efforts to implement a variety of instructional media services.

Problem-Solving Activities

1. Some bright young men at a university who are interested in educational administration are preparing by means of graduate programs to become superintendents of schools without first having had experience as teachers. State your point of view on this situation giving arguments for both sides. When you take the negative side, identify some serious mistakes that superintendents without teaching experience are likely to make. What are some steps that bright young men without teaching experience who wish to enter educational leadership positions in general and instructional media leadership positions in particular could take to gain the essential teaching experience that is recommended in this book?

2. Explain how skills and insights in both instructional technology and teaching would aid the media program director in solving his administrative problems. Analyze one or more problems stated in the chapter as a basis for your explanation.

3. Define as succinctly as you can in a brief statement of fifty words or less the nature of the administrative tasks that have to be carried out by the media program director. Do the same with reference to the school superintendent.

4. Contrast the nature of administrative activity of media program directors in large-city and small-city school systems.

5. Examine the statements about formal preparation of educational administrators and decide if the media program administrator needs to have similar experiences in his own preparation.

6. Identify an innovation of reasonably large scope that you have conceived and wish to have adopted in a school system with which you are familiar. Formulate in outline format the steps you would take from obtaining administrative decision to implementing the change in all schools (emphasize action with people).

7. We have identified and discussed a number of significantly important personal values the development of which may be the means of growth toward administrative competence. Most are broad and pervasive. In the light of that discussion, identify three or four additional values at approximately the same level of breadth, and indicate briefly how each if possessed by you would aid you and others in carrying on administrative activity more effectively.

8. Explain Hagen's statement that creativity may take place in varying degrees. Explain also Hagen's concept of innovation.

9. Explain how, in any job you name or now hold, you could stratify your productivity at a higher talent level (that is, concentrate your activity at a level requiring greater skill and insight). In completing this exercise, do not move yourself out of your present job. What activities you now perform could you omit or turn over to people with less education? If you carried out your plan, what extra help would you require?

10. Locate if you can a recent textbook on educational administration that stresses the democratic process as a characteristic of good administration. Report the viewpoints given in these references to your class or to your colleagues. (If we move away from democratic processes, what alternatives do we face?)

11. Sketch out a plan of formal course work

in connection with your present professional, graduate program that will prepare you for more effective administrative service. What personal values should you pay more attention to in your search for means of growth and development? Be courageous and objective and identify some of your personality needs. This analysis may prove to be your route to innovation in yourself. What image do you believe you are radiating toward your colleagues? To your local community environment?

12. Define the term *democratic conscience*, and state how you believe it is developed. (By all means include the principle of democratic action stated in man-to-man terms.)

13. What is Mort's concept of *Common Sense of the Culture*? How will this knowledge, if used by you, guide your performance on the job?

14. Do you fear the learning of new skills? Name some new skills that you have developed lately.

15. How will the ability to perceive definite and worthy goals and the ability to define problems lend power to your personal performance? Give specific examples.

16. Appraise your own strengths and weaknesses with respect to the personal values for enrichment of administrative activity as discussed in this chapter.

References

Abbott, Max G. and John T. Lowell (eds.). *Change Perspectives in Educational Administration* (Published in cooperation with the University Council for Educational Administration) (Auburn, Alabama: School of Education, Auburn University, 1965).

Adapting the Secondary School Program to the Needs of Youth, 52nd Yearbook of the National Society for the Study of Education, Part I (Chicago: University of Chicago Press, 1953).

Ayars, Albert L. *Administering the People's Schools* (New York: McGraw-Hill, 1957).

Bair, Medill and Richard G. Woodward. *Team Teaching in Action* (Boston: Houghton-Mifflin, 1964).

Baughman, M. Dale. "School Administration: Beatitudes for Beleaguered Bigwigs," *Phi Delta Kappan*, Vol. 47, No. 6, February 1966, pp. 317–319.

Blau, Peter M. and W. Richard Scott. *Formal Organizations* (San Francisco: Chandler Publishing Company, 1962).

Brickell, Henry M. *Organizing New York State for Educational Change* (Albany, New York: University of the State of New York, State Education Department, 1961).

Brown, Edwin J. "Experienced Schoolmen Talk to Beginners," *Phi Delta Kappan*, Vol. 47, No. 6, February 1966, pp. 320–322.

Carlson, Richard O. *Adoption of Educational Innovations*, a publication of the Center for Advanced Study of Educational Administration (Eugene, Oregon: University of Oregon Press, 1965).

Carlson, Richard O., et al. *Change Processes in the Public Schools*, a publication of the Center for the Advanced Study of Educational Administration (Eugene, Oregon: University of Oregon Press, 1965).

Charters, W. W., Jr., et al. *Perspectives on Educational Administration and the Behavioral Sciences*, a publication of the Center for Advanced Study of Educational Administration (Eugene, Oregon: University of Oregon Press, 1965).

Corey, Stephen M. *Helping Other People Change* (Columbus, Ohio: Ohio State University Press, 1963).

De Huszar, George B. *Practical Applications of Democracy* (New York: Harper and Row, 1945).

Dennis, Warren, Kenneth Benne, and Robert Chin. *The Planning of Change* (New York: Holt, Rinehart and Winston, 1962).

Eye, Glen G. and Lanore A. Netzer. *Supervision of Instruction* (New York: Harper and Row, 1965).

Griffith, Francis. "Six Mistaken Meanings of Democratic Administration," *Phi Delta Kappan*, Vol. 48, No. 2, October 1966, pp. 59–61.

Griffiths, Daniel E. et al. *Organizing Schools for Effective Education* (Danville, Illinois: The Interstate Printers and Publishers, Inc., 1962).

Halpin, Andrew E. *Theory and Research in Administration* (New York: Macmillan, 1966).

Harcleroad, Fred F. (ed.). "The Education of the AV Communication Specialist" (Proceedings of a DAVI Seminar), *AV Communication Review*, Vol. 8, No. 5, Supp. 2, September-October 1960.

Harris, Chester W. (ed.). *Encyclopedia of Educational Research*, rev. ed. (New York: Macmillan, 1960).

Leu, Donald J. and Herbert C. Rudman (eds.). *Preparation Programs for School Administrators* (Seventh UCEA Career Development Seminar) (East Lansing, Michigan: Office of Research and Publications, College of Education, Michigan State University, 1963).

Levy, Ferdinand K. *et al.* "The ABC's of the Critical Path Method," *Harvard Business Review* **41**: 98–108; September-October 1963.

Lippitt, Ronald, Jeanne Watson, and Bruce Westley. *The Dynamics of Planned Change* (New York: Harcourt, Brace and World, 1958).

Lippman, Walter. *Essays in the Public Philosophy* (Boston: Little, Brown and Co., 1955).

Litterer, Joseph A. (ed.). *Organization: Structure and Behavior* (New York: John Wiley and Sons, 1963).

Loughary, John W. *Man-Machine Systems in Education* (New York: Harper and Row, 1966).

Meierhenry, Wesley C. (ed.). *Media and Educational Innovation* (in cooperation with the U.S. Office of Education under Title VII, Part B) (Lincoln, Nebraska: University of Nebraska Press, 1966).

Miles, Matthew B. (ed.). *Innovation in Education* (New York: Bureau of Publications, Teachers College, Columbia University, 1964).

Miller, Richard I. (ed.). *Perspectives on Educational Change* (New York: Appleton-Century-Crofts, 1967).

Miller, Van. *The Public Administration of American School Systems* (New York: Macmillan, 1965).

Morphet, Edgar L., Roe L. Johns, and Theodore L. Reller. *Educational Organization and Administration: Concepts, Practices, and Issues*, 2nd ed. (Englewood Cliffs, N.J.: Prentice-Hall, 1967).

Mort, Paul R. and Donald H. Ross. *Principles of School Administration*, 2nd ed. (New York: McGraw-Hill, 1957).

PERT. *Guide for Management Use* (U.S. Department of Defense, Document No. d1. 6/2: P94/2.) (Washington, D.C.: Government Printing Office, 1963).

Saunders, Robert L. *et al. A Theory of Educational Leadership* (Columbus, Ohio: Charles E. Merrill Books, Inc., 1966).

Shaplin, Judson T. *Team Teaching* (New York: Harper and Row, 1964).

Sherman, Mendel. "Training for a Top-Flight Coordinator," *Audiovisual Instruction*, Vol. 3, No. 5, May 1958, pp. 148–150.

Simon, Herbert. *Administrative Behavior: A Study of Decision Processes in Administrative Organization*, 2nd ed. (New York: Macmillan, 1957).

Thompson, Victor A. *Modern Organizations* (New York: Alfred A. Knopf, 1965).

Trump, J. Lloyd and Dorsey Baynam. *Guide to Better Schools: Focus on Change* (Chicago: Rand-McNally, 1961).

Weber, C. A. and Mary E. Weber. *Fundamentals of Educational Leadership* (New York: McGraw-Hill, 1955).

Woods, Thomas E. *The Administration of Educational Innovation* (Eugene Oregon: Bureau of Educational Research, School of Education, University of Oregon, 1967).

3

Acquisition and Deployment of Audiovisual Media

The process of acquiring the audiovisual media that teachers need for accomplishing their objectives requires sophisticated administrative ability, technological knowledge, and a keen insight into teaching and curriculum. At the turn of the century such media were practically nonexistent for purchase, but today the marketplaces are virtually bulging. Nevertheless the task of locating and obtaining the suitable media for specific instructional purposes, regardless of how interesting the job usually is, is both arduous and critical. (Refer also to Chapter 12 relative to the print medium.)

For the purposes of discussion and analysis in this chapter, we must separate the generally used term *media* into two parts, namely, *materials* and *equipment*, and they will be dealt with in that order. A given item of material should be considered as a concentration, system, or body of content of potential value when put to work. On the other hand, equipment or instruments (often referred to as hardware components) should be recognized as the means of presenting such content. Bulletin boards and chalkboards are also means of displaying content. The camera, of course, is a means of assembling content or essential to the making of media or a given medium.

Kinds of Audiovisual Materials

Audiovisual materials is the term commonly used to refer to those instructional materials that may be used to convey meaning without complete dependence upon verbal symbols or language. Thus, according to the definition, a textbook or reference book does not fall within this grouping of instructional materials, but an illustration in a book does. Some audiovisual components, like taking a field trip, dramatizing an event or procedure, or making a diorama, are in the nature of processes and experiences. Some, like the motion picture, require the use of equipment to release their latent value. Still others, like an exhibit or a study print, need no equipment whatever. Some materials have been in use for decades, while others, such as the miniature slide, tape recording, television, and special combinations of them, are relatively new; under the appropriate conditions all may make important contributions to teaching-communicating-learning processes. See Figure 3-1.

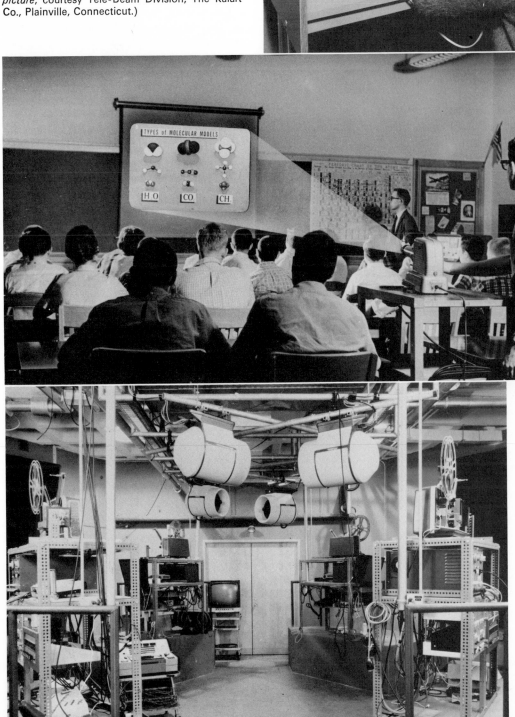

Figure 3-1. These views of an electronically equipped carrel for individualization; a conventional class group; and of a large-group multimedia presentation, projection-pit installation; imply a wide variety of teaching-learning situations, all of which may demand a wide array of media materials, from filmstrip to videotape. (*Top picture*, courtesy Raytheon Learning Systems Co., Englewood, New Jersey. *Middle picture*, courtesy Encyclopaedia Britannica Educational Corp., Chicago. *Bottom picture*, courtesy Tele-Beam Division, The Kalart Co., Plainville, Connecticut.)

The term *audiovisual materials* is not, strictly speaking, a satisfactory one, since it designates in common usage both material things as well as processes. Field trips and dramatic performances are processes, not materials. A field trip is a means of studying and reacting to and using real things and actions in their natural environment; a dramatic performance is a means of representing people, events, and procedures. However, there is dramatic production activity for some pupils but only dramatic observation for the viewers. The camera helps a teacher assemble material for subsequent presentation, and one of the uses of the opaque projector is to help a teacher enlarge material to facilitate observation. It is obvious that an opaque projector, a bulletin board, an exhibit case, a feltboard, or a chalkboard are not materials but are means of displaying materials. Furthermore, the planning and preparation of any one of the audiovisual materials as a joint teacher-pupil project has high potential value as a means of motivating and organizing class activity. The media program director should be aware of this differentiation, since it is his responsibility to keep the wide range of possibilities for experiencing in mind as routes to better learning.

A brief though comprehensive listing of audiovisual materials, together with the necessary related equipment or processes for putting them to work in the classroom, will be helpful to the reader for present and future reference purposes. Such a list is presented in the paragraphs that follow. It should be noted that materials are arranged in order from the most realistic to the most abstract.

Realia in the Social and Physical Environment. These materials, situations, and people have to be visited, studied, observed, reacted to, and worked with, right in their natural environments, schoolroom, schoolyard, city, farm, state, or nation; that is, by means of field trips or in connection with other community study and work projects. Some of these realia, such as equipment, materials, specimens, and objects, both animate and inanimate (and people too), may be brought into the classroom. The study of realia may then demand field trips, demonstrations, experiments, and other direct experiences as processes for getting the meaning. Some realia will have to be brought into the classroom in display cases, preferably in lifelike

arrangement, and some may be suspended in the air or attached to bulletin boards.

Dramatic Performances (Portrayal of People, Events, Procedures). Dramatic performances are obviously not materials, but rather are processes for using properties and representing situations in dramatic rather than graphic form. Actually, pupils become "models" of people. The classroom post office or store in the primary grades is a good example. Often equipment such as tape recorders and photographic and television cameras are called for. Also dolls and puppets are produced for use as dramatic models.

Models, Mock-Ups, Globes, and Relief Maps. These materials may be purchased or produced by the teacher and used as means of communication, or they may be produced jointly by pupils and teacher as a focal point for the learning activity. Many of the models may have moving or removable parts. Exhibits and dioramas made up of models instead of realia may be borrowed, purchased, or constructed.

Television Programs. The use of such materials demands television receivers and antenna systems in schools, and for expanded use of this medium in schools, closed-circuit studios, television cameras, videotape recorders and players, and distribution systems as well. With the necessary videotape players, television programs may be distributed to self-instruction carrels and used in combination with other media materials and equipment. Television programs may also be produced jointly by pupils and teacher as learning experiences.

Motion Pictures. Projection equipment for accommodating either optical or magnetic sound tracks and projection screens are, of course, required. We must also point out that new kinds of equipment may be required by the use of this medium such as push-button mechanisms that operate 8 mm cartridge-type motion picture projectors. Such equipment may be arranged with other display mechanisms as a part of teaching machines, or also in carrels as was mentioned under the medium of television. Production of motion pictures by pupils and teachers is also a possibility as a major learning activity, if cameras, lights, film stock, and other related equipment items are available.

Still-Picture Projection Materials. There is a wide array of still-picture projection materials.

Each requires unique projection equipment, so each is listed and commented on separately as follows:

1. *Transparencies.* Use of transparencies demands overhead projectors of appropriate types.

2. *Slides (handmade or photographic) in all sizes.* Use demands separate or combination projectors for $3\frac{1}{4} \times 4$ inch, $2\frac{1}{4} \times 2\frac{1}{4}$ inch, and 2×2 inch slides, in regular or automatic adaptations. Slides are also widely used in self-instruction carrels and in multimedia presentations. Individual slide viewers with tape-recorded commentary may also be required for special applications. Slides for short-exposure techniques demand special flashmeters and projectors.

3. *Filmstrips (sound and silent).* Use of these materials demands a projector for silent filmstrips; for sound filmstrips, a phonograph, tape player, or some manufactured combination of projector and sound reproducer has to be added. Short-exposure filmstrips demand the use of flash meters and appropriate projectors. Projection screens of appropriate size are also a requirement.

4. *Opaque Projection Material (drawings, objects, illustrations).* The projection of such material requires the opaque projector and projection screens of appropriate size.

5. *Micro-projector Materials (microscope slides and microscopic objects).* Projection of such material, animate or inanimate, requires the micro-projector and nonbeaded screen.

The materials listed may also be produced by groups of pupils for various communication projects as significant, productive learning activities.

Study Prints and Pictorial Illustrations. Bulletin boards and opaque projectors may be required for facilitating observation. Such materials may be photographed and converted to slides for subsequent teacher use, or drawn by pupils in connection with learning activities.

Audio Programs. The use of tape or disk recordings and radio broadcasts demands a wide variety of equipment, such as recorders, record players, microphones, aggregate boxes, earphones, listening response centers, radio receivers, and even radio stations. Students and teachers may produce dramatic and other radio programs; and teachers may produce a series of taped language lessons, or they may analyze speech needs, do remedial work in mathematics, and conduct map-interpretation exercises.

Graphic Materials (Maps, Graphs, Cartoons, Diagrams, and Charts). These materials often require for adequate observation opaque projectors, bulletin boards, flannel boards, chalkboards, and overhead transparency projectors. The use of such materials often demands that they be prepared by teachers for purposes of communication, or by pupils for communicating with others. Cameras, slide projectors, and drawing tools, together with diazo chemical supplies and processing equipment, may be required for their production. Graphic materials may be on canvas, flannel, muslin, paper, wood, glass, and plastic.

Programed Materials. Programed learning sequences are available in many forms. At one extreme is a linear, small-step, no-error, item-by-item presentation in strictly verbal-symbol format. At the other extreme is an automated multimedia teaching system of which several components are richly illustrated presentations using verbal frames, slides, taped directions for responses, 8 mm single-concept film cartridges, and a remote-controled videotape player that fills a special television screen at the push of a button. Some programed sequences use illustrations in diagramatic, or pictorial, forms in both black and white and color to provide explanations of difficult concepts prior to response by students. Such illustrations have a pinpointed role to play in communication, and depending upon the system being used and the available hardware, they may be displayed by means of filmstrips, slides, films, or television, or as picture-panels in a booklet. Thus it can be seen that a programed learning sequence may be considered as a special kind of textbook, or it may be considered to be a kind of audiovisual material, or a complex combination of audiovisual media, incorporating both materials and instruments.

In addition to and now often associated with programed instruction pedagogy we observe the need for computer technology. In fact we may with considerable assurance point to the expanding use, especially in a research-and-development sense, of a wide range of computer-assisted instructional processes. We see clearly that computers may serve teachers in doing some seemingly impossible jobs of analysis and summary of pupil responses, and they may also serve pupils in tutorial and individualization roles. Some of these services loom large on the horizon and in the decade ahead will become commonplace. Chapter 11, *Implementation of Instructional Systems*, includes a section on computer-assisted instruction.

One of the significant signs of maturity in the media field that can be displayed by teachers is the ability to design and prepare or guide the preparation of media for special instructional purposes, and the facilitation of this process is a modern-day concern of all media program directors. Without such facilitation on a system-wide basis, the materials identified in the preceding list will not fulfill their vast potential of assistance in meeting educational objectives.

Supplies for Media Preparation by Teachers. Repeatedly in the foregoing groups of audio-visual materials, reference was made to their production by the teacher and also by the joint efforts of teachers and pupils; by the teachers, of course, for purposes of improving communication, and in the latter case as a basis for organizing learning activities around the hub of vitally interesting projects. To make possible these production activities, a wide range of expendable materials needs to be stocked for issue to teachers, and this becomes a vital aspect of the organized audiovisual-services program. Such supplies need to be centralized in large quantity at the audiovisual service headquarters, or by special arrangements of the director, at a school-system supplies center, or even at both places if a combination serves to facilitate ordering and use. In addition to large stocks of supplies, i.e., large enough to serve school needs for one year, smaller quantities of the more commonly used items may be kept on hand in each school building to meet needs of teachers quickly. Also since some materials deteriorate, the plan for ordering, distribution, and storage should be carefully formulated and periodically evaluated if waste is to be avoided. We shall devote Chapter 9 to the subject of teacher preparation of media.

In the next section the prospective media director is encouraged to tackle the problem of deciding which among the many materials described in preceding paragraphs ought to be procured for teachers as a part of his professional services, both centralized and decentralized in the various school buildings.

Deciding on the Scope of Media Program Services

The director of media services may find it helpful to think of media materials in different frameworks of reference. First he may think of materials as being the means of pupil experiencing. In this case he thinks of materials as new, even though vicarious, experiences—visiting far off places, breaking down the barriers of time and space, backtracking into history, swinging toward the moon and Venus—as opportunities for students to project their beings and ideas into new images of themselves. He may think secondly of materials as a set of slides, a motion picture, a large model of a store or a bank, a dramatic production, as foci for organizing the activities and energies of a class of pupils demanding productive creativity. He may think thirdly of media as cast in their newest role, based on the preparation of special and sequential materials that take over from the teacher under optimum learning conditions laborious tasks of repetitive teaching. In the fourth place, materials enhance the impact of a teacher in carrying out communication tasks in a face-to-face situation for both large and small groups, and thus make possible a whole array of contributions not the least of which is simply to see what the teacher is doing and to hear what he is saying from the back rows of a classroom. All of these modes of orientation, and others as well, are merged in the teaching process, and the media program director must know them well.

The big problem for the director as presented in this section is *which of the audiovisual materials should be acquired and incorporated into the service program?* The answer to this question can be given only in terms of the needs and priorities of the local situation. However, the basic factors that enter into the decision are as follows:

1. What teachers want and need in terms of present and the hoped-for curriculum.
2. Nature of previous local experience.
3. Status of school facilities.

4. Cost and financial support; present, and estimated for the future.

5. Present and future supply for purchase.

6. Predicted service difficulties to be surmounted.

7. Scope of staff coverage.

8. Nature of the roles that the materials will play in meeting instructional needs.

Each of these factors merits a brief analysis.

What Teachers Want and Need

The surest way to make serious mistakes is to ignore what teachers really believe they need. Their needs and wishes should be a basic factor in decision. Directors should get the facts and should elicit the required participation through bulletins and questionnaires or directly through curriculum and other study committees. If the media director insists, for example, on putting all his local resources into prerecorded tapes, and the teachers want to expand into motion pictures and the transparency preparation process, he is heading for trouble.

Nature of Previous Local Experience

Years of previous successful experience with one or more kinds of audiovisual media produce readiness for new experience with others and a good base upon which to build new teacher competencies. Teachers become media minded; that is, they grow in their understanding and ability to put media to work. They are then likely to become eager to try new materials. Thus if teachers have used motion pictures, filmstrips, and slides, they may be willing or even eager to undertake a production program involving Polaroid and 2 × 2 inch slides and tape recordings and 8 mm cartridge-type motion pictures for self-instruction purposes. Unfortunately, unsuccessful previous experience will naturally set up negative attitudes toward new programs of service. In this case reconditioning may have to take place before new developments are undertaken.

Status of School Facilities

Some elementary school teachers—as incredible as it seems—may still be limited, as far as projected audiovisual materials are concerned,

to the use of filmstrips on rainy days because of lack of adequate classroom light-control systems. Or perhaps only one projection room with adequate light control is available, and to add motion pictures to the filmstrip and slide service in the elementary schools would overtax the physical facilities as far as properly equipped classrooms are concerned. Materials that do not require expensive light-control systems, such as dramatizations, realia, models, exhibits, transparencies, and recorded audio programs on records and tape, graphic materials via flannel board, bulletin board, chalkboard, study prints, and television receivers, may thus seem to be the choice. However, the motion picture offers a great contribution to experiencing, and therefore it should be considered along with a number of other factors before reaching a decision.

Cost and Financial Support

With other factors kept constant, the factor of cost and financial support is obviously an important one in the determination of what materials the audiovisual media program ought to include. Any cost analysis made should be complete. Not only does the director need to figure what the cost will be (for example, of production supplies) but he ought also to estimate the costs for related equipment and school facilities, as well as the costs of paying for required commercial laboratory services.

If, for example, the media program director is considering a plan for inaugurating closed-circuit television programing in which video-tapes will be produced and replayed as called for by the school's curriculum, then he will not only have to determine the relatively heavy initial cost of equipment, studio facilities, and additional staff, but the continuing rental charges for distribution cables, and the cost of media preparation facilities for the support of good programing. It is conceivable that in this latter connection additional contractual expense will be incurred because of photographic laboratory services on a commercial basis. As a final consideration it must be determined if strong continuing financial support for any given aspect of media service is likely in relation to the total and continuing contribution to curriculum objectives.

Present and Future Supply

Taking sets of study prints as an example, the question should be asked: What are the present sources for purchase? Probably the most comprehensive and up-to-date source is the Fideler Company, formerly Informative Classroom Picture Publishers, Grand Rapids, Michigan. There are also a number of other less comprehensive sources presently developing new and significant sets. Other questions also need to be raised. Are the sources of purchase likely to increase in number? Are study prints popular with teachers? Are other audiovisual service centers increasing or decreasing their study print libraries? What are their circulation figures? What sources of study prints other than commercial distributors can be tapped? Such data are essential if a good decision is to be reached insofar as this factor is concerned. Other materials being considered for procurement will have to be analyzed similarly. For example, if the use of a listening-response center is being planned for each school building, where will the taped programs come from? Are there ready-made sources? Will teachers be willing to learn to make their own taped lessons?

Predicted Service Difficulties to Be Surmounted

If we discuss study print sets in connection with the service-difficulty factor, the director ought to raise and answer the following questions before he proposes to incorporate them into the service program: How will study prints be grouped? In sets corresponding to teaching units? Other general subject matter topics? How will they be packaged and stored? Can boxes or envelopes be purchased? How can they best be preserved? Should they be mounted with rubber cement or dry photo tissue on mounting boards or laminated in plastic? If the loan period for some prints needs to be longer than for other materials, how many sets on each topic will be needed? How will they be delivered and picked up? Who will do the work of inspection and checking against loss? Similar questions will have to be answered for all materials. As another example, when considering the installation of electronic learning laboratories using taped instruction, the preparation of the necessary high-quality tapes may prove to be a difficult problem. Can tapes produced locally be exchanged with other school systems? Who will teach teachers to produce their own high-quality tapes? What regrouping and rotating procedures may have to be employed to schedule all pupils through the electronic learning laboratories? What repair services for the laboratories may have to be organized and paid for? In the face of such facts, all involved can come to a sound decision for a given local situation.

Range of Curriculum Applicability

Another crucial question in the media director's process of determining which kinds of materials he should supply as a part of the program of services is this: Is a particular kind of material suitable for use at all grade levels in the system? In general, priorities should be given to kinds of material that have wide application over the entire range of the curriculum. The reader should note that the problem of whether a particular title ought to be used in the fourth grade and again in the ninth is not involved in the study of this factor. The problem here being considered is whether or not the motion picture, for example, should be selected instead of some other kind of material, such as micro-slides, because of its wider potential use throughout the curriculum?

Nature of the Contribution to Instructional Needs

In considering this factor the director should seek to estimate along with his teacher colleagues the nature of the experience a given type of material is likely to provide. To explain textbook matter, to provide rich vicarious experience, to facilitate research and remedial work, to overcome physical difficulties of subject-matter presentation, to get students ready for difficult problem-solving tasks such as laboratory work or advanced shop work, and to carry burdensome jobs of presenting repetitive content for the teacher, as in instructional systems, are a few of the potential contributions audiovisual media may make to instruction. Some of the materials are more restricted in their potential contributions than others, and the use of others is so vital as to be required of all teachers in a given grade or subject under specified circumstances.

Figure 3-2. These two views show school building media centers that provide broad services to teachers and pupils. Such centers will be discussed in detail in subsequent chapters. (*Top picture*, courtesy of Public Schools, Dearborn, Michigan, shows the Stout JHS media center. *Bottom picture* shows a portion of one of the Resource Centers at Nova Junior-Senior High School (1966–67 arrangement), courtesy, Nova Schools, Nova Dissemination Project, Fort Lauderdale, Florida.)

Availability of Leadership for Innovation

When recently developed media are to be introduced into the curriculum, such as programed instruction and teaching systems involving regrouping and rotation of pupils in new patterns, teachers need generous and continuing assistance before they develop a desirable feeling of security with the new practices. Therefore, the more radical the departure from conventional and long-established methods, the greater is the need for preparation of the teaching staff for implementing desired innovations. The use of electronic learning centers, television for direct teaching, self-instruction systems are at this time good examples, because of the need for new facilities, equipment, materials, and staff education.

Balancing the Factors

The task of determination of specific media services is a problem of arriving at a wise policy in terms of efforts to help teachers. This policy will have to be the best possible balance between the factors just described. Even in the largest and most comprehensive programs this task is great because it may be better to have adequacy in ten kinds of material than inadequacy in twenty. See Figure 3-2.

Whenever it is decided what kinds of material (from filmstrips to television programs) are to be made available to teachers, consideration has to be given to the problem of balancing centralization of distribution at the audiovisual service headquarters and decentralization at the point of use. A brief discussion of this problem follows.

Centralization and Decentralization of Media

Local centralization of materials under good management is more efficient and economical from the standpoint of maximum use of the fewest number of available units of material, but the usually necessary short loan-periods may work a hardship on teachers as well as on busy central office booking, inspection, and shipping personnel. Some service centers are therefore decentralizing the more inexpensive types of materials such as filmstrips, tape recordings, phonograph recordings, maps, globes, and study prints. Television programs may, for another example, originate at studios in the media center headquarters, and also in decentralized locations such as may be located in one or more elementary and secondary schools. Furthermore, in electronic learning laboratories, the programs involved in repetitive use must be stored in such a way that they are immediately accessible. Again, this is a local decision involving more than just simple arithmetic. It is service to the teacher that is the crux of this matter. Media must be, according to one of the broad principles for organizing a service center, made available to the teacher at the optimum time for their use and with a minimum of inconvenience. Remembering this principle, it may be said that generally the media headquarters controls the distribution of those materials which are relatively the most expensive, most difficult to repair and maintain, less frequently requested, but essential, and those that need to be individually scheduled, issued, received, and sent out under strict control. Decentralization may also be a way of saying that the director of media services declines for the present to organize and supervise the use of certain kinds of material, service, or process. Provisions for field trips may be a case in point. A great deal can be done in setting up a formal organization to facilitate field trips, or the handling of the field trip program may be left entirely to the individual school, that is, to the principal, teachers, and to the instructional

media building coordinator. This type of decentralization is desirable only if the plan reflects careful study and decision by all concerned. However, decentralization of new media services may be necessary if the director fails to get adequate staff and budgetary support, or it may be deliberately planned as a stopgap measure, pending further developments.

A Hypothetical Service Program of Materials

Using the listing of media materials already presented, and assuming reasonably well-developed services, the following hypothetical program may be valuable as an example for present study, analysis, and criticism:

1. *Kinds of Instructional Media Distributed from Central Service Center to All School Units*
   (a) Motion picture films in center-owned collection
   (b) Filmstrips (silent and sound), general collection
   (c) Slide sets (2 × 2 inch size), general collection
   (d) Prerecorded tapes, general collection
   (e) Short-exposure slides and filmstrips for all areas
   (f) Instructional kits, general collection
   (g) Realia display cases
   (h) Models, general collection.
2. *Special Media Service from Central Headquarters Studios and Playback Centers*
   (a) Television programing (live and taped) for direct teaching distributed on schedule to all schools participating
   (b) Remote control video-playback equipment units for self-instruction programs in school buildings.
3. *Kinds of Instructional Media Deposited and Decentralized at Each School Building Unit*
   (a) Prerecorded tapes for electronic learning laboratories
   (b) Slide sets (2 × 2 inch) arranged and stored in magazines for special presentations of a repetitive nature, for use by one or more teachers
   (c) Specialized filmstrip collection, of a basic nature for specific grades, units and problems
   (d) Maps and globes
   (e) Sets of study prints

(f) Transparencies in special teacher collections for specific grades, subjects

(g) Phonograph records

(h) Teaching system components, arranged for specific parts of courses

(i) Models and apparatus for specific classes and units of work

(j) 8 mm single-concept films for specific classes and groups on a self-instruction basis.

4. *Special Media Processes and Arrangements Carried on at Each School Under In-Service Education Promotion*

(a) Bulletin board displays

(b) Exhibits

(c) Field trips and community contacts

(d) Micro-projector materials.

5. *Supplies Available from Central Media Headquarters for Use by Teachers in School Building Preparation of Media Centers for Producing*

(a) Photographic $3\frac{1}{4} \times 4$ inch and 2×2 inch slides in black and white and color—Polaroid film, mount frames and Dippit, cover glass and slide-binding tape, black and white and color film in 35 mm size, mount frames for automatic projector magazines

(b) Overhead transparencies—plastic sheets, mount frames, wet process and dry process photocopier materials, lettering pens, and lettering templates, lettering scribers, sheets of ready-made letters and symbols, inks, small drawing boards with pin-bar registration device, pressure sensitive tapes, binding tape, hinges for overlays, and staplers

(c) Tape recordings—magnetic recording tape, splicing tape, extra empty tape reels

(d) Motion pictures—unexposed motion film stock in both color and black and white, and in fast and slow speeds, spare floodlamps for lighting

(e) Crafts and displays—celotex, plywood, masonite, lumber in assorted lengths, cotton flannel, felt, coarse sandpaper stock, cardboard stock, construction paper, felt-nib pens, colored inks, paints, yarns, confetti ribbon, burlap cloth, metal foil, and wire mesh, to mention a few.

The reader should not draw hasty conclusions from the foregoing hypothetical program to the effect that it represents what the author considers an ideal system of services. The possibilities seem infinite. It is a fact that in many instances the programs and available services vary greatly from school to school within a given school system. This situation is unfortunate for it is to be hoped that all of the learners will have equal opportunity for access to the best that is available, notwithstanding the fact that pilot projects and research studies will probably be conducted on a continuous basis in testing innovations not generally available.

Instructional Materials Programs. It is obvious that in the treatment of audiovisual media in this book, they have been deliberately and forcefully tied to the achievement of valid teaching objectives and to the significant problem-solving, learning experiences of the pupils. Audiovisual media are instructional materials, but as has already been pointed out, the term *instructional materials* when applied to school-system service centers is a broader and more comprehensive one. Hence, looking back over the preceding hypothetical media-service program, it can be seen that to convert this program to an *Instructional Materials Service Program* would require the addition of all materials of a printed nature, such as library and reference materials, textbooks, pamphlets, documentary materials, and professional library and curriculum publications. The entire range of school supplies could also be handled by the director of the *Instructional Materials Service Center*. This type of comprehensive service program will be discussed further in Chapters 7, 8, and 12.

The history of experience in any given community and its setting in relationship to a state's educational policy, legislative and otherwise, will have to be the bases for determining plans for service. The director must seek out the facts, must elicit the participation of the teaching staff and his advisory committee to formulate policy for the approval of, or modification by, the superintendent of schools. He must then execute it in terms of valid educational needs.

Evaluation of Audiovisual Media for Selection

The inexperienced and incompetent have no business doing the important work of evaluation. Evaluation is a critical function and one that carries with it a heavy responsibility. The decisions to accept or reject and to rate high or rate low are in a real sense a public display of competence or incompetence. It must be remembered that producers of materials deserve to be treated fairly, and that to choose poor quality materials is not only a waste of public money but also a source of potential educational injury to learners.

Just as an experienced editor will get a good idea of a manuscript by reading a chapter, an experienced media program director, specialist, or an experienced teacher, will frequently be able to make correct judgments leading to the acceptance or rejection of a motion picture by looking for five minutes at the first part of a twenty-minute film. Of course there is danger in such a hasty examination, and there are better ways of getting the enormous task of evaluating material for purchase completed. There are occasions when not to make a complete and critical examination before purchase and distribution will lead to embarrassment and even disaster. The issue in quick judgments is whether or not enough information can be mobilized to make sound judgments. It is always possible that, to an experienced and penetrating observer, the material being examined will reveal early in its organization such glaring weaknesses or obvious strengths in design and treatment that continuance of the examination is unnecessary. The criteria to be stated later will clarify these possibilities.

Two levels of selection should be identified. The first is at the classroom teaching level. At this level the teacher selects from local or remote sources for a forthcoming unit and carries out an appropriate pre-use examination. The second level of selection is the system-wide, central distribution level. At this level the director of instructional media services must assume responsibility for selection of the best materials that teachers need to carry on their work effectively. The best basis for selection of materials at both levels is their probable contribution to valid teaching purposes (these of course being the best possible estimates of pupil needs), their excellence in technical quality, and their suitability for known groups of learners. The only valid reason for selection at the second level is to facilitate selection at the first. The director himself must therefore be able to evaluate materials for selection and to teach others this skill, and he must be successful in obtaining the willing services of teachers in setting up sound

policy and in getting the work of evaluation and selection done as efficiently as possible. The subjective nature of the task of evaluation demands a usable set of criteria—usable, that is, in terms of effectiveness and convenience.

General Criteria for All Audiovisual Materials

The most fruitful line of attack on the problem of the selection of a wide variety of materials is to develop a set of general standards applicable to all kinds of instructional media, and then add to this set whatever additional criteria are needed in order to judge the value of specific kinds of material. Many statements of criteria appear in the literature. Some of these are general in terms of all materials, and some are very specific dealing with the motion picture, the still picture, and pictures for teaching geography concepts or for motivating reading. On the basis of personal experience and a synthesis of the standards recommended in the literature, the author lists the following brief questions which should be of help to the director in developing his ability to choose wisely such materials as models, study prints, filmstrips, slides, motion pictures, television programs, and recorded audio programs.

Curriculum Relationships

1. Will the material be usable in direct relation to a teaching unit? To a specific experience, or problem-solving activity?

2. Is the content to be communicated by the material useful and important? To the pupil? To the community? To society?

3. Will the material make a contribution to major teaching purposes? (Or toward the major goals of the learners?)

4. Does the difficulty level of the teaching purposes (the understandings, abilities, attitudes, and appreciations) demand the help of the material being examined?

5. Will the material be likely to call for vicarious experiencing, thinking, reacting, discussing, studying?

6. Is the content to be communicated presented in terms of problems and activities of the learners? (Logically arranged subject matter may be called for at advanced levels of study.)

7. Will the uses of the material being examined be obvious to teachers?

8. Is content to be presented by the material sufficiently rich in concepts and relationships?

9. Does the material possess appropriate content that facilitates the process of inference? Size? Temperature? Weight? Depth? Distance? Action? Odor? Sound? Color? Lifelikeness? Emotion?

10. Is the material accurate, typical, and up-to-date?

11. Is the kind of material uniquely adapted to the achievement of the desired teaching objective? When media are in programed format for use in instructional systems, are published try-out results valid and convincing?

12. Is the content in the material in good taste?

13. Is the material likely to be of value for a period of seven to ten years?

14. Could the material be used conveniently within a regular class period?

15. Is the content of the material sufficiently rich in number of examples to warrant sound conclusions? That is, are both sides of an issue explored? If not, is the insufficiency pointed out?

16. If the item duplicates content in material already owned, is it sufficiently superior to warrant supplanting the older item?

Technical Quality Relationships

1. Is technical quality of the material artistic?

2. Is the producer's mode of communication adequate for the purpose? That is, is the message put over clearly, forcefully, in ways that attract and hold attention?

3. Are physical size, format, and color satisfactory?

4. Is workmanship in the construction of the material adequate?

5. Is the content to be presented free of conflicts and distractions?

6. Was careful planning by the producer obvious in the content and structure of the material?

7. Did the producer of the material set out to produce the material for school audiences with competent educational consultants?

The prospective director would do well to supply for each of the preceding questions a specific example, either in the affirmative or negative, and to gain as much experience as possible by screening, viewing, listening, or otherwise examining materials from a wide variety of producers. The preceding general standards, applying to all audiovisual materials, will carry the burden of the evaluation in any case, but there are important specific, supplementary standards that will also aid the media director and his teacher deputies in making correct decisions.

Specific Criteria

Additional criteria that apply to specific kinds or classes of audiovisual media are important to all who select materials on the basis of suitability of content instead of an eye-catching title or a glowing superlative-filled advertisement. Such criteria may sometimes by themselves serve as the basis for a quick and correct judgment.

For motion pictures and television programs

1. Are picture images sharp?

2. Is the sound intelligible and realistic?

3. Is there sufficient action?

4. Is continuity natural and understandable?

5. Is composition satisfactory?

6. Is content free of conflicts in music and speech or dialogue?

7. Are pictorial sequences of appropriate length?

8. Is pacing of the action appropriate?

For models and display cases

1. Is construction sturdy enough to withstand hard usage?

2. Is the size suitable for the material and the nature of the observation activities intended? Is the scale appropriate?

3. Are labels easily readable?

4. Are arrangements of models realistic?

5. Does the material contain sufficient details?

For pictorial study prints, filmstrips, and slides

1. Is the content free of irrelevant material?

2. Are the desirable details shown in proper size and number for optimum observation and correct conclusions?

3. Is photographic quality acceptable? Sharpness? Composition?

4. Are pictures free of distortion because of good balance between the artist's technique and educational needs?

5. Are the colors natural and desirable?

6. Are the pictures available in units or well-organized sets?

7. Do sets of pictures provide adequate continuity and range?

8. Is the designated continuity of pictures appropriate for the teaching objective?

9. Are the captions and explanations readable and suitable for the teaching purposes?

10. Are captions and explanations of suitable length and in proper positions for the pictorial content being presented?

For audio programs

1. Are the sound effects realistic?

2. Is speech crisp and intelligible?

3. Is sufficient response-type action implicit in the content?

4. Is continuity between parts or sections unmistakable?

5. Is the program free of conflicts between background sounds and speech or dialogue?

6. Are programs on tape or disks of appropriate length?

For graphic charts and overhead projector transparencies

1. Are the symbols understandable by the learners who are to observe them?

2. Will it be relatively easy for the teacher to bridge the gap between graphic symbols and the real situation?

3. Does the graphic material present the optimum amount of material for the grade level of the observers?

4. Are labels readable at desirable viewing distance?

5. Is appropriate action implied?

For visualized programed learning sequences and media packages

1. Are the steps in the content small enough to minimize errors?

2. Is the role played by visual stimuli significant? For readiness purposes? For explaining difficult concepts or aspects of an item of content? To depict details of a situation for vicarious experiencing? To serve as source material in making detailed observations for comparisons?

3. Is the balance between verbal and graphic or pictorial symbols optimum for the objectives being achieved?

4. Are try-out data for the program sufficiently valid and complete?

5. Are components of the program such as directions and motivation sections, response sheets, and hardware components, if required, well articulated and simple to use?

6. Is the medium, or are the media, used in the program appropriate to the presented content and required response?

7. Is the length of program sections appropriate for normal usage by class groups?

The questions listed under both general and specific criteria have been phrased to call for either *yes* or *no* answers. However, in actual practice, evaluation forms may be constructed cooperatively which will demand the use of numerical or qualitative rating scales. Since the director of audiovisual services is more of a *methods and media* specialist than a *subject-matter* specialist, he must enlist the help of teacher specialists at all levels of instruction to advise him in the essential process of evaluation and selection. This situation demands consideration of the process of putting the criteria to work by the proper people. (Refer to Chapter 11 for special suggestions for evaluating instructional systems.)

The School-System Process of Evaluation and Selection

The media program director will have to consider, as always, the local patterns and policies for the process and make decisions accordingly, but specific plans of action should grow out of cooperatively formulated policy. If such policies do not exist, then the director should take action to have a study committee appointed by the superintendent, after proper discussion of the matter in a bulletin to the teachers. If policies for selecting textbooks, library books, and other materials, such as *sponsored* leaflets and booklets are already in effect then the study committee should be charged by the superintendent with the responsibility of working with the director of media services to develop a set of recommendations for approval by all concerned, pertaining only to audiovisual media. In the absence of a comprehensive policy regarding all instructional materials, the director should undertake to interest all supervisory personnel concerned in developing a workable, over-all operational plan. One or more of the procedures described in the following paragraphs may be needed in setting up an effective process for selection.

Method 1: Preview Panels. This method of procedure is to organize evaluation groups or preview panels on the basis of subject-matter fields, involving a representative from each grade. Such panels should be as numerous as needed to get the work of evaluation for selection completed. Panel members should, of course, be appointed by top administrative officials or by school principals at the suggestion of the media director. The media director must then

1. Arrange schedules and preview programs for meetings.
2. Compile lists of likely materials for consideration, by circularizing teachers with lists of titles, catalogs, or source books.
3. Prepare appropriate evaluation forms, or see that this is done by the original study committee.
4. Coordinate the preview and evaluation sessions with the help of his audiovisual media school-building coordinators.
5. Prepare a brief but effective bulletin for the evaluators, giving instructions to chairmen and other participants.
6. Arrange schedules of materials for panels so that evaluators will be viewing or examining materials with the same curriculum purposes in mind.
7. Arrange his own schedule so as to meet with such groups periodically to find ways of speeding up the process and encouraging the workers.

Method 2: Classroom Try-out. Another method of procedure is to evaluate new materials by actual classroom try-out in advance of purchase. The more expensive materials, such as motion pictures, can be procured on a rental basis, with evaluation reports being made by students and teachers or both. In this case the director will have to do the necessary preparatory and organizational work of lining up the try-out schedules. Less expensive materials may be purchased outright from sourcebook and catalog descriptions, with multiple copies being purchased as soon as actual try-out evaluation can confirm the predicted value.

Method 3: Preview by Individual Teachers. Under still another method, the director assembles the titles desired on the basis of requests from individual teachers, orders the titles in for preview by the teachers requesting them, and upon an expression of satisfaction, purchases the material and adds additional copies upon confirmation of value.

Method 4: Use All Methods in Combination. It is obvious that the preceding methods may complement each other, and that in some cases it may be economical of time and effort of teachers to organize combination methods by schools, taking due precaution not to duplicate effort by having more than one school preview or examine the same materials on a preview basis.

In considering all of the plans just described there is little doubt that a group judgment by teachers who are to use the material will be the safest procedure to follow. Other instances where group judgments are imperative are

1. In the acquisition of basal media, media in programed format, and sponsored materials
2. When materials are made available by unknown and unestablished producers, and
3. When adequate descriptions of content and published try-out results are unavailable at the time of purchase.

Some Principles As a Basis for Selection Practices

Techniques ought to grow out of valid principles of action. An unusually good example of a set of principles governing procedures for selecting instructional materials is to be found in the public schools of Rochester, New York.[1]

1. Instructional materials are those materials which in themselves have educational content and are used to achieve educational goals.
2. A wide variety of instructional materials— textbooks, charts, maps, globes, periodicals, motion pictures, filmstrips, recordings, models, etc.—are essential for best instruction. The selection of

[1] By permission of the late Paul Reed, Director, Department of Instructional Materials, Rochester Board of Education, Rochester, New York. The policy draft was entitled *Guiding Principles and Procedures for the Selection of Instructional Materials* and was dated September, 1957.

instructional materials should be considered as a whole and in terms of their interrelationships.

3. The single, most important objective in all selection procedures is to locate and make available the best materials that can be found to help in reaching the teaching objectives set forth.

4. Selection of materials should be based upon the judgments of those who are to use them. Group judgments are superior to individual judgments. Teacher judgments are best when they are based upon actual experience in using the materials in classroom situations.

5. The selection of instructional materials should be closely coordinated with curriculum development work.

6. Lists of approved and recommended instructional materials should be under constant revision to assure up-to-dateness. Normally no approval or recommendation should be for a period greater than five years.

7. In the case of basal textbooks, a multiple list of approved books is preferred to a single adoption. Exceptions are made, however, where a sequential program of instruction is fundamental, as for reading and spelling.

8. Textbooks and other instructional materials will be listed as "basal" or "supplementary." Wherever possible these materials will be "written into" the courses of study, and all teachers will be expected to make use of the materials listed as basal. Not all teachers will use the supplementary and enrichment materials.

The reader should take particular note of Principles 4 and 8. The "basal" and "supplementary" classification puts an extra burden on evaluation groups, but such addition demands a closer tie with teaching units at various grade levels. In no uncertain terms Principle 4 demands decisions by groups, but especially by those who are to use the materials. Although selection for purchase in advance of classroom try-out is permitted, Principle 4 also stresses selection on the basis of actual use in classrooms as the ideal basis. The Rochester system of procedure, as would be expected from a study of the guiding principles, includes (1) subject-matter councils with key responsibility working under the assistant superintendent in charge of instruction and with the department of instructional materials, (2) selection committees nominated by the councils and appointed by the assistant superintendent, (3) the stipulation that evaluation plans for textbooks and other materials should be worked out by the committees with the director of instructional materials, and (4) a unique purchase plan for motion pictures,

based on actual try-out. By means of this plan motion picture titles selected on the basis of predicted suitability are ordered, paid for, and tried out under normal conditions. Those titles that teachers designate as being desirable are then purchased in quantity, and the subjects that do not meet classroom use standards are then exchanged for slightly used prints of other films. Such plans are, of course, unworkable in cases where only one print of a subject is purchased anyway.

We must be alert, however, to changing instructional needs and the plans and procedures to meet those needs. We do not intend to give the impression that we are concerned solely with the evaluation and selection of any one kind of media such as, for example, motion pictures. Today and in the future there will be multimedia packages, videotapes, teaching systems designed in various formats to meet the special transmission and display systems in towns and cities throughout the nation. Some of the media will be produced locally according to unique teaching plans formulated by curriculum-revision study groups. We shall deal in later chapters with media preparation, with television, and with self-instruction systems, but for the time being we need to turn our attention to the use of evaluation forms to facilitate the work of teacher groups, or the work of teachers as individuals, as they give invaluable assistance to audiovisual media program directors and school-building media-service coordinators.

Evaluation Forms

To expedite and control the work of evaluation and to maintain adequate records for future reference, the director needs to develop special evaluation forms that fulfill local conditions. It is best to develop such forms with selection groups or panels, and if the director doesn't already know it, he ought to heed the fact that tedious, interminable forms to fill out will kill teacher participation faster than any other single error. Some directors have decided after proper instruction in evaluation techniques and after providing appropriate written standards as guideposts, or after a classroom try-out, to ask participants to fill out an extremely brief form that calls for the teacher to write the title, check the *accept* or *reject* blank, and sign his name. Other directors use longer, comprehensive, analysis forms.

Example 3-1[2]

Teacher Preview Judgment

Type of Film _____ Silent? _____ Sound? _____

Source of Film _____ Name of Teacher _____

School _____ Date _____

I.   What educational purposes can this motion picture assist the teacher
      to achieve.   Rating   Grade   Course   Unit

            1.
            2.

II.   What are the strong points of this motion picture?

III. What are the weak points of this motion picture?

IV.   What changes in the motion picture do you suggest?

V.   Is this film one that predominantly

            _____ 1. Raises questions?   Comments: _____
            _____ 2. Answers questions?   _____
            _____ 3. Does both about equally?   _____
            _____ 4. Does neither?   _____

VI.   What is your judgment of the film as a whole?

            _____ 1. Excellent
            _____ 2. Good
            _____ 3. Fair
            _____ 4. Poor
            _____ 5. Useless

VII. From the standpoint of classroom procedure would you use this picture
      in a unit?

            _____ 1. To introduce   Comments: _____
            _____ 2. To present material during unit _____
            _____ 3. To summarize   _____

VIII. How much, if any, preparation will be needed
            _____ 1. On the teacher's part?
            _____ 2. On the student's part?

IX.   Photography rating
            1   2   3   4   5

X.   Sound or title rating
            1   2   3   4   5

[2] By permission. From Charles F. Hoban, Jr., *Focus on Learning* (Washington, D.C.:
American Council on Education, 1942), p. 170.

Example 3-2[3]

STUDENT JUDGMENT OF EDUCATIONAL
MOTION PICTURES

Name of student _____ Boy?_____ Girl?_____

Title of film _____ Silent? _____Sound?_____

School _____ Grade _____ Course? _____

Name of Teacher_____ Date _____

I.   What did you <u>learn</u> from this motion picture?

II.   What were the <u>strong points</u> of this motion picture?

III.   What were the <u>weak points</u> of this motion picture?

IV.   What incidents, parts, or features of the picture did you <u>like</u> best?

V.   What is your <u>general judgment</u> of this motion picture?

        _____ 1. Excellent
        _____ 2. Good
        _____ 3. Fair
        _____ 4. Poor
        _____ 5. Useless

[3] *Ibid.*, p. 171.

Example 3-3[4]

BRIEF EVALUATION FORM FOR SLIDE SETS AND FILMSTRIPS

Title of set or series_____

Producer _____ Color or B & W _____

Approximate Cost: Each Slide?_____ Each Filmstrip?_____

                      Number in Set?_____ Number in Set?_____

Is medium content significant?   Yes_____ No_____

Is quality (both educational and technical) high enough
to warrant purchase?   Yes_____ No_____

Recommended for use in the following subject _____
grade _____ unit of work _____

Recommended for immediate purchase?   Yes _____No_____

Recommended for basal usage by all teachers involved?   Yes _____ No _____

Is this evaluation based on actual use in class?   Yes _____ No _____

Example 3-4[4]

NEW MATERIALS EVALUATION FORM

MEEKER PUBLIC SCHOOLS - 1964
Meeker, Colorado

TO BE FILLED OUT AS NEW MATERIALS ARE PREVIEWED BEFORE PURCHASE

1. Circle: Film   Filmstrip   Slides   Recording ＿＿ disc ＿＿ tape
   Transparency   Chart   Graph   Map   Other

2. Check: ＿＿＿＿ Sound ＿＿ Color ＿＿ B & W   Length ＿＿

3. Title: ＿＿＿＿＿＿＿＿＿＿＿＿＿＿＿＿＿＿＿＿＿

4. Source or Company: ＿＿＿＿＿＿＿＿＿＿＿＿＿＿

5. Producer: ＿＿＿＿＿＿＿＿＿＿ Copyright Date: ＿＿＿＿

6. Preview Date: ＿＿＿＿＿＿＿＿＿ Grade Level: ＿＿＿＿

7. Subject areas: ＿＿＿＿＿＿＿＿＿＿＿＿＿＿＿＿

8. Evaluation: Check items which apply to the material

	Excellent	Good	Fair	Poor
a. Teacher's guide; captions; narrative				
b. Continuity of outline and content				
c. Vocabulary				
d. Authenticity of content				
e. Quality of:				
1. Sound				
2. Color				
3. Photography or artwork				
f. Total Instructive Value				

9. Remarks:

10. Previewer's signature: ＿＿＿＿＿＿＿＿＿＿＿＿

---

[4] Courtesy of Meeker Public Schools, Meeker, Colorado.

Procedures, if carefully worked out, for media evaluation and selection may serve other extremely important purposes such as (1) in-service education programs where evaluation exercises encourage teachers to think critically about their teaching purposes, student experiences, problem solving, and teaching-unit relationships; (2) promotional programs involving the preparation and distribution of lists and catalogs; and (3) maintenance of adequate record-keeping systems. Thus data relative to grade placement, major teaching purposes for using the materials, course and unit placement of the materials, over-all technical quality, over-all predicted educational effectiveness, and data relative to whether the teaching use will be on an urgent or purely elective basis are of vital importance. In these cases evaluation forms must be more comprehensive in scope. Evaluation often does and should involve the learners, and in these cases forms for this specific purpose need to be made up. However comprehensive or restrictive the scope of a form needs to be, the list of general and specific criteria previously presented should be sufficient as a source of questions.

Example 3-5[5]

PRE-VIEW FILM EVALUATION

TITLE _____

COMPANY _____ Year Made____

Teacher_____ School _____ Date _____

Running Time _____ Cost: Color _____ B & W _____

Previewed in: Color _____ B & W _____ Is Color Necessary? _____

Suitable for:

    Subjects _____

    Grades _____

    Rating: Excellent _____ , Good _____ , Fair _____ , Poor _____

CONTENT:

(Please fill out and return card with film)

[5] Courtesy of Euclid Public Schools, Euclid, Ohio.

Example 3-6[6]

The Sherman Film Evaluation Profile   makes use of a 100-point rating scale for each of the following eleven standards:

1. Relevancy to curriculum

2. Accuracy and authenticity

3. Organization of content

4. Scope (suitable number of concepts)

5. Suitability of film length

6. Coordination of picture and sound concepts

7. Pupil interest

8. Pupil comprehension

9. Technical quality of picture

10. Technical quality of sound

11. Over-all rating of film (not necessarily an average of the other points)

[6] Mendel Sherman, *An Exploratory Study into the Feasibility of Using Television for Evaluating Instructional Motion Pictures*, Doctoral Dissertation, University of Southern California, Los Angeles, California, 1955 (unpublished).

Example 3-7[7]

EVALUATION BLANK

1. Film _____ Instructor _____ Date _____

2. Producer _____ Length_____

3. Source _____ Silent _____ Snd _____ Color_____ B & W_____

4. Used in grade _____ Subject_____

5. With unit on _____

6. For use with this unit the film is

    _____ Excellent _____ Good _____ Average_____ Fair

7. Student interest and reaction to the film:

    _____ Excellent _____ Good _____ Average _____ Fair

8. Comments:

9. I recommend this film for use in grade _____ subject _____

[7] Charles Crombie, "Film Selection and Evaluation," *Audio-Visual Guide*, Vol. 18, No. 9, 1952, pp. 18–19.

In Examples 3-1 through 3-7 and Figure 3-3 we present a few examples of actual evaluation forms that have been used in specific situations and which are indicative of the kinds of compromises that have to be reached by media program directors in the construction of any given check sheet for local schools. As we have said, long forms are excessively burdensome for busy teachers, and forms that are too short may not be sufficiently informative for selection decisions. Examples 3-1 and 3-2 date back to 1942 and have been deliberately included to indicate the earlier thought about the evaluation problem.

Somewhere between the briefest evaluation that it is possible to devise and the form that supplies an adequate amount of information for the important judgments to be made, we need to find a compromise. See Figure 3-3. Busy teachers are simply not going to find the time under present work loads to make intensive analyses of film content and write exhaustive reports. As a minimum we need a valid judgment that a given item is useful because of its potential major impact, and we need a written record of that judgment to file for future reference. We should never fail to ask teachers to check a blank indicating whether or not an item of material is so important as to be *basal* in the curriculum, and hence, warranting immediate purchase. After all, teachers need to spend their energy creating effective utilization techniques. It isn't enough just to locate something suitable.

Locating Sources of Audiovisual Media

Where do teachers find the materials to order for try-out purposes? Where do media program directors find the items that they compile in list form for teachers in specific subjects, grades, and problem areas? We must reply first, in answering these questions, that there is unfortunately no single, adequate, up-to-date sourcebook for media. Hence, we must advocate a continual search in commercial catalogs, listings, distributor's catalogs, such sourcebooks as are available, and professional journals and magazines. Anyone who sets out to build a comprehensive reference file of media catalogs, and endeavors to keep such a file up-to-date, knows what an arduous task it is. It is to be hoped that new and improved comprehensive sourcebooks can be produced in the future that can be maintained and brought quickly up-to-date.

The fact is that the media program director must take steps to keep his teachers informed, and must work with school principals, his own staff, and other curriculum personnel in locating media for specific instructional purposes. At the present time, then, it is necessary to consult many sources. Some of the principal ones are itemized in the following list.

1. Audiovisual media magazines: *Audiovisual Instruction* (Department of Audiovisual

Instruction of the NEA); *Educational Screen and Audiovisual Guide* (415 North Dearborn, Chicago, Ill.); *Film News* (Film News Co., 444 Central Park West, New York, N.Y.); and also subject-field journals.

2. *Audio Cardalog Cards*, evaluation cards for educational phonograph recordings. The service is available for purchase from Audio Cardalog, Max U. Bildersee, Editor, Albany, N.Y.

3. *Catalog of Education Film Library Film Evaluations*, Educational Film Library Association, 250 West 57th Street, New York, N.Y.

4. Catalogs of commercial producers of media.

5. Catalogs of major regional and state film libraries.

6. Catalogs of free films, filmstrips, tapes, and phonograph records, and of free or inexpensive instructional materials, available from Educators Progress Service, Randolph, Wisconsin.

7. Catalogs of producers of scientific equipment, and also catalogs of manufacturing promotional agencies, such as Petroleum Institute, American Association of American Railroads, and American Chemists Association.

8. *Educational Media Index*, a comprehensive sourcebook of many media, published by McGraw-Hill Co., New York, N.Y. First published in 1964. Expanded and revised issue expected in 1968.

9. *Free and Inexpensive Learning Materials.* (Prepared by Division of Surveys and Field Studies.) Available from George Peabody College for Teachers, Nashville, Tenn.

10. *Guides to Newer Media.* (By Margaret I. Rufsvold and Carolyn Guss for The American Library Association.) Available from American Library Association, 50 East Huron, Chicago, Illinois.

11. *Index to 16 mm Educational Films* (First Edition in 1967), published by McGraw-Hill Co., based on the work of the National Information Center for Educational Media.

12. *Landers Film Reviews.* Order yearly service from Bertha Landers, 4930 Coliseum St., Los Angeles, Calif. 90069 (P.O. Box 69760).

13. *Library of Congress Catalog—Motion Pictures and Filmstrips.* Order copies from Card Division, Library of Congress, Building 159, Navy Yard Annex, Washington, D.C. (Annual Service, $8.00).

14. *National Tape Recording Catalog* (and supplements) available from the Audiovisual

DIVISION OF INSTRUCTIONAL SERVICES - LOS ANGELES CITY SCHOOLS

SECONDARY FILM EVALUATION FORM
AUDIO-VISUAL SECTION

TITLE OF FILM _____

SOURCE _____

BLACK AND WHITE _____ COLOR _____ FEET OR RUNNING TIME _____ PRICE _____

SUBJECT AREA _____ GRADE LEVEL _____

UNIT IN INSTRUCTIONAL GUIDE _____

ABILITY LEVEL: REGULAR _____   ACADEMICALLY ENRICHED _____   SPECIAL TRAINING _____

CONTENT AND PRESENTATION	NOT ACCEPTABLE	WEAK	AVERAGE	STRONG	OUTSTANDING
RELEVANCY TO COURSE OF STUDY					
ORGANIZATION					
ACCURACY					
CLARITY					
OBJECTIVITY					
PUPIL INTEREST					
SUITABILITY OF CONCEPTS TO MATURITY LEVEL OF PUPILS					
OVERALL RATING (NOT NECESSARILY AN AVERAGE OF ABOVE POINTS)					

SPECIAL QUALITIES OF FILM (CHECK IF APPROPRIATE):

1. FREE FROM OBJECTIONABLE PROPAGANDA _____   6. PRESENTS CHALLENGING IDEAS_____
2. ACCENTS AMERICAN IDEALS AND INSTITUTIONS _____   7. IS SUITABLE FOR: _____
3. IS INSPIRATIONAL_____   (A) AN OVERVIEW _____
4. DEVELOPS CRITICAL THINKING_____   (B) A STUDY IN DEPTH _____
5. STRESSES ETHICAL VALUES_____   (C) A DEMONSTRATION OF AN IMPORTANT PROCESS_____

IS FILM LENGTH SUITABLE?   YES ____ NO ____   RECOMMENDED FOR PURCHASE?   YES____ NO ____

REMARKS:

PLEASE RETURN COMPLETED EVALUATION CARD INSIDE FILM CAN

_____   _____   _____
EVALUATOR   SCHOOL OR SECTION   DATE

Figure 3-3. The film evaluation form shown is the official form that teachers use in the Los Angeles secondary schools, and it is published and explained in the handbook produced for school-building media coordinators. *Courtesy Los Angeles City Schools.*

Center, University of Colorado, Boulder, Colorado. (Jointly sponsored by two national media organizations, NAEB and DAVI.)

15. *Programed Learning: A Bibliography of Programs and Presentation Devices.* Published by Carl H. Hendershot, 4114 Ridgewood Drive, Bay City, Mich. (Catalog and Supplements issued periodically.)

16. *Sources of Free and Inexpensive Teaching Aids.* (Prepared by Bruce Miller.) Available from Bruce Miller, P.O. Box 369, Riverside, California.

17. *Sources of Information on Educational Media.* (By John A. Moldstad for the Educational Media Council.) Available from U.S. Government Printing Office.

18. *U.S. Government Films for Public Use*, a catalog of films and filmstrips. Order copies from U.S. Government Printing Office.

The acquisition of materials is, of course, a continuous process and one that proceeds more easily as teachers become, through first-hand contact with them, acquainted with an ever-increasing range of available subjects. It is up to the director to obtain these materials, either by purchasing them at a pace permitted by local financial support and the educational demand or by borrowing and renting them. In the smaller school systems, in the case of motion pictures, many more subjects are rented during any one school year than are purchased. Thus, the director needs to develop efficient procedures for purchasing materials as well as for providing a steady stream of materials as requested by teachers from rental or free-loan sources outside the school system. Of course both these aspects of acquisition depend on critical evaluation procedures as discussed in preceding pages. However, selection for rental purposes may proceed by less rigorous evaluation, since weak materials may be detected during pre-use examination or in actual classroom-use situations. Teacher experience with rented materials certainly provides a natural opportunity for building a priority listing of purchase selections. Discussion of efficient procedures for renting and purchasing materials follows in the next two sections.

Efficient Procedures for Renting and Borrowing Media

Efficient procedures for ordering and handling media materials obtained from sources outside the school system will save time, money, and effort and will promote maximum effective use during periods of limited availability. Directors of media-service programs must decide on two basic methods for handling the rental or the loan of materials. They must either centralize or decentralize the process or devise some workable combination of these two methods.

The Centralization Method. By this method, all orders for materials are collected from teachers, sent out to distributors, received, paid for, delivered to teachers in the various schools according to schedule, collected, and returned to the source on time by the media program director or members of his staff. This method provides for full control of all details but causes a tremendous amount of work for the central office staff. Clerical and technical operations are necessary, and the director is likely to get himself bogged down by this one job alone unless his staff is adequate. However, this method may be absolutely necessary unless competent media coordinators, or other representatives in each school, are available and are willing to assist.

The Decentralization Method. By this method a school-building media coordinator is delegated to carry out the processes of collecting and sending in orders to sources outside the school and thereafter following through with arrangements to use the material, pay for it, send it back, and collect teacher reports if, as ought to be the case, a continuous program of evaluation is being carried on. This method obviously frees the school-system media center director for more creative work. However, as is often the case, the process gets out of hand with delayed return shipments, nonpayment of bills, overspent budget allotments, lost or missent materials, and so on. Regardless of the plan developed, one thing is certain, and that is that no system will run smoothly and efficiently unless the citywide media director gives it his regular, periodic attention. Of course, additional clerical personnel are needed as a means of economizing on professional time and effort.

Combination Plans. Local factors will have to be balanced in arriving at an ideal plan of operation. A combination of centralization and decentralization may work. For example, orders for specific materials could be sent through the central office, with deliveries being made directly to the teacher involved or to the school-building media coordinator. Under this plan bills could be paid by the central office upon confirmation of receipt by the school involved. High schools and elementary schools in any combination of numbers, all or a few, could operate their own rental programs, depending on the status of the audiovisual building coordinator. Such coordinators may also carry out just a few selected elements of the total plan of operation. For example, they can arrange for use in the classroom, can pick up materials after use, can collect teacher and student evaluation comments, if necessary, and can return material to the distributor.

Essential Elements of Media-Rental Plans

The rental or contractual borrowing of media (mainly motion pictures) is such an important aspect of the entire service program in most schools that the media program director must formulate and implement the best possible operational plan. It is imperative that his plan of action be based on a detailed analysis of the steps in the operation and that all possible labor-saving procedures be incorporated. See Figure 3-4. Confusion over assigned duties in carrying out the various processes involved must be eliminated, and adequate control must be exercised over borrowed property whose care is the director's responsibility. The kinds of action that need to be taken in setting up a desirable media-rental system are as follows:

1. Provide teachers with information about available rental materials through (a) lists of films and other materials rented during previous years, (b) catalogs of closest distributors, and (c) comprehensive sourcebooks conveniently accessible in the school library, teachers' rooms, office of the principal or the audiovisual media building coordinator.

2. Provide teachers with easy-to-use ordering sheets, one sheet for each teacher, or arrange to mimeograph the lists in the first step as order sheets with blanks for filling in dates for the coming year. Accompany ordering forms by a school-year calendar form by weeks and months, with vacation periods and marking periods clearly indicated.

3. Devise a simple but businesslike mimeographed or printed form letter for ordering titles for needed dates. Make up a form to suit local ordering conditions, giving instructions for invoicing and any rigid stipulations relative to the local business operations. This form could be made up in several copies, or printed as a snap-out form if desirable, so that records of orders for files, for the school media coordinator, and for teachers involved would be avail-

able. Also, a form could be devised that would combine the operations in Steps 2 and 3.

4. Compile lists of materials scheduled for each school for each month of the year for which materials have been ordered. Duplicate this list for principals, coordinators, teachers, and operator crews.

5. Arrange a local bill-paying and check-off system, checking off materials as they arrive from distributors, using code numbers or titles so that bills can be matched according to dates to the lists compiled in the preceding step.

6. Arrange to have a receiving system set up in the central office or at the school's receiving office, using the lists of Step 4.

7. Arrange for a delivery and pick-up system on a regular schedule in terms of the lists in Step 4, checking off the return shipments and entering the insurance numbers used on the return packages.

8. As described under the evaluation section, arrange with teachers and other school representatives to issue and collect evaluation reports from students and teachers regarding their recommendations for future purchase of the material provided. Have purchase recommendations come in on three levels of urgency; for example, (a) buy at once for a specific unit, (b) buy soon, and (c) buy for enrichment purposes.

9. Set up a card file for source-data cards of all materials confirmed for purchase according to regular selection procedures. Once a subject has been marked for purchase, do not call in additional report slips. Free teachers from as much detail work and red tape as possible.

10. Set up the entire ordering plan on a two-level basis. First, order in April and May for the following school year when teachers can predict accurately the need for a subject in advance. Second, reserve a budgetary allotment for special needs that cannot be anticipated in advance.

11. The media program director should personally check the operations periodically to see that all involved in the special local plan are carrying out their assigned functions. Facts should be obtained while there is time to take remedial action.

12. Set up a system for collecting information about new material from teachers and other supervisory personnel. Develop a report slip for use by these individuals who send such

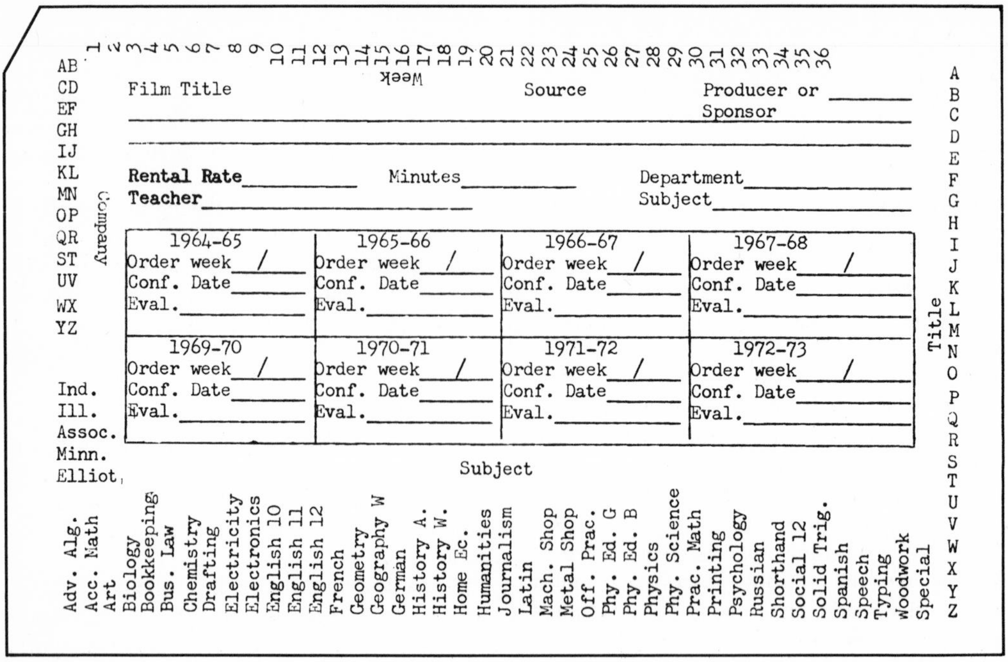

Card 1 (Rental card)

Week: 1 2 3 4 5 6 7 8 9 10 11 12 13 14 15 16 17 18 19 20 21 22 23 24 25 26 27 28 29 30 31 32 33 34 35 36

AB CD EF GH IJ KL MN OP QR ST UV WX YZ

Company

Film Title _____ Source _____ Producer or _____ / Sponsor

Rental Rate_____ Minutes_____ Department_____
Teacher_____ Subject_____

1964-65	1965-66	1966-67	1967-68
Order week ___ /	Order week ___ /	Order week ___ /	Order week ___ /
Conf. Date ___	Conf. Date ___	Conf. Date ___	Conf. Date ___
Eval. ___	Eval. ___	Eval. ___	Eval. ___

1969-70	1970-71	1971-72	1972-73
Order week ___ /	Order week ___ /	Order week ___ /	Order week ___ /
Conf. Date ___	Conf. Date ___	Conf. Date ___	Conf. Date ___
Eval. ___	Eval. ___	Eval. ___	Eval. ___

Ind. Ill. Assoc. Minn. Elliot,

Subject

Adv. Alg. / Acc. Math / Art / Biology / Bookkeeping / Bus. Law / Chemistry / Drafting / Electricity / Electronics / English 10 / English 11 / English 12 / French / Geometry / Geography W / German / History A. / History W. / Home Ec. / Humanities / Journalism / Latin / Mach. Shop / Metal Shop / Off. Prac. / Phy. Ed. G / Phy. Ed. B / Physics / Phy. Science / Prac. Math / Printing / Psychology / Russian / Shorthand / Social 12 / Solid Trig. / Spanish / Speech / Typing / Woodwork / Special

Title: A B C D E F G H I J K L M N O P Q R S T U V W X Y Z

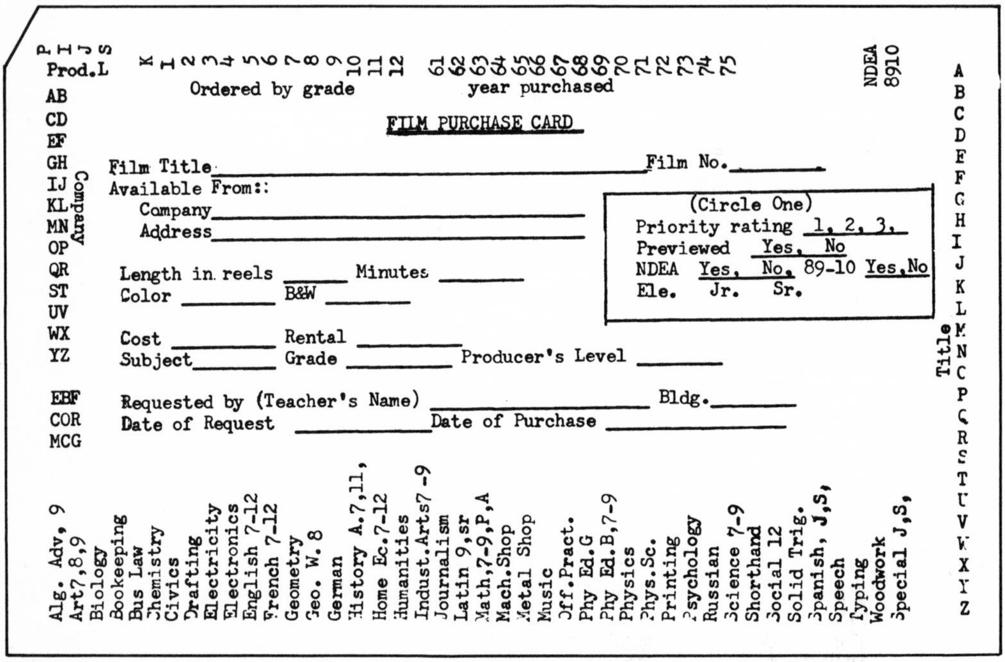

Card 2 (Film Purchase Card)

Prod.L P. I J S Ordered by grade: K 1 2 3 4 5 6 7 8 9 10 11 12   year purchased: 61 62 63 64 65 66 67 68 69 70 71 72 73 74 75   NDEA 8910

AB CD EF GH IJ KL MN OP QR ST UV WX YZ

Company

FILM PURCHASE CARD

Film Title_____ Film No._____
Available From::
  Company_____
  Address_____

  Length in reels _____ Minutes _____
  Color _____ B&W _____

  Cost _____ Rental _____
  Subject_____ Grade _____ Producer's Level _____

(Circle One)
Priority rating 1, 2, 3.
Previewed Yes, No
NDEA Yes, No, 89-10 Yes, No
Ele. Jr. Sr.

EBF COR MCG

Requested by (Teacher's Name) _____ Bldg._____
Date of Request _____ Date of Purchase _____

Alg. Adv. 9 / Art 7,8,9 / Biology / Bookeeping / Bus Law / Chemistry / Civics / Drafting / Electricity / Electronics / English 7-12 / French 7-12 / Geometry / Geo. W. 8 / German / History A.7,11, / Home Ec.7-12 / Humanities / Indust.Arts7-9 / Journalism / Latin 9,sr / Math.7-9,P,A / Mach.Shop / Metal Shop / Music / Off.Pract. / Phy Ed.G / Phy Ed.B,7-9 / Physics / Phys.Sc. / Printing / Psychology / Russian / Science 7-9 / Shorthand / Social 12 / Solid Trig. / Spanish,J,S, / Speech / Typing / Woodwork / Special J,S,

Title: A B C D E F G H I J K L M N C P C R S T U V W X Y Z

Figure 3-4. The rental and purchase of media, particularly motion pictures, demand painstaking attention and management. Time-saving key-punch cards for both processes are used effectively in the audiovisual department of the St. Louis Park Public Schools. Coded information is quickly retrieved, and in the case of rental films, teachers do not have to repeat the process of filling in film data. *Courtesy St. Louis Park Public Schools, Minneapolis, Minnesota.*

reports to the director or to the school media coordinator.

Bearing the preceding essential kinds of action in mind the district media program director will have to formulate an efficient plan for his own local school system.

Efficient Procedures for the Purchase of Materials

It was pointed out earlier that collecting recommendations-for-purchase slips as a result of classroom use of rented materials provided a valuable way of obtaining a priority listing of subjects that teachers believe should be owned locally. Such information, coupled with other continuing programs of selection by evaluation panels, subject-matter or other curriculum committees, facilitates the development of an efficient plan to purchase needed materials.

One of the basic principles for organizing and operating a media-service program is that a variety of materials should be provided for teachers. Most of the audiovisual materials commonly distributed by audiovisual media service centers must be purchased if they are to be made available at all. The first and foremost essential of efficient handling of a purchase program is long-term planning. Elements of such planning require the director to

1. Set up priority lists for purchase in terms of recommendations made by established selection panels.

2. Establish budgetary allotments for purchase on a proposed five- or ten-year schedule, and adjust totals to be spent each year as fluctuations in financial support demand. (See Chapter 13.)

3. Maintain flow of rental materials according to need, and provide for replacement of worn or damaged materials.

4. Set up an ordering format specifying that acceptance is subject to the privilege of exchange of materials if defects are noted.

5. Maintain inventory file cards carrying purchase date, description of content, producer, production date, distributor, identifying number or catalog of item, and a print or copy number in case more than one is on hand. When purchased materials are decentralized, such file cards ought to be transferred to the school

building involved, especially if capable school-building media coordinators are functioning there.

6. Set up an appropriate system for filing the purchase orders for future reference, and incorporate in this an adequate receiving-inspection-report system. The need for such safeguards is obvious, since the cost of replacement copies of some materials (motion picture and filmstrip) is based on length of ownership.

7. Set up a plan for keeping abreast of new materials. Such a plan could include such elements as (a) appointing a group of "spotters" in various subject-matter fields who would check special journals every month, using a brief, special form for reporting new productions to the director or the school-building coordinator; (b) setting up a personal file of up-to-date catalogs and announcements, with titles marked by the media director or a staff member for inclusion in preview sessions of evaluation panels; and (c) encouraging regular study of sourcebooks that are made available in every school library and supervisory office.

A file card for pre-purchase examination of media is used by the Euclid, Ohio, school-district media center. The information collected and saved for future reference is shown in Example 3-8.

Balanced Purchase-Rental Programs

Some audiovisual materials such as maps, filmstrips, and recordings are not generally available on a rental basis. Other materials such as pictorial displays are available only on a loan or rental basis. The director is confronted with the problem of balancing the acquisition of materials through purchase against acquisition by the rental method only in the case of those materials like the motion picture where local, state, regional, and national distributors make them available on either basis. Striking a balance is a matter of being guided by the principle that a variety of materials should be available to teachers when they are needed for optimum instructional value. However, in trying to achieve this objective, the director must consider the following important factors:

1. *Convenience.* It is easier to supply materials to teachers from a school source than to order them elsewhere.

Example 3-8

```
┌─────────────────────────────────────────────────────────────────┐
│                        PRE  VIEW  FILMS                           │
│                                                                   │
│                                         Rec. _____ Rtd. _____     │
│                                                                   │
│   TITLE _____  │
│                                                                   │
│   COMPANY _____ Year Made___          │
│                                                                   │
│   Running Time _____   Cost: Color _____ B & W _____  │
│                                                                   │
│   Previewed in: Color _____ B & W _____ Color Necessary ___ │
│                                                                   │
│   Suitable for:                                                   │
│       Subject: _____   │
│                                                                   │
│       Grades: _____   │
│                                                                   │
│   Rating: Excellent _____ Good _____ Fair _____ Poor ____ │
│                                                                   │
└─────────────────────────────────────────────────────────────────┘
```

2. *Timeliness.* Teachers stand a better chance of getting materials just when they need them when they are in school system or school-building service centers.

3. *Financial Support.* With an adequate budget the flow of rental materials need not be interrupted while school-owned libraries are being built up. On a limited budget, expensive items such as motion pictures should be rented.

4. *Volume of Use and Cost.* If a $60 film is being rented ten times a year and being paid for at a total cost of $40, including postage, it should obviously be purchased as soon as possible. Moreover it can almost be afforded at once. Lease-to-own plans also make sense in this connection, but again budget limitations and demands to maintain a flow of needed materials will determine the point at which purchases can be paid for.

5. *Period of Usefulness.* Materials with limited periods of usefulness such as news releases should not be purchased except for use in self-instruction systems.

6. *Cooperating School Sources.* When nearby school systems arrange to share owned audio-visual materials on a cooperative basis, purchase programs are facilitated. The director should not miss such opportunities for cooperative endeavors. However, agreements and policies need to

be written up in businesslike fashion to protect all parties involved.

7. *Required Maintenance of Materials.* Some materials require more maintenance work than others. Motion picture films need to be inspected after each use, spliced, cleaned periodically, and properly housed under normal conditions of temperature and humidity. Such conditions could conceivably have a bearing upon the number of titles purchased.

The media director must, as experience demands it, strike the most favorable balance between purchase and rental of materials. The preceding factors, considered in terms of the principle that demands timely service for teachers in accordance with valid instructional needs, will help him find the right answer for the local school community.

The Use of Sponsored Materials

A great many materials are available to school people on a free or free-loan basis. Because many of these materials are rich in potential instructional value for teachers and learners, the media director must ascertain whether or not the local school policies permit the incorporation of free materials into the service program. In connection with this decision, two basic principles should be borne in mind. (1) Sponsored materials should be accepted and used only when they contribute to valid teaching purposes. (2) Policies for accepting and handling them should be formulated cooperatively by all concerned. The director must assess such local policies as already exist and if necessary should undertake to encourage the appointment of a representative body to study problems in connection with free and free-loan materials for the purpose of arriving at an over-all administrative policy. The following broad outlines for formulating such a policy for the school system have been stated by the American Association of School Administrators:[8]

1. Define clearly the relation that materials must bear to the basic purposes and objectives of the schools.
2. Provide specific guidelines upon which rules for selection and use can be based.
3. Give assurances to teachers concerning the limits within which they have official backing in the selection and use of materials.
4. Delegate responsibility to appropriate administrative officials or other school personnel for selection and handling of materials.
5. Provide some means of maintaining community confidence in the schools and of safeguarding them against unwarranted pressures.
6. Make available necessary funds so that teachers are not forced to use free materials as substitutes for superior materials that could be purchased.

Whenever appropriate the director should see to it that materials to be deposited for local distribution are properly evaluated and that free materials requested by teachers on a short-term loan basis from distributors other than the school system are previewed before classroom use. Reports of such previews, with the estimate of value, should be collected for the record-keeping system. As a part of over-all school-system policy, or as a part of the audiovisual service policy, selection panels may need to be informed of the necessary safeguards. When such instruction is necessary, it can be provided easily in a widely distributed bulletin. Desirable free materials to be incorporated in the media

[8] By permission, *Choosing Free Materials for Use in the Schools* (Washington, D.C.: The American Association of School Administrators, NEA, 1955), p. 14.

services program should, of course, be listed, publicized, and afforded proper curriculum placement.

The Selection of Media Equipment

The kind and amount of equipment obtained and the way it is made available to teachers is a matter of great importance to the success of the entire media-service program. This section seeks to guide the prospective director in developing his ability to define and solve problems in evaluating, selecting, planning, and purchasing media equipment for instruction. See also Chapters 9, 10, and 11, with respect to media preparation, television, and instructional systems equipment installations.

Earlier in this chapter a listing of audiovisual media was presented, and the kinds of equipment necessary for their instructional use were indicated. The reader should refer to that listing from time to time as necessary. Two important general aspects of the media equipment problem are (1) the process of selection, and (2) the standardization of equipment brands.

The Process of Selection

The media director must bear the responsibility of deciding what to buy, but those who are to use the equipment deserve the right to participate. In inviting and encouraging participation by an equipment committee, the director does not abdicate; rather he needs to use his own specially developed powers of observation in being a leader of the group. Working with a director, a selection panel, if composed of a physics teacher, a machine-shop teacher, an experienced school-building media coordinator or two, a school principal or two, and from two to four elementary and secondary school teachers, ought to be able to come to a sound decision on critical equipment problems. The director should seek this kind of participation, and if the evidence turned up is against his own view of what should be done, he should be open-minded enough to accept the decision as the best policy and then execute it to the best of his ability. The director must realize that the pressures to purchase a specific brand of media equipment may be terrific. Many times local and regional distributors can muster strong forces within a community that can result in extremely embarrassing situations. Hence there is a significant advantage in a pooled judgment using all the facts that can be gained from representative participation by skilled observers in competitive demonstrations.

But the job of evaluating and actually selecting a specific brand is not the whole problem. Prior to or concurrently with such activity, the equipment-study group should be charged with the formulation of an *operational plan* for handling media equipment problems. The director should therefore merge the following or similar elements into the best possible plan for his school system:

1. Secure the appointment by top administrators of an Equipment Selection Panel, and see to it that qualified, impartial, dedicated individuals are chosen.
2. Write up the charge of responsibility for the appointed officials, including authority to reach final decisions in matters of equipment selection.
3. Lead the group to write up and legislate an operational plan including such provisions as (a) procedures for handling competitive demonstrations, (b) procedure for reviewing decisions, (c) a statement of the policy to standardize media equipment purchases, or a statement as to nonstandardization as a policy, how broad or narrow each policy would be, and (d) provisions for expanding the size of the group by calling in additional advisory members from special fields.

These are the crucial matters of process, and the media program director should consider carefully the pros and cons for standardization and be prepared to discuss this matter, guiding the policy-forming body to a good decision in terms of local conditions. This second general aspect of the equipment problem is considered next.

Standardization of Media Equipment

By standardization of media equipment is meant a firm commitment to the plan to purchase the product of only one manufacturer in each category or kind of equipment. Thus a school system under a standardization policy would own only one make of motion picture projector, only one make of tape recorder, and so on. There are a number of important advantages and a few disadvantages to such standardization. The advantages are:

1. It is easier to train teachers and students to operate the equipment; hence less time and effort will be spent by supervisory personnel on this phase of service.
2. There will be fewer operational failures in the classroom because more people will understand how to control the output of the equipment.
3. It is easier to service one make of machine because local servicemen are more familiar with it and understand how to fix or adjust it.
4. It is cheaper to service the equipment since only one set of spare parts needs to be maintained. Therefore, less money needs to be tied up in a stock of spare parts during any one year.
5. There is less clerical and technical work involved in maintaining the inventory of spare parts, and in storing, organizing, and finding space for them.
6. Standardization under school-system policy eliminates wrangling with distributors every time an order is sent out for bids.

The disadvantages are:

1. Other manufacturers may develop a piece of equipment of better quality, and the company whose equipment has been standardized may not catch up.
2. The company whose equipment has been standardized may go out of business, with the resulting need to get rid of spare parts and change to new equipment.
3. Local or nearby dealers who were depended upon for speedy service may change to another brand, or their franchise may be canceled.
4. Dealers for equipment that has been standardized may bid higher in competitive bidding, knowing that their equipment will be specified anyway.

Actually, achieving a high level of standardization may require years in any given community because of the present supply of mixed items and because of the usually low budget for replacement. When a media program director begins his activity in a given school system, he will have to get the facts by means of a survey or by examination of up-to-date records, and if he works with a policy-forming, media-equipment-selection panel, he may have a real opportunity to study this problem for the purpose of a showdown decision.

But such decisions must be a part of long-term planning. In arriving at any special decision about what media equipment to buy, the director must be a penetrating observer in terms of both general and specific criteria. In applying such criteria for the selection of equipment to go on a standardized listing, the decision is all the more critical, and hence the best possible examination conditions ought to be set up, including (1) competitive demonstrations using identical materials and conditions in the kind of room in which it is to be used normally; (2) actual try-out of equipment under rigorous use for a month; (3) study of the manufacturer's manual; (4) actual cleaning processes and adjustment procedures practiced, even to taking the equipment apart and examining its structure; and (5) letting the equipment operate for a few hours if necessary to check temperature and any other critical operating characteristics as clues to proper operation and satisfactory service. These, of course, are the processes for taking action. We turn attention next to the standards by means of which good judgments of value may be made.

General Criteria for Media Equipment Selection

In judging the value of media equipment, a number of standards of a general nature that are applicable to all classes or types of equipment may be used to good advantage. Such standards or criteria apply, of course, only to the usual classroom type of equipment and then only to the more commonly used types. However, one or more of the general criteria apply to units of all kinds of audiovisual media equipment, regardless of their purpose and location for service. Each of these criteria is explained in the following paragraphs in terms of its utility for judgments.

Portability. Is the piece of equipment easy to handle and move around? Is it reasonably light in weight in comparison with others? Is it compact? Are handles placed conveniently for easy carrying and lifting? (Example: A motion picture projector for classroom use should be light enough to be carried, lifted up, and placed on a projection stand by either the teacher or pupils.)

However, it should be noted that not all media equipment units are or ought to be designed for portability. Some items of equipment should be located permanently in classrooms, and also, many items of equipment are highly specialized, such as a videotape recorder or player, a tape deck for a permanent electronic laboratory carrel, or a motion picture projector

on a pedestal for an auditorium projection booth. We should therefore apply this criterion to media equipment that does have to be deployed in a mobile sense throughout school buildings, or for use in specified clusters of learning spaces.

Ruggedness. Will this piece of equipment give good operating service with a minimum of trouble? Does it have a sturdy appearance? Is it free of vibration during operation? Are the joints, supports, braces, and connections tight and strong? Is the construction material appropriate and heavy enough? Are the carrying handles anchored securely? Are the control mechanisms strong? (For example, a slide projector was found to have an insecure base because of a loosely made joint, and another projector was rejected because it had too many plastic parts.)

Cost. In comparison with others, and in terms of other criteria, is the cost reasonable and competitive?

Ease of Operation. Can teachers and students operate the equipment effectively? In general, is operation of the equipment easy to teach? Are the control mechanisms easy to use? Are the control mechanisms few in number? Are the controls accessible, in full view, and plainly marked? Is the equipment free of operating peculiarities such as loose parts that have to be removed and reinserted? (Example: Sometimes control switches are too hard to turn on and off.)

Quality of Performance. How well does the media equipment meet desirable performance standards? That is, whatever the equipment is supposed to do, does it do it well? Can the equipment be depended upon to perform at desirable levels consistently? (Example: A filmstrip projector must project a bright field of light, evenly focused, on the screen. This is its desired performance. Comparisons of both illumination and focus are easily obtained.)

Effective Design. Is the design attractive? Is it free of unfinished or rough exterior parts? Is it free of imperfections and errors in construction? Is the finish functional and attractive? Is the finish easily marred? Was the equipment designed with school use in mind? Does the equipment include desirable safety features? Electrical? Mechanical? Properly balanced? (Example: A tape recorder, slide projector, and a record player designed for home use may not be strongly enough constructed to take daily handling and use in a school without need for excessive repair and service.)

Ease of Maintenance and Repair. Can necessary minor adjustments be made easily and quickly? Are parts that need cleaning frequently conveniently accessible? Are the parts standard and easily available for purchase? Is it easy to remove the sections likely to need repair, that is, without complete disassembly? (Example: Projectors ought to come apart easily for repairs, and lenses need to be kept clean. Some lenses are too hard to get out and too hard to put back correctly.)

Reputation of Manufacturer. Is production of school equipment a major concern of the company? Is the research, planning, and development record of the company favorable? Is it likely that the company will continue in business for the school field? Are the manufacturer's personnel policies and his relationship with dealers commendable? (Example: One manufacturer has introduced and then discontinued the supply of several items of classroom equipment.)

Local Equipment Status. Is it worthwhile to switch to new equipment when switching means replacement of all similar units presently owned? (Example: Turning in equipment ahead of its normal replacement time is expensive. Gains in quality must be commensurate.)

Available Service. Are repair and emergency service facilities nearby? Are adequate stocks of spare parts maintained locally? (Example: It is expensive to ship equipment away for repairs, and if this is necessary, service to schools may have to be interrupted.)

The general standards have to be applied, of course, in full knowledge of how an audiovisual media-service program functions in the schools. Equipment selection problems can be solved only in terms of how teachers use it in their day-to-day work. Some producers design and manufacture equipment units for the "home" market. Since the functional logic of manufacturing procedures is entirely different, directors need to discern the differences in the requirements of the home and school markets, and they must make sure that their own interests are being protected. The media program director obviously has to deepen his understanding of construction procedures, and he ought to gain experience in predicting what will and will not be serviceable in the long run. However desirable it may be, the director cannot organize, maintain, and operate a *bureau of standards.* Hence, he needs to marshal sufficient help in making sure that his value judgments are accurate. He needs also to consider specific criteria for specific kinds of equipment. These are dealt with in the next section.

Specific Criteria for Media Equipment Selection

In this section specific criteria are stated and questions are raised to guide the evaluator in making judgments in connection with various types of media equipment. The important general criteria should not be lost sight of in the subsequent statements.

Criteria for Motion Picture Projectors

1. *Noise.* Does the projector operate quietly? Motor? Film shuttle? Blower? Switches?

2. *Steadiness of Picture.* Is projected picture free of noticeable flicker?

3. *Controls.* Are controls sufficient for the intended use? Does "tone" control bring out bass and treble sounds sufficiently?

4. *Electronics.* Is sound from speaker free of motor and projector noise at high-volume levels?

5. *Threading.* Can the projector be threaded quickly with a minimum of danger of damage to film?

6. *Automatic Threading.* If threading is automatic, can the projector be threaded manually at the beginning, and also threaded and unthreaded at a point within a film, with reasonable ease?

7. *Rewind Process.* Is the rewind mechanism fast, dependable, and reasonably constant in film tension?

8. *Sound.* Is film speed over sound drum sufficiently constant? Are sound quality characteristics, as for other audio instruments, satisfactory? Are output connections for sound distribution available and satisfactory?

9. *Magnetic Sound.* Are provisions for mixing music and voice adequate? Do splices run over playback head without distortion?

10. Refer also to general criteria.

Recommendations for Tests. Employ standard test films for determination of faithful reproduction of wide-range music, picture steadiness, uniformity of picture brightness, flutter, frequency response, and dialogue intelligibility as follows: *Jiffy*, 135 feet, $12; *Sound Projector*, 200 feet, $15; *3000-Cycle Flutter*, 100 feet, $27.50; *Multifrequency*, 150 feet, $60; *Registration*, 100 feet, $27.50; and *Buzz-Track*, 100 feet, $27.50; and others. All tests of competitive projectors should be made under the same conditions with the same films. Other test films are also available from this source.[9]

Criteria for Regular Slide Projectors

1. *Balance.* Is the base long enough to keep the projector in balance even though the bellows is extended?

2. *Tilt Device.* Is there an easy-to-operate vertical and horizontal tilting mechanism?

3. *Ventilation.* If a blower is not provided, is ventilation adequate for normal uses?

4. *Noise.* If blower is provided, does it operate effectively and quietly?

5. Refer also to general criteria.

Recommendations for Tests. Use same test slides for all competitors. Employ slides with critical focusing content such as small letters.

Criteria for the Selection of Opaque Projectors

1. *Size of Opening for Projected Material.* Is a 10 × 10 inch opening approximately correct for the type of material that is to be used?

2. *Size of Projected Image.* Will the projector project a picture in sharp focus of the size desirable for the rooms where the projector will be used? (If not, are extra lenses available?)

3. *Operating Temperature.* Is adequate light output achieved without excessive heat at the reflecting surface? If heat filters have to be used, is adequate screen illumination maintained?

4. *Blower.* Does blower operate effectively? Reasonably quiet?

5. *Accessories.* Are additional lenses available? Are built-in pointers and material-insertion devices available?

6. *Controls.* Are mechanical and electrical controls easy to operate?

7. *Compactness.* Are over-all size and weight reasonably satisfactory?

8. Refer also to general criteria.

[9] Write to Society of Motion Picture and Television Engineers, for catalog of 16 mm test films, 9 East 41st Street, New York, N.Y.

Recommendations for Tests. Conduct the tests during the daytime under conditions intended for use of the projectors. Use a variety of materials (mounted and unmounted pictures and books).

Criteria for Combination Filmstrip and 2 × 2 inch Slide Projectors

1. *Convenience in Change-over.* Are the change-over parts easy to remove and insert correctly?

2. *Accessories.* Are automatic take-up mechanisms for filmstrips removable? May the projector be manually operated with standard slide changer?

3. *Restrictions on User.* Is the projectionist free to project his materials in his own way, with his own selection pattern, without restrictions and extra techniques.

4. *Framing Device.* Are forming mechanisms sturdily constructed, and properly braced?

5. *Automatic Features.* If the projector is of the automatic type, is remote-control operation possible and at the sole direction of the projectionist? If slide magazines are to be used, will they accommodate paper mounts, glass, and metal-bound slides intermixed?

6. *Tilt Devices.* Does projector provide horizontal and vertical tilting devices?

7. *Lenses.* Are additional lenses available to permit a variety of picture sizes as needed?

8. *Ventilation.* Is blower operation adequate? Is projector free of defects that tend to shatter heat-filter glasses?

9. *Temperature.* Is adequate light output achieved, together with desirable low-temperature at the point where slides and filmstrips are inserted? At highest wattage operating levels, are materials spared the effect of buckling and warping?

10. Refer also to general criteria.

Recommendations for Tests. Use slides and filmstrips with small details for sharp focus tests. Arrange for large-screen projection if possible. Take illumination readings, or judge visually the evenness of spread of light and sharpness of focus.

Criteria for Selection of Record Players

1. *Range of Use.* Does player have a microphone input for public address use? An extra speaker output for wider sound distribution? Will the player accommodate records at the

four standard speeds? Are the kinds and number of input and output connections adequate for multipurpose use? Is the stereo or monaural provision adequate for the intended usage?

2. *Controls.* Are controls simple to operate? In plain view? Plainly marked?

3. *Cartridges.* Are cartridges easy to replace? Will the player accept standard makes of cartridges?

4. *Sound Quality Standards* (for each or all components). Is uniform frequency response range adequate for the use intended? (In general, the wider the spread in cycles and the fewer the number of decibels stated, the better.) Is the electronic system free of excessive distortion? (In general, the lower the percentage expressed, the better.) Is the turntable speed free of excessive "wow" or "flutter"? (The lower the percentage figure expressed, the better.)

5. Refer also to general criteria.

Recommendations for Tests. Use voice records for intelligibility tests, sustained musical tones for "wow" or "flutter," and violin tones for frequency tests. Employ, wherever possible, standard audio-test records as follows: (a) Series 10LP, Frequency; (b) Series 12, RIAA Frequency; and Series 300, 301, and 302 dealing with stereo tests (all available from Cook Laboratories, 101 Second St., Stamford, Conn.).

Criteria for Selection of Tape Recorders

1. *Position of Heads.* Can heads be reached easily for cleaning? Are heads easily accessible for realignment?

2. *Adjustment of Control Mechanisms.* Are drive and rewind mechanisms conveniently accessible for cleaning and adjusting?

3. *Sound Quality Standards* (for each or all components). Same as for record players. Also, does the recorder have a satisfactory signal-to-noise ratio? (The larger the number of decibels, the better.)

4. *Range of Use.* Does the stereo or monaural provide for record and/or playback adequate for the intended usage? Does the range of operational speeds provide for flexibility in use, or for the specific use intended? Are the kinds and number of input and output connections adequate for multipurpose use?

5. *Controls.* Are the controls simple to operate? In plain view? Plainly marked?

6. Refer also to general criteria.

Recommendations for Tests. Use voice, sustained musical tones, and violin music tapes for tests as described for record players. Employ also Audio Head Alignment Tape for special tests (procurable from Audio Devices, Inc., 235 East 42nd Street, New York, N.Y.).

Criteria for Selection of Overhead Transparency Projectors

1. *Projection Stage.* Will the projection stage accommodate an 8 × 10 inch (minimum) transparency projection area in both horizontal and vertical positions?

2. *Temperature.* Is adequate light output achieved without overheating the projection stage?

3. *Blower.* Does the blower operate effectively? Is the noise level sufficiently low?

4. *Resolution Power.* Do the projection optics provide for adequate resolution power throughout the projection stage area normally used?

5. *Tilt Mechanism.* Is the projector tilted by means of moving the head instead of the projection stage? Is the projection stage level during normal operation?

6. *Illumination.* Does the lamphouse accommodate lamps up to and including 1000 watts? Is the illumination even on the screen? Is the brightness level satisfactory? Is glare from the projection stage sufficiently low?

7. *Controls.* Are switches easy to operate? Plainly marked? Located in easy-to-use positions during projection? Does focusing arrangement permit easy access from a sitting position? Will the head remain in position at any given focus setting without slipping?

8. *Lenses.* Are additional lenses available as accessories?

9. *Mount Frame Guides.* Are vertical and horizontal mount frame guides either built in on the projection stage, or are they available as accessories? Are they easy to install if they have to be purchased separately?

10. *Light-Weight Models.* Does the projector provide for proper on and off switching? Make possible easy access to lamphouse and socket? Incorporate sturdy metal instead of plastic at movable joints and other points of likely breakage? Are focusing limits reasonable for normal usage? Is light output adequate for intended uses?

11. Refer also to general criteria.

Recommendations for Tests. Conduct the tests during the daytime under conditions intended for the use of the projectors. Use a variety of transparencies and sizes of letters including fine grid sheets.

Criteria for Selection of Classroom Television Receivers

1. *Size of Picture Tube.* Does the receiver meet the recommended minimum tube size of 23 inches for classrooms?

2. *Safety.* Does the set meet recommended safety features for classroom receivers? Permanent glass cover for the picture tube surface? Meet Underwriters Laboratory Standards? Automatic power shut-off feature?

3. *Range of Use.* Is receiver readily usable for both open-circuit and closed-circuit reception with a minimum of adjustment? Does the set have an all-channel tuner?

4. *Mounting.* Is the receiver designed for various suspension and mobile-stand mounting arrangements for elevation?

5. *Sound.* Is set equipped with an adequate amplification and sound distribution system? Is the rated power of the amplifier adequate for the location of the set? Are the loudspeakers located in front-of-set positions? Does sound quality meet satisfactory standards?

6. *Controls.* Are the controls easy to operate? Plainly marked?

7. Refer also to general criteria.

Recommendations for Tests. Conduct comparison tests during daytime under conditions of classroom operation. Use same videotape for all receivers.

Criteria for Selecting Projection Tables

1. *Mobility.* Does table come equipped with 4-inch casters, one for each leg? Do casters have rubber tires? Do two of the four casters have locking devices?

2. *Noise.* Does the table roll quietly without vibration?

3. *Level.* Does the table stand level? Do the casters fit properly so as to make the table stand evenly on all four legs?

4. *Height.* Is the height appropriate for the equipment to be used on it?

5. Refer also to general criteria.

In the preceding examples of specific criteria we have dealt with only those common media equipment units that are purchased in large quantities, the instruments that are deployed in optimum manner throughout a school building. Such equipment units as we have indicated carry the daily burden of use, but equipment needs are constantly changing. We have not included here many instruments such as combination tape-slide units, individual filmstrip and slide viewers, and other items such as headsets and screens and the cartridge-type film projectors. Neither have we dealt with the wide range of teaching machines, remote-control electronic learning laboratory equipment, multimedia projection systems, closed-circuit television studio packages, including lights, cameras, consoles, videotape recorders and play-backs, large-screen television projectors, film and slide chains, or the complex dial-access systems. We deal with a number of these media equipment units in later chapters, and it is there that the reader will gain insights into the problems of selecting such newly developed media instruments. It has been our purpose to introduce the prospective media program director to the essential character of equipment using both general and specific, or the unique, criteria that apply to the various types of media.

The media director who can discuss important differences in equipment in terms of the general and specific criteria described in the preceding pages will obviously have to be quite an experienced equipment technician. Such status and competence, if a director lacks it and wants to gain it, could doubtless be compounded by close observation of exhibits at media conferences, laboratory work in formal audiovisual media courses, and a study of manufacturers' manuals. The director will probably not have the time, but with a minimum of a college course in physics as a background he could accelerate the process by spending a week at a manufacturer's factory, at the nearest audiovisual dealer's repair shop, or at a university or nearby city audiovisual media-service center to study special media installations.

One important word of caution is necessary. Whatever else the director is or is not, he must not become a repairman. Any director who spends his time probing for electronic difficulties should be charged with dereliction of duty. He should organize student crews for minor adjustments and cleaning, employ technicians, or should arrange for service contracts with nearby agencies. To be a repairman himself is to waste the school-system's tax dollars. In one unusual case, a director, capable technically, is employed by a local school authority on the basis of special salary payments during a month of his summer vacation period to give all equipment units a thorough cleaning and overhaul. The important thing to note is that this work is done under a special contract when schools are not in session.

Once a director has made the best possible selection of media equipment, there still remains the critical job of buying it. Getting the specified purchases delivered on time, by the appropriate and desired dealer, and for the budgeted amounts, may in many cases prove to be difficult. The next section, therefore, deals with this aspect of the equipment problem.

Efficient Purchase Procedures for Media Equipment

Although the director must frequently abide by rigidly prescribed purchasing procedures as to format, bids, and awards, he can nevertheless set up controls based on his own specialized knowledge that will achieve his objectives. Each of these controls deserves separate consideration.

Long-Term Planning. A thoughtfully prepared plan for purchasing equipment on a priority basis is one of the most important controls for meeting equipment needs. Getting the right equipment at the right time requires planning, and splitting up an equipment budget allotment ought to be done in terms of carefully selected equipment units that are going to meet specific instructional needs. A five-year purchase plan permits a good deal of perspective, and presents more easily achievable goals than a ten-year plan. A long-term plan, in addition to focusing attention on future goals, facilitates thinking about the important problem of equipment replacement. More will be said about long-term planning and replacement in a later chapter when we deal with the topic of budgeting for audiovisual media services.

Equipment Specifications. Directors frequently make major errors in ordering equipment units by not writing specifications properly. Purchases on the basis of public bids makes this problem a critical one and the director must safeguard his own and the public's interest by

giving due attention to complete information. In case the director can name the manufacturer he has selected, he should include on the requisition or order the following, as appropriate: model, number, acceptable serial number, and names of all accessories with identifying catalog numbers. All details of construction including description of materials, manufacturer, weights, colors, and so on, should be added when items to be purchased have to be fabricated. As is the case with classroom light-control systems, not only construction details should be specified, but strict mounting or installation specifications should be given as well. The media program director who thinks everyone understands what he wants and will give it to him whether or not it is specified is naive and is sometimes in for some severe embarrassment.

Some central purchasing agencies call for publicly advertised bids on all purchases over $1,000 and will not permit the specifying of a brand name unless the term *or equal* is added. This forces the director to (1) write specifications in terms of construction characteristics, that is, include in the specifications such unique features as total weight, switches and controls, and mechanisms, not possessed by competitive products; (2) plan in advance and accompany the requisition with a letter stating the reasons why none other than the particular brand or make specified can be used; or (3) take formal steps to have the product specified made standard officially by the central purchasing authority. Although difficult, step three will probably be most satisfactory in the long run.

Serial Numbers. As is sometimes the case, new models of a particular make are about to be released at the time orders are being placed. Dealers, having bid on old models, may feel no compulsion to supply the newer and sometimes improved product, especially if bids are highly competitive. Directors should, therefore, make sure that serial numbers of current-year models and information about release dates of new models are ascertained in advance. With such facts at hand he can then specify the lower limit of serial numbers of equipment units that will be acceptable.

Conditions for Purchase. A number of interesting tactics may be employed in directing orders to bona fide local dealers who have given notable services to the schools and to the field in general. Chief among these conditions of purchase, and of course wholly ethical, is the specified-service arrangement that metropolitan "warehouse" merchants cannot meet. Conditions of purchase are many, and the director should use imagination in devising them and discretion in using them. Some examples are as follows: (1) specifying free service for six months beyond factory guarantee, except for replacement of parts; (2) specifying free-loan of equipment during emergency repair periods; (3) specifying that the seller must maintain a full stock of spare parts for the equipment purchased; (4) specifying that purchased equipment must be delivered, set up, and operated satisfactorily by the dealer or his salesman prior to acceptance; (5) specifying in the request for quotations that the seller, or one of his salesmen, must conduct a demonstration meeting and/or operation clinic for teachers prior to the acceptance of the merchandise; (6) specifying that seller must pick up trade-in equipment described in the purchase contract; and of course there are many others. The practice of trading in outworn or obsolete equipment units, not necessarily of the same type as the product being purchased, is highly recommended. It clears the storage shelves of inactive items, thus streamlining the inventory, and as an adjunct of the regular replacement plan it increases the purchasing power of capital outlay allotments. Thus, the director ought to save his outmoded equipment for this suggested use And, of course, the trade-in plan might be an important factor in setting special conditions for purchase.

Problem-Solving Activities

1. Using the general and specific criteria for the evaluation of materials as presented in this chapter, construct a long and short version of a form for any one of the audiovisual media of your choice. Members of the class can choose different media and pool their efforts, working as committees. Results can be mimeographed and a set of forms prepared for each member for each type of material.

2. Under what conditions, if any, should the media program director recommend the use of sponsored (free) audiovisual media?

3. What expendable supplies do you as a media program director feel it necessary to stock for distribution upon request to school buildings or directly to teachers?

4. Show how you would elicit, collect, and utilize the suggestions of teachers in matters pertaining to the selection and purchase (or rental) of materials.

5. Devise a plan for efficient handling of rental materials, from the form for ordering them to their eventual return to the source, basing your plan on any familiar situation you name.

6. What are the basic types of material that you would like to distribute in quantity from a public-school service center?

7. Using your own local school system, or hypothetical situation, apply as many as you can of the criteria for determining which of the following services to add to an already existing program: (a) sets of study prints, (b) cases of realia, (c) magnetic tape and disk recordings, (d) television programing (open circuit), (e) closed-circuit television.

8. Make a listing of the major specific difficulties that would be encountered and that would have to be surmounted in connection with the inauguration of a teacher preparation of media program with a newly equipped and stocked production room in each of the elementary schools of the city in which you now teach. Sketch out your difficulties and outline tersely the way to surmount each difficulty you name.

9. Familiarize yourself with at least some major sourcebooks of audiovisual media materials. What are some strengths and weaknesses in these publications? Which sourcebooks would you recommend placing in each school building?

10. Pretend that you are writing an evaluation of a new film for publication. Follow instructions and the evaluation form given in class, or make up a form using the general and specific criteria mentioned in the chapter. The film selected by the instructor will be shown twice. Take notes and then complete the report. Synopsis and teaching-purpose sections are not to exceed seventy-five words each. (Agree in class on the format for stating the teaching purposes.)

11. What are the advantages and disadvantages of "standardization" of equipment? What precautions can you take to minimize the effects of the disadvantages.

12. Using selected general and specific criteria

for the evaluation of equipment presented in this chapter, evaluate in teams two makes of as many kinds of media equipment as you have time for and as many as your instructor feels it important to present for analysis.

13. How would you defend your choice of a particular kind of projector in a "fight" over bids, two years after a "standardization" decision, when *another make of projector* is being forced upon you by a purchasing agent who can get it at a "price"?

14. Use any standard requisition form, or the one supplied you in class, and write out a proper requisition for twenty combination filmstrip and 2 × 2 inch slide projectors of any make specified by you. (Employ all the ethical tactics you know of and can devise to safeguard your own interests and to direct the award to proper distributors.)

15. Using the Rochester Public Schools' principles for selecting materials, formulate any appropriate specific set of procedures for implementing them. Assume for the time being that these principles were developed in your own community. How would the "democratic conscience" influence your procedures?

16. By what system are media materials rented in your school community? How would you improve it?

17. What would be the advantage of arranging to share audiovisual media with a nearby school community? What precaution should be taken? What policies formulated? How would the problems of cooperative use of media differ if television programs produced locally were being shared instead of motion pictures?

References

Allen, William H. "A Scientific Method for Evaluating Films," *Nation's Schools*, Vol. 47, April 1951, pp. 76–78.

Audio-Visual Equipment Directory, National Audio-Visual Association, Inc., Fairfax, Virginia (issued annually).

The Audio-Visual Program, Bulletin No. 218, Department of Public Instruction, State of Indiana, Indianapolis, Indiana, 1956.

Brown, James W. and Kenneth D. Norberg. *Administering Educational Media* (New York: McGraw-Hill, 1965).

Choosing Free Materials for Use in the Schools, American Association of School Administrators, NEA, 1201 Sixteenth Street, N.W., Washington, D.C., 1955.

Crombie, Charles. "Film Selection and Evaluation," *Audio-Visual Guide*, Vol. 18, No. 9, 1952, pp. 18–19.

de Kieffer, Robert E. *Audiovisual Instruction* (New York: Center for Applied Research in Education, Inc., 1965).

Gerletti, Robert C. "The Importance of an Evaluation Policy for Instructional Materials," *Audiovisual Instruction*, Vol. 7, No. 5, May 1962, pp. 289–291.

Hartsell, Horace C. and Richard A. Margoles. "Guidelines for the Selection of Instructional Materials," *Audiovisual Instruction*, Vol. 12, No. 1, January 1967, pp. 23–26.

Hoban, Charles F., Jr. *Focus on Learning* (Washington, D.C.: American Council on Education, 1942).

Index to 35mm Education Filmstrips, based on the work of the National Information Center for Educational Media (New York: McGraw-Hill, 1968).

Rufsvold, Margaret I. "Guides to the Selection and Evaluation of Newer Educational Media," *Audiovisual Instruction*, Vol. 12, No. 1, January 1967, pp. 10–15.

Shaver, John M. and Carlton Fleetwood. "The Audiovisualist and Centralized Purchasing," *Audiovisual Instruction*, Vol. 10, No. 10, December 1965, pp. 770–773.

Taba, Hilda. "Evaluation Techniques? First Some Fundamental Questions," *Audiovisual Instruction*, Vol. 9, May 1964, pp. 288–290.

With the rush of technological development and the consequently high premium being placed on innovation in educational processes, it can readily be seen that meeting the need to retrain teachers becomes one of the great problems of the educational leadership. Actually the task of in-service education is so important that it demands an all-out creative effort. There is little doubt that in most school systems special measures to get the staggeringly large job done will have to be devised and implemented. Not only is the need to retrain teachers staggeringly large, but it is also a difficult task, for teachers do not easily adopt new methods, and do not put themselves easily into situations that add a feeling of insecurity to an already burdensome work load. The implementation of new methods therefore requires many complex changes not only in facilities, in materials, in the organization of subject matter, and class situations, but it requires changes in people. The media program director is consequently a *change agent* of vast importance in every school system, in fact wherever he works. And thus we must consider a variety of frameworks of reference such as leadership and administrative activity, supervisory activity, and change-process activity.

It was stated early in Chapter 1 in connection with the role of supervisor, that the media program director needs to see his mission broadly in terms of guiding teachers in specialized methods to greater valid achievement. Therefore he needs to be an effective teacher himself, needs to understand the nature of learning, the nature of curriculum design, the nature of planning and organizing for teaching, and needs to be able to evaluate instructional processes in action. In education, valid achievement has but one reference point, bona fide educational objectives, and since this is true, then the supervisor, in addition to his technological roles must inescapably be identified as a coworker in the field of curriculum. Every list of duties for the director of media services includes the function of helping teachers use media more effectively, and it is the purpose of this chapter to point out fruitful ways of getting this job done.

In a tour of public school media service centers a number of years ago, the writer found a diversification of activities, a wide range of thinking among media directors about what constituted the most promising procedures for

4

Organizing Effective In-Service Education Programs

the accomplishment of in-service growth of teachers in this area. In most cases the job was carried out in the face of great odds, without needed personnel, financial support, and time. Some directors sought to work through curriculum specialists only. Others felt that good promotional practices including catalogs and subject-correlated listings were sufficient and that skill-building activities were the concern of the subject-matter specialists and methods people. One person actually spent approximately four hours out of every school day visiting schools to talk with audiovisual media school-building coordinators, or principals, and to make visits to teachers' classrooms. Other in-service education programs were operating on the basis of teamwork on a specific schedule of instructional meetings for and with members of the teaching staff.

This chapter cannot undertake, however desirable it may be for the prospective media director, to synthesize the content of courses in curriculum, supervision of instruction at elementary and secondary school levels, and school administration that may be the routes to competence in the field of supervision. The student must prepare himself diligently in these fields if he is to succeed in his leadership of media services, but it is assumed that such effort will either precede or follow the study of material herein assembled. However, as a proper orientation for the learning activity promoted by this chapter the following questions need to be raised and answered.

1. What is the definition of modern supervision?
2. What is in-service education, and what is the role of the local school system in accomplishing it?
3. Is continuous in-service education necessary?
4. When is a teacher competent in the use of media?
5. How can the goal of competence be reached?

The answers to these questions are given in this chapter.

Modern Supervision Defined

Burton and Brueckner[1] define supervision as

[1] William H. Burton and Leo J. Brueckner, *Supervision a Social Process*, 3rd ed. (New York: Appleton-Century-Crofts, 1955), p. 11.

"an expert technical service primarily aimed at studying and improving cooperatively all factors which affect child growth and development." The term *supervision* carries with it the connotations of inspection and "snoopervision" of an earlier day; hence it may be well to expand the above definition by another quotation from Burton and Brueckner[2] pointing up the contrast between traditional and modern versions of the supervision process:

Traditional	Modern
1. Inspection	1. Study and analysis
2. Teacher focused	2. Focused on aim, material, method, teacher, pupil, and environment
3. Visitation and conference	3. Many diverse functions
4. Random and haphazard or a meager, formal plan	4. Definitely organized and planned
5. Imposed and authoritarian	5. Derived and cooperative
6. One person usually	6. Many persons

The media director's role as supervisor must be in line with modern supervision concepts if his work is to prosper.

In-Service Education and the Local School System

What is in-service education and what is the local school system's role in accomplishing it? In-service education is certainly implicit in the term *supervision*. Hass[3] defines in-service education as follows: "Broadly conceived, in-service education includes all activities engaged in by the professional personnel during their service and designed to contribute to improvement on the job." In implementing a program of in-service education, the role of the local school system is vital. The reader should pay close

[2] By permission. From William H. Burton and Leo J. Brueckner, *Supervision a Social Process*, 3rd ed. (New York: Appleton-Century-Crofts, 1955), p. 13. Copyright © Appleton-Century-Crofts.

[3] C. Glen Hass, "In-Service Education Today," Chapter II, *In-Service Education*, 56th Yearbook of the National Society for the Study of Education, Part I (Chicago: University of Chicago Press, 1957), p. 13.

attention to what Weber[4] has to say on this point:

One of the most neglected agencies . . . has been the local school system. . . . Boards of education, school administrators and teachers have assumed to a considerable degree that the chief source of growth of teachers lies in the practice of attending summer sessions, attending extension classes, and otherwise engaging in study outside the sphere of the school itself . . . such activities are of great significance and importance, yet one of the most fruitful agencies for educating teachers in service could and should be the school system itself. . . . Real learning should suggest solutions to real problems which the teacher has the occasion and opportunity to test in application.

The director of media services should work toward the best possible balance between the agencies being used for getting the in-service job accomplished. His own leadership functioning in the natural laboratory of school activities, seems to provide the most direct path to competence. At any rate, the local situation with its unique needs ought to be made the focal point for all such channels as extension classes, summer study, and conferences used in the in-service education effort.

Is Continuous In-Service Education Necessary?

The answer to this question is an affirmative one, but why? Hass[5] answers it this way.

Continuous in-service education is needed to keep the profession abreast of new knowledge and release creative abilities. . . . An additional purpose is to give the much needed help to teachers who are new. . . . At least for the present, a third purpose . . . must be to eliminate deficiencies in the background preparations of teachers. . . . New teachers rarely begin their teaching service at the peak of efficiency. After a few years in college, beginning teachers are often able to do little more than toddle through their new world of baffling pupil personalities and unfamiliar subject matter. . . . In recent years many

school systems have as many as 30 percent of their teachers starting their professional careers or possessing less than two years of experience.

It is not uncommon to hear the claim that the teacher preparation program must turn out at the preservice level an individual adequately competent to put the wide range of instructional media to work in the classroom. Such demands are unrealistic in terms of today's situation. The best teacher-training institutions in the country can do little more than introduce their students to the possibilities. Even in the important endeavor of unit planning and construction, many are the schools that require prospective teachers to prepare but a single teaching unit in their undergraduate training period.

It is unfortunately still a fact that many schools claiming to offer a media training program for undergraduates are teaching equipment-operation skills only. In these cases the beginning teacher is totally unprepared for the creative acts of planning for the use of media to achieve valid teaching objectives.

The prospective media director has but to recall his own undergraduate training experiences with audiovisual media, assess the present status in general of teachers and their technological capabilities, and then review the changes now taking place, and the conclusion will be inescapable. If he is to be successful in his work of implementing change, he will have to deal continuously with both experienced and inexperienced teachers, and his attention to related problems will have to be, or ought to be, continuous.

The Nature of Teacher Competence with Media

No aspect of his professional thinking is more important than the media director's penetrating insight into what constitutes effective utilization of the new media. As a means of stimulating him to think critically about this magnitudinous job of in-service education we must urge him to make an analysis of a cluster of problems and conditions surrounding his endeavors in this field. We need to continually challenge our ideas and commitments in the area of what we consider to be the fundamentals of teaching method, the dependable values in curriculum

---

[4] By permission. From C. A. Weber, *Personnel Problems of School Administrators* (New York: McGraw-Hill, 1954), pp. 72–73.

[5] By permission. From C. Glen Hass, "In-Service Education Today," Chapter II, *In-Service Education*, 56th Yearbook of the National Society for the Study of Education, Part I (Chicago: University of Chicago Press, 1957), pp. 13–14 and pp. 29–30.

Figure 4-1. A penetrating analysis of the activities, real or implied, shown in these three views, is hardly necessary to draw the conclusion that continuous in-service education of teachers is an indispensable element in educational professional life. Moreover, teachers will have to work together in unprecedented fashion. Also as pointed out in Chapter 2, adequate technical assistance for teachers who are willing to use innovative methods and equipment is a basic law of success in implementing the process of change. (*Top two pictures*, courtesy Fountain Valley School District, Huntington Beach, California. *Bottom picture*, courtesy The Advance Products Co., Wichita, Kansas.)

operation and change, the basic needs and difficulties that face teachers daily which media can fulfill or alleviate, and to consider the creative nature of the decisions that teachers have to make in deciding how to put media to work in their classroom activities. So much is being and has been written about good media utilization, yet, how is it defined? In fact it is not difficult to define this term in a general way, but it may not be so easy to determine if any given example of use has been effective because we do not seem to be able to get all the facts we need soon enough. Even if computer systems are utilized and we know the nature of responses of a group of science students at any given minute of time, we still do not know how individuals in that group will react to stimuli during after-school part-time jobs. But these detailed judgments do become available in time, and thus we must make needed changes in the light of our judgments. This is why we define utilization the way we do. We say that *effective utilization is the system of judgments and procedures by means of which instructional media are put to work to accomplish valid teaching objectives, with proper emphasis upon accepted principles of teaching and learning.*

When does a teacher know that effective utilization has happened? How does the program leader know that a teacher is creatively competent with media processes? Is it likely that competence with motion pictures is entirely different from competence with film-strips? Is competence just showmanship with equipment? In what performance does competence become obvious when a teacher is not even in the classroom when media components combined in an effective system are carrying on teaching processes, most probably with the clerical and technical personnel in charge. What observations do we make to determine teaching competence with media on the part of a studio teacher who presents the telelesson to class groups throughout the school district? There need be little guesswork involved because competence exists in the essential beliefs, understandings, and commitments that teachers possess about technological media, and in the definite, identifiable abilities that teachers possess for putting them to work.

In assisting the prospective media program director to pull together some of his learnings from past experience, to provide a point of departure for discussions and reviews that may

be needed, and to stress the need for developing a set of values and one or more approaches to effective work with teachers in bringing about needed changes, we should push a little deeper into several of the basic aspects of teacher competence with media. We shall deal first with some general aspects of curriculum, with some fundamentals of teaching and learning, then more specifically with the roles that media play in assisting teachers, and finally with a set of general principles that will help the in-service education leader identify crucial abilities that teachers need to develop en route to modern-day media competence. The new roles that can be played by technological media today are vastly different from an earlier day. But concepts of what they can do, how they are and can be related to the medium of print and face-to-face teacher-pupil action, in both individualized and mass-communication format are not static and will undergo change. The media program director must prepare himself, as we have said in earlier chapters to meet new needs and implement innovations. The reference point for media use, now and in the future, will be valid educational objectives, and the curriculum will be, as it has been, the sum total of what is going on in the schools to achieve these objectives.

Before we proceed to several more specific and detailed aspects of the curriculum in relation to teacher competence with media, we ought to sense the deep undercurrent of thinking about curriculum change in our modern-day society. In this more fundamental matrix of beliefs about what the curriculum ought to be like, we ought to make year-to-year and day-to-day decisions about our teaching activities. Or, putting it another way, we can make use of this all too brief discussion of the need for curriculum change as a backdrop against which we can view more clearly the media-use changes that ought to be implemented in courses and at teaching stations. It will be in these changes that we may observe the knowledge and skill of supervisors and consultants, as well as the willingness of the teaching staff to undergo the rigorous mental activity of effective in-service education programs.

Some Changing Priorities in American Education

Central Values As Guides for Curriculum Change. As a point of departure for viewing a number of important curriculum aspects of media-use insights and skills, we ought not to miss a fairly recent formulation of some principles to guide the decisions of teachers with specific reference to what the learner ought to be able to do if he is an educated man. We turn to the formulation prepared by the Educational Policies Commission of the NEA and stated as *The Seven Central Values of the Rational Tradition of 1966* in sharp contrast to the *Seven Cardinal Principles of 1918*. The central values are listed as follows:

1. The longing to know and understand.
2. The tendency to question.
3. The search for data and their meaning.
4. The demand for verification.
5. Respect for logic.
6. Consideration for premises.
7. Consideration of consequences.[6]

In many places in this book definitive and complete discussions about the curriculum, past, present, and future, would have been valuable, had space and purpose permitted it, and this section needs such discussions particularly. We must be ever mindful of the fact that curriculum needs determine the quality and the quantity of the contributions that media or any one medium —or any combination of media—ought to make today and in the future. We must take time now, however, to establish a framework of reference, and hence we turn to some of the ideas expressed by James E. Russell, Secretary of the Educational Policies Commission, in his own book, *Change and Challenge in American Education.*[7] Obviously looking sharply at the rational tradition indicated in the Commission's listing of central values, Russell explained that:

... the rational powers of the human mind are playing an expanding role in modern life; that they are basic to individual dignity, human progress and national survival; and that to help every individual to develop those powers is therefore a profoundly important objective and *one which increases in importance with the passage of time.*

Here is the central insight making for the philosophical revolution in education. This is not to say

that the insight is new. After all, schools have always attempted to develop the ability to think. What is new is the recognition of this role as *central* and *growing*, and with it comes a series of concomitant conclusions about the nature of education, particularly with reference to questions of priority.

We do not know what our children will face in the future. All we know is that it will be different from what we have faced. If they are to succeed in establishing the conditions in which they can earn their own dignity, they will have to know how to make responses which we do not today understand. . . .[8]

When we attempt to envision such a pervasive and massive shift in instructional programs toward the development of rational powers, we must consider some difficult curriculum revision problems in school systems at all levels from elementary through higher education. Russell states the need this way:

... Our greater need is no longer how to do things, how to perform, how to act. It is rather to learn how to think, how to judge, how to balance, how to perceive. . . .[9]

In his own pursuit of methods for implementation, Russell calls for great improvement in the elementary school, insisting that:

The elementary school is the basis of all education. It must therefore be the school where the first steps toward rationality are taken. . . . The biggest change, and it will be a lot more radical than it sounds, will be to enable all elementary schools to actually do what many of them are trying to do now. . . .

When we finally treat the elementary school as our first priority, we will have a true revolution in American education.[10]

We ourselves ask the question, "Is it not possible and probable that in the elementary school, long impoverished in media-use leadership, the widespread and effective use of a variety of media from filmstrips to videotape and computer may well spawn the revolution that Russell is talking about?" We do not in any sense mean to slight his analysis of needs that exist at other levels of instruction also, but we wish for the present to add another observation relative to change in the curriculum. We therefore point

[6] Educational Policies Commission of the NEA. *Education and the Spirit of Science* (Washington, D.C.: National Education Association, 1966), p. 27.
[7] James E. Russell, *Change and Challenge in American Education* (Boston: Houghton Mifflin Company, 1965).

[8] *Ibid.*, pp. 22–24.
[9] *Ibid.*, p. 47.
[10] *Ibid.*, pp. 51, 55, 62.

Figure 4-2. What do you believe James E. Russell means by the term *rational powers*? Is it likely that this little boy is being guided into action that will develop rational powers? Should all learning be dis-covery in the real sense? Is thinking a complex, or a simple and single-action process? Should all learning be done alone? How should the conditions for learning be arranged? *Courtesy Science Curriculum Improvement Study, University of California, Berkeley. Photograph by Herbert D. Thier.*

out several common characteristics of the many so-called new curricula.

Major Objectives of New Curricula. It is not necessary for our purposes to examine the nature of the significant changes that have been wrought in the basic courses taught in our schools since 1951 in detail. The work of revision was implemented on a nationwide basis and took place, as had few if any previous curriculum reforms, largely outside of the usual curriculum revisions undertaken through the endeavors of state and local school systems. It was implemented also because of the rare willingness of scholars at collegiate levels to participate in elementary and secondary curriculum revision problems. In the light of our present discussion centering around the future instructional uses of media, it will be interesting to note the two essential characteristics common to the several, separate curriculum revisions. To present these common characteristics, we turn to two excerpts from the book, *The Changing School Curriculum*:[11]

Excerpt 1

Objectives stress the importance of understanding the structure of the discipline, the purposes and methods of the field, and the part that creative men and women have played in developing the field. A

[11] John I. Goodlad, with Renata Von Stoephasius and M. Frances Klein. *The Changing School Curriculum* (New York: The Fund for Advancement of Education, 1966).

major objective of nearly all projects is to afford students an opportunity to explore, invent and discover; to develop some of the tools of inquiry appropriate to the field; and to experience some of the satisfactions of research scholars. A more distant aim is to prepare the student for intellectual and academic survival in a complex, scientific world.[12]

Excerpt 2

In virtually every field the focal point for teachers and students alike is an instructional package: invariably a textbook or series of textbooks (often paperback) and frequently supplementary books, workbooks, teachers' manuals, filmstrips, films, programed materials, and laboratory experiments. Students often learn about subject matter through audio-visual media of instruction and whenever possible by directly observing phenomena and the methods of dealing with these phenomena.[13]

In the first excerpt, we can see the emphasis on rational powers, and in the second we see the influence of technological development on the accomplishment of instructional goals. Both of these aspects of the teaching process are of course crucial and germane to our general topic.

We may properly ask the question, "What does an emphasis on the development of rational powers of learners throughout the years of a learner's formal educational experience have to

[12] *Ibid.*, p. 92.
[13] *Ibid.*, p. 14.

Figure 4-3. In the top picture we see a youngster studying a filmstrip by himself. Equipment is plentiful. He may well have used a filmstrip viewer instead of a projector and rear-projection screen. The reader should ponder whether the boy is just looking or is he truly studying in the valid professional sense? Under what condition is it likely that rational powers will develop? Is the self-sufficiency being gained by the young student in the middle picture, when he procures his own film-study material from the rack, important? Is it more valuable for the young student in the bottom picture to be giving his report than for the young man's audience to be listening to it? When pupils are given opportunity to make and project media, and to procure and study films, filmstrips, and tapes by themselves, does the amount of media equipment have to be drastically increased in the schools? Do teachers need help in becoming effective, or in growing into or up to such levels of media utilization? (*Two top pictures*, courtesy Encyclopaedia Britannica Educational Corp., Project Discovery, Chicago. *Bottom picture*, courtesy City School District, Shaker Heights, Ohio.)

do with the use of media by teachers and the school's media services?" We must answer quickly that it is what learners do and say in response to the teaching situations in which they are placed or which they seek that determine the nature of their contribution. We predict that under a pedagogical strategy that calls for discovery, creativity, and problem-solving activity, the uses for a wide variety of media services will be legion.

When making such predictions, we must make a significant effort to see the relationships existing between the emphasis on rational powers and the day-to-day activities of teachers and pupils. We must observe that teachers have to seek and find ways to undertake new kinds of problem-solving activities, and find new ways to stratify their talents along lines of working with individuals and small groups on time-consuming activities of a creative and productive nature. It is precisely this view of teaching that by emphasis and priority includes the use of guiding principles set forth later in this chapter. Curriculum leaders in a school system, including media program directors and school-building coordinators, must concern themselves with basic values and principles, with the means for implementing new priorities in teaching-learning activities, and with the pacing of such implementation as they guide their school staffs in shifting their directions of accomplishment toward desirable change.

Curriculum Design As a Focus for Media Competence

One of the fundamental reference points for thinking about media competence on the part of teachers is the nature of a given curriculum design adopted locally. The media program director needs to be familiar with fundamental curriculum designs that have been proposed in terms of changing cultural values, and he should be aware of the fact that the curriculum in any given school community is likely to be a unique mixture of such designs with audiovisual and other instructional materials making a variety of contributions. In a simple classification with sharp distinctions, Stratemeyer, Forkner, McKim, and Passow [14] identify the following four major types of design according to the way in which facts, generalizations, and skills are organized for teaching:

First is the organization by *separate subjects*. . . . Second is the organization by *subject fields* or *groups of related subjects*—history and geography as social studies. . . . Third, and in contrast to the two preceding bases of curriculum design, are the

patterns where scope and sequence are still designated from grade to grade but in terms of *broad areas that cut across subject fields*. In some designs these are areas of living or major aspect of life . . . communication, development and conservation of human and material resources. . . . Fourth are the designs in which choice of subject matter for any pupil group, how it is organized, and how it flows in sequence from grade to grade emerge from the *needs or problems faced by the group*, broadly interpreted. This organization is distinct from the other three in that neither scope, organization nor sequence is specifically outlined and preplanned grade by grade.

Inspection will show that curriculum designs, as they are presently operating in schools, are similar in some respects and widely different in others, but all need appropriate instructional media, the best possible teachers, and as this volume suggests, capable leadership and financial support if they are to be effectively implemented. Each locally adopted curriculum pattern will be certain to emphasize characteristic values. The group of curriculum experts [15] just quoted supports the view that the needs and purposes of learners must be central. They indicate desirable values when they say:

These everyday concerns of learners are the sources of situations which have meaning for them in the light of their maturity and experience and which provide strong motivation for learning. Expressed or unexpressed, these immediate problems, concerns, and interests need to be the starting points around which classroom experiences are developed. This is a concept of the curriculum which . . .

recognizes the work of each individual and allows for his uniqueness in needs, concerns, talents, interests.

helps the learner face the world at his level of understanding.

recognizes the nature of his growth and utilizes the meanings experiences have for him.

values the learner's daily living at any stage of his development as important to the society of which he is a member.

relates his in-school and out-of-school experiences.

The way in which facts, generalizations, and skills are organized for teaching, and the emphasis upon particular values, have a definite bearing on the way media are selected and put to work. However, as has been previously

[14] By permission. From Florence B. Stratemeyer, Hamden L. Forkner, Margaret G. McKim, and A. Harry Passow, *Developing a Curriculum for Modern Living*, 2nd ed. (New York: Teachers College Press, 1957), p. 87.

[15] *Ibid.*, pp. 114–115.

Figure 4-4. We ask the reader to make some judgments with reference to the development of good school libraries as related to rational powers and future learning and change. Is not the relationship between student action at this long row of carrels equipped with Craig readers and the school library shown obvious? (*Top picture*, showing pupils at work in the Sedgefield School Library, Charlotte, North Carolina, courtesy American Library Association, Chicago. *Bottom picture*, courtesy Craig Corp., Los Angeles.)

pointed out, regardless of the curriculum design prevalent in any given community, media will make significant contributions to learning and teaching. In the most traditional subject-type curricula, good teachers will feel the need for a wide range of media to present clear explanations and to develop readiness in pupils for new subject-matter areas by defining issues and developing interest in prescribed activities.

Instructional media will also assist in presenting practical applications of content to everyday situations, as well as aiding in evaluation, diagnostic, and remedial work. Selection will of course be by the teacher, and emphasis in utilization may in some cases be upon memorization.

As curriculum patterns move away from subject-centered designs to the psychological organization of learning activity, technological media will be also used in relation to the purposes of pupils—that is, used in helping in the process of finding solutions to problems that they themselves have defined, selected, and cooperatively planned. In this framework of reference pupil concerns will determine both the nature and the quantity of materials needed. Certainly the teacher will be the guide in suggesting helpful items and will have to locate valid materials as needs for them become obvious or are anticipated. Also, in these cases where preplanning for the year cannot be done, scheduling of materials long in advance, as is common in cases where sequential units of work are taught repeatedly, cannot be practiced. It is readily seen that under such curriculum designs, materials that are produced to serve in the capacity of realistic vicarious experiences, or are produced on topics that deal with pupils' life situations, will be of special significance.

As will be described a little later, media can be utilized in subject-matter aspects of various curriculum designs in providing the means of actually presenting content, controlling such presentation and guiding the responses of pupils, thus playing a new role that may free the teacher for use of talents at a higher stratum of professional activity.

The foregoing broad outline suggested ways that media would be put to work in various frameworks of reference, specifically in this case, to serve curricular needs growing out of a particular curriculum design. We need to combine such insights with what is known about basic principles of teaching and learning as a next step in exploring media competence.

Basic Principles of Teaching and Learning As a Focus for Media Competence

A comprehensive treatment of this subject is of course beyond the scope of this book, but we can introduce the importance of this reference base by a single authoritative quotation listing principles of teaching and learning. The media program director who understands such principles will possess increased capacity to make sound evaluations of teacher performance in a wide variety of situations at all levels of instruction. He will in fact have as his orientation for action a dependable theoretical basis for the teaching-learning process. Teachers who are competent decide to take action, that is, they think of what to do and say in the light of these principles. These dependable principles may become the beacons that guide the process of innovation. We need to know them and believe in them and moreover seek to refine them on the basis of new evidence.

We have chosen the statement of principles formulated by the late William H. Burton which appeared in the original version of his first methodology textbook, *The Guidance of Learning Activities*:[16]

...The salient characteristics and principles of learning and teaching ... are brought together for the sake of clarity and ready reference. The summary is not final but subject to revision by students as new research findings appear.

The Characteristics of a Learning Organism

1. *The learner is a behaving organism.* Activity is primary and continuous.
2. *The learner is a goal-seeking organism.* Activity is directed toward and controlled by purposes. The remote general purpose is to restore and maintain equilibrium and comfort.
3. *The learner reacts to whole situations or total patterns* and not to isolated or abstracted parts thereof. . . .
4. *The learner reacts as a whole.* He reacts all over, intellectual, emotional, and physical reactions being simultaneous.
5. *The learner reacts in a unified way.* Unless interference occurs, his total reaction, intellectual, emotional, physical, is coordinated and integrated toward achievement of purpose.

The Characteristics of Learning Processes and Products

General Definition. Learning is the process of acquiring useful controls of response through experiencing them.

1. *The learning process is experiencing, reacting, doing, undergoing.* Scores of different learning activities are utilized.
2. *The learning products are responses and controls of response*, values, understandings, attitudes, appreciations, special abilities, skills.
3. *The learning process proceeds best when the numerous and varied activities are unified around a*

16 By permission of Appleton-Century-Crofts, Inc. From Wm. H. Burton, *The Guidance of Learning Activities*, 1st ed. (New York: Appleton-Century Co., Inc., 1944), pp. 212–214. (Students should refer also to the second edition, 1952, for an excellent sample of a teaching unit. The material quoted above has undergone a revision in arrangement which was not so useful for the author's purpose; hence the first edition material was used here.)

central core of purpose, when the learner's interest is in the activities and products, when the learner identifies himself with the purpose through originating or accepting it.

4. *The learning products accepted by the learner are those which satisfy a need, which are useful and meaningful.* Learning products which are extraneous to need and purpose are either rejected or learned only superficially. (Actually they are not truly learned.)

5. *The learning process proceeds and the learner grows through continuous individuation of new patterns out of original wholes* and the reintegration of the new wholes into the total personality pattern.

6. *The learning products are perfected through a series of discrete identifiable experiences.* The number of experiences necessary for the production of a change in the learning organism will vary from one to a great number, depending upon: the type of learning, the adjustment between difficulty of learning and maturity of the learner, the relativity of the learning situation to the life of the learner, the speed with which insight develops, and many other factors.

7. *The process of organization implied in (5) and (6) may be slow and gradual, or relatively rapid, or sudden.* Good learning situations will stimulate continuous changes in the pattern or response toward an even better organization. The better organized into systems the learning experiences are, the less likely they will be forgotten. Isolated and fragmentary items are soon forgotten.

8. *The learning products, when properly acquired, are complex and adaptable, not simple and static.* They are transposable from situation to situation, or more simply, there is transfer of training.

9. *The learning experiences, to be of maximum value, must possess lifelikeness for the learner.* They must satisfy a current purpose, be continuous with ongoing experience, and be interactive with a wide and rich environment.

10. *The learning experience, initiated by need and purpose, is likely to be motivated continuously by its own incompleteness.* Further stimulation through subsidiary purposes suggested by the teacher may be necessary.

11. *The learning process and its products are conditioned by heredity and environment.* Hereditary factors: a plastic nervous system, glandular balance, chemical composition and secretions, the various physiological systems, organic drives, etc.

12. *The learning process and its products are affected by the level of maturity of the learner* as indicated by various measures of chronological, mental, emotional, physiological, and social age; by the nature and amount of previous experience as indicated by tests of informational background, interests, needs; by fatigue, etc.

13. *The influence of previous experience upon learning is regarded quite differently by the two major schools.* The associationists stress its importance and note the value of knowing the learners background of experience. The principle of "apperception" is important. The field-theory group places more emphasis upon the clarity and organization of the field or pattern, upon subsequent differentiation through insight. The sensible view would seem to be that both emphases are important.

14. *The presence of many errors in a learning experience is usually though not always an indication that the experience is too difficult for the learner's level of maturity.* Better pacing is needed.

15. *The learning process and the aquisition of products are materially affected by individual differences among the learners.*

16. *The learning process proceeds best when the learner has knowledge of his status and progress.* The satisfaction accruing from success, from challenge to overcome difficulties, and to rectify failure definitely aids learning. Failure imposed by others, or by arbitrary standards beyond the control of the learner, is not an educative situation.

17. *The learning process is unified functionally, but distinguishable types of learning may be separated for discussion:* perceptual, sensorimotor, memoriter, problem-solving or conceptual, affective.

18. *The learning products are interrelated functionally but may be listed separately for discussion.* Values, understandings, attitudes, appreciations, abilities, and skills are all interrelated in any one given learning product possessed by the learner.

19. *The learning process proceeds more effectively under that type of teaching which guides and stimulates without dominating or coercing.*

The Characteristics of the Teaching Process

General Definition. Teaching is the guidance of the natural activities of the learner and the stimulation of desired activities, directing them through educative experiences to the acquisition of socially desirable controls of conduct.

1. The teacher will aid pupils in defining their purposes and will set the stage for the emergence of desirable purposes.

2. The teacher will aid pupils in distinguishing between levels and types of purposes and will aid them to choose those leading to outcomes deemed desirable by our civilization.

3. The teacher will guide or direct (sometimes) pupils in planning procedures for the achivement of their purposes; that is, she will guide or direct learners into experiences possessing maximum lifelikeness, which satisfy the selected purpose, which are continuous and interactive. Direct experiences

will perforce be supplemented by vicarious experiences which should be as vivid as possible.

4. The teacher will guide pupils in a sufficient number of these experiences to guarantee, as far as it ever can be guaranteed, the acquisition of desired outcomes.

5. The teacher will guide pupils into, or will provide for, numerous and diverse learning activities; that is, she will provide for responses from the whole organism.

6. The teacher will aid pupils in selecting experiences fitted to their abilities, needs, interest, and levels of maturity; that is, she will adapt learning experiences to individual differences among the learners.

7. The teacher will aid pupils in discovering how to judge their own progress and will encourage the constant self-evaluation of status and progress.

Another very helpful basis for thinking about media-use competence is a listing of 10 conditions for effective learning formulated and elaborated by Tyler as follows:

1. The student must have experiences that give him an opportunity to practice the kind of behavior implied by the objective.

2. The learning experiences must be such that the student obtains satisfactions from carrying on the kind of behavior implied by the objective.

3. The motivation of the learner, that is, the impelling force for his own active involvement, is an important condition.

4. Another condition is that the learner finds his previous ways of reacting unsatisfactory, so that he is stimulated to try new ways.

5. The learner should have some guidance in trying to carry on the new behavior he is to learn.

6. The learner should have ample and appropriate materials on which to work.

7. The learner should have time to carry on the behavior, to practice it until it has become part of his repertoire.

8. The learner should have opportunity for a good deal of sequential practice. Mere repetition is inadequate and quickly becomes ineffective.

9. Another condition is for each learner to set standards for himself that require him to go beyond his performance, but standards that are attainable.

10. The tenth condition, related to the ninth, is that to continue learning beyond the time when a teacher is available, the learner must have means of judging his performance to be able to tell how well he is doing. Without these means, his standards are of no utility.[17]

[17] Ralph W. Tyler, "New Dimensions in Curriculum Development," *Phi Delta Kappan*, Vol. 17, No. 1, September 1966, p. 27.

Some Implications of Teaching-Learning Principles for Media Utilization

In this statement of characteristics and principles of learning and teaching, the list of implications for technological media could be lengthy indeed, but for the present it will suffice to point out that they ought to be used in relation to those problems and purposes recognized, accepted, and planned by the learner; that they be a part of a process that is novel, lifelike, significant, satisfying, and leading to complex learning products; that media ought to be selected in terms of pupils' maturity and experience levels; that learners should be expected to react to them in different ways, contributing to accomplishment by various routes of endeavor; that the introduction and use of media should be characterized by adequate intrinsic motivation; that media may, in the light of newer roles and arrangements for their use, be put to work in a direct teaching mode, used that is without the teacher getting between the medium and the pupil; and that they be used always in connection with the achievement of identifiable and desirable outcomes. The reader should note also that emphasis is given in the preceding set of principles to learner experiences as the focal point for organization of content, and that the learning products are characterized by their usability in meeting other situations. The implications just stated would hardly permit the director to condone some of the unpardonable errors committed all too frequently in the name of media methods.

Later in this chapter a statement of the roles that the new media play in carrying out such principles will be made, and an additional set of five principles that lead teachers to become creative in their decision-making processes, will be provided. Both of these discussions will be helpful in explaining the proper relationships of media to basic teaching processes.

The two preceding discussions dealing with the important professional aspects of curriculum design and basic principles of teaching and learning have been proposed as a valuable theoretical basis for the media program director's orientation to the over-all problem of teacher competence with media. Deliberately the presentation has been offered in broad outline without details and examples to focus attention on the framework of reference itself. Now, looking at this theoretical basis, we need to point out that teachers work on a day-to-day, week-to-week, term-to-term basis in attaining their objectives. Thus we come face-to-face with the fact that teachers, under their own responsibility or according to operational plans firmly laid down by school authorities, must formally organize content, activities, materials, and problems within and for their groups of learners. This job of organizing content should be considered separately from the job of organizing pupils into instructional groups, and of course it is carried on in a number of different ways despite the nature of the curriculum design. We urge the educational media staff members who are working on in-service education aspects of their program to take careful note of the relationships of media to specific patterns of organization of content.

Organizational Patterns and Media Utilization. One of the major methods for organizing content for day-to-day teaching is the *unit method*. Many expressions that refer to organizational patterns are commonly used, such as the activity method, the project method, the problem method, subject-matter unit, experience unit, several of which generally form a sequence within a course, or in a number of courses in a course of study, for example, in a chemistry course in the college preparatory course of study or curriculum. We must be sure to perceive that a teaching kit or media package, a series of films or filmstrips, or a series of practice sessions in an electronic learning laboratory must be related to a larger stream of curricular activity engaged in by the learners. Certainly we cannot as teachers recommend that we fragment the learning activity into discrete facts learned in rote fashion one by one. We may refer to the basic principles previously stated for the reasons why such organization of content would be unprofessional.

Good unit methods are basic to discriminating, effective utilization of audiovisual media specifically, and are basic to all good teaching in general. It is indeed a pity that teachers everywhere cannot find more time to spend on this rewarding and highly professional activity. However, while some curriculum designs demand preplanning of the organizational structure, others demand that the units be developed with the learners in any given situation. In discussing the implications for organization of instruction, Burton[18] emphasizes the responsibility of teachers as follows:

The course of events in a classroom situation cannot be left to chance. A teacher when he steps before a class to participate in and to guide learning experiences, must have some idea as to what should and is likely to occur. This is true in situations which are planned cooperatively with the children as well as those in which the teacher plans by himself. . . .

Steady improvement in book-centered teaching leads to significant assignments and pupil-teacher planning and to effective unit methods as well. Implementing designs where needs and purposes of the learner are central also calls for unit organization of the type developed with learners. In the reference just cited, Burton[19] gives the following definitions of *subject-matter* and *experience* units:

A *subject-matter unit* is a series of educative experiences centering upon subject-matter materials which are arranged around a central core found within the subject matter itself and which are to be studied by pupils for the purpose of acquiring learning outcomes derivable from experiences with the subject matter. The core may be a generalization, a topic, or a theme.

An *experience unit* is a series of educative experiences organized around a pupil problem, utilizing socially useful subject matter and materials and resulting in the solution of the problem and in the acquisition of learning outcomes inherent in the experiences.

The distinction between subject-matter units and experience units is in part arbitrary. The terms are useful to the extent that, in given situations, they indicate the instructional emphasis to be upon organized subject matter or to be upon the total experience of the learner. Again we must beware of the either-or interpretation. The actual instructional organization developed by a teacher must of necessity use subject matter and also experiences.

The subject-matter unit utilizes many, in fact could not proceed at all without, pupil experiences. Reading or studying books, reciting, working examples, and listening are all experiences, even

---

[18] By permission. From William H. Burton, "Implications for Organization and Instructional Adjuncts," Chapter IX, *Learning and Instruction*, 49th Yearbook, Part I, National Society for the Study of Education (Chicago: University of Chicago Press, 1950), p. 217.
[19] *Ibid.*, pp. 219–220.

though somewhat narrow and limited. A wider range of activities will appear in subject-matter situations where policy and supplies permit and good teachers are at work. The experience unit draws heavily upon many diverse sources of subject matter. The evidence seems to show that a good experience unit is likely to use as much subject matter as a subject-matter unit, with a somewhat wider range of activities. The latter fact is, however, subject to modification both ways in terms of teacher competence.

It is obvious that when units of activity are developed with youngsters, only a part of the planning by teachers is likely to be written down in advance. It is not easy in any case to show quickly in desirable detail just how media equipment and materials are related to unit plans. Actually such a theoretical discussion and the necessary case studies are subjects in other texts, some of which are included at the end of the chapter. It is rather the point of view that we seek to emphasize in this analysis. It is not an easy matter either to provide a set of directions for planning units of work for all the representative curriculum designs. However, we turn again to the work of the late William H. Burton [20] in the valuable reference, previously quoted, for an excellent, briefly stated outline of the procedures involved in planning and using good teaching units.

General Outline for Planning and Developing Teaching Units

The unit organization cannot be reduced to an easy series or processes as was the assignment-study-recite-test process. A general outline is, nevertheless, observable.

1. Objectives are stated.
   a. The teachers' objectives are the understandings, attitudes, appreciations, general abilities, and skills which it is desired to develop in the pupils.
   b. The pupils' objectives are questions, problems, topics of interest, and purposes of the learner.
   c. The teacher will participate in developing pupil objectives. Guidance will be exercised in the avoidance of a large list of trivial questions. Teachers will suggest, and pupils will welcome, questions and problems for investigation which are significant and of which the learner could not know on the basis of his present knowledge.

[20] *Ibid.*, pp. 241–243.

2. An overview is given.
   a. The overview is a brief statement of the nature and scope of the unit. It may consist of (1) a description of the unit in running discourse, (2) an outline of leads in terms of topics, themes, or generalizations, or (3) an outline of leads in the form of actual or probable pupil questions, problems, or proposals.
3. An approach is developed.
   a. A probable introduction or approach is outlined. Two or three or more may be indicated. The teacher endeavors to make clear just how she proposes to get the particular teaching-learning situation under way.
   The pupils' objectives usually develop explicitly, whereupon the procedure turns to planning and working out the plans.
4. The working period is outlined.
   a. Two phases are recognized, planning and working. It must be emphasized that in actuality there is a continuous ongoing process. The approach, the planning, and the working period are not separable but merge, one into the other.
   b. The teacher may plan in advance what to do about the questions and problems which were developed and listed during the approach, or teacher and class may plan co-operatively. In either event, questions, exercises, readings, experiments, excursions, reports, and interviews are planned. Group discussions or socialized recitations, and individual and group reports are used as needed. Committees are set up. Study guides and worksheets may be outlined cooperatively. Exercises will appear for organizing, summarizing, memorizing, practicing, or encouraging creative effort. Possible methods of diagnosis of difficulties, of special disabilities, and possible remedial measures are indicated.
5. Evaluation techniques are planned.
   a. The teacher will indicate how he proposes to gather evidence, showing that the objectives are being achieved. Any and all kinds of tests and evaluational techniques will be used as needed. Pupil participation in all evaluation will be encouraged. As indicated elsewhere, careful training in methods of appraisal is necessary either in the pre-service or in-service education of teachers.
6. Adequate instructional equipment will be noted and its specific use within the unit indicated.
   a. A bibliography of books useful to the teacher and one of books useful to the pupil will be included. The books and, in some cases, the passages must be related to given objectives and learning experiences.

b. Lists will be given of materials, exhibits, tools, realia of all types, audio-visual aids available in both school and community, together with sources.

In the preceding outline several operational phases of the unit may be observed. Audio-visual media, ranging from a videotape to a self-instruction, electronic-learning laboratory, may well be put to work in one or more of these main phases, namely, the introductory or approach phase, the planning and working phase, and the evaluative phase. Since the working phase may demand pupil reporting, sharing, discussing, constructing, demonstrating, and both individualized learning activities and work in groups, a wide range of media-provided experience situations would be expected. Some of the media used in the unit method, or in other methods for organizing instruction, will be demanded for both large-group and small-group presentations, and, as we have already pointed out, some of the media will be the vehicles for direct teaching while the teacher is guiding, for example, one or more students in their creative learning activities in the library or elsewhere. Also, pupils and their teachers may need to observe as well as make special media according to their needs. It would be in such operational phases of teaching units, which in themselves provide a framework for competent teaching, that media staff observers would be likely to identify the need for and find expert use of media in relationship to both conventional and innovative roles. In the next section we shall identify what these roles are and provide ourselves with another reference base for discussing the nature of media competence by teachers.

Basic Roles of Audiovisual Media As a Focus for Teacher Competence

Since it is not the intention in this presentation to offer a detailed analysis of the roles that media play we shall identify each of the roles briefly and state a number of examples. The reader is urged nonetheless to explore their meanings and potentialities as far as is needed in the light of his own teaching experience and subject-matter specialities. In-service education activities designed to build true competence will demand a full knowledge of basic media roles. Only when teachers know and understand the many ways

in which media can contribute to their day-to-day efforts, can they be truly interested in and committed to their effective utilization. The basic roles that media play are discussed in the following paragraphs.

Role 1. *Audiovisual media provide the teacher with the means of extending the horizon of experience.* Good teachers sense the need on the part of pupils for actual experience. How can it be provided? Many times, media can become the substitute for actual experience. Examples of media playing this role are the following:

1. A film journey to the jungle, television program of a Gemini blast-off, a film of close-up moon surface pictures.
2. Studying a reenactment of an historic event by means of film.
3. Studying a colonial setting by means of a field trip to a museum.
4. Studying a model of a flower.
5. Studying an Indian arrowhead brought into the classroom.
6. Making a model of a dinosaur.

Role 2. *Audiovisual media help the teacher provide meaningful sources of information.* In this role media go far beyond the verbal symbol of the print medium in presenting stimuli to learners to enhance communication processes. Difficult concepts and complex informational structures demand clarification and explanation. Students may consult such media sources alone as individuals or listen to and view them in large groups under teacher-controlled situations. Examples of media playing this role are the following:

1. A photo enlargement (or study print) of a honeycomb.
2. A diagram of a jet engine.
3. A drawing of a cave-man family or a habitat grouping in a museum.
4. A motion picture of undersea life in the tropics.
5. A film segment showing the underwing gyroscope of a fly.
6. A relief map of the Norwegian fjord area.

Role 3. *Audiovisual media provide the teacher with the means of guiding and controlling the desirable responses of the learner in relation to stimulus materials of the learning situation.* In

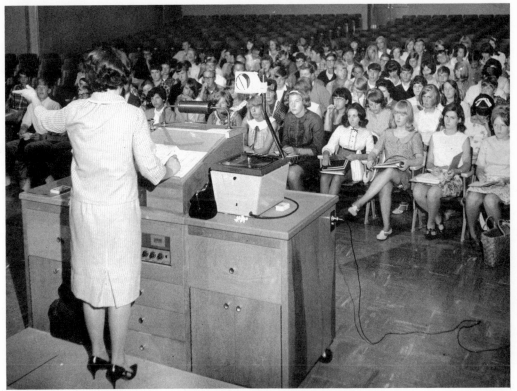

Figure 4-5. Can new and rich, though vicarious, experiences be presented to large groups such as this one at Southwest High School in Portland, Oregon? Can explanations and assignments be given, problems presented and defined, issues clarified while meeting with large groups? Face-to-face? By closed-circuit television? When making instructional presentations to large groups, is it generally recognized that media become indispensable to good communication? Are there teaching situations when independent study may be considered as being highly inefficient? Was this auditorium designed for teaching purposes? Find the motion picture projector. Note several design characteristics of the lectern. For teaching purposes what changes, if any, should be made in the seating? *Courtesy Public Schools, Portland, Oregon.*

playing this role, media materials and equipment units, when appropriately programed and under optimum learning conditions, may take over direct teaching functions without the physical presence of the teacher. It is of course the creative teacher that either prepares the program of media or arranges optimum conditions for learning. Examples of media playing this role are the following:

1. A set of slides and worksheets showing how to make graphs arranged in a self-instructional package.

2. A taped set of directions for advanced students in mathematical computation, for use in an electronic learning laboratory.

3. A programed learning sequence accom-

panied by a set of slides teaching laboratory skills in chemistry.

Role 4. *Audiovisual media provide the teacher with interest-compelling springboards into a wide variety of learning activities.* Media in this capacity assist teachers to open up new units of work through the presentation of problem situations and new possibilities for exploration. Examples of media playing this role are the following:

1. A colorful motion picture introduces a new teaching unit on South American life.

2. A filmstrip is shown and discussed that stimulates students to produce a 17-foot model of a dinosaur, and undertake a three-week study of geological history.

Figure 4-6. In these three pictures students are being taught. They receive instruction. Content is presented, and they write something, or manipulate something. They make responses. All three pictures have something else in common. Normally, a particular person does these things to pupils. What is doing it now? What conditions have to be arranged and managed? What role is being played by media? (*Top picture*, courtesy Educational Laboratories, Huntington, New York. *Middle picture*, courtesy Mast Development Co., Davenport, Iowa. *Bottom picture*, courtesy Public Schools, Manchester, Connecticut, and Dorothy Getchell, first grade teacher.)

3. A motion picture on *Huckleberry Finn* introduces a new teaching unit in the field of literature.

Role 5. *Audiovisual media provide the teacher with the means of overcoming physical difficulties of presenting subject matter.* In playing this role media can be used to perform some very significant tasks for the teacher, some of which are virtually impossible to achieve in any other way. Examples of media playing this role are the following:

1. Reduce the physical burden of lecturing to present information by playing recorded tapes, both audio and video, and by visualized programed learning sequences.

2. Project 2 × 2 inch slides in color to show enlarged views of charts, objects, and live material that cannot be seen in detail from any but the front seats of a lecture hall or other learning space.

3. Use an opaque projector, or make a 2 × 2 inch slide copy of a single picture or leaflet for observation by an entire class simultaneously.

4. Copy and project a cartoon in a few minutes by means of the Polaroid slide-making process.

5. Prepare complicated chalkboard drawings on master sheets and prepare permanent transparencies in color for repetitive presentation.

6. Record content, questions, problems and exercises at three different levels of difficulty for use on three different tape players, for disturbance-free listening and responding by pupils in the same room according to special needs.

Role 6. *Audiovisual media provide the teacher with rich sources of pupil purpose when com-*

municative materials are produced jointly by pupils and teachers. Pupils at almost any level in small or class-size groups become absorbed in organizing themselves as production crews and in making communicative media such as films, slide sets, tape recordings, dramatizations, models and displays, especially for significant purposes. Thus this activity becomes the core of pupil purpose so necessary to absorb the energies of an entire group of students. Examples of media playing this role are the following:

1. Pupils and teacher plan and produce a series of tape recordings on such topics as avoiding colds, good diet, historic shrines of the community, and good communication.
2. Pupils organize a classroom store and really do some business.
3. A high school civics class plans and produces a set of slides in color, accompanied by a tape-recorded commentary, on the topic of bicycle safety, to be used by elementary school class groups.
4. A class plans and produces a series of displays in packaged format for science activities in lower grades.

Role 7. *Audiovisual media provide the teacher with a kit of tools to carry out diagnostic, research, and remedial work demanded by up-to-date instructional purposes.* Emphasis in this role for media shifts to the media instruments themselves, such as the camera, tape recorder, and the projector with a flashmeter. Examples of media playing this role are the following:

1. The electronic learning laboratory records the responses of pupils not only in developing a host of language skills, but also in mathematics and other fields, leading the learner to discover his own difficulties and make responses to correct them under guidance.
2. A camera may photograph eye movements of readers, speech gestures, and facial expressions.
3. A flashmeter and related devices for short-exposure techniques are the means for diagnosing eye-span conditions, and under teacher control may be the means of remediation work in regularized instructional sessions.
4. An audiometer may indicate levels of hearing sensitivity, and optical instruments may test for visual defects.

Competent teachers should be able to make use of media in a variety of roles, thus tapping the great resources available. We should point out, however, that a number of roles may be played at the same time by any given medium. For example, a motion picture may provide a realistic though vicarious experience, and then at the same time serve as a rich source of information, and the observational activity during a realistic film experience may serve to introduce a unit of work, for example, thus serving as a springboard into many and varied learning activities. We should also be sure not to miss the point that teachers may sense the need, and be able to meet it by their own competence in and familiarity with technology, to design and prepare special media for unique purposes. The roles as stated do not imply the sole use of ready-made materials. Some of the media may have to be produced from supplies provided for the purpose in each school building or at media service headquarters. In fact, perhaps, a crew of technicians may be at work meeting just such needs for teachers.

We readily see in these roles, and the few examples listed, assistance for the teacher of such magnitude and importance that it can be given in no other feasible way. We need to see in these roles the possibility of optimum assistance through media already commercially prepared and through media the teacher designs and prepares himself for special purposes and for unique arrangements of learners. We must not miss either the basic difference between two major roles of media that become obvious after careful study of the listed examples. On the one hand there is the basic and seemingly unlimited assistance in helping teachers in personal communicative processes, from providing vicarious film experiences, for example, making observations of automated manufacturing assembly lines, to a multiple overlay diagraming the steps in writing chemical equations, always with the teacher in direct and minute-to-minute control. On the other hand, the assistance of media may be so structured that it offers both presentation of content and guides responses of students as they move toward the accomplishment of valid objectives. Under the latter, teachers may shift a larger proportion of their energies into more talented endeavors, planning new materials, formulating creative problem-solving activities, and guiding students in special

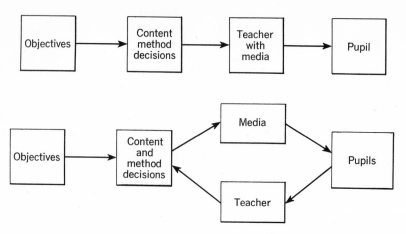

Figure 4-7. The first diagram shows a teacher using media to accomplish specified objectives, being not only responsible but being physically present and in charge of the minute-to-minute, face-to-face process. The second diagram indicates the teacher as a component in the total process, and also media as a separate but related component in direct relationship to pupils in optimum ways as determined by the objectives and underlying conditions, and when the media component is working in the process the teacher may or may not be physically present. *Courtesy Audiovisual Instruction, Department of Audiovisual Instruction of the NEA.*

research and project-completion work. The teacher becomes an expert arranger of conditions for learning, making full use of new components in the teaching-learning process. In a classic position paper, *The Function of Media in the Public Schools*, growing out of the deliberations of a task force organized by the Department of Audiovisual Instruction of the NEA in 1962, edited by Barry Morris,[21] these two major functions were stated as follows:

The first function of technological media is to supplement the teacher through enhancing his effectiveness in the classroom. . . . Educational media are both tools for teaching and avenues for learning, and their function is to serve these two processes by enhancing clarity in communication, diversity in method, and forcefulness in appeal. Except for the teacher, these media will determine more than anything else the quality of our educational effort.

Function No. 2, then, is to enhance overall productivity through instructional media and systems which do not depend upon the teacher for routine execution of many instructional processes or for clerical-mechanical chores.

[21] Barry Morris (ed.), "The Function of Media in the Public Schools" (Prepared by a DAVI Task Force in 1962 as a position paper), *Audiovisual Instruction,* Vol. 8, No. 9, January 1963, pp. 9–14.

Both of these roles are depicted in diagram form in Figure 4-7. The reader should study these diagrams as he ponders the intricate subject of media competence.

Let us pause for a reexamination of the significant aspects in the present exploration of the nature of teacher competence with media. We first focused our attention on curriculum design as a reference base for the use of media by teachers, then we moved to a brief analysis of some major principles of teaching and learning, giving emphasis to teaching plans; next to a consideration of the basic roles that media play in helping teachers with their work; and now we are ready to turn our attention finally to five basic principles that teachers could use with profit in arriving at creative techniques for putting media to work in their day-to-day operations.

Media Use Principles As a Focus for Teacher Competence

One of the standards for judging competence of teachers with media is that the action in general and the decisions about what to do and say in particular ought to be inventive and original in nature. Techniques ought to arise out of a matrix of principles and learnings instead of being utilized as recipes passed along from book or colleague. Insofar as judging and developing media competence is concerned, no aspect of professional thinking is more important than the director's penetrating insight into what constitutes effective utilization of media. This essential must be thought through to the best possible conclusion. The director ought to study the relationship of principles to techniques and then develop from the literature, from his own experience, and from statements of leaders in the field a set of comprehensive working principles that will point the way to effective supervision of media methods in action. Burton and Brueckner[22] stressed this point of view when they wrote:

Techniques are necessary and important—in fact, nothing could take place in any field without ways of doing things. *Principles*—that is, general truths or concepts or accepted tenets—are also necessary. New techniques are constantly being devised which are better ways of carrying out principles and which, furthermore, must be chosen discriminatively to fit given circumstances. Principles are guides that help in selecting techniques. Studies in both industry and education show that workers equipped with the "theory of the thing" are more efficient than those equipped only with sets of techniques which they may not fully understand. . . . The so-called practical teacher is the worst offender, since his level of training and insight is that of the device and not that of intelligent independent invention of techniques based upon principles.

Further on we will state five principles that may form such a matrix of learnings and thus serve teachers well in making their day-to-day decisions about their uses of media. The principles we have formulated demand specific kinds of action on the part of teachers, and the principles are of course infused with vitality only as teachers come to understand valid principles of teaching and learning. The kinds of teacher performance listed with each principle may well become the backbone of any long-term, system-wide program of in-service education in media utilization.

We use the term *audiovisual* in the statement of our principles to focus attention on technological media and the kinds of specific performance teachers need to be able to carry out

22 By permission. From William H. Burton and Leo J. Brueckner, *Supervision a Social Process*, 3rd ed. (New York: Appleton-Century-Crofts, 1955), p. 73.

when they are used. We are well aware that as general statements, with the word *audiovisual* omitted, they apply as well to the print medium which is treated separately in Chapter 12. The principles are briefly stated in the following paragraphs.

Guiding Principle 1. *Teachers should base their selection of high quality audiovisual media on valid teaching purposes and the unique characteristics of a specific group of learners.*

This principle in action becomes the *ability to find and choose audiovisual media.* This ability must be broad enough in scope to encompass the entire range of audiovisual media from field trips to pictograms from bulletin boards to videotape recordings, and from the teacher production of a transparency to the teacher-pupil production of a motion picture. Probably several years of skill-building effort could be expended on this ability alone.

This basic ability demands the subsidiary abilities to:

1. Identify and write out in clear and consistent form the specific valid teaching purposes (the understandings, abilities, attitudes, and appreciations) that are to be developed in the students.

2. Select specific audiovisual media to make optimum contributions to the valid teaching purposes.

3. Use audiovisual media sourcebooks and catalogs.

4. Predict that an identified learning experience among many will influence students in desirable and specific ways.

5. Relate precisely various kinds of selected audiovisual media to specific problems as they are being worked on by individuals and groups.

6. Select technological media for use in new and efficient ways to involve students in self-instruction processes and/or large-group methods.

7. Select audiovisual media to play a variety of instructional roles.

8. Judge the quality and suitability of specific audiovisual media on the basis of the interests, experience, maturity, and powers of comprehension of a specific group of learners.

9. Plan and prepare the more simple, specialized audiovisual media such as slides, transparencies, instructional tapes, and displays for the unique teaching purposes and processes.

10. Design and produce such complex, specialized materials as magnetic sound motion pictures, instructional television programs, and programed instructional packages for classroom and/or school-system utilization.

Guiding Principle 2. *The use of audiovisual media should be preceded by the development of adequate learner readiness for effective participation.*

This principle in action becomes the *ability to build pupil readiness.* When good teaching-unit problems and pupil concerns are the basis for using instructional media readiness plans come easy. However, even though they are tied directly to specific problems and detailed programed responses, teachers need to take proper action in introducing or launching them. The possibilities are limitless.

This basic ability demands the subsidiary abilities to:

1. Develop a specific readiness plan of what to do or say.
2. Guide learners in setting up individual or group needs for the medium or media selected.
3. Relate specific audiovisual media to specific pupil problem-solving activities.
4. Employ a variety of methods for building *readiness* in pupils, including the procedure of setting up a class problem before the materials are presented, and including readiness plans in written form for each pupil for use in self-instruction processes, for any specific audiovisual medium or combination of media.
5. Use a number of sources of information in making decisions about readiness such as teaching purposes and knowledge of pupil characteristics.

Guiding Principle 3. *Details relating to physical facilities and conditions for using audiovisual media should be handled or arranged for by the teacher in a manner that safeguards materials and equipment and provides for economy of time and optimum learner attention.*

This principle in action becomes the *ability to control equipment and physical facilities.* Teachers have to be good organizers and in addition have to know when learning conditions are appropriate. The use of facilities and media equipment ought not to be bungled. For certain kinds of

activities, special equipment know-how is needed.

This important ability demands the subsidiary abilities to:

1. Operate the kinds of audiovisual equipment that are made available by school authorities.
2. Detect improper use or malfunctioning of equipment.
3. Judge the degree of darkness needed for proper viewing of projected images for conducting any specific instructional task.
4. Arrange proper placement of screen, seats, loudspeakers, and other media equipment for optimum pupil attention and participation.
5. Make proper arrangements for viewing and responding to media presentations, and for manipulating or handling models, charts, maps, demonstration materials, and related devices.
6. Plan proper timing for using or presenting audiovisual media within existing schedules.

Guiding Principle 4. *Teachers should guide the learner in the important processes of reacting to, and taking appropriate action as a result of, audiovisual experience situations.*

This principle in action becomes the *ability to guide the responses of students.* The teacher's purpose, namely, the ideas, concepts, principles, conclusions, beliefs, attitudes, appreciations, and abilities, determines the kind of action that learners need to engage in. Seeing a film on hitting a baseball should obviously be followed by some form of physical adjustment and application, or perhaps language activity, or self-analysis.

This basic ability demands the subsidiary abilities to:

1. Identify and call for pupil action in direct relationship to specific teaching purposes.
2. Formulate and use valid provocative and illuminating thought-type questions.
3. Employ good discussion techniques based on known and accepted problems, topics, and issues.
4. Organize pupil action around imaginative, challenging and unique problem-solving project work.
5. Prepare worksheets and arrange media sequences calling for specific programed res-

ponses in the light of (a) objectives, (b) a given audiovisual presentation, and (c) a given instructional environment, or employ commercially prepared programed sequences as available.

6. Organize and manage individualization and/or large-group situations in which media are programed to carry out specific aspects of the teaching process.

7. Organize action of learners around the production of audiovisual materials as significant, class-group learning activities such as producing a sound film, a set of slides, a mural, or a set of charts.

Guiding Principle 5. *Teachers should subject both the audiovisual media and the accompanying techniques to continual evaluation.*

This principle in action becomes the *ability to appraise the value of audiovisual media and the appropriateness of accompanying techniques for using them.* No evaluation can be sound unless valid reference points are known. Such reference points must be the teaching purposes (objectives) underlying organized pupil problem-solving activities, toward the accomplishment of which the audiovisual media will make a contribution.

This basic ability demands the subsidiary abilities to:

1. Engage in the process of self-criticism and be willing to modify previous plans of action.

2. Judge the worth of audiovisual media in terms of specific learning objectives.

3. Scrutinize the procedures used in the light of pupil growth and valid principles of learning.

4. Make use of various sources of data in making judgments of strengths or weaknesses in media and methods.

The influence of such principles is revealed in the work of teachers who have learned to think in critical terms about the *why* of audiovisual media and in terms of principles-techniques relationships. We need also to stress the point that the principles just stated apply to all of the audiovisual media. When teachers apply them to any given teaching-learning situation, their collection of related decisions becomes a unique system for the utilization of a given medium or any combination of media. Sometimes this

collection of decisions is put together quickly a few minutes before the class meets; sometimes decisions have to be made and altered in a continuous fashion as learners and groups respond; sometimes decisions have to be made long in advance as when a teaching system is being constructed for tryout purposes; and sometimes decisions are put together only after painstaking study, as when designing a television program for videotaping with planned repetitive, remote-control usage. These principles are also intended to operate effectively under all curriculum designs, from traditional to modern, and are intended as well to operate in the media director's in-service education programs, as will be seen later. We now turn to the focal point of this chapter as we consider the means by which teaching competence with audiovisual media, and the print medium also may be developed.

The In-Service Education Process

The Need for Good Leadership

First and foremost the media program director must identify the basic tasks to be accomplished. He must then relate cooperatively his own specialized endeavor to the larger stream of activity being conducted by other curriculum, administrative, and supervisory personnel. It is believed that the energies of the director in this field of responsibility ought to bear directly upon teaching teachers to engage in very definite kinds of performance with media without bypassing optimum relationship to the continuous efforts of others who also have important objectives to achieve. The director will have to determine needs in his own field as points of departure, and he will have to seek the help of students, key teachers, principals, and other curriculum personnel for teaching colleagues how to use media equipment and materials effectively. The media director in turn will be called upon to assist others and relate his own efforts effectively to competence-building programs throughout the school system.

The emphasis in this chapter is on teaching audiovisual media skills to teachers, and it is fully intended that the implied action be carried out within the framework of the concepts of modern supervision and good leadership. The goal of teacher competence in any great percentage of teachers in a school system will probably never be reached unless the director is firmly committed to his role as supervisor and is also committed to giving high-caliber leadership. Since the process of leadership is so vital in making progress toward this goal of competence, media program directors should consider some guideposts for action. Weber[23] makes the following helpful suggestions:

1. Possess a thorough understanding of the meaning of democratic control.
2. Have an up-to-date understanding of the nature of learning.
3. Be committed to democratic control, to an abiding faith in people, to the desirability of orderly change, and to the belief that leaders should be parts of groups, not external to them.
4. Approach problems in the inverse order or likelihood of producing controversy. Assume reponsibility for guidance so that aspects of problems least likely to produce strong disagreements are attacked first, more controversial phases last.
5. Be skillful in making inquiry; analyzing situations; discovering attitudes, beliefs, and commitments of members of the group; discovering facts and information; mobilizing facts; and utilizing abilities of group members.
6. Seek to develop teamwork rather than compromise.
7. Guarantee that all persons involved have direct rights to participate in planning in direct proportion to their ability to foresee consequences. Seek continuously to help each individual become increasingly able to assume important roles in planning, policy making, and control.
8. Be imaginative, and be willing to assume calculated risks.
9. Seek always to become a member of the group. The most successful leaders are those who are looked upon as "one of us."
10. Develop such attributes as friendliness and promptness.
11. Be mentally and physically vigorous.
12. Develop the habit of suspending judgment until the facts are in.
13. Possess uncompromising integrity.
14. Measure efficiency in terms of purposes and goals accepted by the group.

The task of teaching and reteaching teachers in a large city is a staggering one, and many

[23] By permission. From C. A. Weber, "A New Look in Leadership," *Audio-Visual Instruction*, Vol. 1, Issue 7, 1956, p. 200.

supervisors make only feeble attempts to get the job done. Other extensive efforts are unfortunately inefficient, and the time and energy spent in these instances should be redirected. To be sure, as the need to increase the tempo of achievement becomes urgent, the job of building competence may well call for extra personnel and the establishment of a higher priority by all concerned.

The countrywide failure to get this job done more quickly should not be overly discouraging, but this failure needs to serve as a challenge because the youngsters in our democracy deserve the best teaching they can get, and to fail in this job may of course be more serious than we generally admit. The truth is that every director of media services needs to reexamine his time and effort budgets to seek more effective ways for reaching the teacher competency goal. In the years ahead it is bound to become even more urgent.

Because each local environment presents a situation that demands unique decisions, no one set of procedures can be prescribed, but this does not mean that there is a paucity of promising patterns for success, and several of these have already been suggested, namely, the *modern supervision* pattern and the *leadership* pattern. Also we pointed out with considerable emphasis the need for growth toward administrative competence with due regard for the value of an innovative personality and other personal characteristics as well, operating in a climate favorable to change. Such patterns of understanding and ability enable directors to work more effectively with teachers in any situation.

Changing the Image. Before we proceed, however, to the next section, which delves more deeply into the parallel between good supervisory action and good teaching, we ought to provide an overview of what may be looked upon as the essence of change in people toward media competence. We have already identified in a previous section the kinds of performance that indicate competence with media, and these we say we should set out to teach. But when media are available with a minimum of inconvenience, why is there oftentimes a barrier of reluctance? We postulate that using media calls for new skills, a readjustment into a new framework of security. A new and foreign image that a teacher has of himself and his action has to undergo change. During a memorable discussion with Henry M. Brickell enroute to a

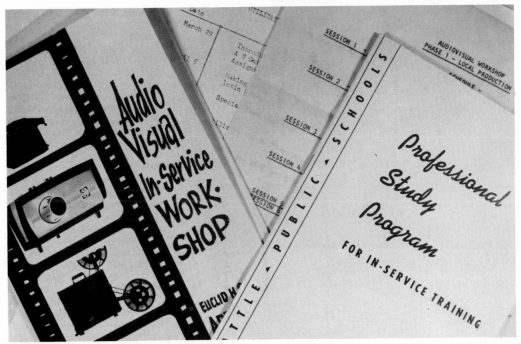

Figure 4-8. Isn't it proper to speak of and plan for the development of new skills in the teaching staff? We need to attack the in-service education problem with a new vigor despite the efforts on the part of some groups to restrict the number of available hours after school to get the job done. The booklets and announcements indicate organized efforts by media directors to conduct fruitful meetings and courses. Samples from a number of booklets and announcements are shown from Euclid, Ohio; Seattle, Washington; and Berlin, Connecticut.

media institute special lecture session from a nearby airport, we discussed his new slant on the change of teachers toward willingness and desire to make use of unfamiliar media. Just how do we see ourselves? What images of ourselves have we developed? And just what would it take to break out of these familiar images of *teaching the book* (like the scrolls of the Middle Ages) to the unfamiliar image of ourselves sitting at an overhead projector without turning around to look at the screen at every change in transparency, or to the image of ourselves in front of a television camera with slides and film clips on call with a flick of a finger or a mark on a script?

Should we not consider this aspect of change in any good in-service education program? Does it require one kind of program, one kind of participation or involvement to become interested, and another kind of activity before a personal commitment develops? Putting this question another way: Is a program that just produces *interest* enough to create the new and positive image? What will move a person to maintain

optimum speed and direction along new paths of activity? What kinds of motives and what kinds of activity? We assert that until the activity develops interest, understanding of value, and the new skill is practiced with an optimum degree of comfortableness and security, or until sufficient help is available to guide faltering steps toward such security, our in-service education procedures will not prosper. We therefore look toward in-service education as a process for teaching teachers, a process that is synonymous with changed behavior.

The Supervision-Teaching Parallel

We therefore assert that good supervision (that is, good in-service education) is parallel to good teaching and that the good *teaching* approach is a promising one. Excellent, modern teaching technique calls for the:

1. Identification of abilities, concepts, and behavior tendencies (attitudes and appreciations) in terms of pupil needs.

Figure 4-9. The task of in-service education of teachers probably can be carried on only at low levels of efficiency unless creative and prolonged effort is expended. One such creative effort was the organization of supervisory districts in New York. Views are shown of the First Supervisory District, Erie County, under the Board of Co-operative Educational Services, with headquarters in Buffalo, New York. Here an in-service education center was set up with staff and equipment for the job to be done. Note the learning carrels for individual study of modern materials using modern equipment including graphic production, teaching machines, and programed media. The heart of the plan was to provide the environment where teachers could explore materials in their own fields of specialization and then as needs were perceived, planning and work sessions were organized. *Courtesy Board of Cooperative Educational Services, Erie County, Buffalo, New York.*

2. Identification of problem-solving activities (learning experiences planned for or planned with youngsters) and the proper introduction of such activities to stimulate desire to participate.

3. Preparation of study guides, plans for action, and the accumulation of necessary materials (instructional materials and supplies).

4. Organization of the group for action.

5. Guidance of activity.

6. Evaluation of the results.

Running parallel to this line of action is the action of a good supervisor who organizes a learning situation for teachers, just as a skillful teacher organizes a learning situation for his pupils. The good supervisor of necessity must:

1. Discover needs of teachers in reaching new levels of competence with media and in terms of the needs, identify specific abilities and understandings which if developed will lead to the desired changes in behavior.

2. Identify problem-solving activities for and/or with the assembled teachers (learning experiences for teachers, taking necessary care in building group readiness to participate) both before and after the group has assembled.

3. Procure and present guides, bulletins, and necessary supplies and materials for the planned learning activity.

4. Organize the group for action, that is, organize voluntary committees or action teams under captains or chairmen.

5. Guide the work of individuals and groups, participate, explain, demonstrate, or arrange for this activity to be done.

6. Evaluate the results and plan for follow-up by questionnaires, bulletins, individual reports, and check lists.

Learning by Pupils and Teachers. Do teachers learn like pupils? The answer must be yes. They, like their pupils, are learning all the time by experiencing, by overcoming some felt need, by solving some problem or deciding what to do in a novel situation. Billett[24] puts it this way. "Types of human learning do not exist. All observable differences between learning in one situation and human learning in any other situation, either in process or in product, are quantitative and not qualitative differences.

[24] Roy O. Billett, *Fundamentals of Secondary School Teaching with Emphasis on the Unit Method* (Boston Houghton Mifflin Company, 1940), p. 471.

Human learning is human learning. Problem-solving is the way of human learning." The same principles regarding teaching and learning ought to apply to teachers also, or the principles need revision. Perhaps this question ought also to be raised: Should teachers be taught differently? The answer must be "of course not." Capable supervisory personnel in any field should plan with teachers what some key problems are (in line with needed abilities) and then guide their work on interesting, significant learning experiences at a satisfactory pace under appropriate conditions. The following specific example shows the supervision-teaching parallel in action.

Application of the Parallel. In studying the following example, the supervisory worker should be aware of the possibility of developing a designated ability in teachers, out of context with its relationship to everyday classroom operations. Collaborating with other curriculum specialists, and placing proper emphasis during the work period with teachers on how the ability can contribute to valid educational purposes, should minimize this danger. The following supervisory process parallels good teaching:

1. *The Need.* Evidence collected from personal observation of classrooms, opinions of school principals, and in talks with teachers reveals poor use of bulletin boards; hence a real need for improvement in display exists.

2. *The Supervisor's Purpose.* The supervisor therefore formulates a specific objective for achievement, *the ability to construct good bulletin-board displays.* To develop this ability in teachers, a learning situation must be organized, and the attention of teachers must be focused on the problem of how to construct effective displays.

3. *Organization of the Learning Situation.* A questionnaire is prepared by the director of media services for teachers of grades 4, 5, and 6 and sent via the school principals after consultation with them and other key supervisory personnel. The questionnaire, of course, has an interesting introductory statement and carries a drawing or two. It asks teachers if they would like to study the techniques of good bulletin-board display in order to be able to guide pupils in this work as a part of significant learning activities, to submit samples of their best displays, and to volunteer to be on a demonstration team. It also asks if teachers would prefer to

meet for a discussion and planning session and when such a meeting could best be scheduled, if they would prefer to work alone by reading suitable references, and if they would rather work on another problem at a later date. The summary of such reactions will determine size of group, degree of interest, and the date of the first meeting. It is now assumed for this example that a short course of three general meetings with groups working as committees on group-determined assignments has been organized, to be taught by the media program director with the art supervisor cooperating.

4. *Some Learning Experiences.* The supervisor (like any good teacher) has several activities already planned, in case they are needed, and is ready to guide the planning of the group as it comes to decisions about participation. In this case it can be assumed that teachers engage in the following learning experiences:

a. They study the motion picture "Better Bulletin Boards" and the filmstrip "How to Keep Your Bulletin Boards Alive" in order to find and evaluate quickly the basic principles underlying good display. (See film list at end of this chapter.)

b. They follow up the observation of visuals by watching a flannel-board demonstration.

c. They work by subject and grade groups in formulating a sequence of headlines for a whole year of bulletin boards in the various participating schools.

d. They bring in pictures and sketches of their own classroom and school corridor displays.

e. They apply the principles immediately to their own classroom and school corridor displays.

f. They study magazines, pamphlets, and textbooks and share their experiences by reporting to the group.

g. They form committees and split up the work of writing a short illustrated handbook about bulletin-board display, which they issue in mimeographed form to be distributed to every teacher in the school system.

h. Months after the experience they check off a questionnaire on the value of their efforts, and they write up descriptions of some of their best bulletin-board displays constructed since their meetings for the local media center news bulletin.

That is the way the supervision-teaching parallel may look in action. When a needed professional skill is lacking, the director should feel committed to take suitable action—capable teaching of teachers who want to learn is a promising pathway of action. Experiencing, problem solving, project completing, and practicing the application of principles will change behavior.

At this point readers are urged to reexamine the foregoing application of the *parallel* and answer the following questions:

1. What was the point of departure for the supervisor's teaching activity?

2. What was the supervisor's teaching purpose?

3. What were the learners' purposes? (Identify several of the problems and activities.)

4. Was the supervisor's emphasis placed on listening or on taking action to apply and produce?

5. Under what circumstances could a supervisor have utilized a bulletin written by him, instead of a *short course*, as has been described?

6. Was the supervisor's purpose specific and achievable with reasonable time and effort?

7. Do you predict that only one regular teacher's meeting with adequate follow-up could have accomplished the objective as well?

8. What other kinds of organization could be developed?

9. How did leadership principles and the democratic conscience operate in the case described?

10. How were the principles of good supervision violated, if at all?

11. Is there a danger in the teaching of skills to teachers, i.e., that the skill may be taught apart from the framework of effective classroom activities?

The preceding point of view in terms of a method for up-grading the performance of teachers on an in-service basis seems to be supported by Miles and Passow,[25] who said:

[25] By permission. From Matthew B. Miles and A. Harry Passow, "Training in the Skills Needed for In-Service Education Programs," *In-Service Education for Teachers, Supervisors, and Administrators,* 56th Yearbook of the National Society for the Study of Education, Part I (Chicago: University of Chicago Press, 1957), pp. 366–367.

We believe that in-service programs can be aided measurably through attention to the improvement of the kinds of skills needed by participants. This means that the need for acquiring particular skills must become recognized, that participants and planners must be willing to take time out for training, that inventiveness during the planning stages must be central, and that efforts to secure data on the effectiveness of the training must be made.

We have a generalized hypothesis which, in our view, needs wider testing: If program planners and participants give careful attention to locating gaps in the teacher's preparedness for instructional services, to planning and carrying out meaningful training experiences, and to research on the effects of the experiences, *then* the in-service program will go deeper and farther, and educational experiences of boys and girls will be improved.

Working with and Through Others

The director of instructional media services who feels that he has to work alone at his job of in-service growth of teachers will get nowhere. Only by teaching others or finding willing individuals already capable enough to help accomplish valid objectives, and by working effectively with and through other key supervisory personnel, can he hope to be successful. Such working relationships need to be clarified.

Top Administrative and Supervisory Personnel. For most effective service the media program director should be on a coordinate working basis with other supervisory personnel. He is most frequently responsible to the assistant superintendent in charge of instruction, if there is one; otherwise he is responsible to the school superintendent. It is vital that the director meet with curriculum and administrative planning groups to report needs as he has discovered them and to make recommendations for action. In proposing large-scale programs for in-service growth, such plans need to be introduced far in advance to secure high priority for action, integration of action with other programs, and cooperation of all concerned. Such contacts and working relations are important, not only for in-service aspects of his work but also for all other phases of his plan for media services. Media program directors who are involved in regular advisory council meetings, weekly administrative report-type meetings, and other kinds of staff meetings indicate that these

clearing houses for action are invaluable. Some media supervisory personnel in public school and county systems go so far as to rely entirely upon the work of other curriculum specialists for their in-service education meetings. Again, the history, conditioning, and needs of each individual situation will have to be accurately surveyed as a basis for decisions in these or any other matters of policy.

School Principals. Because they are key administrative and supervisory officials in school-building units, full support on the part of school principals for the entire program of media services is fundamental to the director's success. Media directors must therefore take the necessary steps to work with and through them in all matters involving their school staffs, plant, and equipment. It is the principal who will arrange for release time for the media building coordinator, who will arrange for the time and agenda for a needed teacher's meeting, and who will be expected to insist on having a voice in policies governing the flow of instructional media and equipment into his school. It is urgent that the media specialist put his department at the disposal of school principals for expert advice and service relative to their public-relations projects, including graphic-production services, building-equipment service, and assistance in programing meetings for their Parent Teacher Associations, or for other civic groups involved. It is urgent also that the media director pave the way for working directly with school-unit coordinators, that is, in assigning duties and planning with them their service roles for the building. For example, it is obvious that if the building media coordinator is going to conduct a meeting or a laboratory session as a part of the in-service education program, he will not proceed without the full knowledge and direction of the principal. It should be remembered that the school principal has direct control over his staff, including teachers, librarians, and custodians, all of whom may contribute useful services to the media assistant in large-scale in-service education programs. This calls for planning in advance by the director so that proposed action will take place at the direction of, or with the knowledge of, or by order of the principal. Meetings and conferences for school principals, special letters, bulletins, simple notices, copies of schedules, and arrangements sent to them in ample time, and the mutual formulation of policies are techniques that will in most cases need to be employed.

Analysis of Needs. Needs for action that are recognized by teachers as well as by media personnel are the only fruitful points of departure for in-service education programs. When needs have been identified by teachers themselves in one way or another, the task of developing interest, of announcing, initiating, and organizing learning situations is made easy. If voluntary participation of teachers is to be the policy instead of a policy of imposition, then the first step to take is the identification of needs by means that they know about and approve. There are a number of important sources of data leading to the discovery of needs, and of course this discovery is not the responsibility of the media supervisor alone. Principals and other supervisors are also involved, and their efforts need to be pooled. Teacher-survey questionnaires, media center records of deliveries to schools, principals' personal observations and accumulated data, and evidence obtained through personal visits to classrooms and conferences with teachers as requested by them are suggested. Each of these sources of evidence of need is now explained, but the point should again be made that the reference base is the goal to develop teacher competence with media.

Teacher survey questionnaires ought to be very specific and brief, but if sent out at the end or beginning of the school year, they may in general be more comprehensive. The director of media services may actually use a check-list type of questionnaire to encourage teachers to define their own problems. This procedure suggests that an assortment of significant problems be sent to teachers in a list, asking them to check off one or more that they feel are germane to their own classroom situations. Such cases need appropriate introductory statements like the following example.

In recent weeks several teachers have sent in requests for materials and references relative to magnetic tape recordings, the making of transparencies, and photographic slides. School-building coordinators and principals have also indicated from time to time that teachers have been asking for help regarding lettering for bulletin boards and the construction of exhibits for school corridors, and that a few teachers have expressed interest in making better use of regular television programs in school

activities. This short check-off sheet is being sent to ask if you would be interested in studying any of these problems, and in case you have other problems in this field that you would like help with, please feel free to add them at the bottom of the following list.

A number of problems could then be stated in "how-to-do-it" form with blanks to check as an indication of interest. Teachers should also be asked how they would prefer to engage in such activities. A check list could be devised that would elicit responses as to choice of teachers meeting, workshop, short course, or committee study, and that would also ask for information about choice of date to begin activity and how many hours of time on such activities teachers felt they would be willing to spend. Summary of such data would leave the door open for a repeat invitation at a later date. Surveys also provide a good means for finding out what formal courses teachers have had in audiovisual media methods and what study experiences or projects they have undertaken in the past. Such data are of great importance in judging the status of over-all need. Of course, whenever opportunities present themselves, such as in the case of a cooperative school evaluation project, teachers may be encouraged to fill out comprehensive questionnaires that ask for responses to detailed, searching questions regarding their competency. Such questionnaires should be formulated locally by directors who have in mind the kind of system of guiding principles and performance that was described earlier in this chapter.

Media center service records provide another important source of evidence relative to teacher competence. Although record keeping is a topic discussed elsewhere in other connections, it should be pointed out here that an analysis of orders for media over a six-month period will reveal whether teachers in any given school appear to be ordering too many or too few, whether media are being used in only a few subject-matter fields, and if supplies for the preparation of audiovisual media by teachers are contributing to learning activities in all schools in equal amount. Such inferences from records will indicate possible weaknesses leading to further study at the school itself.

School principals, because of their daily contacts with teachers and students, are in a unique position to point out special needs in their schools to the director. Office records may show data on teacher interests, and experiences, and the principal himself can point out the nature of learning activities in his classrooms.

Personal visits to teachers' classrooms at their request and the conferences that follow may also provide evidence leading to reliable judgments. Some communities by tradition insist that classroom visits be made and if this procedure can't be changed, the director must thus spend his time and make the most of it. Visits made upon invitation, however, are likely to reveal strengths rather than weaknesses, and the inspectorial visits imposed on a teacher are, according to research, unpromising for growth. It is a matter of simple arithmetic that the director simply can't spend his time on individual visits and do the important group-planning work that is so productive. Of course the director will make visits to school buildings to confer with principals and media building coordinators, and on those occasions he can observe exhibits in corridors and perhaps bulletin boards in classrooms. If an hour can be scheduled at a school, it is better to use this time to conduct or participate in a staff or committee project meeting where the director can make contact with thirty people instead of three. Local situations will have to be the basis of decisions regarding this and other generalizations.

In carrying out the work of collecting evidence of needs, the director ought to make accurate judgments about the way teaching processes are being handled. He must appraise instruction in terms of dependable principles, and hence he must bring to bear his understanding of basic principles of learning and teaching that were presented earlier in this chapter, and specifically those principles that apply to media methods. When needs have been identified, objectives can be defined, and the process of planning and organizing growth activities can be started.

The Need for Planning. As in all policy-making activity, it is the responsibility of the media director as an executive with a democratic conscience to obtain the participation of those concerned in matters pertaining to in-service education. And with evidence at hand it is time to initiate a number of different kinds of planning activities, depending upon the specific complex of circumstances. If there is a system-wide in-service education council that clears the plans, then this group receives proposals from the director or from units in a network of representative groups functioning for this purpose in each school building. Perhaps, as is true in some cases, a central staff council fits all activity of this nature into a master plan for the school year. And in many cases the media supervisor will be free to carry on his own planning activity on his own terms. Painstaking planning ought to be conducted by the media program director at two levels of action, regardless of the local custom.

Level 1. The first level is that of detailed planning in advance for an immediate learning situation. Direct guidance must be given to all media coordinators in their various buildings, to school principals, to other curriculum specialists, and to committees of teachers who are preparing presentations. The nature and amount of such planning will differ in terms of the kind of situation being organized, but the following aspects of his planning are common to all: What his own part in instruction will be; what the opening program will be; details of time, place, date, and record keeping; what specific problems need to be solved; what learning experiences will be likely to achieve the specified objective (the ability defined); how to initiate the program, that is, how should the appropriate people be notified, interested, and gathered together; what help will be needed from what people; what instruction needs to be given to chairmen and leaders; what supplies and materials need to be on hand; what the cost of the activity will be; what obstacles to progress are likely to be encountered; how much personal time and effort will be required to complete the plan; and how the immediate in-service education plan will be related to other routine or special duties and commitments. Several of these items will have to be, or should be, written out for distribution to participants.

Level 2. The second level of planning action will probably have been done in advance of the planning work just described. If not, it should be undertaken as soon as feasible. For relatedness and direction, there should be a long-term plan for the media competency-building program. Such a plan might provide a tentative program in broad outline for a period of five years, with the following elements included: basic reference data on school units, total number of teachers, an estimate of number needing over-all general competence with the various media, and the number of new teachers coming into the system each year; listing of basic recognized needs from the evidence collected; an estimate of number of teachers in each school who it is hoped will participate; the number of group meetings that will be held each year for elementary, secondary, and new school personnel; the nature of such groups as to extension classes, short courses, teachers' meetings, workshops; a listing of needed bulletins and manuals together with a preparation schedule by committees, individuals, and central staff members; and a schedule of activities for teaching new skills to school-building media coordinators and other staff members who will be participating as instructors and leaders in implementing the master plan.

Everyone recognizes the need for planning in connection with the acquisition of materials, equipment, and facilities, but the zeal for planning in-service education activities seems to be all too frequently lacking. True, in-service education is a time-consuming business. It is also a costly business if outside experts are relied upon; and if staff members inside the organization are to be used, they must be adequately prepared in advance of meetings. Whatever particular obstacles arise, media program directors need to determine their own rates of speed and volume of action. Planning is the royal road to maximum accomplishment with minimum time, effort, and staff. But the questions of how much and how fast are complex. They can be answered only in terms of financial support for adequate staff, inclination and skill of the media director, the ingrained traditions of the local school system, and the morale and motives of the teachers.

The director should finally be aware of the important fact that cooperative effort for decision on a plan for action takes time. Therefore he should see to it that large segments of a master plan (for example, six months or a year's work) are developed and approved by teachers of a school or group of schools, so that the same lengthy process doesn't have to be duplicated for each small meeting. One other important aspect of process in connection with involvement of individuals is the balance between face-to-face contact with groups and contact with them by means of written communications, that is, questionnaires, bulletins, and mail ballots, together with summaries of opinions and decisions.

Initiating and Maintaining Action. The important process of initiating and maintaining action in any program of in-service education is facilitated when the important preliminaries of recognizing needs and detailed planning through cooperative effort have been completed. Then teachers will be notified of opportunities to engage in learning activities that they know about and have already made plans to attend. In fact, under conditions of optimum readiness for such participation, teachers with common interests have been preparing themselves on a limited scale through an in-advance reading program. Some plans for initiating meetings may be quite easy to handle; other plans may be more complex. For an example of the former, we turn to the program operating in the public schools of Seattle, Washington, where a printed leaflet is issued to teachers announcing a schedule of courses for professional credit. Entitled *Professional Study for In-Service Training*, this booklet provides course schedules, registration dates, registration blanks, description of courses, and the number of local credits given for completing the course satisfactorily. In this booklet a number of specific audiovisual media courses are listed. Each of the courses meets for twelve 2-hour sessions and carries two professional credits. The organization of such programs, of course, has grown out of policy-making sessions with the staff, and registration for them is a voluntary matter. Whenever proper in-advance planning is lacking, initiating a series of meetings becomes a more difficult matter, needing all the customary development work prior to setting the meeting date.

When initiating in-service learning situations, the director must, as has been said before, work through school principals and other supervisors. When proper plans have been made and the principal has taken the necessary steps or has given the authority, the media program director or building media coordinator is free to make decisions. Once this clearance has been given, the group gathers and, under effective leadership, begins activities already suggested on the agenda, undertaking the planning of others according to expressed needs. In more complicated groups a steering committee is vital to safeguard against imposition of thought and activity not only by an undemocratic, overzealous leader but by overbearing individual members within the group. Steering committees,

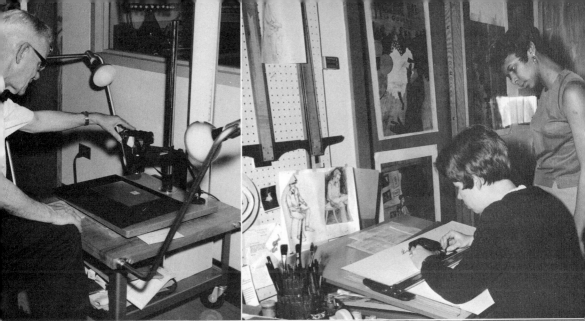

Figure 4-10. One of the most rigorous in-service education courses for the development of skills in media utilization and preparation is the course organized and implemented according to need and interests by Blake Reed at Thornton Township High School and Junior College, Harvey, Illinois. This course runs for 16 three-hour work sessions, approximately one each week during the term. In addition to a number of discussion and planning sessions, most of the time is devoted to project design and completion. Credit given meets professional requirements in the district. The pictures show the group in session in 1966 and two of the many specific practice sessions either in or outside of the class period, in these cases, a special lettering scriber, and a 35-mm single-lens reflex copying camera. See other pictures of the Thornton High School Center in Chapter 7. *Courtesy Thornton Township High School, Harvey, Illinois.*

if guided in doing so, will serve the leader well by carrying on the democratic function as activities proceed, by serving as a liaison body for suggesting activities that the leader feels are urgent, and by exercising other controls as they become necessary, such as calling for the completion of writing projects and possibly rejecting work of unacceptable character.

A system-wide council or committee for in-service education may prove to be helpful to a director of media services in initiating and implementing in-service education learning situations, since such a group, being a representative body of all teachers, may be able to present plans and call for extra attention and effort to meet higher standards of teaching competence. The point for emphasis is that the director need not and must not work alone on planning the initiation and implementation. Principals' councils may in their own analyses of needs, or upon the suggestion of the media program director, undertake to seek staff motivation for study and action.

Organizing Learning Situations for Teachers

The process of improving competence with the various media is not a mysterious affair. Shotgun methods hold out little hope. Teachers, like pupils or anyone else, have no inside track on learning. The simplest statement that can be made is that in terms of time, energy, facilities, and teacher incentives, the media program leader must arrange for teachers to engage in worthwhile, carefully chosen, skill-building learning experiences. Before proceeding with discussions relative to organizing learning situations for teachers, it is suggested that a closer look be taken at some learning activities with a potential for not only building competence in the use of all kinds of media but for other kinds of competence as well.

Experiences for Teachers to Engage in

Planners of in-service education programs need to know what kinds of activities may be useful as vehicles for developing the desired understanding and ability. The author suggests that teachers may be encouraged to participate in one or more of the following under appropriate conditions:

1. Study published literature, pamphlets, and textbooks.
2. Read locally produced manuals, handbooks, curriculum guides, and case studies.
3. Plan, write, and/or edit a handbook or bulletin of directions; write up a case for publication and distribution.
4. Prepare and give a report.
5. Prepare and give a demonstration.
6. Produce audiovisual media for unique class situations and teaching purposes.
7. Watch demonstrations.
8. Listen to speakers.
9. View presentations of audiovisual media.
10. Evaluate various kinds of media.
11. Write detailed teaching plans and teaching units.
12. Evaluate teaching plans, case studies, and teaching units.
13. Formulate basic principles and apply them.
14. Act out a dramatic role.
15. Observe other teachers at work.
16. Take field trips.
17. Evaluate experiences of self and others.
18. Plan and conduct a research experiment.
19. Teach other teachers.
20. Follow directions.
21. Conduct surveys.
22. Participate in a discussion.
23. Formulate valid teaching purposes.
24. Formulate good thought-provoking questions.
25. Fill out questionnaires.
26. Operate equipment and handle materials.
27. Plan programs for meetings.

The preceding learning experiences are, of course, generalized in nature. Each may be stated in specific terms as soon as the ability toward which the action is to be directed becomes known. (The reader is referred to specific examples under the earlier section, Application of the Parallel.) Additional examples of generalized experiences stated in terms of specific objectives will appear in the subsequent pages. Such experiences are the pathways to learning, but teachers won't engage in these activities by themselves, that is, not many will; so, the question needs to be asked: "What are the learning situations in which such experiences may be carried on in proper relation to definite classroom problems?" This question is answered in the following descriptions of seven basic learning situations: regular teachers' meetings, extension classes, short courses, workshops, institutes, reading programs, committee and individual service projects.

Regular Teachers' Meetings

The simplest of the learning situations to organize is the regular teachers' meeting. Despite their long tradition of boredom, the capable media director can find ways to revitalize them. The leader for the media in-service education program should heed the basic principles of learning and teaching, should apply good principles of leadership to both arrangements and content, and of course he must search for ways to eliminate the disturbing flash of knitting needles as they pick up the late afternoon sun. One of the advantages of regular teachers' meetings is the help that can be given by the principal in organizing them. The difficulty is in organizing short, significant activities that can take place within the time allotted. Since the regular teachers' meeting involves all teachers in a school or group of schools, the supervisor's objectives will have to be set up accordingly. Certainly no activity in a meeting should concern a limited group while others sit idly by until adjournment. Some directions for the media supervisor to follow are:

1. Concentrate on a specific objective.

2. Plan activities around identified needs. Set up appropriate problems: What is the nature of? Why? How to plan, construct, use, or formulate. Prepare a brief study and activity guide, or at least an agenda sheet with planned problems on it.

3. Continue action of the meeting through work by individuals or committees, to report later, or to complete a project.

4. Try to run the meeting into a series or on into a new set of related problems for volunteers.

5. Keep people alert by personal involvement.

6. Give full credit for accomplishment of participants.

7. Get follow-up summary sheets out on the specific performance planned, discussed,

Figure 4-11. Regular teachers' meetings need neither be boring nor do they have to be so often bungled. They can lead to continuing action if they are properly planned for that eventuality. Sometimes they may border on conferences and hence may not be so "regular." The two pictures from the Euclid, Ohio, Workshop, may not represent a workshop in the true sense of the word, but the participants in the group shown seem to be responding favorably. Small clinic groups, one of which is shown in this cluster of views, followed the main speaker. *Courtesy Public Schools, Euclid, Ohio.*

Figure 4-12. Pacing of amount to be accomplished in one meeting is an essential for success. Demonstrations and opportunity for action call for painstaking preparation. Action often has to be very specific in terms of goals. Teachers need to get to know new media quickly. Teachers need to become familiar with new pieces of equipment that are available on other than a marginal basis. The success of such in-service meetings with known goals ought to provide a good example to emulate for other training sessions for many other aspects of the teaching process. (*Top picture*, Fountain Valley School District, Huntington Beach, California. *Bottom picture*, courtesy Encyclopaedia Educational Corp., Chicago.)

demonstrated, or developed through the laboratory activity.

8. See to it that the people in charge of the meeting (principal, media coordinator, teacher, or other supervisors) plan cooperatively for selection of capable participants and appropriate activity.

9. Communicate effectively through graphics and other visuals at every opportunity.

10. Develop adequate readiness on the part of teachers by group participation in program plans, through brief check lists, announcements, brief case studies sent out in advance.

11. Make every minute count, and adjourn on time.

12. Carry out similar meeting plans, where

possible and appropriate, in other schools to economize on time and effort.

13. Take precaution in the planning-stage of the program that administrative details and announcements do not interfere seriously with the allotted time schedule. Arrange with the principal to have the committee chairman take charge of the meeting from start to finish.

14. Provide materials and facilities, and limit the activities to be carried out in terms of group size and available time.

The following example of a specific objective and a list of suggested learning experiences that might lead to the accomplishment of the objective, using the regular teachers' meeting as the situation for learning, is now presented for critical appraisal.

Example

The Objective. To develop in teachers the ability to build pupil readiness for the use of audiovisual media.

Suggested Problems and Activities to Achieve the Objective

1. Teachers listen to a short orientation talk by the building media coordinator, which raises several critical questions: Why ought we to pay careful attention to readiness plans? What are some highlights of our experiences here in this school? What are some firm guideposts for help in deciding what to do or say?

2. Three teachers give prepared reports to the group, to answer each of the questions. The second question is answered on the basis of a teacher survey for highlights given without names. The third question is answered by using a large chart with contributions of possible examples being given by teachers from different subject-matter fields and for different kinds of audiovisual media such as audio programs, individualized and large-group videotapes, motion pictures, and filmstrips.

3. Upon the invitation of the principal, a group of volunteers agrees to prepare a brief bulletin on readiness for audiovisual media experiences, with examples from different grade levels and from subject-matter fields, with the media coordinator as editor, for distribution to all teachers in the elementary schools.

4. Before adjournment, teachers agree to *write up good examples* during the next two weeks

for submission to the bulletin committee. (Readers should refer to the listing of previously presented generalized learning experiences for clues to additional specific activities.)

Other more complicated plans could have evolved. A decision might have been made to devote another meeting to the survey and improvement of teachers' ability to formulate valid purposes in relation to the improvement of teaching plans. Another turn of events might have created the need for (1) an analysis of the kinds of problem-solving activities to which students were being led to devote their efforts, possibly resulting in a set of criteria for evaluating problems; (2) a plan for teachers to compare and evaluate sets of problem-solving activities; and (3) a teacher-produced bulletin on the contributions of motion pictures, filmstrips, and study prints to the completion of problem-solving activities. A few other objectives that seem to be particularly appropriate for regular teachers' meetings are the following:

To develop in teachers the ability to:

1. Make improved chalkboard illustrations.
2. Evaluate sponsored materials.
3. Give demonstrations.
4. Use study prints effectively in the teaching process.
5. Construct charts.
6. Construct letters for display purposes.
7. Plan and conduct field trips.
8. Prepare masters for making transparencies.

Extension Classes

It is not uncommon for city school districts to pay course fees for teachers who enroll and complete specified university extension courses satisfactorily. Middletown, Connecticut, authorized its director of media services to select teachers to serve as media building coordinators and then to arrange for them to take a basic course in the media field, with the city reimbursing the teachers in full for books and course fees. The mental calisthenics of good extension courses in audiovisual media may, if properly oriented to local problems and situations, stimulate teachers to develop increased professional skill. Supervisors may make a great mistake, however, if they assume too much and fail to follow up the course work. They may make an even greater mistake if they fail to take a keen interest in the plans and activities of such courses. Directors of media services should certainly encourage teachers to get help through formal courses and should facilitate arrangements for local course offerings according to a long-term plan. Although "kill or cure" is not wise treatment, interested media program directors should seek to arrange through conferences with course instructors for stimulating activities to be organized and completed during a semester's work. If this is done, the media leader will build up in the process a cadre of helpers for in-service education programs, made up of individuals who can penetrate deeply to underlying principles and values and who have the broad, over-all view of the field that is so helpful in planning citywide programs.

Some of the learning experiences, in addition to those that serve purely local needs, that the local director should encourage in extension courses are the following:

1. Study and application of basic principles in classroom plans.
2. Higher caliber planning and writing.
3. Analysis of contributions of media in the learning process.
4. Evaluation of plans and materials.
5. Penetrating thought about the teaching and learning process.
6. Production of audiovisual media for special purposes.
7. Analyzing barriers to communication.
8. Analyzing own teaching competence.

Above all, the media program director should seek ways of putting to work the newly developed talent in his school system. Extension courses provide a unique situation for developing high-level ability—unique because they proceed with an expenditure of minimum effort on his part through a series of concentrated learning experiences.

Short Courses

Not so involved as a workshop, specific in its appeal to interested people, and easy to organize and implement, the short course as a learning situation for teachers merits careful consideration. The inexperienced director may well feel that the short course offers an ideal way to get started, especially if the topics and objectives are in line with his own special interests. Careful planning in advance makes possible the prediction of time to be devoted to the course, and conceivably anywhere from three to ten sessions will be feasible. However, the term *short course* implies a specific interest group ready for study, laboratory, or homework. Local needs will influence decisions; however, busy teachers will be more likely to volunteer for courses of short duration. A few objectives (supervisors' purposes) that seem appropriate for the *short course* learning situation are described in the following list.

To develop in teachers the ability to:

1. Construct good bulletin-board displays.
2. Operate and use a tape recorder.
3. Produce Polaroid slides for teaching purposes.
4. Formulate valid teaching purposes.
5. Operate the audiovisual media equipment available in the school.
6. Produce graphic transparencies.
7. Construct exhibits and dioramas.
8. Use instructional motion pictures effectively.
9. Produce audio programs on tape for self-instruction purposes.
10. Produce motion pictures with magnetic sound tracks.
11. Take good pictures for teaching purposes, both outdoor and indoor.
12. Select and teach map interpretation.
13. Select and use filmstrips effectively.
14. Operate and use "short-exposure" equipment effectively (in any field where this procedure is appropriate).
15. Prepare scripts for the production of audiovisual media.
16. Design and produce visualized presentations for individualized learning activities.

When such objectives as the above are identified, appropriate learning experiences may be planned by the supervisor for or with the teachers who are interested in participating. An example of specific learning activities appropriate for the *short course* situation was given earlier in this section under the heading Application of the Parallel. The example referred to described possibilities for the objective of developing ability in teachers to construct good bulletin-board displays.

It should be noted that the emphasis is placed upon a definite ability so that appropriate learning activities can be selected. Readers should also be aware of the implication that just learning about some process is not enough. Nothing said or implied by this emphasis should be construed as favoring a decrease in responsibility for using democratic methods and high-caliber leadership processes. The lowest common denominator is skillful teaching technique directed toward the accomplishment of desirable outcomes in teachers as a route to better learning on the part of everyday pupils.

With few exceptions, the same directions given earlier for conducting good teachers' meetings apply as well to the organization of good short courses.

Workshops

The author was speaking one day at a three o'clock teachers' meeting. Three other speakers were on the same program. The superintendent of schools and the person in charge of the media services program in getting the meeting started referred to it as a workshop. Somehow they had missed the point of workshops completely and were actually conducting nothing more than a thoroughly bad example of a regular teachers' meeting. Institutes, conferences, lectures, and committee meetings are not workshops. The term *workshop* must not be applied indiscriminately. Burton and Brueckner[26] had this to say:

A workshop is just what the name implies, a shop in which work is accomplished. This meaning was in use for centuries by artisans and craftsmen and has been applied in modern times to university offerings in which objectives are original production and the development of the abilities of the participants. ... The crux is productive work in contrast to listening to lectures ... workshop emphasis is upon the production of end results useful to the participant and desired by them. A second emphasis is upon the personal social development of participants as they work with others on common problems. ... The workshop utilizes the principles which should be used everywhere in teaching; readiness,

personal and social needs as motives, cooperative and participatory process, experimental procedures. ... Workshops are problem-centered.

DeBernardis[27] put it this way:

The audiovisual workshop offers a great deal of promise as a technique for in-service education of teachers. It gives teachers an opportunity to work on individual problems, it allows for flexible schedules, it helps to develop a cooperative work spirit, it provides for more individual guidance, and it helps develop a better attitude toward audiovisual materials. The essential requirements are:

1. A group of teachers who have specific problems on which they want help
2. A capable leader to direct the workshop
3. Enough resources (materials, equipment, consultants) to meet the individual and group needs
4. An adequate work space.

Since the workshop holds so much promise as a learning situation for teachers, and since the term has unfortunately been extensively misused, the student should be guided by the following directions stated by Burton and Brueckner:[28]

1. The length of the session must be adequate. ...
2. The collection of resource materials of all kinds likely to be of value to participants should be as extensive as finances permit. ...
3. The staff should represent a wide diversity of personnel.
4. The full-time staff may be based on the ratio of one staff member for each 12–15 participants. Some of the specialists may be on a part-time basis. ...
5. The physical facilities should permit varied experiences. ...
6. The over-all purpose must be clearly defined.
7. The specific problems of the participants must emerge and be defined without pressure or steering from above. ...
8. Tentative and flexible grouping may be made around common problems.
9. The process of the workshop is co-operative and participatory throughout. ...

[26] William H. Burton and Leo J. Brueckner, *Supervision a Social Process*, 3rd ed. (New York: Appleton-Century-Crofts, 1955), p. 147.

[27] By permission. Amo DeBernardis, "In-Service Teacher Education," *Audio-Visual Materials of Instruction*, 48th yearbook of the National Society for the Study of Education, Part I (Chicago: University of Chicago Press, 1949), p. 117.

[28] By permission. From William H. Burton and Leo J. Brueckner, *Supervision a Social Process*, 3rd ed. (New York: Appleton-Century-Crofts, 1955), pp. 148–150.

10. The personal and social growth of the individual participants should be provided for as well as their growth in the solution of professional problems. . . .

11. The physical facilities should be adequate. . . .

Supervisory objectives of broader scope, such as the following, are suggested as being particularly appropriate for the *workshop* learning situation.

To develop in teachers the ability to:

1. Organize teaching-learning activities centered on the production of audiovisual media.
2. Apply basic principles for utilizing media.
3. Make effective use of community resources in teaching.
4. Construct valid teaching units.
5. Design and produce effective instructional TV programs.
6. Employ multi-group activities by means of taped lessons.
7. Construct models for teaching purposes.
8. Design and produce visualized programed instruction sequences.
9. Operate equipment and use short-exposure techniques (in all fields where procedure is appropriate).
10. Develop plans for designing, preparing, and using teaching systems.

Once more using the list of generalized learning experiences presented earlier, a wide range of specific learning activities, organized around problems defined by the participant, could be suggested for each of the foregoing supervisory objectives. An example will make this clear. (Media specialists should understand that learning activities are to be set up with the group, not imposed upon it or assigned to it.)

Example

The Objective. Organize teaching-learning activities for pupils around the production of audiovisual and print media.

Suggested Problems and Activities to Achieve the Objective

1. Study magazine articles, booklets, and other references describing cases of joint pupil-teacher production of films, slides, dioramas, models, and printed booklets as an organizing center for learning to answer the question: *What unit structures were used if any?*

2. Examine source units from your own and other school systems to find the answer to the question: *What changes need to be made in our present unit organization techniques* if we use a large scale production project as a focal point for organizing learning activities?

3. Formulate lists of suitable production projects for various grade levels to answer the questions: *What are the possibilities for significant learning experiences for children?* How can small-scale production projects be incorporated in present teaching units?

4. Collect samples of direction sheets that have been prepared for pupils in other cases and places to find out: *How can time and energy on production details be kept from overpowering the efforts to gain insight and concepts on the part of pupils?*

5. Watch demonstrations of scriptwriting technique to find out: *How to write picture and narration scripts.*

6. Practice operating cameras, projectors, and tape recorders to answer the question: *How difficult is it to teach youngsters how to operate the equipment for production?*

7. Work with volunteer groups on preparation of a set of bulletins for wide local distribution on the following topics: Hollywood Comes to School; Learning by Producing Exhibits; Slide and Tape Production; Writing and Producing Dramatic Sketches.

8. Preparing and giving reports to the group to provide information for solving these problems: *What will be the cost to produce a schoolmade movie? A typical three-panel exhibit? Set of sound slides? What are some pitfalls in the production method?*

9. Work in groups to write a teaching unit for a particular grade level and unit to find out: *How to organize learning activities around a production project in my field.*

Many more problems and activities without limit could be defined and carried on in terms of time, staff, interest, and financial support. Such a workshop could actually develop a corps of talented leaders, ready to show by example what can be done to enliven classroom practices, and possibly to assist in other workshops as they are organized as teachers and leaders.

Institutes

Whether fifty, five hundred, or five thousand teachers are gathered together, whether the conference or institute is organized on a city, county, or statewide basis, the chances are that the emphasis will be upon *learning about something* instead of *learning to do something*. However, much improvement has been noted in recent years. Emphasis on better communication and action rather than exhortation has induced conference and institute planners to organize clinic sessions, so-called interest groups, and even work groups. Also, institutes have been lengthened from a half-day to a full day, and schools now are frequently closed to permit full concentration by teachers on the in-service program. But long, concentrated, tiring, "broadside" sessions are relics of the "twenties and thirties" when school people flocked by the thousands to statewide conferences to find out what *visual education* was all about. However, some media program directors, especially in recently formed organizations, still find that much interest can be built up by a large group gathering where teachers have ample opportunity to attend several work sessions of their choice after an inspirational keynote speech. The work of planning, staffing, and implementing such an institute must be painstakingly done, and the opportunities for follow-up must be seized upon, or the teachers and pupils might better have stayed in their classrooms. Since teachers have had so much direct experience with institutes and their shortcomings, the media supervisor should be forewarned to make every minute as interesting, provocative, and filled with action by participants as is possible. In his planning, the supervisor should get the history of such activities in his locality from his colleagues and should get all possible teacher participation in setting up the program.

We hardly need to caution the reader that the word, "Institute" has taken on a new aura of significance in its adoption to indicate a 6- to 8-week session filled with strenuous activity in any one of a number of fields from media to social science and economics. This kind of prolonged paid-for-at-government-expense professional activity, such as the NDEA Media Institutes began in 1965, is not to be confused with the Institute Day once every year that we have spoken of in such deprecating fashion.

However, we need to learn to make keen judgments relative to the kinds of learner activity, be the learners nine-year olds or teachers themselves, that will accomplish valid objectives in a professional setting of great urgency.

Reading Programs

Study of professional references constitutes a learning situation of rich potential for individual growth. Some cities at great expense provide centralized professional libraries, curriculum laboratories, and curriculum publication production centers. The director of media services in city systems where such services are offered will need to find ways to guide teachers along short cuts to vital reference material in terms of well-defined needs and specific problem situations. In the absence of central and well-developed professional library services, the supervisor will have to set up his own library of references at his headquarters and to set up a library of selected references at the media center in every school building. Publicity about the availability of such references is, of course, of prime importance.

Such services will not make maximum contributions to in-service education goals until teachers are led to discover their needs, until they define a problem for themselves and take the kind of action where new responses are called for. Therefore, directors of media services and their supervisory assistants need to stimulate desired reading by:

1. Reviews of recommendations growing out of staff meetings, sent out as brief bulletins.
2. Newsletters to teachers, reporting summaries of interesting experiments, or reports of activities tried locally and elsewhere with good results.
3. Statements summarizing school-system survey results, revealing problems considered by teachers to be important and needing concerted effort.

It is certain that the most reading and study by teachers is likely to be done in *case studies, handbooks, how-to-do-it bulletins,* and *illustrated guide sheets for specific skills* that provide short cuts to job success. For example, the following titles, if needs were indicated by teachers, would make contributions to the improvement of implied teacher performance:

How to Make Good Physical Arrangements for Using Audiovisual Media

How to Make Good Tape Recordings for Listening-Response Activity

How to Mount Study Prints

How to Make Sets of Color Slides

How to Make Good Transparencies

How to Prepare Illustrated Direction Sheets for Students

How to Write Scripts for the Production of Television Programs and Motion Picture Segments

How to Plan, Conduct, and Use Field Trips.

Thus, on the director falls the burden of planning, writing, and editing publications for distribution to teachers. Publications of this nature, however, can have such a tremendous impact upon improvement of teacher performance that their production is a prime necessity. How the publication production-load carried by the director of media services may be lightened, short of employing assistants to do the job, is shown by implication in the next topic.

Committee and Individual Service Projects

It has already been shown in earlier examples, described under regular teachers' meetings, short courses, and workshops, that one of the routes to significant understanding and ability on the part of teachers is the actual planning and writing of case studies, manuals, guide sheets, source lists, units, and how-to-do-it bulletins by interested groups or teachers or by individuals. Such activities, if correlated with a plan for production of publications, could make a real contribution to in-service education and could lighten the burden of such writing on the director of media services. However, the completion of service projects by committees and individuals may take place quite outside the framework of a specific meeting or workshop. Hence *committee and individual service projects* constitute a learning situation worthy of careful consideration. Many such service projects have only limited application, but again, if the media supervisor is ready with needs and problems

requiring solutions, coordinators and principals may be in a position to guide teachers into writing and compilation projects that could be duplicated and distributed throughout elementary or secondary schools or both. Certainly ways could be found to give special credit and recognition by school officials. Ways could also be found to spread this work out among different groups. Such production of needed publications could conceivably mount up in a five-year period to a sizable contribution.

An example of the great achievement possible is the one-inch thick, illustrated, mimeographed *Study Trip Handbook* for the San Jose, California, Unified School District, prepared by a committee of twenty-five teachers, principals, and central staff workers, working under the guidance of the Supervisor of the Division of Instructional Materials. This handbook, also referred to as *Curriculum Monograph No. 82*, has the following Contents:

Section I General Information
Foreword
Study Trip Procedure
What Is a Study Trip?
Authorized Trips
Safety Regulations
Arranging for a Study Trip
Procedure for Planning a Trip
Pupil Preparation
Taking the Trip
Follow-through
Evaluation
Suggested Places to Visit by Grade Level
Section II Study Trips to Business and Industry
Section III Study Trips to Community Agencies
Section IV Study Trips to Historical Locations in Santa Clara Valley
Section V Nature Study Trips
Section VI Resource People
Section VII Walking Study Trips in and About Each School

The committee certainly must have taken great pride in accomplishing such a useful service project. San Jose has long used its school buses to facilitate the operation of its Study Trip Program. A well-stated Foreword in this handbook, written by the Assistant Superintendent of Schools, added a fine touch of dignity and importance to that valuable contribution to in-service education. This handbook was recently extensively revised by a summer workshop committee, and was reissued as five separate hand-books, one for each grade, one through five.

Some of the essentials for the success of a service project include the establishment of a master plan of needed publications in terms of priorities; organization of study and writing teams or individuals, cleared through principals, other supervisors, and coordinators; enlisting the cooperation of qualified teachers in getting editorial work done; use of student typists; and the coordination of clerical supplies.

Shoddy work and irresponsible editing would kill the value of such publications, and hence a good precaution to take would be to supply all workers with a simple, brief bulletin on format and then to procure a small reviewing board of teachers that would either accept a bulletin for wide distribution or return it for further editing. An unwieldy, top-heavy organization could also kill the flow of production; so, only when the volume increases beyond the capacity of the supervisor to handle it personally should he expand his editorial organization. Careful thinking, cooperation, deepened insights, up-grading of writing skill, increased recognition of individuals, and wider reading and study are found to result from a well-executed plan for encouraging committee and individual service projects. Such an imposing array of values merits consideration.

This important work by committees and individuals must of necessity involve the direct guidance and supervision of the media program director himself. Final decisions will, of course, be up to him rather than his helpers. A question that apprehensive students often ask is, "How can a director of media services who, for example, has been a science teacher work with a committee of English or Social Studies teachers?" The question can be answered easily. He can work with them successfully if he has adequate understanding of teaching methods in general, of the nature of learning, and of the role that significant experiences play in learning. It is essential that the director inform himself about national thinking in the various subject-matter fields, to be in a strong position to support the work of other curriculum specialists as he works with specific subject-matter and grade committees or individuals. Yearbooks and publications dealing with criteria for evaluation at elementary and secondary levels must be on every media director's personal library shelf.

In the seven basic learning situations just described, the director of the media service program has a potential network for a tremendous range of learning experiences. In tapping that potential, the director must manage to be the supervisor, effective teacher, and dedicated organizer. Learning experiences for teachers have been directly related in this analysis to a group of guiding principles for effective utilization of media. In turn these principles seem to demand specific kinds of teacher ability in the classroom. Such a system should be most helpful to the instructional media supervisor in achieving better balance among the kinds of learning activities into which he and his assistants guide teachers. Such a system also helps in focusing attention on the relationships between the media of instruction and instructional goals. What the director must continually keep in mind is the need for proper balance among the five basic utilization principles and the abilities they imply. If he fails in this, he will likely be driven toward undue emphasis on physical equipment.

Procuring Staff Members for In-Service Learning Situations

In a later chapter the problems of staffing the audiovisual media service program will be discussed, but we need to point out now, at least in a general way, the nature of the special problem of getting the teachers who will teach other teachers the necesssary skills for media utilization.

Teams of Teachers for Learning Situations. If the director of the media program organizes only those situations where he personally will be the teacher, they will be too few in number. The fact is that many learning experiences organized for in-service education in the media field must of necessity be deeply concerned with broad phases of teaching such as the ability to design and construct teaching systems and to plan large-group visualized presentations. Obviously such abilities demand the combined and concentrated efforts of every person on the supervisory staff, principals, curriculum specialists, and the media program director. Thus in any workshop, meeting, or course dealing with this and other broad problems, a team of teachers is the only answer. Or if a committee is at work on a handbook on this topic for use by teachers, then a team of consultants and editors is called for. Actually abilities to use the various media must not be taught at all unless they are taught in the context of professional teaching accomplishment. Hence all that has been said about the nature of media competence now demands attention for the director must be prepared to participate as a member of the team of teachers that teaches others the needed ability and understanding.

The director will, of course, have to select capable, previously trained teachers to carry out assignments in workshops, short courses, and teachers meetings, and in some cases the teachers he selects may have to be given additional specialized training. This is exactly the case with school-building media coordinators and school principals, who if the job is to be accomplished, may have to be urged to participate.

The Value of Additional Supervisory Assistants. The problem of adequate staff is likely to be an ever-present one. However, some school systems, both large and small, have found the means to employ consultants for in-service education functions who work under the supervision of the media director. Such capable, professional assistants greatly increase the tempo and scope of the in-service education effort as they become organizers and planners, as they become members of instructional teams, or as they work with teachers under any of the suggested organizational procedures for guiding growth experiences.

The Use of Visiting Consultants. Many directors believe that the best and most feasible technique for speedy, effortless accomplishment of in-service educational objectives is to employ outside experts, set up a schedule of meetings, and run off the programs, one expert for each meeting. In these cases the assumptions about the learning process and the nature of the objectives should be analyzed. Such activity seems to indicate a belief that if you can get the attention of a teacher at a lecture, that is all there is to it. Development of ability, however, calls for understanding, a desire to take action, practicing under guidance with a desire to meet a standard of excellence, knowledge of progress, and satisfaction. Too often the work of a series of visiting lecturers or demonstrators is not tied together and too many objectives are set up to be accomplished at one time. If the use of experts provides the only feasible method for in-service

education meetings, careful advance planning should be conducted to meet the shortcomings implied in the preceding criticism. We should not overlook, however, nearby sources of available personnel, such as teachers in colleges and universities who may become valuable members of in-service education teams for a given number of hours each week on a firm schedule.

The Media Director As a Vital In-Service Education Staff Member. One other point should be borne in mind by directors of media services. They themselves should not shrink from opportunities to develop their own powers for leadership, their own technical skills, and their own penetrating insights into difficult curriculum problems. Concentrated effort for adequate preparation will, of course, be necessary for giving demonstrations, conducting discussions, and formulating plans for the production of bulletins, handbooks, case studies, and curriculum guides, but this is the road of experience that leads to genuine respect by colleagues.

Media directors need to be much more than skillful moderators. They need to be not only technological experts, but (and this is infinitely more difficult) they also need to provide the mainspring of leadership for the change process to take place through the in-service education program in media methods. The media program director will then truly fulfill his role as a supervisor.

We have pointed out a staggering need for in-service education, and this means a staggeringly large number of hours of staff service in carrying out any given program. As we have emphasized, the job is an urgent one and programs must be organized and implemented by every available means. Cooperative effort by willing and talented teachers already on the regular staff, will need to be elicited, organized, and guided along promising and fruitful channels. We thus see that there will have to be an optimum mixture of staff members, both internal and external with regard to the school system itself, both full time and part time. We must emphasize that it remains for the instructional media leader to find creative solutions to the in-service education problems. Such creative solutions must be effective in every sense of the word, and must be economical of the time and effort of all persons involved—instructors who are teaching the new skills and those who are learning them. We therefore turn next to a discussion of some plans for speeding up the tempo of the in-service education process.

Mass Methods for Building Media Competence

A number of the proposed means of organizing learning situations for teachers lend themselves for what we may refer to as mass methods for developing media-use skills. Specifically we may mention *reading programs*, which in turn involves *individual and committee service projects*. What is needed are methods, either singly or in combination, to involve all teachers who need or are required to participate in new media methods. In seeking these methods, it is obvious that reading manuals, specially prepared bulletins, and even textbooks is one of the promising mass-communication methods, but practice sessions and special help sessions may also be urgently needed in helping teachers make changes in their procedures. Also, a given kind of innovation may call for thought and action of a more difficult and analytical nature within established deadlines of time, obviously demanding group meetings of one kind or another. In such critical circumstances basic to the entire curriculum, it is obvious that the principal goal is to achieve maximum competence with media in the shortest possible time. We shall explore first one possibility of organizing teachers' meetings by first training a cadre of instructors to carry out a specific operation who will then serve as the staff for a series of similar same-content meetings in all of the other schools.

The Train-to-Teach-Other-Groups Method

We either hire a cadre of professional media specialists to carry out the job of retraining teachers, or we procure interested and willing personnel from local ranks and prepare them to carry out repetitive teachers' meeting (workshop) leadership assignments. The latter may actually be the only feasible mass method that will utilize the leadership and technological ability of the media program director. Many

other snail's-pace plans using only the efforts of the media program director are virtually unproductive. An example will make this clear. Let us assume that a full-time media director has 200 teachers located in 10 elementary schools with 20 teachers in each school plant. We shall make the further assumption that each teacher needs 50 hours of instruction either in person-to-person sessions or in effectively organized discussion and skill-building practice meetings to reach the level of desired competence in the desired abilities. Let us for the purpose of this example also assume that there is a part-time or full-time school-building media program coordinator in each of the buildings who could work with the media director as a nucleus of staff for an in-service education program. Now, we ask this question: How many hours of visitation, conference, and person-to-person meetings would the media program leader be required to make to meet the instructional requirement of 50 hours? The answer is obvious, the director would have to hold 10,000 man-to-man conferences. Since schools meet approximately 180 days each school year, and also since teachers would rarely be able to hold such conferences until after-school hours from three until five o'clock, the media leader himself would have to work at this task for about 38 school years. Supposing now that the media program leader arranged to go to each of the schools to hold teachers' meetings during the late afternoon from three to five for the entire staff of 200 teachers, conducting laboratories and organizing instruction effectively. He now would have to conduct 25 two-hour meetings in each of 10 schools to provide 50 hours of "contact" instructional time. The media director would now, at the rate of three meetings each week, and having to conduct a total of 250 meetings to meet the requirement, have to work at his task for two years. Now finally we ought to ask: How many meetings would the media director have to conduct if he were to train his coordinators (ten of them as a group), using specially prepared materials, to duplicate his meetings, in their own schools? The arithmetic would run something like this: twenty-five two-hour meetings teaching media skills to ten coordinators (and also providing them with instructions and materials for their own meetings) would meet the 50 hour instructional requirement. The ten coordinators then in turn would conduct 25 meetings in their own schools, at which each of the 20 teachers in each school would receive the stated 50 hours of instruction.

Assuming that the meetings are properly organized and skillfully taught, we can readily observe the futility of the individual conference method, and that as we move toward effective use of groups for significant and fundamental skill development work, the director's capacity to give leadership and guidance becomes feasible.

We should emphasize a singular criterion of success of the suggested train-to-teach method for developing mass competency. This is that the ability (or the objective) to be taught ought to be sufficiently narrow in scope to be attainable with reasonable time and effort during each repeater-type meeting. Another way to say this is "Do not try to do too much at once." Thus good pacing and better balance between listening to instructions and practicing application are facilitated. For example, it would be wiser when dealing with other than broadly talented media production people to try to teach one method of making transparencies at a time, broadening out to more difficult visualization projects in later meetings.

As this concept is explored, the director needs to bear in mind his coordinate relationships with all other curriculum personnel in his local school system. He must recognize the complexity of a situation in which others are as zealous as he is in reaching competence objectives for which they are responsible. Hence, competence in the classroom use of the various media needs to be examined in relation to other professional needs, with all necessary steps being taken for the cooperative planning that will assure optimum balance of effort and achievement. The need for system-wide curriculum development on the one hand and a need for analysis of such specific though basic aspects of teaching as unit planning, use of print medium services, and pupil guidance programs on the other, may, because of a higher priority, postpone or decrease the tempo of other mass programs. The crucial factor in the eventual success of the type of program about to be explored is that it be accepted as a part of the general program for professional growth and that those who are to be affected by it participate in all related decisions.

Assuming the general conditions for acceptance, it is believed that a mass program for competency, with the tempo optimally established by the local situation, becomes a promising possibility. At any rate the director ought to consider the valuable lesson to be derived from a study of the proposal, namely, the potential effectiveness of group methods. The broad outlines of a mass competency development venture are described in the following paragraphs.

Condition 1. Provide adequate leadership, sufficient clerical and technical personnel to carry on the routine services of the service center.

Condition 2. Develop an incentive system based on in-service education credits for salary purposes for all participants, including some time off from classes, awarding a diploma, entry in personnel records, and so on.

Condition 3. As a result of careful system-wide planning, set up a base of major abilities with media to meet local program needs and changes.

Condition 4. Prepare the staff by appropriate announcements for individual participation in filling out a specially constructed, personnel, media skill-survey sheet to get full data about status of needs. The announcements should be signed by the organizing group, including teacher representatives. Summarize the data and discover both those who because of need should be the learners and those who because of competence already possessed could be the teachers of others. Seek services of the latter.

Condition 5. Make participation voluntary on three levels of activity: (1) as a member of the steering committee; (2) as a teacher demonstrator; or (3) as a learner. Get consensus, but also do an appealing and challenging job of communication.

Condition 6. Enlist the help of student equipment operators, school-building media coordinators, other curriculum personnel, and school principals in building up a corps of teachers. The selected so-called "training" teachers, including the director of the media service center, participating curriculum specialists, and a few carefully selected classroom teachers would on a given day teach the school coordinators, principals, and other qualified teachers. These in turn would hold scheduled (by consent and planning) meetings for their respective school staffs, using the same procedures and kits of material supplied to them in the previous "training" meeting. The "training teachers" could therefore conceivably hold a meeting for a group composed of school-building representatives, that is, twenty or even a hundred principals, coordinators, talented colleagues from elementary or secondary schools in any combination, with the agreement that during the next two weeks each of these representatives would conduct meetings, clinics, or laboratory sessions (skill-building sessions) in their schools for their own volunteer colleagues. This procedure could then continue on schedule according to plan.

Condition 7. The next year a new group of volunteers for this experience could be met by a new corps of volunteer teacher assistants, using the plans and kits from earlier meetings.

Condition 8. Bulletins reporting news of the venture, aspects of progress, names of participants, schedule of group meetings, special speakers, dates for coffees for the group, and the like, would be a necessity.

Condition 9. Maintain an adequate record system to note completion of planned schedules and of specific contributions.

Thus, long-term plans backed up by careful preparation, financial support, full cooperation of administrators, principals, teachers, supervisors, with some staff members being taught and others helping to teach colleagues could facilitate the mass production of competency. Group processes provide the most fruitful technique. Individual visits and follow-up conferences, especially when requested by the teacher, are quite productive but are geared to a slower pace.

Who knows whether such a mass production of competency scheme as outlined would work? Whether tried on a 100 per cent basis or not, prospective directors would do well to give such a plan strong consideration. One point is clear: It is strange that many a city-system media director has taught college and university audiovisual media education courses on a campus fifty miles away but has no course for his own staff in his own school community. The same amount of effort as that expended on a campus teaching assignment, if applied to a plan as just described, would work wonders. The idea contained in *Condition 6* deserves special attention because the group instruction technique,

using teams of teachers to teach school-building representatives for the specific purpose of repeating the instruction at the local school-building level, is promising indeed.

Along the lines of this concept, a highly successful pilot program was conducted under a U.S. Office of Education grant at the Ohio State University by a team of investigators, and was later reported by Catherine M. Williams.[29] Ten kits of special materials, one for each media in-service education workshop topic, were designed, produced, and tried out with entire staffs of selected schools. An additional kit was prepared for the leader of the program. The programs, involving media components in planned combinations, were carried on by leaders in each school after an orientation session in one-hour meetings. The topics for which kits were produced are as follows: bulletin boards and other displays, study pictures and opaque projection, chalkboard, overhead projection, filmstrips and 2×2 inch slides, motion picture, recordings and radio, television, programed instruction, community resources, and the kit for the administrator.

According to the investigators and producers of the kits, all of the media-program packages will be made available for purchase. Since the preparation of such specialized workshop materials is one of the requirements described in *Condition 6*, it is understandable that their commercial availability will greatly facilitate the process which we have presented under the topic of mass production of media competency. The pacing of such programs, as we have emphasized, would have to be determined in the light of local circumstances.

Using Mass Media Methods

Television. In the years immediately ahead, closed-circuit television systems will likely enhance the possibilities for using effective large-group methods for teaching media skills to teachers. In effect, these mass-media methods may be the means of presenting demonstrations of media skills in action with class groups, permit on the spot observation of other teachers carrying on processes that may influence others to

[29] Catherine M. Williams, "Packaged Program for In-service Audiovisual Education," *Audiovisual Instruction*, Vol. 10, No. 7, September 1965, pp. 552–555.

change, and accomplish in one session what may take weeks by a staff of volunteer workers who have to be trained and then organized into a suitable in-service education workforce under conventional methods. Such uses of television for example could be one of the components of well-organized reading programs based on bulletins and handout sheets, designed to provide actual demonstrations and play other large-group information-giving roles. Furthermore, the programs carefully planned, sequenced, and presented could be recorded on videotape and used as needed in later in-service sessions for new teachers or for a refresher treatment. The possibility of exchange with other school systems is a valuable advantage of such arrangements. This kind of cooperative, creative action will need, of course, expert coordination and planning. Teams of presentors, as previously discussed, may plan several programs dealing with the major abilities. Teachers would then be supplied with necessary follow-up sheets guiding subsequent classroom action, and may meet for workshop sessions in their own schools under a media assistant. What we mean to emphasize at this point is that television must be programed in such a way that the information given will elicit the kinds of responses that will achieve the established objective. The television program would then serve its unique purpose with other preprogram and postprogram activity following in optimum order and amount.

Although such mass-media programs as television offer unique opportunities for in-service education under skillful leadership, other mass media also make significant contributions to this process. We refer to programed material that is presented not in large-group fashion but in an individualized instruction sense. Under this heading we shall discuss several possibilities.

Programed In-Service Learning Sequences

Teachers may learn by themselves not only from bulletins and other reference sources, given adequate directions and supplies, but much more effectively from visualized teaching systems involving a combination of media, each component of which makes a specific contribution to the total learning process. Teachers may be guided by means of such programs during "free" periods, or in groups in electronic learning laboratories, in carrels equipped with a television receiver, a rear screen for viewing slides that call for responses in small error-free

Figure 4-13. The laborious job of teaching teachers how to operate new media equipment may be accomplished by programed methods, utilizing teaching systems of an automated nature. It may be well worth the cost to install carrels properly equipped to carry on this job on a self-instruction basis. The carrel shown with 8mm cartridge film and programed slides would teach teachers easily operational skills. Operation of the basic, general-use media equipment units is taught in carrels like the one shown as a homework (extra-class) requirement in the University of Connecticut's automated media equipment operation laboratory. *Photograph by David H. Curl.*

Figure 4-14. This teaching kit for in-service education contains all needed media for visualization, manuals for the learners and the instructors and the needed working materials or expendable items for use in carrying out the prescribed operations. *Courtesy Educational Media Laboratories, Austin, Texas.*

steps, and single-concept cartridge-type films, all of which operate by pushing a button. Such programing again, as for the television program series discussed earlier, requires sophisticated design, preparation, and packaging, and we might add cooperative action by local and regional school systems.

Many prospective teachers in several of the leading schools of education around the country are now operating individualized instruction programs in basic media skills from operating media equipment to such skills as lettering with Leroy scribers and templates, making transparencies, learning spirit reflex master duplicating processes, and mastering photocopier processes, to mention just a few. The possibilities are many and doubtlessly commercial producers will meet to some degree the urgent need for packaged in-service education kits—from a simple programed booklet to a complete teaching system.

We should also discuss at length the need for the preparation of new kinds of materials for presenting problem situations to teachers by means that simulate the real situation. Although such materials—in the forms of videotapes, audio programs, cartridge films on specific teaching skills, and sets of realistic slides in desirable full-view and close-up format showing experienced teachers at work with classes—are urgently needed for teacher preparation programs, they can also be used to advantage for in-service teachers who must undergo retraining. We are presently just scratching the surface in preparing examples of the kinds of new materials that are needed in vast array. Under the stimulation of federal grants to school districts and universities, as well as for in-service education research and experimentation, we can look forward to significant action in this field. When teachers can be guided into such media-controlled learning experiences and can feel the impact of their contributions personally, they will then alter personal images of their own working skills along lines of desirable change. They will be then most likely to put the same media to work to achieve their own objectives.

"Go Slowly" may be good advice for the neophyte media program leader, but trends toward media development and use in the schools indicate in-service education as an on-going process demanding celerity not dawdling. Media program directors should use the media they espouse, and they ought to be imaginative in every phase of the process which is or will be the hallmark of their success.

Problem-Solving Activities

1. Study the definition of *effective utilization of media* stated in this chapter and check it against the list of characteristics or principles of teaching and learning, and then prepare three (actual or hypothetical) briefly stated examples of media utilization at three levels—competent, mediocre, and incompetent. If possible, make the same medium or combination of media common to all three examples. (Base your cases on actual observation, new or recalled, if feasible.)

2. Study the quotations from the DAVI Task Force Position Paper (Barry Morris, Editor) relative to the two broad functions of media, and then identify examples of both functions in Media Roles 2 and 3 found under the section Basic Roles of Audiovisual Media.

3. Explain by using specific cases from your experience, how Function 2 of media according to the Morris paper referred to in the preceding exercise, is related to the definitions of *teaching* and *learning* quoted under the Principles of Teaching and Learning section.

4. We have emphasized the value of valid teaching units as a good framework of reference for competent use of media. Answer the following questions regarding teaching units and media, and the five principles for effective media utilization.

(a) Are clear-cut, behavioral-type teaching objectives (teaching purposes) a crucial part of design for good utilization? Prove it by writing out a brief example (See Guiding Principles 1 and 4). Do valid teacher objectives have anything to do with the independent study activities of pupils? If so, identify several examples.

(b) Are the problem-solving activities of a good teaching unit (one large, or an array of problems as here at the end of this chapter) a good reference base for providing media contributions? Prove your point by writing out a brief example (See Guiding Principles 2 and 4).

(c) How can media-controlled, self-instruction processes, as in Media Role 3, be related to good teaching-unit plans? Explain the relationship by an example, written out and handed in, or presented for discussion in class (see Guiding Principle 4).

(d) Give an example of the need for teacher-prepared media as they relate to a teaching unit, problem-solving assignment.

(e) Identify a realistic example of media production (such as a set of slides with tape commentary) and explain how such an absorbing class activity can be related to valid teaching units of both the *experience* and *subject matter* type.

5. Examine several case studies of media utilization, then write a critique of the teacher action, identifying and giving details about specific strengths and weaknesses revealed. (Use case studies in generally available textbooks, or study specially prepared outline-type case studies handed out in class.)

6. Examine critically several problem-solving activities that elementary- and secondary-school teachers have assigned their pupils as a part of their teaching units. Identify two examples, one poor and one good. Write them out or make photocopies of them and restate the poor problem in correct form.

7. Go over the *Media Program Director and Change* section in Chapter 2, including the discussion of the *Media Program Director as a Change Agent*, and prepare a written statement, for use in class discussion, showing the relationships of the *change process* to developing media competence in teachers.

8. What is meant by an incentive system? (What reasons would teachers have for volunteering to help with the teaching of an in-service education program? What reasons for being willing to attend meetings and practice sessions to learn new skills?)

9. Assume that there is a real need in a school system in which you work for improving the level of skill on the part of teachers in writing scripts and recording tapes for electronic laboratory, listen-response activity in any subject-matter field. Plan out a how-to-do-it bulletin in outline format. Use a step-by-step procedure for specific direction-giving content.

Also indicate the nature of illustrations you would include. Polish your outline and duplicate it for exchange with fellow classmembers.

10. Make two lists of significant, specific projects; one that teachers could work on in groups (as committees), and the other where action by individuals would be most desirable.

11. What are tentative titles for at least five short courses on audiovisual media subjects that you would be willing to give for teachers in your school system? Pool your titles in class. Make an outline of *activities* for any *one* of the courses you listed.

12. Show in a point-for-point comparison that the director's supervision is, or should be, parallel to expert teaching.

13. When is a teacher competent in audio-visual media methods?

14. What is the most fruitful beginning point of all good in-service "growth" programs as far as teachers are concerned? How are these "points of departure" determined?

15. Agree in class upon a specific ability that is an important aspect of competence in the use of media and list under each the *specific* learning experiences for teachers as routes to their development. Pool these in class, or turn over results of individuals' work to a special committee for editing, summarization, and duplication. (Refer to the listing of generalized learning activities for teachers presented in this chapter.)

16. Formulate several plans for obtaining both preliminary and continuing participation of teachers in formulation of policy. Once a policy has been formulated and approved by the school superintendent, who executes it or enforces it? The people who helped make it, or the director who spearheaded its formulation?

17. Examine some reports (or recount your own experiences) of *workshops* and decide whether any actual materials were produced by the people present or whether they just learned *about* something.

18. What criteria would you use to discover if a classroom teacher is using audiovisual and/or printed materials competently?

19. Make up a short questionnaire to determine the status of teacher experiences, formal and informal, with audiovisual media. Duplicate the questionnaire and bring it to class for sharing with fellow classmates.

20. Formulate a questionnaire that asks teachers to indicate their reactions to and their interests in a number of personal problem situations for in-service education. Ask them to return the completed questionnaire, showing their preferred method of study, total time limit (day or week), and the best month for beginning the project.

21. In terms of a stated objective, describe in fifty words a *demonstration of audiovisual methods* that you would personally conduct in a group meeting. Record this description on tape for a critique by the class.

22. How would you make use of a utilization case study of a film in providing "growth" experiences? Mention at least two vastly different methods of using them. (Hint: See list of generalized learning experiences for teachers.)

23. What is wrong, if anything, with classroom visitation by you as a supervisor? What's good about it? How much of your time could you afford to devote to this "growth" technique (assuming you were a full-time media director)? Would you employ an assistant for this purpose?

24. Examine at least one source unit or one detailed teaching unit in published form. Criticize the stated objectives from the following standpoints: (a) correctness of form, (b) comprehensiveness, (c) consistency, (d) significance. Rewrite in proper form several of the statements you claim are weak.

25. How would you apply unit-organization procedure to in-service education planning? How does cooperative effort fit into this system of planning?

26. How would the formulation of your own teaching purposes help you to prepare a talk or demonstration for a group of teachers? For a parent-teachers group?

27. Write an outline-format plan for implementing a specific objective (agreed upon in class) by means of mass program methods. Use teachers' meetings as the organization procedure, and show: (a) the objective, (b) the plan for the meeting for training the trainers, (c) materials and supplies needed for the training trainers meeting and for the subsequent meetings with regular teachers, (d) the number of meetings and the number of people involved. (Use ten elementary schools and 200 teachers as a basis for your thinking and planning.)

28. For any objective you name (and agree upon in class) sketch out a plan in outline form for using self-instruction, mass communication methods to achieve it. (Stick to the electronic

learning laboratory, or electronic carrel with media in combination, as the basis for individuals to listen and respond at their own time and pace.) Assume that all the media you need have been prepared, but name the media that you plan to use as components.

29. How will restrictions on the time teachers may be expected to spend on an after-school basis, determined by decisions of negotiating professional groups, be likely to affect the pacing and implementation of in-service growth programs? How would you as a district-wide media leader propose to meet your objectives? (What would be your line of reasoning in formulating a desirable plan of action?)

References

Allen, William H. "Audio-Visual Communication—Administration of AV Programs." In Chester W. Harris (ed.). *Encyclopedia of Educational Research*, 3rd ed. (New York: Macmillan, 1960).

Association for Supervision and Curriculum Development. *Role of the Supervisor and Curriculum Director in a Climate of Change.* Yearbook, 1965 (Washington, D.C.: The Association, N.E.A., 1965).

Billett, Roy O. *Fundamentals of Secondary School Teaching with Emphasis on the Unit Method* (Boston: Houghton Mifflin, 1940), p. 471.

Blank, Gordon. "Beware the Instant Teacher." *Audiovisual Instruction*, Vol. 9, No. 8, October 1964, pp. 524–525.

Brown, James W. and Kenneth D. Norberg. *Administering Educational Media* (New York: McGraw-Hill, 1965).

Burton, William H. *Guidance of Learning Activities*, 2nd ed. (New York: Appleton-Century-Crofts, 1955).

Burton, William H. and Leo J. Brueckner. *Supervision A Social Process*, 3rd ed. (New York: Appleton-Century-Crofts, 1955).

Cochran, Lee W. "Televised Inservice Training: Iowa Picks Up the Wisconsin Course." *Audiovisual Instruction.* Vol. 8, No. 9, November 1963, pp. 674–675.

Cross, A. J. Foy. "The Unit Method in Modern Teaching." *Audiovisual Instruction*, Vol. 3, September 1958, pp. 168–169.

Curl, David H. "Automated Equipment Operation Training." *Audiovisual Instruction*, Vol. 10, No. 7, September 1965, pp. 564–565.

DeBernardis, Amo. "In-Service Teacher Education." *Audio-Visual Materials of Instruction*, 48th Yearbook of the National Society for the Study of Education, Part I (Chicago: University of Chicago Press, 1950), p. 117.

Erickson, Carlton W. H. *Fundamentals of Teaching with Audiovisual Technology* (New York: Macmillan, 1965).

———. "A Yardstick for Your In-Service Program." *Audiovisual Instruction*, Vol. 8, No. 9, November 1963, pp. 678–680.

———. "Making a Production of It." *Audiovisual Instruction*, Vol. 3, September 1958, pp. 174–176.

Evaluative Criteria, 1960 Edition. National Study of Secondary-School Evaluation (Washington, D.C.: NSSSE, 1960).

Frye, Roy A. "The Texas Plan: A Phased In-service Training Program." *Audiovisual Instruction*, Vol. 8, No. 9, November 1963, pp. 671–673.

In-Service Education, 56th Yearbook of the National Society for the Study of Education, Part I (Chicago: University of Chicago Press, 1957).

Learning and Instruction, 49th Yearbook of the National Society for the Study of Education, Part I (Chicago: University of Chicago Press, 1950).

Mager, Robert F. *Preparing Objectives for Programed Instruction* (San Francisco: Fearon, 1961).

McLuhan, Marshall. *Understanding Media: The Extensions of Man* (New York: McGraw-Hill, 1964).

Miles, Matthew B. and A. Harry Passow. "Training in the Skills Needed for In-Service Education Programs." *In-Service Education for Teachers, Supervisors, and Administrators*, 56th Yearbook of the National Society for the Study of Education, Part I (Chicago: University of Chicago Press, 1957), pp. 366–367.

Miller, William C. "Let's Put Our Methods Where Our Mouths Are." *Audiovisual Instruction*, Vol. 8, No. 9, November 1963, pp. 656–658.

Morlan, John E. "The Team Approach to Large-Group Instruction." *Audiovisual In-*

struction, Vol. 9, No. 8, October 1964, pp. 520–522.

Reed, Blake L. "Constant Contact: An Essential of Inservice Education." *Audiovisual Instruction*, Vol. 8, No. 9, November 1963, pp. 659–661.

Schuller, Charles F. (ed.). *The School Administrator and His Audio-Visual Program*. Year-book, Department of Audio-Visual Instruction of the NEA, 1201 Sixteenth St., N.W., Washington, D.C., 1954.

Singer, Ira J. "Reducing the Research to Practice Gap." *Audiovisual Instruction*, Vol. 8, No. 9, November 1963. pp. 652–655.

Smith, Gordon L. "South Carolina TV Program." *Audiovisual Instruction*, Vol. 10, No. 7, September 1965, p. 560.

Stratemeyer, Florence B., Hamden L. Forkner, Margaret G. McKim and A. Harry Passow. *Developing a Curriculum for Modern Living*, 2nd ed. rev. (New York: Teachers College Press, 1957).

Swenson, Patricia L. "Portland's Professional Growth Series on Radio and TV." *Audiovisual Instruction*, Vol. 10, No. 7, September 1965, pp. 557–558.

Thelen, Herbert. *Education and the Human Quest* (New York: Harper and Row, 1960).

Weber, C. A. "A New Look in Leadership." *Audiovisual Instruction*, Vol. 1, Issue 7, December 1956, pp. 200–201, 218.

Weber, C. A. and Mary E. Weber. *Fundamentals of Educational Leadership* (New York: McGraw-Hill, 1955).

Williams, Catherine M. "Packaged Program for In-Service Audiovisual Education." *Audiovisual Instruction*, Vol. 10, No. 7, September 1965, pp. 552–555.

Audiovisual Media for In-Service Learning Situations

The following list of audiovisual media is not intended to be complete. The standard source-books and the catalogs of regional and local media distribution centers should be consulted for detailed descriptions of these as well as for additional appropriate titles. Titles of motion pictures are marked "MP" and "MPC" if in 8mm cartridge form. Filmstrips are marked "FS" and audio tapes are marked "Tape."

Abbreviations used for producers are identified at the end of the list. Unless otherwise indicated, the subject is black and white.

And No Bells Ring (MP, NEA, 57 min.)

Audio Equipment: Record Player (MPC, Chandler, 2 min., color)

Audio Equipment: Tape Recorder (MPC, Chandler, 3 min., color)

Audio Equipment: Splicing Magnetic Tape (MPC, Chandler, 2 min., color)

Behind the Tape: The Teacher (Tape, 3M, 30 min.)

Better Bulletin Boards (MP, IU, 13 min.)

Bulletin Boards: An Effective Teaching Device (MP, Bailey, 11 min., color)

Bulletin Boards at Work (FS, UWa, 42 frames)

Bulletin Boards for Better Teaching (MP, ISU, 10 min.)

Chalk and Chalkboards (MP, Bailey, 15 min., color)

Chalkboard Utilization (MP, McGraw-H, 14 min.)

Charts for Creative Learning (MP, Bailey, 10 min., color)

Child of the Future (MP, McGraw-H, 60 min.)

Children Learn from Filmstrips (MP, McGraw-H, 16 min.)

Choosing a Classroom Film (MP, McGraw-H, 18 min.)

Cloth Mounting (Roll) (MPC, Chandler, 4 min.)

Community Resources in Teaching (MP, ISU, 20 min.)

Creating Cartoons (MP, Bailey, 10 min., color)

Creating Instructional Materials (MP, McGraw-H, 15 min.)

Demonstration Tape for Elementary Schools (Tape, 3M, 15 min.)

Demonstration Tape for Secondary Schools (Tape, 3M, 15 min.)

Demonstration as a Teaching Technique (FS, UWa, 35 frames)

Diorama as a Teaching Aid (FS, OSU, 58 frames, color)

Dry Mounting (Hand Iron) (MPC, Chandler, 3 min.)

Dry Mounting (Press) (MPC, Chandler, 4 min.)

Duplicating by the Spirit Method (MP, Bailey, 15 min., color)

Effectiveness of Audio-Visual Materials (FS, BSF, 45 frames, color)

Enriching the Curriculum with Filmstrips (FS, SVE, 60 frames)

Example of a Teaching Machine Program (FS, BSF, 71 frames, color)

Facts about Films (MP, IFB, 11 min.)

Facts about Projection (MP, IFB, 11 min.)

Feltboard in Teaching (MP, UWa, 10 min.)

Film and You (Using the Classroom Film) (MP, Bailey, 13 min.)

Film Research and Learning (MP, UWis, 14 min.)

Filmstrips and the Teacher (FS, McGraw-H, 32 frames, color)

First the Ear (Tape, 3M, 30 min.)

Flannel Boards and How to Use Them (MP, Bailey, 15 min., color)

Fundamental Skills in a Unit of Work (MP, Bailey, 21 min.)

Globes: Their Function in the Classroom (MP, Bailey, 14 min., color)

Handmade Materials for Projection (MP, IU, 20 min.)

High Contrast Photography for Instruction (MP, IU, 13 min.)

How to Get the Most Out of a Filmstrip (FS, EH, 50 frames, color and sound)

How to Keep Your Bulletin Board Alive (FS, OSU, 32 frames)

How to Make a Puppet (MP, Bailey, 12 min.)

How to Make and Use Dioramas (MP, SU, 27 min.)

How to Make and Use the Feltboard (FS, OSU, 52 frames)

How to Make Papier Mâché Animals (MP, Bailey, 12 min.)

How to Use Classroom Films (MP, McGraw-H, 15 min.)

How to Use a Teaching Film (FS, BSF, 43 frames, color)

Improving Use of the Chalkboard (FS, OSU, 44 frames, color)

Instructional Materials (FS, Bel-Mort, 50 frames)

Learning from Visuals: The Application of Programing Principles to Visual Presentations (MP, AIR, 36 min., color)

Lettering: The Felt Pen (Applications) (MPC, Chandler, 4 min., color)

Lettering: The Felt Pen (Basic Skills) (MPC, Chandler, 5 min., color)

Lettering Instructional Materials (MP, IU, 23 min.)

Lettering: Leroy 500 and Smaller (MPC, Chandler, 4 min.)

Lettering: Wricoprint (MPC, Chandler, 2 min.)

Lettering: Wrico Signmaker (MPC, Chandler, 4 min.)

Make a Mighty Reach (MP, IDEA, 45 min.)

Making Field Trips Effective (FS, UWa, 46 frames)

Making Geographic Models (FS, OSU, 55 frames, color)

Making Learning More Meaningful (MP, McGraw-H, 12 min.)

Making Your Chalk Teach (FS, UWa, 47 frames)

More Different Than Alike (MP, NEA, 28 min.)

Motion Picture Projectors: Motion Picture Projection Practice, Part 1 (MPC, Chandler, 4 min., color)

Motion Picture Projectors: Motion Picture Projection Practice, Part 2 (MPC, Chandler, 4 min., color)

Mounting: A Cut-Out Picture (MPC, Chandler, 3 min.)

Mounting: Overcoming Dry Mounting Problems (MPC, Chandler, 3 min.)

Mounting: Setting Grommets (MPC, Chandler, 3 min.)

Mounting: Using Laminating Film (MPC, Chandler, 5 min.)

Multifaceted Approach to Teaching Botany (MP, Purdue, 20 min.)

New Dimensions Through Teaching Films (MP, Coronet, 27 min.)

Opaque Projector (FS, OSU, 42 frames, color)

Overhead Television: A New Visual Aid (MP, UCLA, 27 min.)

Passe Partout Framing (MP, IU, 10 min.)

Permanent Rubber Cement Mounting (MPC, Chandler, 4 min.)

Photographic Slides for Instruction (MP, IU, 10 min.)

Pictures and Words (Part 1 and Part 2) (FS, Bel-Mort, Part 1 49 frames, Part 2 52 frames)

Poster Making: Design and Technique (MP, Bailey, 10 min., color)

Preparing Projected Materials (MP, Bailey, 15 min., color)

Probing Mind (MP, USOE, 28 min.)

Quiet Revolution (MP, NEA, 25 min.)

Recording with Magnetic Tape (MP, UMinn., 8 min.)

Relief Models (MP, Lipscomb, 10 min., color)

School Journey (FS, BSF, 48 frames, color)

Selecting and Using Ready-Made Materials (MP, McGraw-H, 17 min.)

Simple Exhibit Technique (FS, OSU, 40 frames, color)

Simplified Filmstrip Production (FS, OSU, 40 frames)

Spirit Duplicator: Operation (MPC, Chandler, 3 min., color)

Spirit Duplicator: Preparing Masters (MPC, Chandler, 4 min., color)

Still Projectors: Opaque Projector (MPC, Chandler, 3 min., color)

Still Projectors: Overhead Projector (MPC, Chandler, 3 min., color)

Still Projectors: 2 × 2 inch Slide Projectors (MPC, Chandler, 4 min., color)

Still Projectors: 35mm Filmstrip Projector (MPC, Chandler, 3 min., color)

Study Pictures and Learning (FS, OSU, 58 frames, color)

Tachistoscopic Teaching Technique (FS, LTS, 51 frames)

Tape Recording for Instruction (MP, IU, 15 min.)

Teaching by Television (FS, BSF, 51 frames, color)

Teaching Machines (FS, BSF, 64 frames, color)

Teaching Machines and Programed Learning (MP, NEA, 29 min.)

Teaching Map Reading Skills in Elementary Schools (MP, Bailey, 19 min., color)

Teaching with Filmstrips (FS, SVE, 59 frames)

Teaching with Still Pictures (FS, BSF, 53 frames, color)

Team Teaching on the Elementary Level (MP, Bailey, 14 min., color)

Television in Education (MP, BTC, 30 min., color)

To Speak with Friends (MP, NEA, 28 min.)

Transparencies: Adding Color (MPC, Chandler, 4 min., color)

Transparencies: Diazo Process (MPC, Chandler, 4 min., color)

Transparencies: Handmade Method (MPC, Chandler, 3 min., color)

Transparencies: Heat Process (MPC, Chandler, 2 min., color)

Transparencies: Making Overlays (MPC, Chandler, 4 min., color)

Transparencies: Mounting and Masking (MPC, Chandler, 3 min., color)

Transparencies: Principle of Diazo Process (MPC, Chandler, 5 min., color)

Transparencies: Spirit Duplicator (MPC, Chandler, 3 min., color)

Unique Contribution (MP, EBF, 30 min., color)

Using Graphs and Charts in Teaching (FS, BSF, 51 frames, color)

Using Individual Learning Procedures in Teaching (FS, BSF, 55 frames, color)

Using Maps and Globes (FS, Rand, 48 frames, color)

Main Sources for the Media Materials Listed

AIR	American Institute of Research, Pittsburgh, Pa.
Bailey	Bailey Films, Inc., Los Angeles, Calif.
BSF	Basic Skill Films, 1355 Inverness Drive, Pasadena, Calif.
BTC	Bell Telephone Company (make local arrangements).
Belmort	Bel-Mort Co., 619 ICO Bldg., 520 S.W. Sixth Ave., Portland, Ore.
Chandler	Chandler Publishing Co., 124 Spear St., San Francisco, Calif.
COR	Coronet Films, Coronet Building, Chicago, Ill.
EBF	Encyclopaedia Britannica Films, Wilmette, Ill.
EH	Eyegate House, Inc., 146–01 Archer Ave., Jamaica, N.Y.
IDEA	Institute for Development of Educational Activities, P.O. Box 446, Melbourne, Florida.
IFB	International Film Bureau, 57 East Jackson Blvd., Chicago, Ill.
ISU	University of Iowa, Audio-visual Center, Iowa City, Iowa.
IU	Indiana University, Audio-Visual Center, Bloomington, Ind.
Lipscomb	David Lipscomb College, Memphis, Tenn.
LTS	Learning Through Seeing, Box 368, Sunland, Calif.
McGraw-H	McGraw-Hill Text-Film Department, 330 W. 42nd St., New York 36, N.Y.
NEA	NEA, 1201 Sixteenth St., N.W., Washington, D.C.

OSU — Ohio State University, Photographic Laboratory, Columbus 10, Ohio.

Purdue — Purdue University, Audiovisual Center, Lafayette, Ind.

Rand — Rand McNally Co., Box 7600, Chicago, Ill.

SU — Syracuse University, Center for Instructional Communications, Syracuse, N.Y.

SVE — Society for Visual Education, 1345 Diversey Parkway, Chicago, Ill.

3M — Minnesota Mining and Manufacturing Co., St. Paul, Minn.

UCLA — University of California, Los Angeles.

UMinn — University of Minnesota, Audio-Visual Center, Minneapolis, Minn.

USOE — United States Office of Education, Du-Art Film Laboratories.

UWa — Wayne University, Audio-Visual Materials Consultation Bureau, Detroit, Mich.

UWis — University of Wisconsin, Audiovisual Center, 1321 W. Johnson St., Madison, Wis.

It is not fully recognized that one of the crucial problems in conducting a media services program is to stimulate the use of media by the teachers for whom and by whom they were selected. Directors should certainly get the facts about the status of their local levels of media use by comparing their present volume of distribution with a potential or desirable volume. If this is done, directors will not be likely to commit the error of taking false pride in what to the uninitiated observer may seem like a commendable volume of requests and service. As others have found out in the past, those who seek information about the potential volume of utilization may be startled to discover that all too frequently the media selected for a given group of teachers may not be having the expected impact because many of the teachers in the group are not using them at all. One would be inclined to assume that once a service is provided, teachers would use it avidly. That this is not the case need not be discouraging, but by knowing it, the alert director may be led to make an analysis that will have a far-reaching influence on the success of his program of service.

In Chapter 3 we discussed the acquisition of media materials and equipment, and in that chapter we raised the problem of selecting materials that are primarily basic to the curriculum. If we choose basic materials, it is obvious that unless teachers for whom the media were purchased or produced use them, the curriculum purposes are not being served. In Chapter 4 we emphasized the identification of needs and the importance of teaching teachers how to use media effectively. If this change process is carried out adequately, teachers will feel a new security because of the skills they have developed, and may therefore be more easily led toward optimum use of the media provided. In this chapter the main emphasis is on the effective and efficient use of audiovisual media by all teachers who *should* use them. The director is therefore confronted with new problems that have to do with giving teachers information about available media materials and making the materials conveniently accessible. The first of these problems is to develop a system for publicizing audiovisual media that meets local needs. The second will be to find effective ways of facilitating and processing the requests made by teachers for the media they need to use at the time their instructional plans will be best served.

Effective Distribution of Media

The reader should recognize the existence of two aspects of the problems identified in the preceding paragraph, namely, the distribution of media materials from the school-system headquarters where the materials are likely to be centralized, and the distribution of media materials that are located at or assigned to the various school-building units. It is the first of these aspects that is dealt with in this chapter, since the problem has to be solved on a system-wide basis and requires both professional and technical personnel efforts of major proportions. The second aspect of this basic problem is treated in Chapter 7 which deals with media services in individual school buildings. The prospective media program director should make sure that the information system he develops will eliminate confusion as to the source of the titles of media material listed. Such information may have to be included in card and list-type catalogs or, as will be pointed out later, on specially prepared lists of the media items or collections available in any given school building. Such items may or may not be made available to other school buildings in the school system.

The System for Publicizing Materials

Adequate information about available audiovisual media is one of the basic routes to the facilitation of their use. Ideally, information about media must be general, specific, up-to-date, easy to use, accurate, and repetitive. Any system developed for publicizing media ought to meet these conditions and at the same time be feasible locally. By *general* we mean that teachers need to know in a comprehensive way just what is available for everybody and for all subjects. Only then will they be likely to know what all the resources are for special plans. By *specific* information teachers may know what materials have been designated for each subject, for teaching units, for specific experiences and problems, or for problem areas. Information about media should be brought to the attention of teachers again and again, probably through different approaches, as, for example, not only in a catalog but also in curriculum guides and special listings. Furthermore, the information must undergo periodic revisions, the entries must be accurately made as to title and descrip-

tive details, and the information must be presented in an easy-to-use format. For example, it is common practice to revise a catalog by a supplement or by listings in news bulletins. Such announcements and supplements after a time, however, tend to pile up on desks or in drawers and file cabinets and become exceedingly difficult to use. Thus new and timely editions of catalogs and listings are essential.

An adequate system for publicizing media may well demand a schedule of the following publications and procedures.

1. Publish a comprehensive catalog and provide a copy for each teacher; revise it and re-issue it every other year, and keep it up-to-date on an annual basis by a supplement alternating with the catalog.

2. Prepare and send to teachers one or more specific listings correlating available titles of material with the teaching units, courses, curriculum guides, and outlines that have been developed for teacher use. Revise such lists by supplement sheets, advising teachers to add subjects to the basic lists for two years. (To make such a detailed and complex program possible, the actual work of writing, listing, and correlating may have to be done by subject matter, grade, or other divisional groups on a cooperative basis.)

3. Prepare or work with others on the preparation of curriculum guides and outlines incorporating the suggested basic and supplementary titles of audiovisual media as available from central sources, and include also, where appropriate, subjects available at each school-building service center.

4. Incorporate topical file cards in every school library card catalog, indicating centrally available filmstrips, picture sets, and motion pictures, and where feasible, also those subjects that are obtainable in each or in a given school collection.

5. Prepare and distribute special lists of materials being rented or borrowed, by grades and/or subject, based on the programs in the individual schools.

6. Publish a news bulletin on a strict schedule, preferably in two editions, one for elementary teachers and one for secondary teachers, four times each school year; this should be prepared at the media service headquarters. This publication should emphasize new groupings of

material, round-ups of new media for grades and subjects, and should report interesting case studies of audiovisual media being used with outstanding results.

7. Encourage preparation of reports and announcements by other curriculum specialists to call attention to audiovisual materials in achieving objectives for special programs and areas.

8. Obtain and distribute a set of commercially available source books to each school library.

Such an extensive system for publicizing materials at first glance may seem to propose an unreasonably increased work load, and it certainly means exactly this if the director is to be a committee of one person to do it all. Since publicizing media information is a necessity, the system for accomplishing it will have to arise out of the local complex of conditions, and the media director will have to strike a balance in taking appropriate action.

Any system for publicizing materials that is developed in any community should start with the first essential, namely, the catalog. Two basic kinds of catalog are in use, and each opens up its own array of possibilities and problems. These are the card catalog and the list catalog. Each of the two catalog methods must be as fully descriptive as is permitted by time, staff, and financial support.

Card Catalog and Processes

When the card catalog method is adopted, the director must arrange to supply appropriate steel or wood file cabinets to each school (see Figure 5-1) together with a complete set of descriptive cards made up of all the multiple copies of cards for each title of every filmstrip, picture set, model, diorama, or other audiovisual media. To make up a master file, the cards should be filed alphabetically according to the first principal word in the title, then filed again and again under other categories such as courses of study, subject-matter fields, grade levels, local topical arrangement, and course units. Thus for any given filmstrip, for example, a card bearing the same information would have to be filed under each of the alphabetically arranged sections. Very rarely, how-

ever, are card catalogs cross-referenced as comprehensively as just indicated because of limitations in the size of filing cabinets, and the time, money, and work required in printing and processing the cards.

For maximum value to teachers, each card should include full data such as synopsis of content; physical characteristics such as running time, frames, or number of pictures in the set, size, and so on; producer and date; and other relationships such as unit, course, grade, and *basal* or *supplementary* designations. Cards for different materials ought to be color coded, that is, blue for one kind of material, white, green, red, and so on, for others. Card catalogs are kept up-to-date by issuing the right number of cards for each new title of material, so that appropriate cross-referencing can be accomplished in the file at each school.

The adequacy of such a method must be judged in terms of the following critical questions: How convenient is it for teachers to use a file cabinet if only one is placed in his or her school building? How many card file cabinets are really needed in each school building? Can provisions be made to send appropriate cards to individual teachers also and thus reduce the otherwise necessary cross referencing in the file? How do teachers react to the system where it is presently in use? What other specific elements in the system of publicizing materials are feasible and necessary with the card catalog method? Are the media cataloged being used

Figure 5-1. This card catalog system for audiovisual media is shown in use at the Hawthorne Elementary School. *Courtesy San Francisco Unified School District.*

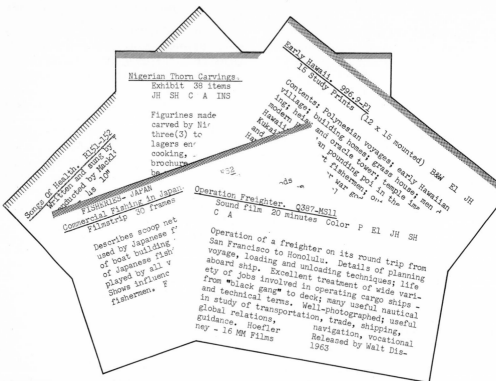

Early Hawaii. 996.9.Pl
15 Study Prints (12 x 15 mounted) B&W El JH

Contents: Polynesian voyages; early Hawaiian
village; building homes; grass house; men ?
ing; heiau and oracle tower; temple imp
modern and ?an pounding poi in the
Hawaii. ?an
Kukai ?t fishermen; on ?
and ?? war go?
Ha

Nigerian Thorn Carvings.
Exhibit 38 items
JH SH C A INS

Figurines made
carved by Nir
three(3) to
lagers en?
cooking, ?
brochure?
be ?
?52.

Songs of Health. R151-152
Written and sung by
?nducted by Meckl?
is 10"

FISHERIES—JAPAN
Commercial Fishing in Japan
Filmstrip 30 frames

Describes scoop net
used by Japanese f?
of boat building ?
of Japanese fish?
played by all v
Shows influenc
fishermen. F

Operation Freighter. Q387-MS11
Sound film 20 minutes Color P El JH SH
C A

Operation of a freighter on its round trip from
San Francisco to Honolulu. Details of planning
voyage, loading and unloading techniques; life
aboard ship. Excellent treatment of wide variety of jobs involved in operating cargo ships -
from "black gang" to deck; many useful nautical
and technical terms. Well-photographed; useful
in study of transportation, trade, shipping,
global relations, navigation, vocational
guidance. Hoefler Released by Walt Dis-
ney - 16 MM Films 1963

Figure 5-2. The San Francisco card system employs color coding for the various kinds of media. Study the cards in each set to ascertain differences in kinds and arrangement of media data. (*Top card set*, courtesy San Francisco Unified School District. *Bottom card set*, courtesy City Schools, Fayetteville, North Carolina.)

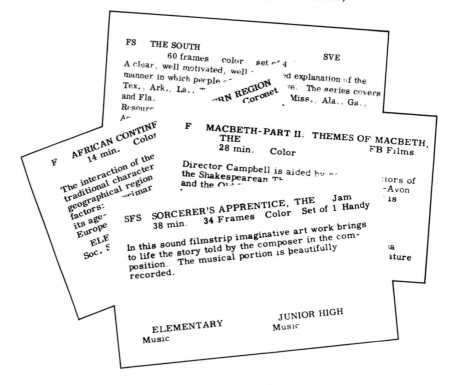

FS   THE SOUTH   SVE
          60 frames   color   set of 4
A clear, well motivated, well-?   ?d explanation of the
manner in which people ?   ?e. The series covers
Tex., Ark., La., ? ?RN REGION   Miss., Ala., Ga.,
and Fla.   Coronet
Resourc?
A?

F   AFRICAN CONTINE?   Color

The interaction of the
traditional character
geographical region
factors: ?rimar
its age?
Europe

ELE?
Soc. ?

F   MACBETH—PART II. THEMES OF MACBETH,
     THE
     28 min.   Color   FB Films

Director Campbell is aided by ?
the Shakespearean T?   ?tors of
and the Ol? ?   ?Avon
                                   ?is

SFS   SORCERER'S APPRENTICE, THE   Jam
       38 min.   34 Frames Color Set of 1 Handy

In this sound filmstrip imaginative art work brings
to life the story told by the composer in the composition. The musical portion is beautifully   ?a
recorded.   ?ature

ELEMENTARY   JUNIOR HIGH
Music   Music

by the teachers for whom they were intended? Are the card catalogs really being used?

The card catalog system may, of course, be combined with the distribution of different kinds of title lists or specialized groupings to aid and encourage teachers to seek additional needed information in the card files. It is obvious that general card catalogs are made specific through cross-referencing techniques; however, the need for other specific lists may prove to be the main disadvantage of the method. Any catalog process is a time-consuming business and unless a plan is set up for the continuous processing of cards that can be handled by clerical assistants, the director will be prevented from performing other urgently needed tasks. In the process of preparing card files, the following are the important elements:

1. Adaptation of a standard format, with all physical properties such as size of picture, running time, number of slides in the set, and so on, being added by clerical assistants.
2. Use of Library of Congress catalog cards or other cards as made available by producers, where available and serviceable.
3. Use of mimeograph or regular printing processes according to local conditions.
4. Utilization of preview and evaluation report forms from teacher selection groups that will provide items of information for immediate transfer to the cards.
5. Establishment of a color-code system for materials.
6. Establishment of a standard cross-referencing code for the director or the professional assistant to use in preparing the cross-referencing schedule for each card, depending on the nature and content of the title.
7. Inclusion of special cards for the materials owned by (or assigned to) a given school within the school system.

List Catalogs

The main advantage of the list catalog is its immediate availability for use by each teacher anywhere, anytime. Like the card catalog method, the list-type catalog may also be made general and specific; that is, general in its comprehensiveness in listing and describing all materials, and specific in its classification system. Of course the more functional and specific the groupings become, the larger the book and the more expensive its preparation. The list catalog, however, lends itself admirably to one other method of issuing a catalog that is specific, which is the method of splitting up the catalog into appropriate subdivisions such as Secondary School Science, Junior High School, Elementary School Social Studies, Foreign Language, or any other combination of specific lists that meets local demands. This, of course, could be done also with the card-type catalogs, and if the card system is to be used effectively, this is what must be done. It is obvious that revising the list-type or bound catalog demands reprinting the entire booklet, whereas with the card-type catalog, obsolete cards are simply removed and the cards for new media are distributed for filing in each card catalog cabinet.

Comprehensive list-type catalogs, in order to be helpful and convenient to use, ought to incorporate the following features:

1. *An attractive, consistent format throughout.* The director should see to it that cover paper and designs are appropriate and that the binding will stand hard usage. See Figure 5-3. Catalog planners without adequate technical supporting staff for publications should not forget that high school art students can be encouraged to cooperate in making attractive designs for covers.
2. *An adequate, introductory section,* detailing the specified ordering procedures and the policies under which service is given.
3. *A topical index* that is as functional for teachers as possible. The director has a real opportunity to make up unique topical headings in terms of local school subjects, courses, grade levels, problem areas, special programs, and so on, or he can resort to a standard classification procedure. At any rate he has but to turn to any of the easily available catalogs or source books to discover examples of procedure.
4. *A classification section* where individual titles of material, properly coded as to type, are listed under each of the topics selected.
5. *One or more sections of color-coded paper* giving descriptions of content of each title in alphabetical order. If the catalog lists all the kinds of material distributed, motion pictures could be in the white section, filmstrips in green, exhibits in red, picture sets in blue, and so on. Descriptions and other details offering helpful clues to teachers as to the value of the

Figure 5-3. Preparing and publishing the necessary catalogs is a major undertaking. Every possible and reasonably available means ought to be used to make this task less burdensome than it always is. Study these catalog covers to make judgments about degree of comprehensiveness, cover designs and size. Refer also to illustrations of mechanized catalog processes. *Photograph by David H. Curl.*

media ought to be as complete as can be afforded in terms of time, staff, money, and other duties.

The director should make the catalog up in terms of a system of information—that is, in terms of other elements of the publicizing program. This is important because the catalog is the largest work assignment in the system. The nature of additional specific listings that are issued regularly will help the director to decide on how broadly or specifically information should be handled. The director may, of course, have to limit the publication to one copy for each teacher. In this case it seems necessary to split the information between elementary and secondary levels.

Examples of Plans to Publicize Media. It is to be expected that media program directors will devise unique designs and plans for their

cataloging procedures, and it will be helpful to study several specific cases in detail. We present the following examples.

Example 1

OAKLAND, CALIFORNIA

The Audio-Visual Section, Division of Instructional Media, of the Oakland Public Schools publishes a total of 18 separate audiovisual media catalogs, all of which are specific in nature. Each of the 3,000 teachers in the school system may have personal copies of these catalogs that are appropriate to the grades and subjects being taught. Typical examples of the titles of such catalogs, each paralleling a course of study, are the following: *Secondary Science—Grades Eight to Twelve, Elementary Science—Kindergarten to Grade Six, Business Practice, Foreign Language, Industrial Arts,* and *Language Arts.* Each catalog is prepared according to a standard format and, as Figure 5-10 shows, is printed by addressograph-plate and offset printing technology. The design of each of the catalogs includes the following features: (1) an introductory section that includes instructions for ordering and returning the media, (2) a separate section for each of the kinds of media circulated (motion pictures, filmstrips, slides, flat pictures, phonograph records, exhibits, and special media for that grade, course of study, or subject) headed by a colored separator sheet that carries the title of the medium being cataloged, (3) each item of a given medium, such as a motion picture, is annotated, appearing in a two-column list on an $8\frac{1}{2} \times 11$ inch page, and included with the main title is a topical reference, production date, producer, grade level usage, and other appropriate physical information.

As is pointed out in the Foreword of each catalog, newly acquired media titles are listed in the *Audio-Visual and Library News* section of the Superintendent's Bulletin as a regular means of keeping the teachers up-to-date. Most of the 18 catalogs are revised annually. The 18 catalogs list, cross reference and categorize about 30,000 items. As an example of the size and scope of the 1965–66 cataloging project, the secondary science catalog was made up of 91 pages, printed one side, and the elementary science catalog had 70 pages.

Example 2

SEATTLE, WASHINGTON

The Audio-Visual Department of the Seattle Public Schools publishes two comprehensive catalogs of media for teachers, one for secondary and the other for elementary schools. Each of these two main catalogs is the same in format, and since motion pictures and filmstrips are cataloged by data-processing methods, each catalog is made up by assembling both offset printed and mimeographed sheets. The design of the catalog incorporates the following features: (1) Title page, Foreword, and a detailed Table of Contents; (2) the twice-each-week delivery schedule to all schools; (3) a section that includes the following instructions: How to Use the Catalog, How to Order, Tips on Motion Picture Projection, Tips on Filmstrip Projection, How to Care for Materials, Teaching with Films; (4) the alphabetically arranged motion picture section where each title is listed and annotated, including such physical charac-

teristics as running time, color, and the curriculum classification and grade level for use; (5) a color-coded section devoted to subject-matter and topical references, under which all of the motion pictures are categorized, together with level and other abbreviated items of information; (6) a single sheet outlining some tips for teaching with filmstrips and immediately following an alphabetical listing of filmstrip titles and, where the title is the title of a set, the listing of each title in the set; (7) in a color-coded section are the curriculum headings with appropriate categorization of filmstrip titles or the title of a set, together with recommended grade levels; (8) four additional sections, each preceded by teaching tips on slides, mounted pictures (together with exhibits and transparencies), records, and tapes; (9) a final section listing, describing, and categorizing of titles in the traveling study collection made available through the cooperation of the Washington State Museum. The final sections, as was the case with preceding sections, supplied recommended grade levels and brief descriptions of content.

The secondary school catalog in 1965 contained 306 pages printed on one side, and the elementary school catalog 198 pages. They are revised and issued to all teachers annually in September. Up-to-date information about media item acquisitions is supplied to all teachers by means of a school district publication entitled *Seattle Public Schools Guide*.

Example 3

WICHITA, KANSAS

The Instructional Materials Center of the Wichita Public Schools publishes one comprehensive catalog including approximately 6,000 media items for teachers at both elementary and secondary levels. Included in the comprehensive catalog of 70 sheets, printed both sides in small type, are motion pictures, filmstrips, slides, tapes, kits and programed materials, categorized under 71 curriculum topics. The approach to the cataloging problem is one of extreme simplicity of organization that stresses ease of handling by teachers, deletion of all content except that which aids teachers to find items needed, narrowing down the area of recommended use, and recognition of the need for an up-to-date information system. The design of this catalog includes a single page providing ordering instructions and a page listing the curriculum topic together with the kinds of media, identifying symbols, and the abbreviations that indicate recommended levels of use. The balance of the catalog lists each item of media under appropriate curriculum headings, subjects, courses, and other functional topics selected in the light of expressed teacher needs. Each item is tersely annotated and coded as to type and order number, grade level, and other appropriate physical characteristics.

In a later section of this discussion, we have described the work of the Wichita media program director in devising and using mechanized cataloging procedures, and the reader is therefore referred to that section in following up this case study. For the time being, it will be interesting to prospective media program directors—and practitioners as well—to read firsthand reports that indicate the rationale behind the catalog described above. The Wichita director's own report is as follows:

We have found there are several factors important in any cataloging system which is designed to be economical and easy to revise. First of all, collating and stapling represent one of the main work loads of any frequently revised catalog. We have found that by using small type (texttype), by making brief annotations, and by using both sides of the page for printing we keep the number of sheets in our catalog to a minimum. This makes the annual assembly and printing of the catalog less cumbersome.

We feel that with the rapid change in instructional materials it is important to have a yearly revision of our catalog so that teachers can go to one source for centrally located materials without searching through several supplements. We also combine all materials, filmstrips, slides, transparencies, programed materials, motion picture films, etc., in one catalog. Only the prefix to the order numbers differentiates the type of material. Secondary materials are grouped as nearly as possible by course. In other words, a chemistry teacher can locate all the materials related to his course in one section of the catalog without searching through several catalogs. We have found this has increased the use of materials other than motion picture films significantly.[1]

Example 4

Los Angeles, California

It has been the policy of the Audio-Visual Section of the Los Angeles City Schools to issue

[1] By permission from B. W. Wolfe, excerpted from correspondence with the author, dated Feb. 11, 1966.

a number of comprehensive and specific catalogs for each of the elementary and secondary instruction levels. In the school year 1965–66 a major shift toward comprehensive catalogs took place and with the publishing of the new elementary school catalog the number of catalogs for that division was reduced from four to two. At the same time the number of media catalogs for the secondary school division was reduced to three. These are as follows: for the elementary schools, one catalog listing and categorizing all media for all elementary grade levels and one additional catalog entitled *It's Worth a Visit*, a sourcebook of approved school journeys suggested for elementary school students; for the secondary schools, a catalog of motion pictures, entitled *Films Secondary Grades*, another catalog listing and describing all other media besides films; and a third, a catalog of school journeys for secondary grades, again entitled, *It's Worth a Visit*.

We shall now turn our attention to the details in the design of two of these catalogs and to the illustrations of them in Figure 5-4 as follows: *Films Secondary Grades* and *It's Worth a Visit* (For Elementary Grades). Both of these catalogs, as other media catalogs and a great number of additional publications of the Los Angeles Instructional Materials Center have been, are of outstanding graphic and journalistic quality. Both, as others have in the past, reflect the careful planning and layout work, as well as the fact that the work of producing school publications is a serious business that merits professional and technical supervision.

Features in the design of the motion picture catalog are the following: (1) the catalog is made up of 545 pages ($8\frac{1}{2} \times 11$), printed on both sides of each sheet, and is bound with an imprinted plastic binder; (2) a section that describes the makeup of the catalog and a detailed table of contents that provides references to subjects and units of work within broad curriculum topics; (3) an attractively illustrated section dealing with tips on using materials, a projection check list, film ordering procedure, and a group of projection pointers; (4) a detailed subject area list of 55 pages; (5) the description section made up of alphabetically arranged film titles with 75-word synopses plus physical characteristics, ordering number, grade levels, and recommended curriculum subjects; (6) a detailed cross-referenced index; (7) a sec-

Figure 5-4. The reader should observe details of format and binding, and in general, the attractiveness of the publications shown. The handbook has been quoted in this book time and time again. *Courtesy Los Angeles City School Districts.*

tion devoted to an alphabetical list of films and their descriptions; (8) a cross-referenced film index for junior colleges. The design of this catalog is based on providing optimally useful film descriptions together with several useful indices for teachers who are seeking the most useful item in a large collection.

Features in the design of the *It's Worth a Visit* catalog include (1) an introduction to explain the make-up of the catalog and a table of contents; (2) Part I, *The School Journey Program*, an attractively illustrated discussion of the field-trip method together with discussions of such topics as Responsibilities, School Bus Regulations, Procedures for Requesting School Journey Services, How to Make a Successful School Journey, Suggestions for Tour Guide; (3) Part II, The School Journey Program, including approved field trips from Airports to Zoos complete with information needed by teachers with many maps and diagrams of processes to be observed; (4) detailed subject and title indexes.

We should point out that because the problem of publicizing media programs is a widespread one and because a solution to it is essential, metropolitan school districts and small communities alike must respond to the need in creative ways according to their local resources. Anyone who faces the problem of issuing effective media catalogs must deal with the always-present problem of cost—costs for the labor of compilation and the actual printing costs. To be sure, many producers of catalogs

in past years have used regular printing methods or have resorted to spirit duplication and mimeograph processes, but recent strides in printing technology open up new opportunities. Hence we can turn to a number of processes that combine new kinds of press work with photographic and electronic techniques employing tapes and computers. We shall now turn to some of the new processes.

Economy in the Catalog Process Through New Technology

Part of the difficulty in economizing is to find a speedy, labor-saving method for compiling and revising media data in addition to inexpensive printing costs. If we consider conventional methods we can still find economy through several expediencies such as using less expensive papers and bindings, having printing done during slack periods, by instructing printers to save the type for one issue until the next catalog is printed, especially where letter-press methods are employed. Naturally, the media program director ought to stretch his dollars for publication costs by suggesting possible economies himself before someone else orders him to do it or before someone reduces his printing budget.

Very possibly some of the newer techniques may actually cost as much for the printing and delivery as the older ones, but nevertheless save many hours of compilation labor, which raises other possibilities.

Figure 5-5. In the Perry Publications system specially typed input is read by a Retina Reader which produces catalog copy in tape form ready for printout by the computer-printer unit. Printout copy is then proofed, and sent to purchaser who checks the copy and returns it for final typesetting, printing, and binding. Top left view is of Olivetti typewriter used to prepare copy with special characters for the scanning process. Next picture at right is the Company's Retina Reader. Lower left is the RCA Computer-printer unit for producing printout copy, and lower right is printout copy being proofread. *Courtesy Perry Publications, West Palm Beach, Florida.*

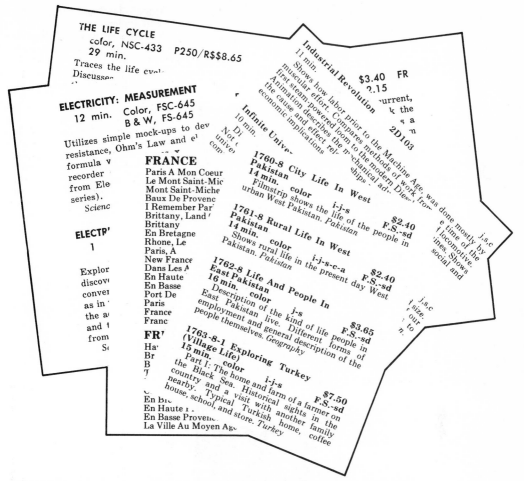

Figure 5-6. One of the advantages claimed for the commercial processes developed by such companies as Perry Publications and Magnetic Library Association (formerly Cafga Associates), is the availability of a variety of type styles and arrangements for cataloging purposes. Some of the usual type styles chosen by purchasers of the service are shown by excerpts clipped from sample catalog pages. *Courtesy Magnetic Library Association, St. Clair Shores, Michigan.*

Punch Cards, Tapes, and Computers. Computer technology is being increasingly applied to the media cataloging process. A number of commercial companies specializing in printout services such as CAFGA Associates (located in St. Clair Shores, Michigan) and Perry Publications (West Palm Beach, Florida), to mention two of them, accept typewritten catalog copy, store it on magnetic tape or on special cards for electronic scanning purposes, then print out the masters from which the offset press work is completed. Subsequent revision is easy to carry out since only new copy and deleted copy has to be supplied for computer processing. In one

case costs for such work for the first year were comparable to the costs of catalogs produced by conventional methods, but the saving in compilation costs of later editions was considerable. The Automated Cataloging Project[2] is another of the earlier examples employing punch cards, tape and computers. The staff of this project began work in 1958 on an automated media cataloging system. Under this

[2] This project was carried on under a grant from USOE Title VII, NDEA, based at Department of Cinema, Film Distribution Division, University of Southern California, University Park, Los Angeles, California, with Glenn D. McMurry, Director.

Figure 5-7. The Automated Cataloging Project process, as late as 1967, used punched cards by means of which the magnetic tape for printout was produced. IBM Tape Drives and the IBM Printer produce copy for printing processes. Top view shows the IBM 1402 Card-Read-Punch which can read the punched cards and produce the master tape. Middle picture shows two different models of IBM Tape Drives and a rack of magnetic master tapes. When these tapes are driven to feed the IBM 1403 Printer, shown in the bottom picture, print-out copy is produced. *Courtesy National Information Center for Educational Media.*

system, data relative to media items, starting first with motion pictures, were key punched onto cards, then transferred from the punched cards to tape for storage as *inputs*. From the master storage tape then come, by computer processes, the *outputs*, or printouts, in any one of several formats, such as camera-ready copy, multilith masters, or paper masters for offset-printing presswork. Many school systems and a number of university film distribution organizations availed themselves of such valuable film-cataloging services and the reader is referred to Figures 5-8, and 5-9, showing the nature of the processes developed and the catalogs produced.

Plans have also been formulated for storing data about all kinds of nonprint media from all sources, present and future, for many and varied applications. For example, the new *National Information Center for Educational Media* (NICEM) under the direction of Glenn D. McMurry, is planning research and development with respect to media cataloging and dissemination processes. Its work will be concentrated in the area of nonprint media items, and one of its eventual projects will be to expand and revise the McGraw-Hill *Educational Media Index*, first published in cooperation with the U.S. Office of Education in 1964. A comprehensive media data bank will have a number of major uses, not only for commercial publications, but for schools and school systems who may wish to apply its services to their local cataloging problems. The new edition of *Educational Media Index* may include as many as 80,000 media items. One can only speculate on the eventual size of such an information bank leading to the preparation of subsequent listings in varied formats. Originally a co-sponsor, the University of Southern California is now NICEM's sole owner with M. T. Risner as Director.

the media director who will always be faced with publicizing problems. We shall need to watch these and other new developments for solutions to this massive problem that is basic to adequate distribution processes.

Addressograph System Equipment. A highly versatile system of metal, tabbed, addressographed plates and special equipment for using them in a number of cataloging and related operations has been developed in the Oakland,

California, Public Schools. Gardner L. Hart,[3] supervisor of the Oakland Audiovisual Media Department at the time, described the situation as follows:

Due to the tremendous amount of new audiovisual materials being added each year and the many changes being made in the curriculum, the Oakland Audiovisual Department found it necessary to develop a faster and more efficient method of producing catalogs.... the Oakland schools, in cooperation with the AM Corporation, determined that the addressograph principle basically met the requirements of the audiovisual procedures.... the first step was to find out just what the equipment should do. It was essential to bear in mind the need to convert a wide variety of audiovisual operations while keeping the operations themselves very simple. Following is a partial list of the tasks which had to be done with one operator and one machine:

AV Catalogs: Make $8\frac{1}{2} \times 11$ offset masters for high-speed duplication.

AV Catalogs and Special Listings: Select materials for imprinting in predetermined categories ranging from 30 to 60 in number.

Bulletins and Classified Directories of Sources, etc.: Change the position of lines so that any one line may be printed in any position. This is possible due to the ability of the machine to pick out any given information from the plate and imprint on any desired position on the form.

Cards: Print catalog and inventory cards, by imprinting full plate on 3×5 cards. Also, print titles and other necessary information on 5×8 motion picture booking cards.

Label AV Materials for Circulation to Schools: Print titles and related information directly on art prints, pictures, phonograph record envelopes, and other audiovisual materials. Also, print titles and related information on gummed labels to be affixed to boxes containing recorded tapes and other audiovisual materials....

Although this equipment was developed especially to meet the needs of the Audiovisual Department, other departments also have found that the same machine can be of benefit to them. The library, for example, has found that library catalog cards, shelf cards, circulation cards, and book pockets can be printed much more efficiently by this equipment than by other methods. Therefore, nearly 400,000 items have been run for the library department of the Oakland schools.

[3] Gardner L. Hart, "Easy and Inexpensive AV Cataloging," *Audiovisual Instruction*, Vol. 9, No. 9, November 1964, pp. 610–612.

Figure 5-8. The film catalogs shown were produced by mechanized and electronic methods. The Center issue was for Riverside, California, upper left for University of Southern California, and the copy at lower left for San Bernardino Schools. Top center catalog was produced by the Wichita Schools, and at right two of the 18 catalogs that are produced annually by the Oakland Schools.

The production of audiovisual catalogs, which formerly took months of careful, painstaking, and time-consuming typing, proof-reading, and reproducing, has now been reduced to a fast and simple mechanical operation. And this in turn has made available to teachers catalogs of up-to-date audiovisual materials to help them toward more efficient teaching.

See Figure 5–10 for additional details.

Automatic Tape Typewriter Technology. B. W. Wolfe, Director Instructional Materials Center of the Wichita Public Schools, tried out three different systems for high-speed cataloging processes. His first efforts were with IBM cards without annotation. The next step as he reported it

. . . was to type the title of the film, plus an annotation, across the top of IBM cards so that the

material could be alphabetized and sorted by IBM sorting equipment. But this necessitated the photographing of the cards onto an offset press master. The cards with the printed information are spaced with a Verifax Tab Card Lister, then photographed with an Ektalith and run on an offset press.

To move to a still faster process, Mr. Wolfe acquired a Friden automatic typewriter with text type that cuts a tape as the catalog is typed. He reported that

to revise the catalog yearly, the tape is fed back through the machine which will type automatically on an offset press master at 200 words a minute. Additions which will be noted in the old catalog will be added to the new catalog by simply turning off the machine at the appropriate time and manually adding the new item. Items which have been deleted are omitted by simply stopping the machine just before coming to the item to be omitted and

Figure 5-9. (Opposite) For the present time at least, the automated processes of NICEM produce a somewhat stereotyped, computer print format. This limitation, though not a serious one, may be remedied in the future. The clippings from sample pages from the computerized punch card and magnetic-tape-process catalogs show the standard format for the *subject matter* and *alphabetical listing* headings.

...iect matter

11 MIN
11 MIN
11 MIN
CARE ... 11 MIN
11 MIN

ARTS, THE - LITERATURE

ENGLISH LITERATURE - THE SEV
HANSEL AND GRETEL
HARE AND THE TORTOISE
LET'S READ POETRY
THREE FOX FABLES

ARTS, THE - MUSIC

ARTUR RUBINSTEIN - HOMAGE TO CHOPI
ARTUR RUBINSTEIN - PERSONAL RECORD
BEGINNING MUSIC READING
GRAND CANYON
LET'S TRY CHORAL READING
MUSIC IN MOTION
OUR COUNTRY'S SONG
REHEARSAL
RHYTHM IS EVERYWHERE
TWO PART SINGING

SCIENCE - GRADE IV

A. CAUSES AND EFFECTS OF WEATHER, CLIMATE AND
   SEASONS   5 MIN
   (SCIENCE GUIDE, VOL. II, PP. 29-35)   11 MIN
   EARTH AND THE SUN'S RAYS   11 MIN
   HEAT AND ITS BEHAVIOR   11 MIN
   OUR BIG, ROUND WORLD - CONCEPTS FOR GEOGRAPHY   11 MIN
   WEATHER, THE
   WINDS AND THEIR CAUSES

B. HOW WE USE POWER DRIVEN MACHINES   11 MIN
   (SCIENCE GUIDE, VOL. II, PP. 36-45)   28 MIN
   AIRPLANES - HOW THEY FLY   16 MIN
   ENERGY AND WORK   31 MIN
   MACHINES THAT MOVE EARTH   11 MIN
   MAN IN FLIGHT   14 MIN
   WE USE POWER
   WHAT IS UNIFORM MOTION

C. GROWTH AND REPRODUCTION OF PLANTS   11 MIN
   (SCIENCE GUIDE, VOL. II, PP. 46-51)   11 MIN
   PLANTING OUR GARDEN
   PLANTS MAKE FOOD
                   MIN
             20 MIN

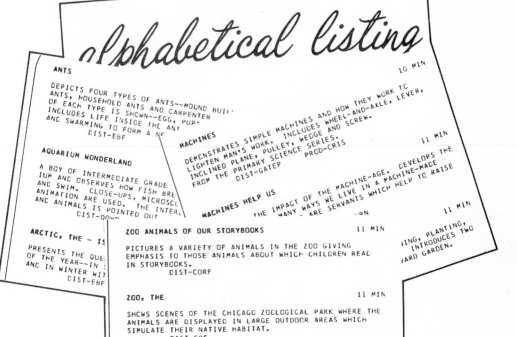

alphabetical listing

ANTS   10 MIN

DEPICTS FOUR TYPES OF ANTS--MOUND BUIL
ANTS, HOUSEHOLD ANTS AND CARPENTER
OF EACH TYPE IS SHOWN--EGG, PUP
INCLUDES LIFE INSIDE THE ANT
AND SWARMING TO FORM A NE
        DIST-EBF

AQUARIUM WONDERLAND

A BOY OF INTERMEDIATE GRADE
IUM AND OBSERVES HOW FISH BRE
AND SWIM. CLOSE-UPS, MICROSC
ANIMATION ARE USED. THE INTER
AND ANIMALS IS POINTED OUT
        DIST-DOWN

ARCTIC, THE - IS

PRESENTS THE QUE
OF THE YEAR--IN
AND IN WINTER WIT
        DIST-EBF

MACHINES

DEMONSTRATES SIMPLE MACHINES AND HOW THEY WORK TO
LIGHTEN MAN'S WORK. INCLUDES WHEEL-AND-AXLE, LEVER,
INCLINED PLANE, PULLEY, WEDGE AND SCREW.
FROM THE PRIMARY SCIENCE SERIES.
        DIST-GATEP   PROD-CRIS

MACHINES HELP US   11 MIN

THE IMPACT OF THE MACHINE-AGE. DEVELOPS THE
MANY WAYS WE LIVE IN A MACHINE-MADE
- ARE SERVANTS WHICH HELP TO RAISE
                             ...ON   11 MIN

ZOO ANIMALS OF OUR STORYBOOKS   11 MIN

PICTURES A VARIETY OF ANIMALS IN THE ZOO GIVING
EMPHASIS TO THOSE ANIMALS ABOUT WHICH CHILDREN READ
IN STORYBOOKS.
        DIST-CORF

ING, PLANTING,
INTRODUCES TWO
(ARD GARDEN.

ZOO, THE   11 MIN

SHOWS SCENES OF THE CHICAGO ZOOLOGICAL PARK WHERE THE
ANIMALS ARE DISPLAYED IN LARGE OUTDOOR AREAS WHICH
SIMULATE THEIR NATIVE HABITAT.
        DIST-EBF

Figure 5-10. In the top view special addressograph plates are being prepared. They will then be appropriately tabbed and filed as shown in the middle picture. In the bottom view, the operator is guiding the printing machine in the preparation of off-set masters which are used in the printing process without further treatment. *Courtesy Division of Instructional Media, Public Schools, Oakland, California.*

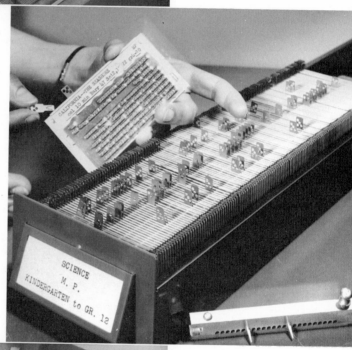

SCIENCE
M. P.
KINDERGARTEN to GR. 12

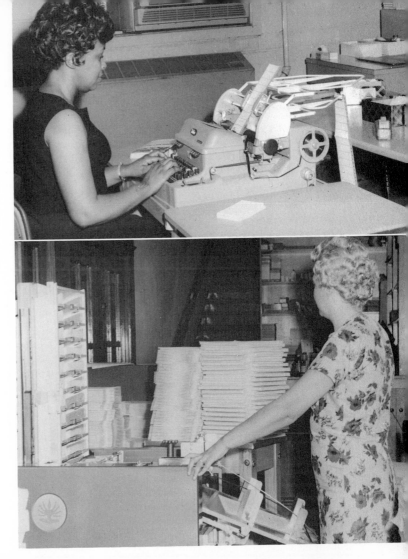

Figure 5-11. The main process in the Wichita system is to store catalog information on a tape which will activate an automatic typewriter that will print small type, thus eventually producing a catalog with fewer pages to assemble, and easier for teachers to use. The Friden Tape Typewriter is shown in the top view. In the bottom picture the operator is using an assembling machine to make up the catalog, the pages of which had been printed directly from the off-set masters made on the Friden Typewriter. Printing is done at the Center. *Courtesy Public Schools, Wichita, Kansas.*

turning forward the tape and restarting the machine. All the time the corrections are being made, a new tape is being cut by the machine.[4]

See Figure 5–11.

Descriptions of Content

Preparing descriptions of material for audiovisual media publications and catalogs, regardless of the cataloging and printing systems employed, is critical and time consuming. Ways must be found to do this job well, however, because of its importance to teachers. Although full-page analyses of content would be valuable, there isn't an audiovisual media budget anywhere that could stand the printing expense to

[4] B. W. Wolfe, "Cataloging Problems," *Audiovisual Instruction*, Vol. 8, No. 3, March 1963, pp. 150–151.

carry out such a plan and the catalogs would be so large and difficult to use that teachers probably wouldn't even open them up. The following suggestions are given for preparing descriptions of a media catalog's contents.

1. Make the synopsis brief, but give teachers clues as to content coverage and usefulness. For example, be sure to mention if the actors are children, adults, or high school students; this is a valuable clue to possible identification of learners with the film action.

2. Include vital data about physical characteristics: running time, number of frames, number of slides or pictures in the set, color or black and white, etc.

3. Include specific grade-level placement.

4. Include producer and production date.

5. Make use of sourcebooks, evaluations, and producers' descriptions.

6. Get other people to help.

7. If the job of writing or obtaining descriptions is impossible, make sure that the selection committee includes an error-free judgment as to subject, unit, and grade-level placement. After all, the description doesn't make the film better, but it does help a teacher predict that a film or other item will help achieve an objective.

Making the Catalog Process Easy

The director will, of necessity, soon realize that the job of cataloging can be divided so that he himself needs to be burdened only with those tasks that require his training and experience. Many aspects, although they are important, are clerical in nature and should be so organized. The basic essentials of a good catalog process are described in the following list.

1. Organize and maintain an alphabetical card file of every item purchased. Enter on each card the proper classification headings or the code that determines the title's appropriate subject relationships for future lists and catalogs.

2. When new titles are announced in a monthly bulletin or list, prepare descriptions and data to accompany them in a standard format, making them immediately available, without further writing or analysis, for subsequent inclusion in a main catalog.

3. Maintain office revision copies of all lists daily. Each new entry in the card file should be made appropriately in the revision copy of the catalog.

4. Devise plans for evaluation and selection that are consistent with the data needed for cataloging processes.

5. Incorporate in cataloging plans optimum use of local automated preparation processes, and/or make arrangements to contract for the supply of needed catalogs with regional or national agencies that maintain banks of stored data about media items.

We turn next to the second major problem presented in this chapter which follows naturally if media are effectively publicized and, of course, if teachers desire to make optimum use of them in their work. Under these conditions teachers will want to order media, and have their orders processed, filled, and delivered at the time they are needed. The system we discuss next is also universal in character and constitutes a problem whose solution is also one of the prime administrative and technological essentials of the media program director's job.

The Ordering, Scheduling, Distributing System

As has been stated before, the media service program should be organized so that a variety of media are available when they are needed for maximum contribution to teaching objectives. Along with this tenet of organization are two other important principles: (1) Convenience in availability of media and equipment increases teacher demands for materials and facilitates effective use, and (2) the media program should be centralized for unity of purpose, planning, promotion of use, and economy. The application of these principles to a school-system media service program demands that an efficient system of ordering, scheduling, and distributing materials be set up to facilitate their use in the classroom. Full attention is therefore given in this section to the essentials of such a system which include (1) ordering forms and procedures; (2) scheduling methods, forms, and control processes; and (3) delivery and pickup of materials. Despite variations in procedure for solving ordering and distribution problems, the demands for certain kinds of action by teachers in their classrooms and by clerical and technical personnel in their offices are the same or similar. We shall therefore describe each of the preceding essential elements by presenting an actual operational system as it has been developed by the Audio-Visual Department of the Seattle, Washington, public schools.

Order Forms and Ordering Procedures

The Seattle order form is a simple, $8\frac{1}{2} \times 11$ inch, triple-copy, snap-out form printed on order by a local business concern, which calls for the teacher to fill out the top form only with his name, school, date, and grade, then to add the catalog numbers and titles of media materials desired, date wanted, and to add a deadline date in a "Not Wanted After" column. The form also specifies that film titles are to be entered at the top of the page and that all other items in the remaining section be clearly marked. The teacher then removes the bottom sheets from the snap-out form and sends the remaining copies to the school coordinator who screens the order and sends it on to the central audio-visual department for processing. See Figure 5-12. The teacher is reminded on the form that no order is to be requested for a date beyond six weeks of the date the order is sent in, and of course the teacher is aware of the delivery and pickup days at his school, allowing use of the material for the school week if necessary. However, orders may be phoned in if they are of an emergency nature. When received at the Seattle media center office, the orders are time-stamped and usually processed the same day.

The methods by which orders from teachers are processed are described in the next section, but first some other possibilities ought to be pointed out. As we have said, order forms and methods have to be designed or selected in terms of unique local conditions and established operational plans. Whenever machine scheduling processes have been established, the ordering process has to be drastically changed. In fact, orders that are processed by automated methods must be sent in by teachers on special machine cards. In some cases orders for a given kind of medium may be processed by machine, and orders for such items as models, slide sets, and filmstrips may be ordered by conventional means. In these instances, two kinds of order forms are needed.

Those who select ready-made forms or who design media order forms for teachers ought to be mindful of the objective of facilitation and incorporate the following standards: (a) demand a minimum of writing, (b) cut red tape to a minimum, (c) be large enough to make possible ordering a number of items of different media at the same time, (d) provide a carbon copy record for the teacher, and (e) be economical of teacher's time and energy.

Figure 5-12. This is Seattle's snap-out-type order form for teachers. After making out the order, the teacher tears off and retains the third copy. *Courtesy Standard Register Company of Seattle and the Seattle Public Schools.*

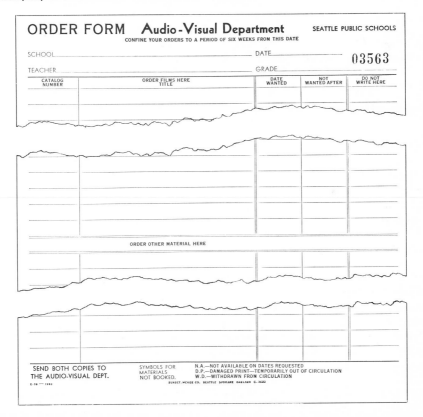

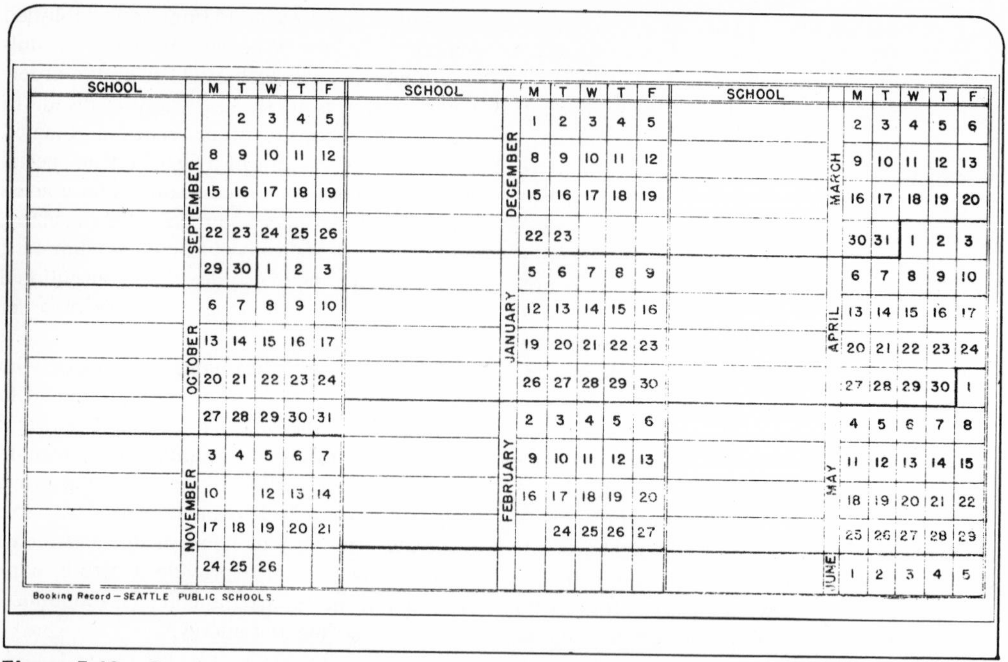

SCHOOL		M	T	W	T	F	SCHOOL		M	T	W	T	F	SCHOOL		M	T	W	T	F
			2	3	4	5			I	2	3	4	5				2	3	4	5	6
SEPTEMBER		8	9	10	11	12	DECEMBER		8	9	10	11	12	MARCH		9	10	11	12	13
		15	16	17	18	19			15	16	17	18	19			16	17	18	19	20
		22	23	24	25	26			22	23						30	31	I	2	3
		29	30	I	2	3			5	6	7	8	9			6	7	8	9	10
		6	7	8	9	10	JANUARY		12	13	14	15	16	APRIL		13	14	15	16	17
OCTOBER		13	14	15	16	17			19	20	21	22	23			20	21	22	23	24
		20	21	22	23	24			26	27	28	29	30			27	28	29	30	I
		27	28	29	30	31			2	3	4	5	6			4	5	6	7	8
		3	4	5	6	7	FEBRUARY		9	10	11	12	13	MAY		11	12	13	14	15
NOVEMBER		10		12	13	14			16	17	18	19	20			18	19	20	21	22
		17	18	19	20	21				24	25	26	27			25	26	27	28	29
		24	25	26										JUNE		I	2	3	4	5

Booking Record — SEATTLE PUBLIC SCHOOLS

Figure 5-13. Seattle's scheduling card provides a record of the reservations for two years, the other side being the same except arranged according to dates for the next school year. *Courtesy Seattle Public Schools.*

Scheduling Methods, Forms, and Control Processes

Now let us resume the story of the triple-copy, snap-out order form used by the Seattle Audio-Visual Department. Starting with the receipt of an order form in duplicate (the third copy having been kept by the teacher for reference), the steps in processing by clerical workers are as follows:

1. The receipt time is stamped on the order for priority in case of duplicate requests.

2. The title for each item ordered is located on an alphabetically arranged, magnetically separated, schedule-control card; the reservation period is marked in the appropriate spaces, if free spaces are available for the dates specified; and the names of the teacher and the school are added. The Seattle schedule-control card, measuring 5 × 8 inches, is of the magnetic-separator type. See Figure 5-13. That is, two thin strips of magnetic material are inserted in the paper in such a way that the cards repel each other at the top. The titles, which are typed at the top of each card, can thus be seen several at a time. This separation speeds up the process of selecting the specific card desired.

The card itself is a two-year schedule card with weekly reservation spaces for all the months of the school year—September to June—on each side. All cards are located in a convenient, deep-well desk. (Such desks may be purchased or fabricated locally.) See Figures 5-15.

3. After the requested item has been reserved, the scheduled delivery date is entered in the appropriate column on the order form. If the requested materials are unavailable, that information is indicated on the order form, or open dates that are close to the date requested are added. The top sheet of the order form then goes to a typist, and the remaining copy of the processed order is filed after being analyzed for purposes of accumulating data.

4. The packaging label, confirmation slip, and order-filling slip are made up from processed order sheets by a typist who uses Seattle's triple-copy, Kant-Slip, continuous, marginally punched forms. See Figure 5-14. For each item scheduled, one of the Kant-Slip forms is typed up on a typewriter with a registrator platen. The top part of the form, carrying delivery date, due-back date, title of material, name of teacher, and school, is the gummed label that is filed with the office copy in the call file under the packaging-for-delivery date; the third copy

Figure 5-14. Seattle's Kant-Slip, triple-copy, marginally punched, combination confirmation and packaging form. *Courtesy Seattle Public Schools.*

Figure 5-15. (Below) Reserving, scheduling, confirming, and order-filling procedures must be planned to save staff time and facilitate service. *Courtesy Pacific Division of the Standard Register Co., and the Seattle Public Schools.*

is sent back to the teacher as a confirmation of the materials he or she is to receive. Each unit of the continuous Kant-Slip form measures $3\frac{1}{2} \times 5$ inches.

5. According to work routines each day, the delivery forms for every item scheduled are pulled from the call files, and the materials are then packaged and made ready for delivery. The office copy of each slip is filed under due-back dates in files for that purpose. Thus when the materials are returned from the borrowers, the slip is checked off. If materials are not returned on the scheduled due date, the corresponding slips that have been pulled from the file are not checked off, and hence the failure is shown up immediately.

Having checked through the Seattle system, we can readily identify the essential elements as follows:

1. Making the reservation.
2. Confirming the order and showing the intent to deliver and pick up on scheduled dates.
3. Filing the packaging slips according to the future call dates.
4. Maintaining a positive check-off control system for the control of each item out on loan.

As with the case of media order forms for teachers, there are variations in the methods by which the important work of reserving, scheduling, confirming, and order-filling are carried out in the many school communities across the country. The differences are, of course, greatest when machine data-processing systems are utilized, and an increasing number of school-system media centers, especially in metropolitan

AUDIO-VISUAL SECTION
LOS ANGELES CITY SCHOOLS

SEND TO
AUDIO-VISUAL

SECONDARY SCHOOLS ORDER BLANK FOR AUDIO-VISUAL MATERIALS OTHER THAN MOTION PICTURES

TELEPHONE ORDERS CANNOT BE ACCEPTED

SEND COPIES 1 AND 2 TO AUDIO-VISUAL SECTION
KEEP COPY 3 FOR REFERENCE

Each teacher may place one order per two week period. Materials are delivered by school truck, and are loaned for two weeks.

SCHOOL_____ NAME _____
(first name)   (last name)

DATE WANTED_____ DELIVERY DAY _____ AUDIO-VISUAL NUMBER_____
(leave blank)   (leave blank)

20 items are the maximum number per two week period allotted to each teacher. Select the title and catalog number from your CATALOG of AUDIO-VISUAL MATERIALS and AUDIO-VISUAL NEWS.

Catalog Number and Title	Catalog Number and Title
FILMSTRIPS	
Example: H-144 Set 1, The Louisiana Purchase	
PORTFOLIOS AND PICTURE SETS	
SLIDES	
WALL CHARTS	
EXHIBITS AND KITS	
RECORDS AND SOUND FILMSTRIPS (Limit: Four)	

DO NOT INSERT CARBON. This paper is chemically treated. No carbon is required.

districts, are converting their distribution systems from manual to machine operations. Before we turn to a discussion of the salient features of automated systems, we ought to point out that for whatever system, machine or manual, that seems best for a community, the prospective media director should know that salesmen and other specialists are available who will help devise the system and the special-

ized forms that are required. Before making a final decision, the director needs to size up his present and proposed system of processing in terms of volume to be handled, available staff, variety of media that teachers can order, materials that do not have to be scheduled for one reason or another, delivery and pickup arrangements, the service procedures in each school plant, the limitations of the system,

```
To be Shipped                              Due Back in AV Office
─────────────────────────────────────────────────────────────────────
                         Do not write above this line
   ▲              REQUEST FOR MATERIALS                    ▲
DEPARTMENT                    OWNED BY                  DEPARTMENT
   ▼            COLORADO SPRINGS PUBLIC SCHOOLS             ▼
   School Number _____ Teacher _____ Grade_____ Date____
```

TYPE*	TITLE	Allow at least three (3) full school days to process this request.				DO NOT FILL IN
		DATE WANTED	NOT LATER THAN	PERIOD	ROOM	DATE BOOKED
	First Choice (ONLY ONE TITLE)					
	Second Choice (ONLY ONE TITLE)					

Give entire completed form, 4 parts, to audiovisual coordinator. A confirmation copy will be returned to you.

```
*F=Film        FSS=Filmstrip,Sound   M=Model
 FS=Filmstrip   T=Tape               P=Portfolio
 S=Slide Set    R=Record             K=Teaching Kit
                                    Coordinator _____   Date _____
```

(right margin, vertical) AUDIOVISUAL DEPT. COPY

Figure 5-16. There are many different kinds of media-ordering forms in use around the country. Media program directors often use an order form to enforce distribution policies. The left form is the regular order blank for Los Angeles secondary schools. The form above was developed at Colorado Springs. *Courtesy of the school districts mentioned.*

and the ease with which the system can be operated.

Automated Distribution Operations. Several metropolitan-area media service centers had already installed film-scheduling processes by machine prior to 1957. The Los Angeles city school system began scheduling motion pictures as early as 1948. Several smaller cities in the one- to two-hundred-thousand population class had converted to machine film-scheduling methods by means of rented local service corporation machine-processing services. In these cases the special order cards are called in at specified times and then turned over to the service bureau for processing and printout sheets from which orders are filled and shipped to the schools. As

has been said, automated processing systems are now common, and equipment is either rented and used full time by the media service center or the service is rented from local commercial agencies. However, many city-governments now incorporate data-processing centers and the schools may arrange to use the equipment and operating personnel for their own purposes on a schedule. Figures 5-17 through 5-19 present examples and supply important details of the various operations developed.

Delivery and Pickup of Materials

The delivery and pickup method is an important link in the chain of services to teachers.

Figure 5-17. There are many different ways of carrying out the ordering, reserving, scheduling, and order-filling processes, and automatic methods must serve these functions. Sometimes limitations are placed on teachers by particular systems developed. Shown in this picture is one of the older models of IBM equipment used for scheduling processes. Note that in this case printout sheets were needed, hence a printer unit had to be used with whatever punched-card sorting machines were required. *Courtesy Bureau of Audio-Visual Education, California State Department of Education.*

Delays in scheduled deliveries cause serious teaching problems and destroy rapport between teachers and the service centers of the schools. Large media service centers find it convenient and desirable to own walk-in trucks, with full-time deliverymen on their permanent staffs. However, small service centers rarely can afford this plan of operation. In the case of Seattle, scheduled deliveries were made once each week to the elementary schools and twice weekly to the high schools. Because of the many ways in which the delivery and pickup problem has been met, and the many unique local conditions that can exist, a list of possible methods follows for the prospective director to consider.

1. Use trucks owned by or assigned to and controlled by the media center.
2. Make use of regular school-system supplies truck.
3. Make use of plant supervisor's trucking system.
4. Employ a local package delivery company on an individual package or daily service contract basis.
5. Send materials to schools via the local Post Office. A post office package pickup station outside the school will facilitate this. The school media coordinator can note the amount of necessary postage and include the same amount of stamps for the return, thus eliminating a trip to the post office. Local post office parcel delivery is regular, but as everyone knows, parcel pickup is not. Only as return packages are ready when incoming packages are delivered can they be picked up at closely predictable times.
6. Use personally owned automobiles of director, or school-building coordinators on a mileage-paid basis. This is found to be expensive if the director is the deliveryman, although it is a deplorably common method of delivery. Sometimes school-building media coordinators return the materials that are delivered by other means.
7. Use older high school students and one or

more center-owned motor scooters. Full insurance will have to be maintained, the working hours will have to be after school and on Saturdays, and all legal requirements must be met adequately.

8. Employ students to serve as messengers where schools are within fairly close walking distance. Employment must be legal on a part-time basis. Directors should be aware of the danger of using students who are not in a fully insured, employed status. In cases of accidental injury, suits for damages may be brought against the schools.

9. Use parents who consent to donate their services and their cars on a rotation basis to deliver and return media to certain schools. This could be a PTA project. (Insurance coverage under most conditions would be needed here also.)

10. Teachers, principals, and custodians can call for and return materials.

So far in this chapter it has been emphasized that teachers need to be adequately informed about available media, and that it is best to develop a system involving both general and specific methods for accomplishing this goal. It has also been shown that publicizing the media is not enough to assure its optimum use but also a system needs to be set up by means of which they may be ordered, scheduled, and distributed. There is much more, however, to facilitating the use of media than this. The prospective director, in addition, must be able to make recommendations to authorities, offer counsel, and seek to provide an adequate environment for the proper and efficient use of the various media. He must also see to it that a service system is established in each of the school units, since these are parts of his over-all service organization. These major aspects of a media director's job are dealt with in the two chapters that follow.

Problem-Solving Activities

1. What are the basic reasons why materials ought to be classified, listed, correlated with instructional units, and properly publicized?

2. Examine several catalogs or sourcebooks, and note the categories or main headings for classification purposes. What are some weaknesses and strengths in these categories as far as busy teachers are concerned? What are some basic attributes of a classification system you would devise for teachers if you were making a catalog?

3. How do you find out if any catalog system you desire to use is going to work?

4. Do you believe individual card systems for information purposes are better than up-to-date mimeo or printed lists? Why or why not?

5. How can the preparation of specific lists of audiovisual materials be tied in with the in-service growth program in audiovisual materials? Make a plan for involving teachers in a publicizing system such as that described in this chapter.

6. Examine several picture stories or verbal accounts of operating procedures in citywide audiovisual service systems, and note the forms used by teachers for ordering materials, for reserving rooms and equipment, and the forms used by the director for saving time and effort. Make a list of the forms you feel are essential for your own school system.

7. Would the Seattle ordering and scheduling system work in your school system? If not, why not?

8. What system for distribution of AV materials and equipment would you recommend for your own school system? How often would you deliver? How long would you allow teachers to keep materials borrowed from the service center?

9. Study selected articles in the literature and examine representative audiovisual media catalogs that have been printed by automated data-processing methods; then summarize, using a step-by-step description, your own plan for producing such a catalog for any school system you identify.

References

Brown, James W. and Kenneth D. Norberg. *Administering Educational Media* (New York: McGraw-Hill, 1965).

Carlin, Kathryn L. "Distribution Is What Counts," *Audiovisual Instruction*, Vol. 5, No. 10, December 1960, pp. 334-335.

Christen, Fred L. "New Tools for Film Libraries—An Overview." *Audiovisual Instruction*, Vol. 12, No. 4, April 1967, pp. 312-313.

Hart, Gardner L. "Easy and Inexpensive AV Cataloging," *Audiovisual Instruction*, Vol. 9, No. 9, November 1964, pp. 610-612.

Holdridge, R. E. "Cataloging Nonbook Materials." *Audiovisual Instruction*, Vol. 12, No. 4, April 1967, pp. 358, 360.

McMurry, Glenn D. "Film Library Uses for the Computer." *Audiovisual Instruction*, Vol. 12, No. 4, April 1967, pp. 314-320.

Miller, R. W. "How to Plan and Control with PERT." *Harvard Business Review* **40**: 93-104; March-April 1962.

Nichols, H. L. *Guidelines to Audio-Visual Cataloging by Means of Data Processing* (Sacramento, Calif.: Bureau of Audiovisual and School Library Education, California State Department of Education, 1966).

Roberts, Tom. "An Efficient Film Filing System," *Educational Screen and Audiovisual Guide*, Vol. 8, No. 3, March 1963, pp. 302-303.

Sanborn, William B. "San Francisco's Audio-Visual Materials Card Catalog." *Educational Screen and Audio-Visual Guide*, Vol. 37, No. 8, August 1958, pp. 384-385.

Shores, Louis. *Instructional Materials: An Introduction for Teachers* (New York: Ronald Press, 1960).

Vento, Charles J. "PERTing the Automated Catalog." *Audiovisual Instruction*, Vol. 11, No. 3, March 1966, pp. 182-185.

Vivrette, Lyndon. "We Put Our AV Catalog on IBM." *Audiovisual Instruction*, Vol. 7, No. 5, May 1962, pp. 302-303.

Wolfe, B. W. "Cataloging Problems? IBM Can Help You." *Audiovisual Instruction*, Vol. 8, No. 3, March 1963, pp. 150-151.

The day of school-media scarcity in the midst of plenty is all but over. Man is fortunately changing once more, as he has many times in past ages, his image of what constitutes a good education. School architects and planners are now generally receptive to the influence of media on the creative designs for schools that they develop. Universally there is a vastly improved climate for educational change, and in this climate modern media are being looked upon as indispensable tools of the profession, tied irrevocably in the public eye to a new concept of how people learn, what they learn, and what the working conditions for teachers and their methodologies ought to be. It is a fact that the physical environment for education has already undergone and is undergoing desirable change, and media are having a new and potent influence on these changes.

Although it would be interesting and highly informative, it is hardly necessary in this book to trace the genesis of the changes in educational method. However, we ought to provide an adequate orientation and point out that many and complex forces have been influencing the direction that new methodologies should take. On the one hand, we have thought about the indispensable process of information giving, and on the other, the essential need to elicit reactions to and provide opportunities for the use of the information and insights gained. We have sought diligently to understand and even elude some of the burdensome repetitive jobs that teachers have been and still are forced to contend with; we have deplored the small amount of time that teachers can devote during the working day to planning and design activity; we have gained insight into the nature of activity that can go on in large groups when new media and programed arrangements are employed; we know that the individualization of learning activity on which we have long placed a high premium is not likely to be achieved unless innovations can be introduced and implemented; and we have long since noted with due alarm the burgeoning pupil enrollments and the looming shortages of teachers.

Educators have taken a keener and more critical look at the nature of educational objectives and have come to realize that valid objectives can be accomplished by new and appropriate operational arrangements that have a bearing on the way a teacher spends his time,

6

The Physical Environment for Media Utilization

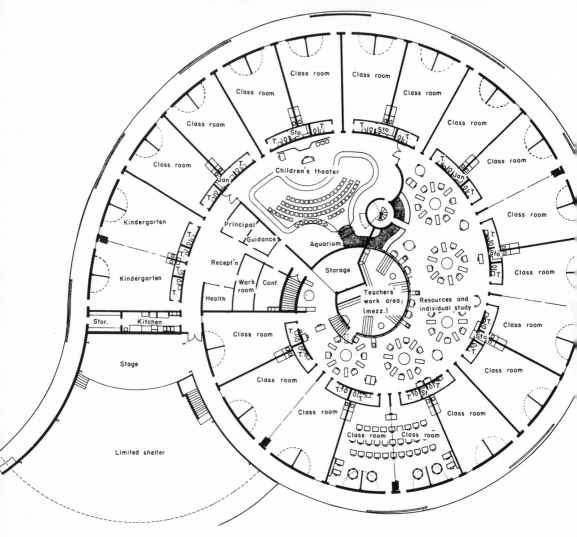

on the tools he uses and has to have at his disposal, and in general on the vital relationships between teacher, learner, materials of instruction, and the ways learners are grouped. J. Lloyd Trump,[1] widely read educational innovator, asked the following significant questions that we ought to note as a basis for planning a modern instructional program: "First, what can students learn largely by themselves? Second, what can students learn from the explanations by others? Third, what learning goals require personal interaction among students and teachers?"

In view of such insightful thinking by educational theorists and planners, technological experts, and teachers, and because we need to provide a basic orientation for the important topics in this chapter, it will be helpful to restate the foregoing questions with media environments in sharper focus, as follows:

1. What kinds of learning spaces should we have and how should we equip them with media facilities if we desire to arrange conditions so

---

[1] J. Lloyd Trump, "Places for Learning," *Audio-Visual Instruction*, Vol. 7, No. 8, October 1962, pp. 516–517.

that pupils can learn effectively by themselves a given portion of essential content?

2. What kinds of learning spaces and media-use facilities must be provided when pupils are organized to learn not only from their own teacher, but from others with teaching roles to play?

3. What kinds of learning spaces and media-use facilities do we need for those educational objectives that we predict demand direct and personal guidance of pupil activity, as well as pupil-to-pupil communication?

4. What kinds of special services do teachers and pupils urgently need when media are to be used effectively in direct and indirect instructional roles?

These questions imply the need for an unmistakable flexibility in a variety of learning spaces, each of which may require in a new and vital way, adequate provisions for media utilization. We perceive also that these questions imply a new and pressing demand for assistance to teachers as they plan and make arrangements for the use of media materials and equipment, and to this latter need for an expanded media service program in each school building we shall devote Chapter 7.

Figure 6-1. New concepts of education in general and of the instructional process in particular are to be observed in these unique, impressive, media-use school designs. The picture of the model of the Lowell, Indiana, High School is shown at the top. This school was under construction in 1967. The floor plan of the much publicized snail-shell Valley Winds school of the Riverview Gardens District, St. Louis, is shown in the middle diagram, and the bottom picture is the two-school complex, the Wilbur Wright JHS and the Senior HS with some of the facilities being shared by both. (*Top two illustrations,* courtesy Shaver & Company, Architects, Salina, Kansas. *Bottom view* courtesy Public Schools, Munster, Indiana.)

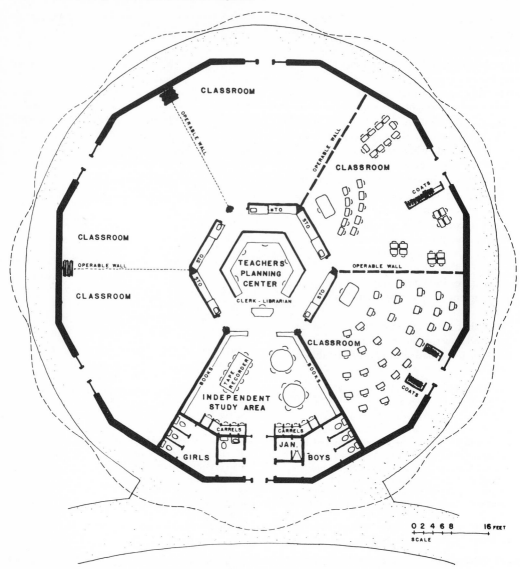

Figure 6-2. What observations may be made in studying this typical cluster plan for classroom arrangement with reference to media use? Independent study? Large-group capability? Individualized work? Small-group areas? Regular size groups? Teacher Planning? *Courtesy Educational Facilities Laboratories.*

It is in this light then that we look with new insight toward solutions to another cluster of problems in relation to increasing the effective use of media in every learning area in every school building both old and new. First we must face up to the urgent need on the part of teachers for a variety of media, projected as well as nonprojected, with which to carry on the essential learning activities. Then we must recognize the fact that one of the greatest deterrents to increased and effective utilization of these essential media is the frequent absence of proper physical conditions in the teaching-learning environment. Naturally the problem of providing the required facilities does not apply to new schools only, but to the massive remodeling needs in old buildings as well.

The fact is that we may have stated the case of new school building construction somewhat overoptimistically, for in the literature and in visits to schools that planners say are designed with media in new and expanded roles, we shockingly observe all too often that the learning spaces do not have, at least at the time they are ready for occupancy, the minimum essentials that we shall recommend in the following sections. Hence, there is a sense of urgency on the part of all media personnel to put their valid and reasonable recommendations before key administrators, building committees, and architects. To do this work well, they must possess the knowledge not only of technology, but also of teaching patterns and curriculum designs. Every shortsighted decision, every omission of media facilities in every classroom will be cause for regret in the years ahead.

The Media Director's Responsibility. In view of the existing need for new school-building construction, and for old-school remodeling also, across the land, the prospective media

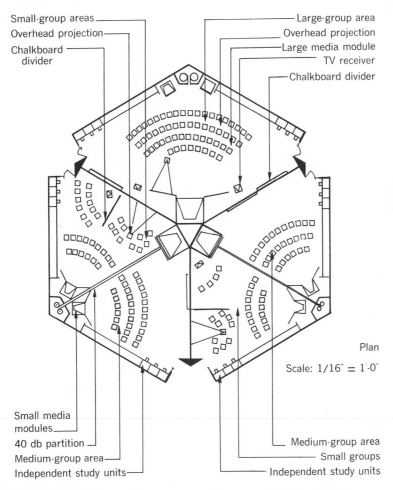

Small-group areas
Overhead projection
Chalkboard divider

Large-group area
Overhead projection
Large media module
TV receiver
Chalkboard divider

Plan

Scale: 1/16″ = 1′-0″

Small media modules
40 db partition
Medium-group area
Independent study units

Medium-group area
Small groups
Independent study units

Figure 6-3. We are fortunate to have the permission to present a number of unique and revealing sketches by Dr. Alan C. Green, of the Center for Architectural Research, Rensselaer Polytechnic Institute, Troy, N. Y., printed earlier in *Educational Facilities for New Media.* The Department of Audiovisual Instruction of the NEA published this invaluable book, the content of which was developed under a grant to the Center for Architectural Research from the U. S. Office of Education. This floor plan makes it clear that flexibility is one of the key aspects of school design, and another is media use. What other features can you identify that indicate a changed concept of learning and learning conditions? Might the actual equipment arrangement in a media module change with changes in technology? In this drawing is the television receiver a part of the media module? *Courtesy Center for Architectural Research, Rensselaer Polytechnic Institute, Troy, New York.*

program director must prepare himself to take proper action in specifying precisely what teachers need and want in their classrooms and other learning areas to facilitate the use of the required media. Although it would be fine if the media director's knowledge of school construction made him an authority on the subject, he need not be the architect. He needs to be capable, however, of advising the superintendent and architect accurately on what the media-use requirements are, and then he ought to be able to scrutinize preliminary plans to see that recommendations have been incorporated correctly in the construction design. A great deal of abuse has been heaped upon certain architects for their designs of school buildings that showed meager concern for the modern-day use of essential audiovisual media equipment and materials. Such storms of criticism should have been more properly directed to school people and laymen who couldn't make up their minds what they wanted and needed. It doesn't seem likely that an architect will defy a board of education's requests and specifications and force it to accept what it doesn't want and won't pay for. There is marked agreement today as to the physical facilities that will make possible the efficient use of instructional technology, and it is up to the prospective director to become familiar with them and to make wise recommendations in terms of local conditions.

Media Utilization in Every Learning Area

Increasing emphasis needs to be given to the principle that media-use facilities are needed in each of the learning spaces where the instructional tasks are being normally and naturally performed. This means that media are needed in libraries, conventional, large-group learning areas, special and general laboratory spaces, and in gymnasiums and auditoriums as well. It is inefficient and distracting to move a class of learners off to a projection room, for example, in order to view a filmstrip or a motion picture, or to evict a teacher from his customary and darkenable classroom to let another teacher use it. Learners need to respond to media in combination and in depth with a minimum of distraction, and it is understandable that when teachers carry, push, and drag equipment units

into position and return them on inconvenient schedules, their own professional work suffers, and consequently media are inefficiently and ineffectively used, or used not at all.

All over the country the problem of improving existing classroom conditions is a serious one. The staggering task everywhere is to backtrack as it were and spend hard-to-get funds to install the needed light-control systems and additional media equipment units in old school buildings that were never properly equipped to begin with. The so-called projection rooms of earlier decades no longer can begin to handle the volume of valid media use in modern instructional programs.

A sustained, herculean effort should be put forth whenever necessary by the director of the media services program in arranging for adequate physical facilities and the required equipment in the construction and equipment plans for every new school building. Unless this is done, the job of dropping back to equip classrooms in older, long-neglected buildings may never be accomplished. The case of West Hartford, Connecticut, is a good example of adequate action in incorporating audiovisual media-use facilities in ten new school buildings, both elementary and secondary. After careful study by school authorities, the media program director, architects, and building committees, it was decided that it would be much cheaper (not to mention the increased efficiency of instruction) to eliminate the proposed special projection rooms, and instead plan to equip every classroom with adequate light-control systems, and to purchase for the school at the time of construction the media equipment units needed to serve the needs of teachers. Although construction costs vary around the country, the cost of an additional classroom to serve as a projection room would run between $25,000 to $40,000. The arithmetic is simple, and if there is any doubt about what action to recommend locally, every prospective or practicing media program director should first perform the following computations: (1) Find out the total cost of providing in each classroom or cluster of classrooms, the media-use facilities and needed equipment units; and, (2) compare this figure with the total cost of adding the additional classrooms to serve as projection rooms. The inclusion of such basic facilities in all new school buildings will make it possible to meet more rapidly the need for modification of old buildings that continue to cripple the present-day curriculum.

We ought to point out, however, that just about the time we decided to do away with projection rooms forever, we discovered a new and extremely significant role for media to play in the teaching process, namely, media in control of presentation-response activities. In implementing this role, we are often forced, as one alternative, to provide new machine-room and electronic learning laboratory spaces as specialized teaching stations. Such installations, as we shall point out in Chapters 11 and 13, are sometimes almost as costly to equip as the rooms to hold the installations are to build.

For the moment let us focus our attention on the problem of installing adequate light-control systems in old schools. In the following paragraphs we report a number of specific situations around the country that indicate highly successful action.

1. San Diego, California

In San Diego a long-range program of installing light-control systems in classrooms has been in operation for many years. According to a recent report from the media program director, Dr. Robert Burgert, we have the following facts: (a) There are 2,208 elementary school classrooms and 1945 secondary school classrooms. Of these learning spaces, 1,550 of the elementary school classrooms had been adequately equipped with window-darkening systems, and 1,046 of the secondary school classrooms, or 70 per cent and 54 per cent respectively, by 1967. (b) The goal, according to Dr. Burgert's report, is to provide every teaching station in the elementary schools with adequate light control for media-use purposes, and approximately 60 per cent to 70 per cent of the teaching stations in all secondary schools.

2. Penfield, New York

In the five elementary and two junior high schools of Penfield, New York, program director James M. Meagher reports light-control systems have been installed in all classrooms. All new schools are so equipped upon completion.

3. Fayetteville, North Carolina

According to a report from media director A. Irving Maynard, all classrooms, totaling 215 in the 12 elementary schools, are equipped with light-control systems and this is also true of all new school buildings recently completed, both elementary and secondary.

4. St. Louis Park, Minnesota

In a recent report from media director Donald Schutte, it was disclosed that all of the 500 classrooms in the school system have been equipped with light-control devices for the projection of audiovisual media.

5. Davenport, Iowa

John Haack, media director for the public schools, reported recently that 70 per cent of the 436 elementary school classrooms had been equipped with light-control systems, that 100 of the 329 secondary school classrooms had also been so equipped, and that classrooms in all new school buildings had been properly equipped with darkening systems.

6. Colorado Springs, Colorado

Jack Prince, media director for the public schools, reported that 80 per cent of the elementary school and 75 per cent of all secondary school classrooms had been equipped with light-control systems. He also reports that all classrooms in recently completed school plants have been so equipped as will the school building units under construction.

7. Euclid, Ohio

Roy O. Hinch, media director in the public schools of Euclid, reports that in eleven elementary schools, and in four secondary school buildings, all classrooms except laboratories and shops have been equipped with light-control systems. He reports additionally that seven new buildings have been completed since 1955.

The list of examples points up a clearly marked trend throughout the country and even though some school systems have not compiled records so enviable, there are many more that are doing equally well. The examples indicate that when striving for high levels of media utilization the earlier projection-room idea is now being looked upon as an interim, makeshift arrangement. Instead, every learning space, large and small, specialized or general, must incorporate the media materials and equipment necessary to achieve the purposes for which the space is to be used. Of course we must be alert to the fact that *classroom* ought now to be used as a term with broad meaning, synonymous with *learning space*, therefore set free from earlier concepts of a small, fixed purpose, fixed chairs and desks, and fixed space

Figure 6-4. These views show several levels of multi-group activity in the elementary schools of the Fountain Valley school district. In this school system the concept of the learning center has been developed to a high degree. In these schools a group of six classrooms has a team of teachers and a coordinating teacher, plus a teacher aide. Media equipment is available to each of these classrooms and complexes on a permanent basis. Teachers plan the schedule of activities and make efficient use of the 1,500 square-foot room that serves each cluster of classrooms. *Courtesy Fountain Valley School District, Huntington Beach, California.*

and constant size always consisting of the same learners for a given course or specified period of time. As we have emphasized, the nature of the program of teaching activity to reach specific objectives, the nature of learners and their needs, staff talents, and available space, may demand that the constituency of groups can and ought to be changed, from large at one time to conventional size and even smaller at another for special purposes. The main point here is that the class group may move to another location, or the small spaces be changed by opening up operable walls for a vastly different program of teaching-learning activity, not at all in the same sense as moving out of an ill-equipped classroom for the purpose of viewing projected media in a so-called projection room.

The Changing Classroom Environment

Concepts of what a good education consists of, how learners get it, and the methods teachers have to use to achieve it, are the main determiners of building design and specifically the classroom environment. This is another way of saying that when we plan our buildings we had better structure them for the program, present and future. We, as media specialists, have too often ourselves acted as though we were saying, "Here are the new media, now let's see what we can and ought to do with them." People who build schools must not say, "Here is a building. Isn't it beautiful? Now let's find out how we can teach in it." We must take seriously our responsibility for matching the schools we plan to the programs, activities, and services we plan to conduct in them. Therefore, as responsible educators and architects have sought wiser and more valid decisions, the teaching-learning environment has undergone drastic revision, in shape, size, flexibility, lighting, electrical power, facilitation of multi-group activity, flow of services, and arrangements for teacher and pupil use of technological media. We shall discuss some of these changes because of their specific relation to the use of media in the classroom, but we shall not deal with problems of design as they apply to the entire school structure, nor shall we discuss the school media service system facilities that support the use of media in the classroom as this topic will be dealt with in another chapter. Instead we

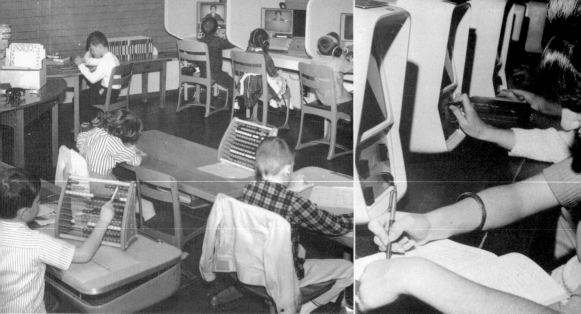

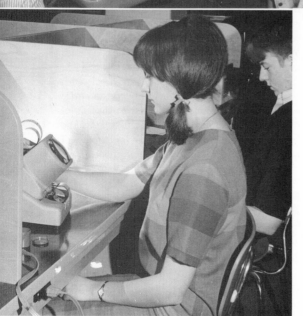

Figure 6-5. Multi-group activity takes many forms, often involving independent and individualized study in other teaching-learning areas, as well as in on-the-spot classroom facilities. In the top left view, youngsters are working in the Midwest Regional Media Center for the Deaf using carrels equipped with Fairchild 8mm sound motion picture cartridges. In the top right picture students are working on reading skill development using Craig reader equipment, and in the bottom picture, students at Southwest High School in Portland, Oregon, are using individual filmstrip viewers as a part of course activity. (*Top view* courtesy MRMCD, University of Nebraska, Lincoln. *Top right picture*, courtesy Craig Corp., Los Angeles. *Bottom view*, Portland Community College, Portland, Oregon.)

shall focus our attention on some of the instructional-program demands that are influencing current changes in teaching-learning areas.

Multi-Group Activity. In many modern-day programs, groups of pupils are engaged in several different learning activities at the same time. Such action is common when the teacher's role as the sole information-dispenser is altered. The rotation of groups through a given activity, with the teacher in control of all learning conditions and materials, is frequently the way the conventional lock-step sequences are broken up. For such activities, rooms should

be more spacious, and furniture should be movable and adaptable. Where presentations involving projection or television are used by teachers, the learning space may be arranged so that a portion of the room where media equipment is most conveniently operated can accommodate the entire class. Other areas in the room should be available for the use of electronic carrels or other individual learning spaces. A regular classroom space would therefore have to be increased in area by 25 to 50 per cent.

Instructional Media in Combination. Teachers may need to use not only the overhead transparency projector for explaining difficult concepts by diagrammatic overlays, but may have to incorporate motion picture subjects or segments, and in addition a Polaroid slide of a map from the morning newspaper, and perhaps play a portion of a tape recording. A videotape may also be scheduled for a given class group in, for example, American History, for all classes in the afternoon at all secondary schools, in which an assignment is presented and explained in detail. Classrooms in which such presentations are a regular occurrence need special facilities such as lighting controls, possibly two projection screens, projection equipment, and loudspeaker equipment that will provide adequate sound distribution. Such a classroom must be shaped for projection-media purposes, longer from front to rear than from side to side, for a more favorable grouping of pupils along the projection axis. The equipment must be maneuverable and located conveniently with respect to the class, with some or all of the equipment under remote control from the front of the room. And since materials are viewed with valid relationship to significant learning activities, work space is essential at desks, for individuals and groups.

Audiovisual Media in Listen-Response Control Situations. Teachers in a given situation may be engaged in guiding the creative and productive project work of individuals while at the same time instructional media are arranged in a control situation, to present and call for specific responses by individuals. Classrooms may have to be arranged so that movable furniture may be changed at will into listening-response-activity stations, with instruction given by the teacher via magnetic tape. Books and other printed media such as specially prepared work-sheets may be keyed into the tape directions, and the responses may have to be written out and self-corrected on the spot. Such specialized work in team-teaching situations may be referred to as total-group areas. Flexibility in classroom size may therefore become a necessity, or groups may be routed into special listen-response learning areas equipped with viewing-response, multiple-media learning stations. Such spaces for complete flexibility must be equipped with large-group viewing facilities. This means that shape is again important for the essential projection activity, in addition to the self-instruction content under the control of media. Teachers may need to make presentations of a motivational, directional, instructional nature, before or after individual study activity. Thus the multi-group activity, media in combination, large-group and small-group pupil activity, and media-in-control activity, call for the most flexible and convenient classroom arrangements possible to design.

Team Teaching Influence. Those aspects of information giving, that need not necessarily demand face-to-face relationships between teacher and pupil may be assigned to media, or to one person in the teaching team who will have a large-group (or total group) presentation. Television or audio systems may be used in such situations, or a highly communicative visualized presentation and demonstration can be given where each pupil may have a front-row seat. Small groups and individuals must also be worked with, and the creative work of assignments, together with individualized, skill-building work, has to be provided for. Thus the learning space or classroom may have to be made flexible, or groups of spaces clustered, being changeable and usable according to need

Figure 6-6. In this teaching auditorium teachers who meet large groups may plan on the use of fixed installations including an overhead projector, a public address system, and a tape recorder in the lectern, and at the rear there is 16mm film, slide, and filmstrip capability. *Courtesy Public Schools, Penfield, New York.*

Figure 6-7. Some listen-response control by media situations are simple, others are complex in so far as technology is concerned. Some involve more complex response functions than others, and some are audio only, while others involve both audio and video. The two views indicate this range.
(*Top view* shows a portion of an electronic classroom in the Southwest High School, Portland, Oregon. *Bottom view* shows video-equipped carrels at one of the Nova High School Resource Centers (1966–67 arrangement), Fort Lauderdale, Florida.) *Courtesy Portland Community College and Nova Dissemination Project, Nova Schools.*

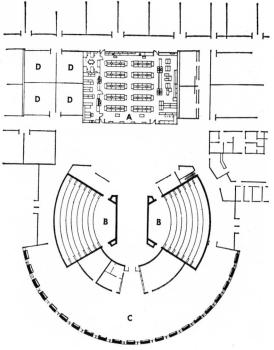

Figure 6-8. In the floor plan of a portion of the Science area in the Munster Senior High School we note space *A* for 80 laboratory positions including special project stations; space *B* for two large-group multimedia presentation facilities; space *C* for independent and individualized work; and spaces *D* for small discussion groups. Each of the large-group spaces, one of which is shown in the illustration, seats 150 students. Projection is from a room behind the students. These spaces are presently arranged for use of several kinds of media and lend themselves for the team-teaching approach. *Courtesy Public Schools, Munster, Indiana.*

and arrangements. It is obvious that all the pupils in the subgroups of a group of a hundred may sometimes have to be assembled together at a given time. Either they will all have to be brought into one large learning area, or they can be taught by closed-circuit television programing in their own learning areas.

Individualized Instruction. We have already described the listening-response station and mentioned the need for individuals to pursue their own learning activity under the guidance of a vicarious teacher. The heart of such instruction may be a set of automated slides, a dial-access videotape, or an audio program, used singly or in combination in what we can refer to as an electronic carrel. Such individualization can also consist of a combination of programed instruction with media used in large groups. Such programs of individualization whether designed by local teachers or other professional personnel simply cannot be implemented without adequate attention to media. Therefore, the facilities in the various learning spaces that make media use possible are essential. But all instruction need not—in fact should not—be conducted on an individual basis. However, this is one of the concepts about education that will greatly influence the design of the whole school as well as the classrooms. We need to

map our programs with care, for we must realize that the school must prepare its learners to seek learning as a life-long process, by themselves, not necessarily in formal courses. But we can be reasonably sure at this time that there are many insights and skills that can and ought to be taught to learners economically and effectively by self-instruction methods. However, classrooms will have to be designed for it, teachers will have to understand it, and media will have to be procured and deployed to implement it.

Small Discussion-Group Spaces. As teachers meet their small groups face-to-face, we are too often prone to believe that only conference or talk situations are required. To the contrary, as teachers grow in their power to use communicative instruments in large groups, they also find new uses for them in small-group situations. Media materials may be the means of presenting situations and calling for teacher-guided reactions to pictorial and diagrammatic content in the fastest possible way. Therefore, it is essential that even small-group learning spaces be equipped for the kinds of activities that have already been planned or will be planned in the future. Electrical outlets for audio tape recorders, overhead projectors, and other projection equipment are essential.

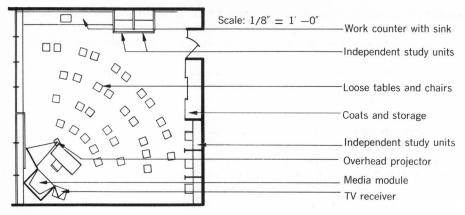

Scale: 1/8″ = 1′ —0″

— Work counter with sink

— Independent study units

— Loose tables and chairs

— Coats and storage

— Independent study units

— Overhead projector

— Media module

— TV receiver

Figure 6-9.   Many small-group discussions may be held in groups of 30 or less students under the guidance of the teacher. Other places should be provided for small informal group discussions. The need for media in all groups is made clear in the hypothetical floor plan shown. What are some possible uses of media for discussion purposes? *Courtesy Center for Architectural Research, Rensselaer Polytechnic Institute, Troy, New York,* from Alan C. Green, *Educational Facilities with New Media,* published by DAVI of the NEA, 1966.

Learner-Activity Influence. Let us ask ourselves some important questions, "What will our students be practicing? What kinds of problems will we have them solve? How deeply should we have them probe into relationships? When has a student learned something? What conditions should we provide? To what degree shall we provide classroom situations in which pupils pool and share their work? What teamwork in the classroom shall we organize? What kinds of research activity? Making observations? Drawing conclusions and testing them? To what degree will we make our social and physical and life science courses classes into listening courses?" Answers to these questions point the way to decisions about changes in our learning spaces, for when we examine in this light the action that teachers and pupils must take, we see the roles of media in the light of their potential contributions. We will not make as many mistakes in our designs as in the past if we turn our attention to the learner and his needs in our society.

Small wonder that architects, educators, and laymen interested in bettering the educational programs of our time, have come up with some striking innovations.

Media-Use Requirements in the Classroom

Light-Control Systems

Regardless of the basic design of the school plant as a whole, we must make sure that in each of the learning spaces proper provisions are made for the use of a variety of media. We do not minimize the use of the print medium. Instead, we use all media—each for its

Figure 6-10.   (Opposite)   As increasing emphasis is placed on significant problem-solving activity on the part of learners, we will have to provide increased laboratory and other kinds of working areas. Architect Green supplies us with another floor plan that points up the important use of media in all of these working areas. Study this floor plan with relation to media services in a school building and in comparison with the plan in Figure 6-8, also. Will the technical staff have to be increased in proportion to the increase in number of fixed installations and rear-projection spaces? How can large-group laboratory spaces provide for individualized student work? How is problem-solving work aided by such additional teaching stations as electronic learning laboratories? *Courtesy Center for Architectural Research, Rensselaer Polytechnic Institute, Troy, New York,* from Alan C. Green, *Educational Facilities with New Media,* published by DAVI of the NEA, 1966.

specific contribution to the teaching learning processes. We know now, that nonprint media are destined to play both old and new roles, that media will be put to work in rooms of different sizes and shapes, in large-group and small-group spaces, in special purpose areas from the cafeteria to the gymnasium, and if a teaching station can be divided into sections, or if it is possible to open up a number of sections into a large area for important instructional activity, then each of the units as well as the whole must be provided with the required basic media-use facilities, and the first of these facilities is an adequate light-control system.

Stand-up/sit-down
laboratory work stations

Demonstration table
with overhead projection

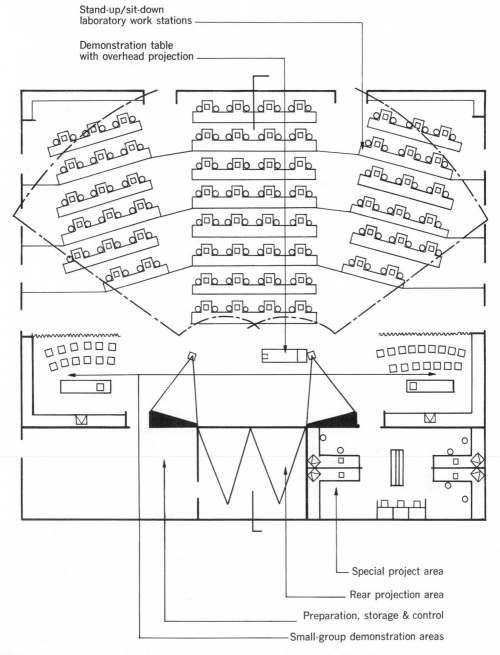

Special project area

Rear projection area

Preparation, storage & control

Small-group demonstration areas

Scale: $1/16'' = 1' - 0''$

Nature of Light-Control Decisions. Good decisions regarding light control depend on the director's understanding of relationships between light exclusion, light diffusion, variation in criticalness of observation tasks, environmental attractiveness, and economy. The media program director should seek a light-control system for each classroom that enables the teacher to keep light out, to admit natural light free of harmful glare or provide it by general illumination, and to keep out enough light to permit the most critical picture interpretation task to be carried on unhampered by uncontrolled stray light. He should choose a system that increases the attractiveness of the room and yet is reasonable in cost. Media-use planners should always keep the following points in mind.

1. Projected pictures are less brilliant for viewers seated at the sides of the room, that is, the same amount of stray light affects a picture differently, depending on where the viewer is seated.

2. Reflective powers of different screen fabrics are not equal.

3. Greater light exclusion is needed for color pictures than for projected black-and-white pictures or black-and-white line drawings.

4. Complete darkening in classrooms is not desirable. Except for special purposes (such as the identification of bacteria by microprojectors), classrooms need be darkenable to the point where only $\frac{1}{10}$ footcandle of illumination falls on the screen.

5. Projectors differ in their efficiency in projecting available light from the lamp to the screen. The opaque and microprojectors understandably are at the bottom of the list.

6. Satisfactory observation of significant details in projected pictures is the criterion for judging the adequacy of light exclusion. When rooms are not sufficiently dark, many details are simply not visible.

7. Projected pictures are more appealing generally under conditions of subdued illumination. This is probably true because distractions are likely to be less intense.

Window Design. Media program leaders should determine whether other school authorities and administrators are taking adequate action to obtain an over-all design of the school plant that will facilitate the use of audiovisual media. If they are not, he should submit recommendations. Unless the school's learning spaces are to be constructed without windows, the architect should design a window structure that will facilitate the mounting and operation of adequate light-control systems. Plans should therefore be made to work with the architect in developing a set of restrictions upon his decisions. The following restrictions, if spaces are to have windows, are suggested:

1. No skylight should be permitted in any classroom.

2. Bottoms of interior glass panes should be located at least one foot above any ventilators, shelving, or other obstruction, if shades or drape traverse systems have been specified as the darkening devices. This restriction may be removed if full-closure Venetian blinds are specified.

3. Window area should be reasonable, not excessive.

4. Appropriate wood or metal mounting strips for all darkening devices should be built into ceiling structures at the required distance from window panes. Ceiling slots and/or window-sill slots for roller shades are to be provided whenever appropriate.

5. Windows should be allowed on one wall only.

6. Clerestory designs should be avoided.

7. Enough wall space should be provided on either side of window-walls to make possible a minimum side overlap of drape systems of 2 feet. This restriction may be removed when full-closure Venetian blinds are specified.

8. Windows should be designed so as to permit opening outward only to avoid interference with present or future darkening-system installations.

Light-Control Systems. Windows are likely to be of the same design and size in classrooms, but different in other areas such as the auditorium and gymnasium. Also, windows in interior or exterior doors ought to be covered. The would-be media program director should note the following suggested applications of darkening systems to kinds of windows and to various sizes and locations:

1. *For window walls, vision strips and glass-brick expanses.* Drape traverse-track systems

Figure 6-11. Double drape systems are very expensive. Are window designs like this desirable? *Courtesy Bureau of Audio-Visual and School Library Education, California State Department of Education, Sacramento.*

of plastic or other serviceable, noncombustible material with nondeteriorating and colorfast properties; overlapped, 3-foot-wide, opaque roller shades, light color preferably for room attractiveness, operating from fixtures in a ceiling slot, or from the Draper XL continuous, angle-iron strip; or full-closure Venetian blinds in appropriate colors.

2. *For windows* 4 *feet or less in width and* 8 *feet or less in height and within reach.* Full-closure Venetian blinds of appropriate colors; opaque roller shades without groove system or enclosures of any kind, except a hinged, wooden shutter.

3. *For windows over* 8 *feet in height and within reach.* Drape traverse-track system, with two

separate systems being used with vertical overlap, if the total weight of the drape system due to the excessive height would stretch the material.

4. *For wide windows* 2 *feet high or less.* Full-closure Venetian blinds; overlapped, opaque roller shades; or fire-resistant cloth, or drape, traverse-track system. Short lengths of plastic of desirable gauge are somewhat stiff, thus interfering with normal hanging and stacking action.

5. *For recessed out-of-reach windows.* Overlapped, opaque roller shades in a Draper XL mounting flush with wall.

6. *For windows in gymnasiums.* Heavy-duty, treated cloth, wood-strip reinforced, folding window cover (Forse Mfg. Co., St. Louis, Mo.),

Figure 6-12. Drape traverse systems are available in a number of different patterns and track-transport arrangements. Experienced drape-installation experts should be employed under contract to perform installation tasks in accordance with specifications. Drapes may be light excluding or light diffusing. Two drape systems are required under direct sun exposure. It may be wise to specify a light diffusing roller shade, or a Venetian blind under the light-excluding drape system. *Courtesy Art Zeiller Co., Allendale, New Jersey.*

Figure 6-13. All-purpose, adaptable, and effective full-closure Venetian blinds are recommended when window dimensions are favorable. Slats have a tendency to vibrate when air currents blow through them, hence they need to be wide open if lowered when windows are open. Note that this classroom is of conventional size and is being used for discussion purposes. How far apart are the side channels? *Courtesy Portland Community College, Portland, Oregon.*

or Draper XL mount, overlapped, opaque shades of heavy-duty cloth. If gymnasium is a combination auditorium-gymnasium, heavy-duty, plastic-drape traverse systems ought to be specified for the sake of attractiveness.

7. *For windows in auditoriums.* Attractive, plastic-drape, traverse-track systems, with an additional recessed traverse system using light-diffusion plastic material if sun exposure is direct during school hours. Window drape should harmonize with plastic or velour-drape systems on stage.

8. *For all windows with direct sun exposure.* Combination diffusion and exclusion systems are essential. That is, use two sets of suitable drape traverse systems on separate tracks, or operating on a double-draw and single-track with the diffusion drape operating when the exclusive drape is stacked; use two sets of roller shades, one set translucent and one opaque, or use all-purpose, full-closure Venetian blinds.

Defective Light-Control System Installations. Many unbelievable errors are made when specifications for light-control systems are written by individuals who do not understand school problems. Media directors, to avoid common pitfalls, would do well to consider the following suggestions when preparing their specifications:

1. Direct orders for light-control installations to experienced school suppliers, not to local department stores, and if this is not feasible, personally supervise or employ a supervisor to see that all specifications are complied with.

2. Locate the best classroom drape-system designer and fitter in the area and get his advice in preparing specifications.

3. Prepare a detailed set of specifications for bids as free of loopholes as is reasonably possible.

Figure 6-14. This is an installation of the Draper XL shading unit. Note the light-diffusion system needed because of the direct exposure to the sun. Try drawing a diagram to explain how the brackets are arranged to permit the observed overlap. *Courtesy Luther O. Draper Shade Company, Spiceland, Indiana.*

Drape-traverse Darkening Systems. To get the best possible installation for long years of trouble-free service, the director of instructional materials at San Diego worked out a set of detailed specifications for bidders on drape systems involving material, hardware, and installation. General items in those specifica-tions included (1) specification as to quality of workmanship and guarantee, (2) the demand that an identity tag of the supplier be affixed to each drape installation, (3) a stipulation that fabric characteristics be fully certified, and (4) that acceptance is subject to inspection. Specific items dealt with material, opaqueness,

Figure 6-15. James M. Parsons stretched his dollars for darkening procedures under a low budget by trying rubberized paint on existing fabric roller shades with good results. Although this was a stopgap procedure, the process holds up well after several years of use. He calls his process the roll-on light-control method. The next step is to discard the shades entirely and implement a more durable system. What permanent method of excluding light should be recommended in the situation shown? *Courtesy Public Schools, Northampton, Massachusetts.*

color, fireproof quality, nontoxic quality, manufacturer and brand name, light leakage, heading construction, hooks, seams, hems, flat construction, tiebacks, fullness, center overlap, return free of obstruction, vertical and horizontal extensions (bottom and sides), cut-outs for exterior doorways, door panels, selvage, track, pull cord, nylon carriers, track splicers, pulleys, floor pulleys, end stops, ceiling brackets, wall brackets, screws, track suspension, separate tracks or track overlap, curves, and mounting battens.

Media directors should make a careful study of the heavy-duty suspension and traverse-track hardware and the required matched accessories. To leave these details to someone who doesn't know classroom requirements is to invite long-lasting trouble. The San Diego school system darkening program also provides the successful bidder with instructions as to placement in each room.

In writing up local specifications the media program director should be guided by the following suggestions:

1. Drape material should overlap at the center of two panels by 1 foot, and at sides and bottom of windows by 18 inches.

2. It is better to use two tracks, one for each drape panel if light-diffusion devices are already provided for. Otherwise, a single, double-draw track can be arranged so that two separately operating drape systems can be mounted on it.

3. Tracks should be of heavy-duty construction.

4. Drapes should be opened and closed by a vertical pull system.

5. Contrary to the opinions of some suppliers, 50 per cent additional material should be added to dimensions of window opening for fullness.

6. Nylon drape rollers should roll on the track system in the same position as train wheels, thus bearing the load on the roller axes while in a vertical position.

7. The drape supplier should demonstrate that his recommended heading construction can bear the weight of the plastic fabric without tearing loose.

8. The suspension device for the track, if it is to be mounted on the wall above the window, should be a sturdy angle iron, and if it is to be mounted to the ceiling, it should be a sturdy

and level wood or metal strip to permit unhampered movement.

9. Mounting brackets for the track must be sufficient in number to keep the track level during operation; near the ends of the drape track, twice as many mounting brackets ought to be installed.

10. Drape fabric must run free of obstructions.

11. It is usually best to mount the track 12 to 18 inches away from the window.

12. Tracks may run in any desired pattern in a room, curved or straight; therefore drape panels can be moved away from a window wall to block off any desired part of a classroom for a desired projection location.

13. Whenever drape systems are to be installed in new buildings, the traverse track should be installed as a part of the construction contract. Drapes themselves should also become a part of the equipment contract.

Opaque Roller Shades. It is a disturbing sight to see new roller-shade fabric half pulled off the rollers at the window-sill level. To prevent this and to make possible many years of trouble-free service, directors should include the following in their local specifications:

1. The finished length should be long enough to reach 1 foot below the sill.

2. Bottom corners should be reinforced by stitching on extra corners of fabric.

3. Light-exclusion shades should be mounted outside of window casing, overlapping it at top and sides by 2 to 4 inches.

4. Light-diffusion shades or other devices should be mounted inside casings.

5. No channels or edge slots should be permitted.

6. The mounting devices for overlapping opaque roller shades on wide windows ought to facilitate easy replacement of shades, such as is the case with the Draper XL unit.

7. Darkening shades should be mounted at top of window, not in the middle as are double-roller systems.

8. Heavy-duty rollers and fixtures ought to be installed for shades wider than 3 feet.

All-purpose, Full-Closure Venetian Blinds. Several makes and models of full-closure blinds are available, and it is up to the director to seek trouble-free operation for the teachers' convenience and for distraction-free learning activities. Therefore the following suggestions should be borne in mind.

1. Gloss-finished slats are easy to keep clean, but they are highly reflective. Light-dimming calls for light absorption by flat, dark tones of paint.

2. Sturdy-structure, built-in, wide sections (up to 7 feet) with unsagging slats should be selected. The many operations required when eight narrow sections, for example, are arranged channel to channel along a window wall may be time consuming and an annoying chore even for youngsters.

3. Channels for the blinds should be so tightly mounted against the wall surfaces at top, sides, and bottom that stray light is excluded at these points of contact.

Channels for Shades. Contrary to the thinking of many, metal or wood enclosures for roller shades are not recommended. Such channels and slots wear out the curtains, and no such system of darkening has ever given trouble-free service for long periods of time. To be sure, leatherette-type fabrics, traveling behind metal plates or in side slots, provide extremely dark interiors, but this condition is not normally desirable in classrooms. Therefore that type of installation is recommended only for clinical or diagnostic laboratories and training situations where such devices as high-power micro-projectors are used.

Lower Limits of Illumination and Light Control. It was pointed out earlier that modern instruction calls for variation in observational tasks with projected audiovisual media, and hence it is sometimes necessary to have the room very dark, while for other classroom activities sufficient light must be available to observe the screen and to write or draw simultaneously. It is therefore desirable that the light-control system be capable of excluding light down to the lower limit where only $\frac{1}{10}$ footcandle of illumination falls on the screen. On the other hand, as demanded by instructional activity, it is necessary to be able to increase the illumination by operating room-light dimmers or by turning on additional lights. Many times it is important to take notes during a projected

presentation, and a minimum of 1 footcandle of illumination on note paper is adequate for this special task. However, it is imperative that such illumination be directed downward and not onto the projection screen during critical observation. When illumination for note taking is properly directed away from the projection surface, it is desirable to strive for an approximation of equal brightness on the note-taking surface and on the viewing screen, approximately five to ten footlamberts reflected from each surface.

Although the reader may refer to his physics textbook for verification, it would be helpful to clarify the use of certain terms normally used in discussions about lighting for classroom activities. *Footcandles* refers to light that is radiating from a source, as from a lamp in a motion picture projector being projected as incident light onto a screen as a field of light. *Footlamberts* refers to the light reflected from, for example, a screen fabric or from a sheet of paper. Luminous energy or quantity of light is expressed as *lumens*. A *lumen* is defined as the quantity of light that shines through a hole one square foot in size at a distance of one foot from a one candlepower light source, often referred to as an international candle. One lumen per square foot equals one footcandle.

Classroom Wiring

The media director must also make certain that his recommendations include adequate wiring requests for present and future instructional demands. Heavy-duty, rubber-covered wiring should be prescribed throughout, together with the following items:

1. Three, double, 2000-watt capacity electrical outlets, positioned as follows: (a) one at front of room, (b) one on side wall, 10 feet from front of room nearest that corner in which a corner projection screen could be hung and tilted appropriately, and (c) one at rear wall center near proposed projection station, all outlets approximately 18 inches above floor. (Side wall positioning favors the location of an overhead projector and/or rear screen as a permanent auxiliary projection station.)

2. In all special learning spaces, such as laboratories, libraries, shops, electronic learning

laboratories, business machine laboratories, multipurpose rooms, ample power supply must be provided for planned and predicted future needs.

3. Each double electrical outlet should have a capacity of 2000 watts, and should be independent of general illumination in any given classroom or learning space area.

4. Standard $1\frac{3}{4}$-inch-diameter conduit system for closed-circuit television and central sound system with a minimum of two junction boxes in the front wall near the baseboard of each classroom, the library, auditorium, central administrative office, and all special purpose, large-group learning areas. As an alternate plan raceways may be run above the ceilings.

5. A three-way on-off power and dimmer control switch should be located on the front and rear walls near the projection stations, thus permitting control of illumination from both front and rear of the room. In the modern-day classroom where the instructor is seated at an overhead projector, and intermittently needs to project other media as well by remote control, light-control switches, including dimmers, ought to be located at that point also. Often, a control station is conveniently located at or near the overhead projection station.

6. A $\frac{3}{4}$-inch conduit line for speaker, with appropriate end receptacles, to run through the floor from rear wall to front of room to connect projector amplifier with speaker. This conduit must be in addition to regular a-c power lines.

7. Junction boxes for central sound system and permanently installed wall speakers must not be located at front of room anywhere within the central area 10 foot wide by 8 foot high above chalkboard-tray level for any given room, preferably keeping the entire front wall free for the installation of large multi-image projection surfaces.

8. A $\frac{3}{4}$-inch conduit for remote on-off film and slide projector control, from projection station at rear to junction box at front of room at instructor station. In large-group spaces where teacher-controlled instructional activity is envisioned, control facilities should be combined at a single instructor station, including lights and dimmer control, and remote control of film and slide projector operation so arranged that the overhead projector is readily accessible for operation.

9. Small-group, face-to-face instructional activity spaces need also to have power outlets according to previously stated minimum needs.

10. Electrical outlets, plug mold on one or more walls, or in the floor as needed to supply individual study stations equipped with electronic as well as electrical devices and projection instruments if included in classrooms or in special learning spaces in large-group spaces or in libraries.

Estimated Power Requirements for Common Media Equipment Units. It is frequently difficult to convince school designers that the amount of electrical power recommended is essential, when media equipment units are to be used in quantity simultaneously in many of the classrooms. The interruption of class activities by the needless blowing of fuses or the tripping of circuit breakers in panel boxes is inexcusable, but this problem rarely gets the attention it deserves. Although the trend toward transistorization will eventually reduce the power consumption in a given unit, we can still use some simple arithmetic in figuring the power consumption for media by adding up the units we intend to put to work and multiplying the total by the estimated power requirements expressed in amperage. To facilitate such work in order to substantiate the power-requirement recommendations we supply the following estimates of needed power for a given kind of equipment unit or package:

Equipment Item or Package	Power Requirement in Amperes
1. 16 mm sound motion picture projector	9
2. Opaque projector	9
3. Overhead transparency projector (heavy duty)	9
4. Overhead transparency projector (light weight)	4
5. Slide projector, $3\frac{1}{4} \times 4$ inch, with blower (auditorium)	7
6. Slide projector, $3\frac{1}{4} \times 4$ inch without blower (classroom)	4
7. Slide projector, 2×2 inch	5
8. Cartridge-type 8 mm film projector	1
9. Tape recorder	1
10. Record player	1

Equipment Item or Package	Power Requirement in Amperes
11. Classroom television receiver	2
12. Videotape recorder	2
13. Independent study carrel equipped with 8 mm cartridge film projector, TV receiver, and automatic 2 × 2 inch slide projector	9
14. TV camera	8
15. CCTV studio, complete, three camera chains, film chain, including 150 amperes for lighting	250
16. Electronic learning laboratory, 36-position, remote control, dial access system	70
17. Public address system for large auditorium	50
18. Central sound system for a school building	15

Projection Screens and the Classroom Layout

Many mistakes have been made in planning the placement of projection screens in classrooms. One general rule is that the screen should be permanently mounted on the front wall or suspended from the ceiling near it so that all the students can see it. When air ducts, clocks, loudspeakers, and flag holders are located in the central area of the front wall above the chalkboard, it can be assumed that the planner is either ignorant of—or acting in defiance of—the need to provide for audiovisual media methods. Not only do projection screens have to be selected appropriately in terms of the shape and size of the classroom, and in terms of the kind of material to be projected upon them, but they also have to be properly placed for optimum viewing conditions. Since the facts about screens are so significant for both teachers and architects, the media director must be prepared to give them good counsel. Careful study of the facts, recommendations, and illustrations that follow will assist him in making correct judgments.

Reflection Characteristics of Screens. The white glass-beaded screen, the matte-white screen, and the silver lenticular projection screen are the generally available screens for classroom use. Each of these has its own characteristics. The glass-beaded screen and the matte-white screen are very commonly known and are frequently compared. Of the two, the beaded screen gives the brighter picture when the viewer is nearer the projection axis (the perpendicular line from the projector to the screen), but the brightness falls off quickly for viewers who are seated to the right or left of the axis. The desirable total observation angle for the glass-beaded screen is 40° to 50°, or 20° to 25° to the right and the same number of degrees to the left of the axis. Light from the matte-white screen is not reflected back along the path from which it came but is highly diffused outward from the screen. Hence, while not so bright from the projector position, light from the matte-white screen is actually spread out more evenly throughout the total observation angle of 60°, or 30° on each side of the projection axis. See Figure 6-16. Under favorable room darkening, the total included angle may be extended to 90° as a fairly acceptable viewing area. Because of the evenness of light over a wider included observation angle, and because of the greater illuminating power of modern lamps and efficient optical systems, the matte-white screen fabric is frequently chosen in preference to other fabrics.

In a 1947 research report publicized by the Radiant Screen Company, it was shown that the glass-beaded screen was approximately 300 per cent brighter than the matte-white screen for viewing positions along the projection axis, but that outside of the recommended 45° total observation angle, the matte screen was superior. According to the same report, the silver-color roll screen, then recommended for three-dimensional projection purposes, had approximately the same reflection characteristics as the glass-beaded screen at about the same observation angles.

The silver lenticular projection screen fabric has somewhat greater reflecting power than the glass-bead fabric and in addition has great light-diffusing capacity. The included observation angle for such a projection fabric is approximately 90°. However, such fabrics need to be stretched tightly for satisfactory reflection throughout the viewing locations. To make

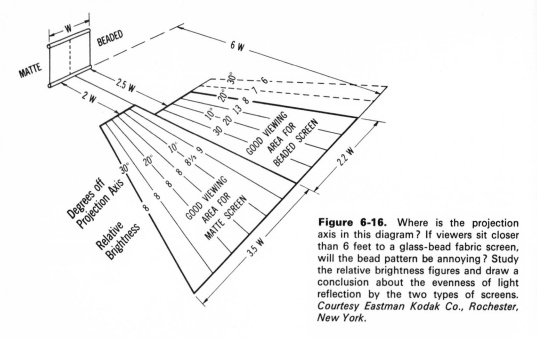

Figure 6-16. Where is the projection axis in this diagram? If viewers sit closer than 6 feet to a glass-bead fabric screen, will the bead pattern be annoying? Study the relative brightness figures and draw a conclusion about the evenness of light reflection by the two types of screens. *Courtesy Eastman Kodak Co., Rochester, New York.*

this needed stretching possible, both the wall-type and the portable-type screens have a fabric-stretching device built into the metal roller case. Also, because the lenticular fabric has to receive the light in a perpendicular line from the projector, it may have to be tipped down properly with the aid of a tilt-bar mechanism. When the silver lenticular wall-model screen is used, it should be mounted on the wall-extension brackets provided. Unless these requirements are met, the brightness of the images projected onto the screen surface falls off rapidly.

The brightness of a given projected image on a particular projection screen may be the result of the reflecting power of the fabric being used, the amount of ambient light, the illuminating power of a given projection lamp, the position of the viewer, and the possible over- or under-exposure of a particular image frame. Hence a number of factors have a bearing on the brightness of a projected image on a projection surface. Brightness is expressed in footlamberts and 5 to 15 such units will be more than satisfactory for most projection purposes.

Projection Screens and the Shape of the Classroom. Because of the narrower observation angle of the glass-beaded screen, it is recommended for long classrooms where a large number of viewers may be arranged along the projection axis. Square rooms, and rooms that are wider than they are long, call for the matte-white screen for the widest possible viewing away from the axis. The silver lenticular screen is not recommended except where no darkening system is feasible and some projection has to be done. See Figures 6-17 and 6-18.

Size of Screen. Recommending the size of a screen is not a matter of guesswork or of what looks best in a classroom. This decision has to be made in terms of adequate visual observation of pictorial content. The size of picture needed by any viewer in the classroom is the criterion. A simple rule of thumb to determine the appropriate size of a picture projected onto a screen uses the last row of viewers in a room as a standard of reference. The width of the picture should be approximately the same number of feet as one-sixth of the distance from the screen to the last row of seats. (Of course, the distance to any other row would be less, but the *size for the last row* is used as the standard.) Viewers need to see pictorial details or to identify symbols, and if the details are not sufficiently enlarged, this process is impossible.

Another rule for arriving at the needed screen size involves the width of the projector aperture in inches. Some of the standard apertures are as follows: 16 mm motion picture projector, 0.38 inch; $3\frac{1}{4} \times 4$ inch slide pro-

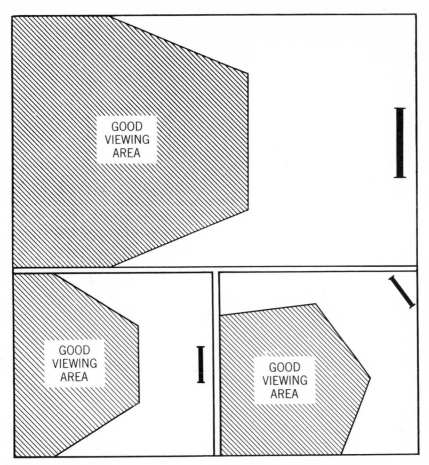

Figure 6-17. What types of wall-mounted screens should be recommended for the above situations? What other projection problems will have to be defined and solved in each case? *Courtesy Eastman Kodak Co., Rochester, New York.*

Figure 6-18. When we view teaching stations in some of the newer schools we note the favorable viewing angles that exist in all wedge-shape rooms, at least for the viewers in a given unit. When operable walls are opened up between such spaces, what new total-group projection orientation may be necessary? *Courtesy Audiovisual Instruction of the DAVI of the NEA and Dr. John Shaver of Shaver Architects, Salina, Kansas.*

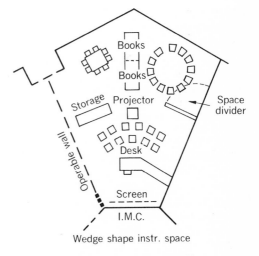

jector, 3 inches; single-frame filmstrip projector, 0.906 inch; and 2 × 2 inch slide projector, 1.34 inches. In order to find the desirable screen width, multiply the aperture in inches (of the projector being used) by the distance of projector to the screen in feet, and divide by the focal length of the lens. One word of caution should be given. Screen width and width of picture may be two different things, and the two expressions should not be used loosely. Many compact devices for projection are available, and some of the small rear-projection screen units, even the media modules being shown in designs for new school plants, may prove to be unsatisfactory for providing the size of image that is desirable for a given group of viewers and the required observational tasks. The size of picture needed in a given room determines the screen size. Would-be and practicing media directors should make sure that this, not the opposite, is the case in practice.

Another factor in selecting a screen of appropriate size is the intended projection usage. The projection of several images simultaneously for study and comparison demands a large projection surface possibly covering most, if not all, of the entire front wall.

Shape of Screen. It is annoying to project the square image of some opaque material onto a motion picture screen and find that important parts of the material are being reflected from the wall instead. This can also be the case with vertical-slide images. The solution is to specify square screens or to move the projector close enough so the vertical images will fit within the vertical dimensions of an improperly shaped screen. Square screens should be specified where various kinds of projected materials are to be used. However, a difficulty arises where the ceilings are not high enough to permit the mounting of a square screen so that the bottom of the screen falls at the eye level of the viewer. In such cases money is wasted on a square screen because the heads of viewers are bound to cast objectionable shadows on the screen area, or the viewers in front will block the vision of those in the rear.

Rear Projection Screens. When rear projection screens are to be used, as compared to front-surface projection screens, a new set of circumstances is introduced into the arrangement and design of classroom space. We can identify the specific conditions as follows:

1. A rear-projection screen, for images of a size suitable for group viewing, may be placed in a corner or elsewhere in front of a mirror that will reflect the image onto the screen's surface. The projector may thus be located to either side of the rear-projection screen, allowing the instructor, in the case of an overhead projector, to stand up and face his class without obstructing the view of his students. Without the reflecting mirror, a rear-projection screen must be placed in front of the room with a large opening behind it through which the images from the projectors are transmitted, or the screen must be placed far enough from the front wall so as to locate the projector far enough behind it to project an image of appropriate size. Short-throw lenses may be used in any given projector thus increasing the size of the image, but even then it may be less than the size desired for viewing if the last row of observers is located more than six times the projected image width from the rear-screen surface.

2. Direct projection onto rear-screen surfaces (from behind the screen) will of course cause the image to be reversed, thus demanding the adjustment of slides and filmstrips before projection. A motion picture will require a mirror arrangement since it cannot be reversed properly prior to projection. When intermediate projection is onto a mirror surface, the image is projected onto the rear-screen surface without image reversal for direct viewing by the class.

3. In general the arrangement of viewers in a classroom using rear-screen projection is approximately the same as for a matte-fabric front projection arrangement with some restriction in the total viewing angle to 70° to 80° instead of the possible 90° for the matte-white fabric.

4. In any rear-screen installation all stray light must be prevented from striking the projection side of the surface, as all such light is transmitted and thus reduces clarity and contrast.

5. As a general rule, rear-screen projection may be carried on under normal levels of room light or ambient light without loss of clarity and contrast. Very little of the ambient light falling on the viewer side of the surface is reflected. The requirement is that the projector should supply as many lumens per square foot of screen as there are footcandles of room illumination fall-

CORNER INSTALLATION LENSCREEN IN-WALL LAYOUT

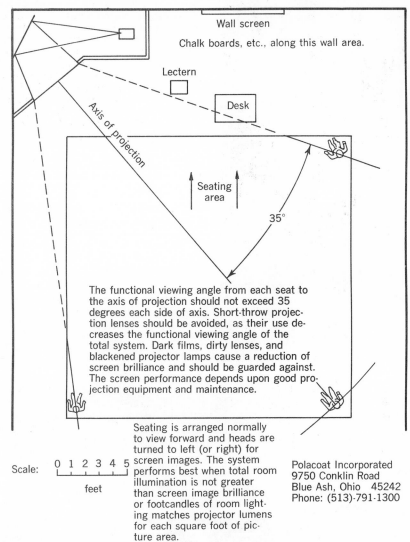

Wall screen

Chalk boards, etc., along this wall area.

Lectern

Desk

Axis of projection

Seating area

35°

The functional viewing angle from each seat to the axis of projection should not exceed 35 degrees each side of axis. Short-throw projection lenses should be avoided, as their use decreases the functional viewing angle of the total system. Dark films, dirty lenses, and blackened projector lamps cause a reduction of screen brilliance and should be guarded against. The screen performance depends upon good projection equipment and maintenance.

Scale: 0 1 2 3 4 5
          feet

Seating is arranged normally to view forward and heads are turned to left (or right) for screen images. The system performs best when total room illumination is not greater than screen image brilliance or footcandles of room lighting matches projector lumens for each square foot of picture area.

Polacoat Incorporated
9750 Conklin Road
Blue Ash, Ohio 45242
Phone: (513)-791-1300

Figure 6-19. Some of the basic arrangements for rear-projection operations. Do mirrors have to be used with motion picture film projection? What adjustments must be made in threading filmstrips for example or loading a magazine or tray with slides in the event that no reflecting mirror is provided? *Courtesy Polacoat Incorporated, Blue Ash, Ohio.*

ing on surrounding surfaces. A range of one half to one third of room illumination may often be acceptable.

6. It is a fact that rear-projection screen surfaces and their mounts are more expensive than glass-bead and matte-white surface screens, and the expense is greatly increased when fairly large mirror surfaces have to be mounted in back of the viewing surface.

7. Aside from corner-of-room installations,

a considerable amount of space should be provided for arranging projection equipment behind a rear-projection screen surface. The rule is to allow in depth a minimum of two times the width of the screen surface. The use of one or more mirrors may save a great deal of space; however, technicians must have convenient access to the equipment to adjust it and load it with media materials. Cramped quarters may complicate the efficient operation of the system.

Figure 6-20. Note the large rear-projection screen installed in this large-group multimedia presentation teaching station. New so-called communication centers of the State University Colleges of New York feature multi-floor clusters of such large-group teaching stations. Rear-projection rooms are connected at each level by exterior curved catwalks. It is important to fit the rear-projection Lenscreen tightly in its wall mounting frame to prevent sound leakage from the rooms behind the screen. This fitting is shown in the top close-up view. *Courtesy Communication Center, The State University College at Buffalo, New York.*

Rear-screen surfaces are generally used in multimedia installations with automatically controlled or programed projection apparatus, in classrooms employing small viewing screens under unfavorable darkening circumstances, in study carrels for viewing single-concept motion pictures, and in other media-module viewing devices.

Focal Length of Lenses for Optimum Picture Size. Projectors are usually equipped with standard focal-length lenses based on average classroom size. For example, a 30-foot-long

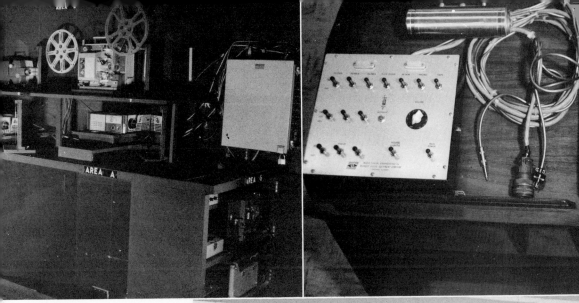

Figure 6-21. In the top picture is the equipment arrangement for the automated, but simplified multimedia system at the North Division, Niles Community Township High Schools, Skokie, Illinois. The top right view shows the lectern with its special control panel developed by Hal Cress, the school's media coordinator, and the large-group teaching station showing the rear-projection, wall-mounted Lenscreen. *Courtesy Niles Township High Schools, Skokie, Illinois.*

classroom requires a 5- or 6-foot screen, and the 2-inch focal-length lens that is standard equipment on the motion picture projector would throw at 30 feet a picture that is 70 inches wide by 52 inches high. Because of seating arrangements, projectors must often be placed either closer to or farther away from classroom screens than is normally desired, thus making the projected pictures too small or too large. Such situations call for lenses other than those regularly supplied. If lens- and picture-size tables are studied, good judgments can be made in specifying special lens sizes or required screen sizes for projection situations normally encountered. See Figure 6-22. Extra lenses may be kept

at school service centers and supplied as needed or, at the time that projectors are ordered, special lenses of the required focal length may be requested as substitutes for the standard equipment. Media personnel should make sure that the following generalizations, obvious in Figure 6-22 Tables, are fully understood; otherwise, costly mistakes may be made and incorrect advice given.

1. The longer the focal length of a lens for a given kind of projector, the smaller will be the picture projected at any given distance. (The reader should examine the screen-size tables, Figure 6-22, and state a similar generalization, using *shorter* instead of *longer*.)

Screen Size Charts

HOW TO FIND EXACT SCREEN SIZE . . . Aperture Width x Projection Throw ÷ Lens Focal Length = width of screen needed. For example: Aperture .38 (16mm movie projector) x 26 feet (projection throw . . . desired distance from screen) ÷ 2 (lens focal length) = 4.94 feet or approximately 58+ inches. Use a 45" x 60" screen.

2¼"x2¼" SLIDES—APERTURE WIDTH—2.1875"

LENS FOCAL LENGTH	SQUARE SCREEN SIZE												
	40"	50"	60"	70"	84"	8'	9'	10'	12'	14'	16'	18'	20'
5"	7.6	9.5	11.4	13.3	16.0	18.3	20.6	22.9	27.4	32.0	36.6	41.1	45.7
6½"	9.9	12.4	14.9	17.3	20.8	23.8	26.7	29.7	35.6	41.6	47.5	53.5	59.4
7"	10.7	13.3	16.0	18.7	22.4	25.6	28.8	32.0	38.4	44.8	51.2	57.6	64.0
8½"	13.0	16.2	19.4	22.7	27.2	31.1	35.0	38.9	46.6	54.4	62.2	69.9	77.7
10"	15.2	19.0	22.8	26.7	32.0	36.6	41.1	45.7	54.8	64.0	73.1	82.3	91.4
12½"	19.0	23.8	28.6	33.3	40.0	45.7	51.4	57.1	68.6	80.0	91.4	102.8	114.3
15½"	23.6	29.5	35.4	41.3	49.6	56.7	63.8	70.9	85.0	99.2	113.4	127.5	141.7
20"	30.5	38.0	45.7	53.3	64.0	73.1	82.3	91.4	109.7	128.0	146.3	164.6	182.8
24"	36.6	45.7	54.6	64.0	76.8	87.8	98.8	109.7	131.6	153.6	175.5	197.5	219.4

(Projection Distance in Feet)

2"x2" SUPER SLIDES- APERTURE WIDTH—1.5"

LENS FOCAL LENGTH	SQUARE SCREEN SIZE												
	40"	50"	60"	70"	84"	8'	9'	10'	12'	14'	16'	18'	20'
3"	6.7	8.3	10.0	11.7	14.0	16.0	18.0	20.0	24.0	28.0	32.0	36.0	40.0
4"	8.9	11.1	13.3	15.6	18.7	21.3	24.0	26.7	32.0	37.3	42.7	48.0	53.3
5"	11.1	13.9	16.7	19.4	23.3	26.7	30.0	33.3	40.0	46.7	53.3	60.0	66.7
6½"	14.4	18.1	21.7	25.3	30.3	34.7	39.0	43.3	52.0	60.7	69.3	78.0	86.7
7"	15.6	19.4	23.3	27.2	32.7	37.3	42.0	46.7	56.0	65.3	74.7	84.0	93.3
8½"	18.9	23.6	28.3	33.1	39.7	45.3	51.0	56.7	68.0	79.3	90.7	102.0	113.3
10"	22.2	27.8	33.3	38.9	46.7	53.3	60.0	66.7	80.0	93.3	106.7	120.0	133.3
12½"	27.8	34.7	41.7	48.6	58.3	66.7	75.0	83.3	100.0	116.7	133.3	150.0	166.7
15½"	35.1	43.1	51.7	60.3	72.3	82.7	93.0	103.3	124.0	144.7	165.3	186.0	206.7
20"	44.4	55.5	66.6	76.4	93.3	106.7	120.0	133.3	160.0	186.7	213.3	240.0	266.7

(Projection Distance in Feet)

2"x2" DOUBLE FRAME 35MM SLIDES
APERTURE WIDTH—1.34"

LENS FOCAL LENGTH	SQUARE SCREEN SIZE												
	40"	50"	60"	70"	84"	8'	9'	10'	12'	14'	16'	18'	20'
3"	7.5	9.3	11.2	13.1	15.7	17.9	20.1	22.4	26.9	31.3	35.8	40.3	44.8
4"	10.0	12.4	14.9	17.4	20.9	23.9	26.8	29.9	35.8	41.8	47.8	53.8	59.7
5"	12.4	15.5	18.7	21.8	26.1	29.9	33.6	37.3	44.8	52.2	59.7	67.2	74.6
6½"	16.2	20.2	24.3	28.3	34.0	38.8	43.7	48.5	58.2	67.9	77.6	88.8	97.0
7"	17.4	21.8	26.1	30.5	36.6	41.8	47.0	52.3	62.7	73.1	83.6	94.0	104.5
8½"	21.1	26.4	31.7	37.0	44.4	50.7	57.1	63.4	76.1	88.8	101.5	114.2	126.9
10"	24.9	31.1	37.3	43.5	52.2	59.7	67.2	74.6	89.6	104.5	119.4	134.3	149.3
12½"	31.1	38.9	46.6	54.4	65.3	74.6	84.0	93.3	111.9	130.6	149.3	167.9	186.6
15½"	39.3	48.1	57.8	67.5	81.0	92.5	104.1	115.7	138.8	161.9	185.1	208.2	231.3
20"	49.8	62.2	74.6	87.1	104.5	119.4	134.3	149.3	179.1	209.0	238.8	268.7	298.5

(Projection Distance in Feet)

OVERHEAD PROJECTION

LENS FOCAL LENGTH	APERTURE SIZE	SQUARE SCREEN SIZE										
		50"	60"	70"	84"	8'	10'	12'	14'	16'	18'	20'
6½"	5"	5.4	6.5	7.6	9.1	10.4	13.0	15.6	18.2	20.8	23.4	26.0
12"	7"	7.1	8.6	10.0	12.0	13.7	17.1	20.6	24.0	27.4	30.9	34.3
12½"	7"	7.4	8.9	10.4	12.5	14.3	17.9	21.4	25.0	28.6	32.1	35.7
8.8"	10"	3.7	4.4	5.1	6.2	7.0	8.8	10.6	12.3	14.1	15.8	17.6
12.5"	10"	5.3	6.3	7.3	8.8	10.0	12.5	15.0	17.5	20.0	22.5	25.0
14"	10"	5.8	7.0	8.2	9.8	11.2	14.0	16.8	19.6	22.4	25.2	28.0
15½"	10"	6.5	7.8	9.0	10.9	12.4	15.5	18.6	21.7	24.8	27.9	31.0
18"	10"	7.5	9.0	10.5	12.6	14.4	18.0	21.6	25.2	28.8	32.4	36.0
22"	10"	9.2	11.0	12.8	15.4	17.6	22.0	26.4	30.8	35.2	39.6	44.0
24"	10"	10.0	12.0	14.0	16.8	19.2	24.0	28.8	33.6	38.4	43.2	48.0
26"	10"	10.8	13.0	15.2	18.2	20.8	26.0	31.2	36.4	41.6	46.8	52.0
30"	10"	12.5	15.0	17.5	21.0	24.0	30.0	36.0	42.0	48.0	54.0	60.0
36"	10"	15.0	18.0	21.0	25.2	28.8	36.0	43.2	50.4	57.6	64.8	72.0
40"	10"	16.7	20.0	23.3	28.0	32.0	40.0	48.0	56.0	64.0	72.0	80.0

(Projection Distance in Feet)

Figure 6-22. These screen-size tables are included to provide opportunity to study the relationship of the focal length of any given lens to a specified kind of projected image at a given distance. Image is approximated in these tables by the size of screen recommended. *Courtesy Da-Lite Screen Co., Warsaw, Indiana.*

OPAQUE PROJECTION
APERTURE WIDTH—10"

LENS FOCAL LENGTH	SQUARE SCREEN SIZE						
	50"	60"	70"	84"	8'	10'	12'
18"	7.5	9.0	10.5	12.6	14.4	18.0	21.6
22"	9.2	11.0	12.8	15.4	17.6	22.0	26.4
26"	10.8	13.0	15.2	18.2	20.8	26.0	31.2

(Project'n Distance in Feet)

INSTAMATIC SLIDES APERTURE WIDTH—26.5MM

LENS FOCAL LENGTH		SCREEN WIDTH								
		40"	50"	60"	70"	84"	8'	9'	10'	12'
1.4"	Projection Distance in Feet	4.5	5.5	6.8	7.8	9.4	10.8	12.1	13.5	16.2
2"		6.4	8.0	9.6	11.2	13.5	15.4	17.3	19.2	23.1
3"		9.6	12.0	14.4	16.8	20.2	23.1	25.9	28.8	34.6
4"		12.8	16.0	19.2	22.4	26.9	30.7	34.6	38.4	46.1
5"		16.0	19.9	24.0	27.9	33.6	38.4	43.2	48.0	57.6
6½"		20.8	26.0	31.2	36.3	43.6	49.9	56.1	62.4	74.8
7"		22.4	28.0	33.6	39.1	47.0	53.7	60.4	67.1	80.6
8½"		27.2	33.9	40.8	47.5	57.1	65.2	73.4	81.5	97.8
9"		28.8	35.9	43.2	50.3	60.4	69.1	77.7	86.3	103.6
10"		31.9	39.9	48.0	55.9	67.1	76.7	86.3	95.9	115.1
11"		35.1	43.9	52.8	61.5	73.9	84.4	94.9	105.5	126.6
12½"		39.9	49.9	60.0	69.9	83.9	95.9	107.9	119.9	143.8
15½"		49.5	61.9	74.3	86.7	104.0	118.9	133.8	148.6	178.3
20"		63.9	79.9	95.9	111.8	134.3	153.4	172.6	191.7	230.1

REGULAR 8MM MOTION PICTURES APERTURE WIDTH—.172"

LENS FOCAL LENGTH		SCREEN WIDTH								
		40"	50"	60"	70"	84"	8'	9'	10'	12'
12.7mm—½"	Projection Distance in Feet	9.7	12.1	14.6	16.9	20.4	23.3	26.2	29.1	34.9
14.28mm—⁹⁄₁₆"		10.9	13.6	16.4	19.1	22.9	26.2	29.4	32.1	39.2
17mm—⁴³⁄₆₄"		13.0	16.2	19.5	22.7	27.3	31.2	35.1	39.0	46.7
18.5mm—⁴⁵⁄₆₄"		14.1	17.6	21.2	24.7	29.7	33.9	38.2	42.4	50.9
19mm—¾"		14.5	18.2	21.8	25.5	30.5	34.9	39.2	43.6	52.3
22mm—⁵⁵⁄₆₄"		16.8	21.0	25.2	29.4	35.3	40.3	45.4	50.4	60.5
25.4mm—1"		19.3	24.2	29.1	33.9	40.7	46.5	52.3	58.2	69.8
27mm—1¹⁄₁₆"		20.6	25.7	31.0	36.0	43.3	49.5	55.7	61.8	74.2
28mm—1³⁄₃₂"		21.4	26.7	32.1	37.4	44.9	51.3	57.7	64.1	77.0
32mm—1¼"		24.2	30.3	36.3	42.4	50.9	58.2	65.4	72.7	87.3

LENS FOCAL LENGTH		SCREEN WIDTH								
		40"	50"	60"	70"	84"	8'	9'	10'	12'
12.7mm—½"	Projection Distance in Feet	7.9	9.9	11.9	13.8	16.6	19.0	21.4	23.7	28.4
14.28mm—⁹⁄₁₆"		8.9	11.1	13.4	15.5	18.7	21.3	24.0	26.7	32.0
17mm—⁴³⁄₆₄"		10.6	13.2	15.9	18.5	22.2	25.4	28.6	31.8	38.1
18.5mm—⁴⁵⁄₆₄"		11.5	14.4	17.3	20.1	24.2	27.6	31.1	34.6	41.4
19mm—¾"		11.8	14.8	17.8	20.7	24.8	28.4	31.9	35.5	42.6
22mm—⁵⁵⁄₆₄"		13.7	17.1	20.6	23.9	28.8	32.9	37.0	41.1	49.3
25.4mm—1"		15.8	19.7	23.7	27.6	33.2	38.0	42.7	47.4	56.9
27mm—1¹⁄₁₆"		16.8	21.0	25.2	29.4	35.3	40.3	45.4	50.4	60.5
28mm—1³⁄₃₂"		17.4	21.8	26.2	30.5	36.6	41.8	47.0	52.3	62.7
32mm—1¼"		19.9	24.9	29.9	34.8	41.8	47.8	53.8	59.8	71.7

3¼"x4" SLIDES (LANTERN)—APERTURE WIDTH—3.0"

LENS FOCAL LENGTH		SCREEN WIDTH											
		50"	60"	70"	84"	8'	9'	10'	12'	14'	16'	18'	20'
6"	Projection Distance in Feet	8.3	10.0	11.7	14.0	16.9	18.0	20.0	24.0	28.0	32.0	36.0	40.0
6½"		9.0	10.8	12.6	15.2	17.3	19.5	21.7	26.0	30.3	34.7	39.0	42.3
8"		11.1	13.3	15.5	18.7	21.3	24.0	26.7	32.0	37.3	42.7	48.0	53.3
8½"		11.8	14.2	16.5	19.8	22.7	25.5	28.3	34.0	39.7	45.3	51.0	56.7
10"		13.9	16.7	19.4	23.3	26.7	30.0	33.3	40.0	46.7	53.3	60.0	66.7
12"		16.7	20.0	23.3	28.0	32.0	36.0	40.0	48.0	56.0	64.0	72.0	80.0
12½"		17.4	20.8	24.3	29.2	33.3	37.5	41.7	50.0	58.3	66.7	75.0	83.3
14"		19.4	23.3	27.2	32.7	37.3	42.0	46.7	56.0	65.3	74.7	84.0	93.3
15"		20.8	25.0	29.2	35.0	40.0	45.0	50.0	60.0	70.0	80.0	90.0	100.0
15½"		21.5	25.8	30.1	36.2	41.3	46.5	51.7	62.0	72.3	82.7	93.0	103.3
16"		22.2	26.7	31.1	37.3	42.7	48.0	53.3	64.0	74.7	85.3	96.0	106.7
18"		25.0	30.0	35.0	42.0	48.0	54.0	60.0	72.0	84.0	96.0	108.0	120.0
20"		27.8	33.3	38.9	46.7	53.3	60.0	66.7	80.0	83.3	106.7	120.0	133.3
22"		30.6	36.7	42.8	51.3	58.7	66.0	73.3	88.0	102.7	117.3	132.0	146.7
24"		33.3	40.0	46.7	56.0	64.0	72.0	80.0	96.0	112.0	128.0	144.0	160.0
26"		36.1	43.3	50.6	60.7	69.3	78.0	86.7	104.0	121.3	138.7	156.0	173.3

35MM SINGLE FRAME FILM STRIPS—APERTURE WIDTH—.885"

LENS FOCAL LENGTH		SCREEN WIDTH												
		40"	50"	60"	70"	84"	8'	9'	10'	12'	14'	16'	18'	20'
3"	Projection Distance in Feet	11.3	14.1	16.9	19.8	23.7	27.1	30.5	33.9	40.7	47.5	54.2	61.0	67.8
4"		15.1	18.8	22.6	26.4	31.6	36.2	40.7	45.2	54.2	63.3	72.3	81.4	90.4
5"		18.8	23.5	28.2	32.9	39.5	45.2	50.8	56.5	67.8	79.1	90.4	101.7	113.0
6"		22.6	28.2	33.9	39.5	47.5	54.2	61.0	67.8	81.4	95.0	108.5	122.0	135.6
7"		26.4	32.9	39.5	46.1	55.4	63.3	71.2	79.1	94.9	110.7	126.6	142.4	158.2
8"		30.1	37.7	45.2	52.7	63.3	72.3	81.4	90.4	108.5	126.5	144.6	162.7	180.8

16MM MOTION PICTURES—APERTURE WIDTH—.380"

LENS FOCAL LENGTH		SCREEN WIDTH																	
		40"	50"	60"	70"	84"	8'	9'	10'	12'	14'	16'	18'	20'	22'	24'	26'	28'	30'
⅝"	Projection Distance in Feet	5.5	6.9	8.2	9.6	11.5	13.2	14.8	16.4	19.7	23.0	26.3	29.6	32.9	36.2	39.5	42.8	46.1	49.3
1"		8.8	11.0	13.2	15.4	18.4	21.1	23.7	26.3	31.6	36.8	42.1	47.4	52.6	57.9	63.2	68.4	73.7	78.9
1½"		13.2	16.4	19.7	23.0	27.6	31.6	35.8	39.5	47.4	55.3	63.2	71.1	78.9	86.8	94.7	102.6	110.5	118.4
2"		17.5	21.9	26.3	30.7	36.8	42.1	47.4	52.6	63.2	73.7	84.2	94.7	105.3	115.8	126.3	136.8	147.4	157.9
2½"		21.9	27.4	32.9	38.4	46.1	52.6	59.2	65.8	78.9	92.1	105.3	118.4	131.6	144.7	157.9	171.1	184.2	197.4
2¾"		24.0	30.2	36.2	42.2	50.7	57.9	65.1	72.4	86.8	101.3	115.8	130.3	144.7	159.2	173.7	188.2	202.6	217.1
3"		26.3	32.9	39.5	46.1	55.3	63.2	71.1	78.9	94.7	110.5	126.3	142.1	157.9	173.7	189.5	205.3	221.1	236.8
3½"		30.7	38.4	46.1	53.7	64.5	73.7	82.4	92.1	110.5	128.9	147.4	165.8	184.2	202.6	221.1	239.5	257.9	276.3
4"		35.1	43.9	52.6	61.4	73.7	84.2	94.7	105.3	126.3	147.4	168.4	189.5	210.5	231.6	252.6	273.7	294.7	315.8

PRINTED IN U.S.A. 6/1/66

2. The closer a projector is moved toward the screen, the smaller will be the picture if the focal length of the lens is kept constant. (Is the effect of moving the projector away from the screen obvious?)

In considering the use of special lenses, media specialists should be aware of some of their limitations. A projected picture using the same projector and lamp becomes brighter as it gets smaller and less bright as it becomes larger. Therefore, a picture may be made only as large as the details of the pictorial content will permit, or as large as the power of the lamp will permit.

Classroom Layout of Projection Arrangement. In the preceding pages a number of important factors have been discussed that contribute greatly to increased use of classroom experiences with audiovisual media. It is now time to relate many of these factors to a classroom unit and to consider aspects of arrangement for carrying on learning activity based on, or making significant use of, projected materials. We can suggest no single arrangement that is best or universal. Neither is it essential to take sides in the issue of whether or not a corner-located projection screen is to be preferred to a front-wall mounted and centered screen. The fact is that we may need more than one projection screen in each of our major learning areas. We may, however, substitute a larger than usual screen, large enough—even covering most of the front wall—to accept two or more projected images, for comparison purposes. It may be advantageous to provide either permanently mounted or portable rear-projection screens to provide for the kinds of presentations that the program and the desired media demand.

The modern-day classroom has been designed for groups of varying sizes and for many and very specific uses that sometimes demand special conditions. It is also true that the shape of any given classroom may not only differ from other classrooms in a given building, but it may be altered at will by operable walls being opened or closed. However, on the basis of viewing needs of the learner—especially as the learner is a member of a group of pupils that will observe and participate together in a learning venture using a projected medium—we can formulate a set of desirable circumstances that we can predict will satisfy the minimum requirements. In stating these recommendations we shall assume that the learning space is itself favorably designed, that the learners are facing a projection screen and that they are arranged or clustered near the projection axis—in other words, the learners are seated within an included viewing angle that is appropriate for the screen fabric being used.

1. If one projection screen of desirable size is available, mount it on the front wall dead center, either on 15- to 26-inch wall-extension brackets or suspend it from the ceiling near the front wall to provide the opportunity to tilt the screen by tying it to the bottom of the chalkboard tray or some other fixture. If a second screen is to be used, mount it permanently in a corner for a specific projection medium such as an overhead projector, and meet the requirements for the particular medium to be used. If rear projection is to be used, make sure that the projected image size is adequate for the group of pupils that must view and react to the content.

2. Flat-top, movable student desks should be positioned within the total recommended viewing angle, with the first row no closer than 2W (two times the width of the projected picture), and the last row of viewers being no farther away than 6W from the screen. Also, no student should have to be seated outside an acceptable viewing limit. The 2W and 6W rules hold true for rear-screen projection surfaces as well as front-projection screens, but not for television tubes. In the case of television viewing the acceptable general rule is 4W for proximity and 12W for maximum distance of viewers.

3. An aisle should be provided for the placement of the projectors in such a way that they may be used in suitable combination (motion picture, 2 × 2 inch slides, filmstrips), or projectors should be placed on 42-inch high movable projections stands with suitable focal-length lenses for the required picture size on the screen. Remote control cords should be provided whenever possible.

4. Screens should be mounted high enough above the chalkboard so that when they are rolled down, the bottom does not extend below the head level of seated pupils. Thus an unobstructed line-of-sight from projector to bottom of screen will eliminate all shadows caused by pupils' heads being in the way. (This means that the top of the screen will in every case be high enough so that the full usable area of the

screen can be covered by one or more images without obstruction.)

5. Because recorded sound components are so important in the communication processes in classrooms, and because teachers use audio media both separately and as adjuncts of motion pictures, slides, and filmstrips, attention must be given to the problem of sound intelligibility. Media program directors, in charge of facilities for teachers and of the design of learning areas, should see to it that all instruments employing sound are properly located, or that extension loudspeakers are positioned centrally, or in ceiling corners so as to beam sound toward pupils for effortless listening. We speak, of course, of group activities with open-group listening as the procedure. (Large and small groups—and individuals too—may of course be in the situation where sound is not radiated openly, but through headsets, but in these situations it is hardly necessary for the teacher to be in face-to-face control, since the medium is in control, as we have described before.) Caution should be exercised in attempting to use central sound system loudspeakers for projection units. Quality may be seriously impaired because of incompatibility.

Tape recorders and record players should be positioned for best results at front center when used alone, or near front corners when used with projection media. Controlling the sound volume and frequency emphasis is a matter of teacher skill and judgment that should receive consideration in in-service education bulletins.

6. As a major point of emphasis, we must not lose sight of the fact that modern classrooms must provide space for other media such as books and documentary materials in the print-medium category, as well as models and other materials that have to be observed and manipulated. Hence, in addition to—and in relation to —projection arrangements, classroom spaces need to be used by individuals and groups in many kinds of problem-solving activity. To meet this condition effectively materials must be displayed, observed at close range, and handled or manipulated. Part of this problem is scheduling pupils for the required study activity. The use of tables for apparatus and models, globes, stands, map rails and rollers for maps, easels for charts, suspension wires and clips for pictures, and display cases all seem essential. Media program directors should not miss the point that the educational objective determines the nature of the activity, and this in turn requires a special set of arrangements. Whenever materials are suspended or displayed on walls or bulletin boards, they should permit eye-level observation.

7. For large-group spaces, one or two screens may serve instructional purposes well, however, in automated multimedia or multi-image installations, one large front- or rear-projection screen capable of accepting three or four projected images at once, plus a separate projection screen for an overhead projector, may be required. Such areas plus all special laboratory spaces, should be equipped to facilitate the learning activity for which they were designed in the first place. The media program director will need to provide advice and counsel for subject-matter specialists and learning-activity planners.

8. Rear-projection devices and other compact arrangements of several projectors combined in mobile or built-in units—often referred to as media modules—may be extremely satisfactory for small-group teaching stations. We must caution against the use of small image-projection devices, however, in medium- and large-size spaces. Media modules and other similar arrangements should never be recommended as a way to avoid the expense of installing suitable light-control systems.

We have considered classroom layout with special reference to projection screens and have emphasized the need for careful arrangements. Although many architects and other school planners are well aware of the need to provide for audiovisual equipment, we must assert that in too many of the designs developed, classroom conditions still do not favor projection installations. We can say with assurance that the larger the group for teacher presentations, the more urgent it is to make effective use of communication media. This is why we say that when operable walls are opened up, we need more than ever to maintain not lose favorable projection conditions.

Teaching Stations Without Walls. Open classroom teaching stations, with shelving or other storage facilities to separate one teaching station from an adjacent one, are not conducive to the use of media involving audio and pictorial elements for group listening and viewing. An

Figure 6-23. Two class groups at work on two sides of a so-called portable divider of book cases and supply cabinets. This new school was barely underway when this picture was taken. In this view we are able to discern few if any new media use arrangements. However, we are not afforded a view of the whole area. It does appear that a wall screen is to be mounted in the chalkboard area in each space. Can you identify the screen? Is there evidence of adequate light control? *Courtesy Edenvale School, Oak Grove School District, San Jose, California.*

exception occurs when student carrels are used for media presentation. In these cases walls are unnecessary because the students use headsets, which prevent the sound from carrying beyond the students' ears, and all needed video elements are presented by means of small television receivers, or by front- or rear-projection surfaces. Therefore, the room stays quiet even though audio equipment is being used. In cases of open planning, light control may pose another serious problem. Even indirect lighting, which is usually employed in such spaces, may provide damaging ambient rays on projection surfaces while in use in one area but not in the other.

Teaching Station Projection Booths. It is reasonable to assert that noise introduced into a teaching station may build up distractive influences that interfere seriously with learning activities. The motion picture projector is the principal offender. To a lesser degree, slide and overhead transparency projectors, with their cooling fans, may also contribute to raising the noise level in a given location. Some of the noise, however, is likely to be distributed unevenly, with mechanism noise from a motion

picture projector being at the rear of a room, and the overhead projector noise being concentrated at the front of the room. As media gain major prominence in instructional plans and procedures, school designers are increasingly recommending the construction of projection booths at the rear of classrooms as a means of noise control. It is obvious, however, that when rear-screen projection systems are installed, as we have pointed out, a space, generally much larger than a conventional projection booth must be included behind the screen. This area serves as a special kind of projection booth, and it is recommended in such installations that the rear screen surface be mounted in resilient, soundproofing material to prevent sound leaks. For front-screen projection then, we must either recommend that the planner include a projection booth that can serve two properly oriented classrooms simultaneously, or that he provide for a space at the rear of the room—or along the aisle—for projection units on mobile stands or on pedestals. Certainly we can rule out, on grounds of practicality, the building of projection booths in any but large teaching stations seating 75 pupils or more. A variety of possibilities exist for operating noise-making projectors without booth facilities. Pedestals can be treated with sound-absorbent material. Also, acoustic shields, similar to folding screens, can be arranged around a motion picture projector to muffle its noise. Whenever booths are utilized, the need for a technician inside the booth must be met. In cases where the remote control of projection equipment is handled from front-of-room podia, booths introduce difficulty in communication, since then an intercom system must be built into the system. Also, teachers—without help from technicians—will have to have keys handy to enter rear-of-room booths when unexpected trouble develops, such as a jammed slide projector, or a parted film splice. We therefore take the position that booths introduce complexity and inconvenience into most of the conditions in which media are generally used. When behind-the-scenes workers are generally available for large-group media presentations, it is doubtlessly desirable to free the teacher from anxieties arising from technical control. It can be readily seen that in large groups, only those near a noise-making device will be affected. In these cases, other factors such as visibility become paramount. When decisions are made regarding the incorporation of projection booths for front-screen projection, all of the factors need to be considered, not the least important of which is the level of technical support staff for continuous duty in the various stations.

Electronic Delivery of Media to Teaching Stations. Under existing limitations of cable connections inside school buildings and the fact that from central studios either one or more 12-channel coaxial-cables, or a 4-channel 2500 mHz low-power radiation system are the means of connecting school buildings, we see an urgent need for only high-priority use of the television medium. It seems obvious that if precious coaxial-cable space is to be preempted by the delivery of teaching activity that is basically under the control of the teacher anyway, the television medium is being relegated to substandard use in relation to its potential. In Chapter 10 we will discuss the curriculum needs for television and we will point out with due emphasis that television ought to be used for those significant contributions to teaching and learning that cannot be made in other ways.

We assert that television programing ought to make use of optimum teacher and media influence, combined in unique ways for maximum impact on formal instructional groups. It is logical and desirable to deliver such programs, loaded as they are with media excerpts or whole units, tied into a basal instructional package, and stored for repetitive use on videotape, by way of television. This constitutes prime usage for maximum instructional impact and, as such, deserves full access to the available channels to all teaching stations. There is one situation that may prove to be the exception to the recommendation we have just made—namely, the often crucial need to combine a number of class groups electronically into a single large group for media viewing. If, for example, a highly significant motion picture on a vital topic needs to be presented to 10 groups of 30 to 90 pupils each in grade 8 social studies, and if such groups were participating in an instructional systems arrangement where the film subject could not be circulated because of resulting delays in carrying on other scheduled learning tasks (as in laboratories and teaching-machine rooms), the motion picture could be electronically delivered to all groups simultaneously. If such a planned film-viewing activity could not be delivered by the television coaxial-cable as a simple transmission medium, a total of 10 film prints, 10 projectors, and 10 operators would have to be organized to implement projection within the same class hour. Timing is sometimes a critical factor for the particular instructional impact desired. These important matters are discussed in considerable depth in Chapters 10 and 11, on the subjects of television and instructional systems. However, we need to bear the concept of electronic delivery in mind, and the conditions under which it is used, as we consider media-use arrangements at teaching stations. It appears at this stage of technological development that electronic delivery ought to be used, if it is used at all, within a school-building unit only, where multiple, 12-channel coaxial cables can be employed, leaving one cable available for incoming instructional television programs from sources outside of the school building itself.

We have already referred briefly to the location of study carrels in classrooms and in large-group spaces. Each of these individual study stations of course needs its own projection surfaces, possibly both front- and rear-projection types. But we shall deal with this subject as we shall deal also with the subject of television and instructional systems in later chapters. At this point we turn to the discussion of a number of important considerations for the use of media in classrooms and in other kinds of learning spaces.

Good Air and Acoustics

Architects must not place ventilating ducts in any place that will interfere with the mounting of projection screens within the central area of the front wall. Ventilating ducts should be placed so that wall-display areas and chalkboards may be arranged at eye level. All who are concerned with effective instruction must call for the best decision possible regarding the ventilation problem in each classroom. Whether the gravity system or some other quietly operating mechanical system is finally installed, it must function adequately during periods when drapes or other light-control devices are closed to darken the room. It should be remembered that in the case of special projection rooms, the ventilation problem may be entirely different than that of a regular classroom where, perhaps, the room will have drapes closed for much shorter periods of time. There seems to be agreement that a good standard for air exchange is 15 cubic feet of air per minute for each pupil, with proper room temperatures and humidity being maintained continuously. Wherever drape systems are used in connection with window ventilating systems, they should be hung from the ceiling approximately 18 inches from the window to permit some flow of incoming air when the drapes are closed.

No one knows better than a teacher how unendurable the air can become in a schoolroom, and how impossible it is to conduct a vital and creative activity when it is too hot, too humid, too noisy, or too smelly. At our technological peak we ought to have the full benefits of engineering knowledge, and air conditioning is possibly one of the vital requirements for the effective use of media. In automated study carrels with television, automatic and electronically controlled projectors, we will be generating more heat than ever before, and we will be incorporating large groups for considerable periods of time in our learning spaces. It appears obvious that we need the environmental comfort, flexibility, and control that air conditioning lends to the learning situation. In his noteworthy article, John A. Shaver,[2] architect, points out that

. . . clustered space is taking on more meaning with the increased acceptance of air conditioning. Air conditioning means that learning spaces need no longer be related directly to the exterior to provide good environment. . . . If air conditioning is used, obviously there will be more freedom of choice in developing design concepts and in organizing space relationships to implement the teaching-learning processes.

In the effort to improve general learning conditions, and to improve the intelligibility of reproduced sound, acoustic treatment should be considered. As a minimum, the ceilings should be acoustically treated to subdue the noise of regular classroom activities which, in the modern program, include multi-group action. Acoustic planning of the entire building is also important in controlling the transmission of noise, from corridor to classrooms, from gymnasiums and band rehearsal rooms to other nearby learning areas, and from one classroom to another.

In discussing the significance of sound isolation, Alan C. Green,[3] Professor of Architecture of Rensselaer Polytechnic Institute, makes the following statements:

To be totally effective, any sound barrier must be airtight. Even the smallest openings, such as open joints or cracks, electrical outlet boxes, back to back, or keyholes, will greatly reduce the sound-isolating value of the partition. . . . A hole of only one square inch in 100 square feet of wall having a 40-decibel transmission loss rating will "leak" as much sound as all the rest of the wall.

It is because of a combination of deficiencies, like mass, stiffness and most importantly, numerous leaks, that until very recently most reasonably priced flexible or folding partitions have been relatively ineffective as sound barriers. In the past several years, however, this situation has improved. Some manufacturers have developed new products which

[2] John A. Shaver, "Build the School to Fit the Program," *Audiovisual Instruction*, Vol. 7, No. 8, October 1962, pp. 518–519.

[3] Alan C. Green (ed.), *Educational Facilities with New Media* (Prepared under a contract with the U.S. Office of Education) (Washington, D.C.: The Department of Audiovisual Instruction of the NEA, 1966), p. C-16.

are better designed and engineered, with careful attention to a better choice of materials and thorough edge sealing, resulting in greatly improved acoustical performance.

Display Area and Chalkboard Space

Bulletin boards and other display areas need to be provided in ample quantity also, and even though there is no single standard except the specific demands of proposed instructional activities, the architect and the director of media services should be concerned with providing well-lighted, uncluttered wall spaces for display activities. Adequate map rails are available that provide devices for mounting charts and hanging cloth-display sections, and these should be recommended for use with chalkboards as a minimum installation. To provide for future increases in display activities, many curriculum workers and classroom design specialists indicate that the use of up to a third of the free eye-level wall space is justified for display purposes. A common practice is to provide for flexibility of display areas by using pegboards, variable area chalkboards, demountable sections of pegboard, tackboard, or chalkboard. Display areas should be located at a convenient height for the pupils to use them. Related to classroom display is the additional need for corridor display cases and hallway bulletin boards.

At least 20 feet of modern, light-colored chalkboard are likely to be needed in every conventional-size classroom, with less in small- and large-group spaces, and authorities recommend that the out-moded blackboards be replaced.

Central Sound-System Facilities

The media program director is often called upon by school-building committees to give counsel regarding a central sound system. Such advice should be based on careful thinking about the uses proposed for the system. Central sound systems, while including tape and record-playing equipment, should not in any way prevent the purchase and use of other tape and record-playing equipment to be handled in the classroom by pupils and teachers. Also, it should be remembered that not all communications from a central office will be directed to the student body. Hence, first and foremost, a telephone system should be provided separately or in combination with a central sound system. Although no standard set of specifications can be suitable for all schools, the following list of criteria may serve as an example of a recommendatian that could be prepared by a director of media services. Local conditions, needs, and decisions will demand modifications in the following set of suggested specifications:

Manufacturer: _____
Model: _____

1. Two-channel models with an additional intercom channel built in as standard equipment.
2. Central console for 45 rooms: (Model _____).
Features to be incorporated:
  1. 50-watt program amplifiers (minimum).
  2. Annunciator indication of room calling the console.
  3. Three low-impedance microphone inputs at console.
  4. Input and output for tape recorder.
  5. Remote telephone line input.
  6. Room pickup for transmission throughout the sound system.
  7. High fidelity AM-FM tuner.
  8. Dual-speed tape recorder (Model————) to be substituted for record player in console.
  9. Classroom privacy feature (two-position selector switch) to be installed in each room.
  10. Telephone handsets as an additional feature of the central sound system, to be installed in each room where a speaker has been located.

Consideration of the functions to be served by school-building communication systems may lead to economy through combination of wiring systems in a single conduit. Kilbride,[4] writing in *School Planning*, pointed out that

. . . with proper advance planning, it is now possible to include in a single set of conduits or raceway, the necessary wiring and basic provisions for six complete systems. . . . Secondary emergency alarm with voice communication for instructions and panic control.

[4] Robert E. Kilbride, "Six Communication Systems in a Single Installation," *School Planning*, Vol. 2, No. 5, October–November 1957, pp. 4–11.

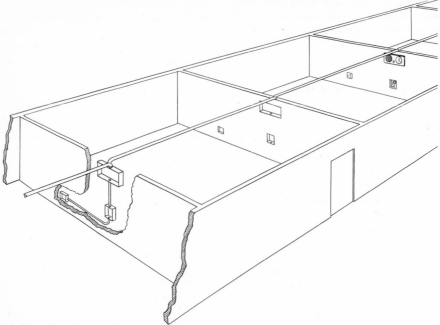

Figure 6-24. This diagram shows the single raceway plan for six communication systems. What modifications in this layout ought to be suggested for proper projection-screen placement? For convenient use of projection equipment? *Courtesy School Planning Magazine, Chicago.*

... The modern system also includes fire sensing and detection circuits. ... Program clock systems with a master clock and secondary clocks in the various rooms and an audible signal to indicate class-break intervals. ... Central sound and program distribution systems, often including an intercom for two-way communications. ... Automatic telephone system. ... Television distribution to the classrooms of "off-the-air" pick-ups from commercial or educational TV stations, and for internal distribution of live demonstrations or audio-visual teaching aids from the school's own studio. ... School-to-home equipment.

The director of media services needs to take a long look to the future, especially in planning communication facilities for new school plants.

Facilities for Media Use in Special Learning Areas

In addition to classrooms a number of other learning areas in the school ought to be equipped for the efficient use of audiovisual media. These areas are the auditorium, gymnasium, cafeteria, and library. Each area needs to be considered in the light of its own program of activity.

The School Auditorium

We can no longer consider the *auditorium* as a place where students are gathered for periodic assembly programs. These spaces now must serve new and additional instructional uses, and these uses determine the shape, size, and multiple-purpose flexibility now characteristic of modern school-building design. Movable, sound-proof walls can divide the total available space into a number of smaller spaces for formal instructional purposes and, as has been emphasized previously, each of these spaces, in addition to the total space, must be equipped to facilitate the utilization of instructional media. This means that separate or connecting power-supply conduits, microphone lines, public address and light-control systems, special central-control lecterns, front- and/or rear-projection screen surfaces, and listening-response connections at seats (when equipped as independent stations) will have to be planned, specified, and provided in accordance with envisoned programs. In addition to these arrangements, we can now consider auditoriums as large and efficient learning spaces that may be flexible in nature, control, and use, or they

Figure 6-25. Many modern schools are designed with flexible auditoriums. Often these are planned for serious instructional activities. The top picture shows the divisible auditorium of the North Division Niles Community High Schools, using Modernfold Coil-Wal. The architectural company was Orput-Orput and Associates. One Coil-Wal unit is shown closed, the other open. Projection booth lights are in the rear of the small section, and the main booth aperture is directly over the right stairway. The bottom picture shows three operable walls open for conversion to full auditorium. Can you identify the projection platform for each of the four teaching auditoriums, and the full complement of equipment? *Courtesy Public Schools, Penfield, New York.*

may be designed with specific media uses in mind where the shape, size, and equipment cannot and should not be altered. Viewing the school auditorium in this light it can be seen that recommendations relative to the following important facilities for media use need to be formulated and transmitted to school planners and architects.

Projection Control Stations: Booth, Niche, and Podium. For small auditoriums seating 300 or less, an elevated projection niche is recommended, but for larger auditoriums a

projection booth is desirable. However, regardless of which is needed, the following items should be specified: (a) switches for control of auditorium lights, motorized screen, and motorized stage curtain; (b) stage-to-booth buzzer signals; and (c) heavy-duty electric current outlets on separate 30-ampere lines. In cases where niches are built, the equipment must be raised up for over-the-head projection to the screen by means of a platform, or the niche itself should be elevated. The niche should be at least 10 feet long and 6 feet deep to permit the convenient operation of several projectors in one program. When projection booths are incorporated in the auditorium plan, the booth should be designed with an adequate number of soundproof apertures for projection and observation, with special exhaust fans for arc projectors, with regular ventilation devices, with sound-monitoring loudspeaker and sound controls for the public address system, and with provisions for feeding sound from tape or disks into the auditorium's sound-amplification system. Projection booths should also provide film rewind and workbench space. We should remember, however, that in cases where projection equipment needs to be automatically controlled, special control stations become necessary. Projection equipment may sometimes have to be located in a projection area in back of a large, rear-projection screen surface. Such equipment may then have to be controlled from a podium under the control of the presenter.

Media Equipment for the Auditorium. For modern-day uses of auditoriums a variety of equipment is essential. Such equipment units as the following are likely to be regularly needed: sound motion picture projectors, a combination slide projector with inter-changeable condenser chests and objective lenses for standard and miniature slides as well as automatic 2 × 2 inch slide projectors with appropriate focal-length lenses, and an overhead transparency projector. However, for large-screen presentations in the larger sized auditoriums seating more than 500 persons, the extra illumination of heavy-duty projectors such as arc projectors or other projectors using high-output lamps is necessary. Sound-producing equipment units should be connected through special input jacks to the auditorium's central sound system, and microphone input jacks should be located in those sound-producing areas such as the stage and the projection stations.

In this listing of commonly needed media equipment for auditoriums, we should also point out the obvious instructional demand for television viewing facilities. Although this medium is the subject of a later chapter, we will mention at this point that built-in conduits for TV coverage by individual receivers or by large-screen projection television equipment should be planned for in advance. The required equipment ought to be provided at the time the building is completed—or at a later date, as the situation dictates. As we have already mentioned, in some auditoriums the media equipment units mentioned above, except the overhead projector, may need to be automatically controlled.

Projection Screens for the Auditorium. What has been said before about projection screens and the placement of viewers applies as well to the auditorium; however, in the case of very large auditoriums the immense screen size called for is impractical because the high illumination demanded is unavailable with the usual 16 mm projectors. CinemaScope screens need not be curved if the throw is in excess of 50 feet. This permits using a motorized roll-up type of screen thus saving a great deal of stage "sky" space. Large frame-type screens cannot be easily taken down once they have been installed, and stage activities are therefore permanently restricted. This is hardly a problem because screens are available in a wide variety of sizes. For example, electrically operated roll-up screens are made up in stock sizes up to 20 × 20 foot size, and rope-and-pulley roller-type screens are made up in a variety of sizes up to 12 × 30 foot and 30 × 30 foot sizes—large enough to take care of almost any school-projection needs. School materials presently available do not demand wide-screen provisions, but large screens become a necessity for multiple-image projection. It should also be remembered that if loudspeakers are to be located behind the screen, the screen must be of the perforated-fabric type. We have already referred to rear-projection screens and automated equipment units for projection, and we should emphasize this provision as being important for one or more of the spaces in any large-group learning area. As we will say again, auditoriums may be several in number for specific purposes, or designed to accommodate an assembly of the entire student body. One or more of the maneuverable areas and smaller auditoriums ought to be equipped with rear-projection facilities or, as a minimum, the appropriate spaces behind walls ought to be planned for future adaptation to such uses.

Auditorium Wiring Provisions. The flexibility of auditorium facilities will be increased if heavy-duty electrical outlets are placed near the front of the auditorium for setting up opaque and overhead projectors near the stage. Such lines should have separate fuses so as not to interfere with lighting and other power needs. Microphone lines, of which there should be several on stage and at each projection station, and amplifier to loudspeaker lines must not be mixed with power supply lines; hence ample conduits must be provided. Television outlets need also to be provided; hence conduits should be included that connect master antenna and the closed-circuit originating studio in the building (if one is included). In large auditoriums an outlet for large-screen TV projection is also a necessity. When special media uses are planned for some portions of or all of the auditorium area, additional wiring and power supply may be needed. In any specified area it may be essential to provide a conduit system to supply each seat, for example, with "dial access" to remote media sources, individual amplifier and headset connections and an electrical outlet. An entirely different wiring system may have to be installed to connect automatic projectors in booths and niches at the rear, or with behind-the-stage projection areas, in the case of rear-projection screens.

Light-Control and Lighting. What has been said earlier about light control applies as well to the auditorium. Now, however, we must consider that in view of technological developments, light-control systems in the auditorium may have to be partially controllable from an additional station such as the lectern, now more properly referred to as a podium. Here an instructor may not only operate the light system for projection but may also control a battery of projectors with prearranged program sequences using a number of media.

Sound Engineering. No media service director, unless he is an acoustic design expert, should undertake to recommend the pattern of loudspeakers or make other critical decisions about design. Acoustical treatment, the decision to employ either high-level, single-source, or low-level, multiple-source sound systems, and the appropriate location of loudspeakers are matters for experts in this engineering field to study and decide upon. The modern auditoriums with flexible areas may now require more than one sound system.

The Gymnasium

The gymnasium is another important learning-activity space that too often goes unnoticed when specifying provisions to facilitate audio-visual methods. Gymnasiums need conveniently located electric-power outlets to supply projectors and record players and tape recorders for instructional and community events. The placement of such electrical outlets will be determined by the shape and size of the activity space; however, power outlets near the center of the floor as well as at the sides of the room are important. Public address systems in large, single, or split gymnasium facilities should be provided for by locating microphone inputs at positions where band leaders, coaches, or instructors are likely to have to stand. Hence ¾-inch conduits should be specified as necessary. Light-control systems, as previously discussed, should also be considered and recommended. Appropriate sections of the gymnasium should be arranged for projection activities, and screens of suitable size should be painted on the wall (a good quality flat white paint will provide a suitable projection surface), or a portable screen should be provided. Wall-mounted screens may interfere with gym activities and they are almost certain to suffer damage.

Cafeterias

The demand for flexible-use space in the modern school is so great that a large cafeteria space normally used only during lunch hours can also be used for a variety of instructional and community purposes. Many of these instructional uses may demand the use of audio-visual media. For example, the cafeteria can be used for large-group viewing of television programs either from open- or closed-circuit sources, rehearsals, group meetings, club activities, community groups, student committee meetings, study and make-up work, of both independent and group nature. Hence provision for television outlets, screens, light-control systems, electrical outlets, and acoustic treatment will extend their usefulness in significant ways beyond the purposes traditionally recognized. Local conditions and plans for these spaces should thus be looked at in the light of other curriculum uses, and especially, as far as the media director is concerned, in the light of possible audiovisual media methods. It would be far wiser to plan such uses as are feasible and provide the requisite facilities than to wait and add the necessary fixtures at a later time.

Figure 6-26. In Wilbur Wright Junior High School Library there are 116 carrels for study purposes, 28 of which are wired for listening to audio-program tapes on the console. *Courtesy Public Schools, Munster, Indiana.*

Some schools today may be able to provide a catering service, and may utilize portable cafeteria service units that will be moved on schedule into other general multi-purpose areas. However these plans are developed, it is advisable to make full effective instructional use of all areas that are idle—but do not necessarily have to be—during substantial portions of the day.

The School Library

As has been repeatedly emphasized, the school library should be designed to serve the instructional program, and in the light of new methods, library services are undergoing and have undergone drastic change. School libraries often provide a one-stop instructional media service for teachers and students. Audiovisual media materials and equipment are checked in and out daily. In other schools the school library and the audiovisual media service center are maintained as separately organized units. We shall deal in considerable depth with the problems of organizing and operating the school's media services in later chapters, but at this point we will focus our attention on the kinds of facilities we need to provide if the school library is to be a place where school groups can make use of the media they need for instructional purposes.

For our present purposes we must emphasize that the library must serve increasing numbers of pupils in both individualized, small-group, and large-group activities of a formal and serious nature, in a concentrated fashion scarcely known before. Libraries will need a special media-equipped, multi-purpose teaching station, work rooms, and independent study carrels, not only of the book-reading type, but also for using other media under remote-control arrangements, storage spaces, flexible-arrangement conference rooms, large reading areas and administrative areas. On the subject of using all of the carriers of knowledge according to needs of the individual student in the library, Ellsworth and Wagener formulated the following list:

He may take a book home for study.
He may sit down and read on the spot.

Figure 6-27. The top view shows a portion of the Nova Junior-Senior High School Resource Center for Language Arts with the charge desk and the micro-form reading equipment shelf in the background. We shall refer to this again in Chapter 12. The right and left pictures show two views of the school library in the Penfield High School. *Courtesy Nova Dissemination Project, Nova Schools, Fort Lauderdale, Florida; and the Public Schools, Penfield, New York.*

He may use the reference collection to verify a date, look up the population of a city, or read a summary of a novel.

He may want to take notes as he reads.

He may want to go into a small group discussion room where he can discuss a book with others, or even practice reading out loud.

He may need to ask questions of librarians or teachers about what he reads.

He may want to use machines—typewriters, calculating machines, teaching machines, phonograph record players, etc.

He may want to take a book to a classroom or a laboratory.

He may want to stretch out in a lounge chair and read in a more "horizontal" manner, as he would at home.

Each of these types of use calls for different kinds of space, equipment, and furniture.[5]

[5] Ralph E. Ellsworth, and Hobart D. Wagener, *The School Library, Facilities for Independent Study in the Secondary School* (New York: Educational Facilities Laboratories, 1963), p. 53.

When working alone, individuals need carrels that are so equipped that media may be dialled or scheduled from remote sources or operated by the student at will, or they work in groups where small- or large-group spaces are equipped with media devices that are operated by technicians or by the pupils themselves. We therefore need to provide sufficient electrical power to the many individual study stations that are needed and also to provide appropriate light-control systems, electrical power, and either portable or wall-mounted projection screens for media use in groups. Microfilm reading, prerecorded tape listening centers, television viewing and the use of many other audiovisual media in programed format are just a few examples of the activities that require special facilities and careful advance planning.

The spaces and media facilities we have mentioned have not stressed another significant aspect of library services, and this aspect has to

Figure 6-28. These clusters of carrels were activated in 1966. They are supplied with videotape and audio programs by cable from the University's own programing and television control center. These carrels are located in the library. See also Chapter 11. *Courtesy Oral Roberts University, Tulsa, Oklahoma.*

do with teaching library skills to all students in a given school building. Hence we should point out the need for television recording facilities that would permit the head librarian to make videotapes of special, visualized presentations, and to use in addition all modern media for distributing such presentations either to selected classrooms throughout the school or for that matter throughout a school district. Thus the capability to originate television programs should be built into the library classroom and into one or more library areas by means of two-way television outlets. The reader should refer for detailed discussions on this subject to Chapter 10. We have also pointed out in Chapter 12 that library skill subjects lend themselves to the use of instructional systems, and therefore, media equipment and facilities will be urgently needed in implementing such programs.

Independent Study Carrels

Earlier in this chapter we referred to the over-all influence of the effort to individualize instruction with regard to the need to provide

an appropriate physical environment for media utilization in the schools. We shall refer to media facilities for independent study in Chapter 11 dealing with instructional systems. It remains for us at this point to emphasize that the study stations or carrels where each pupil may listen, interact, write his responses, view projected images from a slide to a TV program from videotape, must be equipped with the required devices and must be electrically powered. Thus we can see the obvious necessity for power supply lines in underfloor grids and conduits, raceways on the walls, or in wiremold on the floor. The second essential is that the electronic carrels must either be equipped with their own operable equipment units and media materials such as programed booklets, books, slides, tapes and filmstrips for each student to use as he chooses, or they must be connected to remote, central sources which can be dialed or otherwise called for on a pre-arranged schedule. It is also possible that both systems will be needed. Thus additional conduits forming a network between all carrels in a given building or building section and supply centers for such media as taped instruction, television programs, or other media such as slides or program frames transmitted by television facilities will have to be planned and provided. Since speaker cables for sound-reproducing devices (such as headsets) and coaxial cables for TV transmission should not be combined with regular power lines, still additional conduits will have to be installed.

Another ever-present problem is that of designing spaces for clusters of carrels, or arranging such stations in large electronic learning-laboratory rooms for each cluster of classrooms. When arranged in large learning-space areas, consideration should be given to orienting the carrels in rows for over-the-carrel-top viewing of projected images in a large-group, or total group presentation, as a part of a larger teaching process. In such cases, properly located projection screens and projectors should be added. Schools inaugurating such teaching-learning activity tend to provide too few carrels for the students using the system and also tend to spread them out in remote areas—even along corridors, perhaps having a few in classrooms here and there. A plan should be formulated that will provide the required number of carrels near the classroom areas where demand and use is likely to be concentrated. Then connecting conduits and cables can be planned in advance.

The Need to Remodel Old Schools for Media Use

Even if all new school buildings include such facilities as those described, the director will have a tremendous task to equip older school buildings that will continue to be in service for a quarter of a century or more.

Since our old schools cripple and force curtailment of instructional activity and tend to force teachers into unimproved patterns of work, we need to change them. This can probably only be done through extensive remodeling. The urgent need is to elevate old school plants in instructional efficiency and effectiveness to a point as nearly equal to programs that can be conducted in a district's new buildings. This action is the only feasible way to provide equal opportunity for all. Thus it is essential to carry out a remodeling program in line with the kinds of activity that ought to be developed in place of those that already exist. It just may not be feasible to thoroughly reconstruct an old school. In some cases it may be less expensive in the long run to build a new building elsewhere. Hence a plan of priorities in changes ought to be set up in the light of predicted gains from the selected activities envisioned. We are here concerned with provisions for media use, and our recommendations are thus limited to improvement in this aspect of teaching and learning.

The following changes are typical of those which should be set up for every old school building in the system:

1. By using wiremold connections to present light switches, or to nearest live circuits, provide double electrical outlets on front and rear walls.

2. Install wall-mount projection screens of appropriate size, using portable screens as a stop-gap only. Add additional screens to each room as needed.

3. Install light-control systems of a suitable type, depending upon sun exposure and type of window in each learning space or teaching station, and use projection rooms and portable window-darkening devices as makeshifts while the new-facilities goal is being reached.

4. Add new electric circuits and electrical distribution boxes to supply sufficient amperage for each learning area to eliminate fuse-blowing inconveniences, and to provide additional power for new media equipment units.

5. Obtain assignment of a classroom in each building of fifteen or twenty rooms as an audiovisual media service center, and build a media service system as comprehensive as local financial support will permit.

6. Add flexible display space and improve present chalkboard in all learning areas according to need in the various learning areas.

7. Wherever possible, add a three-way on-off switch at the rear of each teaching station near the projector placement area, and also add light dimmers where possible and feasible.

8. Undertake the planning of new facilities such as additional classroom areas and large multipurpose learning areas. Include flexible-space auditoriums with modern operable walls for creating new learning areas for new instructional programs.

9. Convert old classrooms into listening-response (electronic learning) laboratories and add new library space with modern arrangements for expanded library uses.

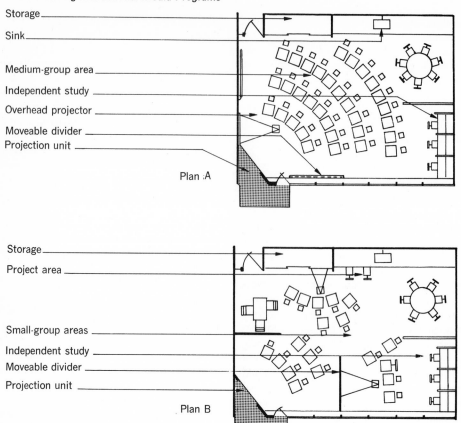

Storage
Sink
Medium-group area
Independent study
Overhead projector
Moveable divider
Projection unit

Plan A

Storage
Project area
Small-group areas
Independent study
Moveable divider
Projection unit

Plan B

Scale: 3/32" = 1' −0"

Figure 6-29. These architect's sketches show two plans for the use of space in a remodeled classroom of conventional size. Note possible rear-projection rooms, additional projection screens, and the multi-group capability introduced by the room dividers. *Courtesy Center for Architectural Research, R. P. I. Troy, New York,* from Alan C. Green, *Educational Facilities with New Media,* published by DAVI of NEA, 1966.

10. Reduce the present classroom areas in old buildings to take over space for expanding facilities in libraries, for providing new technological services and for moving the instructional activities toward newer teaching practices, including team teaching, individualized instruction, better teacher-talent utilization, and more effective pupil groupings.

11. Remove outmoded furniture and reequip to provide a new and up-to-date environment. Movable desks, spaces for larger groups using risers as permitted by probably existing higher ceilings for better views of projection screens, and facilities for independent study, may be planned and incorporated. Outmoded window designs ought to be altered, better light-control systems installed, and improvements made in ventilation and noise control.

In Dallas, Texas, for example, a plan for remodeling old schools was worked out whereby a standard addition was made to each old school building, namely, a gymnasium and a projection room. A policy was also established that while the projection room could be used as an all-purpose space, its reservation for audiovisual media-use purposes would have highest priority. In a report received from H. W. Embry, media program director in Dallas, it was stated that additional classrooms are currently being equipped with adequate light-control systems with priority being given to science classrooms.

Long-term planning and a campaign for adequate financial support for this program will produce maximum results. This problem of adapting old buildings must be solved, and top school administrators are the only ones who can initiate proper action to accomplish this vital task. The media program director, however, must provide the facts and the recommendations. Then, working with and through school principals, colleagues, teachers, PTA, and other community councils, he needs to help build adequate support for the superintendent's public proposals and requests. These matters will be dealt with again in later chapters on financing the media program and on building public understanding and support.

Problem-Solving Activities

1. Identify and list various kinds of professional teaching activities, representing several levels of teacher talent, generally engaged in during the process of achieving educational objectives in any normal teaching situation. Repeat this analysis with reference to using audiovisual media. What teacher talents (kinds of professional activities) are required if pupils are to spend more time learning by themselves?

2. Consider the roles that media play in helping teachers listed in Chapter 4. What media-use facilities must be provided if these roles are to be realized in any specific situation you name in the light of your own teaching experience?

3. What audiovisual media facilities are particularly necessary when team-teaching plans are being employed? What media facilities are required for individualized instruction? What are the alternative methods for implementing this latter process?

4. Explain how media materials, equipment, and special classroom arrangements are related to such expressions and processes as, *multigroup activities, media in combination, independent study activities, small discussion-group spaces,* and *problem-solving activities of learners.*

5. Make a series of sketches of learning-space windows that are most difficult to darken in both old and new schools and indicate how you would solve the light-control problem. Pool the drawings and issue a set of case studies in duplicated format.

6. Study Figures 6–11 through 6–13 (and

Scale: 1/8″ = 1′ −0″

Existing classroom partition

Overhead projection & teacher's station

TV receivers

Media modules

Medium group

TV receivers

Project areas

Seminar

Stepped floor

Large group

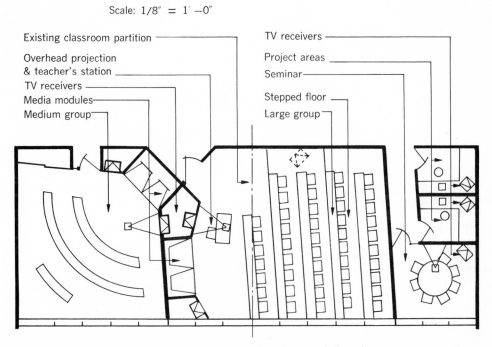

Figure 6-30. A host of new possibilities are indicated by the remodeling of a two-classroom space into new types of facilities. *Courtesy Center for Architectural Research, R. P. I., Troy, New York.*

Figure 6-31. Two top views show the recent addition to the Robertson School in Manchester, Connecticut. A modest media center including a new school library and an area for audio-visual media services, and several new classrooms were added, as can be seen, to the old structure. A portion of the library space is a sample of the new interior. The bottom picture shows part of a new operational area including study carrels at Staples High School, Westport, Connecticut. *Courtesy Public Schools, Manchester, Connecticut, and Public Schools, Westport, Connecticut.*

other illustrations as well) of various methods of darkening windows in both old and new schools and discuss the obvious strengths and weaknesses shown. Also, formulate critical comments about the architectural design in terms of current school-planning concepts.

7. Make a diagram of a regular classroom area and label the provisions you would recommend for wiring and conduits. Make an overlay transparency of your diagram and present it to the class as a simulated presentation before a school-construction planning committee.

8. Study the power requirements included in this chapter and make some realistic recommendations for regular and specialized learning areas.

9. Consult the recommendations in this chapter for projection screens and then make specific recommendations for several classrooms of known size and shape, both regular and specialized, for necessary screens, fabrics, preferred mounting arrangements, both front- and rear-projection types, for both single and multiple-image projection.

10. Sketch out a classroom that is to be used for large-group (100 learners) projection in art appreciation. The instructor desires to use two projected 2 × 2 inch slide images and control the projection from the front of the room with projectors at or near the rear of the room. What projection arrangements, including projectors, lenses, projection screens and their location, would you recommend?

11. Perform the necessary arithmetic computations and report the utilization ratio for any school auditorium with which you are familiar. What media facilities in that auditorium are available? Are they adequate? If not, what are some additional uses to which this auditorium might be put if appropriate media facilities were provided?

12. Remodeling old schools in the light of new media developments is an essential. Make a high-to-low priority listing of media-facilitation recommendations for changes in existing classrooms that have few if any provisions for audiovisual media utilization.

13. State your recommendations for providing makeshift arrangements whereby teachers normally teaching in rooms without proper light-control systems may satisfactorily project motion pictures, color slides, and filmstrips. Weigh your recommendations carefully and critically against the requirements.

14. Make a collection of the literature distributed by producers of darkening systems. Then, formulate a policy regarding darkening installations in terms of a preference list of methods for the following types of windows: (a) regular windows (usually in old buildings) of approximately 3 feet wide by 7 feet high; (b) short-in-height windows located high on a wall, approximately 3 feet high by 8 feet wide, recessed without casings; (c) a window wall 8 feet high by 30 feet wide; (d) a window 8 feet square, recessed; (e) a window 5 feet wide and 7 feet high, recessed; and (f) an auditorium window 20 feet high and 4 feet wide with a semicircular-shaped top section.

15. Your superintendent of schools has written you asking that you participate in a conference with the architect working on plans for several new schools in your community. You have been asked to prepare a letter, addressed to the superintendent, stating the crucial architectural considerations for the use of audiovisual media for the proposed new high school building, and for two new elementary schools.

16. How can the *size of screen* needed for a given classroom be determined? Are there special cases when the generally accepted method for determining this will not be applicable? Explain.

17. Write out a list of facts as they apply to (a) types of screens to purchase; (b) viewing and reflecting characteristics; (c) mounting procedures; and (d) rules regarding placement of viewers, projectors, and screens.

18. Explain how the following factors are related to the size of a projected picture: (a) distance of projector from screen, (b) focal length of lens, (c) projection area of material, and (d) the intensity of illumination.

References

Acoustical Environment of School Buildings. (New York: Educational Facilities Laboratories, Inc., 1963).

The Audio-Visual Program. Bulletin 218, State of Indiana, Department of Public Instruction, Indianapolis, Indiana, 1956.

Brown, James W., and Kenneth D. Norberg. *Administering Educational Media.* (New York: McGraw-Hill, 1965).

Cornell, Francis G. "Plant and Equipment," in Chester W. Harris (ed.). *Encyclopedia of Educational Research* (New York: Macmillan, 1960), pp. 1008–1031.

DeBernardis, Amo, Victor W. Doherty, Errett Hummel, and Charles William Brubaker. *Planning Schools for New Media.* (Prepared in cooperation with the U.S. Department of Health, Education, and Welfare, Office of Education.) (Washington, D.C.: Superintendent of Documents, U.S. Government Printing Office, 1961).

deKieffer, Robert E. *Audiovisual Instruction.* (New York: Center for Applied Research in Education, Inc., 1965).

Design for ETV: Planning for Schools with Television. (New York: Educational Facilities Laboratories, Inc., 1960).

Dombrow, Rodger T. "How to Meet Your Construction Deadlines." *School Management* **7**: 99-103, July 1963.

Ellsworth, Ralph E. and Hobart D. Wagener. *The School Library.* (New York: Educational Facilities Laboratories, Inc., 1963).

Environmental Engineering for the School: A Manual of Recommended Practice. (Washington, D.C.: U.S. Office of Education, 1961).

Erickson, Carlton W. H. *Fundamentals of Teaching with Audiovisual Technology.* (New York: Macmillan, 1965).

Estes, Raymond L. "Effects of Stray Light on the Quality of Projected Pictures at Various Levels of Screen Brightness." *Journal of SMPTE.* Vol. 61, No. 8, August 1953, pp. 257–272.

Gage, N. L. (ed.). *Handbook of Research on Teaching.* (Chicago: Rand McNally, 1963). Chapter 12, "Instruments and Media of Instruction" by A. A. Lumsdaine, pp. 583-683.

Geisler, M. A. and W. A. Steger, "How to Plan for Management in New Systems," *Harvard Business Review* **40**: 103-10, September-October 1962.

Green, Alan C. (ed.). *Educational Facilities with New Media.* (Prepared under a contract with the U.S. Office of Education.) (Washington, D.C.: The Department of Audiovisual Instruction of the NEA, 1966).

Hayman, John L., Jr. "Viewer Location and Learning in Instructional Television," *Audiovisual Communication Review* **11**: 27–31, May-June, 1963.

Hyer, Anna, A. J. Foy Cross, and Don White. "Effective Use of Audio-Visual Aids Through Building Design," *American School and University*, 25th ed. (New York: American School Publishing Co., 1953).

Kilbride, Robert E. "Six Communications Systems in a Single Installation," *School Planning*, Vol. 2, No. 5, October-November 1957, pp. 4-11.

Kinne, W. S., Jr. *Space for Audio-Visual Large Group Instruction.* University Facilities Research Center (Madison, Wis.: University of Wisconsin Press, 1963).

Kolb, Frederick J., Jr. "Specifying and Measuring the Brightness of Motion Picture Screens," *Journal of the Society of Motion Picture and Television Engineers*, Vol. 61, October 1953, pp. 533-542.

Koppes, Wayne F., Alan C. Green, and M. C. Gassman. *Design Criteria for Learning Spaces: Seating, Lighting, Acoustics* (Albany, N.Y.: Office of Facilities, The University of the State of New York, 1964).

Maxfield, J. P. "Auditorium Acoustics," *Journal of the Society of Motion Picture and Television Engineers*, Vol. 53, August 1948, pp. 169–176.

McClurkin, W. D. *School Building Planning.* (New York: Macmillan, 1964).

Moldstad, John and Harvey R. Frye. "Making Room for AV," *Audiovisual Instruction*, Vol. 2, Issue 9, December 1957, pp. 270-271.

Nimnicht, Glendon P. "Windows and School Design," *Phi Delta Kappan*, Vol. 47, No. 6, February 1966, pp. 305-307.

Nimnicht, Glendon P. and Arthur R. Partridge. *Designs for Small High Schools* (Greeley Col.: Colorado State College, 1962).

Palmer, R. Ronald and William Maxwell Rice. *Laboratories and Classrooms for High School Physics*, Educational Facilities Laboratories, Inc. (New York: 1961).

Parsons, James W. "Roll-on Light Control," *Audiovisual Instruction*, Vol. 8, No. 9, November 1963, p. 700.

Planning Schools for Use of Audiovisual Instructional Materials. (Albany, N.Y.: The University of the State of New York, New York State Education Department, 1959).

Planning Schools for Use of Audio-Visual Materials, No. 1, Classrooms, 3rd ed. (Washington, D.C.: Department of Audio-Visual Instruction of the NEA, 1958).

Planning Schools for Use of Audio-Visual

Materials, No. 2, Auditoriums. (Washington, D.C.: Department of Audio-Visual Instruction, 1953).

Planning Schools for Use of Audio-Visual Materials, No. 3, Audio-Visual Instructional Materials Center (Washington, D.C.: Department of Audio-Visual Instruction of the NEA, 1953).

Shaver, John A. "Build the School to Fit the Program." *Audiovisual Instruction*, Vol. 7, No. 8, October 1962. pp. 518-519.

Study Carrels: Designs for Independent Study Space. Western Regional Center, Stanford, Calif. (New York: Educational Facilities Laboratories, Inc., 1963).

Trump, J. Lloyd. *Images of the Future.* (Washington, D.C.: National Association of Secondary Principals, 1958).

————. "Places for Learning," *Audiovisual Instruction*, Vol. 7, No. 8, October 1962, pp. 516-517.

Vlahos, Petro. "Selection and Specification of Rear-Projection Screens." *Journal of the SMPTE.* Vol. 70, No. 2, February 1961, pp. 79-95.

Westley, Bruce H. and Werner J. Severin. "Viewer Location and Student Achievement," *Audiovisual Communication Review* **13**: 270-74, Fall 1965.

The Media Service
System in Each School

The one question frequently asked by new practitioners of media methodology is: How can I promote the use of instructional media in my school? Instead of answering it at once, we should counter with some questions of our own. The implication that is obvious in the original question is that the existing media-use program hasn't prospered, teachers haven't changed along desirable lines of action. We ask, "Why?" What learning-space media facilities have been provided? Do teachers get the assistance they need in changing to technological methods? Have they had reasonably good opportunities to develop a feeling of security with unfamiliar methods? In short, how effectively has the media-service program in the school been organized? We must hasten to point out that *promotion* is hardly the word for the kind of *change process* that should be carried out in every school building in the country today. What media program directors must be able to do is to work with all concerned in establishing the fundamental conditions under which teachers can make use of media naturally and conveniently.

It has been emphasized repeatedly in previous discussions and in illustrations that media-service spaces are and have been included in new schools around the country and have also been provided when remodeling old schools. The reason is obvious, namely, the burgeoning of technology and an increased understanding of the roles that media play in modern education. In view of the essential character of a school's media-service system, this chapter is intended as a handbook for planning and implementation by innovators not only in each school building, but by the prospective school-system media program director as well.

Give Teachers the Help They Need

If we have learned anything about the process of facilitating media use, it is that we as change agents must give teachers the help they need in adjusting to new conditions. Of course teachers must also be motivated to the point of being willing to make innovations, but such efforts are likely to fail unless they can experience success in the new processes and be recognized and given attention along the way. The climate for such success is generated in large part by the

226

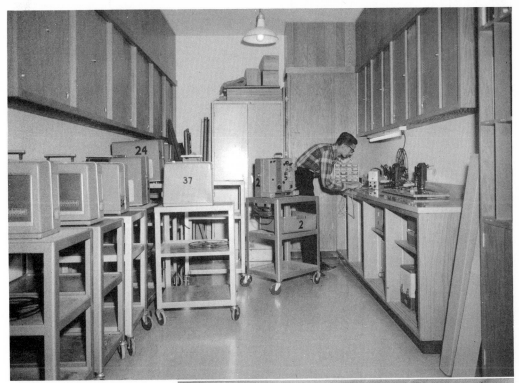

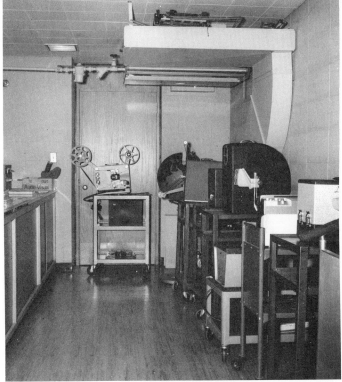

Figure 7-1. These pictures show portions of the audio-visual media service centers in two schools, one secondary, the other an elementary school. Note permanently assigned general use equipment on mobile stands, ready for delivery; storage cabinets; and in one instance, the full use of available wall area for media purposes. The top view shows part of a much larger area in the Thornton Township High School, Harvey, Illinois. The bottom view shows approximately half the available area at the Indian Prairie Elementary School, Kalamazoo, Michigan. Refer also to Figure 1-9. *Courtesy Thornton Township High School, Harvey, Illinois; and Public Schools, Kalamazoo, Michigan.*

service system that is functioning in support of effective teaching.

It can be readily seen that as facilities for technological media are developed in the various learning spaces, teachers need technical and clerical support. For example, as teachers grow dependent upon the electronic learning laboratory as the means of teaching specified operations, such as learning the pronunciation of words or the operation of a microscope, and as such laboratory sessions are scheduled with regularity in the teaching process, technicians will simply have to be available throughout the day to keep the units operating. On the more professional side, it can also be seen that as teachers plan and write scripts for tape-recorded instruction, they need in-service education programs to develop new skills in pinpointing objectives and identifying appropriate pupil responses that will accomplish them. But then as the volume of writing builds up, teachers need additional clerical services. Thus we see that teachers have need of an array of in-school services, from professional skill-building activities and clerical and technical assistance to the ordering and scheduling of materials and mobile equipment.

Some Specific Kinds of Help Needed by Teachers. In the light of conditions already described we can list a number of important kinds of help commonly sought by teachers in carrying out their plans to use audiovisual media effectively. The list that follows would of course vary as the program in each school varies from meagre to comprehensive. Teachers ordinarily seek help in:

1. Obtaining up-to-date information about locally owned materials.

2. Locating and scheduling needed materials from local and remote distributors.

3. Transmitting orders to local distribution headquarters.

4. Arranging for pre-use examination of materials.

5. Arranging optimum conditions for learning when media are to be used.

6. Learning to operate equipment.

7. Obtaining delivery to and pick-up of media equipment at classrooms.

8. Obtaining the assistance of trained equipment operators whenever needed.

9. Finding what the trouble is when physical difficulties with materials and equipment arise.

10. Avoiding conflicts with plans of other teachers for material and equipment.

11. Obtaining supplies and equipment for the personal preparation of audiovisual media such as slides, transparencies, tapes, automatic sequences, and TV programs.

12. Obtaining media materials that are to be prepared by others for specific purposes.

13. Planning classroom presentations that are to be supported by special media productions.

14. Planning equipment installations in learning areas such as libraries, auditoriums, gymnasiums, and in school corridors for both general and highly specialized purposes.

15. Organizing cooperative efforts with other teachers in preparing and exchanging needed media to save time, effort, and expense.

16. Developing special professional skills for making effective use of media in both small and large groups.

A Cooperatively Formed Plan by School Principals and Media Program Directors. Giving such help is no easy matter, and if school principals and the school-system media program directors turn their backs on these needs, their best efforts to have an impact on the learner through modern media contributions fail. Therefore, the media director and principal must cooperatively establish a system of teaching services in each school building—elementary and secondary. The efficiency of this service program depends on a key person, an audiovisual media leader, working at the school-building director level. Although this position has been given many titles, such as *Vice Principal in Charge of Media* or *Audiovisual Building Representative*, the ones most common presently are *Audiovisual Building Coordinator*, *Instructional Media Coordinator*, and *Instructional Materials Coordinator*. It must be recognized that the help teachers need cannot be given by the principal on an unorganized, unsystematized basis. Therefore, the first step in establishing this essential media-service system is to select a qualified individual to work with the principal and the media program director in setting up the service system. In the section that follows we discuss each of the essential operating facilities and conditions under which this school-building media leader can supply the necessary services.

Figure 7-2. Two areas in media-service centers where media-preparation equipment units are permanently assigned. Top shows the area at the Milwood JHS, and the bottom view shows the preparation space at the Northeast JHS, both schools in Kalamazoo. Copying camera and lettering equipment are not shown in these pictures. See also Figure 4-10. *Courtesy Public Schools, Kalamazoo, Michigan.*

The Availability of Media Equipment and Materials

Assign Equipment Units to Each Building

We frequently blame teachers for not making use of media equipment when we should put the blame instead squarely where it belongs on school leaders for not meeting the minimum standard of reasonable convenience. Equipment units should be obtainable with ease according to a well-organized service system. We cannot seriously charge teachers with dereliction of duty in carrying out their methodologies when they cannot make arrangements for using media at the right time and place for optimum learning. The bulk of the equipment needed for classroom use in any school building should be assigned permanently to the building. It has come to be axiomatic that centralization of the most expensive materials is economical and feasible, but that centralization of *equipment* is unwise and impractical because trucking it to the schools subjects it to merciless pounding and, most important, generally puts it beyond the reach of teachers for convenient, frequent use. Another reason is that equipment units need to be on the spot for training students and teachers to operate them. Although decentralization of equipment in every school unit is a clear-cut goal of the media-service program, it may be necessary to establish a central pool of certain kinds of special-purpose equipment that may not be needed continuously and which, if distributed on a loan basis as needed, would permit a more rapid build-up of the inventory of more commonly used equipment such as motion picture projectors, filmstrip projectors, and tape recorders.

In the light of recent technological developments, we now have to emphasize the essential need to locate in each school building a number of permanently installed equipment units. We certainly will not find it feasible to transport television receivers to and from schools, nor would we wish to deliver hundreds of headsets for an auditorium or library listening-response laboratory. The fact is that we see more clearly in both old and new roles of media the vital necessity to equip each school building with the amount and kind of media that teachers need, for now we think less frequently of enrichment, and we think instead of the accomplishment of clearly recognized basic objectives that cannot be achieved without modern methods.

Kinds of Equipment Usually Assigned to Each School. In a well-developed media-service program, one or more of the following equipment

units are likely to be found in every elementary and high school building in the school system in reasonably adequate quantity:

1. 16 mm sound motion picture projectors, with a special auditorium model, or regular model with booster speakers if the public-address system is not designed for projector sound connections.

2. 8 mm cartridge-type projectors, both sound and silent models for both group (possibly rear-projection screen) and self-instruction uses.

3. Filmstrip and 2×2 inch slide projectors (combination model).

4. Automatic and remote-control 2×2 inch slide projectors.

5. Slide projectors, $3\frac{1}{4} \times 4$ inch models.

6. Slide or filmstrip projectors for short-exposure projection exercises.

7. Sound filmstrip projectors, for both disk and tape recorded audio components.

8. Record players, both monaural and stereo, for scheduled audio listening exercises in music rooms and libraries.

9. Overhead transparency projectors, both light weight and heavy duty, the latter for large-group learning spaces.

Figure 7-3. The teacher in this conventional-sized classroom in the John F. Kennedy Elementary School was able to introduce innovative methods because of help in arranging learning environment conducive to change. Small groups of children listen to instructional tapes and look at filmstrips on a projector they can operate. The teacher uses the equipment as a basis for multi-group activity as well as a basis for her own explanations and motivating experiences for problem-solving activity in the class and in the school library. See also Figures 1-4, 4-1, 4-3, 4-6, and 6-4. *Courtesy Consolidated City Schools, Kingston, New York.*

10. Tape recorders, both monaural and stereo, equipped with packaged headsets and plug-in boxes as accessories.

11. Classroom and auditorium TV receivers.

12. AM/FM receiver, depending on audio programing in the area.

13. Microprojectors.

14. Opaque projectors.

15. Portable projection screens, both front and rear-projection types, for learning spaces not having permanently wall-mounted or other fixed screens.

16. Mobile projection stands, ample for moving each heavy piece of equipment on assignment.

17. Copying cameras, 35 mm, in preparation of materials spaces, and related graphic supplies.

18. Polaroid cameras and copymaker stands, and related graphic supplies.

19. Transparency-maker equipment, and related graphic supplies.

Such equipment units will make it possible for teachers to plan for a variety of teaching methods in reaching their objectives, hopefully right in their own well-equipped classrooms. Some of these units will be used so frequently that they should be located in each classroom permanently, and others will be on call from the school's service headquarters. Still other media equipment may be needed on a loan basis for special purposes and such equipment may be centralized at the school system media program headquarters.

Nature of the Centralized Media Equipment Pool. Let us now take note of several kinds of media equipment that individual schools may have need of on a loan basis. We should recognize, of course, that the degree of local development may tend to limit or increase the size of the following list:

1. Magnetic sound, motion picture projector, for recording and playing back, school-made sound tracks.

2. Motion picture cameras, both 16 mm and 8 mm, necessary lighting equipment, and film exposure meters.

3. Flash-meters for filmstrip and slide projectors, for short-exposure work not covered by specialized equipment units.

4. High-fidelity record and tape playing components.

5. Portable public-address systems.

6. Portable TV display system for special learning space uses.

7. Large-screen TV projection system for large-group uses.

Some Fixed Media Equipment Installations. In a school where pupil groupings are flexible and learners learn by themselves under optimum conditions part of the time, additional media equipment units and installations become necessary. The following are among those frequently referred to in remodeling and new construction plans:

1. Electronic learning laboratory rooms as special separate learning spaces, or provided in instructional materials centers, in libraries, or in divisible auditoriums. Also referred to as listening and responding centers and as foreign language laboratories. May have broad or specialized scope through dial-access techniques.

2. Individual electronic study stations or carrels, located in libraries, classrooms, and special learning areas. Equipped with manual control devices, or with dial access to central, local, and remote sources, both audio and videotape, and small projection screens for flexible programing in multimedia format.

3. Closed-circuit television studios in each school or in one school serving a cluster of schools, by means of cable or other transmission system.

4. Television image magnification and display systems in large learning spaces, as fixed equipment.

5. Teaching machines in fixed positions in large or small learning areas. Such teaching machines may possess various kinds of media-use and display capability, and they may or may not be linked or associated with computer terminals for analysis and/or activation.

6. Fixed, remote control projection stations built into classrooms, both large and small, and into teaching auditoriums. Projection stations may be at rear of rooms or behind rear-projection screen installations.

7. Learner-response devices at each student desk, connected to group presentation and analysis equipment, in teaching auditoriums, and in large and small classrooms.

It can be readily seen that the media equipment units appearing in the preceding list are special installations designed for use in modern

Figure 7-4. General use equipment units, such as projectors and tape recorders are commonly assigned to specific classrooms for long-term loans, even built-in permanently on pedestals and raised platforms. Not so common are long-term loans of special-purpose equipment such as the diazo-film exposing unit together with a pickle-jar developing unit. Some of the youngsters in the top view seem apprehensive about the process (especially the smell of ammonia fumes) and the resulting product. In the next two pictures a kindergarten group in the Mercer school of Shaker Heights, Ohio, is using the dry-mount press to laminate some feathers. The young man in the picture has bravely opened the press, and, as can be seen, it is quite a serious business as the teacher guides the hand of the little girl as she uses the tacking iron. *Courtesy Public Schools, Shaker Heights, Ohio.*

programs that possess the capability to delegate to media new roles in the teaching process. Such roles demand unusually talented teachers who know how to analyze the teaching process into the various aspects of pupil and teacher action that will produce optimum achievement in any given situation. Such action must not be subjected to the capricious difficulties that frequently attend the borrow-and-return process, where a delay in arrival of a specific film or filmstrip, or an emergency failure in equipment, can be readily adjusted.

Figure 7-5. Installations like the one shown at Ohio State University (top view) with dial access to a central resource bank employing North Electric Company's Datagram System and the pilot-program, audio-video carrels (bottom view) at West Hartford's old Hall High School, also connected to a central resource bank, are the results of efforts to widen the horizons of technological applications to individualized instruction on the one hand, and the use of media-controlled instruction for large groups on the other. See also Figures 6-26 and 6-28. What will be the general and specific effects on media-service arrangements as such installations appear in every reasonably large school in the land? (*Top view*, Courtesy North Electric Company, Gallion, Ohio ; *Bottom view*, Courtesy Continuous Progress Education, Inc., Norwalk, Connecticut.)

Amount of Equipment in Each School. The problem of formulating standards or guidelines for the amounts and kinds of media equipment units that should be purchased and made available to each school building is a difficult one to solve. Many national groups have worked on solutions to this problem, and from time to time the results of such earnest and arduous deliberations have been published. We must be clear on the point that although guidelines are often helpful to school program planners and to all who prepare budgets for adoption by local boards of education and finance, they may also tend to place lower limits on the thinking of school leaders, and actually may then focus attention on the devices themselves rather than on the learners' needs and the required instructional programs. It is essential to recognize that it is the nature of the school's program in relation to valid objectives that determines the need

Figure 7-6. In large-group presentation centers like this one in the Wilbur Wright JHS at Munster, Indiana, equipment has to be specialized and operated under a different set of technological controls. In this instance the teaching station seats 150 students and the equipment is permanently located behind the rear projection screen 20 feet wide. Equipment is operated by remote control from the lectern. See also Figures 6-21 and 6-25, bottom picture. *Courtesy Public Schools, Munster, Indiana.*

Figure 7-7. Another type of fixed installation is the individual responder system, employed in electronic classrooms, and both large and small groups. More details are given in Chapter 11, but for the present, the reader should note the large, readable percentage meters mounted at the front of a 100-seat teaching station, the special lectern, the rear-projection screen, and the individual responder recessed in the writing surface at each seat. This teaching station is one of many similar spaces at Florida Atlantic University, Boca Raton, Florida. See also Figure 3-1, bottom picture. *Courtesy Raytheon Learning Systems, Englewood, New Jersey.*

Figure 7-8. The Edex System console uses a magnetic tape to program the sound motion picture and the filmstrip projectors. Each student is asked to make responses during the presentation using the individual responders shown on their desks. The responses may be immediately known by reading individual tabulators or reading the percentage meters. The teacher plays different roles in situations like these. What effect will the complexity of programing presentations like the one shown have on existing concepts of teaching load, and on the number of required supporting personnel in every school building that employs the technology depicted in Figures 7-5 through 7-8? *Courtesy Aetna Life & Casualty, Hartford, Connecticut.*

Figure 7-9. A whole new range of both fixed and mobile installations will be needed in school buildings with mature media programs. In these pictures we see the sophisticated television control center in the Nova junior-senior high school, and the use of a portable television videotape recording and playback system. Note also the tilting-screen arrangement that indicates on-going use of other types of projection media. (*Top view,* courtesy Nova Dissemination Project, Nova Schools, Fort Lauderdale, Florida ; *bottom picture,* courtesy General Electric Co., Syracuse, New York.)

for and particular kind or amount of instructional equipment.

We must, however, in the face of an urgent need to make estimates of financial support for media-service programs, turn to the help of the excellent statements of guidelines (notwithstanding their shortcomings). This is especially true in the preparation of proposals in connection with state and federal grants for instructional programs. We shall for the present purposes stress the need to assign to each school the media equipment required for optimum use by teachers under favorable conditions. Then in Chapter 13, in connection with budgeting and

finance, we shall make use of published standards, and use some of our own judgments as well.

Deployment of Media Equipment in Each Building

If we bear in mind the basic principles for the organization and development of a media-service program that were stated in Chapter 1, the kinds of action demanded leave us little choice. The potentially important roles that audiovisual media can play can only be realized when sufficient equipment and materials in good repair are maintained in each school building so that teachers can put them to use with a minimum of time and effort. As we have already indicated, this kind of availability is indeed one of the first essentials of the desirable media-service system in each school building. We shall now examine the several aspects of the problem of deploying equipment.

Equipment at Each Teaching Station. As school leaders and their boards of education work toward adequate support of instructional programs, they will come to realize that audio-visual media utilization is vital and basic to teaching processes, and that thus each class-room, special learning area, and most teaching stations, wherever they are, need permanently assigned media equipment units, either fixed or portable. Various teaching stations may require different equipment units. One particular teacher or classroom may, in addition to equip-ment units assigned to all teaching stations such as an overhead projector, require a remote-controlled 2×2 inch slide projector for daily use. Another teacher in a large-group teaching situation might require the same equipment plus a 16 mm motion picture projector, two tape recorders, a record player, and six TV receivers. Still other special learning spaces may require electronically equipped listening and response carrels accommodating up to ninety students. Teaching auditorium spaces may be equipped with a permanently installed multi-media rear-screen projection system and dial-access equipment for videotape and audio programs accommodating 300 or more pupils. For the present we should emphasize the principle that teachers ought to have equipment for use at the optimum time for maximum learning impact. One of the ways, then, for deploying audiovisual media equipment is to assign urgently needed and frequently used units to each classroom.

Equipment at Media-Service Center Sub-stations. Some effectively organized media-service systems incorporate a plan that locates frequently used equipment units close to clusters of teaching stations. Such decentralized location points throughout a school building can be called substations for media equipment. Thus a group of social studies, science, shop, or business studies classrooms, or a cluster of first and second grade classrooms, for example, may be served by a media equipment pool from which a specific piece of needed equipment can be drawn upon request by simple scheduling procedures. Deployment of media equipment in this fashion cuts red tape to a minimum, and reduces the equipment delivery time from school headquarters, or cuts pick up and return time if teachers are handling the details. In some of the sprawling, one-floor schools, it is readily seen that wheeling a loaded projection stand a third of a mile on wobbly, noisy wheels is an un-pleasant task, even when a pupil on duty does it. Certainly no school principal or school super-intendent would expect a teacher to carry an opaque projector in one hand and a motion picture projector in the other from his office on the first floor to a third-floor classroom. So deploying frequently used media equipment or instruments on their own mobile projection stands or carts to substations close to the teacher is another of the desirable possibilities.

Equipment Units at the School Media-Service Center. Conservation of time in preparation for classroom learning activity is a crucial matter for teachers. Those activities that are clerical or menial in nature should not be permitted to take precedence over those that are professional, insightful, and innovative insofar as communica-tion with pupils and the guidance of their responses are concerned. Thus we need to make it possible for teachers to obtain their media materials and equipment with minimum inter-ruption of class routines and pupil activity. If, for example, a teacher who wishes to project a seven-minute motion picture clip, show fifteen slides, and three overlay transparencies, has to spend an hour locating and setting up the proper equipment, those in charge of the school's instructional program are causing an unfavor-able balance between nonprofessional and professional activities. What we want to do is to provide the time for planning the presentation, formulating questions for guiding student reactions to content, and preparing and sequenc-ing the media materials that are vital to the objectives being attained. Therefore, if media instruments cannot be placed in the classroom on long-term loan, or assigned to substations serving clusters of classrooms, then they must be deployed in the school's service headquarters and an effective system of ordering, delivery, and pick-up established. When equipment units are so deployed several conditions must be created, namely, (1) that each heavy and bulky equipment unit must be in a state of readiness for delivery on its own mobile projection stand; (2) that teachers may order such equipment with a minimum of red tape and advance notice; (3) that the equipment may be made available on the day preceding carefully planned utilization and thus made ready at times most convenient for the teacher; and (4) that teachers who obtain such equipment will have other needed facilities in their own classrooms or other regular teaching stations that will permit easy use of the equipment after it is delivered. We shall of course deal fully with these matters again later in relation to organizing the school's media-use facilitation headquarters.

Assign Some Collections of Media Materials to Each School

Lest we focus too much attention on equipment and thus detract from the true reason for its existence—the content in the media materials—we ought to refer again to Chapter 5 in which we gave proper emphasis to the effective distribution of media from centralized collections. We must emphasize again at this point that good equipment services for teachers must go hand in hand with optimum availability of the materials. We also discussed this important topic in Chapter 3 under the topic *Acquisition and Deployment of Audiovisual Media.* Having already introduced this subject in other contexts, we need merely to point out here that in recent years there has been an increasing tendency in well-developed media-service programs to build up collections of filmstrips, 8 mm cartridge motion pictures, study print sets, maps

Figure 7-10. Many school districts continue to issue filmstrips, audio-program tapes, phograph records, study-print sets, and cartridge films from central depositories. The desirable practice, however, is to seek an optimum balance between centralization and decentralization of media. Depending on the instructional program, it is recommended that many kinds of media, even such expensive media as sound motion pictures and videotapes be located in school-building units. The three pictures show school-building collections, though not necessarily typical ones. Most collections in reasonably large schools should be much larger than these. (*Top view*, courtesy Encyclopaedia Britannica Educational Corp., Project Discovery, Chicago ; *two bottom pictures*, courtesy Fountain Valley School District, Huntington Beach, California.)

and globes, recordings, magnetic tapes, and other special-purpose and repetitively used media materials in each school building. This de-centralization of the less expensive kinds of audiovisual media will doubtlessly facilitate their use, but unless teachers select such materials with due regard for their frequent demand, inefficient usage will result. Some media materials used for self-instruction and other special purposes doubtlessly should be in the teacher's full-time possession or kept at the school's media headquarters for issue to the various learning laboratories, or located in dial-access resource banks. With the decentralization of media equipment and materials a service center in each school is essential, and the organization and development of such a center are dealt with in the following sections.

Organizing an Effective Program of Media Services in Each School

In the preceding section we emphasized the importance of having media materials and equipment close to the teacher to facilitate their use at the optimum time in the teaching process. Now we are confronted by another group of problems that have to do with maintaining conditions that will provide for the continuing flow of media materials and equipment at maximum-use levels with a minimum of inconvenience, and at the same time provide at least a desirable minimum of help that teachers need in order to carry out their work with media efficiently. The goal is clear, but the requirements for that kind of operation are many and are often complicated by inadequate personnel and money, by ineffective operational procedures, and by poor administrative arrangements. We shall therefore discuss these basic conditions and seek to point out some solutions to problems common to school people everywhere.

The System of Services in Operation

First let us take an over-all look at a hypothetical service system as it is functioning in a given school building, and then proceed to deal with some basic questions about the nature of organizational problems. The school-building system in a thriving citywide media organization

with good leadership and financial support may be in operation under the following conditions:

1. All classrooms and other learning activity spaces have been equipped with facilities for audiovisual media use.

2. Equipment units needed by teachers have been assigned to the school for quick, convenient use upon request.

3. Collections of frequently used, less expensive materials have been assigned to the school by the central headquarters.

4. A school building media-service center has been organized and is open for business. This center is the clearing house for all orders for media materials and equipment for the school.

5. A responsible staff of professional media specialists, trained technicians and clerical workers, supplemented by a crew of student assistants has been organized and is on hand to carry out the day's media-use schedule as needed.

6. A professional leader, the school's co-ordinator of the media-service program, has been appointed and is available to consult with teachers, organize in-service education programs, and coordinate the flow of service from both the school building and the school-system headquarters. The coordinator has the necessary professional prestige in the school, and his importance is recognized by top-level school authorities. He sees to it that the system is set up properly and functions efficiently. The school principal helps him accomplish his mission by providing leadership and financial support. The principal has also appointed a media advisory committee to help plan the school's program of service. The services of other teachers have been elicited to help with the media-service work load as needed.

Under such conditions there will be a ceaseless flow of materials in and out of the school according to a well-worked-out system, and teachers will make their plans for suitable learning activities with confidence that they can be carried out without distraction or interruption.

Such an operation in broad outline appears to be workable at a high level of efficiency, but the fact is that several important questions need to be raised to point out the nature of decisions that both the principal of the school and the citywide media program director and possibly other administrative officers have to make. The first question we shall ask has to do fundamentally with the nature and scope of the services to be given. Will the media-service center for the school building be broad and comprehensive in its instructional media service, encompassing the school's library facilities as well, or will its services involve audiovisual media only? Every school principal in the country knows how difficult the answer to this problem can be. He knows full well the need for competent librarians, and he also knows that when teachers want, or are required, to use sophisticated technological methods, both professional and technical assistance are indispensable. In this case, just what do the principal and the citywide media program director do? Although a number of people have taken a firm stand on both sides of this issue as basic methods for organizing school service programs, we can say that local conditions—that is, the sum total of local experience and conditioning, including qualifications and potential of present staff, present operational efficiency of existing media-services facilities, the nature and degree of media use envisioned, and the nature of services needed by teachers—ought to be taken into account in making the decision. But this situation leads us to examine this problem further as we explore the topic of organizational patterns for media services next.

Some Organizational Patterns for School Media Services

Because the media services to be given in any single school building vary in complexity, and because some programs of media use are far more comprehensive than others, there are many possibilities for setting up workable service organizations. We shall of course deal with the problems of providing staff members for any given type of organization and planning and equipping school-building media-service centers separately, in later sections.

In discussing the various organizational patterns for media services, we must focus on the needs that have to be met and the duties that have to be performed. Professional duties should be performed by individuals with professional preparation. If teaching experience is

required for certain duties such as for in-service education programs involving instruction in teaching methods, then only those individuals who have the required experience should be given this responsibility. On the other hand, when technical duties are paramount such as maintaining equipment in operational readiness, and when clerical and secretarial duties are called for, then it is essential that such duties be performed by supporting staff members at their respective nonprofessional levels. Some professional librarians have never had teaching experience in the true sense of the term, but they have taught groups of students to use library facilities. Other librarians have had years of experience in regular classrooms, and in addition have been thoroughly prepared for work in the field of audiovisual media. It is asserted that when trained audiovisual media specialists are assigned responsibility for library activities, they ought to undertake special training courses in the field of library science as well, or library specialists should be provided to carry out these aspects of the service.

Media-Service Leadership in Each School. There is general agreement among school people that media-service programs in school buildings prosper when the leadership function is placed in one person who is sufficiently free of other duties and responsibilities to concentrate a major portion of his time and energy on the media problems that have been identified. Occasionally, school principals and others claim that a media-service school-building coordinator, as a media specialist, is not being used. These people have probably developed other plans for providing services, using, for example, a vice principal, backed up by a head technician, and one or more teacher aides as in a team teaching program. It is true that a number of the identified duties that appear in any listing are clerical and technical in nature. Yet, we assert that school principals themselves are too far removed from the specific media services needed by teachers to undertake either technical or professional duties themselves. To be sure, school principals, as we shall point out later, are the key administrators in their schools. They themselves are the first and foremost media-use facilitators, through their active support for methodological innovations. Thus, throughout the country, in both large and small cities and towns and in both large and small schools, ways are found by good school leaders to provide qualified, professional personnel to carry on the media-service program where it matters most and where it succeeds or fails—close to the teacher at his teaching station. In a later section we shall treat the problems of staffing, but at this point we assert that to provide qualified leadership at the school-building level is one of the most commonly agreed-to, though not always achieved, patterns of action the country over.

This media-program leader, operating as an audiovisual media specialist or as an all-media generalist, seems to be the key to successful technological services for teachers at the day-to-day instructional level. Every existing statement of duties of the school media coordinator that the writer has observed includes the job of helping teachers use media more effectively, a professional supervisory function, as well as organizing and overseeing the purely physical and mechanical details of the building's service program. Actually, this makes the media coordinator a unit director working with and for the school-system director but appointed by and responsible to the school principal.

In a very real sense, therefore, the audiovisual or all-media building coordinator also plays the roles of educator, executive, supervisor, technological expert, and equipment technician. Everyone recognizes the absolutely essential nature of the coordinator's service in the realm of physical details, but some school superintendents and principals are apparently afraid of the implications for higher salaries if they recognize and utilize the services of a talented school coordinator in more professional ways, for example, in supervisory and consultant capacities. School superintendents and other key administrators should "go all out" in attempts to discover talented teachers on their staffs who, through their valuable experience working with colleagues, form a cadre of school-curriculum leaders. Willingness to express open appreciation for this service is shown by Curtis Davis, Assistant Superintendent of Schools in San Jose, California, who wrote the following Foreword[1] in a manual for school coordinators:

Effectively used audiovisual materials represent one of the great advancements in education during the past few years. As a school coordinator, much depends on you as to how well these materials are used. The extra work required and the many coordination duties are well known and appreciated by all.

When you get discouraged at machines breaking down and the schedule going haywire, just stand back for a moment and think about the importance of what you do. It takes you to make the program click. . . .

Curtis Davis
Assistant Superintendent

We would do well to consider the following listing[2] of the major duties and responsibilities of audiovisual media coordinators in the Grosse Pointe, Michigan, school system as part of an adopted operational plan.

Major Duties and Responsibilities

1. Counsel teachers in the wise selection of audiovisual materials.

2. Work with teachers to improve utilization and production of audiovisual materials in the instructional program.

3. Compile teacher's monthly orders for audiovisual materials and forward them to the instructional materials center.

4. Train teachers in the use of audiovisual materials.

5. Organize the scheduling and use of AV materials in the building.

6. Be responsible for the care and maintenance of AV equipment.

7. Serve on the central audiovisual committee:
   (a) Attend monthly meetings with the curriculum assistant in charge of the instructional materials center.
   (b) Help make decisions for the expenditure of the yearly budget for new materials.
   (c) Help select materials that will be purchased.
   (d) Evaluate the function of the AV program in the instructional programs of the entire school system.

8. Maintain an effective liaison between the school and the instructional materials center for the efficient operation of the AV program:
   (a) Inform teachers of available materials.
   (b) Promote participation by teachers in previewing materials for purchase.
   (c) Prepare materials daily for pickup and return to the center.
   (d) Notify teachers when AV materials arrive.

---

[1] *Handbook for Audio-Visual Coordinators.* Curriculum Monograph No. 85, prepared by the Division of Instructional Materials, San Jose Unified School District, San Jose, California, 1955.

[2] By permission. From Wanda Daniel, "The AV Coordinator on the Rise," *Audiovisual Instruction*, Vol. 2, Issue 5, 1957, pp. 100–102.

9. Work closely with and advise the principal on all phases of the AV program.

10. Demonstrate and interpret AV materials and equipment to the board of education, PTA's and others.

11. Be on call on an emergency basis to assist teachers with equipment.

12. Participate in local, state, and national audiovisual programs and conferences.

We would also do well to study the following listing of duties published by the Los Angeles City Schools, Instructional Services Branch, in its celebrated handbook,[3] revised and reissued in 1965. The listing follows:

An effective audio-visual coordinator makes certain that

The principal is kept informed about the operation of the school's audio-visual program.

Teachers are kept informed about development of new audio-visual techniques, technology, and research.

Teachers are notified of availability of new material.

There is effective liaison among teachers, administrators, and the Audio-Visual Section.

Teachers receive advice and instruction in the proper utilization of audio-visual materials.

Teachers are assisted in selecting materials in their subject areas which will enhance learning.

School film orders are properly processed and sent to the Audio-Visual Section.

Teachers are informed of the identity and content of materials present in the school or scheduled for delivery.

Teachers have a convenient, established procedure for previewing audio-visual materials.

Films are scheduled to appropriate classrooms.

Equipment is scheduled for maximum utilization.

Films are skillfully projected by qualified operators.

Films and other materials are returned on time and in good condition.

School audio-visual equipment is inventoried, conveniently stored, and properly maintained.

Another statement from the same publication[4] that shows these duties and the relationship of the audiovisual coordinator to the principal and the central media headquarters is shown in Figure 7-11.

It has been repeatedly emphasized that duties

such as those listed, together with the additional professional and technical knowledge required by television, dial-access and other self-instruction systems in education today, leave no room for doubt as to the need for school-building leadership and supporting staff for the services that have to be given on a continual basis. The title conferred is not so important, but the abilities and insights possessed by those who are responsible are crucial.

Certainly as has been pointed out, leadership personnel at the professional level are essential. This designated professional person may be a part-time teacher or supervisor, or a vice principal who is devoting a specified portion of his energy on solving instructional media utilization problems. It may well be that this leadership will be supplied by a professional working on a full-time media-supervisory job in the central office who devotes a portion of his time and energy to a cluster of schools, working under the cooperative jurisdiction of two principals, or under a combination of administrators such as the system-wide media program director and the principal of the school that gets his services for a portion of the weekly work schedule. As the job of being an audiovisual building coordinator takes on a new urgency in the face of new technologically supported programs, the leadership personnel together with the necessary supporting secretarial and technical staff members will have to be located close to the teachers in every school or be assigned an intermittent schedule in the schools, but be based in a central office or in a cluster of schools, both elementary and secondary. The work has to be done; services have to be given. But we must be mindful of the fact that in many schools both principals and teachers have not yet created in their own minds the image of working effectively in a technological environment. The day when such images will have to be developed is rapidly approaching.

In the light of recently published standards that we shall quote a little later on (see footnote 8), we can insist on the need to employ the following staff for each 500 students in a school: two media specialists (including print and audiovisual media capability), two clerk-aide assistants, and two technician-specialist assistants. When in the next organizational pattern we discuss the audiovisual media center, we must recognize that the need for audiovisual

---

[3] *Handbook for Audio-Visual Representatives, Secondary Schools* (Revised 1965), pp. 4–5, Los Angeles City Schools, Instructional Services Branch, Los Angeles, California, 1965.

[4] *Ibid.*, p. 23.

THE ROLE OF THE AUDIO-VISUAL COORDINATOR

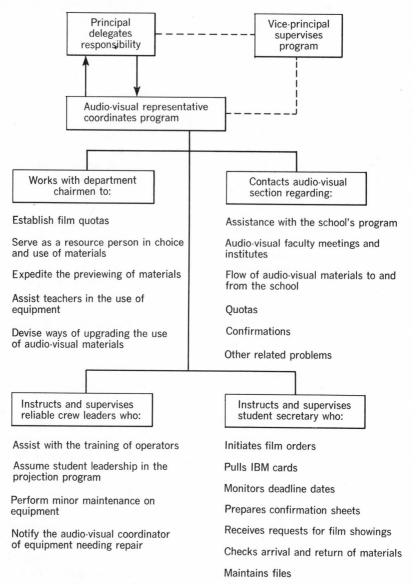

Figure 7-11. This analysis of the role of the school's audiovisual media coordinator is a clear-cut statement based on the Los Angeles organizational relationships between school centers and the district center. *Courtesy Los Angeles City Schools.*

media leadership personnel is in addition to the library organization.

We should not hesitate to assert that unless the right media personnel are provided, the media-service job is simply not done. If school principals claim that the only personnel needed are secretaries and some technicians, then the job of developing professional skills will not be carried out. If the school system provides only central office leadership, the various close-to-the-teacher assistance procedures simply will not be performed because the district-wide media program director cannot cope personally with the specific activity plans in each school. He must therefore expedite action through his administrative and supervisory activities that affect the programs of all schools at or nearly at the same time.

There are many ways to solve the leadership problem, not all of which are as good as others. We shall deal with these problems more fully in another major section to open up a number of possibilities. However, some of these are implicit in additional patterns for organization to which we now turn.

The Audiovisual Media Center Pattern. One has but to examine the various names for school-building media-service centers to note the organizational emphasis. Some of the names applied to the centers are actually misnomers, for although some names may mean one thing in terms of specific operational scope, they may also refer to something else. Regardless then of the name applied, let us identify a widely known pattern of organization that includes in its scope all technological media, all media materials and equipment and related processes except the medium of print. This means specifically that libraries and librarians, and audiovisual media-service centers and their media specialists in individual schools are organized into separate organizations although they may work closely together and may actually complement each other's activities. And, as we have already pointed out, libraries may possess specialized instructional media facilities, such as listening-

Figure 7-12. A floor plan, a close-up view of the drymount press counter, and an array of worktables, storage cabinets, and professional media library in the distance. Altogether these pictures indicate the arrangements in the space allotted to the audiovisual media center of the new senior high school in Munster, Indiana. Adjacent to this area are the projection booths for the large-group teaching stations. See also Figure 6-8. A large staff of students do much of the routine service work. *Courtesy Public Schools, Munster, Indiana.*

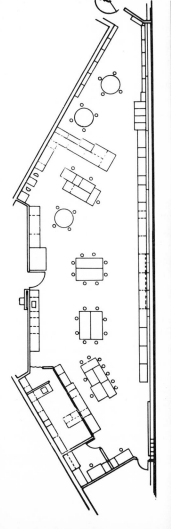

response centers and electronic carrels variously equipped, and may be engaged in carrying on a number of specified media services such as cataloging, storage, and the delivery of information to teachers about available media in local and district collections.

The most commonly used names for a media-service center that is separately organized from the library are the Audiovisual Service Center or the Instructional Technology Center. Other names, such as Educational Media Center, Learning Resources Center, Curriculum Materials Center, Instructional Materials Center, or Instructional Media Center, refer to more broadly based media programs that include *all* media. Not to include the print medium under service center names such as these is to mislead all who have broadened their insights into the roles that media play in teaching. This may or may not be a serious matter. It may even be justifiable. The logic underlying the organizational separation of services, however, is that audiovisual media and their related processes, call for such complex and specialized facilities and for such unique applications to teaching and learning that it is more simple and effective to concentrate professional and technical effort on the tasks that have to be done.

According to the Audiovisual Media Service Center pattern, each individual school would possess a headquarters suite that would be not less than a conventional size classroom in area, with such supporting operational spaces as are needed around the building. Such spaces may include equipment substations on each floor or in the vicinity of clusters of classrooms, electronic learning laboratories, teaching-machine laboratories, teaching auditoriums, listening centers in libraries, television studios, projection spaces with rear-screen projection equipment centers, and multimedia storage spaces for valuable mobile television and videotaping equipment. If we return to Chapter 3 for a look at the items included in a hypothetical audiovisual media-service system in operation, we can see that the nature of the program will demand certain minimal conditions, and as a program waxes in importance and scope of its technological applications, the service organization—from space allotments to personnel and equipment demands—will increase accordingly. A principal may say, "We do not need anyone in our media program besides myself to work with

teachers in teaching methods," until he gets involved in a large-scale television production responsibility. Then it is not only the technical engineer that matters, but also the designer and curriculum worker who understands the roles that media can play, who can break the teaching process down into its components and then advise and guide teachers in using the television medium wisely. When teachers need professional advice in preparing and using audiovisual media, principals—despite their being key curriculum workers and administrators—do not always have the necessary technical skill to help them.

As we look to the future we can see that the technological development of audiovisual media and related processes may become so complex that it may be wise (except in situations where the personnel have the required qualifications) to maintain a separation of the print and non-print media services insofar as supervisory and administrative organizations are concerned. This is particularly true because a head librarian who is carrying on in-service education in television programing, or working with teachers in developing media preparation skills and planning teaching systems for special objectives, will obviously have to be a media-service generalist and have a staff of media specialists working under his supervision. In such cases the librarian may be more an audiovisual media specialist than a print medium specialist.

In the pattern under consideration, it can be readily seen that the service headquarters leader will be in most cases fully responsible to the school principal, but in the light of good central media leadership, this school-building coordinator would also be a cooperating colleague of the system-wide media program director. It is in fact one of the primary concerns of a district-wide media administrator to lead all involved in the formulation of media program policy, and see to its execution. It is at this point that principals and other decision makers work together to implement changes or carry out old plans. We must take care not to conjure up the image of service programs of by-gone days, dating from the turn of the century, when a single city-wide media program leader with a tiny office, and perhaps one clerk, operated a central slide or film lending library. We have instead entered a new age where filmstrips, videotapes, color TV, computers, and electronic

Figure 7-13. This picture is an over-all view of the library at the Casis Elementary School, Austin, Texas, which was built by Page, Southerland, Page, Architects-Engineers. When both print and audiovisual media services are combined in one service organization, we have a true instructional media center. Refer to space-need estimates for all-media centers. *Courtesy American Library Association, Chicago.*

study carrels are no longer a novelty. We must not forget either that schools are being designed for teaching that is vastly different—or ought to be—than it was in the Middle Ages, and that schools as units are larger because more pupils are being taught better than ever before at minimum cost.

But such considerations make possible, and point the way to, other new and effective arrangements for providing vital services. Hence there has been an expansion in the development of another pattern for giving comprehensive media services to teachers. This is the pattern we may call the *Instructional Media Center* service pattern. We shall explore and illustrate this pattern next.

The Instructional Media Center Pattern. The symbol IMC has come to mean Instructional Materials or Media Center, and as such, is the symbol that indicates another of the principal patterns for organizing a school's media-service program. Under this pattern we combine the school's provisions for handling the print medium, usually administered out of the library facility, with a complete audiovisual media-

service program. Such school libraries may or may not be assigned the responsibility for text-book selection. Almost universally, however, they provide whatever services exist for circulating books and documents to students and teachers and, even more importantly, they arrange for the short-term assignment of classroom reference libraries as needed during a given period of special need. The symbol IMC has thus come to represent a comprehensive media-service program that has grown out of an expanded concept of the library function. Thus the library with its former limited focus on the print medium has broadened its service to include all of the so-called audiovisual media from a model to a CCTV telecast. Virginia McJenkin and Bruce Miles [5] have discussed the new library concept in this way:

Virginia: Also, the IMC person is quite aware of the total program and must participate in all types of activities related to curriculum, scheduling, selection of materials, in-service eduction, and so on.

[5] Bruce Miles and Virginia McJenkin, "IMC's: A Dialogue," *Audiovisual Instruction*, Vol. 10, No. 9, November 1965, pp. 688–691.

She works closely with teachers, department heads, and the administration as well as with students in producing a more effective program. In short, the IMC has become a vital part of the overall teaching-learning picture.

Bruce: IMC's will differ widely from one school system to the next and, as a matter of fact, will differ within a given school system. Such differences may stem from philosophy, the unique needs of a school or school system, and always from the budget. Budget is often necessary to accomplish the goals set for a program. Thus, possibly the best thing to say about the difference between traditional libraries and the modern concept of the IMC is that the new service is one dedicated to the necessity and opportunity of providing a wide variety of critical learning resources to many people within the community served. It may be that the word "service" is the all-important word in such an attempt to define this difference.

Regardless of whether the school-building instructional-media center is in an elementary or secondary school, one of its main aspects of service will be the print medium, and hence its existing library facility will serve in whole or in part as the media-service headquarters. The library may be only one of the units along with its workrooms for print medium operations. The spaces for audiovisual media services may be located elsewhere such as in a separate technological center where both professional and technical services are controlled. In some instances, the librarian with the rank of vice principal would head the program, especially when he or she possesses the required expanded media skills, professional and technical, and would presumably have an expanded staff of library assistants or media aides, one or more technicians, and one or more professional assistants. Of the professional assistants, one or more would specialize in nonprint such as television and others would carry out print-medium duties. In other instances, instructional-material centers may be headed by a school-building audiovisual media leader with the rank of vice principal who, if he has considerable insight into print-medium problems and procedures, may supervise the library and all other media services as well. However, his main concerns should be the advanced in-service education programs and other technological systems in the school. This variation of media-program organization is but another instance of the instructional-materials center pattern. We are not concerned here with who is in charge of the school's media services, but rather with the nature and scope of the services that are brought together under unified leadership. If the library, as it has been organized in schools before the need for other communication media developed, is the organizational hub, or is an integral part of the school's media-service organization complex under unitary leadership, the school's media-service organization may be properly classified under the Instructional Media Center pattern.

Patterns of Media-Service Organization. It is not a simple matter to choose an organization of a particular type. School principals working with their staffs and their administrative leaders and the school-system media program director must make this decision in the light of local conditions. What any local group must undertake before reaching this decision is to identify the services that have to be rendered and to find out what changes in personnel need to be made to reach the goals stated.

If there are elementary schools that have no library facilities whatever or if secondary schools or elementary schools have weak library facilities, the decision for action should be deflected toward the unification of all services in the school with new leadership. If, on the other hand, the existing leadership status of the library in any given school seems unreceptive to, or incapable of, expansion into other media efforts, then it would seem best to exert pressure for the development of both print and audiovisual media-service aspects along the lines of separate organizational patterns. As we have emphasized before, the educational need that has to be met is primary. Decisions have to be made as to what means will be employed to achieve the desired ends, and such judgments may not be easy to make.

Relationship of the Media Service Organization to the School-System Organization. A problem of large scope faces the school-system media program director when he plans with principals and other key administrators the best public policy for adoption by the Board of Education. We have reiterated this basic insight repeatedly. As schools are presently organized, individual school principals occupy uniquely powerful leadership positions in their own schools and therefore principals must help make the policy with regard to leadership for the media-services program in each school. It may even be desirable to institute several different patterns of organization throughout the schools of the system, but each of the school-building media program leaders should have the kind of relationship to the central media headquarters that will expedite the flow of leadership forces as well as the flow of media materials and equipment. Thus there ought to be a wide, open line of communication and leadership force from the school-system media director to each school-building media director, yet it ought to be recognized that staff members in any given school may also have to be more directly under the jurisdiction of the school's principal as the school's chief administrative officer.

We should explore one other possibility that changes the nature of the principal to school-building media-coordinator control. This is the case where a principal does not assign one of his own staff members to the media leadership job, but instead holds for himself the jurisdiction of technical and clerical personnel and takes charge of the supervisory and professionally creative aspects of media-use developments. In this case the line of control and jurisdiction from the central media program director becomes tenuous. In some cases, and this was not cited as a basic pattern of organization for media service, the central office staff is expanded to include additional supervisory personnel to move among the various schools on either a flexible or fixed schedule—for example, a professional media supervisor working in a given school two days each week. Many arrangements are thus possible and the need for additional services on a full- or part-time basis will have to be determined in light of the needs in a particular school. It is certain that the more technically complex teachers' uses of media materials and equipment become, the more necessary it will be to add additional supervisory and technical staff members to whatever system of organization has been developed.

We have repeatedly referred to the need for professional and technical staff members, and in the next major section of this chapter we shall deal at considerable length with the problems in and arrangements for giving needed assistance to teachers in carrying on their media-use activities. We have been discussing two considerably different patterns of organizing and grouping the various services that constitute the

prime reason for having a school-building media headquarters. Up to this point we have generalized both teachers' needs and the scope of services rendered, without regard to the level of instruction. Principals of elementary schools are confronted by different problems that confront principals of secondary schools. We now turn our attention to these problems and recommendations for their solution.

Media-Service Problems in the Elementary School

There is little doubt that elementary schools, as a class of schools, are less likely to have well-structured and organized media-service programs than secondary schools. We need not overemphasize this condition, nor should we overlook the fact that in a number of schools outstanding programs have been developed. In some cases the existence of these programs has led some observers to make generalizations that were not true. However, it cannot be said that all secondary schools have good media-service programs. Most curriculum leaders and analysts imply in their writings and speeches that elementary school teachers, working as many do with groups of pupils all day long, tend to focus their attention on the learner and his needs instead of on the act of teaching a subject per se. Perhaps this belief about elementary schools has led some observers to say that the teacher in the self-contained group can handle her own visualization, projection, and presentation problems, and on a more informal basis can manage with whatever audiovisual equipment is available. Many school principals have through sheer necessity appointed one teacher to take care of the record players, another to look after the filmstrips, and still another to handle a cataloging project. The truth is that in any formal or informal survey conducted on a statewide basis, the facts about organizational procedures are often shocking. Many so-called media-service coordinators have little or no time in which to carry out their duties. Moreover, some principals resent the assertion that audiovisual media coordinators should be anything more than equipment clerks or technicians. Yet they themselves in many cases do little to organize and give leadership for needed development. Actually this is understandable in the light of a principal's generally heavy work load. But should they not then do some creative planning, exert a little more administrative leadership in guiding other professional people on their staff to do media work under their supervision? We answer, of course, in the affirmative, but obtaining staff for this program of service poses real problems in the elementary school. Obviously we need to take a look at some of the more serious problems that face the elementary school principal and then make some recommendations as to several possible solutions for them.

The Problem of Obtaining Leadership Services. We have already pointed to the urgent need for additional manpower hours to carry on media-service programs. We assert that despite a few voices to the contrary, what is needed is professional leadership activity for implementing innovations. Yet, some principals and some school-system media program directors, probably in desperation, settle for one or more people to do the work of clerks and technicians. What is a greater pity is that many times teachers who are freed for hours of service, or even other part-time or full-time personnel of professional caliber who are assigned to school-building staffs, are completely taken up with nonprofessional duties. In both cases the effect is to weaken the potential to move to creative and more mature levels of media utilization. Now, just what is the problem? The trouble seems to lie in the difficulty of finding or arranging for professional people to be freed from their teaching duties on a part-time basis. Many principals have resorted to such expedients as relieving teachers from such nonteaching chores as playground supervision during daily recesses, daily cafeteria duty, transportation surveillance before and after school, and other dreaded but necessary chores, and also have assigned media chores to teachers whose classes are instructed one or more sessions per week by special teachers, as is often the case with art and music activities. When we discuss the secondary school situation in the next section, we shall find that there are many possibilities for freeing competent teaching personnel for professional media-service responsibility that do not exist in the conventionally organized elementary school.

We shall direct our attention first to the *conventionally* organized elementary school. Each teacher in such schools is pinned down, by and large, for the entire day at work with the same group of learners. This type of organization is often referred to as the self-contained classroom method of grouping and teaching learners. It is obvious that under this condition teachers cannot be rescheduled for part-time assignments as a part of the professional work load. What are some possible solutions to this problem that we can suggest to elementary school principals who wisely place a high priority on media-service development? We shall list a few of the possibilities, but we shall also make suggestions that are applicable to those situations in which pupils are not scheduled all day in one room and taught by the same teacher all of the available time. Our suggestions follow:

Under Conventional Classroom Organization

1. Using funds from school allotments, appoint a full-time coordinator for the instructional media-service organization, and provide the necessary supporting staff of media specialists, clerical workers and technicians. The coordinator should be in charge of school library services as well, undertaking training in this field. This position could or ought to be rated as a vice principal, especially in large schools.

2. Where a librarian is already on the staff, but is not qualified by experience or training for audiovisual media responsibility, employ a

Figure 7-14. Opposite. At Layton, Utah, in the Davis County Schools District, we point out the so-called saw-tooth-shaped school. The teaching stations are arranged radially around an open court, and three of the conventional rooms may be converted by means of two operable walls into a large-group instructional area which is shown in use. Because of the radial arrangement, each of the classrooms has but one window. This is observable in the middle picture. The Vae View Elementary school, one of many in the Davis County District, has consultant services of two full-time Audiovisual Media specialists employed at County Headquarters. The school has organized an audiovisual media-service program, and media materials and equipment are available in the school's service center. In the picture shown, two teachers are checking out materials and equipment. *Courtesy Davis County Schools, Farmington, Utah, and the Principal of Vae View School.*

media-use coordinator for full or part-time duties along professional technological lines. Some of the professional distribution duties may be assigned to the school librarian.

3. Appoint the current full-time librarian to the position of coordinator of instructional materials center services, and assist him or her in obtaining audiovisual media skills as needed, in order to carry out a well-balanced program of services. Support this effort by additional media specialists, technicians and media aides.

4. Employ an additional professional staff member and assign to him the responsibility for audiovisual media, and also the responsibility of inaugurating a school library service. Employ also a supporting technician and a media aide.

5. Invite (and assist him in procuring support for the policy) the citywide media program director to assign on a part-time basis, a professional audiovisual media specialist who would serve as an organizer and implementor for the use of media by teachers, thus sharing professional media leadership with one or more elementary schools in a given area of the district. Appoint one or more full-time media aides and technicians to support the leadership activity.

6. Find ways to combine extra-teaching responsibilities in the lunchroom, playground, and so forth, in order to free teachers for a specified number of hours to perform professional duties with media-use tasks working under the supervision of the principal or a vice principal. Support this professional activity by a technician and a media aide.

7. Proceed as in item 5, but assign the responsibility for clerical and technical duties in maintaining good control of flow of equipment and materials to specific teachers, with the regular vice principal carrying on in-service education for implementing media-use activities.

Under Newer Pupil Organization Plans

1. Employ an instructional media specialist as a vice principal to take charge of the professional media-use responsibilities, and support this person with media specialists, technicians, and media aides according to need. Assign some of the leadership responsibility to the leaders of teaching teams, and some of the media-use duties to the teachers' aides.

2. Where a full- or part-time librarian is already on the staff, assign media duties to that person, if he is qualified; or employ an audiovisual media person and separate the functions accordingly, on a full- or part-time basis.

3. Employ one or more additional teachers as specialists in science or mathematics, or to meet other needs, and assign these persons on a part-time basis, to carry out media-service duties of a professional nature under the principal's supervision and coordination. Because of the flexibility in scheduling instructional activities under newer organizational plans, one or more teachers in a given team may be scheduled so as to devote up to half-time to a media-use supervisory position. One of these people might well be designated as the school's Chief Media-Use Coordinator, with administrative control over the assignments to one or more part-time media-service professionals. Technicians in media preparation, and for more complicated technological installations such as television and electronic study carrels, would have to be provided according to need.

4. As in item 3, invite a central office media-use professional to provide organizational and innovational services as valuable school-district media-center contributions. School-building staff members may support this effort by carrying on continuing assignments according to local technological needs and developments.

5. Plans of action patterned after items 2 through 6 listed previously under plans for conventionally organized elementary schools.

Providing Technicians and Clerks for Media-Use Purposes. The level of accomplishment of educational goals is diminished when professionally trained workers spend their time on nonprofessional tasks. Obviously it is necessary to employ the necessary technicians and media aides and, on the basis of an adequate task analysis, to assign them duties in line with their training and capabilities.

As the nature of the educational process changes in the direction of technological emphasis, needs for personnel will change—and in fact have already changed. Principals should unite their efforts with those of school-system media directors to exert pressure on other key administrators to increase citywide budgets for an increase in technical and clerical personnel. The existing situation is deplorable, but, as we have said, it should be solved in good balance.

Many schools use students as a whole or

partial solution to the problem of providing media aides and technicians. We shall discuss this procedure more fully later, but we ought to relate the use of students, possibly from fourth grade up, to the need for a nonprofessional work force. Of course, the wasting of professional potential may be due to a lack of administrative insight and organizational ability, but in cases where principals are forced to use teachers as clerks, they may also have to turn to the organization of student work crews. There can certainly be little if any harm done, and very probably a lot of good may come from using student workers. The students will get a chance to practice being a responsible individual, relating their developing personalities to adults, settling conflicts with peers, and budgeting their study time. Special arrangements may have to be made with specially trained and highly qualified high school juniors and seniors to pay either a token sum or a full hourly wage for their services. This is understandable in an age where material wealth has become so highly prized.

The use of student assistants requires close supervision, careful planning, and hence demands a professional person who understands the role of the contribution of work and personal service to the total learning process. We must find ways to avoid overloading students with work that should be organized and carried on in other ways—and here is where the principal and media coordinators must show their administrative imagination in wise decisions. We must never miss the point that students are not being sent to school to do the menial and clerical tasks of the professionals, but to engage in a continuing stream of learning experiences, the specifications for which must not be altered for selfish ends. At any rate, we can point to the fact that in elementary schools organization is generally such that pupils are not scheduled for study halls or free time with any precise regularity, and furthermore, almost all of the youngsters in our kindergarten-through-grade-six schools can learn to turn on switches, volume controls, and manipulate knobs and push buttons for self-instruction purposes. However, it is not generally feasible to organize them into working crews that carry out a schedule of assignments for moving projectors or players, or for operating equipment outside of their own classrooms. Elementary school students may actually serve the teacher best by helping in each classroom situation (see Figure 7-15) rather than being organized as an external group operating during the school day. Older pupils may assist after school with mechanical and clerical chores, and help get equipment into classroom locations for the following day.

There is a definite relationship between an adequate equipment inventory and the need for technical services for teachers. There aren't many teachers who would not be willing to learn to operate and use audiovisual equipment units located in their teaching areas. What most teachers object to is moving out of their classrooms for walks to other spaces, or having to go to an equipment center to pick up and return heavy or even mobile equipment units. Although operating the equipment is a nonprofessional activity in one sense, it may be quickly accomplished once the skill is developed,

Figure 7-15. Youngsters take the job of operating equipment such as shown in this picture seriously. But school hours need to be filled with a balanced diet of activity, and spending too much time on media-equipment handling may deprive them of opportunities to widen their interests and capabilities. *Courtesy Encyclopaedia Britannica Educational Corp., Chicago.*

and moreover, when teachers are in operational command of their situations, they may plan the timing and carry out special uses of equipment in the stream of their teaching decisions. Thus we ought to point out that as the number of equipment units approaches the optimum amount, the need for additional technicians may be reduced. For example, if thirty teachers in a given school are using audiovisual equipment units of one kind or another at the same time on a self-operation basis, one trouble-shooting technician and a clerk for handling communication and note-taking jobs may suffice for surveillance and control; and thirty operators would not have to be at their posts in classrooms. We have already stressed the development of optimum media-use environment in schools, and now we have seen another reason why this optimum condition is desirable.

Lack of Provision for School Libraries. Another possible deterrent to the development of better media-use service programs in elementary schools is the lack of formal library facilities, especially in the older schools. (See Chapter 12 for detailed discussions.) In one sense the difficulty of inaugurating a school library service is almost as great, from the standpoint of obtaining professional staff and financial support, as it is to inaugurate new audiovisual media-service programs. Adding them both simultaneously poses an even bigger problem. Some elementary schools have regrettably solved the library staff problem by adding nontrained, or technically unqualified, "librarians" to their school organizations as a stop-gap measure. Thus the principal has a decision to make as to the direction along which to move in solving his problem of providing what we may again refer to as comprehensive instructional materials center services. Some school principals solve this problem by assigning duties for both audiovisual media and library services to the audiovisual media leader, and other principals start with a part-time librarian and add the audiovisual duties. In either case, leadership for the media services ought to go to the most professionally qualified person. As we have said, expansion of both print and audiovisual media services needs to be accelerated.

Lack of Available Space in Elementary Schools for Media Services. We must refer again to the self-contained classroom concept as it has been applied to school-building design in the past. Since the program was based on a teacher for a specific grade group of a definite number of pupils, schools were made up of just the number of rooms for the predicted enrollment. Occasionally an all-purpose room and an auditorium, and more recently a cafeteria and a gymnasium, were added. Under limited so-called extra or flexible space there was and still is no room to use for media headquarters. A principal in one of these situations is hard pressed to come up with a solution that does not require an addition to the building, or involve shifting pupils to other schools, thus compounding the problem elsewhere. This may be the reason why so many principals operate their audiovisual media programs right out of their office suites, with the equipment under lock and key and almost inaccessible to teachers when desired. In any school of ten teachers or more, where such space limitations exist, it appears that the only solution is to find ways to take over one of the existing classrooms, and to develop a media resources center of a comprehensive nature, or to undertake a remodeling job and add the kinds of facilities for media and other purposes. When we develop the image of modern education and what essential components are mandatory, we will no longer be content with impoverished teaching methods.

Media-Service Problems in the Secondary School

Just as we explored media-service problems in the elementary school we shall also identify some characteristics of conditions that generally exist in secondary schools, and we shall study them to ascertain their influence on media-program development. Such explorations are essential for the assessment of plans to organize, inaugurate, and implement media-service programs by school principals and the citywide media director working cooperatively.

Just what are the basic conditions in high schools that have a bearing on the development of media services? We shall list them first and then proceed to make some recommendations.

1. High schools are large schools, larger by far than most elementary schools and fewer in number in a community.

2. Their instructional programs are vastly

Figure 7-16. The Rock Canyon Elementary School, Provo, Utah, a recent 16 classroom school features a school library, a portion of which is shown in the picture, an audiovisual media storage and service room, with some media-preparation equipment in the library's workroom. There is media-use activity in the library in connection with informal school work. Each classroom has adequate light control, television receivers on stands, and maps and globes. Countless older schools are not so fortunate. *Courtesy Rock Canyon School, Provo, Utah.*

more diverse and flexible than in elementary schools.

3. High school programs are departmentalized, and thus by means of the scheduling process, class enrollment may be shifted, and sections combined, thus making possible the rearrangement of work loads of staff members.

4. Students are sophisticated, independent, and mature.

5. High school principals quite frequently occupy positions that are higher up in the power

structure of a community than do elementary school principals.

6. High schools have, by and large, well-developed and long-established library facilities.

7. High schools generally possess staff members often acclaimed as expert in subject-matter fields, and therefore subjects per se tend to receive great emphasis.

8. Great value is placed on cumulative records, transcripts for college entrance, and satisfactory job applications. A sense of high priority tends to develop from the immediate link with adulthood responsibilities. Financial support for extra services in such schools is easier to get, generally.

9. In the high school environment there is likely to be more movement of teachers to and from facilities because of shifting class sessions. Hence more contacts during any given day, better communication, more action class to class, more activity between administrators and teachers and learners, making a high school more closely knit as an organization.

10. In large high schools there are generally available what we may refer to as flexible-use spaces, even a ground floor area that can be taken over for special uses, multiple-purpose areas that by rearranging the schedule of space use may free a classroom adjacent perhaps to a main library, or a space between classrooms that lends itself for a media-service office or an equipment distribution substation.

11. In our modern high schools there is a sense of urgency to keep people in school, by means of interesting, lifelike, highly practical, and worthwhile activities.

12. Students are often available for special work as a club member or as an after-school paid worker. Independent study and work periods and study halls may thus help in making available a student technical and clerical work force of considerable proportions.

13. High schools universally have a number of electronic installations that require technical services. Electronic learning laboratories for foreign languages, electronic carrels supplied with both videotape and regular audio program recordings, extensive public-address systems, central sound systems, television facilities for CCTV production and distribution and for reception via master antenna systems, and automatic projection equipment.

Having identified several of the major characteristics of and conditions in high schools, we should now proceed to an analysis of the bearing that some of these conditions have on the media-program development.

Size of Building and Scope of Program. Programs in large high schools are so diverse, and the need for media services is so great, that the media leadership, staff support, and equipment inventory are sometimes incredibly large. Such programs may have one or more full-time professional media coordinators and specialists, a staff of technicians and secretaries, together with a crew of projectionists and clerical and media-preparation assistants. The principal may decide to keep the library and staff operating as a separate agency, with new media installations in the library being serviced by the audiovisual technical maintenance staff. In this case the audiovisual media coordinator will have his own service spaces and will work coordinately with the head librarian. In cases where all media services are combined under one head, the principal would be likely to secure the appointment of a media coordinator at the vice principal rank. As we have said before, high schools usually have highly structured organizational patterns, and well-organized staffs. Their media coordinators are generally certifiable and hence possess special qualifications for their jobs. A sizable staff is an essential for the work that has to be done. It is, however, a fact that even though many schools have incorporated television in their media-service programs, they still have far too little service space in which to work. Moreover, some sizable programs are administered on time borrowed from other classroom activities. Extensive developmental action needs to be taken by principals, superintendents, and the school-district media director working together to arrive at sound operating policies.

Finding Suitable Spaces for Media Headquarters. The problem of locating space for an instructional materials center, or for a separate audiovisual media center, in a large school is always difficult unless this problem has been met in plans for new construction. The nature of the space needs is determined as usual by first mapping out the program itself. When the audiovisual media center is to incorporate electronic learning laboratories or remote-controlled resource centers involving videotape recording and audio programs, to say nothing of media preparation, equipment maintenance, storage and distribution areas, areas must be extensive. The problem is even more acute when in the case of instructional media centers, spaces for a complete library service, which now also generally includes listening centers, electronic carrels accommodating a ceaseless flow of students, are also included in the plans. We shall deal in considerable detail with the problems of planning media-service headquarters and show in the illustrations the nature of spaces and operation in both old and new schools. At this point we should emphasize the hope that because of the flexibility that exists in the high school program and because of several of the other factors identified, principals can find—on a stop-gap basis—spaces that are more or less suitable to operate sizable media-service programs. In situations where space is severely limited, it will be necessary to locate storage areas and equipment substations out of which equipment may be deployed to the classrooms.

Obtaining Professional and Technical Staff. In the next major section we deal with staff arrangements in schools for media-service duties, but we must point up this problem here as a crucial one that needs more extensive action. Since high schools are so universally departmentalized, and since newer pupil organization methods with increasing emphasis on independent study by learners necessitate a flexibility in scheduling that may free some teachers for other duties, obtaining a professional work force for media service may not be overly difficult. On the other hand, because the program is so complex in most high schools, and because the work load carried by most teachers is heavy, principals and school-system media leaders cannot expect to superimpose extensive, additional media duties of a permanent schoolwide nature on these people. Hence, a solution to the problem of procuring a full-time media-use leader for the school plus the additional media specialists, media aides and technicians needed should be assigned a high-priority designation. We need technicians to maintain equipment, and also graphic technicians to assist teachers with the preparation of slides, transparencies, and film-clips. Media-service programs in modern high schools can no longer operate as they did

decades ago mainly by student work crews and a teacher as a media leader with two free periods a day and a $200 annual bonus. Now, with adequate leadership and support staff, teachers can be led to cooperate in the preparation of materials, working together on programing for television and electronic carrels, for example, and thus participate in increasing the effectiveness of instruction through media. Under such leadership, student assistants may be recruited and trained for making reasonable though significant contributions to the program of services.

The General Climate for Change in Media Organization in High Schools. We have noted several conditions that appear to be characteristic of most high schools, and some of these have a direct bearing on the development of media-service organizations. Other conditions have indirect relationships, but so far as we can observe, it appears that in schools that lay claim to having an effective instructional program, a well-organized and expanded media-service system is indispensable.

Possibilities for Solving the Media Leadership Problem. In preceding pages we listed several possibilities for action by principals of elementary schools to procure and deploy media leadership personnel in their schools. We presented two lists, one applying to old schools with conventional classroom organization and the other to newly designed schools. Rather than refer to that list we provide here a tersely stated summary of those possibilities that apply as well to the principal of a high school that is in general characterized by flexible scheduling and departmentalized operations. We assume when we discuss leadership arrangements that other staff members such as technicians and clerks will be provided, or other stop-gap arrangements made, until the needed financial support is available. Our brief list is arranged in order from most desirable to least desirable, in our view.

1. Appoint a full-time coordinator for the comprehensive instructional media-service organization, including all library facilities and operations, expanding the existing position of librarian to include full media-program leadership, or make the existing librarian position a subsidiary one in case audiovisual media

insight and skills are lacking. Establish the rank of the position at the level of vice principal. Title the position Vice Principal in Charge of Instructional Media, Coordinator of Learning Resources, or Coordinator of Instructional Media. This person would be directly responsible to the high school principal, but would work through him with indirect lines to other key media and curriculum experts at the school-system level.

2. Appoint a full-time coordinator for the audiovisual media-service center, and organize such services and library services as separate agencies in the school.

3. Invite (and bring pressure to bear in support of the position) the school-system media director to supply a full-time or part-time audiovisual media consultant to work with school-building media specialists in two or more schools.

4. Appoint a qualified teacher to serve as an audiovisual media-service coordinator on a part-time basis. Provide him with one or more part-time qualified teacher assistants who will take charge of specific aspects of the service program, such as in-service education in television programing; in designing slide sets, transparencies, and tape-recorded instruction; electronic carrel installations; the library's listening center; student part-time projection and clerical crew; media procurement and distribution; or, equipment readiness and distribution.

5. Add media aides to the school librarian's staff, and assign all clerical functions of procurement and distribution of media, cataloging processes, and communications with central media headquarters for the school system, and appoint from the teaching staff a qualified part-time audiovisual media coordinator to take charge of the full-time technicians and to carry on all in-service education activities and consulting work.

As we have emphasized, all such plans require technicians and clerical assistants proportionate to the technical complexity of installations in the school, the volume of service given, the degree to which teachers need to prepare their own materials, and the need for extensive television, electronic-carrel, and self-instruction programs. The need for change agents in implementing innovations in the years ahead

seems staggering. The logistics will have to be worked out at an ever-increasing pace until higher levels of efficiency and teaching skill with new media have been reached.

Principals and Their Media-Use Decisions. Principals of schools need to develop a penetrating insight into the nature of learning products and activities and the ways in which media contribute to the effectiveness of learning. Insight into the dynamics of the teaching process whereby components involving specific teacher acts, pupil responses to stimuli, pupil efforts, specific media and their relation to both teachers and pupils, will determine in large part the level of priority that principals place on media-use development. Because principals know so little, by and large, about technical matters, they appreciate the emergency services of a technician. When a microphone is out of order they seem to lay undue stress on the need for a technician—but they sometimes exclude or underestimate the importance of the professional person who helps teachers. School-system media program directors also sometimes make this mistake. Principals need to differentiate between the technician-clerk activities and those activities of professionals who may lead a school staff to use media to achieve educational goals at high accomplishment levels. Principals also must be the ones to develop an insight into the possibility of stratifying talents of their personnel if maximum efficiency is to be achieved. Professional personnel ought not to be permitted through negligence or incompetence to waste time and energy in the face of great need to carry out regularly assigned tasks of menial and clerical nature. Each of us needs to take this responsibility to heart. We must not, in addition, fail to envision the growth and development that will take place in the years ahead in the use of technological media in all phases of instruction. In the fact of this burgeoning development, the stratification of talents among many people, each with his valuable potential contribution to desirable educational results, should be planned and implemented. As we have emphasized again and again, principals are key administrators. They are agents of change, and school-system media directors must unite with them in arriving at sound policies to recommend to chief administrators. The process of change need not be carried out at a snail's pace when readiness for a sound plan of action has been developed and when the people involved in the change understand it and support it. Moreover, such processes of change will demand equally extensive plans in both old schools and new.

Staff for the School-Building Media-Service Program

We have made already many detailed references to the need for both professional and technical staff members in carrying out a modern media-service program in each school building. We have based such discussions on the principle that assistance for facilitating innovation and for unleashing the potential of technology in the teaching-learning process has to be located close to the teacher and should be continuously available. We have also indicated that the physical environment in each learning space must be favorable. We need now to define somewhat more specifically the nature of the work that has to be done in a given school and then emphasize the use of various kinds of personnel that have to be obtained and deployed for accomplishing it. First we shall indicate what has been set up as national minimum standards for providing the professionals who are called upon for guidance in matters of teaching methods and curriculum in each school-building unit.

Minimum Standards for Professional Personnel. We shall point out first that the minimum standards to which we refer were first published as *Tentative Guidelines for Audiovisual Personnel and Equipment*, by Gene Faris,[6] Chairman of the Department of Audiovisual Instruction of the NEA. The quantitative guidelines, published as a part of the Gene Faris–Mendel Sherman study under the auspices of USOE, NDEA, Title VII, Part B Program, were officially adopted by the DAVI Board of Directors in October 1965, and also by the Association of Chief State School Audiovisual Officers of the same year. The personnel guidelines specify leadership personnel only, and the recommendations for elementary and secondary schools are stated separately, and further evaluated as *weak*, *good*, and *superior*.

[6] Gene Faris, "Tentative Guidelines for Audiovisual Personnel and Equipment," *Audiovisual Instruction*, Vol. 10, No. 3, March 1965, pp. 201–204.

The person is described as an *instructional materials specialist*, and is defined as a person with training in both audiovisual communications and library science.

Elementary Schools

One instructional materials specialist per 35 teachers (*Weak*)
One instructional materials specialist per 25 teachers (*Good*)
One instructional materials specialist per 15 teachers (*Superior*)

Secondary Schools

One audiovisual specialist per 60 teachers (*Weak*)
One audiovisual specialist per 40 teachers (*Good*)
One audiovisual specialist per 20 teachers (*Superior*)[7]

In another official publication of the Department of Audiovisual Instruction of the NEA [8] based on the same study, personnel guidelines were stated in more direct fashion with additional reference to a number of different categories of professional and nonprofessional staff members needed for school services. These guidelines, as restated, are quoted as follows:

[7] *Ibid.*, p. 202.

[8] *Quantitative Standards for Audiovisual Personnel, Equipment and Materials* (In Elementary, Secondary, and Higher Education). Developed as part of the Faris–Sherman Study conducted under the auspices of the United States Office of Education, National Defense Education Act, Title VII, Part B Program (Washington, D.C.: Department of Audiovisual Instruction of the NEA, 1201 Sixteenth Street, N.W., January 1966), 18 pp., mimeographed. (As is often the case with formulations of standards in rapidly expanding fields of activity, they become obsolete as soon as they are published. The quoted standards are no exception. In December 1967, as a result of deliberations by a Joint Committee of members of the American Association of School Librarians and the Department of Audiovisual Instruction, it was agreed to recommend an upward revision in the previously published standards of both organizations. Such new standards as are approved by the cooperating associations will appear as joint standards for both print and audiovisual media programs in schools. Many drastic though insightful changes were voted at these discussion meetings, that will, it is expected, be incorporated in a new publication entitled, *Standards for School Media Programs*, to be published jointly by the *AASA and DAVI of the NEA* in 1968. In so far as personnel standards are concerned for a unified print and audiovisual media center in a school, it was agreed that the goal should be to employ for each 250 pupils the following staff members: one professional media specialist, one media-aide assistant, and one technician assistant as a minimum. See also Footnote 8 in Chapter 12 for an indication of other changes in standards proposed by the Committee.)

In schools with 15 teachers or less—half-time audiovisual specialist (specialists may serve more than 1 school).

In schools with 16 to 30 teachers—1 full-time audiovisual specialist.

Add one audiovisual specialist for each additional 40 teachers or major fraction thereof.

One, or the equivalent, semiprofessional assistant (technician, graphic artist, clerk, photographer, etc.) for each 30 teachers.

In schools where audiovisual and library responsibilities are combined (the instructional materials concept), the amount of staff required will be determined by adding the above audiovisual requirements to the personnel standards for libraries set by the American Library Association. It is recommended that the first specialist hired be an instructional materials specialist with training in both audiovisual instruction and librarianship.

Every multiple unit school district with at least one high school and four elementary schools shall employ a district or system audiovisual specialist.[9]

We thus observe that directors of school-system media programs as they look toward the fulfillment of new roles by media must exert great effort to implement teacher-assistance plans at two levels working in each school building. They must seek ways to provide professional help in designing and carrying out media-supported and media-controlled teaching plans, or components of such plans, and they must provide clerical and technician services so that teachers themselves may devote their talents and energies along professional lines for maximum effectiveness. The personnel guidelines just quoted (see footnote 8) reveal that this action has been given full consideration.

To reveal the need for a multi-level staff for media services, we present at this point a statement of duties usually carried on by school-building audiovisual media coordinators together with an analysis indicating the nature of professional and nonprofessional activities.

The Need for Professional and Nonprofessional Staff Services in a School Building

The Nature of the Media Coordinator's Duties. Since media-service programs vary from school to school, the following list of duties performed by audiovisual media coordinators is intended

[9] *Ibid.*, p. 5.

to be representative rather than exhaustive. We should note, however, that the reason for this particular listing of duties is to make it obvious that a variety of personnel are needed if media are to be used effectively to play important roles in the teaching process. Duties in the following list generally apply to both elementary and secondary school situations.

Group 1

1. Design the physical layout of a school building media service suite.

2. Devise a complete media-services program, provide leadership and guidance for its implementation, and evaluate its effectiveness.

3. Write a proposal for decision by the principal and other key administrators and curriculum leaders to carry on an in-service education program for teachers to teach them to prepare their own teaching tapes and guidesheets for large-group, self-instruction processes.

4. Write job specifications, procure qualified personnel, teach them to carry on desired duties as needed, assign responsibilities, and supervise their work with both teachers and students, and as needed carry out the same performance with student work crews.

5. Design a media-preparation workroom for teachers, obtain authorization to spend funds, make decisions as to kinds of equipment needed by teachers, identify needed supplies, develop teacher-assistance programs, maintain inventory of supplies on a continuing supply basis, and teach teachers visualization skills.

6. Organize and conduct in-service education meetings to teach teachers the relationships of media to valid educational objectives.

7. Discuss and demonstrate before teacher groups how to plan and design slide sets, tapes, and television programs to accomplish specific educational objectives as a part of a self-instruction program in both large and small groups.

8. Plan and supervise the installation of electronic learning laboratories, and work with teacher groups as grade and subject-matter specialists in deciding how best to use them in programs of instruction.

9. Work with teacher groups in his school to assist them in planning what special media they need to prepare as a part of a system-wide cooperative exchange program with other teachers of similar subjects and grades.

10. Teach teachers how to prepare scripts and continuities for audio and television programs on tape for repetitive use in classrooms.

11. Design and make self-instruction plans and materials with which to teach teachers to operate equipment to both use and make media.

12. Assist teachers in the selection of media for use in specific teaching situations, for specific teaching objectives, including supervision of teacher evaluational activities.

13. Assist and advise the school principal, teachers and departmental heads as to the proper application of new technological developments.

14. Serve as a media consultant in advising principals and teachers in preparing media specifications for remodeling old and building new classrooms and other learning spaces.

15. Manage the school's budget for media expenditure in the light of central or local allotments.

16. Devise and implement an effective plan for controlling the flow of incoming and outgoing media, from local sources as well as from sources outside the school system, including the proper ordering, scheduling, and confirming actions, and the delivery of materials and equipment.

17. Carry on liaison activities with school-system media headquarters personnel, making reports, conducting surveys, analyzing media needs of teachers, and preparing budgetary estimates for long-range planning.

Group 2

18. Make slides and transparencies for teachers for which design and content have been determined.

19. Maintain inventory records of the school's media collection and equipment units.

20. Inspect and maintain high-quality condition of the school's media materials and equipment that flow in and out of classrooms.

21. Maintain in operational readiness the school's electronic learning laboratories and other fixed technical installations such as CCTV studio production, transmission, and receiving equipment, and both individual and group responding systems.

22. Assist in carrying out promotional activities such as preparing special listings, visual presentations for the principal, and typing, duplicating, and distributing announcements.

23. Keep adequate records of the use of media equipment and materials and maintain work records of personnel who contribute service to the media program.

Analysis of the Duties. Now we suggest that the reader analyze the performance in the foregoing listing and take particular note of those activities that are characterized by (a) design and planning, (b) responsibility for sound decisions, (c) need to evaluate objectives and the means to achieve them, (d) teaching teachers how to apply operational techniques, (e) judging the contribution of teacher efforts in relation to the school's instructional program, (f) perceiving application of technology to instructional systems, (g) leadership activity, and (h) laying out work patterns and activity to be done by others. Such activities are the responsibilities of professionals.

Freeing the Media Coordinator for Professional Service. Such an analysis indicates that the items in *Group 1* demand a concentration of the leadership and design action. Obviously these kinds of performances cannot and should not be permitted to be undertaken by any but professional people. But let's note further that the issue is whether or not the professional because he has no choice in the matter has to work at a nonprofessional level. This will be the case when he has to check off the return of equipment and media, change lamps in projectors, type forms and run off copies of reports, make and post schedules of equipment delivery to classrooms, clean tape heads in electronic learning laboratories, show teachers how to perform simple equipment operations, answer phone calls, type letters, put out supplies in the teacher workrooms, make slides and transparencies for teachers, copy audio programs on tape, or operate a CCTV camera. Thus if we analyze the performance in *Group 2*, we will see the need for both clerks and technicians. We can assert with confidence that so long as the school-building media coordinator is forced through lack of supporting personnel to engage in the types of activities just listed, he or she will be unable to carry on the kinds of performance listed in *Group 1*. Moreover, if we carry the need still further, we can readily observe that in almost any one of the *Group 1* activities the assistance of secretarial and technical staff members would make significant contributions. When clerks and technicians are present and at

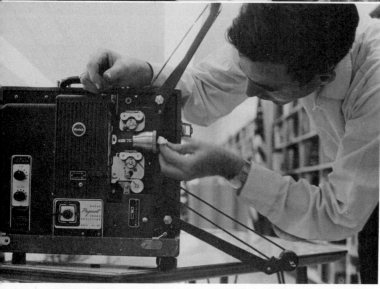

Figure 7-17. Graphic technicians are now in great demand. Many other kinds of media technical personnel are being trained in community and junior colleges and in vocational schools. In these pictures we see a teacher in a Portland, Oregon, High School talking over some needed graphics work at a media center. *Courtesy Portland Community College.*

work under the guidance of a competent professional worker, the school and pupils will gain because more of the leadership and design energy will flow into and through the media-service program to the growth of teachers in their ability to use media in newer and more important roles.

Kinds of Nonprofessional Services Needed for Mature Programs. We have already pointed out that as media programs wax in importance in every school building, highly trained technicians of various kinds will become a necessity. We mention in the following list a few of the kinds of technican workers that will be required as the school-building media service program reaches maturity.

1. Electronic and electro-mechanical equipment repair and maintenance technicians.

2. Television cameramen.

3. Television engineers, licensed and unlicensed.

4. Videotape and audiotape recorder operators and studio technicians.

5. Film inspection technicians.

6. Graphic technicians, and media production assistants.

7. Photographers, and photo-lab technicians.

Coordinators May Need the Assistance of Specialists. When we consider the professional worker in the media field, we look for certifiable individuals who have gained experience in the

Figure 7-18. As media equipment such as shown here is installed for scheduled and integrated use of instructional plans, specialists both professional and technical will have to be added to maintain a steady stream of professional programing activity, and moreover, equipment jams have to be prevented. The carrels at Oklahoma Christian and Oral Roberts Universities are made operationally possible by tape banks such as the one shown in the picture. (*Top picture*, courtesy North Electric Co., Gallion, Ohio. *Bottom picture*, courtesy Oral Roberts University, Tulsa, Oklahoma.)

classroom and who have undergone a program of preparation in the media field. Such individuals may also be highly specialized as in the field of media design working specifically in television, in designing teaching materials for visual presentation by means of slides and transparencies, either partially or fully automated, or for use by classroom teachers in their face-to-face groups. A full-time media generalist may in fact be supported by professional assistants, and by other specialists who are not in the strict sense professional, for example, a television program assistant who may be working closely with teachers in the design of their TV presentations, serving as an adviser in TV techniques for effective communication.

As we have already pointed out, individual schools and school systems have found a variety of ways to get the required man hours of work during the school day needed to assist teachers with their media-supported teaching processes. Sometimes the central media headquarters staff is supplemented by several additional professional and technical persons who work part time at headquarters carrying out assigned duties, and then these people move into the schools to carry on assigned technical duties there under supervision of the school's media coordinator. Many times a staff of pupils handles the clerical work and routine equipment-handling duties that are carried on by adult technicians on a full- or part-time basis in schools that have more mature programs in operation. Since students in both elementary and secondary schools play such important personnel roles in media-service programs, a special section is devoted to common problems in their organization and control.

Obtaining the Services of Qualified Media Coordinators. In the face of a critical shortage of media professionals at all levels of instruction, many school principals and school-system media program directors are forced to select teachers who, though they possess excellent reputations in the classroom and are interested, are not technologically prepared for leadership in this field. School media coordinatorships of course are, or may become, the stepping stones for qualified individuals to system-wide contacts with teachers and citizens, to prestige, and to new jobs as school-system media directors, school supervisors, and principals. No media director or principal should shrink from seeking the most capable teachers that are to be found on the staff for this purpose. They have a duty to select the best obtainable personnel and to bring every professional influence and argument to bear upon getting this leadership. They may have to take less than the best teacher available, but they must select and secure the appointment of a person who at least shows promise to a marked degree, and they must then assist that person to undertake needed training in the media-use field. The reader has but to turn again to the listing of representative duties of the professional media coordinator in a school building with a mature program to realize the need for knowledge and skills in both teaching methods and media technology. In the recently revised *Handbook for Audio-Visual Representatives, Secondary Schools* of the Los Angeles City Schools, this brief description of a media coordinator and his qualifications appears.

The audio-visual coordinator is in a position to exert lively educational leadership. His is a unique place in the secondary schools. To varying degrees, he is a curriculum specialist, in-service training specialist, and media specialist. There is an increasing demand for him to be familiar with an ever-widening field of audio-visual resources ranging from study prints to educational television. . . . To be successful an audio-visual coordinator should possess certain qualifications. First and most important, he should be an expert teacher and should have a genuine desire to serve as a resource person. He must be familiar with audio-visual methods and have the ability to share his knowledge and skill with others. It is also important that he be able to work harmoniously with teachers, administrators, and pupils. Organizational ability is a key to the success of the audio-visual program. Mechanical aptitude is an asset but not absolutely essential. The audio-visual coordinator must be able to accept criticism and to evaluate it objectively.[10]

Today in a number of states, such as Connecticut and Pennsylvania, a media coordinator who is to devote half time to his duties may not be employed by a school department unless he has become certified, or, shall we say, is *certifiable*. Thus in an increasing number of cases principals and citywide media program directors turn to qualified personnel outside of their own school staffs. Therefore it is imperative that those who seek to fill such positions prepare explicit job descriptions and specify the levels of preparation and other qualifications that have to be met by applicants. A more detailed discussion of the problem of preparing job specifications is provided in Chapter 8.

It is expected that one of the duties of a citywide media program director will be to advise school principals as to the present and future nature of duties envisioned for school-building media-use leaders. It is revealing to read a set of specifications written for a high school media coordinator that includes the sentence, ". . . *Must be able to repair and maintain audiovisual media equipment*." If the list of specified duties had stipulated instead "*Devise and supervise an effective equipment maintenance program*," a candidate for the position would have been able to sense a greater concern for the professional

[10] *Handbook for Audio-Visual Representatives, Secondary Schools* (Revised 1965), p. 5, Los Angeles City Schools, Instructional Services Branch, Los Angeles, California, 1965.

aspects of the service system rather than pre-occupation with technician's duties. When we deal with the school-system media program headquarters we shall discuss in detail the nature and importance of equipment-maintenance programs. If technicians are urgently needed, and they will be in all advanced programs, they will have to be employed, deployed to service stations, and supervised. No professional media-use leader should spend his valuable time on maintenance work, except in an emergency.

Remuneration Policy for School Media Co-ordinators. Individuals who have established their reputations as outstanding teachers, who are capable organizers, and who exert significant professional influence on the teaching ability of other staff members deserve more than letters of appreciation and their own personal professional satisfaction in return for their services. The fact is that in far too many schools, remuneration policies are still woefully inadequate. The city-wide media program director as one of the educational leaders of the school system, together with the various school principals, who are themselves respected key school adminis-trators, must put their good influences to work to formulate acceptable local policies governing the remuneration of school-building audiovisual media coordinators for service rendered. Care should be taken in formulating such policies to include an agreed-upon statement of major duties and responsibilities (samples of which have been presented earlier), and to involve school principals, teachers to be served, and other curriculum leaders in the process of developing effective plans of action. It will not be easy to obtain the adoption of adequate remuneration policies, but even though unsuc-cessful, the campaign to do so must be con-tinuous. The combined weight of the opinions of principals, teachers, and other curriculum people should be formally reported to school authorities, and as needed, community support should be enlisted through PTA groups or other local school-community organizations. Reports and requests for action on this matter need also to describe the extra work load normally in-volved, and to provide the evidence and results of the duties performed.

Because school-building media coordinators are professional workers, they should be paid as such. Therefore they should be paid not only as a regular teacher, which they were at one time, but as teachers who give special services that influence the work and results of other teaching personnel. This means that as a vice principal, or as a special teaching consultant, and because of special skills and knowledge, they deserve additional remuneration. Many are the ways in which media workers in schools are paid, some of them, unfortunately, receive small token bonuses at the end of the school year, in addition to their teacher's salary. Schools with advanced or mature service programs will recognize the values in an adequate staff; other schools may somehow arrange for a technician to be on duty to help teachers with equipment problems, but provide no professional service whatever. The following levels of remuneration are presented from inadequate to highly desirable.

1. Reduce teaching load or release from required school routine assignments.

2. Annual bonus payments as salary, starting at $300, in combination with reduced teaching and extra-duty loads.

3. Full-time media-service assignment with rank of teacher.

4. An additional salary payment equivalent to one or two months of extra pay when the coordinator spends two extra weeks at school after school closes in June, and two weeks prior to the opening of school in September on significant service projects.

5. Full-time assignment as an instructional materials specialist, ranking as an assistant principal, or the salary of a regular teacher plus a differential of 10 per cent as a minimum.

We can not and should not ignore the fact that many individuals are indeed willing to accept additional responsibility for unique reasons. Such incentives may be the means of inaugurat-ing service programs, but they rarely serve successfully as a continuing basis for worthwhile and long-range programs.

Employment and Remuneration for the Non-professional Media Worker. Although it is com-mon to employ a wide variety of workers at well-developed city- or countywide media-service centers, it is not so common to find film inspectors, projectionists, electronic technicians, graphic technicians, secretaries, and illustrators in every school building of a given school system, but this is rapidly becoming a prime necessity. Again as before, it is imperative that citywide media program directors work with school principals in preparing job descriptions and specifications, and all school administrators know that it pays to study applicants and their records before, not after, they are employed. Since levels of training and experience differ vastly between professional and nonprofessional personnel, their salaries and wages differ also. Secretaries and clerical workers may carry on a wide list of important duties, and men, who generally demand higher wages for their marketable skills in media-service centers may frequently possess combinations of skills that are very valuable. Some electronic repairmen have been known to possess graphic skills as well, or they may be taught to use cameras and media-preparation equipment. And of course if skilled technicians are available, women may be employed to operate electronic film-inspection machines. As we shall point out in the next section it is also possible to employ skilled students as part-time workers. Such students working on an after-school basis receive varying hourly rates of pay, however not often lower than $1.50. A combination of club activity and a work experience program on a no-pay basis as a part of the school's course work may work to the advantage of media coordinators. The pay range we present for technical workers may prove helpful for purposes of long-range planning but of course the figures indicated may vary considerably across the country according to experience and economic factors. The following are starting-salary estimates for nonprofessional, technician-type media-service personnel:

1. Television engineer or chief technician in a school television studio and transmission facility: $6,500–$9,000.
2. Electronic equipment installation and maintenance technician, with skill in designing systems of components: $5,500–$8,000.
3. Electronic repair and maintenance technician: $5,000–$7,000.
4. Electro-mechanical repair and maintenance technician: $4,500–$6,500.
5. Film inspection and service worker, both men and women: $3,500–$6,000.
6. Graphic technician and media preparation assistant: $6,000–$8,000.

7. Photographer and photographic laboratory technician: $6,000–$8,000.
8. Television cameraman and videotape and audio-control technician, and other studio assistants: $5,500–$8,000.
9. Instructional programing design assistant for school studio operations (nonprofessional or semi-professional): $6,000–$8,000.

We are well aware that in larger organizations supervisory personnel may also be nonprofessional in category, as for example a chief film inspector, and in these cases, additional pay for additional responsibility is well worth it to free the media-use leader from the time-consuming supervisory work of setting up standards of workmanship and planning work schedules and checking on their completion.

We have pointed out previously that school-building media-program leaders, in the absence of financial support for full-time technical and clerical workers, rely heavily on student media-service clubs and work crews. As service programs develop, there should be a steady stream of dependable and continuous assistance by trained, full-time workers. Even though it may be necessary to make use of some student helpers—as long as it is beneficial and not harmful to the pupils—the largest percentage of the needed man-hours of service should come from regular employees. Until that goal can be reached, various kinds of student service organizations will be needed. Therefore we turn to a discussion of this topic in the following section.

Making Effective Use of Student Assistants

A Rationale for Using Voluntary Student Work Crews

We should bear in mind that although donating service to their school may be a rewarding experience for pupils, both socially and educationally, it is for special service to teachers and media coordinators that student work crews have to be recruited, trained, organized, and supervised. Because of their frequent presence in classrooms and laboratories, media coordinators and school principals should persuade the most dependable and capable pupils or those with acceptable potentials for accomplishment, to donate their time and energy to school-building media service. If we were considering in a major way the particular needs of pupils, we would then select those who could profit most from the work experiences, and some or many in that category may bring discredit one way or another on the total service organization, and in addition require unusually large amounts of training and supervision.

Thus, on the one hand we face the personality-development needs of pupils who are recruited for work on media-service clubs and squads, and the need of a media program coordinator to extend highly efficient and well-organized technical and clerical services throughout the school day. A balanced decision will have to be reached on this and other problems. The school-building media coordinator should work with his school principal and also with the school-system media director in formulating and implementing policies and procedures. In fact, we must emphasize that meeting the need on the part of the citywide media director to implement an operational plan for school-building services becomes one of his primary problems. Therefore, the school-district media leader must be prepared to advise and teach, through the cognizant principal, of course, each school-building media leader how to organize and maintain student operational crews. The problem then is both a school-building problem and a school-district problem. The basic assumption underlying the stated rationale is that selected fourth- and fifth-graders and above, both boys and girls, may under favorable conditions be motivated to donate time and energy without detriment to their academic standing and health. It is also important to note that the less the degree to which teachers possess technical self-sufficiency, and the more sophisticated and the greater the volume of media use is in any given school, the greater will be the requirement for student work crews and other full-time technical and clerical assistants.

This student-crew aspect of the total media-service system involves the school-building media coordinator in solutions to the following important problems: (1) selection of crew members; (2) training the crew; (3) organization for efficient service; and (4) developing morale. All these are interrelated, but each needs a separate discussion.

Selection of Crew Members

When selecting members for the crew the coordinator must formulate local policy, but he should bear in mind the following suggestions:

1. There is a need for balance between members at various levels to facilitate progress in capability from year to year. This policy provides a number of top-ranking, capable students for the most difficult jobs, such as training and supervising other workers, and inspecting equipment. For example, strike a balance between a number of fourth-, fifth-, and sixth-graders in elementary school; between seventh-, eighth-, and ninth-grade pupils in junior high school; and between tenth-, eleventh-, and twelfth-graders in senior high school.

2. Superior students are needed for crew members, but above all, students should be capable of excellent workmanship or they should never be accepted, or if they cannot succeed, they should be eliminated. But sometimes membership in the crew, as has already been pointed out, will be good for a student who is maladjusted, and here a real problem exists in balancing the good of the service against what might be good for one or more individuals. Thus, in the selection of crew members, the coordinator should incorporate the advice of his colleagues through the offices of the principal and the guidance counselor.

3. Teachers and current crew members may help in recruitment, although it is imperative that a scale for judgment be formulated for all who make recommendations; that is, a brief, workable scale involving such items as appearance and poise (or capability to develop it), health, character, academic capability and study habits, interest in media equipment, and technical aptitude.

4. Final acceptance of new members should be made only after a specified provisional status period which ends as soon as an elementary though important examination has been passed satisfactorily.

Many times, teachers in both elementary and secondary schools may organize supplementary classroom services by asking interested students whom they themselves train to perform valuable kinds of work in the interests of more efficient use of media materials and equipment. In this era of technological sophistication, many youngsters in third grade know how to operate several kinds of media equipment in self-instruction programs for themselves and for the teacher as well. Everyone knows that in modern-day school teaching, the teacher herself has need for technical and clerical support that is rarely adequately met, so it is not only the media program leader for the school who needs and deserves sympathetic consideration.

Training the Media-Program Service Crew

Training the crew demands an organized teaching program with study materials and laboratory practice sessions. The coordinator should bear in mind the points made in the following paragraphs as he builds a training course for his own situation.

An equipment handbook for each student is an essential. Directors of media-service programs should prepare suitable handbooks as a direct form of assistance to each coordinator. Such a handbook should contain threading diagrams and explanations of how equipment should be set up and handled. An interesting example is the mimeographed *Manual for Student Projectionists*, prepared by the Division of Instructional Materials of the San Jose Unified School District of California. In the front of this manual there appears a Foreword by the Assistant Superintendent of Schools. Similar manuals including appropriate additional materials have also been prepared for teachers and for elementary and secondary school coordinators by the San Jose department. Los Angeles provides another example. The audiovisual department there has prepared an attractively printed and illustrated manual for school coordinators that contains excellent materials for training programs. Many schools follow this practice. In this connection equipment operation manuals and textbooks may be used as a source of content for preparing materials for local use.

Scheduled training-practice sessions are essential. The best training programs are organized on the basis of sessions complete with instruction sheets and practice in an equipment laboratory. Such instruction should be carried on in groups for specific topics and machines and should involve only those who have not passed the required operational tests. This procedure demands a record system that shows on a card, to be carried by the student, the extent of the trainee's qualifications. For example, at the Bloomfield, Connecticut, High School, the operator's qualification card bears the signature of the school's media coordinator and of the school principal. All major pieces of equipment are checked off on the card as performance tests are passed.

Personnel for carrying on training are essential. The school-building media coordinator may not be able to find the time to accomplish the

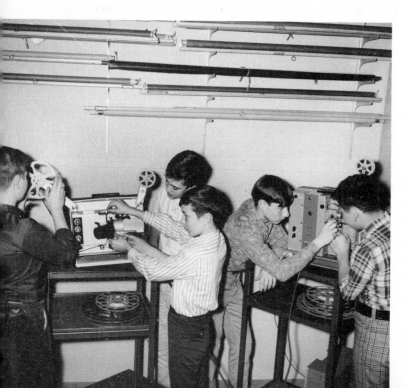

Figure 7-19. New recruits for student service groups have to be trained to perform specific tasks, checked out thoroughly during working periods, and given opportunities to grow in self reliance. These younger boys at the Northeastern JHS are being guided during practice sessions by older and more experienced members of the service crew. See also Figure 7-9. *Courtesy Public Schools, Kalamazoo, Michigan.*

PROJECTIONIST CHECKSHEET

AUDIO-VISUAL PROJECTIONIST PERFORMANCE RATING

CENTRAL HIGH SCHOOL

NAME _____ DATE _____

PROJECTOR MAKE AND MODEL _____ _____

	MEETS PERFORMANCE STANDARDS	BELOW PERFORMANCE STANDARDS	NEEDS FURTHER INSTRUCTION
OPERATE PROJECTOR			
Set up equipment			
Thread film			
Adjust focus, sound, framing			
Start and stop during showing			
Disassemble equipment			
SERVICE PROJECTOR			
Change projection lamp			
Change exciter lamp			
Change fuse			
Change metal belts			
Clean lens, film gate, and film guide			
SPLICE FILM			
Make overlap splices			
Make permanent splices			
KNOW HOW TO CARE FOR FILM			
Explain common types of damage			
Explain common causes of damage			
Explain ways to prevent damage			
KNOW HOW TO SOLVE COMMON PROJECTION PROBLEMS			
Loss of loop			
Jumpy picture			
Dim picture			
No picture and no sound			
Picture but no sound			
Distorted sound			
Sound but no picture			
Sound not synchronized with picture			

Figure 7-20. Many media centers that depend on student service organizations to carry out projection and other operational assignments at teaching stations on schedule, develop and use rating sheets. Such checksheets may be highly specific to check on certain kinds of performance, others are more general. The particular checksheet shown deals with operation of the motion picture projector. It was developed at Central High School, Los Angeles. *Courtesy Los Angeles City Schools.*

required training on a personal-instruction basis. He should take the necessary steps to obtain assistance from colleagues through the principal's office, or he should organize a teaching crew among his best student operators, thus putting the training program on an apprentice basis, or he should turn the training and handling of the crew over to an assistant.

Implementation of programs of instruction designed to develop specific abilities is an essential.

269

The nature of a crew member's duties, whether secretarial or technical, and the standard of efficiency desired, will determine the specific nature of the instructional activity. Objectives, identified as kinds of performance, ought to be written out and then developed by appropriate means in optimum order so as to build one skill on another to facilitate the learning process. For example, from a filmstrip projector to a motion picture projector or from an audiotape recorder to a videotape recorder, thus making use of knowledge learned in preceding steps. Some student crew members may work in electronic learning laboratories, or operate listening centers in teaching auditoriums and libraries. Their work may be operational only and not include maintenance. Other student assistants may be film inspectors and splicers, work in the school's CCTV studio, or clean and inspect equipment for readiness for the next assignment. Training programs may therefore vary greatly. Many media coordinators are visualizing and taping instructions for crew members and thus are moving toward media-supported training systems. Even though the

design and preparation of such systems is an arduous task, the eventual economy in time and energy and the subsequent facility with which future training sessions are handled are astounding. Kenneth G. Skinner, one of the author's students has inaugurated a teaching system of this sort for his crew members in the Manchester, Connecticut, High School. Instruction is presented by means of 2 × 2 inch slides calling for small-step responses. This self-instruction system is designed to teach skill in preparing classrooms for effective projection. See Figure 7-21. Illustrated booklets may also be prepared for similar self-instruction purposes. It is hardly necessary to emphasize the importance of continuing evaluation of crew-member performance by means of tests, checksheets, and teacher reports of action while on assignments.

Organization of the Student Crew for Efficient Service

Organization of the operator crew for efficient service is another matter of great

Figure 7-21. This flow diagram shows the phases of instruction through which the trainee moves. This plan is arranged to be self-instructional in nature. Each main phase deals with a specific kind of performance, and if the student is not successful, he returns to the beginning for a repeat of the presentation of small-step operations, each calling for its desired response as depicted by the media. Each such phase is referred to as a "loop." See Chapter 11. *Courtesy Kenneth G. Skinner,* Manchester, Connecticut.

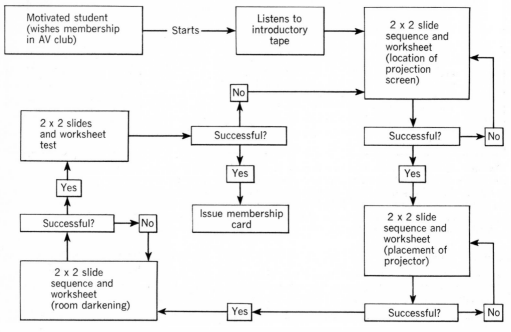

importance, and the following suggestions in the following paragraphs should be considered.

Leadership Force. Each school-building co-ordinator will have to determine how to organize his operational crew so as to maintain control at all times, either on a personal basis, or through students who have been designated as crew leaders. Even when media coordinators have no teaching assignments in regular class-rooms, a leadership structure may serve to free him from excessive direct personal control. A word of caution is in order, since some of the drawbacks in having students give technical and clerical services that full-time personnel could be held responsible for, are the possibilities of absenteeism, irregular performance, and having to use pupils who are neither qualified nor properly trained. It is necessary to understand the nature of the problems involved and to be alert to what is going on. Strict control and full and continuous knowledge of performance is of the greatest importance. A supplementary leadership structure is therefore vital to any student organization. In this case, the service of the operator crew could function with the help of a top-ranking, capable crew member as a captain, together with one or more assistants who could take over during scheduled periods of the school day or when the captain was absent from school. This leader would have specific duties of a supervisory nature, checking on attendance, orders, routing, and so forth. The media coordinator will then have to check up in detail on a fewer number of workers.

Teams or Squads. The organization of crew members into teams or squads for the coverage of floors, or for morning or afternoon sessions, or for certain days of the week—depending on the volume of service and the size of the school —may prove to be helpful. Each team or squad would, of course, have a leader who could report to the coordinator or to the crew captain.

Office Force. Any operator crew should be supported by an office clerical crew; these workers may never go out on classroom assignments, but may process orders, check schedules, prepare materials and route slips, and get equipment ready. Office forces are easier to organize at the high school level, but modifications of such procedure in elementary schools is not impossible. In the case of high schools, students may conveniently report to the audio-visual headquarters during study periods or under other arrangements. In elementary schools when the school media coordinator has a part-time teaching assignment, care must be taken to locate the coordinator's classroom near the headquarters suite to facilitate office-force work under surveillance before and immediately after school. The system for accepting and processing orders may thus have to be restricted to specified periods in advance of the date that material and equipment are needed. Greater emphasis may also have to be placed upon teacher operation of equipment and the training of operators within each class, fourth grade and above, in order to cut down the frequency of separating the same student from his class for a projection assignment elsewhere.

Developing Morale in the Media Service Crew

A highly important factor in developing and maintaining the efficient service of a crew of projectionists is morale. Morale develops as a result of favorable conditions, and although not all these conditions can be covered here, those discussed in the following paragraphs should receive close scrutiny.

Operating according to a well-known, clearly defined set of procedures and commitments develops morale. When working with either youngsters or adults, it pays to inform them about their responsibilities. We need to spell out important requirements in broadly stated rules and regulations. If such statements are too detailed and lengthy, they are likely to be neither learned nor heeded. Rules will make their maximum contribution to morale when they are formulated in a spirit of mutuality and then agreed to by all concerned. Morale grows through understanding and respect for an organization and its leadership and goals.

Check-up and accurate recognition of quality workmanship is important for morale. Co-ordinators must know what is going on and what is being done by each worker. Unless work is being checked, a sense of disregard for good workmanship is likely to ensue. Morale is influenced by the knowledge that what is done will be checked and due recognition given.

Belief by crew members that the work is important develops morale. This belief can be most effectively instilled by expressions of appreciation by someone other than the im-mediate leader. School principals, teachers, and

Figure 7-22. Good administration of student assistants demands selection, training, appropriate assignments, and continuing evaluation. The young lady, a senior at Bloomfield, Connecticut, High School, is shown carrying out office work and receptionist assignments at the audiovisual media headquarters, and at the same school, a group of boys is shown checking and cleaning a filmstrip projector. In the bottom picture two students at the Staples High School, Westport, Connecticut, are assigned to work in the graphic-service area. Young men and women may be trained and organized to do sophisticated service work, but there is a reasonable limit to the man-hours of work that can be performed without curtailing the instructional accomplishment of student helpers. (*Top views*, courtesy Public Schools, Bloomfield, Connecticut. *Bottom view*, courtesy Public Schools, Westport, Connecticut.)

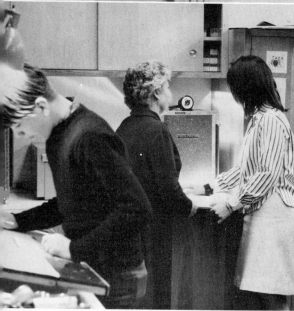

top-level school authorities can speak the right words. The impressive Foreword in the San Jose school system Manual for Projectionists [11] was signed by the assistant superintendent of schools. It is a strong case in point and we quote it here in full:

You are a member of a select group that gives much service to your school.

The morale of your group and the services performed have always been very high. You should always strive to fulfill your obligations, and maintain the highest standards of performance. Your first consideration must be satisfactory service rendered.

A projectionist must become familiar with each piece of equipment, and well trained in its use. Following is a manual that will give many useful and practical hints to help you do a better job of showing audio-visual materials.

Curtis Davis
Assistant Superintendent of Schools

Club or organization procedure and appropriate insignia develop morale. Making a club out of the crew, with elected leaders chosen by carefully taught criteria for judgment, together with appropriate membership cards and badges, is a good pathway to morale. School coordinators may set up a strict procedure for application for a membership card of their own design or the

[11] *Manual for Projectionists*, Division of Instructional Materials, San Jose Unified Schools, San Jose, California, 1955.

Example 7-1   AUDIO-VISUAL SECTION
                      Los Angeles City Board of Education

Date _____

The undersigned has completed a course of instruction in the operation of the 16mm. motion picture projector or projectors named below.

Authorization is hereby given to operate the projector when all rules and regulations of the Board of Education, and all laws of the city, county, and state governing motion picture projection, are fully met.

This card shall be revoked upon evidence of incompetence or for violation of city, county, or state requirements.

Make _____   Name _____

_____   School _____

Model _____   Instructor _____

_____   Approved _____

club may become affiliated with the Projection Club of America,[12] using standard cards and gold pins. As we pointed out earlier, projectionist cards should show special qualifications as a matter of record. The standard student projectionist card as used by the Los Angeles City Schools[13] is shown in Example 7-1.

As a club, the operator crew frequently engages in interesting group activities such as trips to nearby university audiovisual centers, theater projection rooms, and audiovisual production centers, thus adding variety to the training activity that must characterize most of the club sessions. Expenses for such all-day trips, including chartered buses, are frequently paid out of school funds budgeted for the purpose.

School awards and formal personal recognition develop morale. Such awards go beyond school newspaper accounts and over-all recognition by school authorities in publications. At appropriate times, a book award, or some other prize, could be offered in school assemblies to the most outstanding technician of the year.

Other awards, such as certificates of service and letters by school officials stating the period of service and the over-all rating assigned by the coordinator, should go to all participating students annually. Plaques with engraved names of leaders, or with names of crew members who serve a specified number of years, have also been effective in this regard. A tribute could also be given the school's crew by arranging a special exhibit of pictures of members using or delivering equipment. Details such as these should, of course, be discussed with other coordinators in meetings with the director of media services for the school system.

Limitations on Student Responsibility

Having given rather detailed suggestions relative to the implementation of student-assistance programs, we feel compelled to point out that limits should be placed on the kinds of performance that are expected of students. We media people are prone to move ahead in our plans to inaugurate our innovations, and we are many times sorely tempted to work on a shoestring basis until we can establish a better set of support circumstances. Thus we place some of our student workers in critical situations, in which, if unfortunate accidents took place, we

[12] See Phillip Mannino, *ABC's of Visual Aids and Projectionists Manual* (rev. ed.), M. O. Publishers, Box 406, University Park, Pennsylvania, 1955.

[13] *Handbook for Audiovisual Representatives, Secondary Schools* (Revised 1965), *op. cit.*, p. 21.

could be greatly and perhaps permanently embarrassed. Take, for example, the use of minors as messengers, or the assignment of high-school-age technicians on a volunteer basis to make videotape recordings of telecasts during the evening hours. Suppose some of these highly respected workers met with an accident enroute to or from the school. Or suppose that youngsters left doors unlocked, or had impressions made of keys on loan to them, or brought uninvited guests to the media headquarters suite or to the work places, while they worked late. What might the consequences be for the school officials? For the students? For the media-service program?

We raise these doubts in line with earlier suggestions that we use adult, full-time technical employees to handle the bulk of our critical assignments, especially those that involve the need for stable adult judgment. We should not place our volunteer workers in those situations where embarrassment may occur either to them or to ourselves. When such special assignments are necessary, the school's media leader ought to arrange for on-the-spot supervision by regular, full-time professional or technical employees, and to take any other precautions that seem to be called for.

Planning and Equipping the School-Building Media-Service Center

When school buildings that were built many years ago lack complete media-service facilities, they must be remodeled to include them. Influenced by media technology, new school structures, as has been pointed out repeatedly, are virtually complete with service suites—some, of course, more extensive than others. School-system media program directors should encourage school planners to increase the media-use potential of all new buildings in order to provide the best possible service to teachers. When old buildings are devoid of up-to-date media facilities, such facilities must somehow be planned, constructed, and equipped. However, we direct this discussion to both school media leaders and principals, prospective and practicing, and to school-system media program directors as well, because it is an urgent topic to

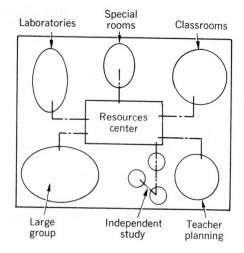

Figure 7-23. This spatial relationship chart indicates the kinds of teaching stations and special facilities that use the services of a school building media or resources center. The sketch is from the book, *Educational Facilities with New Media,* published by the DAVI of the NEA in 1966. *Courtesy Center for Architectural Research, R.P.I., Troy, New York.*

which too many school officials continue to assign a low priority.

Because of the flood of new school construction across the land we will first discuss the nature of space needs. Then with these needs in mind, we can suggest how they may be met in old school buildings. We shall refer to illustrations of school-building media headquarters spaces with some pointed references to both weaknesses and strengths as they appear. We should also explain that because we wish to focus attention on audiovisual media operations in this as we have in earlier chapters, and because we devote another chapter to the print-medium program, we shall not include the subject of libraries in the present discussion in a detailed way. We have stressed earlier that facilities for all media can either be combined in one comprehensive service suite or maintained as separate school departments.

Space Needs

The reader should not miss the main point in this section, namely, that in order to provide adequate media services in school buildings,

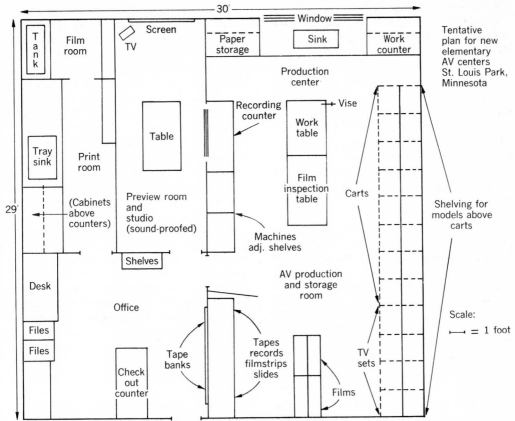

Figure 7-24. The floor plan diagram indicates the planning done by a citywide program director to provide minimum-size quarters in a school building for audiovisual media services. Whether constructed in new or old schools this plan should be studied to identify the various kinds of essential functions that have to be carried out. *Courtesy Public Schools, St. Louis Park, Minnesota.*

specific functions must be carried out, and to do so operational spaces are essential. This same assertion applies at the school district level, and therefore we shall discuss and illustrate in the next chapter space needs that must be met in planning and equipping school-system media program headquarters. It can be readily understood that space needs for media functions at the district level will be far greater, but even so some of the functions are similar in nature. There is no established requirement for the design of school-building media centers, and their actual size will depend on the degree to which spaces for electronic learning laboratories, CCTV studios, and school library facilities are incorporated in the same suite. Many times, specialized spaces are scattered throughout the school plant according to needs in specific in-

structional areas. The basic space needs for the school audiovisual media-headquarters operations are suggested in the followng list. There should be enough room to

1. Store media equipment issued to or owned by the school.
2. Store media materials issued to or owned by the school.
3. Store audiovisual media supplies.
4. Handle the flow of media materials and equipment in and out of the center.
5. Inspect and clean returned media materials and equipment.
6. Handle and process pre-use examinations of media materials by teachers.
7. Prepare special audiovisual media materials for teaching purposes.

8. Administer the service program.

9. Provide and manage the use of fixed technical installations for the school (such as TV studios and electronic learning laboratories).

Directors of school-system media-service programs need to be aware of these elemental needs for servicing teachers in every school and they should plan accordingly with school superintendents, school principals, architects, school media coordinators, and teachers in connection with all new school-building construction. In the absence of citywide media leadership in the schools, school principals and their school-building media coordinators will have to be the ones to exert the necessary leadership force for planning and implementing the acquisition of the needed facilities. A noteworthy example of local planning in the new schools of Portland, Oregon, is what is referred to as the school's Instructional Materials Center. In each new school building, and in all others, a large block of space is being provided as rapidly as possible, for centralizing the services in connection with all instructional materials. In charge will be a vice principal as a curriculum worker able to help teachers with curriculum problems ranging from books to graphics. This kind of comprehensive service, involving all instructional materials, is characteristic of the Portland system.

How Much Space Is Needed? No easy or pat answer is available for this question. We can, however, identify services to be performed and identify levels of media support for teaching in any given field of instruction on a continuous scale from poor to excellent, weak to strong, minimum to saturation at every teaching station. If we look to common practice, we find some programs of media service operating out of remodeled shower rooms; others operate out of book closet spaces where the backs of doors have been equipped with storage shelves for filmstrips. Others, still in cramped quarters for the scope of service, are housed in a conventional-sized classroom that has been carefully planned for some basic services with additional facilities such as electronic learning laboratories and TV studios located elsewhere. In new schools we are more likely to find suites of rooms, either for audiovisual media services alone, or a complete instructional materials center where print medium services and audio-

visual media are combined. It can be readily understood that when these facilities are combined, the square-footage estimates may strike the naive as being enormous. Referring to the preceding list of basic space needs, it is easy to understand that if a school's media-service center space layout includes a TV studio and related control room and storage areas, and two 50-position electronic learning laboratories, together with a remote-controlled bank of programs, the total space requirement would be increased by an estimated 3,250 square feet. The media-service center may in fact have to service special facilities elsewhere in the school, and these we have identified previously, but in cases where classrooms are clustered in such manner as to provide at will a large-group instruction space with a multimedia, rear-projection screen installation, the center's technical staff may have to be on the move to and from such areas on a flexible schedule. Such spaces may be associated with other facilities and hence not thought of as a part of the school's media headquarters suite. Moreover, there are many ways of utilizing floor space efficiently, such as basing floor layouts on time-motion analyses, using floor-to-ceiling storage cubicles, and using the same areas for many uses according to need—for example, using a workroom area for conference groups as well as for the preparation of media for special uses by teacher groups or their aides. Thus, in the light of school size, basic media-service needs, operational level of program, and special-purpose spaces that serve the whole school, we can make some serviceable estimates of space on a square-footage, floor-space basis. We make these estimates for a thousand-pupil school using the previously stated basic needs as follows:

Basic Needs

1. Storage areas for all basic purposes including dead storage (80), media supplies (80), and media equipment and materials (300) for a total of *460 square feet of floor area.*

2. Workroom for processing orders (50), inspecting materials (100), receiving and issuing media materials (50), *totaling 200 square feet.*

3. Cart garage for holding a dozen ready-to-roll equipment units on mobile stands, *totaling 100 square feet.*

4. Workbench area for checking and servicing equipment units, *totaling 50 square feet.*

5. Area for pre-use examination of materials (individual viewers and headsets for sound carrels or benches, individual small screens for projection of films), *totaling 140 square feet.*

6. Area for preparation of instructional media (see also Chapter 9) by teachers, teacher aides, and by pupils for special purposes; and area also for duplicators and central duplicating for the school, *totaling 700 square feet.*

7. Area for administrative activity, including leadership (100), and staff space for related operations (100), *totaling 200 square feet.*

Subtotal, basic need section: 1,850 square feet.

Fixed Media Installations

1. Closed-circuit TV studio for taping and transmitting to intra-school teaching stations: Studio (900), control room (150), storage (100), office (100), *totaling 1,250 square feet.*

2. Electronic learning laboratory (electronic carrels), two 50-position units, and space for remote-controlled banks of programs, *totaling 2,000 square feet.*

Subtotal, fixed media installations: 3,250 square feet.

Library Needs

1. Complete school library (see also Chapter 12) facility for print-medium functions, including professional library, *totaling 6,000 square feet.*

Subtotal for library section: 6,000 square feet.
Grand total of space estimates: 11,100 square feet.

When perusing such suggested space allocations, the reader should bear in mind that many variables must be considered, and that therefore the figures given must be recognized as tentative in light of school needs and operations. The estimates provided are nonetheless serviceable for discussion purposes. The illustrations should be analyzed with care to assess the nature of the services which a given diagram of a center, or its special layout, will support in actuality. Wide variety in available space and the ways in which it is used are readily observable.

Some Guidelines for Designing School Media Centers

We shall of course concern ourselves mainly with basic audiovisual media space needs, since in subsequent chapters we include detailed dis-

cussions of a number of specialized services that may or not be planned as a part of the school's media-service center. We refer to preparation of media by or for teachers, school library services, television, and self-instruction systems. In each of those chapters additional guidelines and illustrations will be provided that will assist the prospective media leader in the school or city to perceive the possibilities clearly for combining any or all of the many desirable services either in the same location or in several locations in the school.

We may now refer to basic media-service spaces as (1) storage areas, (2) order-processing and materials-inspection areas, (3) equipment-maintenance area, (4) mobile-equipment (cart-garage) area, (5) media-preparation area, (6) pre-use-examination-of-materials area, and (7) administration area. Each of these areas will be discussed briefly, with the understanding that in the next chapter much additional information will be given to the planning and design of the citywide or district-wide media-service center. First, let us turn our attention to some general considerations.

Some General Considerations. In their notable booklet,[14] published in 1961 as part of a project pursuant to a contract with the U.S. Office of Education, DeBernardis, Doherty, Hummel, and Brubaker formulated several statements in the nature of broad guidelines for the planning of the instructional-materials center in each school building to meet the needs of both teachers and students. We quote those guidelines as an introduction to the more specific recommendations that follow:

The storage, cataloging, inventory, and distribution of books and of all other teaching materials should be combined in one center, designed to assure coordinated, efficient use of its resources.

The instructional materials center should be located centrally for the efficient distribution of equipment and materials and for convenient use by teachers and students.

In buildings of more than one floor, elevators or ramps should be provided so that books, materials, and equipment can be transported easily. Floors and entry-ways through which carts must pass should be

---

[14] Amo DeBernardis, Victor W. Doherty, Errett Hummel, and Charles W. Brubaker, *Planning Schools for New Media*, in cooperation with the U.S. Office of Education (Washington, D.C.: The Superintendent of Documents, U.S. Government Printing Office, 1961).

free of obstructions. Kickplates and jamb-protection should be provided where equipment must be moved through doors.

Due to the weight of materials and equipment needed in the center, and due to problems of handling and distributing supplies and equipment, a ground floor location is preferable.

All features of the center should be planned for flexible arrangement. Storage, cabinets, shelves, and walls (where acoustical considerations permit) should be designed to be movable so space may be rearranged to meet the changing functions of the center and make possible multiple uses of space.

The arrangement of the center should provide for isolation of noise-producing areas from classrooms and reading rooms. Those activities of the center that generate noise are previewing, testing and repairing equipment, auditioning, preparing teaching aids and materials, and distributing supplies and equipment.

Provisions should be made for future expansion. The ultimate size of any school or school district cannot be foreseen with certainty; neither can the degree of increase in use of new educational media. Therefore, the materials center should be planned so it can be expanded with a minimum of cost and disruption to adjoining areas.

Space requirements for storage, distribution, and preparation of materials will depend on the degree to which these functions are shared between the center and the classroom.

Adequacy of storage is paramount. Long-range requirements for storage of equipment and materials must be considered.[15]

One of the authors of the booklet just referred to was Amo DeBernardis, then Assistant Superintendent of schools, of Portland, Oregon. Because of subsequent formal planning work completed by a coordinating committee of Portland School System administrators including that author, and which was published in 1964 as "Educational Guidelines for Southwest High School,"[16] we can trace the influence of the general guidelines previously quoted in the formulation of specifications and also in the actual architectural plans. We therefore quote the entire section under the heading *Instructional Materials Center*. The reader should bear in mind that the Southwest High School was being designed for a starting enrollment of 1,200 with plans to expand to 2,400 pupils.

15 *Ibid.*, pp. 12–13.
16 "Educational Guidelines for Southwest High School" (Portland, Oregon: Public Schools, 1964), pp. 127–132.

Instructional Materials Center

Effective teaching and learning require many and varied teaching materials and equipment. Books, periodicals, films, filmstrips, microfilms, recordings, programmed learning materials, television programs, models and displays, and data banks are some of the teaching and learning tools available to teachers and students. The school must be organized to make these materials easily available to teachers and students. The facilities must be planned not only to make these tools available but to efficiently store, distribute, and repair them. The instructional materials center is the central focus for the handling of these materials and equipment. It should provide the following services to students and teachers:

To catalog and inventory all types of teaching and learning materials—books, pamphlets, films, recordings, models, exhibits, art prints, slides, filmstrips, microfilms, community resources.

To maintain and service all of the teaching tools used in the school.

To inform teachers and students about new developments in materials, equipment, and teaching technology.

To produce materials which are unique to a specific teaching situation.

To provide assistance in the locating of needed teaching and learning materials.

To assist teachers and students in the use of teaching equipment and materials.

To provide space and facilities for teachers and students to preview, audition, review, and try out various teaching media.

To serve as a comprehensive learning laboratory in which students can learn to use all types of learning materials and equipment.

General Considerations for the Planning. The center should be located centrally so that it can serve the various components of the school. It should be designed to make it easy to change partitions or expand areas such as reading and storage. Acoustics and ventilation should be carefully planned to take care of the work being carried on in the area. Floors and doorways should be designed to facilitate easy movement of carts, materials, and equipment.

Reading Area. This area should provide the following:

Reading space for 150 students (preferably not more than 80 to 100 in any one area).

Storage space for 15,000 volumes.

Spaces for individual reading and research.

Display space—cases, tackboard.

A browsing area.

Materials Stack Area. This area should provide the following:

Storage for books, periodicals.

Storage of microfilms, slides, films, recordings, tapes, programmed learning materials.

Circulation Area. This area should be centrally located to facilitate checking of materials and supervising of the various spaces. It should provide spaces for card catalog and reference files and be easily accessible from office and work area.

Multi-purpose Area. This area should:

Provide adequate lighting for television production.

Be accessible to the production area.

Provide storage facilities for television camera, lights, console, etc.

Accommodate 120 students for large group instruction.

Provide folding partition to allow room size to be changed easily.

Be accessible from the corridor.

Be adaptable to the production and distribution of closed circuit television programs.

Provide adequate power and outlets for television cameras, projectors, etc.

Conference Area. This area should:

Accommodate small groups of 6 to 8 students.

Be adaptable to use of all types of learning materials and equipment, films, recordings, slides, programmed learning materials.

Be conveniently located to the materials.

Provide for supervision.

Have a folding door to permit combined use of adjacent room.

Have adequate ventilation, light, and acoustical control.

Provide shelving for storage of books and equipment.

Individual Study Spaces. The individual study spaces should:

Be equipped to use all types of learning materials and equipment, books, machines, recordings, etc.

Provide some visual and sound separation from general reading area.

Have adequate lighting and ventilation.

Individual Preview and Audition Spaces. These spaces should:

Accommodate one student.

Have adequate acoustical and ventilating treatment.

Provide space for using recorders, viewers, microfilm readers, projectors, teaching machines.

Provide temporary storage for books, tapes, films, recordings.

Storage Area. The storage area should:

Provide for adequate storage of all types of materials—maps, globes, projectors, exhibit screens, recorders, displays, tapes, carts, etc.

Be located near the general receiving area for the school.

Be easily accessible to all parts of the center.

Be arranged for ease of handling material.

Provide shelving and storage space which can be easily changed to fit new equipment and materials.

Maintenance and Service Area. The maintenance and service area should:

Provide space for the repair and servicing of all types of teaching media such as books, audio-visual equipment, science equipment, maps, globes.

Provide work bench and tool cabinet.

Provide space for grinder, test equipment, bench drill press and small tools.

Provide storage for equipment needing repair.

Production Area. The production area should:

Provide space for production of all types of teaching materials, such as transparencies, slides, motion pictures, models, charts, dioramas, signs, posters, mock-ups, etc.

Provide space for jig saw, table saw, and other small tools for model making.

Provide darkroom which can be used for production and instruction.

Provide space for artist.

Provide space for storage of paints, papers, wood, etc.

Provide adequate power and electrical outlets to run small shop equipment.

Provide sinks with hot and cold running water with clay traps.

Provide space for editing films, slides.

Provide space for photocopy equipment.

Office Area. The office area should:

Be located to facilitate supervision of the materials center.

Provide space for desk, books, files, and storage space.

Be adjacent to a work area.

Receiving Area. The receiving area should:

Be located near loading area for the school.

Provide doors which allow carts and equipment to be delivered with care.

Provide shelving and spaces for temporary storage of materials and supplies.

Textbook and Supply Area. The textbook and supply area does not need to be in the IMC complex, but could be adjacent to it. This area should:

Provide space to house textbooks.

Provide for the distribution of books to students. Be easily accessible to a corridor and receiving area.

Provide space for receiving, storing, and distributing educational supplies.

Multi-purpose Learning Lab. The multi-purpose learning lab should:

Provide electrical and communication facilities for all types of audio and visual instruction.

Provide seating for 40 students.

Be equipped with 40 student stations with facilities for listening to tapes.

Provide for a master console.

Provide two individual listening rooms.

Provide for showing of all types of visual materials.

Provide for adequate ventilation, sound, and light control.

Provide chalkboard and tackboard space.

Future Expansion and Development. All partitions in the center should be of a removable type to allow for future expansion and rearrangement of the space. Power facilities should be designed so that it would be easy to use any type of new electronic teaching device. Lighting and ventilation should be so designed as to allow for the division of spaces into any size from small group to large group.

The final result of such planning was a combination of one central instructional materials center for the whole school and eight additional so-called unit-instructional-materials centers, one for each unit school. See Figures 7-25 and 7-26.

Some Specific Suggestions for Designing Each of the Working Areas. We shall now give consideration to those space arrangements that contribute to the effectiveness of the media-service program and which may facilitate future changes to meet new developments. We shall make these suggestions in relation to each of the seven basic space needs previously listed, and also in direct relationship to the Portland, Oregon, specifications which should be borne in mind as the additional following information is analyzed.

Storage Areas

1. Provide five kinds of storage:

(a) For media materials such as films, tapes, globes and maps, slide sets, filmstrips.

(b) For media equipment units not on long-term assignment to teaching stations for issue on request. See Figure 7-27.

(c) For media supplies: spare reels, film leader, cleaning fluids.

(d) For infrequently used equipment units and stocks of accessories, and equipment awaiting trade in, commonly referred to as "dead" storage.

(e) Bulk storage for summer or other non-use periods.

2. Provide for additional space to store materials used for preparation of media, and spare parts for equipment such as tubes, belts and lenses in or near areas of such activity.

3. Arrange flow diagrams of operations and use storage area spaces as sound barriers, and also in line with economy of time and effort to retrieve needed materials.

4. Supply adequate lighting, ventilation, and dehumidification when storing electrical and electronic units that may deteriorate over long periods of idleness.

5. Allow space for workers to move freely when returning or retrieving materials from shelves and bins.

6. Refer also to *The Storage Area* list in the Portland, Oregon, example.

Order Processing and Materials Inspection Areas

1. Economize on time and effort by locating order-filling and packaging processes near storage and pick-up or delivery areas.

2. Incoming and returned media materials such as films, disks, filmstrips and filmstrip sets, slide sets, tapes and kits need to be visually inspected for signs of damage and errors in repackaging in the classroom. Special electronic and/or mechanical equipment may be required. Such inspection stations ought to be located in optimum relationship to storage areas.

3. Provide electric power for inspection devices, and sufficient space for both worktables on which to lay out materials and mobile carts for returning materials to storage or stacks.

4. Filling orders for filmstrips and other materials becomes an arduous task when shelving units are too close to the floor. Provide convenient to use storage units for efficient handling.

5. Provide space for shelving, or a long table or bench, on which to place packages ready for pick-up and delivery.

6. Media materials should be returned from classrooms to the same location, a central receiving station, where they may be routed conveniently to inspection area.

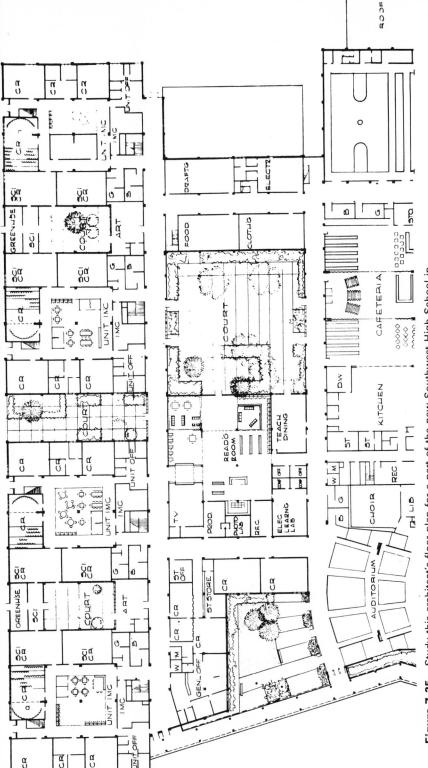

Figure 7-25. Study this architect's floor plan for a part of the new Southwest High School in Portland, Oregon. Note the reading room to the left of the court near center of diagram. Note also electronic learning laboratory, television studio facility, and photographic laboratory. Now note the subsidiary instructional materials centers (to use the Portland, Oregon, expression), four of them at top of the diagram, one for each cluster of classrooms. Note the large-group teaching station near the top wall, one for each cluster. Supposedly a small specialized library facility is to be made available in each of the classroom clusters, thus implementing a decentralization of the main library as a resource center. *Courtesy Public Schools, Portland, Oregon.*

281

Figure 7-26. The main reading room portion of the Main Instructional Materials Center for the school. With the facilities shown, this school should be able, with the continuing support of school leaders, to have a fine instructional all-media service program in the years ahead. *Courtesy Public Schools (Photograph by Portland Community College), Portland, Oregon.*

7. Refer also to the *Receiving Area* and *Maintenance and Service Area* lists in the Portland, Oregon, example.

Equipment Maintenance Area

1. Provide a waist-high work bench equipped with adequate electric power in plug mold, constructed so as to include storage bins for equipment units being worked on.

2. Repair materials need to be handily stored in drawers and bins, and one or more pieces of test equipment may have to be placed on the workbench or on appropriate shelves nearby.

3. Maintenance area needs to be supplied with mobile stands for moving equipment to and from storage areas, or mobile stands each with its own piece of media equipment should be located adjacent to the maintenance bench with easy access to school corridors.

4. Locate the maintenance area in close proximity to media equipment return stations.

5. Refer also to the *Maintenance and Service* list in the Portland, Oregon, example.

Mobile Equipment Area (Cart Garage)

1. Provide an accessible row of mobile projection stands each with its projector, tape recorder, portable electronic learning laboratory,

Figure 7-27. There are many storage functions, as indicated in the list, and some of these have been shown or implied in the previous illustrations. In Portland, Oregon, secondary schools, bins are provided for equipment units that are not kept in a state of readiness for classroom delivery. By examining the various cubicles, we can make some inferences. What inferences can be made from the number tab on the overhead projector? What inference may safely be made from the fact that a microphone is stored with a record player, bottom, second left cubicle? What special use is planned for the tape recorder middle right? *Courtesy, Instructional Materials Center, Public Schools, Portland, Oregon.*

stereo tape or record player, portable television display or transmission system, ready for delivery to teaching stations upon request.

2. Locate mobile equipment-stand area near corridor to avoid traffic through workrooms.

3. Locate the mobile equipment storage area adjacent to equipment repair and service area.

Media Preparation Area

1. Special attention should be given to the problem of storing supplies for the preparation process. Stocks of supplies ought to be visible to teachers using the facilities, and good organiza-

tion is essential. That is, supplies for a given process such as making Polaroid slides (in either 2×2 inch or $3\frac{1}{4} \times 4$ inch size) ought to be arranged together and labeled properly. Shelves and cabinets with sliding doors may have to be used in combination.

2. Waist-high workbenches, or flat-top student desks for sit-down processes such as binding slides, should be provided, making possible convenient arrangement of all equipment from copy-cameras to lettering sets.

3. Provide special working stations where equipment is in a state of readiness for immediate

Figure 7-28. Media-preparation centers require special arrangements of space and furniture, with emphasis on counter space and storage for supplies that is easily accessible. Spaces vary greatly in operating area. The functional space needs are analyzed in Chap. 9. In the bottom picture we note a portion of the new and spacious media preparation section in a secondary school service center. Note the tilted screen, the light box for viewing media masters in preparation or after processing. Note in the top view the graphic technician and his working area in one of Portland's high schools. *Top picture*, courtesy Instructional Materials Center, Public Schools, Portland, Oregon. *Bottom picture*, courtesy Thornton Township High School and Junior College, Harvey, Illinois.

use, with needed supplies nearby or at the station.

4. Refer also to the *Production Area* list in the Portland, Oregon, example, and to Chapter 9, *Implementation of Media Preparation Services.*

Pre-use Examination of Media Materials

1. Provide flexible area for simultaneous examination of all media by individuals and small groups, by means of small projection screens and headsets for individual or small-group listening.

2. Provide plug-in boxes for sound, and projectors and players arranged on optimum-size tables. Provide possibility for group viewing of a single projection screen and an additional person viewing his own screen using an additional projector.

3. Suggest using nearby classrooms for large-group evaluation of media.

4. Previewing space should be easily usable for other work groups on occasion for recording instructional tapes as an example.

5. Refer also to the *Individual and Audition Spaces* list in the Portland, Oregon, example.

Administration Area

1. Usually, the criterion uppermost in the minds of planners of offices and administration areas, is privacy. This is not generally in keeping with the great need of school-building media center administration activities. Although some planners surround an office area by wall-to-ceiling partitions, it may in fact be far more effective from the standpoint of getting work done to strike a balance between privacy and visibility of as many working spaces as possible. This would be especially desirable when reliance is placed on student assistants.

2. Conference spaces may be associated with office areas and media literature files for professional study-committee use.

3. Far too much space is devoted in general to the office area. When space allotment is at a minimum, the size of the office for the school-building media coordinator should also be at a minimum, and emphasis should rightly belong on the contact with operations as needs dictate.

4. Management activity by assistants needs consideration, and hence desk and file space must be provided in proper relationship to the media coordinator's office.

5. Refer also to the *Office Area* list in the Portland, Oregon, example.

We have presented space estimates in consideration of essential functions, and we have presented some guidelines for designing such operational areas. However, the prospective media-center designer needs far more information than he has received to this point. We therefore assure the reader that we shall discuss and illustrate in detail many aspects of media-use operations and needs in the chapters that follow. We ought to stress the point, now, however, that not all of the media-service

Figure 7-29. This area for pre-use examination of media is also a multi-purpose space that adjoins the media-preparation area shown in Figure 28. Instructional television services are a part of this school's media program. *Courtesy Thornton Township High School and Junior College, Harvey, Illinois.*

SCHOOL AUDIOVISUAL ROOM

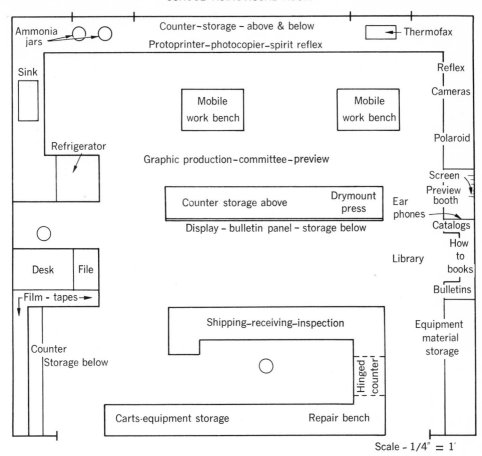

Figure 7-30. One of the author's students developed this floor plan for a minimum-size audiovisual media service center that could be set up within the space of a classroom area 30 feet by 26 feet. What flaws in the planning can you identify? How remedy them? *Courtesy Marilyn McNab, Glastonbury, Connecticut.*

facilities have to be located in one suite. It is often highly desirable to move equipment and materials into substations and also into several more specialized service stations such as electronic learning laboratories and TV studios.

Some Suggestions for Planning Media Service Centers in Old Schools. It is rarely possible to find large unused spaces in older school buildings that can be taken over for developing a media-service center. The probable alternate methods of providing needed space are to construct an addition to the building or to take over one or more classrooms. In the former case, the previous general and specific suggestions may be helpful. In the latter case a great deal can be done with imaginative layout of space available in a single classroom, which may provide more

than 675 square feet of area. Planners would make a serious mistake if they recommend the use of wall-to-ceiling partitions in such classrooms. Emphasis placed on work-flow diagrams, over-all administrative surveillance capability, and on maximizing working space for teachers and crew of assistants, plus the location of possible smaller substations and additional cart garages to serve clusters of classrooms on additional floors that older buildings are likely to have, will pay dividends in increased service effort.

Further discussion of details and specifications regarding the school-building audiovisual media-service center and its equipment are unnecessary for the present, since the school-system audiovisual center will be discussed in the chapter that follows. Significant parts of that discussion will be applicable to service centers within each school building. Such plans as have been described indicate the kind of service center that each school should be provided with. The instructional programs in some schools demand that these centers be larger and more comprehensive than in others.

Having viewed in detail a number of the pertinent aspects of organizing, planning, and staffing good audiovisual media-service centers in school buildings, we should focus our attention finally on a problem that relates to over-all operation, namely, the management of control systems. We need not present such management systems in great detail because it is doubtful that any given system that is devised will be applicable in a universal way to all school programs. We must, however, stress the importance of giving due attention to the nature of the problem, and call for creative and high caliber action on the part of the citywide media program director, the school-building media leader, and the principal.

Management of Audiovisual Media-Service Systems

We have pointed out in an earlier chapter the difference between leadership and management, and we emphasize here again the great need for professional leadership for perceiving and setting goals and designing good service systems for achieving them. Good management in the implementation of policy is also an essential phase of the on-going, developing media-services program. In preceding sections in this chapter and in earlier chapters we have discussed a number of organizational problems, and by suggesting desirable procedures for the acquisition and distribution of media materials, and deployment of equipment, to mention just a few topics, and in the duties that have been listed, we have implied the necessity of effective operational systems. It remains for us at this point to identify some of the systems that should be set up and managed efficiently. We again deal with audiovisual media processes common to the programs in most schools with the knowledge that many variations exist in the degree of media emphasis and comprehensiveness, and that new developments are certain to appear in the future that will require new control procedures.

Distribution of District- and School-Owned Media Materials

Nature of the Problem. Schools that are units within a school district that has an organized, district-wide media-service program, are likely to have available many resources upon which to call, located in central school-district headquarters. They may also have their own collections of media materials, either on long-term assignment or owned outright, located in the building for daily use. Materials needed by teachers may therefore have to be ordered from the citywide center or from the school-building center, or on a free-loan or rental basis from sources outside of the school system, but this procedure will be treated as a separate system. Such materials must be ordered, delivered to the teacher or teachers, used according to need, and returned to school district headquarters on time. How can this clerical process, that involves high-cost materials, be routinized and handled in a safe manner by other than professional employees?

Suggested Management. Procedures may naturally vary according to local arrangements with a given citywide media center's scheduling system, but the process in rather general terms is clear-cut. Hence the following suggestions may be made:

1. Provide teachers with a statement describing the step-by-step procedures that have been officially adopted by the school and school system, having to do with deadlines, quotas, delivery and return dates, and other items characteristic of the local system.

2. Distribute sample order blanks or ordering forms for materials available only from the citywide headquarters, and remind teachers of deadline dates for submitting orders for materials.

3. Distribute catalogs or specialized listings to each teacher.

4. Collect orders on due dates and forward them to citywide center for processing.

5. Return confirmations of scheduled materials to teachers involved, but a listing is made by dates of use for the entire school for each week, for those media that may have multiple uses by several teachers—for example, motion pictures and tapes.

6. When motion pictures and such materials as are likely to be used by more than one teacher

arrive at the media center of the school, they are logged in or checked off on the incoming list and placed on suitable shelves or racks pending delivery and/or pick-up by the teachers who wish to use them.

7. Media titles and/or packages are noted for return according to lists that have already been prepared and then made ready for return to city headquarters.

8. Make some centralized media materials available directly to teachers by special procedures, using a different ordering form. Such materials should be noted by means of carbon copies of original orders, and should be delivered directly to teachers who are to return them to the school's media center for pick-up by school-system's trucking service.

9. Make available school-building-owned materials by using a separate multiple-copy ordering slip. Such media as maps, globes, filmstrips, tapes, may be picked up or delivered to teaching stations, and upon return by the teacher are checked off on the order slip.

10. Organize full- or part-time staff members or students to handle clerical aspects of materials processing. Write out specific instructions and post them, and give copies to personnel concerned.

11. Deploy a staff member to make daily checks on the system's operation.

12. The media leader should make periodic evaluations of all aspects of the process, including analysis of flow diagrams and motion-time observations.

Any system must be as nearly foolproof as possible under the enforced limitations; however, a professional leader must not become enslaved to clerical and menial tasks. Thus good procedure must be painstakingly worked out and delegated to appropriate workers.

Independent Short-Term Procurement of Media Materials

Nature of the Problem. In addition to obtaining media materials from district headquarters and from school collections, teachers are permitted by means of budget allotments to make use of materials from sources outside the school system on a rental or a free-loan basis. Because of their high cost, potential value, popularity, and often limited local availability, motion pictures are the most frequently rented medium. Aside from the problem of providing

financial support to each school media coordinator for this purpose, the heart of this problem is locating the right film, getting it for use at the right time, and then returning it to the distributor on time to be sent to the next rental customer.

Suggested Management. Since film procurement through rental arrangements is such an important method of acquisition for so many schools, this problem was discussed in Chapter 3 under the topic *Efficient Procedures for Renting and Borrowing Media*. Systems may of course vary greatly from school to school, but nevertheless operational systems are made up of essential elements, and these were set forth in considerable detail in that previous chapter. Therefore, at this point we shall assume that the school is operating an independent system of rental procurement limited by specific budget allotments involved. The following briefly stated suggestions as to management constitute a review of the earlier treatment.

1. Provide check-off lists of previously regularly rented film subjects for teachers, including space for new film requests and dates desired for use.

2. Provide simple ordering forms together with a school calendar that includes vacation periods, marking periods, and other pertinent regulatory information.

3. Maintain card file of preferred distributors with related code numbers included on lists sent to teachers.

4. Use a labor-saving printed form letter for setting up rental orders with distributors.

5. Compile and distribute to teachers involved, the list of rental motion pictures scheduled for each month of the school year.

6. Check monthly master list for rental films (formal log sheet) as soon as films arrive, and fill teacher requests for equipment and service. Notify teachers if necessary to confirm arrival of expected film shipments.

7. Inspect films in every shipment prior to use to determine print condition, and then place them on the separate, rental-film ready rack or shelf (to avoid mix-ups with district-owned and school-owned media).

8. Locate films, if not returned to ready rack on due date, and inspect them for damage, repackage them in original containers, label properly, and enter on log sheet the return shipment data and post office insurance number.

9. Notify distributor of any irregularities in the film shipment, and save log sheets for handling the bill-paying process.

10. Note evaluations from teachers regarding future film rentals and/or purchase recommendations, filing them appropriately. Refer also to Chapter 3 content included under *The School-System Process of Evaluation and Selection.*

If we scrutinize this process carefully it can be seen that once the system has been established, only clerical functions are carried out to implement it. Hence, helping teachers to choose and evaluate media in light of their objectives, and evaluating the entire system constitute the higher-level processes usually carried out by the professional school-building media coordinator.

In some districts, the rental film process is carried on only by personnel working in the district-wide media headquarters. In these cases, some of the elements of the above operational system are still desirable, particularly those that have to do with the control of the film at all times while it is being used in the school-building audiovisual media center.

Handling Media Equipment Breakdowns

Nature of the Problem. In any good-sized elementary or secondary school that has a well-organized and supported media program, anywhere from ten to fifty audiovisual media equipment units may be functioning in as many rooms at a given time. Teachers may be operating this equipment or, in some cases, students in the class or assigned student operators from a media service-center crew. What happens when there is a breakdown? Who will be Mr. Fix It? The teacher? The operator? Will the audiovisual media coordinator be called out of a conference, or even his own class of pupils, to diagnose the difficulty? What operational plans ought to be implemented?

Suggested Management. The answer is not too difficult. If we follow the principles already enunciated, we can see that there are several alternatives, but one thing is certain, the remedy has to be administered fast. Contrary to some common practices, it does matter to a lot of people that time is wasted because of defective equipment or because equipment is sent out in a poor state of readiness. The following essentials should be present in any good system formulated:

1. Send out to teaching stations only those equipment units that are fully ready for use.

2. Organize an emergency operational equipment pool, with standby projectors on mobile stands ready to dispatch to a teacher in trouble.

3. Assign a student technician to trouble shooting and equipment-dispatching duty near the office phone. (Such calls will hopefully be so few that students assigned to this duty may study most of the time.) In larger schools, trouble-shooting duty may be handled by full-time technicians who are working regularly in graphics or maintenance, or doing other technical work in electronic learning laboratories, and who may be absent from such a post for a few minutes on an emergency assignment.

4. Undertake to develop organizational plans for locating equipment pools near clusters of classrooms so that standby units are available a large percentage of the time close at hand.

In trouble-shooting situations, especially when technology becomes complex as it does with automatic and remote-controlled equipment, technical personnel become indispensable. Such personnel may then be made available for training purposes, and hopefully teachers and some of the student technicians will be able to handle most, if not all, of the minor difficulties that are almost certain to arise.

Distribution of Media Equipment

Nature of the Problem. This problem is directly related to the problem of procuring media from all sources for use by teachers, and also directly related to the assignment of operators. Once the needed tapes, films, and filmstrips, to name just a few media, are at hand, coordinators are then faced with the problem of providing the right equipment (and operators if necessary) to make possible the effective use of the media. In large schools this problem is a serious one and one that may have to be resolved by placing restrictions on the volume of service. The equipment may have to be operated by teachers themselves when enough technicians or student workers are not available. As soon as teaching stations are equipped with

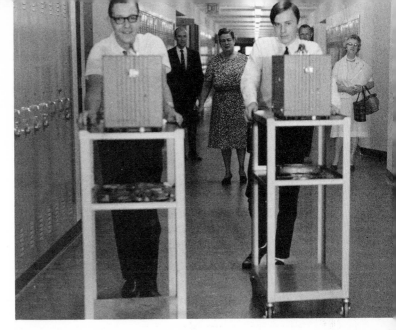

Figure 7-31. These two boys, members of the efficient media-service crew at the Bloomfield High School, wind up some late afternoon work at headquarters by making some equipment deliveries for early morning classes. They even blocked a little faculty traffic while they had their picture snapped. *Courtesy Public Schools, Bloomfield, Connecticut.*

all needed equipment units, and teachers can operate their own equipment, then coordinators will have to deal only with the problem of media delivery and pickup. Hence the problem is one of degree of self-sufficiency of teachers in their own teaching stations. The more self-sufficient they are, as far as media equipment is concerned, the less serious the problem of equipment distribution becomes. Since one of the basic principles to be followed in providing media services is that of timeliness of use by the teacher, and since teachers should have materials and equipment conveniently available, we suggest that the equipment-distribution problem be solved without fail.

Suggested Management. As guidelines for media coordinators with similar problems we suggest several essential parts of a system to handle the distribution of equipment units from an equipment pool or substations, as follows:

1. Collect and organize requests for equipment service from teachers, up to the limit of equipment and personnel available, using suitable order forms, sign-up chart, equipment-allocation board, or sign-up sheets for the week posted at the media center, in the office or library or at any suitable location.

2. Assign equipment units as requested entering notations on a master request sheet.

3. Schedule operators, if teachers need them; otherwise deliver the requested equipment at or before the appointed time.

4. Post a daily schedule for movement of equipment units according to assignments and work orders for operators. Provide standby equipment units for substitution.

5. Issue assignment slips to each operator specifying jobs to be done. (Slip to be given to teacher for signature and report on quality of personnel service and operational efficiency of equipment assigned.)

6. Pick-up all equipment units that are due back at end of the day for a complete readiness check-up and reassignment to mobile equipment pool, to regular substation, or to the next day's teaching stations.

Unless teachers can operate their own equipment, and this will always be the case a certain percentage of the time, the media coordinator has no choice but to organize a student technical crew, employ full-time clerks and technicians, or work out some optimum combination of supplying the needed personnel services for a predictable number of hours of classroom service each school day. In the Los Angeles City Schools, a simple and workable procedure is recommended in the handbook for audiovisual media coordinators who, in released time from teaching assignments, organize service programs in their respective schools. This suggested six-step procedure is as follows:

A six-step procedure is recommended to achieve this self-scheduling effect:

1. Five teacher sign-up sheets, one for each day of the week, are posted with the confirmation sheet in a central location. . . .

2. Days and periods when service cannot be provided should be crossed off the schedule. Some

PROJECTIONIST'S REPORT FORM

Projectionist's Name _____

	Film Code_____	Punctual		

Film Code _____   Punctual

Projector _____   Efficient

Room _____   Cooperative

	YES	NO
Punctual		
Efficient		
Cooperative		

Remarks _____

_____

Mark (circle one)   A   B   C   D

Teacher's Signature _____

Date _____   Period _____

Figure 7-32. This check-off evaluation form for the teacher to fill out on each occasion of service, or during selected periods of the month, unknown to the student, if record keeping becomes burdensome, is a model of desirable simplicity. *Courtesy Los Angeles City Schools.*

coordinators note reasons for limitations on service, such as holidays and assemblies. . . .

3. Teachers sign up for film showings on days and at times desired. They should be secure in the knowledge that films will arrive on schedule unless they are notified to the contrary. . . .

4. At the end of each day, the sign-up sheet for the following day is transferred to the audio-visual room. . . .

5. The sign-up sheet is used as a worksheet to program the movement of crews with projectors and films. The coordinator will:

   a. Assign projectors and crews to rooms where they are first needed during the day. . . .
   b. Reassign each projector, period by period, for the balance of the school day, scheduling it to the nearest classroom where a film is to be shown. . . .
   c. Assign a crew to each projector for each period. . . .
   d. Schedule additional projectors to and from storage areas if necessary.

6. Worksheets are filed as a record of film use within the school.[17]

[17] Los Angeles City Schools, *Handbook*, pp. 31–33.

As the reader studies the preceding six steps, he should consult also the illustrations that show the special forms and processes that were designed to make the system work. See Figure 7-33.

Another part of the equipment-distribution problem is the long-term-loan aspect of supplying classroom needs such as portable tape recorders, filmstrip projectors, individual viewers, headsets, automatic slide projectors with programed tape accessories, short-exposure equipment, and the like. Equipment may be needed for extended periods of time, and in fact such units may either be picked up by teachers or it may be delivered and set up after school and left for specified periods of time. Request forms, assignment records, and a filing system for due-back dates, at which time the return of equipment units is checked and irregularities noted and action taken, are the essential elements. Limitations in assignments may have to be announced and strictly adhered to for the good of all concerned.

Again it can be seen that the work to be done is largely clerical and technical in nature, and the need for sufficient assistance is self-evident. The media coordinator must find ways to procure needed hours of work, devise a workable plan of operation, assign the jobs to the right people, and check on and correct weaknesses in the system.

Maintenance of School-Owned Media Equipment

Nature of the Problem. The problem of maintaining audiovisual media equipment units in a state of operational efficiency becomes acute when they become worn and outmoded. Therefore all operational equipment ought to be scheduled for replacement according to an optimum time schedule. Essentially, equipment needs to be given regular care and kept in good running order. This demands regular cleaning, a readiness-for-next-use check-up after each assignment, periodic inspection for signs of wear, and an immediate check-up upon receiving reports of malfunction. A stock of spare parts and maintenance supplies should be maintained so that proper adjustments may be made quickly and conveniently. Major repair work should probably be done at the central repair service, or by local equipment dealers, depending on policies. All cleaning and inspection work and considerable minor adjustment work can be handled on the spot in the school's media-center maintenance area. Equipment on loan to classrooms, and all fixed equipment installations, such as multimedia, projection booth, TV studio, and electronic learning laboratory installations must be given the same meticulous care to make possible trouble-free service at the time of need. Such action calls for a good maintenance-management system.

Suggested Management. Elements of an equipment-maintenance system are as follows:

1. Assign technical personnel on a daily basis to check and prepare mobile equipment units for issue. Prepare and issue to personnel involved a list of specific jobs to be carried out for each kind of equipment.

2. Make minor repairs, replace parts as needed, and make notations on equipment-record card for each unit handled.

3. Maintain a stock of repair and servicing materials, using a stock card to describe each item as to part number, source, and price.

4. Maintain a file of service manuals.

5. Post a set of instructions regarding the handling of equipment in need of major repair service (e.g., tag and send equipment unit to central media headquarters; prepare a requisition and fill out a form letter covering shipment to local or regional equipment dealer; or, pull defective equipment out of service and substitute standby equipment, pending repair in the school's own center by qualified technical personnel working on an overtime basis).

6. Set up a schedule for periodic check-up of all fixed equipment installations, noting action required, substituting replacement equipment units as needed.

7. Using suitable equipment control cards for units issued on a long-term basis to teaching stations, carry out a periodic check-up including cleaning, operational efficiency analysis, and repairs as needed.

This technical work may be carried out by qualified students working after school, but supervision of all operations, including the record-keeping aspects of the work, is essential. Such supervision may have to be given by a specially qualified member of the student crew, but preferably by a full-time technician who may be performing more difficult tasks while student helpers are carrying out routine checks. No professional teacher-coordinator or other leadership personnel should be using time and energy to carry out technial operations on equipment.

Reservation and Scheduling of Media-Use Teaching Stations

Nature of the Problem. When fixed media-equipment installations are organized and administered by the school's media center personnel, the media coordinator must set up an efficient control system for the flow of students and teachers on a daily basis. Many schools today have one or more electronic learning laboratories, multimedia teaching stations, large-group TV viewing areas, TV studios, audio production studios, and teaching auditoriums. In some schools, the fixed installation may be an integral part of a cluster of teaching stations, as for example in the Foreign Language Department. In such cases, the school's media

USING TEACHER SIGN-UP SHEETS

1

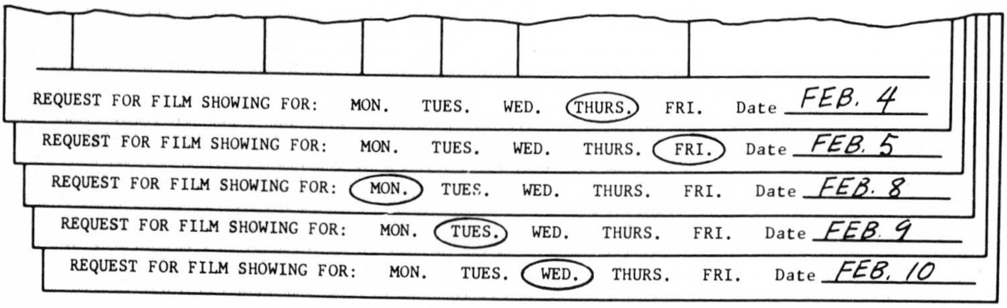

| | REQUEST FOR FILM SHOWING FOR: | MON. | TUES. | WED. | (THURS.) | FRI. | Date | *FEB. 4* |

REQUEST FOR FILM SHOWING FOR: MON. TUES. WED. (THURS.) FRI. Date *FEB. 4*

REQUEST FOR FILM SHOWING FOR: MON. TUES. WED. THURS. (FRI.) Date *FEB. 5*

REQUEST FOR FILM SHOWING FOR: (MON.) TUES. WED. THURS. FRI. Date *FEB. 8*

REQUEST FOR FILM SHOWING FOR: MON. (TUES.) WED. THURS. FRI. Date *FEB. 9*

REQUEST FOR FILM SHOWING FOR: MON. TUES. (WED.) THURS. FRI. Date *FEB. 10*

One sheet for each day of the showing week is posted so that teachers may sign up for films.

2

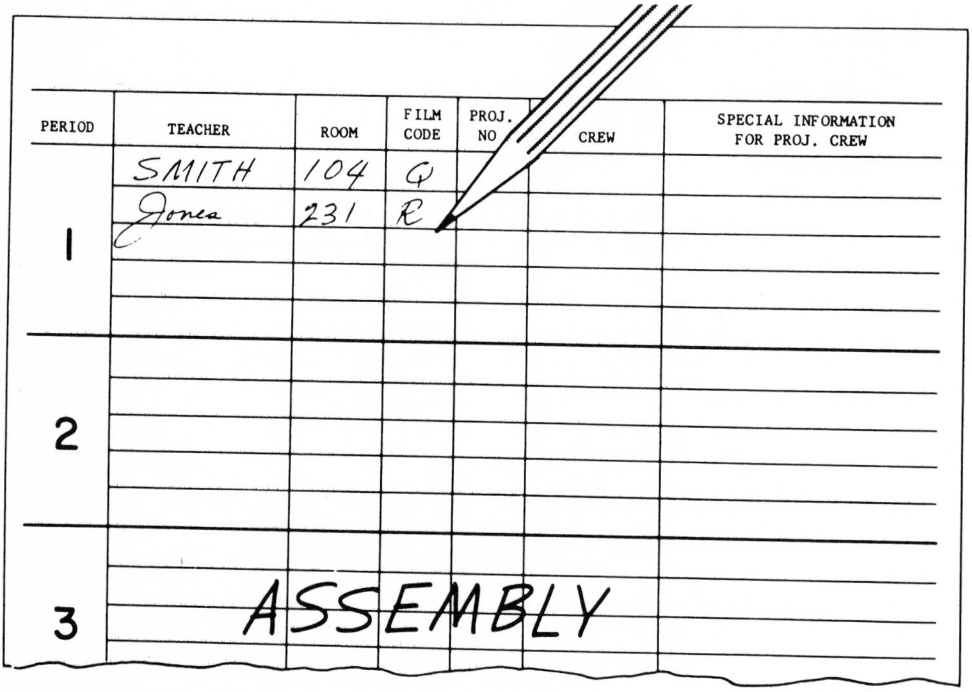

PERIOD	TEACHER	ROOM	FILM CODE	PROJ. NO	CREW	SPECIAL INFORMATION FOR PROJ. CREW
1	SMITH	104	G			
	Jones	231	R			
2						
3	ASSEMBLY					

Teachers request films, using code letters appearing on the school confirmation sheet. In the example shown above, the audio-visual coordinator has indicated that he cannot provide service during third period because of an assembly.

Figure 7-33. The four numbered parts of this illustration show how the six-step procedure quoted for making use of the sign-up-sheet procedure is implemented in the Los Angeles schools. *Courtesy Los Angeles City Schools.*

3

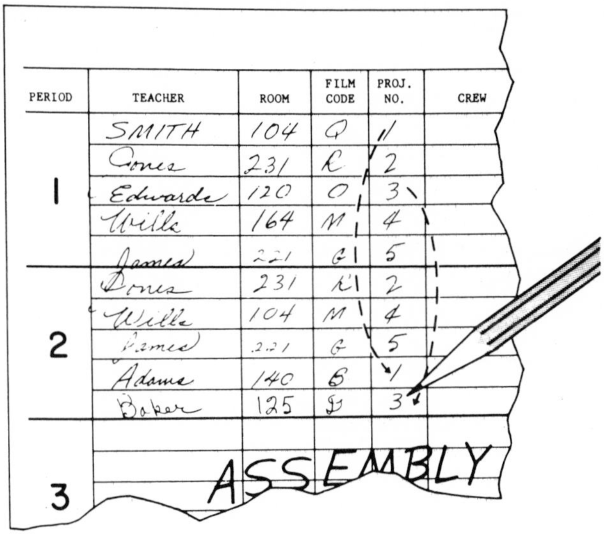

PERIOD	TEACHER	ROOM	FILM CODE	PROJ. NO.	CREW
1	SMITH	104	Q	1	
	Jones	231	R	2	
	Edwards	120	O	3	
	Wills	164	M	4	
	James	221	G	5	
2	Jones	231	R	2	
	Wills	104	M	4	
	James	221	G	5	
	Adams	140	B	1	
	Baker	125	J	3	
3	ASSEMBLY				

At the end of the day, the coordinator uses the sign-up sheet as a worksheet, first scheduling the movement of projectors.

4

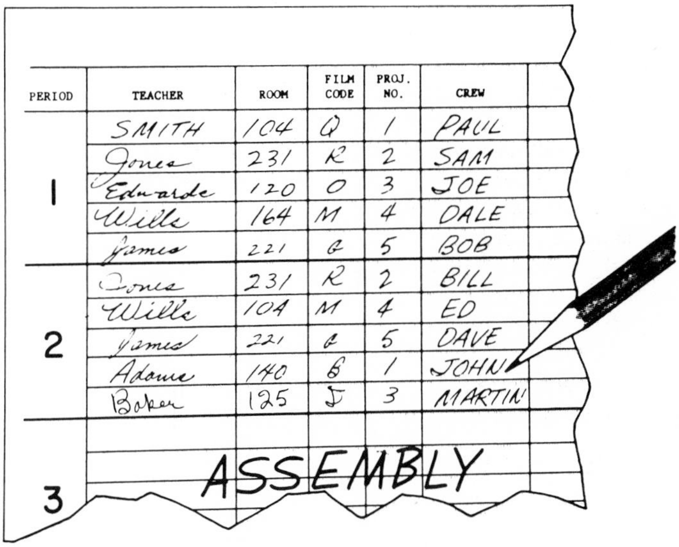

PERIOD	TEACHER	ROOM	FILM CODE	PROJ. NO.	CREW
1	SMITH	104	Q	1	PAUL
	Jones	231	R	2	SAM
	Edwards	120	O	3	JOE
	Wills	164	M	4	DALE
	James	221	G	5	BOB
2	Jones	231	R	2	BILL
	Wills	104	M	4	ED
	James	221	G	5	DAVE
	Adams	140	B	1	JOHN
	Baker	125	J	3	MARTIN
3	ASSEMBLY				

After the projectors are scheduled, he assigns projectionists.

coordinator is responsible for maintenance and possibly for operation but not for scheduling. In other cases, as for example the school's auditorium, facilities may be scheduled only through the principal's office, or through the principal's office and the media coordinator's office, personnel in the latter being called in to render service on a routine operational basis. In most of the technological installations, the media coordinator will be involved with not only routine service, but with the scheduling as well, since some limitations may have to be placed on the degree of service that is available on a given day or in any given class period. Therefore we can readily see that a management system needs to be formulated.

Suggested Management. Essential elements that must be incorporated in the management system are the following:

1. Establish limits on operational service in light of present technical staff for the operation of fixed installations, and distribute procedural statements to all teachers who use the specialized teaching stations.

2. Post sign-up sheets which incorporate the operational service limits for any given installation, that is the number of periods in a day or week that can be reserved, at the media center, and accept telephone orders as staff permits.

3. Arrange schedules of service for operational staff, students, or full-time technicians, and write assignment work orders.

4. Call in operator report slips on the operational efficiency of equipment used.

5. Maintain a log sheet (or use original sign-up sheets) of installations scheduled.

Maintaining the Inventory of Media-Equipment Process

Nature of the Problem. In the modern school the number of pieces of media equipment may become enormous. We think of course of electronic laboratories where headsets, tape-recording units, and TV receivers may have to be listed separately. We think also of teaching stations where there are individual filmstrip and slide viewers, and teaching machines, and then there are the larger pieces of media equipment that are either assigned to teaching stations or distributed on a mobile basis. Hence, whereas media materials are generally purchased and

listed in catalogs, or entered on various types of file cards, equipment units are purchased and placed on shelves for distribution without being listed in the same manner. We therefore face the problem of setting up an adequate system that will reveal what equipment is on hand, where it has been assigned or stationed, and whether it is where it is supposed to be at any given time.

Suggested Management. The management of inventory is essentially a problem of devising and using a control card that carries adequate information and keying each of many cards to an inventory list if such listings are required in the school system. A master inventory may be automated so that print-out processes for each school are periodically possible. In fact, the management of an inventory-control system may be simply the management (maybe not so simple either) of a system already established and being implemented on a school-district basis. At any rate the essential elements of a control system are as follows:

1. Log in each piece or unit of equipment as it arrives at the school from a vendor, if purchased, or from the district media center if assigned.

2. Ask the central media headquarters office to supply standard transfer inventory cards, or fill out an inventory card for each unit of equipment received, noting as called for on the card, date of purchase, make, model number, cost, and dealer's name or code. On this card also indicate the school's identifying number, such as MP 15, indicating that this unit was motion picture projector number 15. Refile the cards in appropriate categories.

3. Using appropriate stencils and a paint sprayer, stencil the school's name or code and equipment unit type number, for example, Smith School MP 15. Stencil both the equipment body and the case.

4. Make additions, or corrections as to replacement when appropriate, to list-type inventories.

5. Use each inventory card as a maintenance record card with suitable maintenance check-off lists on the card.

6. Indicate on the inventory card the teaching station assignment, if part of a fixed installation, or indicate equipment pool, as the case may be.

7. Periodically, as is feasible or as demanded by school-system policies, complete an actual unit-by-unit physical inventory, indicating completed date on each card or school list.

Systematizing Routine Processes

A larger number of operations are carried out in a well-organized media-service center than those that have just been discussed in detail, not necessarily demanding a multiple-step control system. Yet, we can think of no better way to manage these operations than to routinize them and develop easy-to-use request or check-off forms. The main idea is to get the work done conveniently and effectively without sacrificing prudence. Every good manager knows that there is a time and place for a specified kind of work to be completed, that deadlines have to be met, and that to get work done, it has to be systematized. We can apply this need to the more extensive control systems just discussed, and we can apply it as well to other operations such as issuing media-preparation supplies to teachers. We will discuss this problem fully in a later chapter, but we should point out here that at least a simple log sheet showing the items issued and to whom issued ought to be maintained. Evaluation forms for media used should be collected and processed for their contributions to purchase and subsequent rental plans. Expenditures against the school's budget allotments should be checked weekly and monthly and carefully noted. Records should be processed monthly for reports and some or all of these processes need to be carried on according to the school calendar to maintain proper relationships to system-wide business operations.

The citywide media program director will have a great deal to do with the formulation of workable policies by school coordinators and their respective school principals. He can also help to inaugurate systematic procedures that will assist all people involved. Once again we refer to the supervisory booklet, *Handbook for Audio-Visual Representatives*, published by the Los Angeles City Schools, which urged school media coordinators to carry out specified duties according to a schedule. We quote this schedule as follows:

First week of school
Train projectionists.
Take all equipment out of storage and re-inventory.
Acquaint new teachers with available audio-visual equipment.
Acquaint new teachers with ordering procedures.
Establish a calendar on which are noted such dates as those for distribution and return of departmental film orders and for mailing IBM film-order cards to the Audio-Visual Section.
Meet with the principal and department heads to establish departmental film quotas.

Daily
Before school:
Check availability of equipment.
Review the day's showing and delivery requests.
At the close of the school day:
Pick up the film sign-up sheets and equipment requests for the following day.
Schedule projectionists and sound projectors.
Schedule the movement of equipment other than sound projectors.
Account for all equipment.
Check security of storage room.

Day Preceding Delivery Day
The following duties often are delegated to students to be performed under careful supervision:
Rewind films. . . .
Inspect films for damage to determine need for additional training.
Make certain that any beginning and ending leaders which have become detached are returned in the proper film can.
Make certain that each film is in the right can.
Place the films in their proper bags, and return bags to the established delivery point.

Delivery Day
Supervise the cleaning and inspection of all machines and equipment. (Refer to the *How to Operate* manuals for guidance.)
Supervise the checking of titles of newly delivered films.
Assign each film a code letter which can be used for identification on confirmation sheets and sign-up sheets.
Notify teachers of previously confirmed films which do not arrive in the school.

Delivery Day Plus Two
Duplicate copies of the following week's film confirmation sheet.

Delivery Day Plus Three
Post the following week's film confirmation sheet and distribute copies to teachers.
Post the following week's film sign-up sheet.

Monthly
Assist department heads with departmental film orders.
Process IBM film-order cards for mailing to the Audio-Visual Section.
File IBM order cards when they are returned.

Notify department heads of titles which have been ordered but are not confirmed.

Biannually
Order supplies and equipment.

Last Half of Each Semester
Select projectionists to serve during the following semester.
Begin training new crew members before or after school.

Last Week of the Spring Semester
Collect and store all audio-visual equipment and materials for which you are responsible.
Provide the principal with an inventory of this equipment and material.
Supply information about missing equipment.[18]

Lest the reader assume that we have given consideration to all of the duties of the school-building media program leader, we hasten to point out that this was not our intention. We have dealt with major topics such as in-service education of the staff in earlier chapters, and other chapters follow such as the budgeting process in its entirety, which have a bearing on a number of other processes that involve the media leader in carrying out his responsibilities. We have at this point dealt with a few basic, more or less routine control systems that have to be carried out on a continuing basis. Other systems are bound to be demanded as technological processes become more complex and comprehensive in their application. The school media coordinator will be successful only when he has learned to be a good administrator, for without good management of day-to-day services, the results of his good leadership with teachers will not prosper.

We must point out finally that the optimum balance must be found by citywide media program directors between adequate material and personnel services located in a central headquarters structure, and the capability growing out of the organization of school media centers to give teachers the technological help they need on a day-to-day basis. What we are emphasizing is the major point that leadership energy, that makes the formulation and implementation of adequate systems possible, must be fed continuously in optimum amount into each school unit.

[18] *Ibid.*, pp. 7–9.

Problem-Solving Activities

1. Just how do you strike a favorable balance between creating and meeting demands for audiovisual media services? What is likely to be the result if a school principal or media coordinator oversells his program?

2. Formulate a plan for providing system-wide equipment facilities. Show how you will strive to make use of both centralization and decentralization in assigning equipment units.

3. Explain by a series of diagrams how you would deploy the media equipment units in a 28-classroom elementary school in order, for example, to avoid wasting instructional time when a motion picture presentation is desirable? (This question demands that you identify and relate the different ways of supplying equipment to teachers when they need it.)

4. Refer to the section of Chapter 3 relative to the decentralization of media materials in school buildings and discuss the merits of such decentralization. Under what conditions would you say that decentralization would be unwise?

5. Prepare a proposal for a school principal (your choice of elementary or secondary school with the guidance and approval of your instructor). Specifying type and pupil enrollment, lay out in outline form the nature of the desired audiovisual media-service program. Specify the desired (a) need for media services; (b) pattern of organization; (c) need for professional leadership and how to supply it. Show diagrams of relationship of media leadership to school principal and to city media director.

6. Identify the principal difficulty in obtaining part-time professional assistance for the service media program in elementary schools. State in outline form the ways of surmounting the problem. Be sure to state what the provision must be at advanced stages of media service.

7. Why has it been possible to operate audiovisual media-service programs in the past with such limited professional, technical, and clerical assistance?

8. Identify several basic circumstances under which it would be wiser to separate the library and audiovisual media services organizationally? Under what circumstances ought the two branches of service be combined or unified? Can you cite cases in support of your points?

9. Identify a school system of your choice with which you are familiar and in view of your knowledge of the teachers on the staff and the number of school plants in the district, use the minimum standards for personnel quoted in the chapter to work out the number of professional and technical media personnel that ought to be provided. (See also Footnote 8.)

10. Analyze the list of professional duties stated by the author under *Nature of the Media Coordinator's Duties* (*Group 1* and *Group 2*, p. 260) and identify the potential contributions of technicians and clerks in carrying them out.

11. Write out a list of specifications for a qualified full-time, audiovisual media coordinator for a school principal to use in procuring a professional media coordinator.

12. Write out a proposal for a school principal requesting budgetary support for a complete staff of professional and support personnel to carry on a mature media-service program. Show in this proposal the degree to which you propose to make use of student workers.

13. Sketch in outline form a training program for fifth- and sixth-graders in a new audiovisual crew. Develop an apprentice system for this training and show how the training sessions become progressively more difficult, based on previous learning. Indicate how automated, self-instruction may be employed in the process.

14. You do not have permission of the principal to use student workers because of tight scheduling and team-teaching operations. You therefore have to provide full-time technical help for which budgetary support will not be forthcoming for another year. Explain in a proposal what your plan for action is and how you would execute it.

15. Assume you have been assigned a normal size, 30-foot by 26-foot classroom, in each of ten elementary schools, for remodeling as a school audiovisual service center. Make a scale drawing of your planned layout. Label your diagram fully as to utilization of the space to facilitate audiovisual services in the building. (Study the illustrations in the text and attempt to avoid in your own sketch any weaknesses you find. Do not use code numbers or letters for identifying your spaces. Use readable labels for quick identification.)

16. Some teachers refuse to exchange classrooms with other teachers to share darkening facilities. Do you blame them? Is the central projection room the most desirable way to provide facilities for projecting pictorial materials? Defend the negative view by giving at least three good reasons for your opinion. What are the arguments in favor of the projection-room method?

17. (A) You have been asked by your principal to submit a rough sketch of a complete audiovisual media-service center for a new elementary school that will enroll 1,000 students. He wants you to indicate the space requirements and area and to show particularly how the different space requirements are related. Make this sketch and label it. Use words and abbreviations in the labels, not a coding system.

(B) Carry out the same assignment for a 1,200-student high school.

(This assignment should be carried out by groups of students, each working on a part of the specifications. Some groups should choose elementary schools and others secondary. At the discretion of the instructor, blocks of unlabeled space may be indicated for media-preparation and television operations with the intention of completing the diagrams with special reference to topics in Chapters 9 and 10.)

18. Discuss in class and agree on the space requirements for a modern school library facility as a separate unit from the audiovisual media-service center, for an elementary school for 1,000 pupils and for a high school housing 1,200 students as a starting enrollment.

19. Analyze any two of the control systems that have to be devised and managed by audiovisual media-service leadership and fill in the details in a flow diagram showing the number and kinds of workers required to get the job accomplished. Include the nature of supervisory personnel as well. Label the diagram fully and include notes where essential.

20. In the management of control systems at a media-service center as depicted in this chapter, select any one of the systems depicted and indicate how the system could be replaced—that is, eliminated entirely—by substituting a different set of circumstances. Identify the system and then report the new circumstances that would eradicate the need for the operations.

21. What are the alternatives to building up a strong service system carried on by school-building personnel in each elementary and secondary school? Support your points by diagrams or convincing arithmetic.

References

American Association of School Librarians. *Standards for School Library Programs*, 1960 (Chicago: ALA).

The Audio-Visual Program, Bulletin 218. (Indianapolis, Indiana: State of Indiana, Department of Public Instruction, 1956).

Brown, James W. and Kenneth D. Norberg. *Administering Educational Media* (New York: McGraw-Hill, 1965).

Burgert, Robert H. and Ben L. Gumm. "Keiller Elementary School." *Audiovisual Instruction*, Vol. 10, No. 2, February 1965, pp. 140–141.

Cobun, Ted and Hal J. Cress. "North Division, Niles Township Community High Schools," *Audiovisual Instruction*, Vol. 10, No. 2, February 1965, pp. 136–137.

Coleman, Jean and Margie Gonce. "Wilbur Wright Junior High School," *Audiovisual Instruction*, Vol. 10, No. 2, February 1965, pp. 138–139.

Daniel, Wanda. "The AV Coordinator on the Rise," *Audiovisual Instruction*, Vol. 2, No. 4, April 1957, pp. 100–102.

DeBernardis, Amo, Victor W. Doherty, Errett Hummel, and Charles W. Brubaker. *Planning Schools for New Media*, in cooperation with the U.S. Office of Education (Washington, D.C.: The Superintendent of Documents, U.S. Government Printing Office, 1961).

DeBernardis, Amo, David M. Crossman, and Thomas E. Miller. "Media, Technology, and IMC Space Requirements," *Audiovisual Instruction*, Vol. 10, No. 2, February 1965, pp. 107–114.

Educational Facilities Laboratories, Inc. *The High School Auditorium 6 Designs for Renewal.* (New York: EFL, 477 Madison Ave., 1967).

Ellsworth, Ralph E. and Hobart D. Wagener. *The School Library: Facilities for Independent Study in the Secondary School* (New York: Educational Facilities Laboratories, Inc., 1963), 139 pp.

Estes, Nolan. "Valley Winds Elementary School," *Audiovisual Instruction*, Vol. 10, No. 2, February 1965, pp. 142–143.

Faris, Gene. "Tentative Guidelines for Audiovisual Personnel and Equipment," *Audiovisual Instruction*, Vol. 10, No. 3, March 1965, pp. 201–204.

Faris, Gene and John Moldstad (assisted by Harvey Frye). *Improving the Learning Environment* (A Study on the Local Preparation of Visual Instructional Materials). In Cooperation with the U.S. Office of Education. (Washington, D.C.: Superintendent of Documents, U.S. Government Printing Office, 1963).

Finn, James D. "Professionalizing the Audiovisual Field," *AV Communication Review*, 1:6–17, Winter 1953.

Ford, Harry J. "The Instructional Resources Center," *Audiovisual Instruction*, Vol. 7, No. 8, October 1962, pp. 524–526.

Gardner, Dwayne E. "Prescribing Educational Specifications," *Audiovisual Instruction*, Vol. 10, No. 2, February 1965, pp. 98–100.

Giesy, John P. "A Working Relationship," *Audiovisual Instruction*, Vol. 10, No. 9, November 1965, pp. 706–708.

Glenn, Magdalene. "Organizing a Materials Center," *National Elementary Principal*, Vol. 40, No. 1, January 1961, pp. 28–30.

Goldberg, Albert L. and Richard A. Darling. "Is the Instructional Materials Center the Answer?" *Audiovisual Instruction*, Vol. 6, No. 5, May 1961, pp. 194–195.

Green, Alan C. (ed.). *Educational Facilities with New Media.* (Prepared under a contract with the U.S. Office of Education.) (Washington, D.C.: The Department of Audiovisual Instruction of the NEA, 1966).

Greer, Phyllis. "A Materials Center That Really Works," *Audiovisual Instruction*, Vol. 5, No. 10, December 1960, p. 332.

Guerin, David V. "Media's Influence on Design," *Audiovisual Instruction*, Vol. 10, No. 2, February 1965, pp. 95–97.

Handbook for Audio-Visual Representatives, Secondary Schools (Revised 1965), Los Angeles City Schools, Instructional Services Branch, Los Angeles, California, 1965.

Harcleroad, Fred F. (ed.). "The Education of the AV Communication Specialist" (Proceedings of a DAVI Seminar), *AV Communication Review*, Vol. 8, No. 5, Supp. 2, September–October 1960.

Larsen, John A. and Jewel Bindrup. "The Library Curriculum Center: Hub of the School Program," *Audiovisual Instruction*, Vol. 5, No. 10, December 1960, p. 332.

Mannino, Phillip. *ABC's of Visual Aids and Projectionists Manual*, rev. ed. (University Park, Pennsylvania: 1955).

Martin, Ann M. and C. Walter Stone. *A Study of Regional Instructional Media Resources, Phase 1—Manpower*. (Prepared under contract OE-3-16-027, with the U.S. Office of Education.) (Pittsburgh: Graduate School of Library and Information Sciences, University of Pittsburgh, 1965).

McMahan, Marie. "Building Coordinator: Professional Partner?" *Audiovisual Instruction*, Vol. 7, No. 8, October 1962, pp. 662–665.

Mesedahl, Leroy K. "The IMC: Contribution to Individualized Instruction," *Audiovisual Instruction*, Vol. 10, No. 9, November 1965, pp. 705–707.

Miles, Bruce and Virginia McJenkin. "IMC's: A Dialogue," *Audiovisual Instruction*, Vol. 10, No. 9, November 1965, pp. 688–691.

Mitchell, Malcolm G. "What's Going On in the School Library?" *Phi Delta Kappan*, Vol. 45, October 1963, pp. 44–47.

Moldstad, John and Harvey R. Frye. "Making Room for AV," *Audiovisual Instruction*, Vol. 2, No. 10, December 1957, pp. 270–271.

Nicholson, Margaret E. "The I.M.C.," *School Libraries*, Vol. 13, No. 3, March 1964, pp. 39–43.

Phillips, Murray G. "Instructional Materials Center: The Rationale," *Audiovisual Instruction*, Vol. 5, No. 10, December 1960, pp. 326–332.

Pryor, Robert L. "Speedy Repair Equals Good Utilization," *Audiovisual Instruction*, Vol. 8, No. 3, March 1963, p. 153.

Quantitative Standards for Audiovisual Personnel, Equipment and Materials (in Elementary, Secondary, and Higher Education). Developed as part of the Faris-Sherman Study conducted under the auspices of the United States Office of Education, National Defense Education Act, Title VII, Part B Program (Washington, D.C.: Department of Audiovisual Instruction of the NEA, 1201 Sixteenth Street, N.W., January 1966), 18 pp., mimeographed.

Rufsvold, Margaret. *Audio-Visual School Library Service* (Chicago: ALA, 1959).

Sharp, J. Stanley. "Architectural Steps in Facilities Planning," *Audiovisual Instruction*, Vol. 10, No. 2, February 1965, pp. 101–103.

Sherman, Mendel. "Training for a Top-Flight Coordinator," *Audiovisual Instruction*, Vol. 3, No. 5, May 1958, pp. 148–150.

Taylor Kenneth I. "Instructional Materials Center," *The Nation's Schools*, Vol. 66, December 1960, pp. 46–50.

Wartenberg, Milton. "A Comprehensive Service Center for Randolph High School," *Audiovisual Instruction*, Vol. 7, No. 8, October 1962, pp. 542–543.

Winston, Fred and others. *Guiding Students in the School AV Club*. (Washington, D.C.: Department of Audiovisual Instruction, NEA, 1201 Sixteenth St. N.W., 1962). 73 pp.

Readers may well wish to ask a searching question after painstaking analysis of content in the preceding chapter. They may wish to ask, "Why, with well-developed media-service facilities and systems advocated for each school building, should there be a need for a district-wide or citywide headquarters suite?" We must have unitary leadership and responsibility for the citywide media program, and we must also have operational facilities, staff, and financial support to provide those inevitable centralized services that are or will be demanded in light of local needs. We assume therefore that as we build strong school-building service systems, our efforts will prosper because of the energizing action of a strong citywide media organization, which will not remain static in its own development but will alter its service programs at various stages of technological progress.

In setting up an audiovisual media center, the director must blend professional, clerical, and technical services, and must therefore bring to his job a thorough understanding of appropriate physical arrangements, adequate technical control of materials and equipment, and adequate inventory controls, and he must possess the ability to build an effective staff organization. Therefore, the purpose of this chapter is to aid the prospective director in making wise decisions and recommendations in setting up these processes and procedures.

Emerging Patterns of Media Center Organization

The single most important first step that a school community takes on the route to providing effective audiovisual media services is to create an agency to provide services to the schools as units of a viable, citywide or district-wide organization. Hopefully an operational plan such as the one described in Chapter 1 would have been legislated into action as a fitting start for the program of service. However, even though there is universal agreement on the need for citywide service organizations, there is not universal agreement on a single pattern and structure. We shall therefore discuss first the need for such centralization of services and leadership and then undertake to describe the nature of the media-service organizations that are presently being established in school systems.

8

Organizing The Citywide Audiovisual Media Center

Need for Centralized Leadership and Services

A citywide media center, as we have pointed out already, is not just a suite of offices that houses the media program leader for the district, plus collections of media, but it is the heart of a system-wide organization. It is also a symbol of the energizing force for external action being taken, and it is the scope and quality of that action which really matters. If we return to Chapter 1 we note that principle number one, first in a series of broad principles for the organization for audiovisual media services, is stated as follows: *The work of organizing and developing instructional media services will proceed most effectively under specialized, centralized leadership, working coordinately with other curriculum personnel and under adequate system-wide financial support for auxiliary staff, equipment, materials, and facilities.*

The alternative to such action, as implied by the *leadership* principle, is to do what school systems without formally organized media programs do—develop a separate media-service program in each school building. The higher cost through duplication of facilities, the wasted effort of innovating individuals who make decisions without sound technical guidance and standardization of procedure, the hodgepodge of operations, procedures, and points of emphasis that develops within a school system (even though the program is carried on under the control of school principals and other administrators talented in other aspects except technology) can lead only to inefficiency and eventual disaster.

No one knows in exact detail what the media-service center in any given district or city ought to be. How large it ought to be, what services ought to be given, how fast the development ought to proceed, where it should be located, and how much financial support is required are relative matters that depend on local conditions. We insist that "pipelines" of service and leadership energy ought to feed every school-building unit, fulfilling through such units specific obligations in each teaching station or learning area. We do know that the technology for teaching and learning is growing in complexity. We know that many changes will have to take place, some of which may proceed at a steady rate, and others which must be accelerated according to local developments. We know that the planning and design for action and the responsibility for study and recommendation is a vital part of the leadership force that helps groups discover and formulate their purposes, then guides them in the process of implementing changes in good balance. And we know that many of those changes need to be made according to long-term plans in all the schools to benefit all of the learners, and that help for teachers must be organized and implemented according to an optimum schedule. We know also that the needs of learners are paramount and that appropriate technological tools of increasing complexity are increasingly the only means of meeting those needs. Learning situations involving their use in modern-day schools require an extensive and dependable service system for teachers. There can be little doubt that some of those services may have to be generated first out of central locations, while others such as those described in Chapter 7 ought to and have to arise in each school building on a day-to-day basis.

Thus we assert that we can see the need for centralized facilities in which a thriving media organization can operate effectively for the good of all concerned. We can also postulate the working principle, based on more than a half century of experience, that a centralization of audiovisual media leadership and services with an ensuing optimum decentralization of facilities, services, staff, and financial support is the right and proper point of departure for audiovisual media development. And it is this particular development with which we shall be mainly concerned in this chapter, postponing important emphasis on print-medium problems to Chapter 12.

We therefore now turn to a description of the emerging patterns of organization for centers of media services. The base of the organization problem is whether services will include all media, both print and nonprint, within the media service center. We shall not deal in the following pages with a resolution of the issue, mainly because we wish to focus attention on the audiovisual aspect of media services and the unique problems to be faced by those who are responsible for providing them. However, we realize fully that one of the emerging patterns of organization is that in which all media services are developed, both centrally for the district, and then further decentralized in each school building. In the discussions that follow, the reader should also refer to the previous chapter which dealt with the organization and development of school-building media-service centers. In actual practice it is possible that the district-wide center will differ in organizational pattern from those that are developed in each school. For example, the district center may specialize in audiovisual media but one or more of the schools may develop an all-media service center including library services. We shall deal first with the pattern of organization that separates the print and nonprint media problems and services.

Organizations Separating Print and Nonprint Media Services

This pattern of organization was the first to develop, as we pointed out in Chapter 1, and it has continued to serve well in cities and towns around the country. Under this pattern the audiovisual media program director is a co-ordinate curriculum leader with full responsibility for the development of all nonprint media services including facilities, staff, and planning for financial support programs. Print-medium services, both central and decentralized as units in each school building, come under the jurisdiction of other administrative and supervisory personnel. If we take note of the pressure exerted by special-area supervisors for their own programs, for financial support, additional operational space and staff, we can see that, given a situation where there is an understanding of the urgency for audiovisual media development on the part of Board of Education members and key administrators, rapid advancement of the system-wide audiovisual media program is likely to result under this pattern of organization. On the other hand, as school systems search for new methods to provide administrative control over increasingly complex organizations and services, it becomes feasible to regroup departments and divisions under knowledgeable and skillful leadership. Hence, under this arrangement, all media agencies are likely to be brought under unitary leadership. Department heads or chiefs of specialized services under such circumstances with adequate budgets and staff may proceed to the development of exemplary and comprehen-

sive media services for the enhancement of modern educational programs.

Organizations Combining Media Services

Under recent pressure to change the name of technological service agencies from *Audiovisual Education* to *Learning Resources, Instructional Media, Instructional Materials,* or *Audiovisual Communications,* and as various professional groups have sought to expand their skills and services, we see a movement toward an all-inclusive media organization. We see great merit in the unification pattern, but we see also the possibility of an unfortunate imbalance in the concentration of effort on one branch of media service or the other. This possibility would be more likely to occur if a bias has developed because of training and experience, or the lack of it. We must note that favorable conditions are needed for each type of media organization, that is, unified or separate, if the release of potential values is to take place.

We can state the situation in summary fashion by pointing out that the media program director, or the print-medium specialist, when possessing required qualifications, ought to be sensitive to instructional needs that demand new or modified services leading to greater comprehensiveness and efficiency. As needed, then, either or both of these qualified teaching methods specialists may be called upon by school-system administrators to

1. Coordinate the centralization of all print-medium processes and development.
2. Coordinate the centralization and decentralization of all nonprint media processes and development.
3. Coordinate the development and operational use of electronic learning laboratories, dial-access systems and other self-instruction systems.
4. Coordinate the ordering, storage, and distribution of school supplies.
5. Centralize and distribute maps and globes.
6. Coordinate the use of community resources, including reciprocal activities and field-trip programs.
7. Centralize   and   distribute   museum materials.

8. Provide a centralized and decentralized service for the production of still and motion pictures, charts, and other graphic materials.

9. Organize and coordinate a school-owned educational radio station.

10. Coordinate the use and production of closed-circuit television programs for instructional purposes.

All this appears to be a formidable undertaking, but it need not be when staff and financial support are adequate, and if this is not the case, the media program director must use his own good judgment by saying "No" until conditions for success are more to his liking.

The combination of audiovisual media with print-medium services makes possible the broadest unification of media services, and names such as *Curriculum Materials Center* and *Instructional Materials or Media Center*, or *Learning Resources Center* become applicable.

Such a center in Portland, Oregon was early recognized as one of the most comprehensive of its kind anywhere. "The main idea back of this unification," said the center's director, Amo DeBernardis,[1] in 1949, "is to provide for the Portland teachers one resource center from which they can obtain any and all teaching aids that fit their instructional needs, and also receive professional help in their use." In Portland, book services[2] not only include a centralized organization for the ordering, distribution, and repair of textbooks and supplementary books, but they also include a library of professional books, periodicals, resource units, and other curriculum publications. Insofar as school supplies are concerned, all school supplies from construction paper to science, music, art, industrial arts, and gym equipment are centralized under instructional materials center management. The points that DeBernardis[3] makes regarding the advantages of a unified center are worth noting.

1. It minimizes the tendency to look upon certain instructional aids as entirely unique and therefore unrelated to the general process of education.

2. It provides better coordination of service functions of purchase, distribution, and maintenance.

3. It has elicited more coordinated effort on the part of staff in the in-service growth of teachers.

4. It makes for greater economy, both in use of materials and in effort by staff and the classroom teacher.

5. It has provided more effective coordination of aids within each school.

6. It has made possible a more efficient inventory.

7. It has made possible a better implementation of the curriculum.

Not all Instructional Materials Centers are really what the name implies. Instead, some centers are little more than audiovisual service centers with limited additional duties involving one or more phases of print-medium service. Those that do have library functions to perform carry them out in a great variety of ways. In some cases textbooks and library reference books of all kinds are handled centrally for elementary schools only, since school libraries and librarians are not available there. At the secondary level, textbooks and other reference materials are sometimes decentralized at each secondary school library. Other instructional materials centers exemplify truly unified media-service centers and both selection and supply of reference books and the distribution and use of all other media are coordinated on a system-wide basis. In larger instructional materials centers a number of supervisors or assistant directors are placed in charge of the various divisions such as book-services, television, media design and preparation, and nonprint-media distribution.

Any media program director should realize that he could easily let himself become, more than anything else, the manager of a warehouse. This will be inescapable if he permits himself to be saddled with extensive media services without necessary increases in staff and budget. Each situation will demand a careful analysis and a wise policy decision.

Location of Media Centers

Some media centers are to be found in new school-system administration headquarters, and others in old and abandoned schools that have been taken over with a minimum of remodeling. Classrooms in outmoded buildings may still serve as film vaults, media production facilities, publication printing shops, and office suites once they have been air-conditioned for year-round comfort. However, for central, closed-circuit

[1] Amo DeBernardis, "Portland's Instructional Materials Center," *Educational Screen*, Vol. 28, No. 1, January 1949, pp. 13–15.
[2] *Ibid.*, p. 15.
[3] *Ibid.*

television studios and control rooms, such space may be totally inadequate. Other media centers may be located in spaces provided in new secondary schools that can be made large enough to support the media services for the district as well as to support in a sizable area the special school-building services described in Chapter 7. So it can be readily observed the country over, that media directors take their centers to places where, above all, operational spaces are adequate, both horizontal and vertical. But there are many factors that should be considered and which will come to light in later discussions or have been indicated already in Chapter 7. For the time being we suggest the following scale of priorities.

1. Design the audiovisual media center, or an all-media center, with adequate space, to be housed in a new and separate building, centrally located with reference to schools in the district.

2. Design the audiovisual media-center suite in combination with, or separate from, the system-wide print-medium services as dictated by local conditions, with adequate space, as a part of a district-wide administrative center.

3. Design an adequate district-wide audiovisual media center, or an all-media center in combination, to be housed in a new school building, separated spacially and operationally from the school's own media center.

4. Take over as much space, in light of justified needs, as can be allotted in an older building to be shifted from instructional to administrative service in the district, and plan required remodeling activity to adapt the space to be used for efficient audiovisual or all-media services.

5. Remodel a number of classrooms in an existing school building still in active instructional service to meet audiovisual and print-media service needs.

As media-service programs develop, the focus for service will shift into the individual school, and because of this situation, there is little point in trying to merge the center for a school building with a district-wide center in an attempt to economize on personnel and space. The two services are likely to be vastly different, therefore they should be kept separate. It does not seem right that one school in the district should be given the kind of preferential treatment generally thought possible in connection with the com-

bination of district-wide and school-building service centers, and the prediction is that one or the other is likely to be at a disadvantage. The main service center should be free for specified services to all schools.

We should not fail to mention that any one, or any combination, of unique circumstances may influence, and rightly so, the decision to move to a lower priority in the preceding list of situations for locating the citywide media-service center. For example, in West Hartford, Connecticut, it was voted to inaugurate an individualization of instruction project by means of what is referred to as dial retrieval of television and audio programs for both large-group and carrel utilization. The installation was planned originally for a new high school that had been authorized by the Board of Education. Since the new high school itself was to be the hub of the project for subsequent interconnections with other schools, it was decided to locate the new citywide media-service center there also, along with the installation of retrieval- and program-preparation facilities in specially designed spaces. To serve the school's own media program, an additional school-building media-service suite was also designed in close relationship to the citywide suite. Such a school-building center could well have been an entirely separate suite, for example combined with the school's library as an instructional media center.

Emerging recently is the pattern of regional services, which, after all, has been in existence for a long time in the large-scale and comprehensive media-service organizations established in a number of county school agencies. Federal and state-supported programs are now appearing that involve a number of school districts. Such regional media-service centers include television and dial-access systems together with computer processes and curriculum and in-service education leadership forces.

It is likely that specialization will develop within such large organizations to carry on those media services that can be handled effectively, but not in any way causing the emphasis on strong school-building services to be eroded. Staff, both professional and technical, and adequate financial support are of course prerequisite to such action. New patterns of service may thus be looming on the horizon where school-building, citywide, and regional service centers may be the only means by which all of the services needed by teachers in the modern school may be available.

Planning the Layout and Use of Audiovisual Media-Service Spaces

In Chapter 7, we pointed out that there seemed to be no pat answer to the amount of space needed for any given operation because there were so many variables. We assert, however, that even though there are some educated guesses as to how much space will be needed for a given school-building center, it is the nature of the services provided to teachers and the inclusion of special facilities, such as electronic learning laboratories and the entire library facility as well that should determine the layout and amount of space needed. We may ask: How large should a district media-service center be, and how much space is required by each of the component spaces required? We make the same assertions as for the school-building media-service center: The nature and quantity of services will determine the various space needs. See Figure 8-1. Knowledge of the processes by means of which media materials and equipment and assistance in their effective use reach teachers at their teaching stations helps us in making sound judgments as to how much space is generally required to provide any given service. And it is on this basis that we estimate space needs in district-wide audiovisual media-service centers.

Some Observations about the Differences in District and School-Building Media-Service Centers

Except for those situations where citywide and school-building media centers have been combined for special reasons, we can see a number of differences in spaces, services, and functions. Bearing in mind the possibility of special circumstances, we state these differences as follows:

1. School-district centers serve teachers, not pupils. For example, district centers are not generally called on to provide electronic learning laboratory facilities. Nor do they issue books, as a school library would, directly to children. On the other hand, school-building media-service centers are more likely to serve both teachers and provide direct services to pupils as well.

2. District-wide media centers almost always organize and implement television programing services. School-building service centers develop TV studio facilities, and/or videotaping and distribution facilities as a means of expansion. The exception would be a decision to conduct a pilot project, tried out in one or more schools prior to organization on a system-wide basis.

3. District centers are not generally called on to distribute equipment units on mobile stands. Hence little or no cart garage space will be needed.

4. Properly equipped meeting rooms and conference rooms are more likely to be called for by school leaders and by executives for planning in-service education and innovational programs at school-district headquarters. For example, meetings in school buildings are likely to be held not in the media-service center, but in other properly equipped spaces. But district media centers, especially in school-system administrative headquarters, may have to maintain special meeting-room facilities.

5. District media centers generally require better and larger loading and pick-up facilities.

6. District centers generally need to set up media design and preparation facilities and often combine design services with the preparation of publications to greater extent than do school-building centers. District centers are more likely to carry on graphic production services that demand support of full-time, sophisticated technicians, but graphic or media-preparation services in each school building are likely to demand teacher work-room space with some technical and artistic support.

7. School-district library services to schools are likely to be administrative and distributive by nature rather than pupil-service oriented as are school-building library or print-medium service centers.

8. School-district centers are likely to demand extremely large storage areas for media materials and equipment in contrast to school-building centers.

9. School-district media centers will generally demand much larger areas for administration and personnel, equipment-and-materials inspection, and for repair, shipping, and receiving areas than will school-building media centers.

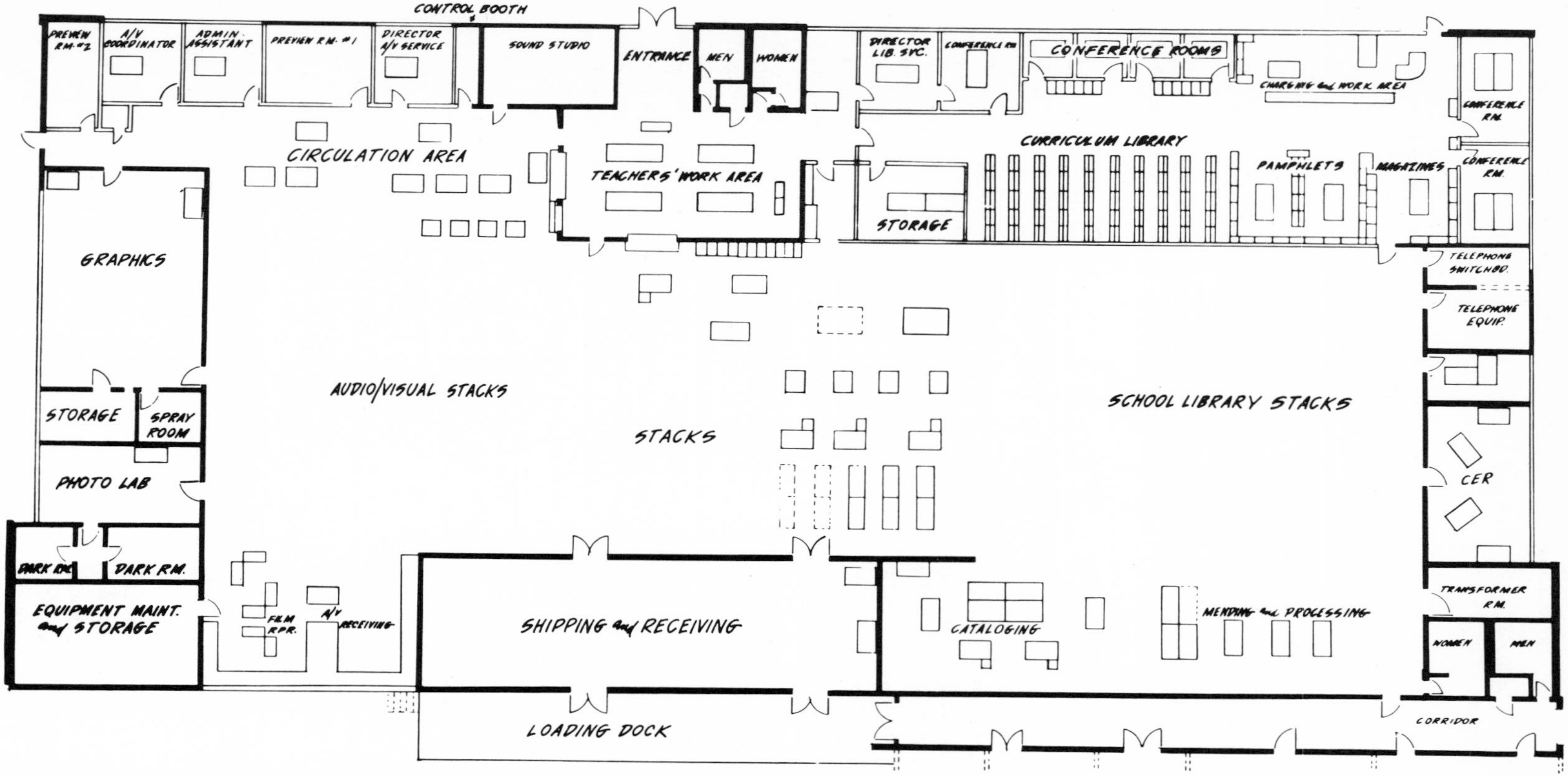

Figure 8-1. We provide in these floor plans for district media centers an opportunity to identify and study a variety of specific functions and the ways these functions are related in terms of space arrangements. Many details necessary for precise analysis are lacking. Nevertheless, these diagrams will serve as valuable examples of the ways in which media-service programs are developing. Some features are common to all. Others are unique. Two of the programs provide library services, one of which offers a unified program organizationally. The other operates with dual directors, one for audiovisual media, the other for print-medium services. Two of the diagrams represent programs in county school districts, the other a union high school district encompassing five high schools. See also Figures 1-1 through 1-8. (*The full-page diagram*, courtesy San Diego County Schools; *the following diagram*, courtesy Fremont Union High School District, Sunnyvale, California.) ; and *the bottom diagram*, courtesy Jackson County Schools, Medford, Oregon.

furniture and floor plan
audio/visual and library building
DEPARTMENT OF EDUCATION
SAN DIEGO COUNTY, CALIFORNIA

Scale: 1/8" = 1'

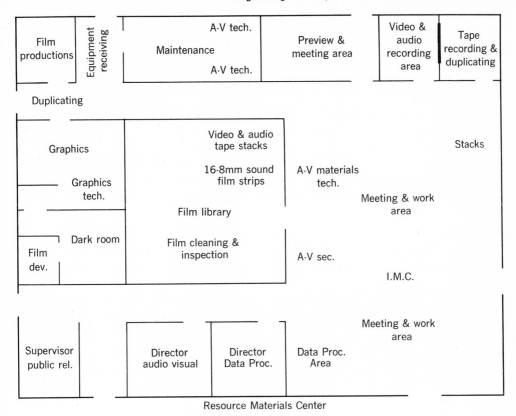

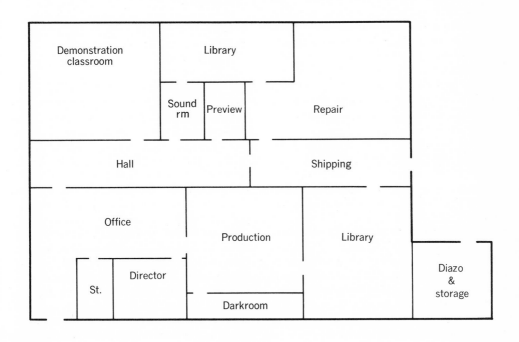

10. School-district centers generally require more space for reception and display area, bearing as it does a greater burden for good school-system public-relations responsibility as well as system-wide promotional activity in the field of media.

11. School-district centers generally require more space than do school-building centers for the work of programing and mass-producing audio and videotape programs.

Looking back over the preceding list, we must insist that the greater the emphasis is on building up services in each school, the less will be the need for space at the central headquarters. However, this generalization is relative, depending on an optimum balance, for as services mount in each school, more and more of the instructional periods in every teaching station will demand media support. Therefore, because of the pressure for increased central services of specific types, the space needs and requirements may still be greater rather than less as the previous generalization would seem to suggest. But the balance at that point would arise from a different set of circumstances. We would then state four guiding generalizations as follows:

1. Optimum space for known services will increase the efficiency of the work done by the available personnel, and conversely, crowding causes working efficiency to deteriorate.

2. Media-center space requirements should be planned to meet educational needs of a given school system for a 15-year growth period.

3. The need for space for any given area depends on the nature and volume of a known or predicted service and the specific operations to be carried out.

4. Until services can be predicted, no valid estimate of space needs can be made.

We have already dealt in depth with the problems of establishing school-building audiovisual media-service centers, and although we need not repeat here all of the guidelines mentioned previously, we shall nevertheless proceed with an enumeration of the space needs in the present section and deal with them briefly. However, we wish also to caution the reader to apply what he has learned in the previous chapter to the design and organization of school-district media-service suites.

Specific Space Needs and Suggestions for Layout in a District Audiovisual Media-Service Center

In the light of known operations and desirable services to meet instructional needs, the following comprehensive list of space needs is suggested as a basis for local planning and reference:

1. Reception and display area.
2. Administrative and clerical offices.
3. Storage space for materials.
4. Storage space for equipment.
5. Blind storage.
6. Shipping, receiving, inspection of materials, and work space.
7. Loading and pickup space.
8. Equipment inspection and maintenance space.
9. Professional library, committee study, and conference room space.
10. Preview and pre-auditioning space.
11. Graphic production space, including publications.
12. Photographic laboratory and work room.
13. Recording studio and control room.
14. School-system FM radio station space.
15. Closed-circuit, or low-power radiation, system-wide television studio, control room, and storage space.
16. Remote-controlled, system-wide resource bank for audio program tapes and videotapes for use in self-instruction services.
17. Rest rooms.

If it is desirable to change the emphasis from audiovisual media service to a comprehensive media service the following additional space needs should be added to the preceding seventeen items: (a) operational spaces for all print-medium services including the school-library program, (b) expanded publication production and distribution center coupled with a curriculum laboratory area, and (c) space for the possible storage and processing of school supplies.

In subsequent sections and paragraphs the layout of centers will be discussed in terms of functional groupings of space needs, as previously listed. However, since desirable production, telecasting, and print-medium facilities will be discussed more fully in Chapters 9, 10, and 12, respectively, emphasis will be placed upon the more commonly known facilities that may well have a high priority in starting a service program. Possible future expansion should, of course, be borne in mind when planning current operations.

Layout of Office Space and Reception Area

These areas obviously need to be together so that a member of the office staff can efficiently receive and route visitors to proper people and places as a part of regular secretarial and clerical duties. Sometimes the reception area has to be too small to include display and browsing areas, and in these cases interesting displays at or near entrances ought to be arranged as, for example, in corridors adjacent to the office. A few brief possibilities and adjustments in layout of these facilities follow:

1. The director's office should be close to the center of operations, not on another floor or at the end of a corridor away from his staff operations. If possible, his office should provide for privacy, but if necessary he may find a quiet corner in the main office or in the central work rooms, if office, storage, and workroom is a large block of space. In metropolitan centers where there are a number of department heads, the director needs a private administrative suite. Sometimes the director is separated from the center of operations by being located in another building provided for supervisory staff members. In general, this is not recommended, but such arrangements will work if a competent manager for the clerical and technical services is located at the central distribution unit.

2. Where adequate space is unavailable, space priority should be given to working areas, cutting the space allotments for reception and the director's office to an operational minimum. In such cases, it is better to combine all functions in one operating area without partitions.

3. Reception areas ought to have a reading table for catalogs and handbooks, and this area could also be arranged to include space for committee meetings.

4. The director's office space should be expanded and arranged to serve as a part of the professional library and committee study area whenever the reception area is extremely small.

5. If other places are available for waiting and browsing, it will be better for the sake of control

to have the reception area attractively fenced off, with a gate leading to other offices and operating spaces. Directing individuals to recording, consultation, and study activities on schedule is obviously an important function, since confusion and embarrassment are otherwise unavoidable.

6. In large centers, various divisions such as photographic production and broadcasting and telecasting would of necessity have to maintain their own reception and administrative offices.

7. Provide ample space for assistant director or manager's office and for secretarial and clerical workers according to volume of services.

Space-Need Estimates. Some space-size estimates are as follows: office or desk and work space for the director, 200 square feet; office and work space for the assistant director or manager, 160 square feet; desk and work space for secretary and clerks, 140 square feet for each; space for scheduling and general office work, 200 square feet, and reception space 150 square feet. Most of the estimates presented are minimal.

Layout of Storage and Distribution Spaces

In this section suggestions will be made regarding methods of storage for each kind of audiovisual media and the use of available space for the following operations: handling the work of filling orders, inspecting materials, packaging, returning used materials to storage, loading and unloading, and issuing equipment and materials. Sometimes it is necessary to issue equipment to users in the same school building where the center is located, and when this is the case, it is essential to provide a convenient, mobile, projection-stand storage area with easy access to a corridor. The main considerations in the arrangement of allotted spaces are the efficient use of staff services, and the protection of capital investments in materials and equipment by adequate provisions for their storage, care, and handling. The prospective media director must be prepared to adjust this entire operation to local conditions by either improving an existing operation in an old or recently remodeled building or, as opportunity presents itself, by planning a modern media-service center in new construction. Without being pessimistic, he should be prepared to make the most of what

Figure 8-2. Rarely do media program directors have enough space. Plans are usually made that at the time seem adequate. Allotted spaces often become totally inadequate in five to eight years or sooner. Careful planning of space use should include the analysis of work-flow patterns. Overcrowding of storage is certain to have deleterious effects on the service efficiency. (*Top view* courtesy Public Schools, Kalamazoo, Michigan; and *bottom view* Public Schools, Euclid, Ohio.)

space he can get, since actual allotments will rarely be as much as he needs or requests. Basic directions and suggestions for space planning are:

1. In planning space needs for the storage and handling of audiovisual media, the director ought to look ahead ten to fifteen years in order to provide for the type of program realistically envisioned as developing during that period.

2. The director should arrange operations within spaces allotted in terms of a natural flow of work to economize on the time and effort of personnel. The only profitable way to attack this problem is to construct a flow diagram showing the relationships between the essential processes that must be carried on. The first diagram should cover the process of receiving materials, and it must include the following flow of activity, beginning with the rear-door loading zone or the front-door parking area: (a) materials are carried or wheeled to a receiving bench in the center's work area where packages are opened and the materials are placed on a mobile table or rack; (b) return slips are checked off against original delivery records; (c) materials are wheeled to inspection benches for cleaning and repair, and after such processing they are (d) wheeled to storage vaults, shelves, or racks, and properly filed for subsequent requests.

Another natural flow pattern is the process of filling orders for media. This flow-of-work diagram is as follows: (a) media material such as a film, chart, filmstrip, exhibit, videotape, or audio program tape are pulled from storage racks or cabinets and placed on a mobile table; then (b) they are wheeled to shipping benches where they are packaged and labeled; then (c) they are placed in canvas delivery bags or in boxes marked with the name of the school awaiting delivery; and finally (d) they are moved to the loading platform on scheduled delivery days. It can be seen that efficient flow-of-work patterns should be planned in great detail before specifications are stated for amount and shape of spaces being requested.

3. Arrangements for adequate light and ventilation should be made to facilitate the proper inspection and cleaning of materials because matching picture frames and sound tracks of motion pictures require accurate observation of small details, and some cleaning

fluids have annoying odors even if they are not toxic.

4. It is urgent also that film materials be kept at normal humidity and temperature conditions; hence a separate room is advised where humidifiers can be operated to keep the air from getting too dry, as it does for instance, in overheated rooms in winter. Brittleness of film materials must be avoided. Such vaults according to suggestions in (2) should be conveniently located with respect to the inspection and packaging benches. Doors into film vaults should be wider than usual to permit mobile film racks and tables to pass easily. Sliding doors are best for space economy.

5. Equipment storage spaces should be near loading and issuing areas. These storage areas could be in the repair shop, but generally the shop should be free of this storage function. However, equipment should be stored as close as possible to the individuals who inspect it, that is, to those who will check its readiness for the next use. Whenever equipment is stored during damp summer months, ventilation in the spaces is needed, or silica gel must be provided to remove excess moisture from the air. When these precautions are not taken, mildew is likely to damage cases and electrical insulation.

6. Loading and unloading zones should be on ground floors with access to loading ramps, and since trucking carts should be available for hauling packages, floors and floor coverings should be able to stand up under hard usage.

7. Although other than ground-floor locations for storage and distribution are commonly found, they should never be specified unless private freight elevators are available. If necessary, the prospective director should compute the tonnage of materials handled annually, adding both incoming and outgoing materials, to prove his point if there should be conflicting requests for ground-floor spaces.

8. Optimum working space should be provided around the packaging bench, and ample space should be provided around the film-inspecting benches for mobile film racks or tables. The packaging bench ought to be a comfortable height for workers; such benches should be constructed to provide underneath storage space, and should be of such size that they can serve as table tops for numerous construction activities if other workbench space for these purposes is unavailable. A width of

Figure 8-3. District media maintenance operations often include in addition to equipment repair, the handling of repair service under contracts, issuing equipment units for special purposes, analysis of technical problems, issuing repair supplies, and maintaining the equipment inventory, to mention just a few. Space allocation is thus determined in accordance with availability and specific functions. *Courtesy Public Schools, Euclid, Ohio.*

24 to 30 inches, length of 7 to 12 feet, and height of 38 inches for stand-up work are desirable general measurements for the combination packaging and work bench.

Space-Need Estimates. Some space-size estimates are as follows: Assuming two automatic film-inspection machines for each station, 200 square feet per station, counting access area from and to storage (the more motion picture prints that are used per day or week, the more stations and personnel will be required to get the film-inspection work done); storage of media, such as tapes, films, filmstrips, slides, exhibits, and picture sets may run from 1,500 square feet in a small district to 10,000 in a metropolitan center; for equipment a minimum for general purposes, would be 1,500 square feet; for receiving and packaging, depending on volume, a rough estimate for moving media materials and equipment would be a minimum of 1,500 square feet; and for a loading zone and docking area other than driveway space, a minimum of

1,000 square feet, with unobstructed areas for moving mobile stands and rubber-tired trucks and hand-carts.

Layout of Equipment-Inspection and Maintenance Space

In general, college and university and metropolitan audiovisual media-service centers maintain the largest and best-equipped equipment maintenance shops; however, many small and medium-sized cities provide school shop facilities for inspection, cleaning, and minor service work. A few centers have been fortunate in discovering a technical person who repairs materials and equipment, and who serves as a photographer or in some other capacity besides. Again, the emphasis in this section is upon the spatial arrangement of the shop and not procedures and equipment, since these will be treated later in the chapter. It should be remembered that in the preceding chapter, shop facilities were recommended as a part of the school-building service center, and the reader should recheck the recommendations and illustrations given there. Therefore, the following suggestions and directions apply to the layout of shop facilities in the school-system audiovisual media center, where facilities need to be more complete and the space allotment greater.

1. Because the job of issuing and controlling materials and equipment is not a shop function (although in small audiovisual media centers these functions may have to be combined), the various units of equipment should be stored elsewhere. However, the repair shop ought to be located near the equipment-receiving area to minimize the work of carrying equipment to the shop. If the shop is near the receiving area, all work of inspection in addition to cleaning and servicing ought to be done in the shop space.

2. If mobile equipment carts are available, and day-to-day inspection of incoming equipment units can be done at an inspection station near the issuing and loading zone, the shop functions may without undue hardship be assigned to space located at a considerable distance from the distribution center but always on the same floor.

3. The most efficient flow pattern is (a) inspection of equipment near receiving point; (b) to storage for subsequent issue or (c) to shop for repair; and finally (d) back to storage for immediate assignment. Another flow pattern could be (a) referral to shop from a city school building via receiving room for needed repairs, and (b) return to issuing room for cartage to its original school location via regular delivery channels.

4. When laying out equipment spaces, a sink and a separately vented exhaust fan should be provided to facilitate cleaning operations.

Space-Need Estimates. Again, an estimate of space requirement is difficult to make when the variables are unknown. We can say that the equipment-service facility should not only be considered as a workbench well equipped with test equipment, but also as a staff of technical personnel that can move to locations where decentralized facilities are operating in each school building, or to telecasting facilities or important dial-access resource banks where automatic installations may be in need of a periodic check-up or emergency service. Hence a good technician needs a tool kit, high-level

diagnostic ability, and speedy conveyance for himself and his instruments. We must think of the space for a maintenance area in terms of the amount of service to be rendered, but as a minimum we suggest a range of 400 to 1,000 square feet. A technician ought to have a small desk, to keep his service manuals, equipment-service diagrams, and maintenance records in.

Layout of Blind Storage Space

The importance of so-called blind or dead storage space is frequently overlooked in planning the layout of operational spaces for audiovisual services. Every center should have at least one storage area in the main office and one or more additional storage closets measuring at least 6 feet wide by 8 or 10 feet deep. In new construction, such spaces may serve also as "expansion" space—for example, as additional preview rooms. These storage areas need not necessarily be located close to operational centers, but they could be located off corridors in such a way that they would serve to stop undesirable transmission of sound. That is, a preview room or recording studio could be located between such storage rooms, thus protecting that space from noise. Small blind storage rooms make possible an uncluttered appearance in regular storage spaces, since obsolete equipment units or infrequently used materials may be stored out of sight. It should be recalled that obsolete equipment units may be used as trade-ins on new equipment units—hence the recommendation to store them. If the possibility of deriving trade-in value is remote, outworn equipment should, of course, be discarded. If such storage areas are not possible in the main center, rooms in other school buildings should be found for that purpose.

Space-Need Estimates. The estimated range of space needed for so-called dead storage should run from a minimum for every service center of 150 square feet to possibly 700 feet of floor space well utilized by floor-to-ceiling racks in large school-system media-service centers. This space estimate is of course relative to other space allocations in regular equipment storage areas. The more unused space there, the less dead storage space needs to be planned for. Here again, a word of caution is in order. Both central and decentralized storage spaces will be required as media-service centers expand their operations in all schools, and an optimum balance is called for when the build-up of services in individual schools is emphasized.

Layout of Professional Library and Committee-Room Space

An audiovisual media center must have space to house its professional library, equipment literature, catalogs, and curriculum listings for teachers, as well as its reference materials for the director. In smaller centers these items may be kept in the director's office, a small consulting office off the main office, or an attractive corner of the main office. These materials should be located in or close to the main office area, since materials on file should be subjected to a control system to assure their usefulness at the time they are needed. Some centers have well-developed areas for these purposes, while others have to make the best of a single shelf and a couple of file cabinets.

If it is remembered that the professional library can be an important factor in mass communication—for example, in in-service education programs for the school system—it can become more than a reading room for a few staff members. It can become a well-developed service center for teacher groups and planning committees at all levels. See Figure 8-4. If the curriculum-development center is a part of this facility, the space and the personnel involved may be extensive. The job of staffing it and providing space for it would be less difficult if it were only a storehouse for audiovisual media publications.

Space-Need Estimates. If a committee room —or a room we may refer to as a conference room, fully equipped for projection and sound recording—is included in this facility, we must allow considerable additional space. In good-sized school systems, especially when audiovisual media centers are located in or near administrative headquarters, a small auditorium should be set up in such a way that conference tables could be installed to suit the purpose of the meeting being held. As a minimum we would estimate the need for 1,000 square feet in a medium-sized school system for the professional library facility with an additional 500 to 1,500 square feet for a conference room or small auditorium.

Layout of Preview and Preauditioning Spaces

If obtaining space is a problem, the allotment for a large-group preview facility should have a low priority. This viewpoint is not heretical at all because many large preview rooms sit idle a large percentage of the school day. Suggestions and directions for allotting such space are discussed in the following list.

1. Small preview and pre-auditioning rooms are urgent, and two to four of these rooms, involving approximately 36 square feet each, need to be located where sound emanating from them will not disturb other operations.

2. A large preview room seating thirty to forty people is not necessary at a school-system center unless it can double as an equipment laboratory, a production center for slides and transparencies and other graphic materials, a picture-mounting workroom, a recording studio, or some other operational area that can be shared by the center and other school agencies.

3. The work of previewing for selection purposes must necessarily go on continuously in every school building in the system, since materials need to be routed to teachers, analyzed, and reported on in accordance with system-wide plans.

4. A projection room seating ten to fourteen people should have high priority, however, and perhaps one of the small, booth-type projection and sound auditioning facilities recommended in (1) should be expanded into one of these.

5. All preview rooms need to be located close to equipment and close to center personnel who can operate the equipment and check on fulfillment of schedules and appointments. This means locating such spaces near office and equipment-control areas, at least on the same floor for convenient supervision.

6. When necessary for elimination of noise, listening to audio materials may be done by individuals or small groups using earphones. In fact, we should give highest priority to providing an area seating fifteen to twenty individuals who could examine films and listen to audio tapes in special analytical situations, possibly looking at ten different films at the same time. Such work may be conducted efficiently only when small projection screens and headphones are available

Figure 8-4. This is Portland's Professional Library for the teaching and leadership staffs. It is located at the Administration Headquarters and is an integral part of the Instructional Materials Center Program. *Courtesy Instructional Materials Center, Public Schools, Portland, Oregon.*

in a bench-type or carrel arrangement. Such work is required when film clips are being sought in connection with automation and self-instruction systems work. However, here again, not all of this work can go on at the school-system audiovisual media center. Most of it will be carried on in school-building media-service centers as already described.

Space-Need Estimates. In a district-wide audiovisual center we believe that the minimum of space to be laid out according to suggested plans and priorities for use would be 700 square feet.

Layout of the Graphic Production Area

Graphic production departments in audiovisual media-service centers often provide diagrams and pictorial illustrations for a wide array of school-system publications, but we think of such departments more particularly in connection with the design and preparation of media for teachers to use in their fundamental professional work. In this modern-day technological development, we need to produce or modify and revise self-instruction teaching systems, and make in addition, or help teachers make, a variety of media from a 2 × 2 inch slide sequence and audio-program tapes for an individual study carrel, to overhead transparencies and 8mm single-cartridge-type motion pictures, or even a set of models for a television program. We have also insisted that each school building have its own media production facilities at a level consistent with central media-service policies.

Space-Need Estimates. The specific program being developed will determine the recommendations for space, but it is difficult to envision a media-preparation program that operates in a facility area less than 1,700 square feet. We arrive at this figure in the next chapter which is devoted to this important subject of media design and preparation operations in schools and school systems. Photographic darkroom services and facilities are included in that discussion and in the over-all space-need estimate.

Layout of Recording Studio and Control Room

Another operational space need is an area where recording work may be done. Today, with magnetic sound motion picture equipment and with the rapidly advancing technology of magnetic tape and its special relationship to telecasting and self-instruction programs, a recording studio and control room merits careful consideration. Such a room, even if it is only 400 square feet, can be serviceable. An adjoining control room with a glass panel and with connector plugs in the partition separating it from the main studio, of 100 square feet minimum, will enable better recording of sound for all purposes. The studio, being acoustically treated, may serve as well to record audio programs and short talks by school officials in connection with school public-relations programs. Also, the control room may house tape re-recording equipment for preparing multiple copies of tape-recorded materials loaned to the school system for that purpose. The work of re-recording, however, does not demand the special conditions of a studio facility. The location of studio and control room is a critical matter from the standpoint of external and internal noise. Only by an analysis of local conditions can the decision to include a sound recording studio be judged practical or impractical. In designing such spaces particular attention ought to be given to acoustic treatment, to quiet air-exhaust and air conditioning systems, and to suitable floor coverings. As with the subject of graphic production facilities, we shall include valuable, considerably detailed information relative to sound recording and audio-program production facilities in Chapter 9.

Space-Need Estimates. It has already been indicated that at least 400 square feet would be needed for a small recording studio and this space should be so arranged that a control room

of 100 square feet could be provided to give the facility additional flexibility and to increase the sound quality of the eventual productions.

Layout of School-System FM Broadcasting Space

The development of magnetic tape technology and new transmission systems has greatly facilitated radio broadcasting, and while FM broadcasting has not generally prospered as an instructional medium, there are many possibilities for significant contributions, some of which may be utilized in the future in large-group teaching activities as a supplement or combined with television components. Space needed for school radio production and broadcast activities must be determined, of course, by the nature of present and future program schedules. Broadcasting on whatever scale, large or small, requires the following spaces:

1. One main studio and control room.
2. One auxiliary studio and control room as a minimum to facilitate rehearsals and taping processes.
3. Main transmitter equipment room (may be located near or remote).
4. Administrative suite and production offices for staff and director.
5. Combination workroom and tape and disk library.
6. Exterior space nearby, or on roof, for FM tower and antenna.

The instructional needs for school-operated radio stations will have to be correctly analyzed, and the wisest possible decisions must be made concerning recommendations as to the best method for meeting them. FM facilities may be combined with an audio program remotely-controlled audio resource bank, or may be a part of a general transmission facility including television.

Space-Need Estimates. Space-size estimates would be as follows: main and auxiliary studios in combination with a single control room that houses a tape-duplicating process would run from 650 to 1,000 square feet or more; supervisory and secretarial space, approximately 300 square feet; a workroom and tape and/or disk library space would run to 900 square feet. (If an automatic audio and videotape resource bank were included an additional 700 to 1,500 square feet ought to be provided.)

Layout of Closed-Circuit, System-Wide Telecasting Facilities

We have already suggested that school-building units may in addition to central tele-casting services maintain their own closed-circuit television studios. And also we have referred repeatedly to videotape services for both large-group and self-instruction activities. At this point we can, for the sake of completeness deal with the layout of telecasting facilities super-ficially in view of the fact that in Chapter 10, the subject of television services will be dealt with in considerable detail. Again, the envisioned use of television, programed and used locally and possibly in combination with other school systems in a given region, will determine the space requirements, but we will at this point emphasize the need for some very basic facilities and arrangements. Primary facilities will include spaces for studios and control room, preparation room which may include film previewing devices and the means for preparing visual media in support of good programing, conference tables for planning productions, storage space for sets and props, storage for videotapes, films, slides, charts and exhibits, maintenance area, an equipment storage area for remote equipment, large-screen projection systems for loan to schools, receiving and unloading area, adminis-trative and secretarial areas, and a suite of offices for program personnel, technicians, and tele-vision studio teachers. The problems of layout will be dealt with in a later chapter.

Space-Need Estimates. As hazardous as it is to estimate the nature and amount of space needs, we can state some approximations based on the kinds of spaces that are generally needed by school systems that go into television seriously. On the basis of the assumption of a system-wide program we can suggest the nature of space-sizes as follows: Main studio, 1,650 square feet; auxiliary studio, 800 square feet; control room serving both studios, 500 square feet; program and media preparation room, 1,200 square feet; storage areas for all purposes, 1,650 square feet; receiving and unloading area (building spaces only, not driveway or truck space), 800 square feet; administrative and secretarial office space, 300 square feet; techni-cians and program personnel, five desk and operational spaces, 500 square feet; desk spaces for participating television teachers in a pro-fessional headquarters, for five studio teachers, 1,000 square feet (approximately 200 square feet for each desk and operational space).

Arrangements for Rest Rooms

Planners unavoidably have to put certain spaces in wrong places. In the case of rest rooms, the availability of water supply and drains may dictate the placement of rest rooms in locations where they obviously do not belong. This word of caution is included for media directors who may wish to provide every convenience for their colleagues and visitors, but who ought also to avoid recording the sound of flushing toilets in their teaching tapes, or avoid subjecting guests to embarrassment by having them walk through storage and maintenance areas enroute. When problems of rest room location arise, it may be expedient to seek usable spaces off outside corridors but adjacent or near audio-visual media service centers.

As we pointed out earlier, we shall not at this point begin the discussion of the problems of implementing print-medium programs in school systems. We will devote Chapter 12 to this subject, and there we shall include ample illustrations as to layout of spaces and the recommended space allotments for the processes that are required. We shall also amplify fully in other chapters solutions to problems associated with media preparation and television services.

At this point we need to turn to the problems of providing adequate storage facilities for handling and distributing the media materials needed by teachers and pupils.

Storage Facilities at the Center

Planners of audiovisual centers need to understand that the nature of storage facilities is usually determined not only in terms of available space, but also in terms of the way materials are, or ought to be, packaged. It should be recognized without fail that the way materials are packaged has a bearing on their protection against damage, both in storage and in transit, on the convenience with which materials are inspected after use, and on the ease with which they are returned to storage to be identified again for order-filling processes. Specific suggestions and illustrations for proper treatment follow.

Motion Pictures

Open film racks should be purchased or fabricated locally whenever it is expected that a film library will eventually grow to several hundred reels or more in size. Such racks should be so spaced in the film vault that mobile carts can be brought to within an arm's length of the racks. See Figure 8-2 and also 1-2 and 1-5. Metal, enclosed cabinets are often used to house small film libraries of a hundred reels or less, but cabinet doors are often in the way because swinging space must be provided. Care should be taken that the film separators in the racks are wide enough apart to hold film cans, although some libraries discard the film cans and store just the reels.

When cans are used, labels must be affixed to the outside of each can that match the label on the film leader. When can covers become bent, or are jammed on, film inspectors have a difficult time opening them. Films lost because of being incorrectly placed in film cans may be difficult to find. On the other hand, if film reels are damaged in transit, then costs for new reels will have to be met, and this offsets the time and trouble saved by the film inspectors when they do not have to open a can first before putting the film on the inspection machines. In most cases the 400-foot cans or just the reels are kept separately in their own racks for convenience in filling orders. Some film libraries keep all sizes stored separately. This is hardly necessary, since all other film cans or reels other than the 400-foot size can be reached and handled easily if stored side by side. Plans for identifying films are many, but in general, cataloging procedures and ordering systems have a bearing on the final decision. Some of the most common systems for locating motion pictures on the racks and identifying them are the following:

1. *Alphabetizing by Title Only.* Write a brief title and the print number on the can, or if no can is used, write the title on the film's white or colored leader strip with a felt-nib or nylon-tip pen. Also type up a brief title and print number on a small label and fasten it to the film rack to indicate the permanent storage position of a particular film.

2. *Using a Numbering System.* Write a code number for the film title on both leader and can and possibly again on the rack. For example, film numbers could run from one to a thousand with a prefix of MP. Such code numbers would then appear in catalogs, subject listings, and on film cards.

Filmstrips

Many ingenious devices have been devised for storing filmstrips, from the commercially available shallow-drawer cabinets to the home-made drawer with separators made of piano wire stretched taut after being threaded through appropriately drilled holes in the drawer frame. Other devices range from hanging wall frames to ordinary shelving where filmstrips are stored in cardboard boxes. Many filmstrip libraries are now storing filmstrips in small sets and are distributing them accordingly. Also, the new plastic filmstrip container with unlosable cover is a popular development. A number of libraries dislike filmstrip drawers because of the packaging problem, preferring to inspect and return filmstrip cans to a cardboard package, and to store the package on a marked shelf ready for delivery, thus avoiding the separate packaging operation of placing the filmstrips in a suitable carton or cardboard tube every time an order is filled. Coding with catalog numbers or other suitable identifying numbers should be affixed to both can and shipping package. Sound filmstrips with their accompanying records need extra coding numbers to indicate disks or tapes that must be packaged separately or in combination. Large fiber cases for records are recommended.

As we have pointed out in previous chapters, filmstrips can usually be assigned to individual school buildings as a part of a standard collection. The assignment of such collections becomes a local policy matter.

Slides

We should first note that slides of various sizes need different storage treatments. The 4 × 7 inch slide is largely available commercially in connection with short-exposure techniques.

Figure 8-5. Plans for filmstrip storage need to be worked out to provide convenient order-filling processes. This extensive filmstrip collection is stored in stacked metal drawers and on slanted shelving units. Refer also to Figure 7-10. *Courtesy Fresno County Schools, Fresno, California.*

Another slide, often referred to as the standard lantern slide, $3\frac{1}{4} \times 4$ inch is now rarely found for purchase commercially. Such slides are made by teachers for special purposes for repetitive use. This size is in fact made by the Polaroid Land camera process using 46L and 146L film. The 2×2 inch slide in color and black and white is the most popular size of slide today because of its frequent use in automatically controlled slide projectors in television studios. They are also made by teachers from a great many sources, making up as they do sequences for self-instruction use in carrels, or used by teachers in classrooms by means of remote-control processes in front of a large or small group. Black and white Polaroid slides are easily made for use in the 2×2 inch size and these of course are made up in a few minutes as the need arises. Other 2×2 inch slides in color are made up by teachers from their own sources and are developed by local or regional commercial processors. Such slides are returned in one to five days depending on the processing contract. Special processing services may be obtained in some metropolitan areas that would return mounted slides in a matter of a few hours.

Instructional media program directors may choose to store slides in sturdy wooden, cardboard, or metal boxes, by topic keyed in topical listings to subject-matter headings, books, and units of work, or they may be arranged by and for teachers in, for example, carousel magazines by topics and given to teachers, or assigned to school-building collections for repetitive use.

The days of storing slides in drawers, or in visible file cabinets seem to be gone. The great difficulty is that teachers do not have the time to search long and complicated listings for content for their presentations. Once found, and used, such materials ought to be duplicated and filed by magazine, for a given teacher's use or duplicated for each teacher in a subject or at a specific grade level. Appropriate code numbers for available sets of slides should of course be in the catalogs sent to teachers.

The only alternative would be to employ random-access devices that would locate such specific slide topics by means of automatic-selection devices. Slides are extremely valuable in self-instruction, and in large-group processes. Ways must be found to make them available on a long-term custody basis for teachers who key them into their daily teaching activities. It is obvious then that the storage of slides becomes pretty largely a problem of storage in a given school building, or in a teacher's room or television studio. More details about slide-making processes and services are to be found in Chapter 9 in connection with media design and preparation processes.

Study Prints

Pictures distributed by a center should be stored in sets, with the possible exception of large-size art prints. Legal-size filing cabinets or appropriately sized shelves are needed to house the sets, and additional protection must be

Figure 8-6. As with other kinds of media some ingenious methods have to be devised to provide adequate protection for fragile paper-print media during transit and also for handling during order-filling processes. A means for rapid identification is also a necessity. Sturdy boxes made up according to specifications may be purchased, perhaps locally. See also Figure 1-2. (*Top picture,* courtesy San Diego County Schools; and *bottom picture,* courtesy Fresno County Schools.)

given by specially fabricated cardboard boxes or by accordion-type folders with tie strings. Tying a set of pictures together and storing them in cabinets with exposed edges and surfaces is not recommended. Paper-box companies will turn out boxes according to local designs and measurements, using sturdy clasps, hooks or other cover fastening devices. Mounting procedures are discussed in a later section on care of materials; however, mounting according to standard sizes of mounting-board material will be a help in standardizing the sizes of transit boxes needed. When individual pictures are distributed, sturdy covers and clasps are

necessary for protection. Figures 8-6 and 1-2 point out desirable procedures.

We should point out that in view of today's technological development, we may well agree to turn over to school buildings sets of pictures urgently needed in their day-to-day teaching. Such use of materials ought not to be left to chance, and curriculum guides ought to stress that such materials are either *basic* or *supplementary.* When it makes little difference whether a given medium is used or not, and if indeed, the use of media is not stressed by those in charge, there seems to be little point in the laborious and expensive processes worked out to get them to the right classrooms at the right time. The days of such laxity with regard to the use of media are about over.

Disk Recordings

Vertical storage cabinets or shelving are easy to fabricate locally, or they may be purchased. Heavy-duty record sleeves should be procured in quantity and used to give records adequate protection. Transit containers may be of the fiber-film-case type with cardboard fillers to keep the record from sliding during periods of transportation. If space permits, disks may be stored vertically in their shipping containers, thus providing more room for appropriate code numbers or appropriate labels. If stored as individual disks in original covers, protruding adhesive cloth tabs may be used for identifying numbers.

At this point of technological development, it seems obvious that teachers who use disks for specialized instruction ought to have them either in their own possession or have access to them in a school-building collection. Again the curriculum guides for a given grade and program of instruction will determine the need for the expansion of this medium. The convenience (subject of course to copyright law stipulations) of taping a section of a disk, and properly relating it to required instructional tasks—thus preserving it for repetitive use—is obvious in many fields of teaching endeavor.

An essential service with regard to disk recordings that could be given by a media center would be the continual supply of standard sleeves and album covers so that school-building media coordinators could keep their disk recording collections in the best condition possible. The replacement of album covers together with new labels will make the use of disks by teachers more convenient. Hence the necessary supplies should be stocked in quantity at headquarters.

Taped Audio Programs and Videotape

Audio-program tapes and taped television programs referred to as videotapes are easy to store since regular metal or wood shelving units will suffice. The best way to store tapes of all kinds is to keep them in their original cardboard boxes to which explanatory labels may be attached. If there is any chance that tapes may be mixed up in their containers, then each tape ought to be labeled with adhesive-backed labels, commercially available. Since there is no way as yet to examine the condition of tapes without playing them through, or spot checking them by actual playing, extra care must be given to prevent erasure, and mixing up the subjects in their containers. Tapes may be distributed in canvas bags, but care should be taken to keep audio-program tape packages from opening in transit allowing tape to unwind and become damaged. The larger sizes of videotape reels would not be likely to open up during local delivery trucking periods. Masking tape, or a rubber band may easily serve in the former case as an adequate precaution. Tapes should be stored vertically for easy accessibility during the order-filling processes, and label strips may be easily affixed to the edges of the boxes. See Figure 8-8.

Realia, Exhibits, Kits, Models, and Dioramas

No center should consider distributing such materials without adequate space and staff for proper handling. Mounted animals need specially designed wooden boxes, and dioramas with glass or clear plastic covers need adequate transit cases of sturdy cardboard or wood to prevent excessive deterioration. Ample shelving or bins will be needed, and storage in their regular transit cases of all large items will, of course, expedite delivery processes. Figure 8-9 indicates processes that centers are presently using.

Maps, Globes, and Charts

As indicated earlier, models, dioramas, and exhibits need only appropriate storage shelves against a wall. The same arrangement will suffice for globes if they are stored in transit containers of heavy-duty, reinforced cardboard or fiberboard with straps. Globes will have to be stored in their fiberboard or corrugated cardboard cases and separated from accompanying metal floor stands. Flat maps and charts may be stored either in a series of drawers of suitable size or in vertical slots made by arranging metal or wood partitions 2 to 6 inches apart in a large

Figure 8-7. Many kinds of prefabricated metal storage cabinets been have designed especially for media. In general it is cheaper to buy such storage cabinets than to design and build them out of wood. Several of the standard units are shown in this cluster of illustrations. All cabinets except lower right, *courtesy Neumade Products Corp., Scarsdale, New York;* lower right, *courtesy H. Wilson Corp., Chicago, Illinois.*

Figure 8-8. (Above) Master audio-program tapes are stored and duplicated in this area of the audiovisual media center at Euclid, Ohio. Tapes are stored in their own cardboard boxes and are plainly labeled. *Courtesy Public Schools, Euclid, Ohio.*

bin. When vertical storage is used, all flat materials should be placed between masonite or heavy paper covers. If charts and maps are of the roll-up type, whether on spring rollers or not, they may be stored in long, reinforced cartons of the type portable screens come in, or in heavy cardboard tubes. Storing these tubes or cartons at the center requires shelving or bins arranged so that code numbers or titles are in full view.

Storage of Equipment

Ordinarily, equipment units are decentralized in the schools; hence, equipment storage-space requirements at a city school-system center are not large. Appropriate metal or wood shelving and bins need to be built into the available space. Consideration should be given to a modular construction of bins that can be stacked up in horizontal or vertical fashion. This is possible if over-all measurements of height, width, and

Figure 8-9. The Instructional Materials Center in the Flint Public Schools, also distributes a wide array of models and apparatus. Metal book-shelving units are used to store them awaiting orders from teachers. In the bottom picture we note the type of flexible wooden shelving units designed many years ago for storing media in the San Diego center. (*Top view*, courtesy Public Schools, Flint Michigan; *bottom view*, San Diego City Schools, San Diego.)

depth are accurately figured. The main purpose is to provide shelving against a wall or in tiers of bins back to back in the center of a storage space. See Figures 7-27 and 8-3.

Applicability of Storage Procedures to School-Building Centers

We discussed at length in Chapter 7 the problems of organizing school-building audiovisual media centers, and urged their operation as a means of supplying the help that teachers need in using technology in its more complicated forms. We should emphasize here that storage facilities will have to be planned as for the district-wide center, but it is likely that storage problems will not be as great, nor the space for handling the media demand in a given school anywhere near as extensive. The previous suggestions, however, will have to apply to school-building centers as well.

Care of Media Materials

Audiovisual media materials must be maintained in first-class condition or their deterioration will accelerate. Teachers lose interest quickly when the materials they receive from central depositories are outworn in appearance, when film materials break during projection, and when materials look dirty. The district media program director must know what kinds of care and handling processes to prescribe, and he must be able to supervise operational plans as carried out by workers. In the preceding section proper packaging for transit to and from schools was stressed in connection with storage and ease in handling. In this section the proper care in terms of inspection and processing is emphasized, and specific suggestions are made for each of the basic kinds of media.

Motion Pictures

After a film is projected, it should be tactually inspected, using standard motor or manually operated rewinds, or mechanically inspected by means of automatic inspection machines. Where such machines are used, it is frequently reported that a pair of machines and one full-time inspector is a very efficient working combination. See Figure 1-3. Inspectors themselves may be part-time or full-time adult workers, men or women, or students who come to work after school. Women are increasingly being used to get this important work done. Specific suggestions for caring for motion picture films are discussed in the following paragraphs.

Equipment Needed. It is quite obvious that in cases where film collections are small, less than 600 prints, the expensive automatic, electronically controlled film-inspection machines may not be practical. If the school building or the school system can afford it, however, it would be a matter of great convenience, and perhaps a means of utilizing a one-man technical force very effectively, since the inspection of incoming films from outside sources, and the inspection of films before being returned to distributors outside the school district, are sizable jobs. High-speed inspection machines would be a means of saving the technician's time for other important jobs.

Because inspecting films by hand opens up such opportunity for error in judgment, it is better for the films distributed, regardless of the size of the collection, to inspect them by machine. We therefore urge an effort even on the part of small school-system film libraries to acquire the automatic units that even students can operate with greater certainty of spotting defects in film condition. The machine itself may cost approximately $3,000, and a good quality splicer with high-speed film cement costs an additional $175.

In case schools and school systems are forced to use hand film-inspection methods, we suggest that the following equipment be acquired: film rewinds, preferably motor driven; a good quality splicer, preferably a model where the emulsion is scraped off without the application of moisture; a sturdy inspection table where workers may be comfortably seated while working; good overhead lighting; a motor-driven film cleaner, or a small fluid applicator for manual use with the film rewinds; a small light-box for sound-track and frame-matching purposes; and, a magnifying glass. But as we have emphasized the trend is toward machine detection of defects in both large and small film-distribution agencies. Of course, a couple of motor- or hand-driven film-rewind devices may be easy to use for the insertion of replacement film footage sections where soundtracks have to be accurately matched.

Film-Care Supplies. The prospective director needs a few words of advice about supplies. Frequently these will have to be purchased in quantity as needed. Because of possible alteration in characteristics through evaporation, film cement should be purchased by the carton in the smallest container offered that will not allow the fluid to evaporate. Other supplies needed are cellulose pads (commonly used in connection with mimeo and ditto duplicator machines) for applying fluids manually; colored "head" and "tail" leader stock; heavy-duty colored cello or masking tape for fastening down loose film ends; film-cleaning fluids such as Renovex, and Protect-O-Film; and, felt-nib pens and ink for writing on leaders and cans. A word of caution is in order at this point, since not all fluids may be used as effectively as others in the automatic-electronic film-inspection machine with film-cleaning attachments. When such machines are utilized, the manufacturer's recommendations should be followed.

Film-Care Processes. The main processes or film-care jobs are as follows: inspecting visually, electronically, and tactually; splicing to eliminate all defects (avoiding notching since notches do not pass through electronic film-inspection machines); cleaning with chemicals; treating new prints before projection; analyzing print condition; reporting specific and general conditions on control cards; and, replacing damaged footage. When inspecting tactually, the inspector must be taught to let the film slip through his fingers in such a way that defects in film edges, perforations and film blisters will be consistently detected.

Splicing is, of course, an extremely critical operation and must never be done in a slipshod manner. In general, this task needs close supervision because errors in workmanship lead to more serious damage to the film during later projections. If moisture is used to loosen the film emulsion, the film ends must be thoroughly dried before applying film cement. Another critical aspect of the splicing process is the deft application of the cement by one stroke of the brush, with the immediate lowering of the film press into its clamped-down position.

Films may be cleaned while rewinding them, using a cellulose pad dampened with one of the recommended cleaning fluids. As has already been mentioned, inexpensive applicators or motor-driven film cleaners are available, but machine methods are preferable. When films are inspected by machine, defects are automatically detected. When a defect is found the machine stops automatically, calling for personal observation to identify the defect and to take remedial action.

Another essential process is the treatment of new film prints. This process is identical to the cleaning process except that the fluid is applied to the new prints for the sake of pliability, not cleanliness. Since all film prints ought to be projected before acceptance to check physical print conditions, the film-pliability fluids can be added by allowing the film to pass from the feed reel along a loosely pinched, chemical-dampened, cellulose pad. This job is more effectively carried out on automatic machines.

The only efficient way to obtain up-to-date information about film condition is to maintain an adequate film-condition report card in a special file on the film-inspection bench. Each splice and each damaged footage replacement should be recorded, as should each film cleaning. Unfortunately, this is a job for clerks, and clerks and other technical workers seem to be all too scarce.

Replacing footage need not be so difficult a job as generally thought. Actually, the only difficulty is the proper matching of the sound track of the new section with that of the old. This job is made easy by ordering replacement footage in units of whole scenes. Thus the splice may be made by joining the last frame of one scene with the first frame of the new scene, and the sound tracks will then be automatically matched. The light-box and magnifying glass aid this process. When other than scene-to-scene replacement has to be done, the section containing the newly spliced-in footage should be projected to ascertain if sound and pictorial continuity has been maintained.

Slides

The first essential of slide care is to bind the slide properly between cover glass. No slide in any size is ready for distribution until this has been done. Miniature slides, the 2×2 inch size, may be quickly protected by glass, using the special metal, snap-on or insertion-type mounts, or they may be bound by using bulk supplies of clean cover glass, standard masks, and $\frac{3}{8}$-inch binding tape of the plastic variety. Usually a slide-binding vise is needed for this work if it is to be done in any quantity. The second essential is to keep slides clean. This is a tremendous "window-washing" job if the slide library is large, and precautions must be taken by students or others who are employed to do the work to keep cloths just damp enough with water to rub off the fingerprints and smears, and then to dry the washed glass thoroughly. If moisture is allowed to get between the glasses through breaks in the tape binding, the emulsion and hence the picture may be seriously damaged. The third essential is maintaining good physical condition of the binding. This process demands that cracked cover glass and loose or sticky binding be replaced in time to prevent damage to the picture. Whenever possible, binding materials should be standardized and stocked in quantity. The advantages of such a procedure are obvious.

We have already indicated under the subject of storage that slides should be stored and arranged for projection in such a way that they receive a minimum of handling. Cautioning users to handle slides by their edges is hardly sufficient. The way to prevent handling is to store slides in their automatic magazines or trays ready for repetitive projection. Where one or more slides in a single presentation must be repeated, duplicates should be made on the spot or obtained commercially. The kind of care made necessary by selecting sets of slides for a given presentation or self-instructional exercises, only to break up the selection for return to a master file or storage rack is unworkable in most schools. To facilitate control of slide materials that are subject to reordering, a master file card for each set should contain the number and title of each slide and its source, not only to facilitate replacements in case of loss or damage but also to make a quick check-up on the number of slides returned after each use. Slides get mixed up with other sets, or often a slide is forgotten in a slide carrier at one of the schools; hence each slide needs to be correctly coded by set and item number.

Study Prints

The newest and most effective method for taking care of study prints is to laminate the entire picture between two clear plastic sheets. The Audio-Visual Section of the Los Angeles city schools owns its own machines for this process, by means of which the necessary heat and pressure are applied. After trimming to desirable dimensions, the pictures are packaged in cardboard containers for storage and transit. In the St. Louis audiovisual center, pictures are obtained in sets and then sent to a commercial concern which supplies the plastic-laminating process service. When embedded pictures get soiled, it is an easy matter to wash them off with a dampened cloth. Another way of preserving study prints is the standard mounting procedure that uses mounting stock of suitable color, weight, and texture, together with photo dry-mount tissue. Such pictures must, of course, be replaced when soiled or damaged. It is also extremely important to show teachers how to use thumbtacks, display hooks, clamps, and tabs for displaying instructional pictures properly.

Filmstrips

Although 35mm film splicers are available, this process is not recommended for torn filmstrips. Arrangements should be made with producers or distributors to replace all worn prints at a reduced price. Filmstrips may be visually inspected, but they should be handled by their edges and then rolled up without cinching, since this may result in scratching by dust particles. Filmstrip cleaners, using the same fluids as for motion pictures, will remove dirt and keep the film base pliable, which of course is essential. When cleaning filmstrips, film fluid should be used sparingly. Jagged corners of torn perforations may be cut off with a film notcher or scissors to prevent further tearing during subsequent use. It is generally true that the job of caring for filmstrip prints is not carried out sufficiently well, with resulting dissatisfaction on the part of teachers and pupils. Since the volume of use of filmstrips is so high, a new and critical look should be taken at this aspect of the media maintenance service in both school-system and school-building media-service centers.

Disk Recordings

Disk recordings have to be kept clean or they will soon be worthless for instructional purposes. Visual inspection will generally show when cleaning is needed, or when damage by scratching dictates immediate replacement. Cleaning by standard chemical cloths that facilitate dust removal by freeing disks temporarily of static electricity charges is recommended. Such cloths, available at any record shop, tend to dry out and deposit a fine chemical dust on the record. When they are in that condition, dampening them with water will usually restore their usefulness; however, they should be replaced when they get dirty. A cloth dampened with warm, slightly soapy water is also recommended for cleaning records. One other aspect of record care is the determination of groove wear that may not show to the unaided eye. When high-quality sound is mandatory, records should be checked by playing them, preferably near their center areas, on a record player in excellent physical condition. Records should be stored vertically without being allowed to remain in a slanting position. Also, disk recordings should never be stored near steam pipes or in direct sunlight.

Tape Recordings

Prerecorded audio-program tapes should be periodically checked for the distortion that may result from what is called magnetic "print-through." This is a slight modification of the original magnetic patterns, made by the interaction of the fields of magnetic force on the adjacent layer of tape on the reel. These transfer patterns have considerable intensity, so that the net effect is a faint echo that may be annoying. "Print through" is less likely to occur in 1.5-mil (standard thickness) tape. It is also less likely to occur, or is less noticeable, if the tape is stored under cool conditions, since it increases proportionately with the temperature.

Polyester base tape is not affected by temperature and humidity as is regular cellulose acetate tape, and therefore this somewhat more expensive tape is recommended whenever tapes have to be stored under other than normal conditions. Best long-run temperature conditions for tape storage to prevent embrittlement are 60° to 70°F. and 40 to 60 percent relative humidity. Another aspect of the proper care of prerecorded tapes is the use of leader and trailer tape to eliminate the gradual shortening of footage due to the almost inevitable breaking off of end pieces. Also, standard splicing tape ought to be used with regular tape splicing machines instead of the regular varieties of plastic adhesive materials.

Videotapes present a different care problem when it comes to splicing. Splicing must be electronically done, using a second tape recorder equipped with an electronic editor, either built into the tape machine or attached as an accessory. A videotape that is damaged will therefore have to be replayed and reedited into a shortened version of the program originally recorded. Storage conditions that apply to polyester tape apply to videotapes as well.

Ideal Storage Conditions

It has been emphasized again and again that storage under ideal conditions is a prime essential in safeguarding the quality and life of media materials for classroom use. Dust and excessive dryness will work havoc on some items, and moisture will have adverse effects on others. Hence, air conditioning may prove to be the most important of all care essentials. Properly designed boxes and packages for the storage and transit of kits, globes, realia, and models should be provided, or else the public money spent on the material will be wasted. Media-service program directors are responsible for bearing in mind these important details and should make sure that appropriate action is taken.

Care of Media Equipment

We must now turn our attention to the job of taking good care of audiovisual media-equipment units. Several recommendations have, of course, already been made that have a bearing on how this work is to be done, and it would be well to recall them before proceeding to specific suggestions. First, it has been recommended that every school plant have assigned to it for the year, and perhaps permanently, as many of the frequently needed projectors, recorders, record players, and other equipment as the school's program demands; second, that centralized pools of equipment be set up at the school-system audiovisual service center to meet special needs, and even to meet regular needs until adequate or complete decentralization is feasible; third, that each school building establish its own fixed media-equipment installations such as TV studios, electronic learning laboratories and the so-called teaching auditoriums with permanent media-equipment fixtures; and fourth, that each school establish its own school-building service center, including a school media program coordinator and technical service crew. Insofar as adequate care of equipment is concerned, these recommendations, made in Chapter 7 in connection with facilitating the use of materials in each school, mean that

1. Certain equipment-care essentials should properly be carried out in each individual school-building unit, while other maintenance jobs should be referred to the school-system media center. In this connection, minor operations of cleaning, lamp changing, and other adjustments ought to be done at the school-building center, and all other major repair work should be carried out at or through the main school-system media equipment shop.

2. In cases of equipment breakdown, temporary replacement equipment units should be arranged for, either from the centralized school-system pool of equipment or from the nearest, reputable equipment repair agency.

3. The central equipment-servicing and maintenance shop must be related to the care and inspection programs in each school building in very definite ways. In this connection it is recommended that the school-system audiovisual maintenance technician be the chief technician for the school system and that the main shop serve as a distribution center for all maintenance of equipment supplies.

Whenever full- or part-time center technical assistants are lacking, the director will have to formulate with his school-building media program coordinators the best possible plan of action for the superintendent's approval. Such a plan may call for the negotiation of a flat-fee service contract with the nearest instructional media equipment dealer; immediate action by each building coordinator to order repair work to be done by business firms, up to a specified expense limitation for the year; the emergency replacement of equipment by the central service center or by the local equipment dealer; the use, on a part-time or overtime basis, of a school-system electrician, physics teacher, or industrial education teacher, and the use of preventive

maintenance procedures by the periodic overhaul of equipment by a reputable service company. Or the plan may call for the use of a talented crew of high school students on a part-time basis to check tubes, lamps, and do other needed work short of a major overhaul job.

The job of caring for equipment is made easier when the kinds of equipment used have been standardized. One thing is certain, if the equipment units that make possible the use of media are not maintained in good condition, then the service program may just as well be liquidated. Beginning media program directors must find ways to solve this over-all problem and must check this service-program aspect continuously if their services are to be held in high regard. The prospective director, therefore, needs to be a technician up to a point. Although he *should not* be a repairman himself, he needs to be able to hire one, he must be able to identify operational deficiencies in all kinds of equipment, and he needs also to be an organizer and overseer of technical services and activities.

Space is not available to undertake a detailed descriptive treatment for the operation and servicing of specific makes of projectors. For this detailed analysis of operation, the reader is referred to the manufacturer's service manual for each specific make of equipment. Such manuals must not be confused with the booklet of operating instructions supplied with equipment units upon purchase. The media program director will have to write to the manufacturer for them, and this is an indispensable reference file that every audiovisual center shop should have. Such service manuals enable the media program director, or chief technician, to order commonly needed spare parts by manufacturer's standard catalog numbers, enable him to write better technical bulletins for coordinators and teachers, and also serve as the director's self-teaching guide. Actually, such service manuals for each type of equipment owned ought to be in the hands of each school-building coordinator as well. The prospective director needs to see the servicing and maintenance jobs in a general, over-all perspective in order to make proper local decisions. It may be necessary for him to increase his own skill in this connection as opportunities become increasingly available. The next topics deal with general-care essentials for equipment servicing and for setting up shop facilities.

General Care Essentials

Cleaning Lenses of Projectors. Dirty lenses are common causes of defective picture projection, and the only remedy is to set up proper lens-cleaning procedures and routines. Similar optical elements are included in all projectors. These are as follows: lamp reflectors (unless reflectors are built into the lamps), condenser lenses, and objective lenses. Some projectors, such as overhead and opaque projectors, have front-surface mirrors and reflectors. The following procedures and precautions should be noted.

1. Optical elements in motion picture projectors, because of high-speed mechanisms and high operating temperatures, accumulate dust and oil particles rapidly. Hence, the back of the projection lens should be wiped with lens tissue before each use of the projector. Unless this is done, the collection of dust particles and an oil film on the back of the objective lens will cause an objectionable picture-halo of haze.

2. Front-surface mirrors and reflectors pose another problem, since they must be brushed off lightly with camel's-hair brushes to avoid scratching. No lens-cleaner solutions can be used because some of them contain chemical agents that will mar the top surface of the mirror. Fingerprints on front-surface reflectors cannot generally be removed except by a water-dampened cloth; however, seriously impaired mirror surfaces may be replaced at the factory. Regular mirror surfaces may, of course, be washed or wiped off in the manner prescribed for other optical elements.

3. Service manuals published by manufacturers should be studied to ascertain the nature and exact positioning of optical elements, so that when they are removed for cleaning, they may be accurately replaced.

4. Regular schedules or routines should be established for cleaning lenses. Except for daily inspection of objective lenses, weekly, monthly, school-term, or end-of-year schedules should be decided upon according to local needs. A spot check by any supervisor, student, coordinator, media director, or chief technician is needed to see that routines are being followed.

5. Lens tissues and lens-cleaning fluids should be stocked in quantity.

6. The director needs to issue one or more illustrated bulletins on the topic of cleaning lenses. Such bulletins or manuals may be prepared by the director himself, by technicians, or by a committee working under his editorship.

Proper Oiling. Again the manufacturer's service manual must be consulted and exact oiling procedures noted. Record players, tape recorders, blower fans and motors in all kinds of projectors, and so on, should be carefully checked for oiling requirements, since failure to comply with the manufacturer's instructions nullifies warranty provisions and decreases quality of service. The tendency is often to oil either too much or too little, and the only safe procedure is to follow stated requirements by attaching a service card to each equipment unit for a visual check on service or to maintain a file of such cards at each school building. Wherever an equipment pool is based, service cards should be maintained, and the director or equipment supervisor must take this job seriously. Strict orders on oiling, and clear instructions on ascertaining if too much oil has been added, should be issued and then compliance noted. In general, motors in new projectors, record players and tape recorders are self-oiling, but this should be definitely ascertained. In the extremely critical case of older models of motion picture projectors where oil cups are provided, oiling about every month, or if use is very heavy, oiling after every four hours of projection, or every sixteen uses of the projector, may prove to be more satisfactory. When optical elements show excessive accumulation of oil film, or if projectors smoke a little during operation, the amount of oil should be decreased. Proper oiling cans for adding one drop at a time and the recommended grade of light oil should be stocked in quantity by the central shop. New models of mechanical equipment units require little if any oiling, hence the word of caution of ascertaining the manufacturer's specifications.

Changing Lamps. Prefocus base lamps of all types are easy to change, and the only caution is to avoid finger burns by cooling off the burned-out lamp before replacing it. The best way to do this is to run the motor, thus using the blower to cool off the hot glass. It will be necessary in motion picture projectors without the stop-on-film feature to disengage the film before the motor is turned on. Exciter lamps of bayonet-base and pin-type are even easier to change because their operating temperature is low.

The director should take care that correct specifications are given when ordering lamps, since the life of a projection lamp is shortened considerably when line voltages are higher than the lamp was made for. It is recommended that the local line voltage be ascertained and that the lamps ordered should be manufactured for use at slightly higher line voltage than is maintained by local power companies. For example, if the local line voltage is usually 115, then lamps should be ordered that are marked for use on 120-volt circuits. The slight drop in illumination is negligible and the life of the lamp is increased by several hours on the average. However, all lamps should be replaced when they become blackened and blistered even though they haven't burned out.

Adjustment and Alignment of Optical Systems. It was pointed out previously that projectors generally make use of the same kinds of optical elements, and it is obvious that such elements have to be centered and lined up on the optical axis for evenness of the projected field of light. Projecting a focused field of light on the screen permits an immediate visual inspection of defective alignment because dark corners or unusually bright areas will appear within the field. Since as many of the optical elements as possible are lined up and centered in fixed positions, adjustments have to be made at specified points.

Usually trouble arises when the lamp socket becomes loosened in the process of changing lamps and is either lowered or turned clockwise or counterclockwise in its clamp. The first of the two changes in the lamp socket just mentioned will cause a darkening of the lower part of the projected field. The use of asbestos gloves and dark glasses will, of course, be required for the process of loosening setscrews on the socket clamps and raising the socket (while the lamp is burning) to the proper position where the field of light is uniform once more. The turning of the socket, darkens the left or right portions of the projected field of light. The rule to apply here is that the plane of the lamp filament should be parallel to the lens elements. In making such adjustments locally, a light shield should be held by a helper or mounted in such a way that the worker's eyes are protected from the bright light of the lamp.

One other adjustment that may have to be made is the moving of the reflector and lamp socket assembly closer to or farther away from the condenser lenses. This operation must also be done with shielded eyes. Always, the test is an even, sharply focused, field of light on the screen. Bright center spots, darkened corners, and vertical streaks of light and shadow through the screen are symptoms that reveal trouble with optical alignment. The trend in manufacture is away from all adjustments by users—in other words, to minimize the amount of work by local technicians.

Sometimes condenser lenses are positioned and held parallel by coil springs. In checking for trouble, make sure that even the fixed optical elements are positioned properly as intended by the manufacturer, but sealed-in optical elements should never be opened. Service manuals should be studied carefully to note special instructions about optics, but in general it is best not to move the lamp reflector or disturb its distance from the lamp, and none of the lens elements should be touched while they are hot.

Replacement of Optical Elements. This is another equipment-service job well within the usual school-system audiovisual center's service routine. Here again is a case in point revealing the advantage of standardization, since with projectors of only one manufacturer on hand, it is easy to carry a stock of spare lenses and heat-filter glasses. To carry a stock of spares for several different makes and models would be difficult and uneconomical. All that is required is to proceed according to diagrams in service manuals of the manufacturer and replace lens elements according to standard part numbers. Care should be taken to work out a labeling system whereby spare lenses are clearly and accurately marked to avoid later mistakes. A card system for the easy ordering of spare parts as supplies run low is an urgently needed aspect of the *shop supplies* plan.

Testing and Replacement of Electronic Tubes. With an increasing number of record players, tape recorders, and motion picture projectors, all using amplifiers, the job of testing tubes and transistors is an urgent one. It may be done in two ways: Either testing equipment must be purchased that will handle the kinds of tubes and transistors specified in the electronic schematics used, or a commercial audio-radio-television service company will have to test them. In the latter case, electric components should be taken to the local dealer for checking and the replacements purchased there as needed or standard space components kept in stock. If equipment and staff are available, it is best to maintain a stock of components and replace defective ones without delay. Although not all amplifier troubles are caused by defective tubes or transistors, the checking and replacement job is simple and can be done with a minimum of technical training. Searching out other amplifier-circuit troubles is a time-consuming task, and unless the large volume of electronic equipment on hand warrants the addition of trained technicians to the school staff, it is advisable to have this repair work done by audiovisual media equipment dealers who specialize in service to schools.

Equipment Switches and Electrical Cords. Media equipment units demand different types of control switches and electrical cords. Except for battery-powered tape recorders and picture viewers, all have power cords usually fastened to the equipment internally by clamps and soldered connections. Such cords may have built-in on-and-off switches, and when this is the case, spare switches should be on hand for replacement purposes. A good soldering iron should also be on hand to facilitate arrangements for the quick repair of faulty power lines. Also, because loose connections and broken lines that are such frequent sources of trouble are not easy to discover by visual means, a test lamp with appropriate connectors, and a short speaker line cord with alligator clamps ought to be handy for checking purposes. Since on-and-off power switches and volume and tone control switches often cause annoying trouble, such units should be stocked for fast replacement. Sometimes these switching units get dirty, in which case cleaning them by brushing with carbon tetrachloride may correct the difficulty. This is a job for a full-time or part-time technician, if available; otherwise, for a local repair agency. Proper care of switches and cords is an element of maintenance that makes a big difference in the satisfactory performance of equipment. Many different connectors are easy to make up, or they may be purchased from equipment service companies. Local conditions and preferences for operations will determine the scope of connectors needed.

Some schools have developed simple connector devices by means of which automatic slide projectors and other types of equipment may be turned on and off by remote-control switches. Other connectors are for copying disk recordings onto magnetic tape. Standardization of equipment and types of connectors for any given operation in the schools will facilitate technical performance by both technical and professional personnel.

Inspection of Equipment after Use

One of the main essentials in taking good care of equipment is the discovery of operational defects before they can disrupt teaching plans in the classroom. Whenever equipment has been used, it should be checked for faulty performance before it is used again. One of the most time-consuming service jobs is the one where technicians have to open up an equipment case, set up the projector or tape recorder, actually try out test materials of familiar pictorial and sound content, and then proceed to clean the lenses, tighten control knobs, repair cords and switches, and so forth. However, this job of readying equipment for the next borrower is a detail of such importance that to fail to get this work done properly is to endanger the whole service program. The importance of good care of media has been stressed previously, and the care of media equipment is directly related to the prevention of damage to materials.

In order to decrease the time involved in checking media equipment and materials after classroom use, some coordinators and media program directors require the teacher and/or the operator to fill out a short check-slip, stating the equipment performed satisfactorily and that the material itself was in good condition and was used without interruption. Dependence upon such forms is dangerous, and an inspection schedule must be set up in conjunction with such a reporting system to catch trouble before it catches teachers and pupils. It is this inspection and reporting system that sets in motion the process of referring to school-building or school-system audiovisual equipment maintenance shops the equipment units that need repair services. The discussion of general care essentials has preceded, and now some specific considerations for taking good care of equipment will be discussed.

Motion Picture Projectors

Good care of motion picture projectors involves a few special considerations.

1. Fuzz and dust particles must be removed from the aperture by means of a bristle brush and lintless cloth, taking extreme care that no metal object comes into contact with metal parts of the film channel.

2. Remove excess oil and dirt from around the filmgate and lens barrel. Complete cleaning of these parts calls for a brush, cloths, and carbon tetrachloride.

3. Spring and fiber belts must be repaired or replaced as needed.

4. Sprockets must be checked to ascertain if hard-packed dirt and oil has built up in back of the sprocket teeth. Such accumulation should be removed by a wooden object (never metal), otherwise film perforations will be enlarged and perhaps torn as film tension pushes the tooth and its enlarged base through the opening. Carbon tetrachloride may be used to soften this hard-caked deposit if it cannot be pushed away with a match stick or a hard wood splinter.

5. Jumpy film motion on the screen and noisy operation may indicate that the intermittent movement needs adjustment or that film claws have become grooved and need honing down on the under side of the claws. Such work must not be attempted except by expert technicians, but overhaul and repair work of this nature must be carried out on schedule.

6. The SMPTE test film *Jiffy*, as well as other test films, are useful in checking pictorial and sound elements of projection performance. Exciter-lamp focus and speed governors need particularly to be checked, and test films are extremely valuable for this work.

7. Magnetic sound motion picture projectors need to have erase and record heads cleaned cautiously with lens tissue. Metal objects, as was pointed out earlier, should never be inserted for cleaning purposes where film guides may be scratched.

The extent to which audiovisual equipment maintenance facilities are developed will depend on the size of the equipment inventory and the availability and adequacy of local repair service agencies. Simple arithmetic—comparing costs of repair by agencies outside the school system, cost of cartage, and cost estimates for a center-staff technician and spare parts if a shop facility were to be established—will establish the need for increased facilities. Maintenance costs for motion picture projectors, record players, and tape recorders will be highest, because of their moving parts and electronic components.

Magnetic Tape Recorders

What we have said about amplifiers, tubes, and transistors also applies to tape recorders, but the maintenance of tape recorders requires a few characteristic tasks that may well be carried out in a school-system audiovisual shop. The following suggestions should be considered.

1. Drive and rewind belts and rubber-rimmed wheels need to be checked for proper tension and wear. They can often be replaced by individuals with a minimum of technical training.

2. The squealing of pressure pads on tape can be stopped by cautiously roughing up the matted-down surface of the pads that press the tape against the recording and play heads.

3. Magnetic heads should be wiped free of accumulated iron oxide.

4. Magnetic heads should be checked for proper alignment and for this purpose a test tape procurable from Audio Devices, Inc. is indispensable (mentioned previously in Chapter 3, under equipment selection).

5. Tape recorders need to be protected from dust at all times and all accumulations of dirt around rollers and capstans should be removed frequently.

Record Players

Record players are generally available in large numbers in almost every school system, and it is sad that they are not cared for in better fashion, since damage to disks is so frequently the result. Although the correction of serious trouble in amplifiers is the job of expert technicians, many maintenance tasks can be carried out in the local school and school-system inspection and repair shops. Special suggestions are:

1. One of the first essentials of care is to convert all existing styli and cartridges to the diamond type. Though higher in cost, diamond styli are the most economical in the long run. Stocks of replacement cartridges and styli of the appropriate type should be maintained for

ready use. Standardization, wherever possible, is recommended to simplify inspection and replacement.

2. Styli and cartridges collect dust and dirt. A camel's-hair brush is needed to brush away this accumulation. The dirtier the records, the more often this has to be done.

3. A microscope should be used to examine styli for wear.

4. Pickup arms must be fastened down to keep them from banging during transit. Such screws, hooks, or clamps must be continually checked and tightened.

5. Turntable speed checks should be made by means of stroboscopic card-type disks; other audio-test disks are available from Cook Laboratories (mentioned in Chapter 3 under selection of equipment).

6. Because of moving mechanisms, dust and dirt accumulate in hard-to-reach places; hence special cleaning and inspection routines must be set up to keep machines in good condition.

Projection Screens

Those in charge of the inspection and maintenance of audiovisual media equipment should not forget the projection screen. Whether mounted permanently on walls, or carried as a portable unit, screen fabrics and tripods or other support systems need to be kept in first-class shape. Tears, smears, wrinkles, and adhesive tape have no place on a reflection surface, and jagged metal corners, bent support rods, and weakened fasteners are equally objectionable in the tripod or wall-mounting system. A full stock of replacement units and parts, including fabrics, should be on hand to keep screens clean and in good repair. Standardization of screen makes, sizes, and types will facilitate inspection and maintenance.

Overhead Transparency Projectors

This frequently used piece of media equipment, the overhead transparency projector, is often assigned to each teaching station and placed in ready-to-project positions on low projection stands or pedestals. Many times there is a separate tilted projection screen. This means that it is likely to be assigned to and cared for at an individual school building. Cleaning, installing new connecting cords and fixtures, and

replacing lamps as maintenance processes will be done at each school-building media service center. More serious maintenance work will be done at the district media center. Special suggestions are as follows:

1. Lamp reflectors and lamp sockets should be checked periodically and replaced by standard parts.

2. Motors and thermostats that control on-off switches should also be replaced when defects are observed.

3. Thorough cleaning of optical elements should be done at scheduled times.

4. Standard switches and connecting cords should be stocked in quantity and maintained in satisfactory condition for quick replacement.

Electronic Learning Laboratories

District-wide media-service centers may be called upon to provide special services with regard to servicing equipment units operating as basic components of electronic learning laboratories. Although we have already recommended providing the needed technical workers in each school building to take care of such services, we pose it here also as a responsibility of the main media center. Such equipment may range from a simple passive listening device to a combination of media-use operations involving tape recorder, automatic slide projector, 8mm cartridge-type motion picture projector, and a television receiver, all or some of which may operate by student dialing or by other selection mechanisms. Such learning centers must be the object of periodic inspection on an optimum schedule or be constantly attended by technical personnel, and must have immediate attention when malfunctioning of equipment is detected. A maintenance force must be available to report to one or more schools for what we can call continual coverage. Special suggestions for action are as follows:

1. Maintain a stock of spare knobs and control buttons and replace them at once when they are removed by students using the facilities. Students who spend scheduled periods in such facilities are likely to either deliberately, or unconsciously try to remove or loosen such devices. Continuous action of that type results in havoc, and hence an instructional program to

guide students toward better care of the equipment is essential. Teachers who route students to self-instruction must recognize the relation of "equipment destruction" to lack of both general and specific motivation.

2. The best way to service electronic learning laboratory equipment is to provide replacement units, as projectors, receivers, amplifiers, and recorders and to repair observed defects in media equipment repair shops where stocks of parts and test equipment are available. The value of standardization is again obvious in expediting such work.

Television Receivers

We recognize the need for technicians and adequate supervision in the important work of maintaining media equipment and materials. Television receivers, both for use in closed-circuit systems and for program reception via master antenna systems from sources outside of the school system, must, like projectors and recorders, be kept in excellent working order. So again, like servicing electronic learning laboratories, an on-the-job work force must be provided, or sets must be replaced at the first sign of defect and returned to adequately equipped servicing centers for repair. In large-scale programs the need for trained and qualified technicians in each school-building media program is an obvious essential. Special considerations are the following:

1. Provide for the immediate replacement of defective television sets sent to a testing and repair center.

2. Stock spare parts and provide the necessary tube and transistor testing equipment for facilitating service.

3. Arrange for periodic check-ups and an efficient reporting system by teachers as to operational efficiency.

4. Make periodic checks on mountings, castors, and other support systems to spot loose connections and possible weaknesses as a precaution against accidents in classrooms.

5. Defects in television sets may have to be traced to defective television studio equipment such as cameras, transmitters, and videotape recording units. Thus the maintenance system for television receivers and for electronic carrels utilizing television programs arising in studios

and in automatically controlled program-source banks must include the availability of qualified studio technical personnel for proper operation and control of complex equipment. (A test film, TV 16, 367 feet, $35; a television alignment and resolution slide, AR Slide, $6; and several videotape test tapes for multifrequency and primary audio level are available from SMPTE, 9 East 41st Street, New York, N.Y.)

The Media Equipment Shop As a Supply Center and Clearing House

In the foregoing paragraphs the media equipment shop has been pictured as a supply center for spare parts, lamps, styli, screen fabrics, oil cans, belts, switches, electrical cables, special connectors and cleaning fluids. The shop, as has also been implied, is the headquarters for maintenance activity that can be carried on locally. This activity has been implied by discussions under the headings of general care essentials and under additional specific processes and suggestions for a few of the major kinds of audiovisual media equipment. One aspect of the supply problem has not been mentioned in sufficient detail, and this is the construction by the central technician of a supply of needed special connectors. In complicated programs, such as those conducted in schools today, a variety of connectors need to be made up and supplied to the various school buildings. Short speaker-to-projector cords, cord adapters for various jacks and fittings, "Y" cable connectors for feeding two microphones into one tape-recorder input, and special remote extension cords for operating equipment from the front of a teaching station, are just a few of the many items needed in quantity. Also, maintaining a stock of projection lamps and electronic tubes, transistors and condensers is no easy problem to solve. Certainly, a stock-card system is called for to facilitate inventory control and periodic ordering.

Some metropolitan school systems maintain supply depots or agencies known as central stores from which teachers, school principals, audiovisual technical, and professional personnel draw needed supplies that are purchased in large quantities annually. The audiovisual media program director should take whatever steps are necessary to inaugurate as many economies as are possible by central purchasing. Under central-purchasing conditions, the problem of adequate inventory procedures is eliminated for the media director; however, a system should be worked out whereby appropriate lamps and other supplies may be identified by standard code numbers. Here once more the advantage of standardized equipment lists is made clear.

One other aspect of the media shop activity is the clearing-house function. Equipment inventory cards with purchase dates, repair and assignment data, and serial numbers must be maintained. Furthermore, equipment units that have to be shipped out for extensive repair work ought to be processed by the central shop staff, that is, logged in, sent out for repair according to contractual arrangements, inspected upon return from the repairing agency, and delivered to the school building as originally assigned. This work, when it is handled by the shop as a central routing and clearing-house agency, relieves school-building personnel of annoying details. Much of the extensive repair work, however, should be planned and carried out during months when the schools are not in session.

The director who sets out to organize the kinds of procedures and processes for handling, caring for, and utilizing media materials and equipment described in the preceding pages of this book, must realize the necessity for a clerical, technical, and professional staff that can get the work done in terms of effective teacher service. National and state organizations are giving this problem the serious attention it deserves.

Staffing and Organizing the Audiovisual Media Center

Building a comprehensive staff organization, not only to carry on the work of the audiovisual media center as a headquarters unit but also as a system-wide service force reaching into every classroom, is a formidable problem, and when reasonably adequate financial support is unavailable for fast-pace development, it may have to be solved in unconventional though hopefully creative ways. We have already mentioned the problem of arriving at an optimum balance between the development of strong, well-staffed central service facilities and strong, well-staffed decentralized school-building service units. This

becomes a critical issue as technology increases in complexity and scope, and we may postulate the principle with confidence that as instructional technology moves toward newer roles where media make important and scheduled contributions to the process of presenting substantive materials to students and guiding their specified responses, both in large-group and individualized situations, the balance between centralized and local service centers must shift toward decentralized facilities and staffs. In an earlier day, the problem was to create loan services, but now the emphasis is on media installations operating permanently and on firm schedules, where a tenuous loan that may or not be cancelled at the last minute will not meet the teaching requirements.

The citywide media program director has the responsibility to meet and deal with this problem. This so-called media director as an executive must identify specifically just what work must be performed, how expertly it must be carried out, and then he must seek the help of individuals to exert the necessary effort for the tasks at hand.

Staff for Audiovisual Center Operations

Since we have dealt at length in a previous chapter with the problems of providing staff for school-building services, we can concentrate on staff for the audiovisual media center at the school-district level. But we must remember that smaller school districts have the same needs for media that large school systems have, and they therefore need similar services without being able to afford the media specialists that larger operations demand. We must consider in every case, be it large city or small town, the nature and demand for services and the ways to provide them, rather than concentrating on the number of specialists the present budget and the potential tax dollars will support. It appears quite obvious that whether the center consists of one small office or a whole building, or whether the media director of the citywide program of service is a full-time worker or not, he must acquire a central staff proportionate to an allotted personal-services budget. His own time, however little he has at his disposal, must be used to the best advantage, and the way this time is spent will determine the nature and scope of the success of the program at any operational level.

An earlier reference was made to personnel guidelines for staffing media programs in schools and school districts, but in this regard we can also quote the statement made by the State of Indiana, Department of Public Instruction, in its Bulletin No. 218 relative to initiating and expanding audiovisual programs,[4] that suggests the following standards for staff:

Each school system should have someone responsible for the audiovisual program. He may be called a director or supervisor. School systems with 50 or more teachers and all counties should have full-time professionally trained audiovisual supervisors. . . . Also, he should be provided with sufficient clerical and technical assistance to permit him to devote his major energies to professional administration and assistance in the utilization and preparation of materials. . . .

It is this citywide media director or supervisor that must systematize and organize personnel forces to the limit of his local resources and ingenuity. It is certain in this stage of development of technology that he will have to bear in mind that his own center staff may have to be deployed in unique ways for services throughout the school system, and also that he can work with school principals in achieving mutual objectives for improving instruction, but that his own center may be the originating point and the only available service center for any given time period. Let us make no mistake about it, however, that it is what goes on or ought to go on in each school that really matters. With what we have discussed in Chapters 1 and 7 particularly in mind, we may turn to an analysis of basic staff needs at the district-wide media center.

Staff for Administrative and Supervisory Functions

First we should consider the range of administrative and supervisory positions of a professional nature. We need to recognize the expanding role of media in modern education, and the increasing need for specialized staff members as smaller audiovisual media programs expand and as programs develop in the

4 *The Audio-Visual Program*, Bulletin No. 218, State of Indiana, Department of Public Instruction, Indianapolis, Indiana, 1956, p. 127.

metropolitan school districts. The need for professional assistants and specialists will be inevitable. Additional staff members beyond the leadership of the media program director may well be placed in charge of divisions or departments, or they may be given the title of Consultant, Associate Director, or Coordinator to provide leadership energy for areas of activity at the center or to energize system-wide programs of service. Their functions are to

1. Supervise media-service activities for each level of instruction as elementary or secondary school activities.

2. Energize selections of kinds of media, such as textbooks and library books, or of projected or nonprojected media.

3. Administer and supply leadership for departments or divisions such as radio, television, photographic and graphic production.

4. Take charge as a coordinator of service functions such as in-service education, distribution, business management, and the school-building coordinator program, and television programing for elementary and/or secondary school telecasts.

5. Supervise media-supported teaching systems development.

6. Manage a central facility, such as the instructional materials center.

Positions such as those mentioned may have to be filled by professional people on a part-time basis, making full use of interested teachers who are willing to undergo special training for new duties. Individuals are often anxious to do such work for various types of rewards. The main consideration is that people who are selected must be professionally prepared and well qualified for the duties they undertake.

Staff for Technical Functions

We have only to review the staffing requirements set forth in Chapter 7 for school-building programs to realize the need for such personnel working at the district-wide media center. We must recognize that in the present state of development, unless technical personnel are available, such functions as installing and operating and maintaining television studios and electronic learning laboratories of a sophisticated level are out of the question, and any stopgap, intermediate steps may be classed as foolhardy and wasteful of the money appropriated for the organization of the media program.

Carrying on the work of a citywide media program, as we have said before, is largely concerned with providing services to all schools, all teachers, and through them to all learners, but it is the schools as units that must possess fixed facilities and make full use of media materials and equipment assigned to them from media headquarters. The technical work must therefore be oriented not only toward technical work required at the center, but toward the school-building units themselves. Some of the major functions to be carried on by technical workers are the following:

1. Maintain media materials and equipment at the center and assist in the schools as demanded by local arrangements and needs.

2. Install, operate, and maintain school-system television studios and assist as assigned with the same function in the school-building TV operations, including transmission and reception.

3. Assist with the installation and maintenance of electronic learning laboratories in school-building units.

4. Prepare media of all kinds at the Center according to specifications and designs supplied by curriculum planners and teachers, and assist with similar operations in each school-building unit according to local plans.

5. Supervise the work of media-center and school-building technicians.

6. Maintain adequate inventory of school-system media equipment.

7. Maintain a stock of spare parts for the servicing of school-system-owned media equipment units.

8. Maintain adequate inventory and a stock of media-preparation supplies for use at the center and for issue to school-building units.

As programs develop, shortages in staff will be inevitable, and when new positions are created it will without doubt be difficult to fill them, yet it will be urgent to get work done on time to prevent deterioration of both media materials and equipment. Many centers have turned to the physically handicapped for part-time and full-time work much to their complete satisfac-

tion. However, obviously the work assignment should be one that is appropriate. In addition to full-time workers especially trained for their jobs, the part-time employment of capable students during after-school hours and on Saturdays to inspect media materials and carry out prescribed maintenance procedures is also a possibility. Because closer supervision of the work of part-time workers is generally needed, the director ought to make the most responsible individual of such crews an operational supervisor, inspector, and checker. However, in no case should minors be permitted to work without on-the-spot supervision of responsible adults.

Staff for Secretarial and Clerical Functions

It is little wonder that some school systems with low secretarial-support budgets have difficulty in obtaining and keeping citywide media program directors. This is also true, as we have already pointed out in Chapter 7, at the school-building media-service level. Professional people should not be burdened with the volume of clerical details inevitable in the media-service field. We are not talking at this point of getting out of hard work, but what we are emphasizing is that the leadership force for energizing programs for the involvement in media-use development must not be cancelled out because available time is not used profitably.

Although it is not recommended because again too much time is required for laying out the work and subsequent supervision, part-time clerical workers may have to be recruited from local high school commercial departments. Students can give good service, especially if the work is laid out with clearly stated instructions, and several students on a well-planned schedule can provide continuous service during most of a school day. Media program directors who are themselves on part-time assignment ought to arrange, if at all possible, for the employment of a qualified part-time worker (student or non-student) during the period when they are free of teaching duties. But if significant developmental progress is to be made at any school-system or school-building media service center, then adequate secretarial and clerical staffs will have to be provided, in optimum balance with other personnel forces.

Staff for Media Mobility Functions

Although we recognize a wide range of skills and required training and experience within the technical-function personnel, we also see the need for support staff in the nature of a labor force. The main function of such a force will be to make it possible to move media materials and equipment between the center and the schools where they are put to work. Thus the media program director must see to it that the required labor force is adequate to meet demands for mobility in the light of the local level of utilization.

Custodial services are also necessary, and this part of the labor force may be provided under other budgets, and this may also be true of the trucking units that may operate on a system-wide basis for all divisions and hence may be under supervision of other agencies. The fact is that such services, both trucking for pick-up and delivery, and custodial in nature, are mandatory.

Staff for School-Building Assignment

We have already discussed in detail the problems of school-building media-service organization, and in this connection great emphasis was placed on the need and procurement of adequate staff members—professional, technical, and clerical. We emphasized the value of adding to the school principal's staff the needed personnel, and when this is done, such personnel certainly would be working with the citywide media program leader, but would be on the staff and be located at a given school building. In some instances, staff members are located at the media headquarters, but are assigned on a part-time basis, or other optimum schedule, to perform specified tasks at one or more of the schools. In such cases, the understanding is that the service is performed for the school principal for the good of his program, but not under his responsible surveillance.

Employing Needed Staff

In Chapter 1 a number of lists of duties were provided detailing the nature of the media program director's professional responsibility. Also in that chapter an operational plan was described that pointed toward a strong legal basis for appointing the chief media program administrator for a school system. The importance of employing a qualified professional person for media-leadership responsibility can hardly be overemphasized, yet all too frequently too little attention is paid to the preparation of specifications for the position. Once the media director himself has been employed by other school administrators, it will be up to him to prepare adequate specifications for every new position he is able to create, whether professional, technical, secretarial, or skilled or unskilled labor. We shall turn next to this important topic for the emphasis that it deserves.

Specifications for Media-Service Positions. Major duties need to be clearly in mind as a part of any given set of specifications, but they are by no means the only topic to receive attention in a prepared statement of personnel qualifications. Certainly an applicant wants to know just what he has to do on the job to be successful, and we want to prepare an announcement to locate qualified people and to urge the right individuals to apply and become active seekers for any given position that is open. But we need to state precisely what requirements must be met by the successful applicant in addition to possessing the special abilities to carry on the work described. Thus if we view the problem as one of preparing a written statement that can be duplicated and distributed as deemed advisable, then we should include the following information:

1. Position title and description.
2. Major duties and responsibilities.
3. Specified requirements to be met by applicants:
(a) Desired professional preparation and specialization (including specific courses).
(b) Desired personal qualifications (hobbies, personality, health, habits, and appearance).
(c) Desired educational experience in the profession and related activities.
(d) Desired scholastic record level, degrees, and certifiability.
(e) Desired age and sex.
(f) Nature and number of letters of recommendation desired.
(g) Desired social competency, vitality, and character.
(h) The level of special abilities desired.

4. Salary, and other working arrangements as to time committed, vacations, and to whom responsible.

5. Special job requirements, if any.

6. Instructions for application.

7. Unique inducements for applicants.

Naturally wide variety is found in formats of announcements and in the details of the specifications set forth. See Example 8-1, 8-2, and 8-3, one of which covers the employment of a media school-system program director, another deals with the search for a qualified person to serve as a media specialist working at the elementary school level, but responsible to the school-system audiovisual media center, and the third covers the announcement of a position of television producer-director.

Writing a good set of specifications is not only applicable to the employment of professional personnel. The media program director who fails to devote adequate attention to the analysis of job requirements and to make use of desirable personnel-recruitment policies and procedures is guilty of making some dangerous assumptions. Public school administrators and leaders know well the difficulties and embarrassments of dismissal proceedings. Two additional examples, one from the Board of Education in Hartford, Connecticut, and the other from Geneseo State University College in New York, will show the attention devoted there to the employment of qualified individuals for newly created technical positions. Since the additional examples are related to those preceding, we shall refer to them as Example 8-4 and Example 8-5.

Example 8-1

BOARD OF EDUCATION
Stamford, Connecticut

June 14, 1966

ANNOUNCEMENT OF VACANCY - COORDINATOR
OF AUDIO VISUAL EDUCATION

It is the intent of the Stamford Board of Education to employ a <u>Coordinator of Audio-Visual Education</u> for the year 1966-1967 who shall be responsible for directing and coordinating the program of audio-visual education and instructional materials for the whole school system by providing leadership in determining the objectives, policies, plans, and programs for the long-term and short-term successful operation of the audio-visual education and instructional materials program, in order to implement improvement of the instructional program.

MAJOR DUTIES AND RESPONSIBILITIES

1. To initiate and improve the use of audio-visual materials throughout the school system.

2. To inventory and assign audio-visual equipment in the schools and classrooms.

3. To work with the teaching staff in the more effective use of multi-media materials of instruction.

4. To be knowledgeable of and be able to recommend specific audio-visual equipment.

5.   To conduct in-service courses on the use and operation of audio-visual materials.

QUALIFICATIONS

The audio-visual and instructional materials coordinator must:

1.   Possess the training and experience which will enable him to fulfill his function in the instructional program. The minimum of a Master's degree is required. At least five years of teaching experience at the elementary and/or secondary level is desirable. Experience as a coordinator or director of audio-visual aids and curriculum materials on a building or system level is desirable.

2.   Be a well-versed equipment technician responsible for the selection, operation, inspection, maintenance, and inventory of all equipment and materials.

3.   Be able to meet all State certification requirements for this position.

4.   Have had graduate courses in the organization and administration of an audio-visual program; in the proper utilization and evaluation of materials; in the production of materials; in the production and utilization of educational radio and TV programs; in learning theory expecially as it applies to self-instruction; in the fundamentals of curriculum development; and in general supervision.

SALARY AND WORKING CONDITIONS

The salary for this position is based on what a candidate would receive as a teacher multiplied by 1. 28. The work year is twelve months with one month vacation.

FILING AN APPLICATION CONSISTS OF:

Letter of application detailing education, experience, and personal qualifications for this position.

Applications for this position must be filled by July 15, 1966.

NOTE: It is expected that the appointee will provide sufficient notice to his present employer.

All correspondence should be addressed to:

>   Dr. Joseph B. Porter, Superintendent
>   Stamford Public Schools
>   151 Broad Street
>   Stamford, Connecticut

Example 8-2

PLEASE POST

Hartford Board of Education

Administrative Offices
249 High Street
Hartford, Connecticut 06103

NOTICE OF VACANCY
MEDIA SPECIALIST

A full-time position will be available as a media specialist on September 1, 1966.

DUTIES
1.   Working primarily on the elementary level, grades k-8.

2.   Providing assistance to all members of the teaching staff with utilization and production of instructional material both during and after school hours.

3.   Providing assistance to other staff members working as Curriculum Materials teachers.

4.   Assisting in the design and implementation of in-service workshops for all staff.

QUALIFICATIONS
Applicants must have or be able to obtain by September 1, 1966, State of Connecticut certification as a supervisor in a special subject field, with a recommendation as an audiovisual specialist.

This position is authorized under the State Act for Disadvantaged Children of 1965. The position is approved until June, 1967, and will continue as long as funds are available.

SALARY
The salary will be the regular teacher's schedule plus 5%, for the normal school year.

APPLICATIONS
Candidates should apply in writing to Mr. Thomas H. Skirm, Director of Certificated Personnel, Board of Education Office, 249 High Street, Hardford, Conn. Applications close June 30, 1966.

THS:ba
6/21/66

Example 8-3

STATE UNIVERSITY COLLEGE GENESEO, NEW YORK	POSITION AVAILABLE:	Television Producer-Director
	APPOINTMENT DATE:	Apr. 1, 1967 or after
	DATE OF THIS NOTICE:	January 26, 1967
STAFF VACANCY NOTICE	SALARY:	$10,000 - 11,000

POSITION AVAILABLE:	Television Producer-Director
APPOINTMENT DATE:	April 1, 1967 or after
RESPONSIBILITIES:	1. Initiating and conducting faculty orientation and training in Instructional Television.
	2. Working with faculty members to incorporate multi-media material into their course curricula with a concentration on instructional television.
	3. Studio television directing.
	4. Training and supervision of student crews.
	5. Limited teaching of some broadcasting course segments.
QUALIFICATIONS AND EXPERIENCE:	1. Masters Degree.
	2. Interest in the overall media approach to learning, including programmed instruction, dial access retrieval systems and computers.
	3. Preparation and experience in Instructional Television producing and directing.
	4. Some knowledge of lighting and set construction.
	5. Some teaching experience preferred.
SALARY:	$10,000 to 11,000
APPLY TO:	SEND CREDENTIALS TO:

Example 8-4

THE BOARD OF EDUCATION
Administrative Offices, 249 High Street
Hartford 5, Connecticut

May 16, 1962

AVAILABLE POSITION

AUDIO-VISUAL TECHNICIAN

NATURE OF WORK

The work requires skill of a technical nature, primarily in repairing and maintaining mechanical and electronic equipment.

DUTIES

1.   Tests, maintains, repairs, and converts a wide variety of mechanical and electronic equipment and components, such as sound motion projectors, filmstrip-slide projectors, record players, tape recorders, radios, television receivers, and amplifiers.

(The above duties are performed at the Audio-Visual Department or at a school, depending upon the situation.)

2.   Maintains inventory of replacement parts and tools.

3.   Duplicates tape recordings for classroom use.

4.   Prepares and produces graphic layouts for instructional use through photocopy or diazo process.

5.   Performs related work as required.

QUALIFICATIONS

1.   Considerable knowledge of the technical and operating principles and applications of equipment, tools, and materials used in the testing, maintenance, and repair or projection, amplification, and related electronic equipment.

2.   Ability to read and interpret schematic diagrams of electronic equipment.

3.   Ability to repair electronic circuitry.

4.   Ability to repair mechanical equipment or have high mechanical aptitude.

5.   The following qualifications are most desirous, though not mandatory:

   a.   Knowledge of graphic layout and art ability

b. Knowledge of photography

c. Knowledge of diazo reproduction

EXPERIENCE AND TRAINING

1. Two years experience in servicing and repairing projection, sound, and electronic equipment, preferably in the audio-visual field, and/or

2. Graduation from an academic or technical high school supplemented by technical courses in the theory of repairing sound and other electronic equipment, and some practical experience in this field.

SALARY FOR THE POSITION

This is a full-time position with a salary range of $4200.00 - $6000.00. The starting salary will depend upon the qualifications of the applicant.

In addition, the Board of Education offers a number of fringe benefits in the way of paid insurance and liberal paid vacation policy.

APPLICATION PROCEDURE

Applicants should write or contact Mr. Edwin M. Manson, Coordinator Audio-Visual Materials, Board of Education, 249 High Street, Hartford 3, Connecticut.

Applicants should be prepared to submit a short synopsis of past training, experience, and places of related employment.

The starting date for this position will be between August 27 and September 1, 1962.

Edwin M. Manson, Coordinator
Audio-Visual Materials

In Example 8-4, it can be readily seen that the media program director entertained the hope that he could locate a qualified person with a combination of abilities that would enable him to broaden the base of his services. He was searching for a person possessing maintenance skills and skill in graphic arts as well. Combining functions in one person is highly desirable in small media centers, and in centers just beginning a program, but as service expands, such individuals must specialize, thus having to choose one or the other of several fields of work. Certainly men and women who possess a wide variety of skills in media work are extremely valuable. Those who have limited skills, but who are willing to learn can eventually serve their school systems or school-building unit more effectively.

Remuneration of Audiovisual Media Center Staff. It is understandable that great variety exists in the pay scales around the country for various types of media personnel, but nothing prevents the estimate of a range in remuneration. In Connecticut for example, according to a 1965 survey, full-time school-system media program directors, by whatever name they are designated, earned from $9,800 to $14,800. The acute shortage of personnel is certain to accelerate salary increases for full-time supervisory salary scales. It seems quite obvious that lower salaries are paid in some small communities where a full-time person is employed without benefit of a supervisory salary differential. Such practices are not destined to be widespread in adoption. We are, of course, well aware also of the range in pay scales for technical workers for various

Example 8-5

STATE UNIVERSITY COLLEGE GENESEO, NEW YORK	POSITION AVAILABLE:	Technical Specialist II U-6
	APPOINTMENT DATE:	Approx. Apr. 1, 1967
	DATE OF THIS NOTICE	February 10, 1967
STAFF VACANCY NOTICE	SALARY:	Approx. $7500

POSITION
AVAILABLE:

Technical Specialist II U-6

APPOINTMENT DATE:

Approx. April 1, 1967

RESPONSIBILITIES:

The Language Laboratory Technician is responsible to the Director of Instructional Resources through the TV Chief Engineer and must work closely with the personnel in the Language Department. He is responsible for the day-to-day technical operation of the laboratory, and assists the instructors in the operation and use of the equipment. He is to be responsible for the technical preparation of tape sources and other similar functions related to dial access facilities. He is responsible for the upkeep of equipment and performs repairs where needed. He supervises those students assigned to help him.

QUALIFICATIONS
AND EXPERIENCE:

1. Ability to handle Tape Recorder circuitry, audio circuitry and switching circuitry including those common to Dial Access Systems.

2. Ability to maintain and repair audio equipment associated with the above.

3. Ability to instruct students and instructors in use of equipment.

4. Ability to supervise assigned help.

5. Experience in the operation of tape recorders including editing and dubbing.

6. Experience in basic electronic theory and in the use of test equipment.

7. Knowledge of program distribution and retrieval.

8. Experience with basic switching systems and in wiring audio cables.

9. Ability to study and learn new developments in associated electronic equipment.

10. Good personality and ability to work well with others.

SALARY:

Approx. $7500

APPLY TO:

SEND CREDENTIALS TO:

levels of ability and for work of increasing technical complexity.

If we refer to statements of pay given for personnel needed in school-building units, as discussed in Chapter 7, we note that technical workers are likely to be paid from $3,500 to $9,000. Supervisors in any given category would probably receive an additional $1,000 or more per year. In addition, we may well find that some combinations of skills and experience would call for adjustments in pay scales that would add several hundred dollars to the announced salary schedules.

Organization of Staff for Control of Media Center Activities

Considering the staff needs at a school-district media center as presented in this chapter and in Chapter 7, we get a good idea of the system-wide scope of the formal work that has to be carried on. However, a great deal of informal work throughout the system has to be done also. Only the media program director himself can serve as the spearhead for getting this wide variety of formal and informal tasks performed by a relatively large number of participants. Since he can never contrive to do this work himself, he has to elicit the cooperation of teachers and others to get it done. An overview of this informal work required by the media center in its day-to-day operations will be of interest to the reader and is presented in the following list.

1. *The Work of Formulating Policy for Recommendation to the Superintendent.* Voluntary participation of members of an advisory council or special study group is essential. Such a council needs to be widely representative and may include one or two lay participants in addition to one or more curriculum leaders, school principals, teachers, and school-building media coordinators.

2. *The Work of Analyzing Media-Use Needs.* This valuable work is called for by the director on a voluntary, individual-response basis through school principals and other curriculum specialists. In addition to deriving data from questionnaire methods, school-building or system-wide committees may have to be organized to study and compile relative information.

3. *The Work of Selecting Materials.* This colossal work load demands considerable individual and group effort. Since this vital group activity needs to be formalized, staff for the selection panels or committees ought to be recruited for definite periods of time and made a part of an important professional organization even though the work is done voluntarily. The selection of instructional materials is such important business that other supervisory leaders must also bring influence to bear in getting this job done expertly. The procedural basis for this work was described in Chapter 3.

4. *The Work of Selecting Equipment.* This technical work calls for a group of qualified individuals to participate according to need in solving equipment problems. Participation should involve a definite term assignment and should provide for continuity of personnel.

5. *Other Work Needed.* Many other individuals and committees will be needed on an intermittent basis to do the work of writing manuals, preparing lists of materials, preparing handbooks of instructional procedure and to do the work of teaching colleagues as recommended and described in earlier chapters. Such services will be entirely voluntary, and the media program director need but ask for it. However, he must always see to it that proper credit is given for the completed results. In some cases experts outside the school system will have to be called in. Some of these experts should be paid, while others need only to be reimbursed for expenses or entertained locally, depending on the circumstances.

From the preceding discussion, it can be observed that the system-wide staff organization is based at the media headquarters, and that some staff members are organized formally in a highly structured way, that other staff members are loosely organized in an informal way while they are working for varying periods of time—under media leadership—on vital school problems. Thus we need to caution the media leader to examine his lines of control, and to keep on the one hand from developing an autocratic climate that will block creative participation and service by others unless he himself can command it personally at each step of the way, and on the other from starting so many things and having so many processes and projects going that he finishes nothing. This latter kind of loose control is unproductive and dangerous. The good administrator will therefore seek patterns of structure that will expedite the accomplishment of his goals and yet will maintain, through a combination of delegation and check-up on action, up-to-date information about what is going on, by whom, and at what quality level. The following suggestions are made as guidelines for appropriate action:

1. Define the duties of each staff member in light of the processes to be carried out, and delegate them officially by duty charts or other official communication. Through conferences, work out detailed specifications and check on accomplishment.

2. When two or more people are at work on similar processes, delegate supervisory responsibility to one of the two or more workers, and while maintaining wholesome contact with all workers, call for and get control through the supervisor of the process involved.

3. Create divisions or departments by grouping similar or related duties, as soon as specialization is feasible.

4. By working with principals, the school superintendent, and curriculum leaders, establish several working groups with defined responsibilities. Set the lines of responsibility to properly appointed steering committees, and to the delegated chairmen. Steering committees with their respective chairmen should be responsible to the media program director or his delegated supervisor. In-service education programs for innovations and selection panels for media materials are examples.

5. Set up a school-building media program coordinator council for supervisory functions, and if program expansion warrants it, appoint a supervisor for each division, elementary and secondary, making the supervisors, or the council chairmen responsible to the media director.

6. Write out official plans with the approval and endorsement of the chief school administrator, and delegate by authority, the responsibility for the actions taken under assignment. Write out the description of the problem to be solved and also the letters of appointments to groups, to be sent by school authorities, and follow through to send bulletins of detailed instructions, and assist in laying out suggestions for final plans.

7. Sketch out in attractive format a clear and precise chart showing the formal organizational relationships, and show in plans for action that recognition of and credit for will be noted and reported to cognizant officials. Duplicate and distribute, and make necessary revisions as needed and redistribute, to all involved.

8. Write up in as attractive a manner as possible a recommended policy statement for all assistants, participants, and authorities, obtaining the approval of chief school officers before publishing it.

Such involved suggestions without a final and specific program in mind or on paper may appear to be irrational, yet implicit in the list is a sensitivity to the people, goals, and processes for accomplishment. It may appear that one goal is to fabricate a program of activity that eliminates any arduous mental or physical work on the part of the media director. Nothing could be further from the truth, for if we now reconsider the earlier chapters we see administrative problems in their true light, and the director must find ways to budget his time for important professional leadership activities. We have already discussed the desirable nature of administrative duties and have shown that *designing*, *planning*, *proposing*, and *deciding*, are the hallmarks of top-level action.

In Chapter 1, we showed several diagrams of strong organizational structures relating the citywide media leader to other school officials. At this point we need to show a number of cases where the media program leader relates his own activity to the structure he has created for his own system-wide operations. To do this we turn to several examples of actual cases where operations are sufficiently complex to show the problems that exist. First, let us turn to Los Angeles, admittedly a large, complex, and comprehensive media organization, for a diagram and brief comment. Before studying the Los Angeles diagrams in Figure 8-10, the reader should know that the administrator of the Instructional Services Branch has the rank of Assistant Superintendent, and is directly responsible to the Head of the Instructional Planning and Services Division. He works

Figure 8-10. These two organization charts contain clearly marked out relationships and functions existing at various administrative levels. See also Figures 1-5 through 1-7 and make comparisons between the charts in the following figures on the opposite page and page 350. (*Courtesy Los Angeles City Schools.*)

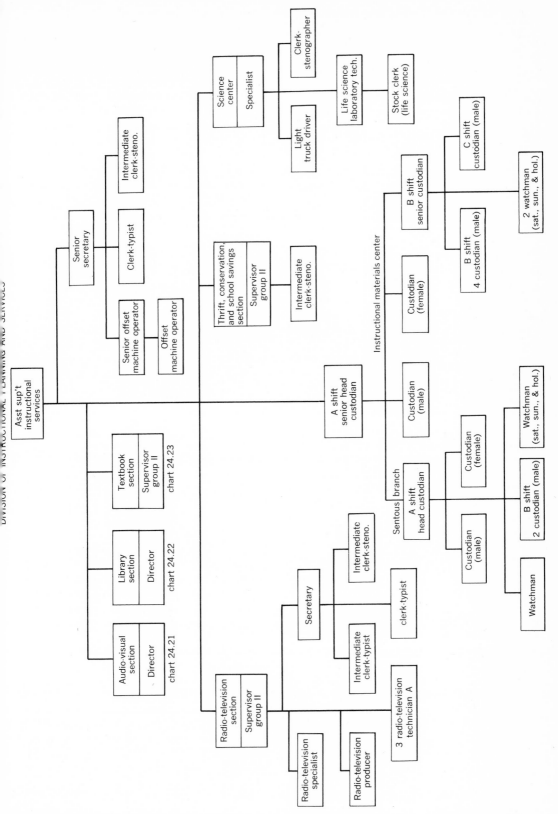

AUDIO-VISUAL SECTION
INSTRUCTIONAL SERVICES BRANCH
DIVISION OF INSTRUCTIONAL PLANNING AND SERVICES

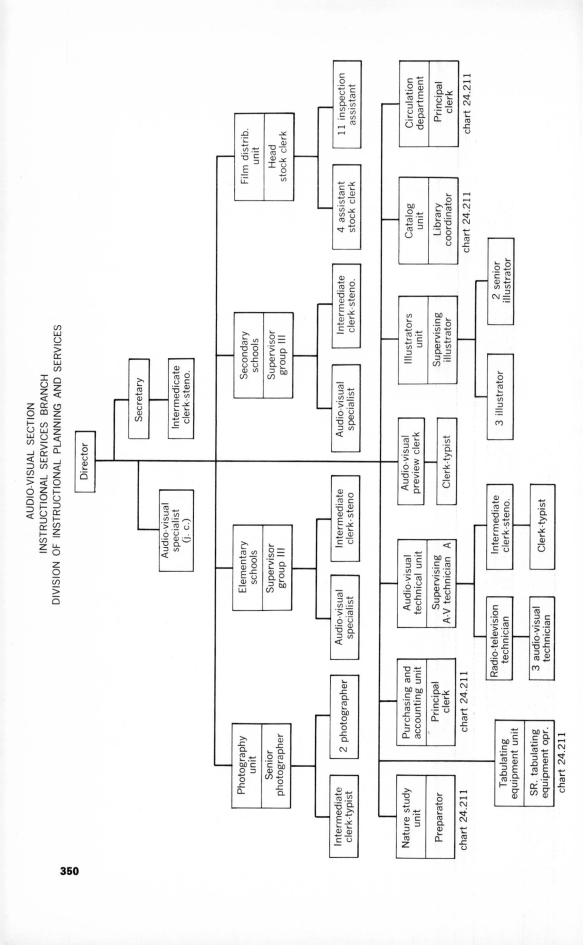

ORGANIZATION CHART DEPT. OF LIBRARIES AND AV EDUCATION
NEWARK, NEW JERSEY

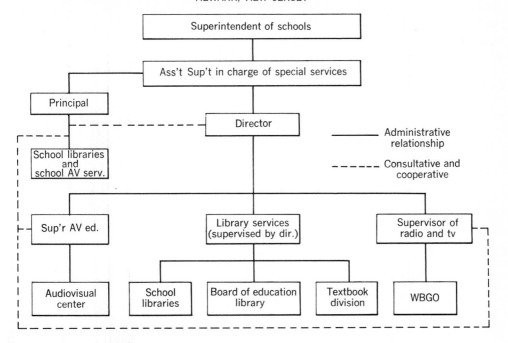

Figure 8-11. This organization chart was redrawn from the original appearing in the official handbook of the department. Questions relative to salient features of the chart should be referred to in the text. (*Courtesy Public Schools, Newark, New Jersey.*)

coordinately with the chief administrator of Curriculum. In this organization we focus attention on salient characteristics and unique features by means of the following questions to be pondered by the reader:

1. How many Sections are identifiable in the chart? How many of these have a Director in charge? How many have a Supervisor Group II in charge?
2. Does the Chief Administrator of this branch act as supervisor of both professional and technical personnel? In which case is the supervision direct instead of indirect?
3. Does the Administrator and all Section directors or supervisors appear to have adequate secretarial personnel?
4. Why do you suppose the Library Section is separate from the Textbook Section? (Function? Scope of service to over 500 schools?)
5. Refer now to the detailed chart that shows the Audio-Visual Section operationally organized under a Director. Note that although not

provided here for analysis, still other charts have been made to pinpoint staff relationships.

Next we shall examine the organizational structure that marks out the pattern in operation at Newark, N.J. See Figure 8-11. The reader is asked to answer another set of questions that points up unique features of the plan of organization:

1. In the city of Newark, as shown in this diagram, are all instructional media services combined under the leadership of a single professional person?
2. Is the Director of the Department directly responsible to the Assistant Superintendent of Schools? Does he work coordinately with school principals?
3. What are the three branches of the Library Services section? In this instance who acts as the head or supervisor of the Library section?
4. What school official is in charge of the school-building libraries and audiovisual services?

5. Are the ranks for TV and AV Section-Heads equivalent?

6. What flexibility exists in this organization with regard to the talents and experience of the Director? Would the Director have to be a specialist in library science?

7. Does Newark have an audiovisual center? Is a professional specialist in charge?

8. Does it appear in the chart that all media are combined in school-building media-service centers? Who is directly in charge of such units? What is meant by consultative and cooperative relationships with the principals and with the school-building media-service centers?

Before leaving this problem for additional creative thought by the reader, we should examine a few additional samples of structure that represent both medium-size and smaller city school systems. We therefore turn to the organizational patterns in effect in the public schools of Portland, Oregon, Colorado Springs, Colo., Pawtucket, R.I., Penfield, N.Y., and Great Neck, N.Y. See Figures 8-12 and 8-13, to note their status of development and salient features.

Chapters 1 through 7, and the present discussion of citywide media-service headquarters, provide content in abundance to stimulate readers to develop administrative insight into media-use problems—which is the nature of this book. Media directors must realize the sweep of development in the past decade and must look ahead to vast implementation, even as new developments loom on the horizon. The fact is that we must note trends in media activity in

DEPARTMENT OF INSTRUCTIONAL MATERIALS, PUBLIC SCHOOLS, PORTLAND, OREGON

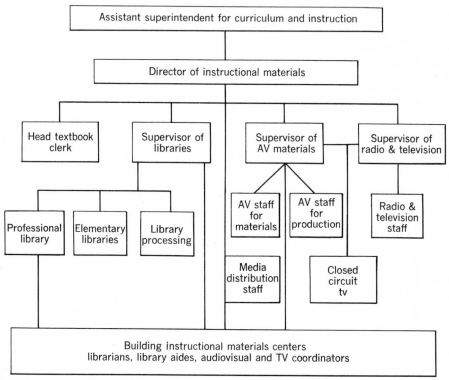

Figure 8-12. This is the organization chart for the comprehensive Instructional Materials Center for the Public Schools in Portland, Oregon. Using the same or similar questions as were raised in connection with Figures 8-10 and 8-11, study the staff specialization in this system. Note the joint effort implied between the Audiovisual and Television Sections with regard to CCTV. Make some comparisons between the Newark and the Portland charts relative to functions being carried out. (*Courtesy Public Schools, Portland, Oregon.*)

response to teaching needs, and continuously analyze the nature of the system-wide contributions being made to instructional effectiveness. Therefore before we leave these problems to attack others, we should emphasize the importance of keeping vital records of services rendered and problems identified in day-to-day routines. The next section discusses this aspect of the media center organization and activity.

Media Center Records and Reports

Prospective and practicing media program directors need to realize the importance of keeping their superiors well informed about the services, activities, and trends of their organizations. Most chief administrators will demand periodic reports but if they don't, the media administrator who fails to submit them regularly each year misses a great opportunity for piling up evidence of need. Furthermore, he fails to place squarely where it belongs the responsibility for failure to take action on pressing needs. Although this may be of little consolation to a harried director, it is nevertheless wise tactically. Moreover, effective reporting inspires confidence for future action. An effective reporting process, however, requires an adequate record-keeping system, and some suggestions for keeping records are therefore discussed next.

A System of Records

It would be an easy matter in a media center to keep so many people busy checking on what the others do, that other important work would go undone. What kinds of records are likely to be useful? This question is difficult to answer because future needs for information can only be predicted. Records may actually, however, make the difference between success or failure, or they may go unused for a decade. In general it is the uses to which records are put that must be the basis for the decision to keep them. To be worthwhile, some of these uses would have to include: (a) historical reporting, (b) reporting growth and development, (c) predicting outcomes and identifying trends, (d) evaluating contributions, (e) providing publicity for developing community understanding and support, (f) identifying instructional and personnel needs, (g) obtaining

additional staff and budget allotments, and (h) good business requirements.

The director needs to decide what records will be likely to be significantly useful, and then he needs to set up a process for summarizing them monthly and annually. Cluttering up the files and wasting valuable hours of labor on unnecessary figures is an unpardonable error. The media director will do well also if he keeps in his desk an out-of-sight summary sheet for each month on which to note important major decisions, meetings attended, and unexpected developments. At the end of a term or year, such notes become valuable. The media leader is also urged to develop his system during his first year on a new job, or at any rate, as early as possible, to provide maximum continuity of the data based on the operational level in effect at the time of his arrival or appointment. The following suggestions merit consideration:

1. Preserve original organization directives, annual budget expenditures, records on classrooms darkened in each school, inventories of media equipment units and materials, purchase requisitions, and other vital information such as employment and work records summarized in man-months of service or in some smaller unit of measurement.

2. Tabulate for each month the total number of media orders received from each school building in the system.

3. Make a tabulation of the number of each kind of centralized item distributed for each half year to each school.

4. Set up a tabulation of the use for each month for those media materials that are decentralized in each school and ordered from the coordinator's office by teachers. (Coordinators report this information to directors.)

5. Set up a summarization system in each school through the school-building media coordinator for the projection requests in order to tabulate the average number of items for each projection order. Such records are to be totaled at end of year or term as average length of the projection period, number of times classes were combined, and names of teachers who reveal highest competence in using materials. (These records are to be kept at the school coordinator's office only.)

6. Also in each school building obtain a tabulation of the times each term or year that

PAWTUCKET, R. I., ORGANIZATION CHART

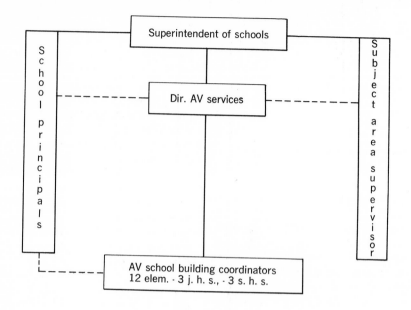

AUDIOVISUAL SERVICES ORGANIZATION CHART
PUBLIC SCHOOLS, COLORADO SPRINGS, COLORADO

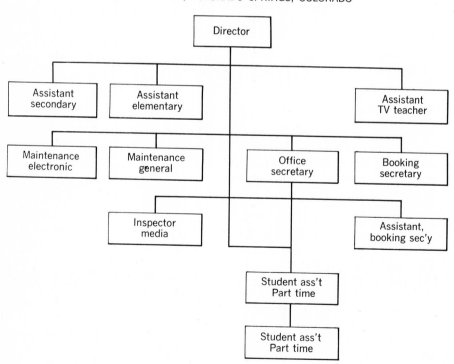

ORGANIZATION CHART — PUBLIC SCHOOLS, GREAT NECK, L. I.

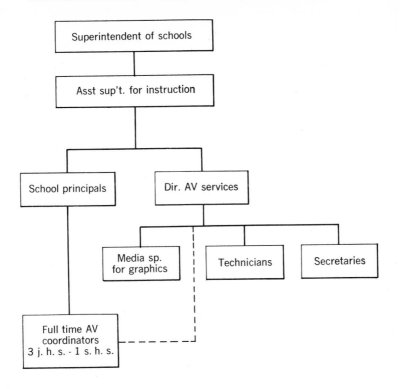

PENFIELD ORGANIZATION CHART — PENFIELD, N. Y.

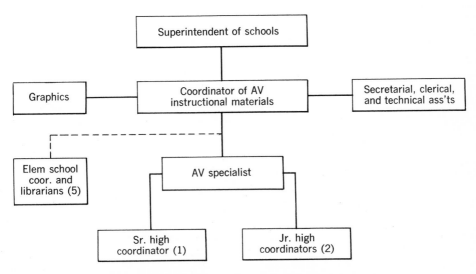

Figure 8-13. Organization charts for the following cities, arranged in order of population ranging from 80,000 to approximately 18,000: Pawtucket, Rhode Island, Colorado Springs, Colorado, Great Neck, New York, and Penfield, New York. The directors of these programs are responsible for audiovisual media services only. All of the charts have been resketched. (*Courtesy of the Public Schools of each city named.*)

nonprojected audiovisual materials are utilized, such as bulletin-board displays and audiovisual production activities involving tapes, transparencies, slides, and models.

7. Make monthly estimates of the number of pupils using electronic laboratory facilities as fixed installations, and such other media uses as regular participation in school-system, closed-circuit telecasts.

8. Maintain accurate records of school meetings conducted for in-service education purposes, including location, attendance, and nature of participation and action.

9. Maintain a listing of individual and group service projects completed as contributions to a program in a particular school and also to the system-wide program.

The media director needs also to consider unique ways to obtain qualitative evidence of the use of materials, and although this is a responsibility of other supervisory personnel as well, he needs to tackle the problem in his own area of operations. It can be seen in the foregoing list that tabulations of qualitative data are set up at the school-building level where continuous observation may lead to reliable evidence. Of course the preceding items of information may be handled and summarized in various ways. Some may never be made use of; other combinations of data may be added. It will be interesting to the reader to study a number of recent listings of types of data collected and utilized in school-system media centers. Several examples follow.

Example 1

In the audiovisual media center at Niles Township Community High School, North Division, Skokie, Illinois, data collected and tabulated for use in the Annual Report are as follows:

1. Number of teaching periods during the day, month, and year.

2. Number of periods various kinds of media equipment units were scheduled, day, month, year.

3. Number of machines available.

4. Per cent of periods using audiovisual media equipment.

5. Number of pieces of instructional materials produced at the audiovisual center.

6. Total volume of specific kinds of audiovisual media used by teachers.

7. Number of in-service education programs offered.

Example 2

In the audiovisual media center at Colorado Springs Public Schools, Colorado Springs, Colorado, data collected and tabulated for subsequent use are as follows:

1. Number of in-service meetings held.

2. Number of television and radio programs produced and telecast each week.

3. Number of TV program brochures distributed.

4. Number and kinds of audiovisual media produced for elementary and secondary schools.

5. Number of teacher evaluations of media items completed.

6. Number of consultative meetings held with teachers.

7. Number of consultative meetings held with administrators.

8. Number and kinds of audiovisual media used in secondary schools.

9. Number and kinds of audiovisual media used in elementary schools.

Example 3

In the audiovisual media center at Penfield, New York, data collected for both regular and special reports are as follows:

1. Number of media material titles distributed to each school during ten-week intervals.

2. Number of media material titles distributed to each school for the school year.

3. Number and kinds of media items produced for teachers.

4. Media utilization by departments and grades.

5. Number of in-service education meetings held with records of teacher participation.

6. Degree of use of fixed media installations in school buildings.

7. Number of staff visitations to schools for media purposes.

Such data are particularly useful, when summarized and tabulated by years, in showing

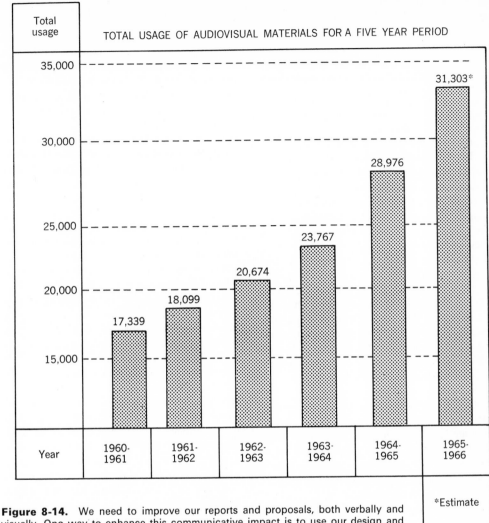

Figure 8-14. We need to improve our reports and proposals, both verbally and visually. One way to enhance this communicative impact is to use our design and operational skills. This chart was easy to make because the appropriate data had been collected and processed regularly. (*Courtesy Public Schools, Colorado Springs, Colorado.*)

trends and rates of development. Systems for keeping records are, of course, indispensable in connection with programs for public understanding and support and in connection with evaluation activity; however, more will be said about these topics in Chapters 14 and 15.

Audiovisual Media Center Reports

A record system should be based on well-defined uses, and one of these is, of course, reporting progress to all who are concerned. Reports to the public, as well as to the staff organization spread out among the various school units, are of great significance, but the reports considered here are the reports made specifically to the chief school-system administrators, who in turn use them as needed for their own analysis and reporting purposes. Reports to administrators should be factual, terse, succinct, graphic, comparative, free of errors, and attractive in format. The use of a summary check-off sheet for the media directors' desk has already been mentioned as an indispensable item in the record system because the director needs to show clearly his own efficiency as well. His annual report may, of course, have to conform to local requirements, but the following suggestions as to procedure may be helpful:

1. Set up a novel introductory section, emphasizing some major highlights of activity.

2. Report major changes in policy.

3. Report vital statistics according to media materials and processes of distribution in comparison to figures for a base year, graphic or tabular in format. Continue such comparisons during a five-year period; then subsequently report the current year with base year and preceding year only.

4. Organize a section of the report to deal with the two following major aspects of operation, namely, *special needs* and *continuing needs*. Include under each of these the date on which the need should be met, and also include the progress made toward meeting it in the current year. Special needs have to do with pressing personnel problems, urgent new facilities, new demands that have appeared, and how such demands should be handled. Continuing needs are the year-to-year problems like improving the media-center quarters, increasing the size of equipment and material inventories, installation of fixed technological facilities such as outlets and light-control systems in classrooms, and the problem of appointing and training additional school-building media coordinators.

5. Set up a strong concluding section for the report, one that summarizes important aspects already mentioned or makes a strong recommendation pointing to the over-all operational progress for the year to come.

6. Use graphic illustrations.

Although these suggestions may apply in many ways to other administrative uses, they are specifically intended for audiovisual media-use reports. Telling the media-service story to the public necessarily involves other points for emphasis and other techniques. The media director is advised not to wait until reports are called for, but to set up a record system and reporting process at once. The media expert must be prepared to facilitate the thinking of top administrative officials by providing sound proposals and recommendations for action.

Problem-Solving Activities

1. An older, two-story school building has been taken over by the school department as its administrative headquarters. You, the director of a growing audiovisual media-services program, have been assigned three classrooms at the rear of the building on the first floor. Your classrooms are adjoining and on the same side of the corridor. Each measures 32 feet long by 26 feet wide. You are told that this space assignment will have to last for the next ten years. Television service programs are envisioned, but textbooks and other reference services are handled by other agencies. You have been permitted to build an addition to the building to house television facilities. Partitions separating the classrooms are load-bearing walls that cannot be removed, although openings may be made in them. On the basis of the operations described in this chapter, prepare (a) a labeled scale drawing of how you would remodel and use this space and the building addition; (b) a labeled scale drawing showing your layout of furniture, cabinets, and so forth, to control the flow of work for the inspection, storage, and distribution area, and indicating the relationship for the present of the television addition to the total media center; (c) study the commercially available storage facilities mentioned in this chapter or as shown in catalogs, and then specify their location in another scale drawing of the storage areas; (d) make a list of the furniture that would have to be built for the new facilities (do not include photographic darkroom furniture in this exercise); and (e) prepare detailed construction specifications for any two of the major items listed in item (d). (The television facilities plan should be delayed until Chapter 10 has been studied.)

2. As time permits and your needs demand, engage in a thorough study of the main types of audiovisual equipment to develop operational and adjustment skills. Use the manufacturer's service booklets for each piece of equipment, and plan a time schedule for what you need most to do.

3. Outline procedures for an effective stock control, ordering, and inventory process for the audiovisual media-center shop. Make a list of the major supplies that will have to be stocked if schools are going to be well served.

4. Assume that you have been appointed to

the position of media program director in a small city where there are ten school buildings. Assume further that you have a reasonably sized audiovisual media-service center in the high school where your own office is located and that you have been hired to develop a system-wide organization. Sketch out your plan to develop this organization as to full-time staff, duties, service units, use of student crews if deemed necessary, and advisory councils. Draw a line-of-responsibility chart for the organization you have established.

5. What characteristics would you like your media school-building coordinators to possess? What recommendations would you make regarding their training, services, and remuneration?

6. Why should directors be concerned with maintaining adequate records of activities and services? Why should a record system be devised soon after a media director's appointment? Formulate the kind of record system you believe would be of maximum helpfulness.

7. Examine a number of annual reports as prepared by media directors, and identify their strengths and weaknesses. Of what value are annual reports to the media program director? Would you write them even if not requested to do so? Why, or why not?

8. After studying Chapter 7 and 8, what conclusions do you draw about the prime responsibility of the citywide media program director in terms of his ultimate accomplishment? What shift in balance between central and school-building center as to facilities, staff, and media budget, do you envision? What organizational structure to achieve this goal would you need to develop in light of modern roles of media?

9. How will decentralization of media collections in school buildings be likely to reduce recommended storage areas at media headquarters?

10. Describe in a succinct summary the nature of professional and technical duties carried on in a *centralized* print-medium service area as it would exist in relation to a citywide comprehensive instructional media center.

11. State clearly in an itemized listing several major ways in which citywide and school-building media services are likely to be different.

12. Make a listing of generally needed media-service center areas, as presented in this chapter, and total the estimates of required space for the functions given. If you wish to take issue with the total square footage you have discovered, make adjustments in terms of your own specific recommendations. Report this to the class and see if your colleagues will agree.

13. Formulate a plan in outline format for the system-wide maintenance of conventional projection equipment. Be thorough. Do not *fail* to take into account personnel, stocks of spare parts, and central and school-building service programs.

14. Suggest a method for handling technical control and maintenance of fixed electronic carrels and TV studios in school buildings to guarantee continuous readiness for use.

15. Sketch out one employment specification sheet for one media position of your choice. (Each member of the class group should do one of these announcement-of-position and job-specification sheets. All should then be turned over to the instructor and an editing committee for final polishing, rewriting, and duplication for issue to classmates as a package.)

16. You are employing one new assistant media director for the Center, and one new maintenance supervisor for system-wide functions. Suggest your plans for screening and interviewing as follow-up procedures to the use of the announcement and job-specification sheet you prepared in a previous exercise.

17. Criticize the pay ranges presented in this and the preceding chapter for required professional and technical personnel in citywide and school-building media centers, and up-date them in light of local or changed conditions. Make your own estimate of need and cost for media personnel in any situation you name.

18. On the basis of discussions and guidelines developed in the text and in class make a list of the kinds of data about audiovisual services and processes that you as a media program director would recommend keeping for the purpose of preparing annual and interim reports.

References

The Audio-Visual Program, Bulletin No. 218, State of Indiana, Department of Public Instruction, Indianapolis, Indiana, 1956.

Brown, James W. and Kenneth D. Norberg. *Administering Educational Media.* (New York: McGraw-Hill, 1965).

Cobun, Ted and Hal J. Cress. "North Division, Niles Township Community High Schools," *Audiovisual Instruction,* Vol. 10, No. 2, February 1965, pp. 136–137.

Cohen, Samuel (Interviewer). "What Does Audiovisual Mean to You?" *Audiovisual Instruction,* Vol. 9, No. 1, January 1964, pp. 40–60.

———. "The Import of the Wantagh Interviews and a Modest Proposal for Next Steps," *Audiovisual Instruction,* Vol. 9, No. 1, January 1964, pp. 61–63.

DeBernardis, Amo. "Portland's Instructional Materials Center," *Educational Screen,* Vol. 28, No. 1, January 1941, pp. 13–15.

DeBernardis, Amo, Victor W. Doherty, Erret Hummel, and Charles W. Brubaker, *Planning Schools for New Media,* in cooperation with the U.S. Office of Education (Washington, D.C.: The Superintendent of Documents, U.S. Government Printing Office, 1961).

DeBernardis, Amo, David M. Crossman, and Thomas E. Miller. "Media, Technology, and IMC Space Requirements," *Audiovisual Instruction,* Vol. 10, No. 2, February 1965, pp. 107–114.

Faris, Gene. "Tentative Guidelines for Audiovisual Personnel and Equipment," *Audiovisual Instruction,* Vol. 10, No. 3, March 1965, pp. 201–204.

Faris, Gene and John Moldstad (assisted by Harvey Frye). *Improving the Learning Environment* (A Study on the Local Preparation of Visual Instructional Materials). In cooperation with the U.S. Office of Education (Washington, D.C.: Superintendent of Documents, U.S. Government Printing Office, 1963).

Ford, Harry J. "The Instructional Resources Center," *Audiovisual Instruction,* Vol. 7, No. 8, October 1962, pp. 524–526.

Gerlach, Vernon S. "The Professional Education of the Media Specialist," *AV Communication Review,* Vol. 14, No. 2, Summer 1966, p. 185.

Glenn, Magdalene. "Organizing a Materials Center," *National Elementary Principal,* Vol. 40, No. 1, January 1961, pp. 28–30.

Goldberg, Albert L. and Richard A. Darling. "Is the Instructional Materials Center the Answer?" *Audiovisual Instruction,* Vol. 6, No. 5, May 1961, pp. 194–195.

Green, Alan C. (ed.). *Educational Facilities with New Media.* (Prepared under a contract with the U.S. Office of Education) (Washington, D.C.: The Department of Audiovisual Instruction of the NEA, 1966).

Handbook for Audio-Visual Representatives, Secondary Schools (Revised 1965). (Los Angeles: Los Angeles City Schools, Instructional Services Branch, 1965.)

Lehman, Frederick M. "A Study of a Small Audiovisual Community," *Audiovisual Instruction,* Vol. 9, No. 1, January 1964, pp. 37–40.

Martin, Ann M. and C. Walter Stone. *A Study of Regional Instructional Media Resources, Phase 1—Manpower.* (Prepared under contract OE-3-16-027, with the U.S. Office of Education.) (Pittsburgh: Graduate School of Library and Information Sciences, University of Pittsburgh, 1965).

Mesedahl, Leroy K. "The IMC: Contribution to Individualized Instruction," *Audiovisual Instruction,* Vol. 10, No. 9, November 1965, pp. 705–706.

Miles, Bruce and Virginia McJenkin. "IMC's: A Dialogue," *Audiovisual Instruction,* Vol. 10, No. 9, November 1965, pp. 688–691.

Mitchell, Malcolm G. "What's Going On in the School Library?" *Phi Delta Kappan,* Vol. 45, October 1963, pp. 44–47.

Moldstad, John and Harvey R. Frye. "Making Room for AV," *Audiovisual Instruction,* Vol. 2, No. 10, December 1957, pp. 270–271.

Nicholson, Margaret E. "The I.M.C." *School Libraries,* Vol. 13, No. 3, March 1964, pp. 39–43.

Phillips, Murray G. "Instructional Materials Center: The Rationale," *Audiovisual Instruction,* Vol. 5, No. 10, December 1960, pp. 326–332.

Pryor, Robert L. "Speedy Repair Equals Good Utilization," *Audiovisual Instruction,* Vol. 8, No. 3, March 1963, p. 153.

Quantitative Standards for Audiovisual Personnel, Equipment and Materials (in Elementary, Secondary, and Higher Education). Developed as part of the Faris-Sherman Study conducted under the auspices of the United States Office of Education, National Defense Education Act, Title VII, Part B Program (Washington, D.C.: Department of Audiovisual Instruction of the NEA, 1201 Sixteenth Street, N.W., January 1966), 18 pp. mimeographed.

"Sample State Certification Requirements" (A collection of reports). *Audiovisual Instruction*, Vol. 10, No. 10, December 1965, pp. 787–794.

Sharp, J. Stanley. "Architectural Steps in Facilities Planning," *Audiovisual Instruction*, Vol. 10, No. 2, February 1965, pp. 101–103.

Stone, C. Walter (ed.). *The Professional Education of Media Service Personnel.* (Pittsburgh: Graduate Library School, University of Pittsburgh, 1964).

Taylor, Kenneth I. "Instructional Materials Center," *The Nation's Schools*, Vol. 66, December 1960, pp. 46–50.

9

Implementation of Media Preparation Services

When a school or school system provides its teachers with convenient facilities for the preparation of their own slides, transparencies, tapes, films, and other instructional materials, it may be said that it has reached a high level of maturity in the development of its audiovisual media services. Unusually skillful teachers today are adding to their communicative skills the power to select, arrange, construct, photograph, visualize, and record ideas that help teach more effectively. Fortunate indeed are teachers who have in their schools the necessary supplies, equipment, and the assistance of media coordinators, principals, or talented colleagues to carry on high-caliber planning and preparation of creatively conceived materials, and infinitely more fortunate are their pupils. Such teachers have a greater impact that stems not only from increased pupil understanding, but from the increased teacher-pupil contacts, as for example with tape-recorded instruction that can be presented to one group while the teacher is working face-to-face with another. We must quickly point out also that such teachers are the ones who will be most likely to utilize locally prepared materials, in combination with ready-made ones, in the newer teaching roles of media which are generally referred to as instructional systems.

The truth is that all of us ought to accelerate our progress toward this maturity in media services. In the light of over-all teaching needs, however, we need first to build our media-service program for teachers on the solid base of adequate facilities for ready-made media for then, since we will have at hand the needed equipment units, we are at least partially equipped to use the various materials produced locally. We need to work next or concurrently toward facilities for the preparation of unique materials planned and made by teachers themselves. Some teachers are fortunately working in situations where materials such as 2×2 inch color slides, Polaroid slides, acetate transparencies, together with spirit masters and stencils, are available and upon order will be prepared and delivered according to schedule. Such services provide teachers with either centralized or school-building technical personnel who serve as consultants and producers, thus freeing teachers for other creative planning activity. However, a great many teachers the country over would feel privileged indeed were they

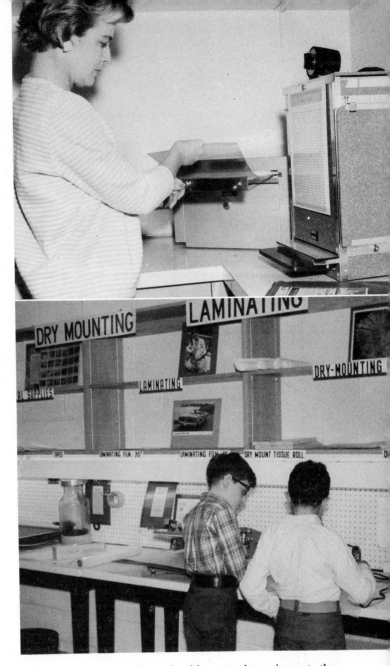

Figure 9-1. Teachers develop keen insight into visualization processes, especially when they design their own media. Media-making facilities should be provided to an optimum degree in each school. Teachers and their aides will demand the bulk of the services; however, the allotted area ought to be increased for its additional use by pupils for instructional activities. The teacher in the top picture is developing a diazo-film print from a master that has been exposed in the Protoprinter. In the next picture two young students use the drymount press. The other part of this work counter has photocopier machines, which in this case are also available to students for teacher guided activity. (*Top view*, courtesy Fremont Union High School District, Sunnyvale, California. *Bottom view*, courtesy Public Schools, Shaker Heights, Ohio.)

permitted to make the materials on a do-it-yourself basis, if the supplies and facilities were in their schools.

As teachers learn to select and prepare their own instructional media materials, they invariably develop new insights and skills that are increasingly being associated with the best modern-day teaching methods. Today's technology makes such maturity possible, but maturity of this caliber arises at two levels. First, there is the operational level of maturity, that is, a level of maturity residing in the teacher who strives to execute his or her ideas about instructional media. Second, this maturity arises at the administration level in the school system that strives to organize and maintain facilities for teachers to use. These are the basic levels of maturity without which team teaching, automation, large-group instruction, and instructional television will never fulfill their promise, since their successful use is uniquely tied to effective communication.

In the face of the rapidly developing technology for the local preparation of media, and because of the newer roles of media that demand systematic and scheduled use of media in combination, we assert that one of the significant problems that a school-system or school-building media director will have to deal with effectively is the organization and implementation of media-preparation services. We therefore turn to a discussion of the problems that will have to be met and solved. To view the media-preparation problem in perspective we present the following questions which we shall attempt to answer: Who needs locally produced media materials, and why is there such an urgency for media-preparation facilities? Who should design and prepare special-purpose media—teachers or supporting technical staff? What spaces for media preparation facilities are required? Should media preparation services be centralized at media headquarters, or decentralized in each school building, or should an optimum combination of facilities and services be organized? What control systems need to be set up for providing media preparation services? What in-service education programs will be needed? What new staff members will be required to provide needed services?

Nature of the Need for Local Media Preparation

Who Needs Locally Prepared Media Materials?

We have already pointed out that teachers are in large part the ones who have need of media in order to communicate effectively with their students—either in large or small groups or with individuals. But we must not overlook the need for in-service education media for use by curriculum specialists and by school administrators. Administrators throughout the school system often require specialized materials for use with both lay and professional groups. Hence we can readily see the need for a wide range of media from television programs to audio tapes, and from slides to charts for a wide variety of school-system purposes.

Why Are Media-Preparation Services Urgently Needed?

Expert teachers who develop keen insights into their subject-matter specialties often need to prepare up-to-date media that reveal recently formulated relationships. Talented teachers also wish to present content in diagrammatic and pictorial form to supplement commercially prepared media to make specific local applications. Such efforts to improve communication have been increasingly put forth by teachers in schools everywhere with the aid of rapidly developing technology. However, in recent years the appearance of new media and the increasing emphasis on new arrangements and conditions for teaching and learning have brought a new urgency to the need for local media-preparation facilities. We shall explain how a few of these changes and developments have a bearing on the need for unique media.

Large-Group Instruction and Team Teaching. Although large-group instruction is generally a part of any team-teaching operation, we can treat both items as separate changes. In large groups, students simply cannot see what is going on during classroom demonstrations with apparatus, and are sometimes lost during referral to charts and maps in the front of a large teaching station. Means for enlargement are a necessity. Therefore, either television or other display systems become a prime necessity. A teacher can hold up for inspection a crystal, a flower, or a skull, but students in back of the first few rows, even if they have 20/20 vision, cannot make the observations required. See Figure 7-6. Thus we see a new urgency in presentations in front of large groups for projection techniques with close-up views made possible by 2×2 inch color slides, for example, of any content desired. Also, diagrams can be drawn and displayed by means of television receivers arranged so as to give every pupil a front row seat. In team teaching we not only have large-group presentations that demand attention-holding media materials, but the teacher making the presentation is likely to be an expert in a particular field and hence will be in a position to use an optimum combination of commercially available and locally produced materials, carefully worked out in the light of desired objectives and required pupil responses. Furthermore, media that control the presentation of content and guide the responses of the pupils (even when the teacher is at work elsewhere) will as a rule have to be locally adapted, or made locally in their entirety. See Chapter 11.

Television. The widespread use of closed-circuit television programing in schools, either on a system-wide, groups-of-schools, or subject-matter and grade-level basis, demands the kind of studio-teacher performance that is richly communicative. One of the great new reasons for providing media-production facilities is to build the kind of television programs through creative media use that will accomplish goals effectively. Although many potentially valuable commercial materials are available for this purpose, television teachers insist that they have a wide variety of media with which to get their message across to students.

Self-Instruction and True Individualization. The development of programs for teaching machines, and the use of pictorial and audio media in carrels for individualized teaching demand locally produced media from video and audio tapes to slide sets and film clips. In fact, as will be pointed out later, both pictorial and audio media may be combined in programs recorded on videotape and transmitted to both large and small groups and to individuals. See Figure 7-5.

Multimedia Presentation Techniques. Multimedia or multi-image and multi-screen-presentation techniques, using either front- or rear-projection surfaces, are also likely to demand sophisticated local media-production resources. See Figure 6-21 and Chapter 11. We expect that in the future many such presentations will be commercially prepared and packaged for local use, but we believe that when such installations are available in schools, unique use will demand the power to organize or reorganize and combine up-to-the-minute local media for teaching the groups involved.

Teaching Systems. The modern teacher is no longer enslaved from hour to hour by the need to confront a group of students and control them second by second. There are newer ways to present content and elicit desired responses of an interacting nature. The modern teacher turns over to media, properly produced, structured, and presented, a number of burdensome though vital teaching tasks. Even though teaching kits and instructional packages will be commercially available in increasing quantities, it is obvious that in a great many cases, teachers will still need to use their own personally designed and structured media as a part of modern instructional systems. Refer to Chapter 11.

Administrators and Their Public-Relations Programs. The desire of school leaders to communicate effectively coupled with the expectancy of the public to receive messages by up-to-date technology, demands that public relations presentations be enhanced by specially prepared media. We must also consider, however, in addition to personal appearances of school speakers at public or executive meetings, the wider audiences that should be reached through audio and television programs and through effectively illustrated school stories in the press. Such uses of special media productions constitute another aspect of the urgent need to inaugurate media-preparation programs in the schools and to expand them according to demonstrated needs.

We can therefore see that for both conventional and new roles of media materials and equipment, the need to organize and implement local media-preparation services is of prime importance. Media program directors will have to take action in this vital area and struggle with problems having to do with policies, staff, supplies, financial support, and in-service education. One of the most important policy matters has to do with the amount of technical service to be provided to teachers. That is, should teachers be expected to spend time planning their own media materials, or should technicians and student crews make the materials for teachers? Perhaps there is no pat answer to this question. To answer it we need to explore the nature of media-preparation processes, and a number of other important questions.

Nature of Media-Preparation Processes

Considering the speed with which technological processes in the preparation of media are advancing, many of the processes referred to in this section will probably be outmoded before this manuscript goes to press. However, this section does not need to be a penetrating analysis of the state of the art, nor does it have to include a handbook on preparation techniques. What we must point out is the nature of the processes we consider necessary in any school-system

Figure 9-2. Books of masters for black and white and for color transparencies are available for purchase in great variety. Printing masters that have already been prepared may be referred to as routine operations. Making these masters calls for far greater insight. This process is more properly referred to as visualization. (*Courtesy Fremont Union High School District, Sunnyvale, California.*)

media design and preparation program. We therefore wish to present a basis, however incomplete, for the purpose of the identification of problems and the implementation of program plans.

Two Basic Aspects of the Media-Preparation Process

Before we present more details relative to the state of technological development for media preparation, the kinds of media needed, and the processes required for their production, we ought to set forth two aspects of the process, the understanding of which will help the reader think more clearly about these problems. These problems involve content and design, as well as the mechanics of making the medium, the operation of the equipment involved, the way supplies are used, and the artistic quality and physical excellence of the final result. We shall discuss each of these main topics briefly to give needed direction to subsequent suggestions.

Visualization and Design. When a set of slides, overhead transparencies, or an audio program on tape for business education or biology is produced locally, it is quite obvious that it is the teacher—the professional—who ought to be responsible for the content. Teachers must decide first what concept or process needs to be visualized, and this decision must be made in the light of specific objectives as they are being achieved in the teaching-learning environment. What is diagramed or printed on a transparency involves decisions about the effect or impact of the message on the learner—and the impact on the learner is a function of his personal responses. Basic, then, to the process of media preparation are the decisions of the teacher who must bear the responsibility for his professional activities. It is he who identifies a specific need in light of an instructional situation. The design of the message and often the medium selected will depend on the advice of a number of curriculum workers, who may be involved because they themselves will use the medium in subsequent presentations. The design of a given message will obviously depend on the nature of the roles to be played, what the learner already knows, and what he is supposed to do when he perceives the content of the medium. These are complicated professional matters and therefore we can separate them from the often complicated but nonprofessional activities referred to as operational techniques.

Operational Techniques. This aspect of media preparation involves equipment units, devices and supplies, mechanical skills, wide knowledge of processes, difficulties, adjustments, and the ability to make judgments in the light of the limitations inherent in any given medium or combination of media. Many of the operational techniques such as exposing a master with diazo-coated film and developing it in an ammonia-filled "pickle jar" may be performed by a fifth-grade student. Other processes like making an overhead transparency of a chart constructed on logarithmic graph paper that is 12×14 inches in size is an entirely different matter. Thus technicians need to be widely skilled, and problems often arise that require unusual insight as to how a message can be presented to obtain the reaction desired and clearly set forth by the teacher in preconstruction conferences. We see in any graphic center both the operational side of media preparation and the message-and-design side of the whole process.

Because of these two basic aspects of the process of media preparation, there will always be a number of people involved, some professional and some not. At times, teachers who are willing to struggle with content-and-design problems may need a professional media specialist (experienced in teaching methods) to counsel him on matters of message and design. After the critical decisions have been made, the actual operational work should be turned over to an artist-technician for completion.

A View of Media-Preparation Technology

We have shown the basic aspects of a process involving both teachers and technicians, and in preceding sections we have shown the need for an organized media preparation service. We shall now introduce a view of current media preparation technology.

Kinds of Media Generally Needed in the Modern School. When we consider the many roles of media in the modern school, we can easily understand why teachers, especially those who have developed maturity in communication skills, have need for specially prepared media. With increasing frequency, teachers who have been able to concentrate their efforts and energies at higher levels of professional activity are engaged in creative planning-and-design activity, and are finding ways to turn over to media several direct teaching tasks. Little wonder then that teachers are facing up to the need not only to use ready-made media, but are designing their own for a variety of roles in the teaching process. We therefore state that many kinds of media are being prepared locally in the most advanced media programs around the country, and we can list these commonly reported types of media as follows:

1. Printed matter: instructional sheets, booklets and school publications.
2. Photo enlargements.
3. Overhead transparencies.
4. 2×2 inch color slides.
5. Polaroid slides, $3\frac{1}{4} \times 4$ inch.
6. Filmstrips.
7. Audio programs on tape.
8. Television programs on videotape.
9. Motion pictures, 8 mm cartridges and 16 mm film footage.

When we consider this array of media productions by schools in their media-preparation programs we can perceive the underlying content and decisions that are faced by teachers as they either explain to others what to make, or make the materials themselves. We now turn to a specific aspect of the operational process, which we need to consider because it emphasizes the preparation of source materials that are often the basis for the media-preparation process.

Making Masters for Media Production. When teachers wish to have sets of slide transparencies made up that are based on their unique needs, the first step is often the making of source materials such as graphs and pictorial arrangements which will then be photographed in color, or converted into multi-color overlays in overhead transparency form. This work must be done either by teachers themselves or by other audiovisual specialists and their supporting technicians. These processes of making what we may refer to as *masters* involve a number of specific operations and often a great many supplies. We shall list the following operations as examples:

1. Use lettering materials such as pens, brushes, scribers, drawing boards, inks, crayons, and pencils.
2. Use pressure-sensitive sheets, tape, symbols, patterns, and other drawing aids.
3. Use stencils, stamps, and pre-cut letters.
4. Use assorted papers and acetate sheets.

Operational Techniques with Equipment. In any well-organized and comprehensive media-preparation program it is possible to observe many kinds of equipment that must be operated in carrying out the basic constructional steps required in the making of instructional media. We shall now list some of the common operational techniques.

1. Make overhead transparencies from masters by the
   (a) photocopier method
   (b) diazo-ammonia method.
2. Duplicate print-medium masters (spirit-master and mimeo stencils).
3. Use photography to produce still-picture media:
   (a) use regular and Polaroid Land cameras
   (b) copy masters (handmade flats, layouts or paste-ups)
   (c) make negatives
   (d) make film and paper positives
   (e) make slide duplicates and alter camera angle and light values.
4. Use photography to produce motion pictures:
   (a) 8 mm cartridges, both sound and silent
   (b) 16 mm footage, with magnetic or optical sound tracks.
5. Mount instructional material on paper by dry-tissue methods.
6. Laminate instructional materials in plastic.
7. Mount slides in frames and between glass plates.
8. Mount transparencies using suitable cardboard frames.

9. Put film footage in cartridges and on appropriate reels.
10. Record sound on magnetic tape.
11. Record television programs on videotape.
12. Program pictorial and sound components.
13. Select, sort, splice, and edit film and tape.

This listing of operational techniques, partial though it may be, constitutes a formidable number of skills for any teacher or audiovisual specialist and his supporting technicians to possess. Yet in modern programs, these and many more increasingly sophisticated skills are essential. We therefore ask the question: What personnel in any given school system should prepare the media required by the instructional program?

Who Should Do the Work of Preparing Locally Made Media?

In their report of a national study of the local production of media by school personnel, carried out by Indiana University in cooperation with the U.S. Office of Education, Faris and Moldstad answered this question using opinions expressed in their interviews with a sampling of teachers. They summarized their findings as follows:

The classroom teachers had differing opinions concerning the best method of getting visual materials prepared. Approximately one-third preferred to prepare their own materials if given adequate time. The remaining teachers preferred that someone else do the actual production work. When asked who this production person should be, they tended to prefer the audio-visual supervisor or student assistants.

All of the television teachers interviewed expressed a preference for engaging a specialist to prepare the visual materials desired. The great majority thought that a hired artist should be employed to do the work while a very small proportion preferred an audio-visual specialist. In no instance did a television teacher express a desire to do his own production work.[1]

[1] Gene Faris and John Moldstad, assisted by Harvey Frye, *Improving the Learning Environment* (A Study of the Local Preparation by Visual Instructional Materials), carried on with the cooperation of the U.S. Office of Education pursuant to a contract under Title VII, Part B (Washington, D.C.: Superintendent of Documents, U.S. Government Printing Office, 1963), pp. 105–106.

It is very interesting to note the major deterrents as reported by the same authors, based on a questionaire and also on actual interviews with teachers as follows:

... respondents to the nation-wide survey indicated that lack of time to prepare materials was the greatest deterrent to an expanded use of local preparation facilities. The classroom teachers confirmed this finding, with thirty-four of the fifty-six teachers interviewed indicating lack of time as the greatest deterrent and lack of knowledge or ability to produce materials as the second greatest deterrent. Television teachers placed lack of time as the second greatest obstacle with lack of knowledge or ability to produce materials as the greatest.[2]

It will be up to the media program director for the school system, or the media coordinator in a single school building, to formulate workable plans in line with principles already stated in connection with needed services for teachers and pupils. Teachers ought to be brought into the planning deliberations, their roles in local production discussed, facilitating equipment purchased, space allotted, and optimum staff in light of local media-use development employed and deployed. This means that if we consider such professional processes as deciding on what needs to be produced, how and when it is to be used, how it will be designed and what media are selected, we know that teachers will have to be involved in some of the preparation work. But teachers may or may not be willing to devote hours of work to such routine technical processes as lettering, exposing, printing, duplicating, binding, and the like. Optimum balance, therefore, between professional work and the semi- or nonprofessional work, is the key to effective programs of media-preparation services. We therefore conclude that if there is no media program director in a school system to organize central media-preparation facilities, staff, and materials, and advise teachers as to professional ways of meeting their special needs for media, and no media coordinator to carry on the media-preparation work at professional levels and to organize supporting technician services, then media preparation activities will not be feasible. As we have already pointed out in Chapters 7 and 8 under school-building and centralized media services, the need for technicians, artists,

and film and tape editors is an urgent one, and both full-time and part-time adult employees, some of whom may be teachers with reduced teaching loads, as well as student crews, may have to be utilized if school instructional programs of modern, technological character are to develop and prosper.

Space Needs for Media Preparation

The difficulty in specifying the amount of space needed for media preparation lies in the number of variables that have a bearing on the operations that have to be carried out. The list would be too large to deal with here, but we ought to point out a few of the items as follows: the degree to which operations are carried out in more than one place; the number of people who will be working simultaneously in any given location or on any given process; the degree to which media prepared have to be used by teachers throughout the school system on schedule, or the quantity required; the speed with which the media must be produced; the complexity of the technological situations in which the media are to be used, as in television production, electronic learning laboratories, or in multimedia presentations; the degree to which equipment units are ready for immediate use; the number of teachers desiring to use the services (the volume of the total demand); the commitment on the part of media program directors to giving adequate services; the degree to which ready-made media become systematized; and a host of other factors as well. Therefore, the estimates of space requirements are based on a number of factors, experience with actual operations, or predicted needs as school programs become more complex and teachers become more sophisticated. Knowing then that this discussion is neither precise nor comprehensive in scope, we present in both text and illustration the nature of space requirements that are likely to have to be met by media coordinators as they embark upon programs of media preparation. We shall refer to space needed for both specific media operations and service areas such as photographic darkrooms and general storage areas. We shall turn first to a discussion of the amount of space needed to prepare 2×2 inch color slides, Polaroid slides, overhead transparencies, audio-program tapes, and videotapes.

[2] *Ibid.*, p. 103.

Figure 9-3. In this illustration we see views of a 28-foot by 23-foot room that was planned and equipped for media preparation by teachers. A full-time media specialist directs the operation of this center which has been organized to provide services to the South Park Independent School District in Beaumont, Texas. There are 70 running feet of combination cabinet and workbench for equipment and supplies around the room's perimeter. Worktables are arranged in the remaining space. As can be seen the emphasis is on visualization. The work of preparing needed audio-program tapes is done in the schools. The media center was developed with the aid of Title I funds under the Elementary and Secondary Education Act. (See also Figure 7-30.) *Courtesy South Park Independent School District, Beaumont, Texas.*

2 × 2 Inch Color Slides

When 2 × 2 inch color slides are made by teachers, or by technicians working to carry out slide-making processes at their direction, space must be available for a camera mounted on a table or bench, on which can be placed a stand with separate or attached lights. Also needed will be space for source material such as magazines, books, and periodicals, and also space for a box or case the size of a book, in which to store copying lenses, filters, adaptor rings, and attachments. In some schools, instead of laying a book or magazine flat on a bench under the camera, a camera is mounted on a tripod and the source material is placed on a shelf or tacked on a wall and photographed in an upright position. This procedure may be necessary in copying large charts and posters. The working space for two people in front of a bench would be normally the same as for the bench and camera itself. *Hence we estimate that an always-ready photographing unit would require a minimum of 15 square feet and working space for personnel would be an additional 15 square feet for a total of 30 square feet.* Not included is normal access space for moving up to and away from the equipment unit. Access space is best provided by locating such operational units in an optimum-size general service area or workroom. The estimate of 30 square feet for a copy-camera unit could then be considered in light of a need for mass production, the degree of decentralization and centralization in the school system, and the number of teachers and pupils that need to work on the equipment. There would be a minimum of one such camera for each school-building unit in any media-preparation program envisioned, and in a central-headquarters-type of organization, multiple units with full-time workers would have to be provided.

Polaroid Slides

Because the Polaroid slide process requires no darkroom operations, many schools have need for such a rapid, on-the-spot process. Where 2 × 2 inch slides in black and white are a necessity—as in television—the larger Polaroid Reflex copying units would be required. A special lens is required for making an image of an 8 × 10 inch picture or diagram on film small enough to fit a standard 2 × 2 inch mask-and-slide mount. *The total operational space requirements for such a unit would be a minimum of 36 square feet.*

Overhead Transparencies

As with other media-preparation areas, when we discuss overhead transparencies we are forced to make assumptions as to the nature of the equipment. We shall therefore limit the equipment to the following types and assume that together they constitute an operating unit: a dry-process photo-copier unit to make transparencies directly from single-sheet source materials, one similar unit for the production of transparencies from sources appearing in books or booklets, and one set of equipment components for exposing and developing diazo-coated acetate sheets for multi-color *static* or overlay transparencies. These three kinds of equipment could obviously serve three persons simultaneously, and each would require bench or table space over which or under which there could be an on-the-spot storage area for needed operational supplies. This bench space for equipment and working room would amount to 12 square feet for each of the first two components and 18 square feet for the third. The room for personnel in front of the three components would be a minimum of 42 square feet. *Therefore the total space requirement on an operating-unit basis would amount to 84 square feet as a minimum.*

Audio-Program Tapes

Magnetic tape has become the workhorse of the electronic learning laboratory, and has served as the basis of dial retrieval systems in individualization programs at all levels of instruction from first grade through college. Teachers who use audio-program tapes need not only write the scripts and add the sound effects, but they need to record them and then often have them duplicated in quantity for all the teachers of any given grade or subject. Where can these operations be performed? It is quite obvious that teachers can make their recordings in their own homes, in their classrooms, or in the ideal environment of the recording studio either in their own school centers or at media headquarters for the school system. It is necessary to point out the importance of high quality in tape recordings to facilitate distraction-free listening and responding, and high quality means, among other things, freedom from noise. The personality of the teacher must also come through or the instruction may lose its effectiveness.

With these conditions in mind it can readily be seen that space for the preparation of tapes, whether for individual use or for use by all teachers of a given grade or subject at a specified time during any given unit, will be needed for two distinct operations, namely, the recording operation and the duplicating operation. We have pointed out that recording may be carried on in a wide variety of localities. This is also true of duplicating. Tapes may be duplicated in some electronic learning laboratories by the flip of a switch at each student recording station or carrel. They may also be duplicated by a string of individual tape recorders connected together with the first one serving as a tape player, and the others simultaneously recording and feeding the next recorder in line. Also, tapes may be duplicated in quantity on sophisticated equipment especially designed for rapid, mass duplication. Therefore it is difficult to make estimates of space needs, especially in view of the special need to edit existing tapes and disk recordings for combining sequences. We can point out, however, that to make proper use of audio-program tapes, space will be needed for

1. Listening and editing, preferably with headphones.
2. Copying from disk and tape to the tape being produced.
3. Straight copying to produce multiple copies of a given prepared subject.
4. Recording by teachers.

If we assume that one or more teachers may be working at the same time in one of these multi-purpose audio stations, we can estimate that each unit should include an audio-recording and playback workroom (or what may be referred to as a workroom) as well as a suite of two to four isolated, acoustically treated sound-recording booths. Such a suite would facilitate good technician services that would expedite the work once the professional work of planning, design, and scripting had been completed.

Such recording stations should preferably be connected to a control room for technical surveillance. Estimates of space needs for the unit proposed are as follows.

1. Audio workroom space (for listening, editing and splicing tape, for combining excerpts, and for straight copying of a tape master) including control-room space *would amount to a minimum of 244 square feet.*
2. Two recording stations would measure approximately seven feet by ten feet each, and would therefore require *140 square feet. We thus see a workroom-recording combination suite requiring 384 square feet.*

Videotapes

Inasmuch as television-program implementation is the subject of the next chapter, we shall treat the need for space for videotaping in this chapter only briefly. Videotaping involves the recording of a television program (either with or without people being shown). Thus a classroom teacher may record an entire lesson, as it was taught on any given day, for subsequent use, or he may bring together a combination of visual and audio components such as slides, film, models, and narration. A studio may be required for some programs, whereas a videotaping workroom may suffice for others. Therefore we can assume that teachers can be recorded in their own classrooms or they can work in studio complexes with control rooms for technical services. Nevertheless, quality in videotapes demands an adequate environment providing proper lighting and acoustic conditions. We must assume in making space-need

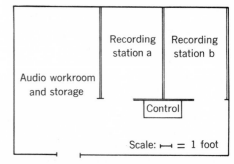

Figure 9-4. This is an author's sketch of functions for which space has to be provided. The space allotment indicated here is at a minimum.

Figure 9-5. While school-building television studio facilities may, as we point out in Chapter Twelve, become a necessity as use of the medium expands, we must point out that compact videotape recording units such as shown reduces the need for extensive studio spaces for certain kinds of instructional television programing. (*Top view*, courtesy Ampex Corporation, Redwood City, California. *Bottom view*, courtesy Continuous Progress Education Corp., Norwalk, Connecticut.)

estimates that appropriate equipment is available and it must be further understood that we are considering only minimum operational space to record a studio teacher with adequate media-support facilities. This means then that we ought to provide at least one small studio, one control room in which the videotape recorder would be operated, and in which such media as slides and film clips could be combined electronically as needed by the studio teacher. It should be emphasized, even in this superficial treatment of the subject, that adequate storage space and media-production space must be included in the plans for any desirable studio facility. We should therefore include in this special videotaping unit, which might well be a part of a large-scale television production and multi-channel transmission center, areas for listening, viewing, and editing, plus preparation space and storage. This videotaping unit in any broader scope of service would have to be vastly increased in size, but here we may consider the possibility of incorporating this estimated space as a unit in several elementary and secondary school buildings in a school system. We shall now make some hazardous estimates of what the space needs of a minimum unit would amount to.

1. A small studio accommodating one teacher as a presenter, with simple set capability and with media-support facilities, would demand *a minimum of 200 square feet.*

2. The required control room housing console, camera controls, videotaping units, multiplexer for slides and film would demand an additional *200 square feet as a minimum* for simple videotaping operations.

3. For a minimum area in which to set up a workroom for editing, viewing, and media preparation for a specific program, the requirement would be *approximately 180 square feet.*

Thus for this limited-use television-taping operation the total space need would be *580 square feet.*[3]

[3] The reader should not misunderstand the attempt in this limited-use superficial treatment of the television program-production and telecasting process, to focus on a minimum-size operating unit. No claim is made that such facilities constitute a feasible operational unit for a full-scale instructional television program in a school system. We can categorically state that had we

Multi-Purpose Working Area

In any media-preparation program, either centralized or decentralized in each school building, there is need for multi-purpose working space. We have already pointed up the process of making masters for many media-making processes, involving various lettering materials and devices, but also there are the important processes of design and layout, binding and mounting, programing, sorting, and selecting. Some processes such as editing, listening, recording, and copying have already been discussed in relation to specific processes with audio-program tapes and videotapes. But we must be sure to consider in addition to the specific space needs already identified, the urgently needed areas to serve in support of such equipment-operating stations as slides and transparencies, together with the arrangement of pictorial displays, printing and duplicating processes, and the production of motion picture film cartridges and clips. Hence we must provide space for drawing boards, flat-top tables, workbenches, a sink or two, and a small desk and chair for each of the technicians and staff artists. Presumably the leadership staff would have office space provided in other areas of the school's or school system's media-services center. In this general service area we need also to provide adequate storage for hundreds of items of bulk supplies. The necessity of providing storage areas is often lost sight of in the plans to meet other operational needs. The lack of storage areas located in good relation to the functional uses of the available space may actually be so serious as to cripple media-preparation operations. We shall therefore give this need the prominence it deserves. It has already been pointed out that along with each equipment-operating station there should be shelf or table space for the supplies that have to be used as a part of the actual operation, but the storage of bulk supplies, and the necessity of having a space to be used as an issuing center or stock room constitute another problem.

Now, as we contemplate this kind of planning, stipulated the school-system operational system in any degree of comprehensiveness of curriculum coverage, we would have estimated a carefully planned suite as is described in Chapter 10. At this point, without going into detail about the facilities, we could justify the need for a suite calling for 9,220 square feet.

GENERALIZED SPACE NEEDS FOR A MULTI-PURPOSE WORKING AREA

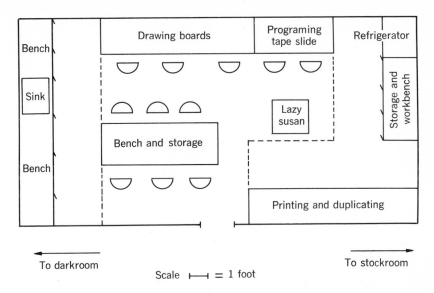

To darkroom

To stockroom

Scale ⊢——⊣ = 1 foot

STORAGE ROOM FOR MEDIA PREPARATION
SUPPLIES

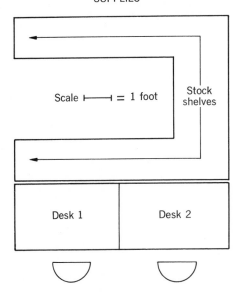

Figure 9-6. One of these author's sketches indicates minimum space allotments for working areas that are needed in connection with the use of basic media-production equipment units. The lazy susan is suggested as a means of putting needed supplies for basic processes in a conveniently accessible place. The other shows a simple diagram for arranging a stockroom for bulk supplies that would be conveniently accessible to the main working areas, but which could be kept locked.

we see again the relationship of comprehensiveness of media-preparation programs to the number of teachers desiring services, and also the degree of decentralization among the various schools. We shall again seek to depict space needs in light of predicted functions and operations and then further in the light of a number of teachers and technicians at work on the processes in question. The estimates of required

space for this general service and working area are as follows:

1. A work bench with space for three drawing boards and operational area, *36 square feet*.

2. One slide-selecting, sorting, and programing bench space and operation area, *25 square feet*.

3. Multi-purpose workbench (pedestal type

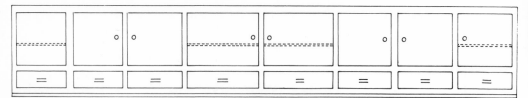

Figure 9-7. The handling and storage of supplies (aside from getting the needed money to buy them) is a major problem in designing and operating a media preparation facility. This illustration shows the kind of media cabinet-workbench unit that was built for use around the perimeter of the space described in Figure 9-3. The photograph shows the arrangement of some of the shelves in the cabinet. *Courtesy South Park Independent School District, Beaumont, Texas.*

with storage underneath) and two-side working area, *64 square feet.*

4. One binding and mounting workbench with sink, plus working and access area, with underneath and overhead shelf storage areas, *66 square feet.*

5. One working and access area for refrigerator and workbench space largely for printing and duplication processes, with storage underneath and on overhead shelves, *35 square feet.*

6. Space for locating spirit duplicator and mimeo machines, offset printing press, plus working-access area, *45 square feet.*

7. Lazy-Susan-type storage rack, five feet tall, with access area for choosing labeled supplies for prescribed processes, *15 square feet.*

8. Two desk-and-chair units for technicians, *45 square feet.*

9. One stock room with floor-to-ceiling shelving and bins for bulk supplies and film stock, *44 square feet.*

10. Space for one 2 × 2 inch slide duplicating and modifying unit (Heiland Ropronar or similar) and access area, *30 square feet.*

Summary of General Service and Working Area. Operations in the working area that were

identified in the preceding items would amount to a total of 400 square feet. See Figure 9-6 for a check-up on the generalized space arrangements to show the requirement for personnel space in relation to equipment and materials operations.

Photographic Darkroom Services

In discussing the general service area we have not yet mentioned the need for a photographic darkroom suite in relation to all of the processes we have identified. There is always the possibility that darkroom procedures will be eliminated by the use of commercial photographic laboratory services. Later when we discuss the possibility of designating which media-preparation functions may be assigned to media headquarters and to school-building media-service centers, we may feel compelled to call for a critical decision as to whether or not in school-building centers it is essential to provide complete darkroom services. However, we can point out that there are a number of significant contributions on-the-spot that darkroom operations can make. Such processes, for example, as making Kodalith negatives and positive film prints, or sharp high-contrast paper prints as parts of masters from which 2×2 inch slides are made, are vitally important. We should also mention the production of photo enlargements and the possibility of contributing to the process of illustrating school publications. Naturally all color film developing ought to be processed by pre-paid commercial mailers. But this has been emphasized before. What we need to do now is to specify some space needs based on reasonable standards and functions.

The reader should bear in mind that we are considering operational space needs instead of giving procedures for carrying out specific tasks, and also that we are not concerned with where such darkroom services should be made available. We now face the question as to who will use the darkroom. We assert that if darkroom services are to be made a part of media-service centers, either in each school-building or at school-system media centers, technicians ought to be available to carry on the required operations. We can no more recommend that a professional media coordinator or director of a media program spend his time in a darkroom developing film rolls and making paper or film prints than we can recommend his spending a whole day or more probing a sound system amplifier for a defective circuit.

We believe that in any large-scale media-preparation program at a school-system center a photographic darkroom service suite should be planned and staffed. If the decentralized program is sufficiently well developed then each school may also need a smaller darkroom service suite, yet as we have already pointed out, some significant media-production processes may be carried out by means of commercial photofinisher companies. We have in mind the duplication of sets of 2×2 inch slides, for example, for twenty or thirty science teachers in any given grade, all of which may be needed at the same time. Therefore, a whole range of possibilities opens up for photographic facilities at both central and school-building media-service headquarters. This subject will, however, be discussed in a later section. For the present, what are the possibilities for getting photographic work done?

Some Plans for Photographic Operations. The plans given here start with those most desirable operationally from the director's standpoint and end with those that provide a minimum of continuous, high-caliber service, and hence are least desirable.

Plan 1. Provide a photographic laboratory suite consisting of workroom for dryers, mounting presses, and so on, and at least two small darkrooms to facilitate simultaneous developing and printing work by more than one person at a time.

Plan 2. Provide one darkroom, approximately 9 feet by 12 feet and a small adjoining workroom consisting of a central workroom 12 feet by 20 feet (including two drawing-board tables, storage workbench, photo dryer, and workbench for picture trimming and mounting).

Plan 3. Provide a small darkroom, 9 feet by 9 feet, with an adjoining workroom of about the same size.

Plan 4. Utilize on an arranged schedule the darkroom in a new school building as close to the central media or school-building headquarters as possible.

Some Examples of Photographic and Graphic Facilities. Several methods for arranging facilities were implicit in the possible plans for action in the preceding section. Basically it is the teacher who ought to have a high priority for photographic and graphic services. Hence, media-service centers in both elementary and secondary school buildings ought to include at least one small photographic darkroom together with working areas.

In planning such photographic laboratory spaces, the following items are critical and need careful description:

1. Light-tight characteristics of the room, including proper light locks.
2. Electrical outlets near workbenches and near sinks.
3. Exhaust fans with proper light traps.
4. Regular lights and safe lighting.
5. Running hot and cold water, and sometimes sinks ought to have double-mixing valves and double drains.
6. Equipment such as trays, tanks, thermometers, timer clocks, enlargers, printers, light table, dryer, mounting press, sinks, and storage cabinets need to be selected and specified by make and size.

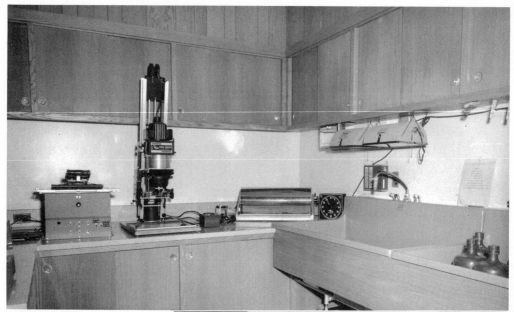

Figure 9-8. Regardless of size, arrangement of darkroom equipment must be planned with care for the kinds of photo-processing work identified. When should several small darkrooms be provided instead of one of large size? Why is it essential to incorporate in plans for doing photographic processing, an adjoining workroom? The pictures in this illustration show parts of two darkrooms, and an adjoining workroom for one of them. Note the multiple use of the workroom area for taping and photo copying. (*Top picture*, courtesy Thornton Township High School and Junior College, Harvey, Illinois. *Remaining photographs*, courtesy Fremont Union High School District, Sunnyvale, California.)

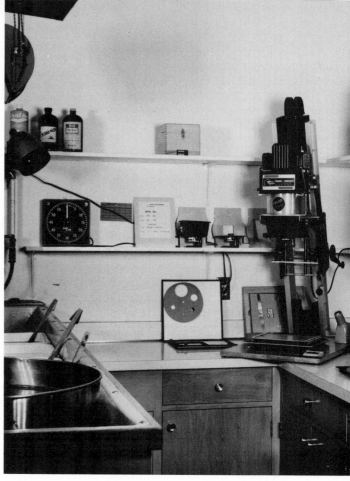

Even though the planner of the photographic suite may have the good advice of an architect, he should be forewarned that:

1. Two small darkrooms rather than one large one are needed if developing and printing processes need to be carried on by more than one person simultaneously.

2. Large prints demand more handling and sink space.

3. Ventilation is a necessary feature.

4. Stainless-steel sinks are recommended.

5. Formica covering for dry benches is serviceable, but maple wood with a coating of wax is preferred by some.

6. Floor coverings of tile with surfaces that are impervious to moisture are desirable.

7. A space-saving type of light lock ought to be designed and incorporated as an essential. See Figure 9-9.

Space Requirements. It is conceivable that a school system would have demands for a large volume of photographic developing and printing with all the necessary related work of drying, trimming, mounting, and labeling, for various instructional uses. Hence the space requirements estimated here may have to be considered as totally inadequate for such an operation. Rather,

we are considering here a suite that may be considered as a minimum operational unit to be expanded as the volume of demand increases. In any event we may say that providing darkroom space is not enough. Additional space is generally needed as a working area for photographic darkroom services. We have already described the need for space in which to make masters, mount, bind and select, sort, and label, and a part of this general service area could be located in such a position as to be handily used by darkroom technicians. Thus if we already have a general service area of adequate size for media-preparation work, we need not provide a completely separate working area for the darkroom. Yet for the purpose of this estimate, we must include the workroom in order to give the need for daylight working area the emphasis it deserves. We therefore estimate the space requirements to be as follows:

1. One darkroom of 9 feet by 12 feet minimum.

2. An additional working space also of 9 feet by 12 feet for *a total of 216 square feet.*

This recommendation is essentially the same as described in *Plan 2* in the preceding discussion, and this plan may be considered as the

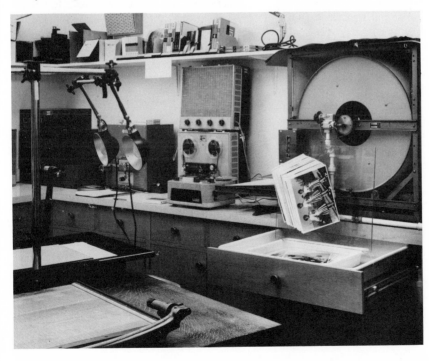

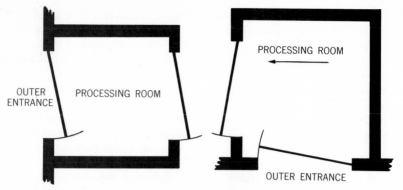

Figure 9-9. An appropriate light lock is a vital part of every photographic darkroom. In addition to those shown, planners should consider revolving-door and labyrinth-type entrances, especially when multiple-room suites are required. (*Courtesy Eastman Kodak Company, Rochester.*)

minimum for incorporation in plans for media services in every school building. We of course see this minimum facility as an integral part of a media-service center, and not as a science club suite to be used by groups. When such use is envisioned, greatly expanded and multiple-use spaces will be required.

Motion Pictures

As we consider space needs for the school and school-system production of films, both 8 mm and 16 mm—possibly employing both magnetic and optical sound tracks, depending on the intended usage—it is easy to visualize the completely equipped and spacious commercial film production studios for television and the movies, and to make some startling though expected comparisons with the cubbyhole spaces used by some schools. It would seem obvious that schools need not go into the kind of film-production operations envisioned in comprehensive, large-scale film making. Yet we must face the need for making film clips and film cartridges for a host of teaching situations from special films for chemistry laboratory introductions to automated self-instruction systems where media play direct teaching roles. We should also recognize the fact that in most audiovisual media centers there are spaces such as television studios, audio-program recording studios, film editing and inspection stations, equipment storage, vaults for storing films, photo-service dark-rooms, and general service areas, all of which may contribute space for the many processes of

film making. Although this situation makes it difficult to state what the minimum space requirements are, we shall attempt to itemize some of the operational needs for space even though such space may be available in other sections of a media-service center. One more fact we should note before estimates are given, namely, that according to predicted school needs, some of the footage needed will be shot in outdoor places, possibly at the bank of a poluted river, in a slum area, or at a town meeting. Studio sets will also be needed, and animation stations as well, but space for shooting will be shared with the world outside the school.

Specific Space Needs in Relation to Operations. The space-need operations listed include basic indoor filming and related activities, based on the assumption that processing, printing, and sounding are done by commercial laboratories. Estimates are as follows:

1. Indoor filming activity under lights, *400 square feet.*
2. General service and working area for lettering, mounting, and chartwork; for storage of filming supplies; and for storage of cameras, accessories, and lighting equipment, *400 square feet.*
3. Space for the preparation of animation sequences, isolated from other operations to permit maximum exposure control, *40 square feet.*
4. Viewing of workprint footage, *40 square feet.*
5. Editing, splicing, and conforming footage,

and for packaging footage for laboratory shipments, *54 square feet.*

Summary of Space Needs for the Production of Motion Pictures. Totaling up the operational spaces specified we see that such a minimum-sized facility as seems reasonable for predicted school-system needs would be likely to amount to *978 square feet.* We point out once more that the specified operational spaces are often combinable creatively in carefully laid plans.

Grand Total of the Space-Need Estimates for Media Preparation

As soon as we total up the various estimates that we have made, the reader is likely to observe that such needs as we have indicated seem unreasonably large and generally unattainable. This is of course not true. If we point to industrial plants, we may assert that the only industrial plants that are operating under crowded and inadequate space limitations are those that will soon be going out of business. This observation naturally applies to the entire media-service areas in each school, not just for media-preparation processes. Just what is the total of our estimates? We add up the specific space-requirements as follows to answer the question:

1. 2 × 2 inch color slides (a single operating unit), *30 square feet.*
2. Polaroid slides (a single operating unit), *36 square feet.*
3. Overhead transparencies (a three-process unit), *84 square feet.*
4. Audio-program tapes, *384 square feet.*
5. Videotapes, *580 square feet.*
6. Multi-purpose working area, *400 square feet.*
7. Photographic darkroom services, *216 square feet.*
8. Production of motion pictures, *978 square feet.*

Total   *2,708 square feet.*

The reader may now review the space need for a school-building media-preparation area given in Chapter 7, and conclude that the estimate of 700 square feet indicated there as a minimum is woefully inadequate. We should point out, however, that the estimate given was for what is referred to as basic needs, not inclusive of additional fixed and special-purpose facilities.

Possible Use of the Space Estimates. Naturally all of the space estimates made are relative to special and local needs. If a school system has inaugurated a program of rear-screen multimedia presentations as a part of firm plans for using instructional systems, then media-preparation facilities for specified types of media preparation must be provided on a priority basis. If a school has a dial-retrieval television or an audio-program tape system, then facilities, staff, and budget considerations for audio programs and videotape preparation will be necessary. Moreover, any one of the estimates may have to be increased radically, and other space estimates in the list decreased by a factor that is arrived at by balancing the many demands. For example, it may be realistic and necessary to increase single-station estimates by a factor of three or more depending on the number of personnel (teachers, teacher aides, pupils, and graphic technicians) to use them during a given school day. If a comprehensive media-preparation program is to be provided, the total space estimate suggested should be considered as a minimum requirement for the district media center with additional media facilities required in each school-building service area.

Combining Functions to Reduce Space-Need Estimates. Before we discuss the possible combination of operational spaces for multi-purpose uses, we should point out that the estimate for space to prepare videotapes should not be included because such a suite would naturally be a part of a larger television program-production complex; however, we have already stated the assumptions underlying the need for videotapes as perhaps separate from television programing in the usual sense. Yet, if television activities in any given school system are comprehensive in nature, it may well be the headquarters for the special video-taping processes as well as the general program-producing capability. We can also point out that the motion picture production space, stated as a minimum of 978 square feet—which is less space than is usually allotted to a fairly large classroom in an elementary school—could be in part combined with multi-purpose working areas, with film splicing and packaging areas,

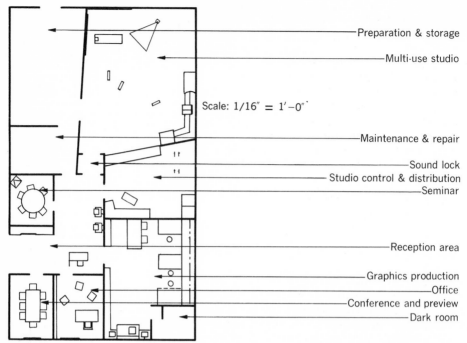

Scale: $1/16'' = 1'-0''$

Preparation & storage

Multi-use studio

Maintenance & repair

Sound lock

Studio control & distribution

Seminar

Reception area

Graphics production

Office

Conference and preview

Dark room

Figure 9-10. Note the multi-use studio in this sketch from the book by Green, *Educational Facilities with New Media,* published by DAVI of the NEA in 1966, usable for television, audio, and motion picture production. Note also that this sketch does not include the other spaces that we have stressed in connection with the school's broad media distribution and use program. It is likely that some large school plants in the future will include such a media-preparation facility; it is possible that such a comprehensive facility as this sketch depicts will be more applicable, for the time being, to school district organization. (*Courtesy Center for Architectural Research, R.P.I., Troy, New York.*)

with viewing and listening areas, with office space areas, and with television studios, provided the spaces are already available and can be spared for sufficient time to accomplish the work that needs to be done within the specified time limitations. Thus it may be feasible to increase certain operational spaces to accommodate additional functions, or to provide additional conveniently accessible equipment-storage space, so that equipment units needed for a given operation may be assembled and placed on available workbenches and then dismantled and put away in designated places for the next assignment. We must not lose sight of a condition already stated, namely, the possibility of including the entire media-production facility in the plans for a large, school-system television facility, where we have already suggested that the preparation area should be as large as 2,000 square feet, thus serving general as well as specific needs. The problem of combining functional spaces into workable arrangements

is not an easy matter. Each case is unique and no pat answer is available, but planners may well consider the following guidelines:

1. When full-time technical personnel are employed, fewer operational spaces will be required. This means that part-time personnel, such as teachers and students, will not have to be working simultaneously at a greater number of stations. And additionally, various equipment units will not have to go unused for many hours during a given school day. That is, each available equipment station or working area will be used more efficiently.

2. When teachers, teacher aides, pupils, and part-time technicians must use equipment units and working spaces during the school day, the greater will be the number of equipment units and working spaces that will have to be provided, and the more equipment-operating stations maintained in a state of readiness.

3. The fewer the equipment stations that are

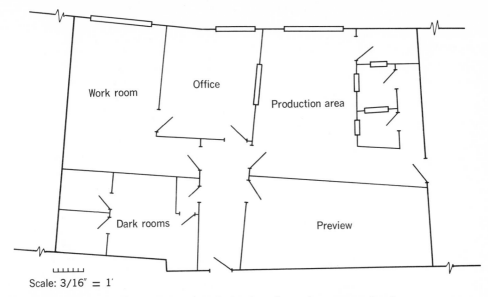

Scale: 3/16″ = 1′

Figure 9-11. This is the floor plan of the audiovisual media service center at South Junior High School, Great Neck, New York. Note the allocation of space to the media preparation program. See also Figures 7-2, 7-28, and 7-30. (*Courtesy Public Schools, Great Neck, New York.*)

in a state of readiness, the greater will be the waste in productive capability on the part of technicians and teaching personnel, and the less the desire on the part of teachers to participate or use the services.

4. The fewer the ready-to-use equipment stations available in media-preparation suites the greater will be the need for storage areas.

5. When work spaces assigned for specific functions are available only by appointment, and when media-preparation projects in process cannot be left in a secured state conveniently for later resumption, the less the chances are that vital needs will be fulfilled.

Organization of District-Wide Media-Preparation Services

As we look at the problem of organizing media-preparation activities on a district-wide basis, we need to focus attention on the many different kinds of services that media-preparation centers are frequently called upon to give. The following list is not comprehensive, but is presented in rather broad outline to exemplify the possibilities.

1. Produce study print pictures in sets for classroom distribution, such as local pictures of historic sites and manufacturing processes.

2. Produce slides and filmstrips on topics needed for school use but unavailable for purchase, such as materials for social studies, language arts, business skills with local adaptations, and materials for science-laboratory skills, including emphasis on media in self-instruction systems.

3. Make motion pictures of special processes for classroom teaching purposes such as are needed for musical processes and techniques, and athletic-skill development, including film sequences and cartridges for self-instruction processes.

4. Produce pictorial materials for student diagnosis and remedial work, such as materials needed for improving reading and speech skills.

5. Produce pictorial and graphic material for more effective communication at public-relations meetings, and also programs for radio and television.

6. Handle picture-mounting processes for all pictorial materials acquired for distribution.

7. Produce study displays, and exhibit material such as dioramas.

8. Make up illustrations for school publications, including improvement in design of

mimeo bulletins as well as of formal printed publications for wider circulation.

9. Offer advisory and consultative services to school media coordinators, to school-club groups, and to teachers for their own photographic, graphic, and self-instruction projects.

10. Microfilm important records.

11. Provide such photocopying services as are needed for the school's record-keeping system.

12. Provide photocopier services to include paper and reflex spirit masters for instructional worksheet applications.

13. Prepare overhead transparencies.

14. Make photographic plates for photo-offset printing processes.

15. Make mimeo stencils and provide duplication services.

16. Plan and produce audio-program tapes for electronic learning laboratories at all levels of instruction.

17. Duplicate audio-program tapes in quantity.

18. Plan and produce videotapes for transmission to all schools via closed-circuit facilities for both large-group applications and individual uses in electronic carrel situations.

19. Mass produce printed labels for media items to be distributed to all schools.

20. Provide photographic darkroom services to meet school-building instructional needs.

Location of Media-Preparation Facilities

Where should the services we have mentioned be performed? In the preceding section the various spaces were described in relation to specific media that teachers need, but we must be quick to recognize that there are also what we may refer to as administrative needs, and a glance at the foregoing list will reveal such items. The issue is, to what degree should media-preparation services be centralized? To what degree should they be carried on in school-building media-service centers? We turn to a discussion of this cluster of problems, with attention devoted first to the centralization pattern of organization.

Organizing Media-Preparation Activities at Headquarters. Since media-preparation programs are common, although differing widely

as to scope and volume of service, a large number of administrators and media people have come to grips with the problems of where to locate facilities and how to get the work of media-preparation accomplished. One of the patterns of organization for getting this work done is to locate the facilities at the district-wide media-services center. The main advantage of this placement falls to the district office staff, since over-all district problems are more easily given highest priority. Under this arrangement, services for specific instructional needs for specific teachers and specific schools may not be as easily or speedily met. In other words, it appears that when media-preparation services are set up in central media headquarters it is easier to control the processes that get priority, and also those that do get highest priority are likely to be the ones that meet general needs that may or may not be purely instructional in nature. The following examples will make this clear.

1. General services like photostatting and microfilming school records, making up illustrations for school publications, catalogs, and curriculum guides, making photographic plates for photo-offset printing processes, producing media for public-relations meetings, making sets of slides for self-instruction processes on a system-wide supply basis, and handling production of study-prints for a given curriculum topic for distribution to all schools are all district-wide media services that may choke off many other vital needs for specific uses.

2. When a citywide school system has inaugurated a special program such as dial-retrieval television, media-production programs may be so controlled as to give complete staff and financial support to one kind of medium to the exclusion of others.

3. The citywide center is likely to be less conveniently accessible to teachers who need to discuss specifications for media sequences, therefore the headquarters program is likely to function on a longer time-lag basis between request date and fulfillment date, or not function at all in relation to specific teacher requests.

Need for Central Media-Production Services. The generalized listing of common media-production services indicates many activities that are best carried on by centralized facilities, staff, and responsibilities. We can identify such specific operations: (1) supplying photographic darkroom services in connection with school-system and school-building instructional needs; (2) providing an advisory and consultative service to school-building media coordinators; (3) mass producing media items in sequence for all schools; (4) systematically producing videotapes to meet over-all curriculum plans; (5) providing mass duplication of audio-program tapes for electronic learning laboratories in all subjects where the use of this medium has been systematized and scheduled firmly as in individualization programs; (6) producing media for administrators' presentations; (7) handling the work of printing school publications, including preparation of illustrative materials. There are also many other uses, some of which have been indicated at the beginning of this section. All of these generally applicable services are vital, and it would appear that many of them cannot be feasibly handled by school-building media-preparation centers. It seems quite obvious then that in the face of burgeoning technology, a centralized media-production facility is inescapable. The problem in this case will be to supply the staff and facilities needed to expand services to the point where specific teacher needs are being met in addition to those district-wide services that are generally available.

Organizing Media-Preparation Activities in Each School Building. There are many who insist that the only way to get specially prepared media items for pinpointed uses in each school building is to organize media-preparation services on the spot. Then and only then will teachers as individuals get the fast service needed. Teachers say, "We need to be able to make our own media, and if the necessary supplies are at hand we can make them as soon as we can design them in response to a specific need." In the preceding section space needs were discussed in light of known operations and in this connection we must note that teachers may have to have convenient arrangements under which to work for short periods of nonteaching or nonscheduled time. Student crews and even full-time technicians and clerks, as teacher aides, may never get what they need if they have to submit requests through media coordinators to media headquarters. This is especially true in extensive metropolitan areas. It appears simply impossible to consider 500

school-building staffs calling for specific media-preparation services on a day-to-day or week-to-week basis. Yet it also seems next to impossible to set up 500 media-preparation suites staffed with technicians and stocked with supplies, but it may not be impossible after all to develop arrangements where most of the needs can be met. We ought to consider the nature of the school-building media-preparation service needs. Teachers, as we have already pointed out, want others (students, the media specialist, and coordinator) to make their slides and transparencies, and one can hardly blame them, but we also know that many teachers will carry out their own media-making operations if the environment is conducive. Therefore, we have the responsibility to provide a climate in which teachers can and will participate at an optimum level in this necessary instructional activity. On-the-spot facilities and assistance constitute one route to such desirable participation.

Some Important School-Building Media-Making Operations by and for Teachers. Earlier we considered media-preparation services and related them to centrally operated facilities. Now we consider several of those services that seem to be best carried out at the school-building level. Some of these are as follows:

1. Make transparencies according to day-to-day or week-to-week needs, such as would be made by teachers themselves, or student helpers or technicians, or by teachers' aides in team-teaching situations.

2. Design, make masters, and run off instructional sheets using reflex spirit masters, or other duplicating stencil or master processes

3. Plan and prepare 2 × 2 inch slide sequences for visual presentations using current events, maps, and pictorials.

4. Use lettering devices to make posters, captions, display titles, as parts of student research and creative project work.

5. Plan and produce audio-program tapes for electronic laboratories, and for classroom multi-group activities.

6. Plan and produce videotapes for school-building closed-circuit television transmission, using inexpensive equipment for special self-evaluational purposes, or more sophisticated taping equipment for classroom or school-building studio-recording situations.

7. Plan and make sketches, diagrams, mounted pictures for use with classroom television-display (or image-magnification) systems.

8. Mount pictures and caption materials for classroom displays.

9. Produce audio and visual materials to meet specific teaching needs both for large- and small-group use for exchange with other teachers of similar grade and subject interest, such as bulletin board displays, audio-program tapes, slide sets, transparencies, and instructional sheets.

10. Use motion picture cameras for making film clips and cartridges.

Need for School-Building Media Preparation Services. As team teaching techniques develop, and as electronic learning laboratories and other technologically supported teaching methods become a firm part of the daily teaching process, we shall have to face up to the need for media-making facilities, staff and supplies. We have already pointed out the effect of newer roles of audiovisual media on the urgent need for special-purpose materials which take on new significance when teachers communicate with large groups of students. Nor do students go into carrels today just to read a book, but also to listen to audio-program tapes, or to study a videotape, or to be programed through a set of slides that teaches them how to carry out basic skills. Without school-building facilities, many of the week-to-week instructional needs for media will not be met. As we have said before, the availability of the right climate, close at hand, means that teachers can learn new teaching methods and try their fledgling wings until a new and desirable security develops.

Optimum Decentralization and Centralization. If we blend the ingredient operational processes of the foregoing centralized and decentralized patterns of organization we have the answer to our problems for making media for modern teaching needs. It is obvious that most centralized media-making programs cater to general school-system needs, or generally get lost in them because of lack of financial support. It is equally understandable how school-building media-making facilities and programs cater in concentrated fashion to week-to-week teaching needs of the school's professional staff. When these basic patterns are blended in optimum balance, school-system media centers concentrate on district needs and on the needs that can be met for all schools according to carefully laid plans, and leave to schools, after facilitating the development of adequate services, the operation of programs designed to help teachers carry out their various instructional tasks. Such localized programs may therefore put proper emphasis on both teachers and their presentations and on pupil needs as well, to make sure that the carrels and machine rooms are properly supplied. How best to separate the services that are to be given will depend on the status of local technological development, on budgetary support, and on the innovative needs of a given school system. Priorities will have to be established in the light of valid plans, with additions of new services being made year by year as the means become available. Although we shall not rule out the possibility in our own deliberations of a strong and comprehensive, centralized, media-making center, we shall now look toward an optimum balance between the assignment of media-preparation functions to media headquarters and to school building media-service centers. The media program director has a difficult job on his hands to set up this balance, and an even more difficult task to obtain financial support to implement his plans. When this has been accomplished, he may move by appropriate stages toward the acquisition of the needed equipment and staff, and undertake the in service education programs that will speed teachers on their way to desirable change.

Acquisition of Needed Equipment for Media Preparation

Since the purchase of equipment units goes hand-in-hand with local instructional needs and available operational spaces, we need not set up at this point a massive listing of desirable equipment and supplies. Instead we shall stick to some high-priority items in line with generally needed media for school uses, concentrating attention on visualization processes rather than on audio-program and videotape preparation. Audio-program production, which is generally related to single-medium audio presentations, is often tied to visualization processes through tape cartridges or by means of tape-slide programed sequences. In Chapter 10, videotape processes and needs will be added since that chapter will deal with implementation of television-program services.

The Nature of Equipment Needs for Media-Preparation Services. In their national survey report, published in 1963, Faris and Moldstad[4] reported that, "The most frequently produced visual instructional materials for classroom or television use were 2 × 2 slides, photographs, graphic materials, mounted pictures and overhead transparencies." As a part of this survey, the authors developed a listing of categories and items indicating the nature of equipment and supplies that merits restatement here to focus attention on some of the basic media-preparation operations being carried on by schools.

No listing for purposes of our discussion, least of all an index of the technological state of the art, can be formulated that would state with any degree of certainty the relative merits or priorities for acquisition by schools and school-system centers for their proposed media-making services. The list just quoted is no exception. We have already pointed out that darkroom services may be neither necessary nor feasible, since so many desirable processes can be carried out without on-the-spot film developing and printing. Also in the quoted list, several of the processes and materials may be eliminated or substituted in favor of local production needs. For example, small offset printing presses, and such operations as silk-screen and multilith reproduction may be or possibly ought to be handled centrally. Under photography processes, schools may wish to add a slide duplicating unit, and eliminate all except 35 mm, Polaroid, and the 16 mm motion picture cameras.

One of the values of the list is its categorization of processes, for any school system or school-building media-making center will inescapably be engaged with some of the processes mentioned under each of the categories. Another important point to keep in mind while studying the list is to treat each equipment item or process as a category for listing specific items of supplies that would have to be procured and kept in stock to carry on the processes. For example, what kinds of supplies would be needed for making use of the dry mounting press, the 35 mm camera, or for reproducing transparencies by the reflex process?

Since we are focusing attention on instructional needs rather than on how the functions will be assigned to either (or both) central or decentralized media-making service centers, we ought to make a straight equipment list without including at this time any reference to supplies or the media to be made. With the list, we have provided a cost estimate—with the knowledge that prices may vary greatly. The following list is an arbitrary one, excluding darkroom equipment entirely, but will nonetheless be helpful, especially in the light of everyday instructional needs of teachers.

Mounting	Coloring
Dry Mounting Press	Air Brush
Laminating Equipment	Commercial Adhesive
Mounting Cloth (Muslin	Materials
or Chartex)	Plastic Inks
Materials for Framing	Other Inks
with Tape	Slide Crayons
Mounting for 3-D	Tempera
Materials	Water Colors

Lettering	Photography
Mechanical Lettering	35 mm Camera
Devices	4 × 5 Camera
Cut-Out Letters	Enlarger
Felt-Point Pen	Polaroid
Rubber Stamp	Darkroom
Primary Typewriter	Copy Equipment
Stencil	16 mm Camera
Paste-Up Letters	$2\frac{1}{4}$–$2\frac{1}{4}$ Camera
Embossograph	Filmstrip Camera

Reproduction

Reflex Copy
Other Copy Processes
Mimeograph
Ditto
Diazo
Silk Screen
Multilith
Line-O-Scribe
Xerox[5]

[4] Faris and Moldstad, *op. cit.*, p. 30.
[5] *Ibid.*, p. 35.

Equipment Items	Cost Estimate[6]
1. 35 mm Single Lens Reflex Camera, plus adapter rings and close-up lenses, direct-reading light meter, blue filter, suitable copy stand with lights.	$280
2. Polaroid Industrial View Camera, plus extra lens for 2×2 inch slide images, copy stand and lights.	800
3. Polaroid (Regular Copymaker) Camera, plus stand, lights, and close-up lenses ($3\frac{1}{4} \times 4$ inch slides).	250
4. Slide Duplicating Unit (such as Heiland Repronar) and accessories.	360
5. Reflex Photo-Copier, single sheet unit.	400
6. Reflex Photo-Copier, book copier unit.	380
7. Diazo-Coated Film Transparency-Making Equipment (one operating system complete).	300
8. Mimeograph Duplicating Equipment Unit (electrically operated) and stand.	450
9. Spirit Master Duplicating Unit (electrically operated) and stand.	370
10. Primary Typewriter, manual.	250
11. Dry-Mount Press (24-inch min. model, open on three sides).	300
12. 16 mm Motion Picture Camera and three-lens turret, plus suitable tripod.	750
13. Two Paper Cutters, one 24 inch, the other 15 inch. Two units.	80
14. One Set of Lights (consisting of five reflector type flood lights each on a tripod).	100
Total	$5,070

In the foregoing listing we have omitted audio-program and television-program taping equipment. Neither have we indicated items such as special lettering pens. These we shall refer to later under supplies. The equipment units just listed seem to be the most necessary items for a media-making center in each school building.

[6] Adjust cost estimates for price increases and local conditions.

Reference to the space-requirement sections will reveal an estimate of how much space will be needed for these items.

General Equipment Selection Problems. It can readily be seen how the purchase of equipment has to be specified in light of special needs and operations. Hence in some instances multiple units have to be purchased and installed, while in other situations but one operational unit of a kind such as a 35 mm camera and stand needs to be specified. Centralization and decentralization policies will strongly influence equipment-selection decisions. It seems almost certain that the equipment needs at media program headquarters will include at least one each of the basic items of equipment to meet the needs of media leadership personnel and for curriculum and administrative staff members as well. It is doubtful that smaller media-producing school-building centers would or should be called on to divert their specific-need programs to handle additional services for headquarters. Media program directors will doubtlessly have to develop printing press and sophisticated illustration-producing units, very possibly also sophisticated and comprehensive darkroom and motion picture production services. Hence we see the need for a wide variety of equipment units, and the additional vexing problem of finding enough space in which to arrange and operate them.

Acquisition of Supplies Needed for Media Preparation

The Nature of the Media-Making-Supplies Problem. In preceding paragraphs we have discussed the need for equipment units and space in which to operate them, but we have barely mentioned the most burdensome problem of all. This is the problem of providing the raw stock items out of which media materials are fashioned. Providing needed raw materials is a burdensome problem for it is complex, continuous, and very expensive. Even when a good system has been worked out for purchase, there is the ever-present problem of inventory and safeguarding against theft and waste. It is not generally realized by teachers, principals, and other administrators, how expensive high-volume use of transparency film, photographic film and even assorted papers is. It is relatively easy to locate a unit of equipment on a table in

Figure 9-12. In these pictures we note the variety of equipment units that are in use in various media-preparation centers. Some of the spaces in which teachers and technicians work are small, others are large. Equipment units as in the top picture may be crowded into limited bench space only when worktables are near. We left the waste basket in the picture for a good reason. Equipment units should be increased in number when teachers instead of technicians are going to do the work. Copying-camera arrangements depend on the purposes envisaged and the skill of people who are to use them. Shown in this illustration is an expensive lighting fixture. There is a wide range of desirable copying cameras, including 35 mm and the Polaroid models. See also Figures 1-9 and 4-10. (*Courtesy Fremont Union High School District, Sunnyvale, California.*)

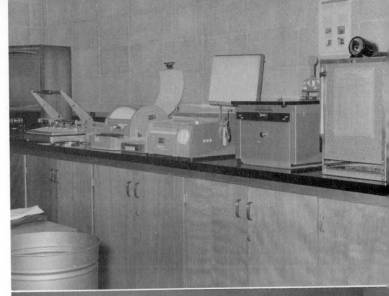

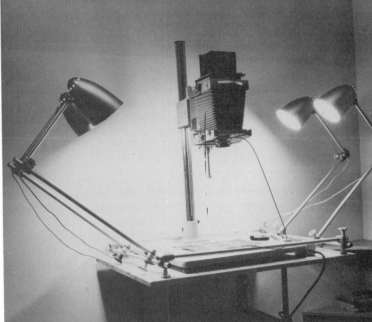

Figure 9-13. Illustrations have emphasized the acquisition of equipment for graphic media, but other kinds of equipment are urgently needed in the entire media-making spectrum. Audio-program and videotape needs are well known. In this picture a combination clerk-technician is participating in the preparation of a tape. Refer also to Figures 8-8, 9-5, 7-9, and to Chapter 10. (*Courtesy Fremont Union High School District, Sunnyvale, California.*)

a production area and schedule its use, but to supply the unit with raw stock from a bulk-supply stockroom, or order weekly supplies from a central warehouse using correct identification codes, and to keep waste to a minimum, are operations that need to be worked out with care. Media program directors and school-building media coordinators should be aware of the cost relationship that frequently exists between a given equipment unit and the supplies to keep it operating. Using reasonably high-quality equipment, such as a $140 (low bid quote) single-lens reflex camera solely for 2 × 2 inch slides, and a $400 reflex photocopier (dry process), used solely for transparencies as examples, we can predict that each year the cost for but one kind of basic supply item for each equipment unit will equal or exceed the original cost of the equipment.

Identification of Needed Supply Items. Media program directors for school systems are faced with the job of identifying raw materials for making special media for distribution to each of the school-building producing centers as soon as they are organized for service. If his own center is organized to produce media as

needed for all teachers, the director must identify items and stock them in appropriate quantities at headquarters or in a central school-system warehouse. If school-building media coordinators are themselves in charge of ordering their supplies, using budgeted allotments for the purpose, then they must identify those items that are essential for meeting the basic needs of the teachers under their guidance. The mistake is sometimes made of identifying a wide range of items to make possible variations in procedure, many different color combinations, many styles and sizes of letters, many sizes, colors, and patterns of pressure-sensitive tapes, for making masters and flats as are essential for transparencies and 2 × 2 inch slides. The point is that it is better to maintain an adequate, continuous stock of a smaller number of basic items, than to try to have on hand great variety but be out of stock at critical times. Another example would be stocking color film and processing mailers for making 2 × 2 inch slides. It would be far better to stock a generally serviceable 20-exposure roll of film and an equal quantity of prepaid processing mailers than to stock many different kinds of film for color slides. Also, it may be unwise to stock for general use black and white 35 mm film for the 2 × 2 inch slide process, since in this case darkroom services to make negatives first will be a necessity. When the immensity of the list of supply items is recognized, it will become obvious that restrictions of one kind or another may become necessary in light of basic operational needs at both citywide media headquarters and at school-building media-preparation centers. We now turn to some lists of supplies related to basic operations; however, the reader should not think of this listing as generally applicable to all school situations. Furthermore, new items will have to be added and other items substituted from time to time. Also, the reader should recognize that not all of the specifications and information needed for reordering are included. The reader may note that since the present listings are based on actual inventory cards, a categorization process is displayed that may not fit other situations.[7]

[7] The listing being shown was developed in part by the writer. It reflects the objectives of the media-preparation service being given, and of course reveals certain limitations. The categorization shows an attempt to organize the inventory functionally, hence while the list is by no means complete, there are enough excerpts to show relationships to basic processes being carried out.

Dry Mounting Process
1. Tissue, Dry Mounting MT-5, 8″ × 10″
2. Tissue, Dry Mounting MT-5, 11″ × 14″
3. Cloth, Dry Mounting (Chartex), White 11″ × 14″
4. Cloth, Dry Mounting (Chartex), White 36″ × 50′ Roll
5. Laminating Film, Seal-Lamin, 11″ × 200′ Roll
6. Laminating Film, Seal-Lamin, 20″ × 200′ Roll

Thermo-Fax Process
1. Transparency Film, Black Line Positive, Type 127 (General Purpose)
2. Transparency Film, Black Line on Blue, Type 129 (Special Stock)
3. Transparency Film, Blue, Red, and Green, Type 888
4. Transparency Film for Book Copier, Type 628
5. Thermo-Fax Copy Paper, Type 15
6. Thermo-Fax Book Copier, Copy Paper, Types 607 and 627
7. Thermo-Fax Color-Lift Film, Type 702

Paper Stock
1. Paper, Construction, Bull's Eye:
   #1 Brown, #4 Black, #52 Light Blue, #19 Red, #50 Blue, #30 Yellow, #20 Orange, #28 Green, #100 White, #21 Violet
2. Paper, Cross Section, Quadrille, $\frac{1}{4}$-inch Ruled, #411, White
3. Paper, Mechanical Drawing, Detail, Extra Fine Grade, 18″ × 24″, White
4. Paper, Newsprint Sheets, White, 18″ × 24″, Pads
5. Paper, Kraft, 24″ Roll, Brown
6. Paper, Illustration, Torchon Board, #831 White, 22″ × 28″
7. Paper, Railroad Board, 6-Ply, 22″ × 28″:
   #1978 Green, #1979 Buff, #1980 Yellow, #1982 Red, #1983 Blue, #1985 Black, #1976 White
8. Paper, Mounting Board, Melton, 12-Ply, 22″ × 28″: #1260 White, #1213 Red, #1215 Chocolate, #1224 Dark Gray, #1239 Green, #1261 Cream

Diazo-Coated Film Transparency Process
1. Paper, Tecnivellum, 8$\frac{1}{2}$″ × 11″ Pre-Punched, TV
2. Paper, Texpaque, 214XXG, 8$\frac{1}{2}$″ × 11″ Pre-Punched

3. Paper, Texray, 214-T, 8$\frac{1}{2}$″ × 11″ Pre-Punched
4. Cardboard Mounts for Transparencies, Holson Co. Model, Punched to Fit Tecnifax System (7$\frac{1}{2}$″ × 10″ Aperture)
5. Cardboard Mounts for Transparencies, Tecnifax Co. Model, Type 267, Pre-Punched (For Special-Purpose Usage)
6. Clear Acetate Sheets, 8$\frac{1}{2}$″ × 11″ (Min. order 1000)
7. Stapler, Tecnistapler #84641 (Or Bostitch P-6-8)
8. Staples (Box of 5000) Bostitch #STH 5019-$\frac{1}{4}$″ or Tecnifax #84502
9. Transparency Mounting Hinges, Techinge, #84501 Silver Foil
10. Tracks, Projectual, Plastic for Sliding Masks, Technifax #84532
11. Diazo-Coated Film Sheets, 8$\frac{1}{2}$″ × 11″ Pre-Punched, Pkg. of 25:
    RF Reversing, KX Superfoil, KBKXXD Dense Black, KBKD Dense Black, KBKP Black on Pink, KBKYL Black on Yellow, KCY Blue Cyan, KMG Magenta, KGN Green, KOR Orange, KYL Yellow, KBL Blue, KBR Brown, KRD Red, KBK Black, KVT Violet
12. Gridmaster Kit, Tecnifax #88202

Tapes (Pressure Sensitive for Graphics)
1. Masking Tape, Tan $\frac{1}{2}$″ × 60 yd. Roll
2. Masking Tape, Tan, 1″ × 60 yd. Roll
3. Tape, Matte, Non-Bleeding 3M #810, $\frac{1}{2}$″ × 1296″ Roll
4. Tape, Cloth (Fastape or Mystic Binding Tape), 1$\frac{1}{2}$″ × 15 yd. roll:
   #4211 Black, #4351 Dark Red, #4271 Dark Blue
5. Tape, Labeling, AC 23 #5201-2, Dymo Black (to fit Dymo Labeler), $\frac{3}{8}$″ wide Roll
   Same: Dymo Red
6. Tape, Chart-Pac, Matte, #1-1, Black, 1″ × 324″
7. Tape, Chart-Pac, $\frac{1}{2}$″ × 324″, Transparent Colors: TC5002 Red, TC5003 Blue, TC5004 Green
8. Tape, Chart-Pac, $\frac{1}{2}$″ × 324″, Matte, Solid Colors:
   #5001M Black, #5005M Orange, #5006M Purple, #5010M White, #5011M Yellow, #5012M Silver, #5014M Brown, #5025M Black on White, #5025M Brown on White, #5025M Blue on White
9. Tape, Chart-Pac, $\frac{1}{4}$″ × 324″, Transparent Colors:

TC2502 Red, TC2503 Blue, TC2504 Green
10. Tape, Chart-Pac, $\frac{1}{4}'' \times 324''$, Matte, Solid Colors:

#2501M Black, #2502M Red, #2503M Blue, #2504M Green

11. Tape, Chart-Pac, $\frac{1}{8}'' \times 324''$, Transparent Colors:

TC1252 Red, TC1253 Blue, TC1254 Green

12. Tape, Chart-Pac, $\frac{1}{8}'' \times 324''$, Matte, Solid Colors:

#12510M White, #12512M Silver, #12513M Gold, #12514M Brown, #12521 Brown on White, #12521 Red on White, #12521 Green on White, #12521 Black on White

13. Tape, Chart-Pac, $\frac{1}{8}'' \times 324''$, Matte, Solid Colors:

#1251M Black, #1252M Red, #1253M Blue, #1254M Green, #1255M Orange, #1256M Purple

14. Tape, Chart-Pac, $\frac{1}{32}'' \times 648''$, Matte: #3101M Black (5 roll pkg.)
15. Tape, Chart-Pac, $\frac{1}{16}'' \times 648''$, Matte #6201M Black (5-roll pkg.)

Slide Supplies

1. Mounts, Polaroid Plastic Frames, Type 633, $3\frac{1}{4}'' \times 4''$ (Box of 16)
2. Dippit Solution, Polaroid Type 646 for $3\frac{1}{4}'' \times 4''$ Slides
3. Binders, Metal for $2'' \times 2''$ Slides, Kodak Type B350 (Box of 50)
4. Masks for $2'' \times 2''$ Slides, Kodak Type B355 (Box of 50)
5. Glass, Cover, for $2'' \times 2''$ Slides, Kodak Type B351 (Box of 50)
6. Mounts, Cardboard, Kodak Ready Mounts for $2'' \times 2''$ Slides, Type B255
7. Glass, Cover, for Slide Binding, $3\frac{1}{4}'' \times 4''$, Kodak Type 324 (Box of 24)
8. Paper Masks, for Slide Binding Purposes, $3\frac{1}{4}'' \times 4''$, Ideal #4 or Burke & James #5901-A(W)
9. Tape, Slide-Binding, Kodak B303, Yellow, $\frac{3}{8}'' \times 30$ yd. roll
10. Mounts, Cardboard for Mounting Filmstrip Frames, Armme Type S1-4, Kwik Mounts
11. Glass, Etched for $3\frac{1}{4}'' \times 4''$ Slides, Keystone View Co. (Box of 25)

Films and Processing

1. Film, Photographic, Kodak, EK-X-135-20, Ektachrome (general purpose)
2. Film, Photographic, Kodak, KRA-135-36, Kodachrome 2, Professional Type A (special purpose)
3. Film, Photographic, Kodak, KRS-135-20, Kodachrome 2 (daylight)
4. Film, Photographic, Kodak, FX-135-20, Panatomic X (special purpose)
5. Film, Photographic, Kodak, FX-135-36, Panatomic X (special purpose)
6. Film, Photographic, Kodak, KRA-459, Kodachrome 2, Type A (8 mm motion picture film, 25 feet)
7. Film, Photographic, Kodak, Tri-X Reversal, Single Perforated, Winding B (16 mm), TXR 455
8. Film, Photographic, Kodak, Type 3 Kodalith Ortho, $4'' \times 5''$ sheets
9. Film, Photographic, Kodak, Type 3 Kodalith Ortho, $8\frac{1}{2}'' \times 11''$
10. Film, Photographic, Polaroid 46L, $3\frac{1}{4}'' \times 4''$ (Transparency)
11. Film, Photographic, Polaroid 146L, $3\frac{1}{4}'' \times 4''$ (Transparency)
12. Film, Photographic, Motion Picture, Kodak, Plus-X 16 mm, Single Perforated, Winding B, Type 7276, SP455
13. Film, Photographic, Motion Picture, Kodak Commercial Ektachrome, Single Perforated, Winding B, Type 7255, SP 449
14. Film Processing Mailers, Prepaid, Kodak, for 20-Exposure Rolls

Lettering Supplies and Devices

This category contains 101 specific items including scriber pens, ruling pens, speedball pens, compasses, heat-resistant adhesive-type letters and numbers, adhesive patterns and symbols, stencils, inks, nylon-tip pens, LeRoy templates, Wrico templates, Wrico brush and manuscript pens, grease pencils, Keuffel and Esser transparency marking pencils, tweezers, scissors, rulers, triangles, and assorted styli.

The foregoing list indicates the content on inventory cards, one card for each item mentioned, for eight of the fifteen categories in this particular system. Each card has a seriatim number and also a category number. Within each category a decimal numbering system is used. Stock cards can then be turned over to a typist in any grouping according to need and then resorted for filing in the inventory card box. The other categories in the system that has been excerpted are *Flannel Board Process, Dark-*

room Supplies, Display Supplies, Dispensers, Sprays, Cements and Thinners, and *Equipment*. Care must be taken to not duplicate inventory cards in any system devised, and thus since some items are used in many ways for a number of purposes, it seems best to categorize multiple-purpose items under useful headings such as *paper, tapes, lettering supplies* and the like where materials have several characteristics in common.

Citywide media program directors and the media coordinators in school-building centers cannot help but realize that unless the right supplies are on hand at the right time, little if any media-preparation work will be completed. We shall turn our attention to several management problems a little later, but right now we ought to bring up again the matter of obtaining staff members to give needed assistance in the media-making program. We have learned by observation how complex the problem is of getting the right supplies for the right processes, and we know that media directors and coordinators themselves will not be able to devote more time than that required for supervision of a system already designed and established. Therefore we must look for help from a number of people who may possess varying degrees of talent in the media-making process.

Staff for Media-Preparation Activities

As teachers begin to increase their uses of media, and even begin to design and fabricate their own, they will not be backward in making known their demands. This is true regardless of the level of instruction. When the writer organized a do-it-yourself media-preparation program at the university level, not only instructors, but full professors came to learn how to make their own slides and transparencies. Teachers at every level will do the same—not all, but some will. Sometimes professors said, "Let me send my graduate assistants, I am busy on research and teaching. Won't you make these slides for me? May I send my secretary?" We know that even though some teachers would make their own media, they prefer to get help, the more the better. Television teachers, because of their sophistication in media-use techniques and the time-consuming nature of the TV program, demand more insistently and more consistently

that artists be assigned to their support. We have already pointed out the findings of Faris and Moldstad[8] in this regard. They found in their survey that 37 per cent of the teachers queried would make their own media, 41 per cent felt the most satisfactory arrangement would be to have the audiovisual specialist make them, 14 per cent would accept the work of students as a satisfactory arrangement, and the remaining 8 per cent believed that a hired artist would be the best plan for getting their media-making work done. By comparison, all of the television teachers wanted full media-making support, with 77 per cent being in favor of having an artist do their work.

The reader is well aware after the discussions in Chapters 7 and 8 that modern-day media-service programs simply cannot be operated by a one-man combination of leader, manager, technician and clerk. Personnel standards have been quoted and emphasized. But now we reiterate that to embark on a media design-and-preparation program without staff assistance, especially in light of the other duties already set forth, is sheer nonsense. So we wish to state what some of the possibilities are, bearing in mind the various levels of activity and possible patterns of organization.

1. Organize first a media-making center at headquarters and employ a media design-and-preparation specialist, in a professional position. Supply him with a graphic technician to handle darkroom and other technical operations in providing needed services. Employ a crew of part-time high-school students on an after-school basis. Make as many services as possible available to all schools.

2. Organize a central media-making facility, and carry on limited district-wide services at headquarters. Organize additional media-making facilities, equipment units, and staff in each elementary and secondary school, and expand school-building operations at an optimum pace to the following satisfactory levels:

(a) Start with services to teachers who will make their own media, with a part-time technician, or preferably a teacher released from half-time teaching to head the program. Such a staff member would train a crew of student workers and personally assist the teachers with

[8] *Ibid.*, p. 105.

the work of designing and planning media, and with equipment operations and supplies. Hopefully, teacher aides may be trained to carry on routine processes under this arrangement.

(b) Move to a level of operations involving a part-time graphics technician who will expand the service program from a do-it-yourself to a we-will-do-it-for-you basis, restricting available operations to such commonly needed media as overhead transparencies and slides. Teacher aides where normally available will assist specified groups or teams of teachers as needed.

(c) Develop a high-level program using a part-time or full-time professional person to aid teachers in their design and planning work to develop special instructional systems, using in addition a full-time technician in large schools to carry out equipment operations, maintain inventories, and meet standards of quality. A part-time secretary will work as a part of this staff to handle clerical operations. Teachers will handle design, planning, and sequencing work after school or during free periods, and the technical staff, assisted by available teacher aides, will handle routine construction on work during times when the preparation areas are relatively free. The media program coordinator for the school will provide leadership and management services, and maintain proper connections with the citywide media program director. The media program leader at headquarters and the school-building media coordinator will have to make sure that all phases of the media-preparation program are being balanced in light of system-wide curriculum needs, such as the need to mass produce audio-program tapes and scheduled multimedia presentations. They will have to arrive at an optimum balance in separating media-preparation functions at their respective centers.

Such plans are proposed in light of burgeoning technology. Electronic learning laboratories in each school, large-scale and comprehensive television-service programs, and the scheduled use of media-supported instructional systems, operating for individualization as well as large-group presentations, are all a part of a new and seemingly inescapable environment. We have already indicated the problems that will attend such technological advancement in schools from the standpoint of providing facilities, equipment, materials, and staff, but if teachers are to make their own media, or design and plan media materials for technicians to produce, then the implementation of in-service education programs will have to go hand in hand with the solution to the other problems mentioned. We have of course already discussed the significance of this aspect of the media program director's duties in general. Now we turn our attention to the need for in-service education as it is needed by media-making activities and programs.

In-Service Education for Media-Preparation Activities

Technological mindedness does not come easy to some teachers. We discussed the *change* process earlier in this volume, and emphasized that teachers who undertake innovative methods either of their own volition or as a result of encouragement from supervisory personnel, need continual assistance. When we look at the nature of this assistance we recognize at once the need for instruction on the one hand and environmental facilitation on the other. Inviting facilities to undertake new kinds of activity appeal to many, and although we once felt that all we had to do was to help the willing, this may have been a way of saying that it really didn't matter if innovative methods were used or not. We should look therefore to effective methods of in-service education that pinpoint the objective to be achieved in all who by some previous agreement are to engage in any given new process.

Pinpointing Needed Performance. When facilities, supplies, convenient arrangements, and a service organization are provided for carrying on a number of operational processes, then it is essential to analyze the processes to determine the skills that are needed by teachers. In any of the operational processes for making media, there are difficult and highly professional skills, and simple constructional skills easy enough so that they may be developed by fifth-graders. If, for example, we consider the making of overhead transparencies, or Polaroid and 2×2 inch color slides, should teachers be taught to concentrate on the professional job of selecting and visualizing ideas and relationships and on the making of *masters* and *flats*—or taught mainly to carry on routine equipment-operation processes? When a crew is made available for the routine processing, then of course teachers as professionals may put more time in on the former instead of the latter. This means, then, that in in-service programs an optimum balance will be developed between needed creative work and the routine work of equipment operation. Under these conditions of balance, demonstrations of equipment operation for the purpose of showing results and standards will suffice in a great many cases. Teachers need to work together on image-changing activities, the most fruitful of all of which will be creative work on masters and flats and the creative work of selecting source materials and arranging symbols. Many teachers will need help in the process of designing visual presentations, for these in essence are the stimuli that elicit pupil responses. This process calls for extreme sophistication when the stimuli and response phases are arranged by the teacher to operate apart from overt teacher control. When only those teachers who will consent to do their own work are entitled to use a media-making facility, then of course the two instructional goals must go hand in hand. This is the kind of skill identification that must be carried out by planners of in-service programs, but this and other kinds of vital action have already been given the emphasis they deserve in Chapter 4. However, in this specific framework of reference we ought to deal with the identification of in-service education target groups.

Pinpointing In-Service Education Groups. In this vital process of instructing teachers in new methods, in-service education planners must make decisions on a priority basis. In-service education in media-making processes may have to proceed along priority lines within groups of teachers of a given grade or subject. Such priorities are of course arrived at by effective cooperative action between media-program and other curriculum and administrative personnel. Hence, although we need to instruct teachers in general, groups may have to be arranged and taught (see Chapter 4) in an established sequence, marshaling all of the available capability to inaugurate innovative programs of wide application in the curriculum. Curriculum revision in science and social studies programs, or the inauguration of videotape production demanding heavy media support, or the activation of multimedia presentations for large-group instruction in both elementary and

secondary schools are good examples of processes that may demand priority arrangements. Such needs may not exist one year, but may burgeon the next with the completion of new school buildings containing hitherto unavailable spaces requiring new procedures. Target groups may therefore have to be identified early and organized by methods set forth in Chapter 4.

Increasing the Impact of Media-Making Activities Through Exchange. In-service education planners and teachers have not yet widely applied methods for gaining maximum benefit from in-service education in the field of media-preparation activities through cooperative exchange efforts. The need to buy ready-made media will of course become acute in the years ahead on an unprecedented scale, but this is also true of the process of making audiovisual media for special purposes. Thus we emphasize the need for the coordination of teacher efforts along priority lines. Teachers and in-service education activity planners may, if they choose to organize such cooperative efforts, make great gains in the availability of special-purpose media. Audio tapes may be rerecorded easily, slide sets may be duplicated inexpensively, and once the masters have been made, additional sets of transparencies may be produced in quantity. Such media production may, through in-service education planning, be made by different groups of teachers or by several teachers working as individuals, and thus one teacher may make five transparencies for a unit in third-grade science and get back fifty for the remaining units in the subject, all of which may be coordinated with the same subject in the next grade. Or as another example, each teacher in the group of ten sixth-grade social studies teachers, after appropriate planning activity, could make five masters for subsequent color-slide photography. The slides could then be combined into the originally planned set, duplicated and given to each teacher permanently as a set of fifty 2×2 inch color slides in a carousel projector tray ready for repetitive projection. The possibilities are many, but the process demands leadership and management skill, coordination, and willing teacher cooperation. As we have said, technical assistance in carrying on the routine processing is essential, otherwise such valuable projects bog down and get lost, not for lack of professional creativity, but for hours of routine drudgery. As we have also mentioned before, we need to move toward the stratification of teaching talents, and the foregoing example is one way of emphasizing high-level professional activity and adding to it the massive cumulative effect of well-directed cooperative endeavor.

Some Observations on Cost

We need not treat the subject of cost in precise detail, nor can this be done, since there is no standard by which we can predict what a media-making program will cost a school system. The variables seem infinite. Yet there is no reason why we should not continue the process so frequently used of making a reasonable estimate based not so much on common practice, but on some conservative views of the future. We ought to be forgiven if we (1) eliminate from consideration the cost of operational space in a school building, (2) assume that each school will devote enough space in which to operate the basic equipment units listed earlier, (3) assume that the citywide media-program headquarters has twice the equipment and materials allotment and twice the staff for media-making purposes as each of the school building centers, (4) assume that each elementary and secondary school would have equally extensive media-making programs with equal staffs, (5) assume that the volume and comprehensiveness of operations are equal in all schools, and finally if (6) we use a media-making facility in a school building as the base unit on which cost is estimated, thus making possible a total estimate for any school system of a given number of school plants.

Cost Per School Operating Unit. We shall now make estimates for each of the following basic types of expenditures (see table).

Now we can at least approximate the cost of a reasonably sophisticated operating media-preparation unit. According to our original assumptions, we might reason that the headquarters unit would pay out $12,800 for its equipment, going more heavily into publication printing activity or into other special forms of media-preparation work, with the recurring annual expenditure of $35,200. In the school-building estimate, equipment would cost (according to our estimates and assumptions) $6,400 with a recurring annual cost of $17,600.

Such estimates as these may be shocking to

Equipment and Supplies

Operating equipment units (one each) as previously listed, plus two additional 35 mm SLR camera units, one additional Thermo-Fax photo-copier unit, and one additional spirit duplicator	$6,400
Bulk Supplies for media-making processes	5,000
Subtotal	$11,400

Staff

(a)	Media Coordinator, $\frac{1}{4}$ time	$2,500
(b)	Secretary, $\frac{1}{2}$ time	2,100
(c)	Graphic artist and technician full time	7,000
(d)	Part-time helpers, students, hourly basis, after school	1,000
	Subtotal	$12,600
	Grand Total of Initial Expenditures	$24,000

some school administrators and even to prospective media program directors and coordinators. Media preparation costs need not be disturbing at all, and probably wouldn't be, except for the fact that until recent years, any increase in school-operation costs was cause for alarm and preventive action on the part of the so-called citizens and finance-control boards to keep the taxes down. We of course have not attempted to be a source of shock to anybody; but rather we set out to probe the future quite realistically, even though we did exceed perhaps the present central tendency. Now as we look ahead to a school system and count the cost for operating media-making centers in 500 school plants, or 20, or 10, we can come to grips with ideas of over-all costs. Whether in actuality media-production costs will be over or under the figures we arrived at is a matter of variables in the day-to-day operation. We have said before that trained staff members, equipment, and materials are not inexpensive, but in the biggest and most crucial business in our time, we had better not be lacking in vision.

Management of Media-Preparation Control Systems

Any school-building or citywide media program leader will soon realize that media-preparation services may prove to be the tail that wagged the dog as far as time and work schedules are concerned. This is why we have repeatedly emphasized that this media program leader cannot allow himself to tackle another burdensome job such as media preparation is, without adequate support. Those who believe that a media leader can spend hours operating graphic equipment, lettering instructional media for teachers, or assisting teachers make their own, possess little if any insight into the difficulties of meeting a broad spectrum of demands for service. We therefore now consider some of the management processes for media-preparation services that the director or coordinator must organize and implement. First, we shall consider the control system that restricts the degree of choice in different media that can be made, or the processes usable in any given media process.

Control System for Restricting the Range of Media-Making Processes

Nature of the Problem. Earlier we attempted to provide an opportunity for the reader to develop an idea of the tremendous number of items that have to be stocked in order to carry on media-preparation activities. Even though we consider factors other than expense in connection with supplies, it is not always feasible to provide teachers with every known material. We can use as an example, the case of a teacher who wants to make quickly a transparency of a single sheet or map from a periodical. We shall assume that she will use the dry-process photocopier. Should she be provided with blue negative Thermo-Fax film Type 128; black line on blue background, Type 129; or black line on colorless background, Type 127? Take as another example, the case of a teacher who wishes to copy a black and white diagram in a book, making it a 2×2 inch slide. The teacher normally makes up color slides. Now since the color film employed may generally be used to make a satisfactory black and white slide by the regular color reversal process, the use of black and white film requiring darkroom processing and printing from negative to positive may well be denied. We may well also ask the question as to whether both diazo-coated film and dry-process transparencies ought to be made available as basic processes, and if diazo-coated film

is made available, how complete should the stock be? Polaroid film for slides, the types of marker pens, the size and style of lettering sheets, kinds of slide-binding frames and mounts, all may have to be limited in availability. Once the identification of specific items has been made, sufficient stock must be maintained to permit wide use under quality-control conditions.

Suggested Management. The school-building media coordinator, and the citywide media director should take joint action on this plan. The citywide director may implement such plans for limitation on a system-wide basis. He would have to set up, in this case, a plan to standardize a stock list. Once such a list has been created, the media coordinator at the school-building center will issue the stock as needed. The coordinator may, of course, be in a position to make his own selection, basing his decisions on the advice of key teachers and assistants. The implementation of such a plan is dependent on a number of factors, such as financial support, the number of technical and clerical assistants available, and the degree of sophistication of teachers in design and visualization.

System for the Control of Media-Making Supplies

We now turn to another problem in control that must be solved, namely, the control of media-preparation supplies.

Nature of the Problem. The most vexing problem of all in connection with media-making activities by teachers or technicians, is the handling of supplies. To order, arrange, inventory, issue them to teachers constitutes a clerical job of such magnitude that to disregard it or treat it lightly is to bring the program to ruin.

Suggested Management. We shall indicate a number of steps that can be taken by leadership personnel which may constitute a suitable plan of action. Actually, the steps imply the kinds of conditions that must be maintained if the problem is to be solved. The essential steps are as follows:

1. Install shelves on open walls near operating equipment units to provide a limited supply of needed items.

2. Maintain one or more mobile carts with an assortment of supplies for specific media-making jobs.

DEPARTMENT

PRODUCTION REQUEST

DEPARTMENT OF AUDIOVISUAL SERVICES

COLORADO SPRINGS PUBLIC SCHOOLS

DEPARTMENT

DATE	DATE WANTED	DATE COMPLETED

PURPOSE OF REQUEST ______________________

PERSON MAKING REQUEST ______________________

	QUANTITY	TYPE OF MATERIALS USED	EST. COST
TRANSPARENCIES			
DITTOS			
COPIES			
SLIDES			
MOTION PICTURES			
TAPE RECORDING			
TAPE DUPLICATION			
MISC. GRAPHIC			

WORK (DESCRIBE)••••• ______________________

REMARKS

COMPLETED JOB RECEIVED BY ______________________ TOTAL COST

BY ______________________ TIME SPENT

DEPARTMENT OF AUDIOVISUAL SERVICES

CHARGE TO ACCOUNT

9/65

Figure 9-14. Management of media-preparation processes requires an optimum balance between freedom and restriction. Certain kinds of record keeping activity are essential. This *Production Request* form is a sample. It was developed for use when media are made for teachers at the School District Media preparation facility. *Courtesy Public Schools, Colorado Springs, Colorado.*

3. Provide for bulk storage that can be under lock and key. The most desirable way to do this is to provide a stockroom cage, or other room set aside for the orderly arrangement of supplies. Such arrangements as separate stockrooms are usually found where programs are characterized by comprehensive and high-volume services. Under these circumstances, however, there has to be a stockroom clerk. Without the clerk, a responsible individual has to unlock the area for resupply of equipment units.

4. Inventory cards, one for each item must be typed out with full information for reordering. Such cards may then be turned over to a secretary for ordering. Content on the cards would be copied on order forms and sent to media-supply headquarters or to the school-system central warehouse. Suddenly running out of stock is an ever-present problem that must be solved by setting up a workable inventorying process. Schools may not for a while build up their support personnel to the point wherein the media-production-center inventory control will be 100 per cent effective. Arrangement of items in stock so that visual surveillance is convenient, helps, but a rigorously followed system of periodical check-up on the available stock, especially insofar as key items are concerned is a prime essential. To this end, a running inventory may have to be maintained on log sheets posted in a central place, so that when film rolls, for example, are issued, the quantity is indicated together with the remaining number of items in stock at that issuing point.

5. Media-making supplies should be arranged so that similar materials are together—for example, pressure-sensitive tapes, lettering pens, and paper. Such plans for arrangement and storage make it possible to develop a high degree of neatness control as well.

6. Stock item arrangements, both bulk-storage and operational-station supplies, such as Thermo-Fax Type 127 transparency sheets in readiness at the photocopier machine, have to be checked once or twice daily.

7. Set up strict policies for issuing media-making supplies. For example, a set of rules and regulations, as simple as possible for execution by technicians and clerks, ought to cover the conditions under which rolls of color film will be issued. One suggestion is that cameras and rolls of film are not to be issued for use outside of the media-making center. A possible exception to this rule could be the use of a camera for field-trip expeditions or for pupil productions under the immediate supervision of the teacher. Safeguards should be set up against the abuse of equipment and especially unauthorized use of materials and equipment.

Control System for Providing Assistance to Teachers

Quite apart from in-service education programs, such as special workshops, there is a need to set up a control system to give assistance to teachers.

Nature of the Problem. Teachers need a number of different kinds of assistance. They need help in operating equipment units, and they need to be guided through processes that sometimes they do not do frequently enough to maintain speed and error-free performance. In order for teachers to do high-quality work when using media-making equipment, the units must be in a state of readiness. The need for continual adjustments on the equipment ought to be kept to a minimum. Also, clearly stated step-by-step directions for procedure ought to be posted near each equipment unit. Unless these conditions prevail, there is liable to be a high percentage of poor-quality work and excessive waste. Another aspect of the problem is the need to give assistance, on a priority basis, to specified groups of teachers who must meet teaching schedules in specified programs. Large-group presentations, media-preparation work for television, multimedia presentation commitments may give rise to problems in giving all the help that is needed to meet deadlines. Also, teachers who are competent at equipment operation could work alone, but may find that space is not available, or that the equipment is in use.

Suggested Management. In order to maintain the efficiency of the media-preparation facilities and meet instructional needs, we suggest the following kinds of action:

1. Make an analysis of each equipment-operation station and write down specific instructions, even to posting a photograph of required arrangements for stock items and pieces of equipment. Students and technicians

will then follow the directions at each station when checking through the entire media-preparation suite. Such readiness check-ups must be made daily, and preferably following the use of the equipment station by each teacher. This check-up work must also be carried out for all shelves on which media supplies are arranged. Use tape printers to make labels for the location of supplies on shelving units or on readiness tables.

2. Make plans to post specific step-by-step directions that will help teachers recall previous action taken. Label operational parts in full view.

3. Set up an appointment system to handle priorities, or make schedules after getting advice from the staff, for hours for work by specific groups at specified stations.

4. Post samples of work done as standards for performance, and also show samples of defective work as a result of common errors.

5. Assign members of operational technical staffs to specific jobs. Write out instructions to technicians as well as for teachers.

6. See that proper check-ups are carried out by the right personnel as assigned.

There are other control systems that may be worked out according to local conditions and situations. Although they should recognize the need to cut red tape for teachers, media leaders need also to recognize that without controls of such complex and often understaffed establishments as media-preparation facilities, the program of service may suffer. Regardless of the problems that usually attend media-producing activities, we can assert, that since media are playing newer and increasingly important roles in greater volume, media leaders will have to find ways to implement these inescapable and essential media-preparation services.

It is not by chance that the chapter dealing with the important, system-wide implementation of media-preparation programs has been completed at this particular point in this book. It is generally recognized by all who understand new uses for audiovisual media in both television programing and as direct teaching components that special-purpose media have to be produced on the spot by a wide variety of operational techniques. These uses of media will be abundantly clear as we move ahead into

the following chapters, the first of which deals with television and the second with self-instruction systems.

Problem-Solving Activities

1. Identify several teaching processes such as large-group presentations, self-instruction systems, and television programing, and prepare for each one you name, a brief statement describing the relation the process bears to the media-preparation services needed by teachers that are involved.

.2. State the old and new roles of media as repeatedly mentioned thus far in this book and explain the need for local media-preparation services in relation to these media roles.

3. Why is the visualization and design aspect of media-making processes so important? How is it related to communication by the teacher or by the medium itself? How is it related to information theory? How is it related to instructional objectives? To the nature of the learning process? To the goals of pupils?

4. What is the role of the graphic artist in visualization and design? Is it educational? Purely technical? If media are being made *for* teachers, what duties must teachers themselves carry out?

5. What basic media generally need to be produced by school systems today? How does your list differ from the one supplied in this book? Can you agree in class, or in a group of teachers, on a listing of media arranged in order of priority, as may be necessary when inaugurating a new media-preparation service? Do you agree that restrictions may have to be placed on what kinds of media, and how many varieties of each kind, can be made in any given media-making center?

6. Your school superintendent has asked you to write him a letter to inform him how many square feet of floor area in the system-wide media-service suite in the new school headquarters building you will need for media-preparation activities. Write him a two-page proposal in which you state the following: (a) a listing of specific operational space needs, if all forty schools in the school district are to be served, and (b) an alternate plan for decentralizing the media-producing process to carry

on specific operations in each school. List each of the space needs in square feet for the operations to be handled at each school, and (c) supply a revised listing of space needs for the centralization plan, or add the new and reduced figures to the listing prepared in (a) under the heading "Centralization with Optimum Decentralization."

7. Prepare a floor-plan sketch to scale showing generalized space needs for basic media-producing operations for a school-building media center as follows: (a) label to show equipment-operation stations, (b) show how each station is related to the general access and working area, (c) base operational space needs on estimates given in this book, (d) indicate the various operating area figures and also the total area allotted, and (e) indicate by arrows flow-diagram patterns as from stock supply to working spaces. (Note: Try to economize in space wherever possible without eliminating specific operations, or unreasonable crowding.)

8. Using the generalized space-need figures for operations identified in the sketch completed in Problem 7, make a new sketch of operational spaces to the same scale after having been ordered to submit a new plan for each school in the district limiting the media-producing area to 600 square feet. Label clearly and again indicate a flow diagram and show relationships of equipment operation stations to work areas. (This sketch calls for a combination of specified functions and drastic limitation of operational space. In cases like these, what media do you produce? What media-producing processes, can be carried on in teachers' classrooms? What kits of media-making materials may be supplied to teachers? What personnel can be allowed to use facilities and when? How could full-time paid staff members compensate for reduction in operational spaces?)

9. Your proposals for operating media-producing facilities in each school building have been turned down in favor of a centralization scheme. You know what the disadvantages of such a plan are, but you must write a new proposal outlining a plan for central media-making facilities in light of new staff-space-service relationships. Include in your outline-format plan the following: (a) a statement as to the possibility that extra technical staff working full time can produce more media in

less space per hour than in school-building centers, (b) a statement as to the possible effect that teachers will not visit and consult with artists and technical staff to the same degree that they would visit school-building units, (c) an estimate of the volume of media items that may have to be produced at the central headquarters, (d) a statement that cost of supplies may be reduced for an equal number of media due to waste reduction, since more full-time technicians will be handling the materials rather than teachers and students, and (e) a listing of operational space needs in terms of the required central staff to carry on *all* media-producing services.

10. In tabular format, identify basic criteria and make comparisons to show advantages and disadvantages of centralization versus optimum decentralization of media-producing processes as a basis for recommending adoption of school district policy.

References

Bowers, Kenneth L. "Filmstrips for Local Needs," *Audiovisual Instruction*, Vol. 9, No. 3, March 1964, pp. 179-180.

Brown, James W. and Kenneth D. Norberg. *Administering Educational Media.* (New York: McGraw-Hill, 1965).

Darkroom Construction. (Rochester, N.Y.: Eastman Kodak Co., 1951).

Faris, Gene and John Moldstad, assisted by Harvey Frye. *Improving the Learning Environment* (A Study of the Local Preparation of Visual Instructional Materials). Carried on with the cooperation of the U.S. Office of Education pursuant to a contract under Title VII, Part B. (Washington, D.C.: Superintendent of Documents, U.S. Government Printing Office, 1963).

Frye, Roy A. *Graphic Tools for Teachers*, 3rd ed. (Austin, Texas: E. and I. Printing Co., 1965).

Gaskill, Arthur L. and David A. Englander. *How to Shoot a Movie Story.* (New York: Morgan and Morgan, Inc., Publishers, 1960).

Johnston, Roy J. "University of Miami Learning and Instructional Resources Center,"

Audiovisual Instruction, Vol. 11, No. 2, February 1966, pp. 91-93.

Kemp, Jerrold E. *Planning and Producing Audiovisual Materials.* (San Francisco: Chandler Publishers, 1963).

———. "Planning for Local Production," *Audiovisual Instruction*, Vol. 8, No. 5, May 1963, pp. 296–298.

Kemp, Rodger L. and Clarissa Sunde. "Video Tapes for Teaching the English Language," *Audiovisual Instruction*, Vol. 10, No. 4, April 1965, p. 303.

Liechti, Alice O. and Jack R. Chappell. *Making and Using Charts.* (San Francisco: Fearon Publishers, 1960).

Magnetic Recording for 16 mm Motion Pictures. (Rochester, N.Y.: Eastman Kodak Co., 1958).

Mascelli, Joseph V. *Five C's of Cinematography.* (Hollywood, California: Cine/Graphic Publications, 1965).

McVey, Gerald F. "Multimedia Instructional Laboratory," *Audiovisual Instruction*, Vol. 11, No. 2, February 1966, pp. 80-85.

Minor, Ed. *Simplified Techniques for Preparing Visual Instructional Materials.* (New York: McGraw-Hill, 1962).

Morlan, John E. *Preparation of Inexpensive Teaching Materials.* (San Francisco: Chandler Publishers, 1963).

Roberts, Alvin B. and Don L. Crawford. "Multiscreen Presentations: Promise for Instructional Improvement," *Audiovisual Instruction*, Vol. 9, No. 8, October 1964, pp. 528-530.

Veenandaal, Wilfred L. "The Visualization of an Idea," *Audiovisual Instruction*, Vol. 2, No. 9, December 1952, pp. 260-262.

Weisgerber, Robert A. and Warren Rasmussen. "A Teaching System for Music Listening," *Audiovisual Instruction*, Vol. 11, No. 2, February 1966, pp. 106-109.

Because of its tremendous potential value in achieving instructional efficiency, because of its unique capabilities, because of its many applications to large-group as well as individualized instruction, and because of its potential as a vital component for the teaching methods referred to as instructional systems, television is a medium that every media specialist should gain experience with. This chapter cannot be a guidebook or even a major resource for those who want to learn about the many past, present, and future uses of television, or for those who seek to develop penetrating insights as they set out to become television specialists. What we desire to accomplish in this chapter is to prepare prospective media program directors and school-building coordinators for some sound thinking about the curriculum contribution instructional television can make, the way it fits into the stream-of-learning activity, and the problems that must be faced before the medium can be used comprehensively, or even in limited ways, by school systems or in individual school buildings. We need to understand the problems we face in using this medium— problems of personnel, new equipment, the rapid strides being made in the technology, the space required for television programing activity, the possible costs, and the patterns by which television is being put to work around the country.

One of the problems we run into at once is whether or not we can invest in television equipment one year without having the equipment become obsolete the next. We may be discussing the ways of using videotape one year only to find that a new technology of video disk recording has replaced or may replace it. We may find some entirely new and more convenient ways for the transmission of programs to where the learners are waiting. We may find in the copyright laws some blocks to our highly desirable electronic reproduction of materials for classroom uses. So as this chapter is being sent to press, we hazardously refer to studio equipment, tape copying and editing equipment, and show pictures of operational uses of television on both closed and open circuits, knowing that the state of the art is an ephemeral condition. We do not apologize therefore for the presentations we make, for we realize that it will become a necessity to retool our operational establishments again

10

Implementation of Television Services

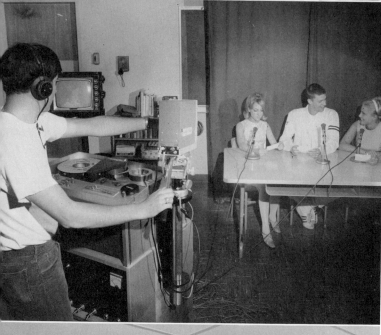

Figure 10-1. In these pictures youngsters of various ages are associating themselves eagerly and naturally with instructional television operations in a number of capacities. Youngsters become performers, producers, cameramen and technicians. (*Top view*, courtesy Audiovisual Media Department, Public Schools, Los Alamos, New Mexico. *Middle view*, courtesy Instructional Materials Center, Public Schools, Portland, Oregon. *Bottom picture*, courtesy Northern Highlands Regional High School, Allendale, New Jersey, and Sylvania Electric Products, Inc., New York, New York.)

and again and continually find solutions to problems as they arise. We need most to point the way to some promising solutions to a present-day cluster of problems that have to do with implementation of television services. When prospective media program directors move into their new positions, they must assess their local television situation in the light of existing needs and operations. They may be called upon to make recommendations for the future, and of course may have to procure the help they need from experts in mapping their future aspirations. They may thus inherit the mistakes of others, or they may have the good fortune to find a thriving and effective organization in full swing. It is the wisdom for guiding change in promising directions that we earnestly seek.

Television and Its Teaching Uses

We shall first identify the unique characteristics of the medium. Many who discuss this topic tend to confuse unique characteristics with possible effects of the medium when used certain ways for instructional purposes. We must separate the communicative effects of any given program on an individual who reacts to it from the basic characteristics of the medium as differing from any other medium.

The Television Medium

Unique Characteristics. When we refer to the unique characteristics of television, we must, as we have just urged, separate program content from television technology. Thus we must mention basic capability of television as a vehicle for communication, display, and transmission, to use a few of the terms commonly used to describe what television does for those who use it. Looked at in this light we can point out three special capabilities:

1. The television medium through what is called electronic reproduction may combine visual and audio components of other media such as motion picture films, slides, and photo enlargements into a single display system.

2. It possesses the capacity to reach an audience of unlimited size, simultaneously for all viewers.

3. It possesses the capacity to transmit program content immediately from the point of occurrence to the point of reception.

Taking a closer look at each of the three characteristics of the transmission system, we can give an example that involves them all. A studio teacher explains a difficult concept for all classes in social science in grade five meeting in thirty different school buildings. The voice and views of the teacher, the pupils' television teacher, provide verbal explanation, and then as a novel experience is needed, takes students on a journey into hot, desert lands by means of a motion picture clip, then identifies the area by means of a map slide, and provides opportunity to make observations relating the slide to the previous film scenes. The television medium has thus served to combine two different media with audio and visual stimuli from the teacher, has served to reach all pupils in the total group at the same time, and whatever the teacher did was transmitted immediately from the point of program origin to the receiving area. Thus these three capabilities open up to the school systems the means to apply in many ways the medium of television to teaching-learning processes. We shall discuss general patterns of uses as have appeared in schools around the country and also point the way to some future possibilities, but first let us identify several basic aspects of television operational technology that have a bearing on its educational applications.

Some Basic Aspects of Operational Technology. The medium of television as a system may operate in classrooms in many different technological ways.

1. Each classroom may have its own television transmission system under the control of the teacher for special and general display purposes, thus producing program content on the spot to provide immediate visibility of the teacher's behavior.

2. Program content may reach schools from remote sources outside of the local school system, thus making use of open-circuit transmission, for direct reception by individual school buildings.

3. Each school system may own and operate its own television systems with origination and reception capability in any or all regular and special teaching stations.

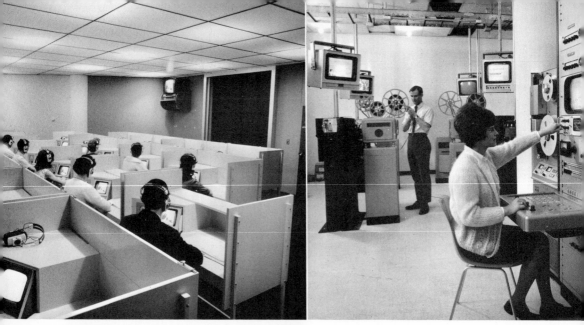

Figure 10-2. This special teaching station depicts program-retrieval technology. The development of videotape recorders and dial-access switching controls provide a new dimension for individualization of teaching-learning activity. The video receivers in carrels are just a part of the complex installation that has to be designed and installed to activate the system. See also Figures 6-7, 7-5, and 7-9, indicating similar activity in high schools. *Courtesy Oral Roberts University, Tulsa, Oklahoma.*

In addition to such basic arrangements for utilizing television in the schools, we can also identify a number of specific aspects of operational technology such as the following, some of which greatly enhance television's instructional contributions.

1. The capability to preserve television program content for repetitive use by means of low-cost, easy-to-operate videotape equipment (with other processes in the offing).
2. The capability of editing videotapes electronically as an important adjunct of television production processes.
3. The capability of automating the retrieval of preserved and stored program content.
4. The present capability, made possible through videotape and other recording processes, to transfer and/or combine source material from a number of audiovisual and print media to whatever video storage system is most conveniently usable in a given education application.
5. The present capability of transmitting television programs by a number of transmission systems, each with its own unique characteristics.

The application of such basic operational technologies will be explained in later discus-

sions and illustrations regarding program production, transmission and viewing at teaching stations. We turn now to television and the curriculum.

Teaching Uses of Television

Most of the nation's educators have not yet been willing to experiment with television in teaching. This unwillingness is certainly typical of education's traditional response to new ideas but anyone who is familiar with the history of instructional television knows that this instructional innovation was launched first among educational decisionmakers, with an unprecedented financial support for centers of experimentation throughout the land. Not all of the experimental centers gave rise to permanent and comprehensive programs of television utilization in schools of the area, yet television has nevertheless prospered to a degree. It has by no means, however, resulted in the television establishment, nor has it had the educational impact dreamed of in an earlier decade. Murphy and Gross, in *Learning by Television*, had this to say:

That televised instruction has achieved even its present modest success is, perhaps, a miracle. The achievement has taken massive pump-priming from private foundations and government. The Ford Foundation alone has made grants in the neighborhood of $100 million to all phases of educational television, at first through the Fund for Adult Education for educational television stations and programing, and later through the Fund for Advancement of Education to schools and colleges. The federal government's support has added approximately another $100 million in equipment to the country's ETV facilities.[1]

In the face of burgeoning media technology, a new feeling toward change on the part of both professionals and the lay public and in face of the changing image regarding education and education's processes, television may be viewed in a new climate of activity. To catch a glimpse of this new future, not only for television, but for other media as well, we turn to the preface of the book just mentioned for quotations from a statement by Alvin C. Eurich:

... the use of television in the classroom for a decade and more has demonstrated incontrovertibly that students can and do learn quite as well from television as they do from conventional instruction. However, the practical experience of school and college educators with the television medium has been quite mixed. As a result, televised instruction has not taken a central position in education. Rather, it is still a marginal enterprise. . . .

As applied to education thus far, television has largely put current modes of teaching on the screen. The result has been widespread disenchantment as the mediocre level of much instruction has been exposed to professional and public scrutiny for the first time. The need for imagination, ingenuity, and innovation in the whole process of education has been forcefully demonstrated.

The primary goal of ITV in the future must be to raise quality and improve classroom utilization. Here, as elsewhere in education today, mere expansion of present practices is not enough. The way forward is necessarily a new way. To create the new some of the old must be constructively destroyed.

... television now stands at the most significant crossroads in its history. Recent developments—governmental, technological, educational—have set the stage for advance to a new level of usefulness and excellence. Opportunities have opened to apply television fruitfully with other new media, and to undertake new experiments with augmented research funds.

... We are now ready for the next stage, which calls for a thorough, dynamic effort to improve the quality of instruction, not just over television, but throughout our entire educational system, with television as one of the many instruments that can be used to give each child, wherever he may live, the opportunity to become all he is capable of being.[2]

Millions of students around the country have been under instruction by television methods. And it is because of this use of television in teaching that we can identify several patterns for putting television to work formally in the curriculum of our schools. Some of these patterns will doubtlessly continue to make contributions of major proportions in the schools of the future. The patterns we have identified, and we are purposely attempting to separate one from the other for purposes of clarity, are as follows:

1. The use of an outstanding television teacher to make direct presentations to pupils in conventionally organized classes of approximately thirty pupils in specified curricular subjects and to guide the regular teachers for the participating groups in their implementation of teaching plans in direct relation to the firmly scheduled telecasts on a required-participation basis.

2. The use of an outstanding television teacher to make direct presentations to pupils in reasonably large groups of 75 to 100 students, in specified curricular subjects, and to guide the participating teachers in each group (possibly two teachers and one teacher's aide) in their implementation of teaching plans in direct relation to the firmly scheduled telecasts on a required-participation basis.

3. The use of an outstanding television teacher to make direct presentations to pupils in formally organized large groups of 300 to 500 students in specified curricular subjects, and guide the participating teachers (usually two or more) at the viewing stations in implementing their teaching plans in direct relation to the firmly scheduled telecasts on a required-participation basis.

4. The use of an outstanding television teacher to teach a specified course in the school's

---

[1] Judith Murphy and Ronald Gross (The Academy of Educational Development, Inc.), *Learning by Television* (New York: The Fund for the Advancement of Education, 1966, pp. 11–12).

[2] *Ibid.*, pp. 6–7. Alvin C. Eurich was formerly vice president and board member of the Fund for Advancement of Education. He is presently the president of the Aspen Institute for Humanistic Studies.

REDEPLOYMENT PLAN

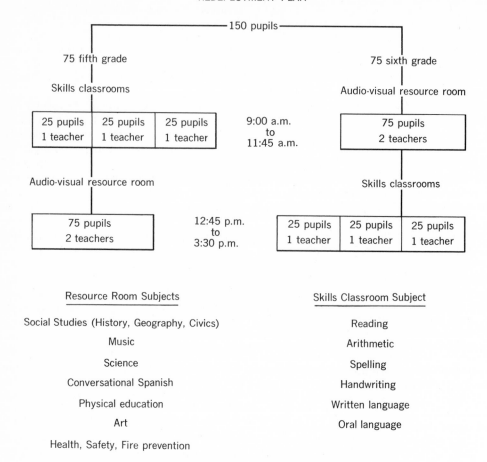

Resource Room Subjects	Skills Classroom Subject
Social Studies (History, Geography, Civics)	Reading
Music	Arithmetic
Science	Spelling
Conversational Spanish	Handwriting
Physical education	Written language
Art	Oral language
Health, Safety, Fire prevention	

Figure 10-3. This diagram of the Redeployment Plan developed and implemented in Anaheim, California, schools concentrates on providing the best instructional personnel throughout the day by combining the benefits of television's characteristics with continual guidance of regular teachers in each classroom. Compare the diagram with patterns 1 and 2 in the list. *Courtesy Public Schools, Anaheim, California.*

curriculum to all organized classes in large groups of 300 to 500 students, meeting at scheduled teaching stations, giving direct guidance to pupils for study and preparation of assignments, with guidebooks, textbooks, and assignments to be handed in as required for grading by assistants. A supervising teacher, and a clerical aide to serve as managerial assistants to the television teacher, with final examinations being taken as scheduled at designated stations.

5. The use of television programs from sources outside the school system broadcast into the classrooms of participating, regular teachers, who use the program content as a resource on a voluntary basis. Such programs

may be single programs or programs in a series as a part of a course. The differentiating factor is in the degree of control over the program presenter. In this pattern, the originating agency has control over the presenter, not the receiving school system. The school system may arrange to take all programs on a series or course basis, paying a per-pupil fee, and by internal agreements may have all teachers in a system make use of the series, carrying on agreed-to procedures.

6. The use of automatically controlled television programs that are maintained in a state of readiness for retrieval by individual students in electronic carrels or on call by teachers for

instructional use by the whole class. In the case of team teaching, large groups may be called together for viewing programs especially prepared by the teacher or programs that had been previously produced, described, and announced for use by teachers in specific grade levels, subjects, and units of work.

7. The use of television facilities to transmit —to specified teaching stations—special program content to expedite administrative processes in schools and school systems. An example would be the administration of a testing program where a specialist or an administrator assumes control of groups to give directions, such as for testing procedure, or makes a series of significant announcements, and has arranged for assistants at the receiving stations to supervise the prescribed operations.

8. The use of television facilities to deliver audiovisual media presentations—such as motion picture, filmstrip, overhead transparency and 2×2 inch slides—to selected teaching stations on demand as teaching and learning resources according to predetermined schedules, thus eliminating the need for projectors, light control systems, and operators for projection equipment.

9. The use of television equipment in a given teaching station to ensure that diagrams, pictures, realia, and instructor demonstrations with small objects and apparatus are visible to all viewers in a large or small group. This process is referred to as a classroom television-display system, or an image-magnification system.

10. The use of television facilities to present programed sequences to specified groups of students, calling for individual responses on group response-measuring instruments. Thus verbal frames may be presented with reference panels displayed and student responses called for and either measured immediately or computerized for later print-out for teachers' records. Such programs may be in videotape format and individualized as described previously.

The ten patterns of television usage in schools around the country are by no means a definitive and inclusive listing, nor are they a guide to the future roles of this medium. We do, however, see in some of the patterns already discernible, strong possibilities for new and greater impact in teaching-learning activities of the future.

The Future of Instructional Television

Although we need not gaze too earnestly into the crystal ball, it may be revealing to explore more fully the thoughts and hopes previously expressed by Alvin C. Eurich. But we dare not make the often-made mistake of treating television as a gift to the schools by technology and then asking, "Here is TV, what shall we do with it?" We should ask instead, as Alvin Eurich asks, what are some great needs of the curriculum of our time that television technology can help educators meet? This is not an easy question to answer. So we go back in our thinking to a solid base of desirable learning activity. We may ask what kinds of activities do youngsters need in order to build into themselves the insights and abilities that the technological climate of our time demands? What will suffice to help our present-day learners come to grips with the massive changes that lie ahead? How can youngsters come to grips with the explosion of knowledge and keep abreast of the changes in concepts once they start their formal learning process? To put the question another way: What do teachers need to do every day to teach the insights, abilities, attitudes, and commitments that their professional duties demand? Indeed, let us put the burden on the teacher, and thus onto his curriculum leader and chief administrator, for proper and adequate action. If we assume that the study of our society and its problems, our philosophical outlook and value system, enables us to decide on what we ought to do, what are the resultant processes like? To answer this question, we shall pose a listing of teacher activities that seem inescapable.

Some Inescapable Generalized Teacher Activities

We have often asserted that before teachers and curriculum leaders and planners can decide how to use audiovisual media, or any medium for that matter, they have to be able to take the teaching process apart, then stand off and look at the components objectively. When we can engage successfully in such analytical thinking, we can begin to pinpoint our choice of media. We can then proceed to build systems of combinations of media and the teacher in proper relationship to elicit the responses of pupils that will achieve instructional objectives. The list we pose does not have to be complete to fulfill our purposes, but we must be sure of the teacher tasks. The reader can use his own experiences to add to the following list.

1. Provide real and vicarious experiences in natural settings for purposes of operations, inference, and generalization.

2. Display illustrations.

3. Provide information to: give detailed directions for action; explain difficult concepts; demonstrate processes; present and define problems; make assignments; ask questions; present case studies and tell stories.

4. Enlarge an illustration or object for all to see.

5. Move learners elsewhere for looking and listening.

6. Give personal guidance to another pupil, group or several groups simultaneously.

7. Motivate students for sustained activity.

8. Provide a common, standardized experience for analysis and evaluation.

9. Get pupils to work independently on creative projects using desirable behaviors.

10. Give continuing guidance to each student.

11. Evaluate the work of students.

12. Prepare media or supervise their preparation.

13. Organize pupils into cooperative groups.

14. Organize reference libraries and facilitate access to them.

15. Organize optimum working conditions that are safe, clean, and wholesome.

We have, of course, not even mentioned one of the most important of all of the professional tasks and that is to formulate valid teaching objectives as a basis for planning action at any teaching station—small-group, large-group, or in an electronic carrel. Looking back over the list of the processes that teachers need to carry out every day by one means or another, we perceive that instructional television possesses the potential to give some strikingly important assistance to teachers. We shall turn to a prediction and an elaboration of what some of those major roles might be in the following section.

Some Promising ITV Roles in the Curriculum

Curriculum Needs as a Basis for Television Services. We know now that the year 1971 is not likely to usher in the full fruition of the instructional developments and uses predicted ten years earlier for instructional television.[3] Men who tried to foresee the future for the television medium then, appear to have been somewhat overoptimistic. But there can be little doubt that ITV can and will move toward more significant contributions toward curriculum fulfillment in the years ahead, although just what the format will be is difficult to predict. Such predictions as we care to make are based on what we have stated regarding the kinds of performance that teachers have to engage in, or that school administrators have to prescribe for them in light of system-wide instructional designs and programs, and also on the long-term view of changing philosophical concepts of American education. In making the following statements, we hold the reader responsible for wide sensitivity to a number of curriculum relationships. Let us first state a few very important needs at all levels of instruction:

1. The pressing requirement of making the most of each pupil.

2. The urgent need to deal with each individual in a personal way, to individualize instruction, some aspects of instruction, such as diagnosis and remediation, and to free pupils for in-depth study.

3. To provide a wide range of experiences in near and far places.

4. To provide challenging opportunities for each student to engage in problem-solving activity, to inquire and question.

5. To provide opportunity for stimulating co-operative endeavor in producing, testing, and evaluating.

6. To save hours of time for teachers in which to give needed guidance to pupils.

7. To provide a range of resource experts in

3 Lester Asheim. "A Survey of Informed Opinion on Television's Future Place in Education," *Educational Television: The Next Ten Years* (Stanford: Stanford University, Institute for Communication Research, 1962).

various disciplines, such as mathematics, social, physical, and biological sciences for demonstrations, explanations, defining issues and problems.

8. To motivate students to study independently in a wide range of situations in electronic carrels, laboratories, libraries, at home.

9. To expand the range of the curriculum according to local needs.

10. To establish contacts with rich sources of content, regional, statewide, and beyond.

11. To give needed preparatory information, directions for action to expedite work of students.

12. To free teachers from the drudgery of routine, repetitive teaching of needed factual content and the checking for mastery of conceptualization processes.

Uses for Television to Meet Curriculum Needs. As we look toward changing concepts of education, particularly along the lines of priority mentioned earlier in Chapter 4, we can envision the use of the television medium by itself and in combination with other media, and with one or more levels of face-to-face teacher guidance. However, we must not fail to specify the particular instructional need that is to be met, and to subject that need to critical scrutiny. As new uses are predicted in the following list, we must also bear in mind the advancing technology that, in light of the present state of the art, is reflected in later sections that deal with operational processes and facilities. We must also caution the reader to beware of possible complexity in a simple statement of a possible use of television in the curriculum, because we see new sources of content from business concerns, museums, city gardens and parks, and libraries, all outside the school. We also see new transmission systems for such taped and stored content, but we must emphasize the ways to integrate such new content with the processes by which students interact and learn. Hence in our suggestions, although we do not deal with each in detail, many relationships of the various television techniques employed in and at our teaching stations are implied. The reader is again held responsible for supplying a wide range of examples, and is also urged to devise combinations of the uses presented as well as new and detailed curriculum applications of his own. Our suggestions follow.

1. Use superior teachers in special programs to get large groups of students (300 to 500 or more), in any field, grade, subject, unit, or stage of work, ready to undertake independent study. Such programs would be designed to expedite work in libraries, laboratories, open up problems and issues, organize students if necessary into cohesive working groups or small teams and task forces. Programs would be fully supported by needed media, could be taped for repetitive use, would be in a daily series of perhaps forty minutes or longer, three or four sessions, to enable students to then move in to blocks of work lasting three to five weeks, meeting in smaller groups for guidance, and in the total group again for the next phase or unit. This would appear to be the use of a television teacher as a member of a team, in which facilities for learning were used as components to maximize the use of rational powers.

2. Use television in new courses for large groups with massive efforts on crucial areas of needed change such as communications and mathematics, which call for the work of truly superior teachers in special fields. Such programing would demand intensive efforts to organize independent study according to needs with available staff qualified for the type of guidance activity called for.

3. To make experts available in various disciplines who are able to give guidance in a series of programs to aid pupils in coming to grips with problems in special areas of endeavor according to existing weaknesses in local teaching staffs. Programs may take the form of whole courses, parts of courses as in item (1) preceding, or may be introduced to give guidance in initiating creative, problem-solving activity in supplementing good teachers already available in mathematics and sciences, for example.

4. Videotapes may be replayed as parts of new curricula as components of whole courses, in any desirable sequence, with the television programs contributing any identifiable part of a specific teaching process from motivation to preparation for laboratory action, explanation of difficult concepts, defining issues, freeing teachers from the repetitive job of presenting basic content.

5. Use television more widely in team teaching presentations for all pupils in the

total group, using existing staff and school-building television installations—thus permitting replay for some groups needing reteaching and make-up work because of absence.

6. To make available to students in large groups programed instruction in the form of presentations calling for individual responses in varied written formats and/or by means of group response systems. Such content may be presented to large groups as a means of releasing a number of teachers from information-giving phases of instructional systems.

7. The use of television as a means of individualizing instruction by dial retrieval of special programs stored on videotape and/or disks, tied expertly according to need into teaching stations for both formal and informal relationships with learning activity. Interconnected schools increase range of coverage by content for both elementary and secondary schools.

8. The use of television to procure and preserve for immediate and/or delayed use, sources of content from regional, statewide and national sources as by means of communication satellites, or by other linkages ending in closed-circuit uses of the content to meet curriculum needs, on a large-group, small-group, or individual basis.

9. Use television to accelerate the program of youngsters in any field of need according to curriculum surveys, employing creative programing to make assignments, giving directions for self-study work, and to organize both school and home activities on appropriate time schedules. Large-group as well as small-group programing are both implied.

10. Use television in packaged in-service education programs to up-date teachers in new curriculum developments and to teach teachers new roles in using teaching systems, for example.

11. Use television facilities for administrative processes such as conducting mass testing programs, compilation and viewing of pupil records, orientation and guidance activities, and facsimile transmission.

12. Use of the medium as a channel for personal contact by school leaders with both pupils and teachers for improved communication about the values and purposes of education, and about new arrangements, plans, and schedules. Such program content would involve both central office and school-building personnel.

13. Use television programing for up-dating postgraduates in vocational retraining activities, as parts of night-school program using school-building facilities and other community resources. Develop methods for using the potential of television for presenting informational aspects, but utilize other means for guiding the use of rational powers.

Some significant Aspects of the Suggested Uses. Repeatedly in the foregoing list the following crucial aspects of television have been stressed explicitly or implicitly:

1. The use of television in proper relationship to other supporting media during and after the programs.

2. The assignment to television of those aspects of the teaching process that can be handled by that medium, with other assignments being made to additional personnel or to media and machines in other locations for the accomplishment of valid educational objectives.

3. The imaginative use of people in television program content, for valid instructional objectives.

4. The breaking away from teaching as usual.

5. A swinging away from the erroneous concept of learning as absorption and memory to the use of rational powers: problem solving, productivity, evaluation.

6. The increased emphasis on independent study, improved interaction with what has been presented and with resulting spheres of activity.

7. The increased use of television in or as one of the components of teaching systems.

8. The valid use of the medium of television to expand the range of school curriculum, to provide experience, and to stimulate and guide organized learning activity.

9. A move away from the lock-step television programing leaving large groups of learners as sitting ducks to waste time on "fill-in" activities.

10. Increased use of libraries and laboratories. (Libraries will have to expand their services to teachers and pupils far beyond anything we have dreamed of in the past.)

Some Observations About ITV Facilities. We must point out that when television uses such as we have suggested are implemented, we shall have to recommend great flexibility in production, transmission, and reception capabilities.

It is obvious that there will have to be not only centralized, citywide capability, but also several school-building production and transmission centers, otherwise such massive uses as we have mentioned cannot be scheduled as needed, as for example team-teaching presentations with several schools interconnected. Great use may be made of videotapes (or other newly developed technology for storing programs) for the immediate retrieval of these program sources when the required equipment is provided. Moreover, as we shall discuss in the next chapter in connection with self-instruction systems, computer capability may have to be used in several phases of the instructional process. We therefore turn next to a discussion of operational facilities for production, transmission, and reception. But once more we must stress the basic concern that it is the curriculum that must determine the uses of the medium, and not the reverse.

Operational Facilities and Equipment: Program Production

Media program leaders will almost certainly be called into action in any insightful deliberations over curriculum change involving television. We have stressed these important curriculum decisions as a basis for the use of all media, not only television, but we should point out that a highly qualified media program director may indeed be the school-system staff member who can best explain how ITV can serve the specified curriculum needs. Therefore, he ought to be considered as an indispensable member on the team of curriculum leaders and school administrators. Once agreements are reached the media director must be prepared to give sound advice on the nature of operational facilities and equipment by means of which desired results can be achieved. The recommendations for implementing television services in all or a part of a school system ought to be worked out as a unified and carefully integrated plan for production, transmission, reception, and viewing of programs. We emphasize this total solution to these problems lest a specific problem such as transmission pose difficulties so great as to jeopardize or preclude successful operation of the instructional television system for the school district. For the purposes of this discussion we shall deal first with operational facilities and equipment for the production phase of the program.

In dealing with these operational problems of production we shall attempt to point out from time to time some of the technological developments that seem to be on the horizon but we shall have to suggest reasonable plans in light of the present technological capabilities. It will be a responsibility of the media director to see to it that he keeps informed and seeks advice from both professional and technical specialists in the field before final decisions are made. We cannot overestimate the importance of getting assistance from qualified specialists before prescribing a given package of equipment. It may be far safer to employ a qualified consultant to check thoroughly the preparation of specifications and to supervise installation. It is with these basic implementation techniques in mind that we now present a number of possibilities for producing, or procuring, and handling the presentation of the programs, up to the point of transmission. Since not all programs are presented *live*, nor do all of them originate in the local system, the aspect of preserving or the handling of program content in the sense of storage or availability must be treated in this phase of program production.

Providing Instructional Television Program Capability

The heart of any instructional television system is the program content. The patterns for putting such content to work in the minds of learners, as well as all aspects of the content, are vital curriculum matters. It is obvious that we face monstrous needs for program material, and because of this we turn to all available sources for desirable programs. We organize facilities, staff, and supporting media and produce programs locally, and we link up with many sources, already alluded to in earlier discussions, external to the school system, in order to meet identified needs. Therefore in a real sense we face the most crucial problem of all in the processes of program production or program availability. We properly refer to all of the means by which we provide needed programing as program capability, and the prospective citywide, or school-building media leaders must consider all phases of such activity in order to recommend the appropriate facilities and equipment required in any particular

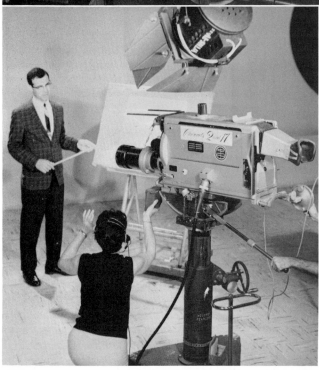

Figure 10-4. In this illustration we focus attention on studio space and equipment, cameras, consoles, and tape recorders. The sum of the impact of it all in the curriculum may be expressed in one word—*program*. In this picture we note the large dual studio complex of the Anaheim Schools, and in the bottom picture we note the action in the main studio at the Dade County Schools television center. (*Top view*, courtesy Public Schools, Anaheim, California. *Bottom picture*, courtesy Dade County Public Schools, Miami, Florida.)

instructional television system. See Figures 10-4 and 10-5. Basic program capability is generally achieved by organizing and equipping one or more local studios, and by procuring additional productions from agencies outside the school district. Ordinarily then, program capability may be developed by one or more of the following program-producing arrangements and processes:

1. *The Central Studio*. A central studio generally implies the transmission process in

Figure 10-5. Are the ITV programs implied by the three views of studio production action in the main stream of teaching activity? Study the program settings shown and make valid judgments as to the amount of effort required for program preparation and production. What professional and technical activity are implied. Should not every program that demands the effort indicated be videotaped and stored for repetitive use? *Courtesy Dade County Public Schools, Miami, Florida.*

addition to production. However, we must concentrate our attention on the process of producing television programs for immediate use *live*, or for storage in a desirable form for retrieval and use according to local plans, both automatic and manual—that is, to be transmitted on schedule to all schools or to a selected circuit of schools, or to be delivered in the form of videotapes, for example, to specific school-building television-service units for use over their own cable transmission circuits.

2. *The School-Building Studio.* As a supplemental program-originating unit, the school-building studio also produces television programs, along lines already suggested, possibly for team-teaching purposes, and also for possible system-wide use among selected schools, grades, and student groups. Such programs may be transmitted *live* or may be also preserved and stored for replay according to local plans, either at the school building, at the central studio storage facilities, or at both.

3. *Teaching-Station, Program Recording Units.* Without the use of studios in the usual sense of the word, classrooms may be equipped with movable recording, viewing, and transmitting units that record off-the-air television presentations for subsequent instructional uses. With the addition of a television camera for image magnification and another camera for viewing the teacher, programs that combine a number of program-content sources can be taped and stored.

4. *Procurement of Programs from External Sources.* When we consider the program capability process, we must look to rich sources that lie outside the school system. A few of the possibilities are videotape (and, as it appears, video disk banks also) for exchange purposes, filmed television programs, and program content from regional, state, and national television services, live, or from stored sources.

What operational spaces and equipment are needed if the program capability we have defined is to be made available to teachers? We shall attempt to answer this question in light of each of the foregoing program availability processes as a means of aiding the prospective media program leader to analyze the problems he must face and solve if television is to fulfill its promise in the curriculum. We anticipate that with the great strides being made in technology new and radically different processes will also be forthcoming.

Program Capability at the District-Wide Studio

Reduced to its simple terms, the process of making and preserving an instructional television program, regardless of how it is to be distributed, or under what conditions, would generally demand two television cameras, a film chain, one videotape recorder, lights, microphones, a control console plus the related operational parts and controls, including audio tape recorder and audio amplifier and mixer control units. The space requirements for better control over quality would be for two separate but adjacent and connected rooms, one to serve as an acoustically treated studio and the other with glass panels for direct visual surveillance to be the control room. As we have already pointed out, studio facilities will also have transmission equipment units. In any studio process, whether *live* telecasting or videotaping, supporting services are required such as graphic production for media support. See Figure 10-6. Also the presentor will likely wish to use apparatus, perform demonstrations, work at tables or desks, and refer to books, maps, and realia. It is therefore essential that adequate workroom and storage spaces be provided.

In the preceding chapter estimates were given that would indicate that limited videotaping operations might be possible in a studio suite of 580 square feet. However, it was also pointed out in that connection that a system-wide comprehensive-service, instructional television studio may need to be as large as 9,200 square feet in area. The variables being so many in local situations, it is not possible to prescribe a standard area without specific information at hand. However, we can make some estimates in terms of the volume of programing needed to meet some of the curriculum needs discussed earlier, and in terms of space needed to carry out known functions. If one program is to be produced each day and transmitted later, a minimum-size suite can be used to good advantage, but if four programs are to be planned, rehearsed, and recorded in one day, additional spaces, a larger studio with room for several separate sets and lights will be a necessity. It is

Figure 10-6. Supporting services are essential for good television programing. Do we not believe that they are just as essential for good teaching in general? The facts are that good communication is important anywhere and everywhere. But unless we get it in instructional television we will waste heavy investment in the technological instruments. In the top view, Dade County ITV staff members prepare film clips for upcoming programs. In the next two views, the art director for the Spring Branch Independent School District television center is preparing a chart and a set of 2 × 2 inch slides. (*Top view*, courtesy Dade County Public Schools, Miami, Florida. *Bottom photographs*, courtesy Spring Branch Independent School District, Houston, Texas.)

also obvious that if the load on a central studio is heavy, the area will have to be greater, and cases where central studios are already large, optimum decentralization to permit special uses of instructional television at individual school buildings will be necessary. If we assume further that the central studio and the school-building supplementary studios will operate videotape resource banks on an automatic retrieval basis, then additional spaces will have to be planned, recommended, and justified.

When central studios are transmitting programs simultaneously, as when several videotape players are feeding multiple channels in cable connections to selected schools, it is obvious that either additional space is required in a central control room, or such videotape machines will be operating with necessary modulators and booster amplifiers in a separate transmitter room. With this brief overview of operational possibilities in mind, we shall now turn to separate treatments of such problems as space needs, equipment needs for both production and preservation, and program-retrieval processes.

Some space needs. Of necessity the estimates of spaces required in which to carry on operational processes are generalized estimates. For our purposes we shall assume fairly comprehensive multichannel television services rather than deal in limited, superficial, and crowded environments.

1. *Three Studios.* Three studios will permit several program-producing activities simultaneously. Videotaping, transmitting a *live* program, taping a presentation for later transmission, the evaluation of a given performance by the presentor, and rehearsing the next program are good examples. Such multiple studios coupled with film and slide chains would permit combination of media with presentor using videotape equipment in the control room. *Estimates:* Studio A, 1,300 square feet; Studios B and C, 1,000 square feet, with a three-studio total of 2,300 square feet.

2. *Control Room.* This space would service three studios and serve as headquarters for all videotaping and transmission, providing also space for consoles, transistorized camera controls, audio control, three multiplexer units, space for maintenance work, and would provide space for automatic-relay equipment for the

retrieval of stored programs. *Estimate:* 1,950 square feet.

3. *Media Support Preparation Area.* Operations in this area include videotape editing and playback; audiotape editing and playback; film footage search; slide making, sorting, and sequencing; and chart and model making. (See Chapter 9 for media preparation.) This space may also serve some dual media-making purposes on a system-wide basis. See Figure 10-6. *Estimate:* 1,950 square feet.

4. *General Storage Area.* This area is vitally needed to store sets and properties, re-usable media, video and audio tapes, and serve also as a blind storage area. *Estimate:* 900 square feet.

5. *Videotape and Other Forms of Program Storage.* Such storage shelves as are used for videotapes and disks and for ITV film programs should be located adjacent to control room area, so as to provide ready access. Shelves could be located on the walls of an access corridor. *Estimate:* 200 square feet.

6. *Library and Workroom for ITV Teachers.* Such space should be conveniently adjacent to media-preparation area. *Estimate:* 460 square feet.

7. *Ready Room for ITV Teachers.* This space should be equipped with desks and some lounge furniture and work or conference tables. *Estimate:* 460 square feet.

8. *Two Rest Rooms. Estimate:* 100 square feet total.

9. *ITV Director's Office. Estimate:* 250 square feet.

10. *Two Offices for ITV Technical Staff. Estimate:* 380 square feet.

11. *Office for Secretaries. Estimate:* 270 square feet.

Summary of System-wide, Comprehensive-Service, ITV Space Needs. When we total the space estimates, made on a functional basis, we arrive at a figure of 9,210 square feet. Needless to say, in connection with other school facilities, it may be possible to combine some of the recommended spaces with other space needs. However, again and again we must insist that the space-pinching days of the past, insofar as education is concerned, are or ought to be over. In connection with the analysis of space needs just completed, the reader should refer to a plan formulated by the author in support of the claim for operational space. It is presented here not as the planner who studies a specific location, but as a challenge to the prospective media director to apply what he knows about television operations to a criticism of the generalized needs identified. See Figure 10-7 and also Figure 10-8.

A Few School-System Examples. Before we finish with the section on equipment and the illustrations, we shall understand that some rather simple methods may be used to produce, procure, and distribute instructional television programs. In fact, some kinds of program content of great value may be made up and stored on videotape without a sophisticated studio. But now since we have discussed in a general way what the nature of the space needs are like for instructional television operations, we ought to temper our demands by referring to the reality of a number of actual examples of school-system operations. Hence we turn to two school systems—Elmira, New York, and Plainedge, New York—examine the nature of their production spaces and perhaps refer as well to some related operations such as, for example, transmission systems (although this problem will be the topic of another section). We turn first to operations in Elmira, New York.

Example 1 : Operations at Elmira, New York

In this example the instructional television facilities are housed in the Beecher school as a part of the audiovisual center. In-school programs are sent by microwave and cable owned and operated by the Elmira Video Company, the local community antenna system (CATV). The school-system television programing plan involves local experienced teachers whose presentations are videotaped and stored for later transmission on one channel of the cable that the company has set aside for exclusive

AUTHOR'S ESTIMATES OF GENERALIZED ITV SPACE NEEDS

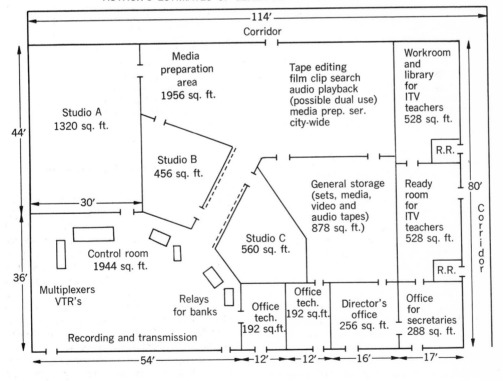

Scale: ⊢—⊣ = 4'

Figure 10-7. This is the author's sketch of space-need estimates for a thriving ITV organization at the district level. Many school-district ITV centers have far less. Space is needed in relation to the rate of program production and transmission.

Scale: $1/16'' = 1' -0''$

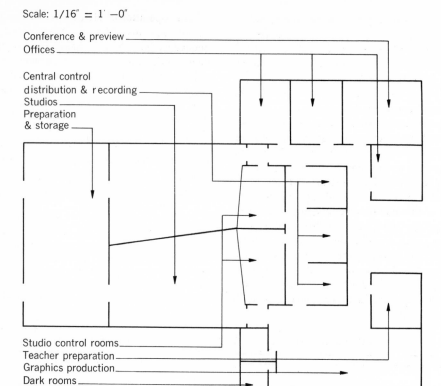

Conference & preview

Offices

Central control

distribution & recording

Studios

Preparation
& storage

Studio control rooms

Teacher preparation

Graphics production

Dark rooms

Figure 10-8. We present in this illustration the analysis of space needs as it appears in *Educational Facilities for New Media* prepared by Alan C. Green and his group and later published by DAVI of the NEA. This sketch indicates an extensive district center for the media preparation support of instruction. The serious student of television processes will do well to study this diagram carefully. (See also, for comparison, Figure 9-10.) *Courtesy Center for Architectural Research, R.P.I., Troy, New York.*

use by the school districts. J. Gerald Loughlin,[4] former school principal, director of Elmira Instructional Television and the Audiovisual Center, has this to say about his present facilities: "Our studio is equipped with three General-Electric vidicon cameras, a film chain, and two Ampex 2-inch video tape recorders. Although somewhat crowded, we find it possible to set up for three or four programs simultaneously, if necessary." Director Loughlin has also reported the following space allocations: Studio production area 900 square feet; and control room, recording, and transmitting area, 150 square feet. Additional operational spaces include staff offices, storage and program-preparation area, 900 square feet and an audiovisual media-production center of 630 square feet, a space that also serves citywide general media-preparation services. Mr. Loughlin has also reported the addition of three one-inch videotape recorder units for placement in schools not yet reachable by cable connections.

[4] J. Gerald Loughlin, "CATV in Education," *View*, Vol. 2, No. 4, August 1966, pp. 16–18.

Example 2: Operations at Plainedge, New York

The Plainedge school district television plan has been operating for a number of years on the FCC-established Instructional Television Fixed Service that became effective in 1963. This service utilizes the 2,500–2,690 megacycle band (also referred to as megaHertz) for on-the-air broadcast of fourteen programs weekly to Plainedge schools. The transmitter sends out a private television signal that is received and converted at each school. We shall be concerned with transmission systems in a later section, thus for the present we shall identify the nature of the operational spaces and the equipment units by means of which the program capability is developed. In the Plainedge system, the Director of Instructional Television reports that the total area is about 1,500 square feet. Of this space about 200 square feet make up the control room, and one end of the program production studio is a media-preparation and workroom area. The transmitter is located in a nearby auditorium stage area storage closet amounting to about 40 square feet, and additional general storage space is found in the studio area. Thus we can see that the total operational area amounts to a total of 1,540 square feet, and there is only one main production studio. Lights are suspended and are controlled by means of a switchboard for the lighting circuits.

The Plainedge instructional television programing capability is maintained by making videotapes of the programs and then transmitting them on an announced schedule. The various equipment units include

(a) Two Sarkes Tarzian Vidicon camera chains, lenses, tripods, console, and video monitors.

(b) One film chain with motion picture capability only.

(c) Microphones, audio tape recorder, and mixer and audio amplifier.

(d) One Ampex broadcast quality video tape recorded and modulator-amplifier.

(e) One 2,500–2,690 mHz band transmitter for one channel operation.

(f) Lights and control board.

According to reports of additional activity, the Plainedge, Plainview—Old Bethpage, and three other school districts (Bethpage, Farmingdale, and Massapequa) are combining their instructional television services in a five-district, South Oyster Bay, Long Island, New York television project. Thus rapid expansion of services in the area seems assured.

We have seen in the two examples limited, one-channel ITV services, operating in crowded and far from ideal environments. Yet we must recognize the value in such endeavors to experiment and gain valuable knowledge and experience for future expansion.

Some Equipment Needs for Program Capability. The nature of the uses made of instructional television and what is done with any given ITV program during or after it is completed, determine the kinds of equipment required. As we have said before, we are concerned in this instance with program availability from a central studio facility and our equipment needs are being estimated in that specific orientation. The following list indicates the required equipment units grouped under operational functions.

Producing Instructional Programs for Live Transmission, Minimum for One Studio

1. Two television cameras, broadcast-quality vidicon, with electronic viewfinders, lenses, and tripods.

2. Camera controls, console, 4 video monitors.

3. Microphones, audio tape recorder, audio mixer and amplifier.

4. One optical multiplexer for 16 mm film and 2×2 inch slides.

5. One RF modulator and transmitter unit for combining video and audio for RF transmission on a given channel frequency.

6. Lighting equipment and a control board.

7. Headsets and intercom system.

Additional Equipment for Program Preservation

1. One broadcast-quality videotape recorder.

2. One modulator for combining video and audio signals for transmission on a specified channel frequency.

3. One additional video monitor for the videotape unit.

Additional Equipment for Videotape Program Editing

1. One broadcast-quality videotape recorder with modulator.

2. One electronic editing accessory (preferably built into one of a pair of recorders).

Additional Equipment for Simultaneous Transmission of five ITV Programs
(For example, one *live* program, three videotape programs, and one film program)

1. Two additional videotape recorders, video monitors and modulators. (Assuming that at least one of the two VTR units listed previously ought to be free for other recording and playback activities.)

2. One additional film chain, video monitor, and modulator-transmitter-amplifier unit. (This assumes that the previously listed film chain will be used during the *live* broadcast.)

3. Amplifier for each modulator for feeding each of four extra channels.

4. External cable and connections from studio control room.

5. Two additional broadcast-quality vidicon camera units with zoom lenses, lights, camera controls, console controls, microphones, audio-control mixers and amplifiers, and additional video monitors for at least one additional production studio for rehearsal and actual, simultaneous, program-recording activity. This additional studio would be a minimum essential to produce programs for a five-channel transmission plan.

Figure 10-9. These pictures show action at the console, the 2-inch videotape recorder equipment to store locally produced programs, and the one-channel 2500 mHz transmission system being checked over by the center's technical staff. Program activity is expected to increase greatly in the immediate future with the implementation of the South Oyster Bay Television Project underwritten by a federal grant. *Courtesy South Oyster Bay Supplementary Education Center, Bethpage, New York.*

Additional Equipment for Remote Pick-up Programing

1. Two portable vidicon cameras, electronic viewfinders, lenses, portable switching unit.
2. Portable lighting units.
3. Microphones for videotape recorder.
4. One one-inch videotape recorder, portable model.

Additional Equipment for Off-the-Air Videotape Recording

1. A high-quality television receiver for tuning in an off-the-air RF signal.
2. One or more high-gain antenna systems feeding one or more of the videotape recording units.

Additional Equipment Units for Automatic Retrieval of Stored Programs

1. Dial-access system involving telephone-type relay circuitry.
2. Automatically activated videotape players arranged in program resource banks (or other recent automatically controlled transmission units).
3. Transmission equipment units for supplying all receiving stations in a given school, selected schools, or in the school system.

Considering again the space requirements stated earlier, we can see that as additional processes are added and the volume of programing activity increases, meeting the need for multiple studios, media preparation space, workroom and service areas, rehearsal and readying space, becomes essential. When centralized television services must carry a full citywide programing load that involves the use of several channels, the space-need estimates given should be considered as minimum, not maximum. The equipment units listed should also be considered as minimum for the functions indicated. Also, it is essential that all equipment components be interconnected to provide flexibility and ease of control. For example, four videotape recorders could be interconnected so that video and audio outputs could be switched by means of a patch board to the modulator for another desired channel.

Program Capability at the School-Building Instructional Television Studio

We now turn to a discussion of school-building ITV program production spaces and equip-

Figure 10-10. This important piece of programing equipment makes it possible to feed slides and film clips into the program continuity at the call of the director. When purchased film is put onto videotape for subsequent repetitive use, the copyright law calls for clearance from producers. Makeshift devices such as projectors and television pick-up from either front- or rear-projection screen surfaces may have to be used, but hopefully only as a temporary measure. *Courtesy Dade County Public Schools, Miami, Florida.*

ment. Since we must be prepared to make creative uses of the television medium in the curriculum, one of the first essentials for planning an internal school-building cable-distribution system is to make sure that two-way service connections are installed. Such two-way closed-loop installations will permit the origination in and distribution from any given classroom or school-building studio. Thus we point out that while we may refer to a program production and transmission studio as a supplementary unit, we may also refer to any number of connected classrooms that may serve as improvised studios for a number of different program production jobs. For the time being we shall consider the school-building studio as an operating center for the school's production and distribution activities.

Some Space Needs in the School-Building ITV Studio. In earlier paragraphs we have indicated the need for school-building studios and therefore we need not repeat this justification. In the next section we shall point out that program capability may also be enhanced by the use of improvised classroom originating facilities for special purposes. For the time being we indicate some estimates of space needs assuming that the local program demands such expansion into school-building units. We face two situations in recommending studio space in any given school building. In one situation we think of remodeling a classroom turned over to the audiovisual media-service center for operating television services, and on the other we think of recommending space for a new school that is being planned. In both cases the actual space needs would be the same, but in the latter case we might be hopeful of getting a larger and more suitably arranged area. For our present purposes, we shall assume that we are dealing with a classroom unit that has been made available for remodeling, hopefully one that has at least a twelve-foot ceiling. We can also assume for our purposes that the classroom would be in an elementary school where the nature of activity usually calls for a somewhat larger classroom measuring 36 feet by 28 feet. Thus we have as a total area a little more than 1,000 square feet of space. As we think about the utilization of such an area, we may also assume that other departments in the audiovisual media-service center will be able to give certain kinds of special support such as making slides and transparencies and providing film clips for programing uses. With these assumptions in mind we list some estimates for good use of the available space indicated as follows:

1. *Studio Presentation Space.* This area would be the main program production center providing good quality sound and lighting. The limited size of this area would permit only minimum camera maneuverability, but it is assumed that a zoom lens will be available on one camera. Two separate program sets may be utilized, if urgently needed, one being used for limited action such as narration for combining and/or transferring other media to videotape. The studio area may have to be diminished by some 70 square feet for media-making activities plus a small area for a shelving unit or metal cabinet for supplies. *Estimate:* 480 square feet.

2. *General Storage Area.* This area ought to be curtained or partitioned off from the rest of the studio. It is needed to store extra sets and backgrounds, rear-projection screen unit, overhead projector and low mobile stand, special charts, and apparatus that needs to be maintained in a state of readiness for ITV use. *Estimate:* 80 square feet.

3. *Workroom and Ready Room for Teachers and Office for Secretary.* This space may be needed for a part- or full-time secretary, teachers' aides, or for study and work space for teachers to use prior to making presentations to be taped. A few library-type carrels, a worktable, and a typing desk for a secretary or for teachers to use. *Estimate:* 112 square feet.

4. *Control Room Area.* In this space there should be room for tape storage, taping operations, the film chain with both slide and film projectors, media table near the multiplexer, the camera control racks, transmitter equipment if separate, a maintenance workbench and underneath storage. The console for both video and audio control would be elevated to provide visibility of the studio area. *Estimate:* 336 square feet.

Some Observations About the Estimates for School-Building ITV Studio Spaces. We refer the reader to Figure 10-11 where he may study the relationships of the spaces identified in the preceding items and draw his own conclusions about the limitations that a small-size studio places on its potential volume of operations. As we pointed out earlier, the total space for this particular analysis of functions amounted to only 1,000 square feet. As we can readily see, the studio under operating conditions would be cramped, yet given time to get ready, a number of separate programing and transmitting operations could be carried on simultaneously, such as:

1. Transmitting a live presentation as for total-group instruction by a teacher in mathematics or communications to three large groups in a school.

2. Taping the live presentation simultaneously on one recorder for subsequent, repetitive use.

3. Making a videotape recording of an off-the-air program for subsequent and repetitive use, as from a regional network for schools.

DIAGRAM OF SCHOOL BUILDING ITV STUDIO LAYOUT

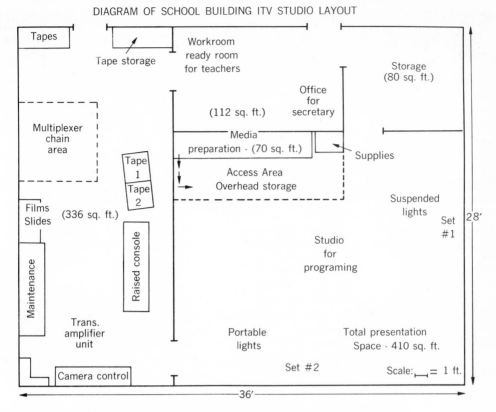

Figure 10-11. In contrast to Figure 10-7, this author's sketch is an analysis of space needs for an ITV studio at the school-building level. We assume that the media center will support this ITV endeavor with assistance in many ways, even to supplying leadership and staff and being responsible for its operation. We believe that for serious and mature programing efforts at the building level an operational area of 4,400–5,300 square feet would be a more realistic requirement.

4. With additional equipment units such as a videotape recorder, a separate program on tape could be sent out simultaneously with the live presentation, but this would require also a two-channel cable operation with an additional modulator-amplifier unit for the second channel.

Such operations as we have mentioned are meant to be considered only as possibilities, although they may be valuable supplements to ITV system-wide utilization plans in the modern media-oriented school. We must emphasize the important possibility that the school-building studio would not only be used to increase the program capability in direct relationship to the school's own teaching purposes, but such facilities as we have listed would greatly enhance the production capability of any system-wide studio operation as a pro-

graming resource. We are not saying that each school in any given system would have to have a studio facility such as we have just discussed. However, it would be highly desirable to organize, as a minimum, one such supplementary studio for each level of instruction—elementary, junior and senior high schools, and junior or community colleges. As volume of ITV programing increases, as the use of ITV on both firm and flexible schedules makes major curriculum contributions, and as teaching systems demand the use of videotapes or programed instructional television sequences, the ITV district-wide plans will have to encompass decentralized as well as centralized program capability.

Some Equipment Needs for ITV School-Building Studio Unit. For the kind of capability desired in a school-building studio, we can

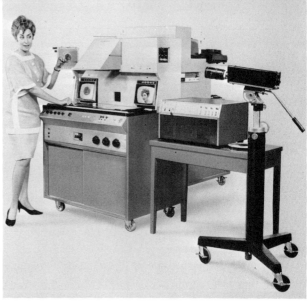

Figure 10-12. These pictures indicate the nature of either automatic television studios or mobile studios. Packages such as these may fill a growing need for the installations in school buildings, for program production, largely for videotape recording, and local distribution. The top picture shows a studio package that was made for limited budgets. Even so, this package was priced at $22,000. Notice fixed cameras, console, and lectern with controls. The bottom picture shows a mobile studio package that has a built-in multiplexer with slide and film capability. Teachers who can design a good television continuity can make their presentation and record it right on the spot. (*Top picture,* courtesy Packard-Bell Company, Newbury Park, California. *Bottom picture,* courtesy Westinghouse Electric Corporation, Metuchen, New Jersey.)

suggest that if school-system needs are also to be met on a contributing basis by such programing, then broadcast-quality equipment ought to be specified. At any rate, every effort ought to be made to provide maximum quality from equipment units that are compatible with the school's and district's purposes. See Figure 10-12. Later on we shall discuss transmission systems and we emphasize now the need to provide maximum quality throughout all phases of the television operation from production to reception. The equipment units we suggest as a minimum are as follows:

1. Two broadcast-quality vidicon camera chains with electronic viewfinders, lenses, tripods, console, and video monitors.

2. Microphones, audio tape recorder and mixer-amplifier at the console.

3. Optical multiplexer chain using film and slide projectors.

4. Suspended lights and a switchboard control.

5. Headsets and intercom system.

6. Two videotape recorders with electronic editing feature on one of the units.

7. Appropriate modulator for RF transmission and supplementary transmitters and amplifiers for multi-channel operation.

8. An antenna receiving system for receiving and taping programs from external sources.

Program Capability by Means of TV Equipment at Teaching Stations

We have come to look upon teaching stations as a means of supplementing program production for instructional television purposes. We note first the possibility of connecting a videotape recorder, for example a high-quality, one-inch tape recorder, to a classroom receiver which may be viewed by some thirty pupils. Since the tape recorder in this case is equipped with a modulator unit a number of receivers can be supplied with the taped program, thus making possible the effective use of the unit by a large group as a total group in team-teaching presentations. With the addition of the appropriate amplifier or amplifiers, and the needed splitters, the tape-recorded program can also be transmitted throughout the school on the internal coaxial cable system generally used for programing from the school-building or school-system studio facilities. We see in this process the capability of receiving via the school's master antenna system, off-the-air program content from many different sources of supply. Videotapes of such centralized local, regional, state, or national sources, could also be distributed to the school building for transmission within the school unit as scheduled.

Mobile units of conveniently packaged classroom receiving, recording and transmitting equipment, may be moved, for example, from one science room to another, or from a nearby social science classroom for special program-production uses. The packaged units may also be equipped with a camera that may be moved or fixed in a classroom where lighting is adequate and be used to record a particular

presentation by a teacher. Such presentations may then be combined later with film clips and slides at the main studio as a part of a teaching system that will be copied and used repetitively, and even exchanged with other resource banks. Teachers who use television display or image-magnification systems in their classrooms to make use of minute objects, a wide variety of diagrammatic content, or demonstrate laboratory techniques, for example, may also combine views of themselves and the illustrative material they utilize on the videotape of the classroom unit we have just discussed. We have not yet mentioned that in classroom situations, teachers may make presentations that are immediately transmitted to other classrooms, but we have repeatedly emphasized the value of repetitive use of a presentation by videotape recording methods. When ITV programs are good they are good because of what they do to pupils. When they are preserved, they may be used again and again with equal results, provided that the systems under which they are used are valid, and the conditions for learning are optimum. See Figure 10-13 for examples of processes and equipment packages.

Some Observations About Space Needs for Classroom Television Program Operations. It can be readily understood that in a studio situation we can engineer quality control over programing efforts. We cannot generally match either the audio and video quality achieved in the studio in the classroom program production activity. However, with installation of a camera, pre-set and fixed lights, and teacher-controlled camera-switching devices (to permit switching from one overhead camera for diagrams and apparatus demonstrations to a camera that shows a close-up view of the teacher), some highly desirable programs may be recorded that will serve valuable uses in the curriculum. If we have a desirable teaching station to begin with we can say that little if any extra space will be needed for developing the kind of programing capability that we have just described. If we consider equipment units such as Tri-Video, Tele-Center, the Ampex Videotrainer, and the Norelco TV School Master, it becomes obvious that space in front of a teaching station area would be approximately 25 square feet if camera and lights are mounted in the ceiling. If the camera is on the floor some 20 feet of additional space would be needed, and if we figure 15 additional square

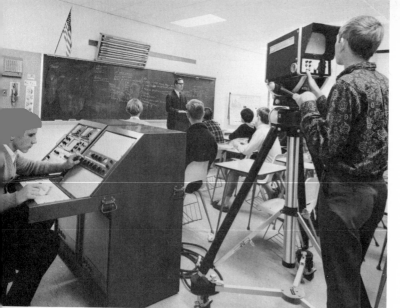

Figure 10-13. Television equipment may be utilized in classrooms for various instructional uses, including live transmission throughout the school, the recording of presentations, and special uses in connection with pupil learning activities. In the top view we depict the use of mobile camera and console equipment, with or without a videotape recorder component. In the second view we show one of the mobile, compressed packages consisting of camera, one-inch videotape recording unit, and a monitor. This unit can also record off the air, and can transmit to other classrooms via the school's coaxial-cable distribution system. The third photograph shows what is called a Tri-Pak Unit that again consists of a videotape recorder (this time a one-half inch model), a monitor and a small camera with a fairly sturdy tripod mount. See also Figures 7-9 and 9-5. (*Top view* courtesy Northern Highlands Regional High School, Allendale, New Jersey, and the Sylvania Electric Products Corporation, New York, New York. *Middle view*, Ampex Corporation, Redwood City, California. *Bottom view*, courtesy General Electric Company, Syracuse, New York.)

feet for portable lights, the total space requirement for the equipment would be on the order of 60 square feet. If we assume that a teacher is working part of the time with an image-magnification television camera mounted on a six-foot long table as an additional component, then the total would be increased by 30 square feet. We now have a total figure of 90 square feet taken up by classroom television equipment. All of this may or may not be in addition to space used by the teacher normally.

Summary of Classroom TV Equipment Needs. At this time a good case could be made for classroom use of ITV equipment as a supplement to other centrally located studios. We must add that the several available ITV record-playback systems vary in price, but for the level of sophistication we assume in general, the cost would run to $6,500 including a view-finder camera. The front-of-room image-magnification system would of course be in addition. The various classroom equipment units envisioned are as follows:

1. One closed-circuit TV and videotape recording-playback system (with the possibility of using the TV camera in a suspended fixed-mount position).

2. One image-magnification television camera with fixed lights and accessories, located on a demonstration table. See Figure 10-14.

3. Additional transmission and amplification equipment to take care of long cable runs to various classrooms and to make possible the use of several splitters as would be necessary to supply classrooms with one or more receiving sets.

Program Capability Through Procurement from External Sources

This is the fourth aspect of potential program capability. We have mentioned rich sources from regional, state, and national agencies and distributors, and when schools are properly equipped, these sources can be readily made available. We can summarize these means as follows:

1. Regional telecasts on appropriate schedules from museums, other school systems, and from statewide networks, *live* or already on videotape.

2. Using videotape (or other program capsules) that are distributed as units, or in series, as parts of instructional packages, directly to school-building and school-system studio transmitting facilities.

We have mentioned earlier the possibilities just listed, but we have not yet afforded them the attention they deserve. We can point out, however, that if such sources are to be useful, school-building, district-wide, and classroom videotape playback facilities will have to be provided and used to the fullest extent. School-building and classroom transmitting centers will become obviously more important and even indispensable for meeting specific needs when multiple-channel operations and crowded facilities at central studios begin to interfere with curriculum needs. Facilities and spaces in addition to capabilities already described are not required for procurement and use of programs from external sources. However, such procurement demands master antenna systems

Figure 10-14. In this television equipment for classroom use we see probably the first method of using instructional television ever to be devised strictly for the classroom. Here we have an image-magnification system arranged for use with a microscopic image. Techniques for using *overhead television* as it is often called have been well worked out with devices for viewing slides that were designed for projection. With this system, provided receivers are appropriately placed, everyone, even when seated in the back rows has a front-row vantage point. *Courtesy Radio Corporation of America, Camden, New Jersey.*

or other transmission and reception systems. In fact we cannot consider the use of ITV programs from outside the school until we have the capability to receive them off the air or via cable, or until agencies send them by parcel post to telecasting agencies in the schools.

Some Hints for the Design of Studio Spaces

Before we leave the discussion of programing capability in general and the subject of studio spaces specifically, we ought to suggest in summary form a number of major critical recommendations that should be made regarding the design of these program-producing areas. We have referred to both centralized and decentralized studios and have mentioned the use of space in old buildings. We wish now to highlight a few factors that should be borne in mind when discussing studio-space specifications regardless of where they are located.

1. Floor-to-ceiling heights in studio-programing areas should be at least twelve feet—and preferably even higher. In other than studio areas, excessive heights may be converted to overhead storage areas, or mezzanine office and other auxiliary spaces.

2. Lights should be suspended on tracks or grids to provide unhampered mobility of cameras and to increase the amount of operational floor space for programing activity.

3. Acoustical treatment should be provided to improve sound quality.

4. Air conditioning installations that employ low-level motor and fan noise are an essential in both studio and control rooms.

5. Studio floors should be smooth and hard. Soft tiles may become pitted from table legs and camera tripods, thus interfering with ease of camera handling.

6. It is essential to provide sufficient AC operating power, and to also provide a sufficient number of outlets for present and expanded uses of any given facility. Such power requirements should be identified specifically.

7. Optimum access areas to multiple studios, in which to carry on auxiliary services of related operations, are necessary for flow of activities and personnel. Doorways should be wider and higher than normal.

8. Studio and control room must be related spacially to provide visual surveillance, with proper connectors for camera cables and audio lines, located in the walls that separate them.

9. Provide for intercommunication between television programing, control, and auxiliary spaces. Elevation of console will not only provide better direct visual control, but will enable the program director to operate the console himself as needed.

10. In plans for new construction, specify a four-inch raceway, or trough, covered by a metal plate along the base of each wall of the control room and as required also in studio spaces. Conduits for power ought to be considered additionally. Floor troughs are essential, particularly in control rooms where large cables and connectors tie console, camera controls, multiplexer, videotape recorders, audio lines, and transmitter lines together for both safety and convenience.

11. Suitable backdrops of gray and blue ought to be mounted on traverse systems for use in areas of the studio where programs are to originate.

An often difficult and vexing problem for the media director to solve when planning to make use of television, especially on a citywide basis, is that of making a wise decision on the adoption and implementation of a television program transmission system. Regardless of whether the ITV programs are to be scheduled for large-group use, or dial-selected by individual learners, one or more systems must be employed in transmitting the program from a studio site, or from a videotape resource bank, to the viewing station. A thorough discussion of the facets of such a problem lies beyond the scope of this book, but we shall discuss the main systems that are presently in common use. In this discussion we shall consider the delivery of ITV programs from the output of the transmitter in the main studio to the input of the building where it is received. We shall also discuss in another section the problem of reception, distribution, and display.

Operational Facilities and Equipment: Transmission Systems

Before we proceed to a description and a brief analysis of some of the main possibilities that are commonly used for ITV systems, we will provide the reader with a summary listing of a few basic facts about the nature of television transmission. We can then emphasize the nature of the problem that the prospective audiovisual media director will have to deal with before deciding what system to recommend. Some of these main facts and considerations are as follows:

1. Television programs (television signals) are ordinarily made up of two separate components, the picture signal from the TV camera and the audio signal from the microphones.

2. Video and audio signal components may be combined and transmitted on a single carrier wave. When this is done the signal is called an RF signal (radio frequency) and this signal can be transmitted through space by means of broadcast or open-circuit procedures, or it can be transmitted by a coaxial cable.

3. Standard television receivers are generally used in classrooms to produce both picture and sound.

4. RF signals may be transmitted over long distances by cable, but amplifiers along the way must be employed to maintain signal strength. A number of factors need to be considered in any transmission and distribution system. What is the length of cable? How many schools and their receivers are being tapped off from main coaxial lines? What is the quality of the devices by means of which the incoming signal to a school is split? What is the quality of the modulator-transmitter unit? How many channels are being used?

5. A cable handling RF transmission will carry all of the 12 VHF channels, simultaneously with each channel signal operating on its own pre-set frequency level. Thus each program source, *live* or taped, will require its own modulator-transmitter unit. Several so-called subchannels may currently be activated because transmitters and amplifiers are available for controlling the frequencies. Special receiving equipment may have to be used, however, if the best possible image resolution is to be obtained.

6. The video component alone, coming directly from a TV camera, may be transmitted over a cable directly to a television receiver. Such video signals are understandably of highest possible quality. Since they are not tuned to any particular channel, the entire coaxial cable is used solely for one video program at a time. Television monitors have to be used for receiving such signals, or a regular television receiver has to be modified to eliminate or bypass other circuits such as the audio, for example. Thus when a cable is used for video transmission only, it has to be scheduled, or a separate cable has to be provided.

7. When the video signal is transmitted over a coaxial cable, a separate audio component line has to be provided from the microphone to an audio amplifier and thence to a loudspeaker or sound distribution system at the viewing station.

8. Intercommunication cables are not coaxial. They are essential for communication between studios and classrooms or between crew members, and have to be separate from the coaxial cables that carry RF signals.

9. RF broadcast transmission may be so controlled (low-power broadcasting) in its radiational effects that it becomes to all intents and purposes a closed-circuit system as does the coaxial cable system. This is particularly true of the point-to-point control possible in line-of-sight transmission with microwave equipment.

In the light of these basic facts and conditions, we shall proceed to a brief description of some of the generally available transmission systems being used by schools for their ITV programs.

Transmission by Coaxial Cable

We turn first to coaxial cable systems of transmission and to the ways in which this system is likely to be handled. We have already mentioned in other connections the fact that coaxial cable systems provide two-way RF signal capability when classrooms are looped into a continuous circuit, and in the preceding section the general applicability of the RF system was pointed out. It is also important to emphasize the reliability of the cable method and to note that no FCC license is required for such transmission linkages. It should also be borne in mind that the main transmission cable may possess a wide range of capability characteristics so that it may function in an ITV transmission system in a number of different ways. We are suggesting that new uses for RF signal cable may be developed that will not

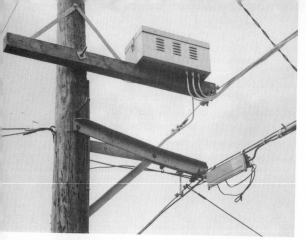

Figure 10-15. This method of closed-circuit transmission seems to be the only one that will provide more than four channels for simultaneous telecasting. This system should be studied in comparison with the advantages of the 2,500 mHz Instructional Television Fixed Service established by the FCC. *Courtesy Jerrold Electronics Corporation, Philadelphia, Pennsylvania.*

only link up computerized operations, but utilize additional channels as well for unusually high-definition content with special receiving equipment.

Some Advantages of Cable Transmission. Since the Bell System cable-leasing plan is one of the two basic and reasonably available transmission possibilities open to school districts, we ought to deal at least in summary form with its advantages. The following list of advantages for this transmission system has been compiled by Deuel.[5]

1. A consistently high-quality signal at all locations independent of distance or terrain.
2. Facilities which can provide large numbers of TV channels operating at the same time and under most situations, and which are also capable of handling color transmission.
3. Inclusion of all repair and maintenance in the monthly charge, on a twenty-four hour basis, if necessary.
4. Facilities which require no license or regulation of any kind to operate.
5. A private system which is not subject to interference due to obstructions, buildings, or external signals.
6. Freedom from engineering and right-of-way problems, which are the responsibility of the Telephone Company.
7. Experienced personnel locally who are readily available to serve the systems on a moment's notice.

[5] Richard E. Deuel, Jr., "A Reaction: The Plainedge Instructional TV Fixed Service," *Audiovisual Instruction*, Vol. 9, No. 8, October 1964, pp. 558–559.

8. A system which does not require the construction of towers or antennas on school buildings.
9. Provision of facilities constructed to the highest technical standards and maintained with the latest type of test equipment.
10. A minimum of capital funds required to establish an effective system, thus making funds available for other school projects.

It is with these advantages in mind that we regretfully note that coaxial cable as a commodity is expensive in the sense of stringing up and using a twenty-mile network, for example; the need for amplifiers over long runs is essential; and the technology of transmission, maintenance, and reception processes is not only complex, but is undergoing rapid change and development. Since the media program director in a city school system can rarely get permission to string a coaxial-cable line on poles owned and operated by other agencies, even if his school system desired to have him do so, he has little choice but to lease TV cable-transmission services, and to these possibilities we now turn.

Leasing Coaxial-Cable Facilities from the Bell System. With the Bell System all needed equipment units, cables, and connectors are supplied, installed, and maintained by the local telephone service companies for a monthly rental charge. Price estimates have to be based on cable distances, number of channels utilized on the cable, number of connectors at the school sites, and other factors that have to be determined locally. Even though technology is changing rapidly, and costs are too, a generalized rate table (subject of course to change for specific situations) will be helpful to reveal the nature of the process as well as to give some idea of the method by which price estimates are figured as shown by the chart on the following page.[6]

Having pointed out the basic items generally used in arriving at cost estimates, we must now reiterate the fact that technological advancements dictate the development of an entirely new rate scale on a 12-channel basis that in specific situations may prove to reduce these rates by 50 per cent. Even though prices may change drastically, we can see that given a specific number of schools, the number of classrooms to be served, and the airline miles

[6] Based on information from Bell System relative to 1966 operations.

Main Cable Monthly Rental Charge for One Quarter Airline Mile of Each Leg Between Schools

1st Channel,	$15.00
2nd Channel,	5.00
3rd Channel,	3.00
4th Channel,	3.00
5th Channel,	2.00
6th Channel,	2.00

Cost Estimate for a $2,000 Modulator at Each Signal Source

Monthly Rental Charge for Each Channel :

1st Channel,	$45.00
2nd Channel,	35.00
3rd Channel,	30.00
4th Channel,	20.00
5th Channel,	20.00
6th Channel,	15.00

Cost Estimate for Each Output at Each Receiving Point

Monthly Rental Charge for Each School Served :

1st Channel,	$10.00
2nd Channel,	5.00
3rd Channel,	3.00
4th Channel,	2.00
5th Channel,	1.50
6th Channel,	1.00

Cost Estimate for the Connector Outlet in Each Classroom

Per Classroom per Month, $1.25

between each school-building unit, this rate table could be used to develop approximation of cost. In light of included maintenance to provide trouble-free service, low capital- equipment expense, depreciation, and replacement costs, the case for cable-leasing arrangements appears strong. We shall discuss one other cable-leasing possibility, which may not be generally available, and then proceed to describe a low-power broadcast system that is nevertheless referred to as a closed-circuit operation.

Leasing Coaxial-Cable Facilities from the Community Antenna Television Company. The possibility of leasing a cable-transmission facility from Community Antenna Television companies may not be legally permissible. Yet, in the case of the ITV program of Elmira, New York, Public Schools, this is the method by which twenty of Elmira's twenty-two schools receive ITV service. It has been reported that the Elmira Public Schools System has contracted for the exclusive use of one of the Elmira Video Company's channels at an annual cost of $5,000.[7] However, according to FCC controls governing their organization and operation, Community Antenna Television companies are organized solely for the broadcast of commercial programs, and therefore may not offer facilities on a lease basis as a common carrier would do, for other purposes. State legislation in the various states may also prevent the rental of cable space by CATV companies, and moreover, state public utility commissions may set up rigid controls over transmission conditions within and across their borders. Unique situations have of course arisen around the country, and hence some exceptions to basic rules have apparently been made. Just what turn these matters will take in the years ahead cannot be predicted, but it seems highly improbable that what has come to be known as CATV will enter generally into the common carrier field unless some drastic changes are made in the technology of handling electrical power and telephone cables on poles or running them through trenches or tunnels. If and when school districts organize themselves into corporate agencies for inaugurating CATV systems for their own ITV transmission activities, they are likely to encounter some major problems in suspending or burying their cables. At the present time it is common practice for CATV organizations to either rent poles from utility and common carrier companies, and then string their own coaxial cable linkages or lease the cable they need from the Bell System companies.

In view of the preceding discussions, it seems obvious that a school district has two main possibilities for interconnecting schools for ITV programing, namely, leasing cable from the local Bell System company, or owning and operating its own 2,500 mHz FCC-controlled, Instructional Television Fixed Service transmission system. Under this system, an RF signal is radiated on a maximum of four channels, using repeaters and microwave point-to-point transmitters as required to reach all of the schools in a given school district. We describe this transmission possibility next.

7 Based on information for 1966 operations.

Figure 10-16. This is the first 2,500 mHz transmitting antenna ever installed. The antenna is on top of a tower that elevates it to a height of 75 feet above the ground. This antenna radiates the signal to all schools in the five districts included in the recently formed South Oyster Bay Television Project. The antenna was erected and used in 1963. The Robert E. Picken School shows its receiving antenna that is the only means of getting the signal from the transmitting antenna. Hence the system is in fact a private one for the schools involved. *Courtesy South Oyster Bay Supplementary Education Center, Bethpage, New York.*

Transmission by Instructional Television Fixed Service

The FCC-assigned frequency band for this service is 2,500-2,686 mHz in the microwave portion of the spectrum. The frequency of this band is much higher than the familiar UHF channels in which the highest channel is only 890 mHz. Since the FCC has assigned this band for educational use only, this portion of the spectrum is in a sense a private band with its transmissions not being receivable on TV sets using regular channels. One of the difficulties in the use of this broadcast band is that the signal has to be telecast in a line-of-sight path from the transmitter antenna to the receiving equipment, and hence, interference by terrain, buildings, and distance limitations have to be considered and accurately surveyed. Where distance is too great, for example, beyond an obstruction-free twenty-mile path,

repeater stations have to be set up, or new paths set up around obstructions, or a point-to-point microwave link constructed.

The system operates by transmitting an RF signal through space in direction-controlled areas at something like ten watts of power. Special receiving antennas pick up the signal at each school building, convert it to VHF television channels and then distribute it via a master antenna coaxial-cable distribution system to all classrooms. The main advantages of such a system are as follows:

1. Up to four channels may be used simultaneously.

2. The system is private.

3. The system operation requires only a second class FCC technician license, and participating teachers and students may need only a third class license.

4. The system is owned outright by the

Figure 10-17. These three photographs show one of the receiving antennae in the 2,500 mHz ITV Fixed Service installation that is a part of the Diocesan system of Miami, Florida; the three major components of any 2,500 mHz Fixed Service installation; and a close-up view of the Micro-Link Corporation's receiving antenna with the converter unit that feeds the proper signal into the school's coaxial distribution system to each teaching station. (*Top views*, courtesy Radio Corporation of America, Camden, New Jersey. *Bottom view*, courtesy Micro-Link Systems, Varian Associates, Copiague, New York.)

school district and claims are made that cost for the system when schools are widely separated is much less than for cable linkages.

5. Each new school in the area of the transmitted signal may be added to the system by providing the antenna and the distribution system.

As we have already pointed out, interference may result from obstructions, and installation costs may be unusually high when sites for repeater towers have to be acquired, roads constructed for servicing, and preconstruction engineering surveys carried out. Competitors point out that all long-term expenditures should be figured in before net costs are established. FCC licensing may or may not prove to be a disadvantage, but the fact remains that a maintenance staff is essential. It seems obvious that there are significant advantages that could accrue, but as with any proposed transmission system, the decision must be based on thorough study. It is doubtful that teachers and students ought to take over any great portion of the technical operation of such a situation. Teachers have significant professional work to do that takes a high priority, and even though some students might find valuable experience in such technical work, full-time personnel are recommended so that most of the time of students can be given to serious study activities.

Some Examples in the Schools. Considerable experimental work was carried on in the Plainedge, New York, public schools by the Adler Educational Service. It was there that the low-power broadcast system was successfully demonstrated on June 14, 1962. Subsequently, the FCC established the Instructional Television Fixed Service in 1963. The cost of the Plainedge [8] transmission equipment amounted to approximately $28,000 for the one channel in operation. Six elementary schools, two junior high schools, one senior high school and the central administration building (seven airline miles of cable) were within the transmission area at the time. Added to this figure is the maintenance cost, for either a permanent technical staff member or for a private maintenance contract with a commercial company. The cost for Micro-Link Systems' (Varian Associates) installation [9] of a four-channel system for the Mifflin County School District in Pennsylvania, serving 340 classrooms and 10,000 pupils, was $264,195.

Just outside of Houston, Texas, the Spring Branch independent school district is operating a 24-school, 2-channel, 2,500 mHz network. Studio and transmitting equipment amounted to approximately $70,000. The cost for each school's receiving antenna, signal converter, distribution circuit, plus 325 television receivers in the classrooms amounted to $142,000. Rochester, New York, also transmits instructional programs over three channels to 46,000 pupils in 52 city schools. Rochester's television studio staff includes an executive producer, producer-director, director, chief engineer,

technician, artist, and a secretary, all full time. Part-time workers include six production assistants, six cameramen, an artist, and a typist. For field maintenance work, the crew includes a field maintenance supervisor and two television repairmen. The 2,500 mHz system of Newburgh, New York, transmits instructional television programs over two channels to some 500 classrooms in 25 public and parochial schools. Also in its first stage of development, the Fresno County 2,500 mHz system serves 47 schools within sixteen miles of the county seat of Fresno, California. Repeater sites will be developed as the service is extended to all schools in the county.

The Jerrold Electronics Corporation in its valuable booklet for school personnel makes the following generalized estimates for 2,500 mHz fixed service installations:

	Cost Range
Transmitter, Tower, and Antenna, One Channel (depending on height)	$15,000 to $30,000
Each Additional Transmit Channel	$10,000
Each School Receiver-Converter, Antenna and Mounting (assuming 20 feet above roof)	$1,250 to $1,500

Maintenance (for ten years, per year percentage of initial cost) amounts to 5 per cent. It is recommended that an independent consultant conduct a site survey . . . A budgetary figure for this service can be estimated at $50 per school, and would include path profiles, sketches, and necessary photographs . . . The survey will determine the best location for the transmitting antenna; which schools will receive satisfactory signals with standard equipment; and which might require more powerful receiver-converter units, larger antennas, higher towers, or alternate arrangements. [10]

As we have emphasized previously, the citywide media director has several vexing problems on his hands, the solutions to which may be anything but easy. Thorough study at the engineering level will be needed, and he will also find the cooperative effort of many other colleagues to be of inestimable value in formulating recommendations for action.

One other operational aspect of using ITV in

[8] Jay M. Brill, "A New Television Service for Educators," *Audiovisual Instruction*, Vol. 9, No. 4, April 1964, pp. 220–221.

[9] Reported in *View*, Vol. 2, No. 4, August 1966, p. 4.

[10] *1966 Schoolman's Guide to ETV Communications* (Philadelphia: Jerrold Electronics Corp., 1966), p. 19.

the schools remains to be discussed, insofar as equipment and facilities are concerned, and this is the aspect of reception and viewing. We look at the process of reception as picking up a received signal at the school by whatever means it comes, and distributing it, after optimum electronic treatment, to teaching stations or to individual study carrels, for planned and significant viewing.

Operational Facilities and Equipment: Reception and Viewing

We are aware at this point of the various sources of program content and the means by which they are transmitted to the schools in any given district. Thus we visualize one kind of antenna for the 2,500 mHz fixed-service transmission, and another type of antenna for transmission via statewide broadcast facilities. Of course, no antenna at all is required in cases where transmissions are received by coaxial cable. In the former case, we need two different types of antennas, each of which may feed signals into its own converter, then out to a mixer where they are subsequently split and distributed to receiving sets. When coaxial cable is used, we have a directly usable signal that is amplified and split, and then amplified again as required during long cable runs to all sections of a school building. This situation leads us to treat first the topic of reception by a master antenna system, referred to as MATV.

Reception via MATV

Regional and statewide educational television stations generally have large school populations that use their programs which are almost always broadcast on either UHF or VHF frequencies. Schools that use these programing services must install one or more receiving antennas, must convert UHF signals to VHF signals by means of a converter, and must then mix signals from various channels to supply a composite signal throughout a coaxial cable in a school building to each classroom receiver where a given participating teacher tunes in. Other teachers in other classrooms would similarly tune in the same program on the same channel

Figure 10-18. ITV Coordinator of the Spring Branch Independent School District is shown observing the controls of the Micro-Link two-channel transmitter. This system broadcasts 10 hours daily to 24 schools. In the bottom picture the chief engineer of the Spring Branch ITV center is threading the videotape recorder in the control room. *Courtesy Spring Branch Independent School District, Houston, Texas.*

or tune in another program coming in on another channel in an entirely different subject field. Now, just what facilities are likely to be needed in the operation of such a reception linkage? We can answer this question in considerable, yet not complete detail, since information about conditions such as local signal strength, number of channels available, directions of the various sources, and interference with transmitted signals is lacking. However, since the media program director must sense the need for expert advice, and must himself make some sound recommendations, it is most important to have knowledge and insight into how the process works. He should get any extra help he needs from dealers, state department of education consultants, engineers, and technical specialists as to just what special arrangements are required.

The Basic MATV Equipment Arrangements. We shall start first by assuming that we have coming in at a given school building at a given hour of the day one UHF channel program and three VHF channel programs. We shall further assume that the three VHF programs originate from different sources and are of different strengths, hence need transformation and separate amplifiers (a strip amplifier instead of the broadband type) for better signal control. We now start with the antennas and show the component parts needed for reception and a two-way distribution loop to all teaching stations as follows:

1. One UHF antenna with a transformer (balun) and a converter to change the incoming UHF signal to an appropriate VHF signal, to be carried by an appropriate channel, and a strip amplifier. (UHF signals suffer such losses in strength on coaxial cable as to preclude their use.)

2. Three single-band antennas, one for each VHF channel, properly rotated and fixed for optimum signal strength, each with a transformer (balun) and an appropriate strip amplifier. (Signal strength on each channel must be equal for the system.)

3. One coupler for the system by means of which the four VHF signals (originally one UHF and three VHF signals) are mixed, split, and fed to the coaxial-cable loop.

4. A complete coaxial-cable linkage system for connecting each classroom with every other classroom and with the main coaxial line on a two-way basis, with additional line amplifiers as required.

5. Each classroom to be equipped with a two-way ITV connector, such as the Jerrold J-Jacks, so that each teaching station can become an originating as well as a receiving

station for ITV programs. The so-called *closed loop* hook-up makes this possible. One teaching station would originate and distribute on one channel while another classroom would receive a program simultaneously on a different channel.

6. One or more standard television 23-inch receivers in each classroom.

Looking at the preceding list of components, we can now suggest that under different transmission circumstances such as equal signal strengths and with channel sources lying in the same directions, it is likely that a single broadband VHF antenna and broadband amplifier could be substituted for the three VHF single-band antennas and matching strip amplifiers in the preceding list. The UHF channel would require a separate antenna and a converter and amplifier as listed previously. Otherwise the components would be largely the same. Broadband amplifiers amplify the signals of all VHF channels equally, and this action may preclude their use in some situations.

Reception via 2,500 mHz Television Fixed Service

Since this system of transmission has already been discussed, we have but to relate the reception system to the MATV system just described. If we assume that all of the components in the preceding list have been installed, then we have only to add the special school-building 2,500 mHz antenna, tower, and converter which changes the low-power channel to a specific VHF channel signal. This signal is then fed into an appropriate VHF strip amplifier and on into the coupler for mixing, splitting, and routing to the school's coaxial-cable loop. This antenna would therefore operate in the system described much as the UHF antenna-converter unit would work. When two to four channels of low-power radiation are being employed, the composite signal on the school's antenna has to be converted to the several VHF channels, each sent to a strip amplifier or to a broadband amplifier and thence into the coupler and to the classroom cable.

Reception Via Coaxial Cable

We have already noted the advantages of transmission by coaxial cable and considered its possible high cost for widely separated schools. We now point out that when signals arrive by cable to the school building being served, they need no conversion since they are already being transmitted on appropriate VHF channels. Such signals are directly usable at the teaching station outlet. Some amplification may be needed along the coaxial lines, but such systems may have already been installed as a component of an MATV reception system. The problem of receiving such signals at the school signal input is the mixing of school-district produced signals with MATV sources. Antenna-received signals would be mixed with cable-received signals in the coupler-splitter equipment unit. If only cable signals are to be received into the school, no additional equipment will be needed with the possible exception of supplementary booster amplifiers. When such systems are leased on a monthly-fee basis, the cable and auxiliary equipment, such as tap-off and J-Jacks connectors are included, much as is the telephone instruments in the school's central offices.

Equipment Units and Arrangements for Viewing ITV Programs

We come now to that operational aspect of the citywide or school-building instructional television process that is the reason for it all—viewing by the learner. If we mention trouble-free equipment, solid-state circuitry that requires but a 5 per cent outlay for maintenance, or if we debate at length the disadvantages and advantages of a given transmission system, it is to make the viewing so free of distractions that the program can have its intended instructional effect. In this discussion we must limit ourselves to equipment and arrangements for its use, since what learners do, or how they react, because of what they see and hear on television is a curriculum matter that we have already dealt with. We therefore present three categories of equipment arrangements at teaching stations, namely, for individuals, for small groups, and for large groups.

Viewing by Individuals. To provide this kind of viewing or display capability we must visualize an individual learner in an atypical environment, namely, at a teaching station prepared for one person. This means a carrel or booth in which he can receive a special program

that meets his unique needs. Technology has been developing rapidly to meet such individualization needs, and there are vastly different ways by which the display can be effected, through scheduling, dialing, or some other form of selection process. In fact, as we shall point out later, media other than television may be desirable and essential. The programs may have to originate in the school building itself, or at central studios and resource banks. In the latter case, transmission systems involving multiple-channel RF and straight audio-program tapes have to be developed, and we shall mention these possibilities in the next chapter. For the present we must point out that viewing stations for individuals must be arranged in special rooms, in viewing areas of the school's library, or in selected classrooms according to grade, subject, and learning activity, or even set up in especially adapted corridor spaces in old school buildings. Wiring for ITV-viewing carrels poses some problems that may be difficult and costly to solve because of the complexity of interconnected cables that are required. Therefore it may not be feasible to spread them out in widely separated locations. Electronic learning laboratories fully equipped with television receivers and headsets, as well as with audio-program sources and other pictorial sources, may prove to be the most feasible means of meeting special needs within a given school building. Thus the television-viewing devices may be only a part of a total media capability for individualization applications. The reader should study Figure 10-2 and also 6-7, 7-5, and 7-9, to make pertinent observations as to needed facilities.

Some General Considerations for ITV Viewing. Before arrangements and equipment units are specified it would be well to list some of the major viewing conditions that should be borne in mind when making decisions about the classroom use of instructional television. In Chapter 3 we discussed the physical environment for the use of audiovisual media, but we have delayed our discussion of matters pertaining to television until now. In fact, we must not proceed even now to consider television only, for then we shall certainly make some hideous errors such as blocking a rear- or front-projection surface with one or more television receivers suspended from the ceiling. We therefore must balance the recommendations for ITV usage in optimum fashion against the urgent need for a wide variety of learning activities. The facts and conditions in the following list will serve as a basis for later decisions and recommendations.

1. No viewer should sit farther away from a television screen than approximately twelve times the width of the image. This means that for a 20-inch wide TV image on the tube the last row of seats should not be farther away than approximately twenty-feet. The 6W rule for projected images can be altered to 12W for television viewing. (However this modification assumes close-up video composition.)

2. The rule for the minimum distance is that the viewer should be seated not closer than approximately three times the width of the image. Also, based on unobstructed viewing by learners in a row, the maximum viewing angle (the angle the normal eye level line makes with a line from the viewer's eye to the top of a television screen) of the closest seated viewer should not exceed thirty degrees.[11]

3. The total included horizontal viewing angle may be as high as ninety degrees, that is, forty-five degrees on each side of the axis perpendicular to the television screen. This is approximately the same viewing angle permitted by matte screens, although the nature of content may preclude the placement of viewers within such wide viewing angles.

4. The nature of the learning activity determines the amount of space required for seating a given number of pupils. Thus television receivers may be required in laboratories, and in both large and small teaching stations, where furniture may range from a tablet arm chair to a desk and flat-top work tables. With normal seating in front of a 24-inch receiver, using desk and chair furniture in a five-foot front to rear spacing, thirty-four learners could be accommodated.[12]

5. Television receivers should be elevated for unobstructed viewing. The height generally recommended is a minimum of five feet from the bottom of the television screen to the floor. Actually, if the students are arranged in a row, the bottom of the screen must be above the normal four-foot eye level of an adult. Thus it is recommended that heights up to seven feet[13] from bottom of screen to floor be used, and moreover, when ceiling heights cannot accommodate the proper placement of receivers, that risers be used to elevate student seats, or that seats be arranged so that viewers do not have to sit in rows directly in back of each other.

6. In teaching stations where television is being used, closing regular light-diffusing shades or blinds and turning off overhead lights provide acceptable light-level conditions.

With these basic insights in mind, media specialists can plan the kinds of installations in schools that will facilitate the effective use of instructional television. We turn now to several typical arrangements of equipment in various kinds of teaching stations.

Viewing by Small Groups. In accordance with generally accepted standards for television viewing, which of course may change radically in the years ahead, we can assume that for a great many conventional-size classrooms in both elementary and secondary schools, one 24-inch receiver, placed either in a corner or at the front, center of the room, will be the minimum arrangement. This television receiver may be mounted on a side wall, on a suitable high mobile stand with 4-inch, rubber-tired castors, or it may be suspended from the ceiling. In many situations, a mobile stand will be desirable so as to make room for one or more projection screens. Mobility may be very important in those situations where the space is to be used for multi-purpose activity. In learning spaces where small- and large-group arrangements are possible and desirable, additional small, portable television receivers may be usable and the addition of headsets and a plug-in strip will permit listening and viewing without distracting other groups. But the means by which programs are to be repeated, or new programs called for, must be precisely defined before such recommendations can be made. For example, one to four students may have the need to retrieve a program from the central or the school-system's bank of video tapes, or several carrels may be available in the teaching area, with the possibility of two students making use of each one. The reader should examine the television-viewing conditions depicted in Figures 10-2 and 10-19.

[11] Based on research reported in *Design for ETV* by Dave Chapman, Inc., published by Educational Facilities Laboratories, New York. See pp. 32 and 88.
[12] *Ibid.*, pp. 34–35.
[13] *Ibid.*, pp. 36, 37.

Figure 10-19. Note the height of this television receiver and its sturdy floor stand and cradle mounting. What particular fixtures besides camera and accessories would make it possible for this teacher to originate in and distribute a program from this classroom to other teaching stations? *Courtesy Ampex Corporation, Redwood City, California.*

Viewing by Large Groups. By the sixties, the need for large-group teaching stations became obvious. Teaching auditoriums became common, and clusters of smaller classrooms surrounded total-group instruction areas as for team-teaching operations. Many early instructional television teaching stations seated 300 to 500 students, and even auditoriums were divided and especially equipped for formal multimedia presentations. Television could serve large groups seated in one place or it could serve them seated in an unlimited number of conventional size classrooms. We must reiterate the need to provide viewing capability for all learners in these large groups without sacrificing the capability to utilize other media in any desirable sequence. We therefore recommend a variety of mountings for 23- and 24-inch receivers, including mobile stands, permanent floor-pedestal mounts, and ceiling mounts. Such multiple receivers should be interconnected

by means of a panel at the front of a teaching station so that the teacher or technician may turn them on and off, switch to video-channel reception from RF, and use intercom circuits to talk to studio personnel. Sight lines to all receivers must be ascertained to avoid obstruction. When up to 25 TV receivers may be required for a group of 450 to 500 viewers, the advantage of a single large-screen viewing process becomes obvious. This advantage will be fully realized when quality in projection television is assured. Such projection-television systems require critical light-control arrangements, adequate sound, and expert technical surveillance. Advancing technology may soon bring about a substantial increase in the popularity of this method of large-group viewing. Scurrying about a 500-seat auditorium to make fine adjustments to 25 TV receivers in time for a telecast is one chore we can eliminate with a projection-television unit. The use of this process

Figure 10-20. Facilities for large-group viewing of instructional television. Note at the top the arrangement of television receivers in one of the special teaching stations at Foothill College. Note also the provision for the use of other kinds of media. In this case, projection is from behind the students. One other feature should be pointed out, namely, each seat in this room is equipped with an individual responder device. In this case the responder is a rotary knob. In the middle picture, we see a large group in session at Florida Atlantic University. This rear-projection screen has large-screen-projection television equipment behind the screen. For a view of the projection pit and television projection equipment, see Figure 3-1. In the bottom view the Tele-Beam Large Screen TV Projector is in use with a large group at Northeastern University. (*Top view*, courtesy Raytheon Learning Systems, Englewood, New Jersey. *Middle photograph* and *bottom pictures*, courtesy Tele-Beam Division, Kalart Company, Plainville, Connecticut.)

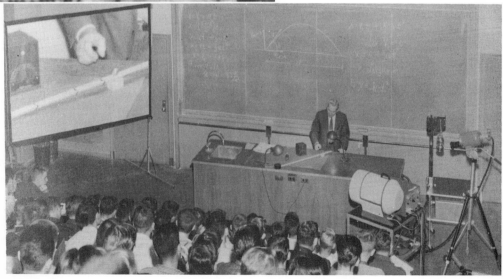

by means of rear-projection screens will doubtlessly become increasingly important.

One problem that needs special attention is the provision for high-quality sound. In present-day media-supported presentations, it is more essential than ever to provide audio-distribution capability for large groups. In small groups a single television receiver with adequate sound distribution from front-mounted speakers may be sufficient. However, in large-group situations, either well-spaced multiple receivers will have to provide this same coverage, or an auxiliary high-fidelity sound distribution system will have to be planned and installed—for example, throughout the ceiling area. The use of sound from the multiple receivers would have the effect of a low-level sound system that is very effective generally. High-level systems that operate from one central source may not provide the quality needed, especially for instructional television presentations. When teachers switch from one medium to another—as to an overhead projector—it is necessary that they use a lavalier or yoke microphone to project their voices out over a large group of learners, and in these cases, the sound system employed may be the one already set up in the television receivers. Care must be taken that such use of audio components follows a careful check-up to ascertain that amplifiers are compatible.

Some Standards for School Television Receivers. Increasing emphasis needs to be given to the purchase of high-quality television receivers for school applications. However, more than a high-quality receiver is required to effect the improvement of picture definition. Advancing technological development will make such quality possible in all of the components involved. To summarize a few major characteristics, a good school television receiver:

1. Has maximum resolution capability commensurate with transmission and origination systems.
2. Produces high-quality sound.
3. Has its loudspeakers located in front instead of on the sides.
4. Has been designed for school use: has sturdy construction, is electrically safe, and easy to maintain.
5. Has safety glass features.
6. Is tiltable.

7. Is equipped with simple, permanent, operational controls, properly placed for convenient action.
8. Is equipped with a variety of safety-engineered mounting frames and cradles.
9. Has been adapted for school closed-circuit wiring systems.
10. Includes jacks and switches for audio distribution adaptations.

Such television receivers, especially on quantity purchase may be obtainable for $150 to $200 in the 23-inch size, with the most inexpensive though acceptable mobile stands starting at approximately $45.00.

Formulating Local Instructional Television Policy

We have placed great importance throughout this book on operational procedures based on sound policies. We have suggested a variety of study committees for formulating recommendations for policy adoption by those who are held responsible for making decisions, and as we contemplate such programs as audiovisual media services that involve major departments such as instructional television, media preparation, and media distribution, we need to formulate realistic policies that apply to all phases of their operation from curriculum contribution to staff and finance. It is in this process that we seek to use the combined experience of teachers and school leaders in the application of *administration* and *change*-process principles. It will be these decisions that will determine the direction, comprehensiveness, and uniqueness of the contribution of television services to the school district's instructional program.

In this section we shall consider several aspects of the policy-formulating process, that will emphasize promising routes to success of the program, but such advice will of necessity have to be general inasmuch as the number of variables is too great for a full analysis. A specific and detailed analysis will have to be an essential of the local study and action process. Media program leaders must not ask to be excused from deliberations because the school system is so small that television services will not be feasible. Neither must they say that the pattern of organization and implementation of such programs ought to be patterned after metropolitan school-district operations. We advise a search for a unique approach to the television-service plan with such equipment units and staff as can be procured. With this general innovative and courageous attitude in mind, we turn to the critical areas of operational policy formulation.

Using Curriculum Needs As a Basis for ITV Plans

The strongest base upon which to formulate television policy is instructional need. Anyone who seeks to participate in the planning process must first be able to determine the needs that exist. If television can neither meet these needs nor make major contributions to the process of meeting them, then it would be a wise decision to use other means. Therefore we recommend as a basis for planning activity the study of curriculum and a succinct statement of the way the television medium will fulfill its promise along these lines. In light of this guideline, we suggest that the audiovisual media program director refrain from listing the facilities and equipment needed until he can relate them to a valid basis for thinking and action. We have already given proper emphasis to the curriculum basis for thinking and planning earlier in this chapter.

It is obvious that the thinking about curriculum matters involves not only the school curriculum leaders, principals, and teachers, but the superintendent and board of education members as well. The plan for system-wide involvement in this process may involve participation of several varieties that will not only develop interest and insight but also commitment to action. Visitation, demonstrations, program production, videotape recording activities, large-group and small-group meetings with staff and specialists should be organized and carried out. It may be wise to initiate a pilot ITV usage project before reaching a major decision to adopt its use on a specified level of comprehensiveness. Effective ways should be found to elicit the participation we advise, and out of such participation should come the broad outlines of operational policy regarding additional staff and their duties, the acquisition of facilities and equipment (both centralized and decentralized), the provision for required financial support, and the relationship

of such a program to the existing audiovisual media services in the district.

Planning for Operational Staff Members and Organizational Relationships

When schools and school districts plan for instructional television programs, they move rapidly toward firm and scheduled use of the medium in a vital relationship to the curriculum. Plans for operations involve many teachers, not just one, many groups of students, not just one isolated class, and the technological equipment units employed for such presentations demand the kind of adjustment and control that calls for technical training and know-how that is continuously available. This applies not only to the more simple television equipment packaged for use in a single classroom, but also to the sophisticated studio equipment packages that are involved with transmission to teaching stations and buildings on a district-wide basis. In addition to the technical staff, we readily see curriculum workers at a number of levels of involvement. It is inescapable that as instructional television programs move from limited to comprehensive scope the planning for full-time personnel becomes essential. Moreover, this vital need encompasses both professional and technical supervisory personnel. We see, for example, the need for a supervisor of district-wide television services who is a professional worker in the sense of his background of teaching ability and insight; and we also see a technical supervisor who takes charge of the additional technicians. In some cases, a television-process supervisor may not be a teacher at all, but a television specialist who has had wide experience with television production, perhaps having worked widely with teachers. In any case we must see clearly that it is not the television-process supervisor or manager who makes decisions as to content and teaching pedagogy, but curriculum and teaching personnel. Thus the problem is to provide both professional and technical capability for the programing, transmission, and display processes to reach curriculum objectives, and to solve this problem we must seek unique solutions in light of local media-development conditions and resources. At any rate, we must determine what staff members we need and how they should be organized and supervised.

The Need for Staff Members Based on Functions. Since variables are so numerous in instructional programs and services, it is difficult to treat specifically the need for staff members, hence we shall, as has been done earlier in this book, use function as a basis of making suggestions. These basic functions with suggestions for providing staff are as follows:

1. *The Teaching Function.* Select and use unusually talented teachers on the staff to handle program design, preparation, and telecasting, or employ special television teachers to act as supervisors of program-design and utilization processes, according to need. Massive programing projects may demand temporary full-time personnel to plan and produce taped programs, write guidebooks and instruction sheets. Only expert teachers can be used for this critical work. They will have urgent and continuing need for supporting personnel. The salaries for ITV teachers and curriculum supervisors, however, hardly need to be charged to television-operation budgets.

2. *Administration Function.* Leadership and management functions may be handled in various ways depending on size and scope of the services rendered. A full-time administrator will of course be essential in metropolitan organizations, and in these cases his title may be director, coordinator, or supervisor. This staff member may or may not have had teaching experience, but if not, then arrangements for program decisions of a teaching nature will have to be handled by personnel with such experience working with him as team members. An overall television-services administrator may be a part-time position in the sense that the audiovisual media director would supply the needed leadership and exercise the required administrative control. In other cases, work loads and the qualifications of present staff may be such that the administration of the instructional television service ought to be a separate organization with its own part-time or full-time administrator, responsible to the district's curriculum director or assistant superintendent of schools. The need for such leadership and management exists at each central or decentralized service facility. Qualified teachers who have developed special interests and skills along these lines may serve

admirably in many of these positions, and in addition assume other programing functions. A number of organizational plans may therefore be developed at various supervisory levels that would involve citywide media directors, school principals, and others.

3. *Production-Direction Functions.* It would be well to treat such important functions as production and direction separately from administrative leadership. However, under some school-district conditions, it is necessary to combine some of them. We must recognize the needs to coordinate production activities and to direct cameramen, floor managers, and audio-control technicians in telecasting a live program or taping it for later use. Once a significant instructional program has been designed and scripted, producing it according to high standards of technical quality is of course another essential. Teachers may carry on such activities on a part- or full-time basis, thus calling for a readjustment in their regular teaching assignments. Experienced technical personnel may also, and most frequently do, carry on the production activities. Staff must be provided for such activities in every studio, large or small, at headquarters or in school-building facilities.

4. *Equipment Operation and Control Functions.* There is little point in purchasing equipment units for instructional purposes unless they can be installed, controlled, operated, and adjusted for optimum performance. We therefore must provide staff members whose training and experience are primarily technical in nature. Some types of equipment under control of the FCC must be maintained by licensed personnel. We cannot recommend the control and operation of ITV equipment except by people with the right skills and insights, and we may need to think of a chief technician, and a group of assistants, fully qualified to handle the technical operation of all required equipment items including cameras, videotape recorders, amplifiers, transmitters, and related testing apparatus. There are many who still believe that students may be the only technical and operational personnel needed. Nothing could be further from the truth. We have already discussed these matters in an earlier chapter. Part-time technicians may be available from audiovisual media-service centers, and technicians with proper qualifications

may be obtained to give over-all technical supervision of electronic learning laboratories, audiovisual media equipment, and television studio and control room equipment. Expert planning must be done to assure that the needed technicians are employed for specific operational tasks. Under appropriate supervision, some students may work on a voluntary basis or on an hourly basis after school.

5. *Media Preparation Functions.* Teachers who are responsible for program production realize the essential character of media preparation for good communication. They know also how much time is required for design and production, and therefore they insist that a graphic artist be employed to give this special service. We may also refer to the need for graphic technicians who can develop the skills for carrying out routine production processes in connection with slides, transparencies, and charts. Students may have to be used in some capacities for this work, especially when audiovisual service centers are in each school building. Technicians may also expand their scope of service by developing photographic skills as well as electronic skills. In comprehensive programs, however, such combinations of functions are not likely to be required.

6. *Secretarial and Clerical Functions.* Unless the secretarial staff of the school-building or central headquarters media centers can handle additional duties in connection with their television programing services, separate full-time or part-time staffs must be arranged for. It is possible that secondary schools with secretarial training programs can supply part-time typists to alleviate the usual shortage of clerical workers, but certainly such assistants would require a full-time secretary who could give on-the-spot supervision. Secretarial-worker pools for a school or for district headquarters may be the source of needed services, yet the volume of work due to scripting, bulletin preparation, and the writing of guidesheets for teachers is likely to be heavy.

Minimum Staff Requirements. It may be helpful in analyzing staff needs to consider the make up of a studio crew that handles the actual telecasting or videotaping of an ITV program. We shall assume that the television teacher is the principal presenter and that he is supported by a variety of media. Members of the on-the-job operational crew are as follows:

1. Chief technician to start, check, and adjust all parts of the equipment system, including the transmitter; operate the camera controls at the console; operate the optical multiplexer; start the videotape recorder if the program is being recorded; and, punch up the cameras using the fader and special-effects amplifier and other equipment as required.

2. An assistant technician to carry out on-the-spot technical assignments or to relieve the chief technician at the console if unexpected adjustments have to be made; assist with handling slides and film clips for use in multiplexer projection equipment; and, primarily, to operate audio tape recorder, audio mixer, and maintain adequate audio control.

3. One cameraman-technician for operating camera 1.

4. One cameraman-technician for operating camera 2.

5. One floor manager, linking the program director with presenter, and assisting with needed changes on the floor in ways dictated by the director.

6. One program director, to direct all operations according to production plans, including control of console cameramen and all video and audio effects.

If, for example, three programs are being telecast *live*, or are being recorded simultaneously, then we must insist that something like a nonteaching crew of eighteen people would be required. Now, it is true that not all television programs call for this kind of action. Some programs are made up of film clips, slide sequences, or combined with instructional narrative. Others may be made up of one film, as would be the case where audiovisual media are being "delivered" via cable. Thus varying degrees of need for crew members exist depending on the program. But what about the need for other staff members who may not even have to be present when a given program is produced? We refer, of course, to the leadership and curriculum supervision personnel as well as to the external maintenance staff members if, for example, the school system's transmission is by the low-power radiation method. Certainly such personnel must exist in optimum amount and capability. Another way to examine the problem of minimum staff requirements is to consider the number of hours it takes to plan and produce an ITV program. Diamond[14] has reported an example of such an analysis, with specific reference to a half-hour ITV program for elementary school science, as follows:

	Hours
Television teacher	22
Producer	$13\frac{1}{2}$
Director	$12\frac{1}{2}$
Visualization specialist (graphic artist-photographer)	20
Engineer*	8
Student Assistants†	15
Total	91

* Time includes setup and teardown of set.
† Includes two cameramen, floorman, and assistants for the visualization specialist.

Perhaps we ought to be bold enough to ask how much time a science teacher spends in preparing to teach a regular class. How much time would he spend preparing face-to-face large-group presentation using a set of ten self-prepared color slides, a 200-foot film clip, and four overhead overlay transparencies? As we ponder such questions and seek their answers, we should also ask ourselves what we consider the teaching process to be. Only when we have determined this can we identify the character of the staff members we will recommend for a particular local situation.

Some Suggestions for Solving the Problem of Television Staff Organization. The media program director may be asked to make recommendations relative to a feasible and promising organization for the operation of a district-wide instructional television service program. Up to this point we have been considering the need to acquire a qualified and talented operational staff on the basis of required functions. However, the media director himself should be ready to decide what organizational structure is possible. He may be asked to take over the leadership function himself, or his superiors may bypass him, and rightly or unwisely place the responsibility for organizing the ITV program in the hands of someone else. There are many possibilities for organizing such services, and one of the crucial issues involved is whether the

[14] Robert M. Diamond (ed.), *A Guide to Instructional Television* (New York: McGraw-Hill, 1964), p. 45.

media director is qualified at the time the need for leadership arises? But even if he is, there are still unique conditions that may militate against the appointment, which may or may not be desired by a given individual. Sometimes, even though such an appointment is desired, the pressure of present work may be so heavy that to devote any significant amount of time to a new program would be difficult if not impossible. In such cases, and they are frequent, it is urgent that the media director arrange to be relieved of some of his routine duties so that he may devote adequate time to planning and implementing the new program. This, of course, may or may not be feasible. But modern administration demands a number of unique arrangements, not all of which depend on the addition of a specified number of new and permanent people. Hence, we see the need to be ready to undertake innovative tasks, to be willing to tackle new projects and reorganize present assignments and work loads to permit emphasis on new activities. In such instances, should the present director be released to plan the new activity, or should a new person be brought in to do it? Many times this question is answered by chief, citywide, educational administrators who may have their own convictions about these problems. The media director may not get his own way all of the time, but he can be ready with a proposal. In the following list we have summarized some of the possibilities and we ask the prospective media director to consider the consequences of each choice in light of his local conditions.

1. Make the ITV process a branch of the audiovisual media-service organization, and provide a supervisor of the centralized as well as decentralized television facilities and operations. The supervisor as the chief ITV administrator would then be responsible to the media program leader. In the school-building units, the media-service coordinators could also be involved, as would school-building technicians, in carrying out over-all service policies for optimum balance in the instructional program.

2. Separate the audiovisual media and ITV services into two service units, making both leaders coordinate workers in curriculum under the assistant superintendent of schools in charge of instruction. In such cases, it is likely that media-preparation services for scheduled

television programs would take the highest priority in the audiovisual graphic-production suites. ITV studios could also develop their own media-preparation capability, and the kind of television-teacher demand that we have mentioned earlier may be just the pressure needed to add full-time graphic artists as essential service personnel, either under ITV control, or under control of the district media director.

3. Organize the audiovisual media-services center and the instructional television unit under a citywide instructional media director who is also responsible for libraries, who in turn would work under an assistant superintendent for instruction. We face in such situations the need to stratify the various directors at a level of responsibility that will attract creative personnel into the various media sections.

All of the possibilities mentioned may be directly related to the size and comprehensiveness of the ITV program, and the previous importance attached to the curriculum contributions by conventional audiovisual media. In smaller school districts, we see similar types of control and coordination, but using interested and qualified personnel from the teaching ranks on a part-time basis. Such part-time positions may be less easy to organize at the elementary school level than at the secondary, yet the possibilities do exist as we pointed out in Chapter 7 under staffing arrangements. In many ITV programs the interservice use of technicians, graphic artists, and student crews will be essential, and the kind of organization that facilitates that cooperative endeavor is recommended. Again we must consider ITV services at two levels, namely, district-wide control, and school-building supplementary services to meet specific needs. Decisions regarding the nature of the ITV organization should be made before, not after, staffing procedures have been inaugurated.

Planning for the Acquisition and Installation of Equipment

We have repeatedly emphasized the relationship of equipment needs and specifications to curriculum plans. Planning for instructional television involves identification of stages by which these plans will be carried out, and

equipment procurement should then follow these requirements. Committees charged with responsibility for preparing basic plans and recommendations should consider and treat in detail the following aspects of equipment acquisition and installation.

1. Identify and arrange for the specific locations in which each equipment unit will be placed and operated. This means that studio and other operational spaces, in both centralized and decentralized service centers, will have to be designated, procured, remodeled, and readied for the work of installation.

2. Employ a consultant to give advice relative to needed space, to assist with the work of preparing detailed, written equipment specifications, and to serve as a supervisor to check and certify that installation has been carried out in terms of the specifications.

3. Assess the quality levels of equipment being specified in the light of curriculum services by means of committee observation of actual operation of equipment under studio conditions. Thus visits to observe operations which include transmission of both *live* and recorded programs to reception areas will be essential.

4. Stress present and future compatibility of various components of equipment packages.

5. Whenever possible, require in the requests to bid that the vendor install and demonstrate successful use of the equipment specified for the intended curriculum purposes for completion of contract.

6. All phases of the ITV equipment-purchase program should be identified in order to insure that production, transmission, and reception systems will operate as needed under existing local conditions.

7. Identify the stages by means of which the various equipment packages will be procured, in light of the various contemplated service functions.

Planning for Financial Support

No proposal for the inauguration of an instructional television system in a school district should be presented until the required financial support is specified. Hence, community study and planning activity may have to proceed through several stages until the school board takes official action. Special bond issues may have to be floated, additional taxes levied, or school-district appropriations increased to match state and federal grants. Regardless of the nature of local action that has to be taken, the plan for capital outlay and the plan for providing continuing support for the ITV programs can be implemented. Although the educational need must be specified first, some estimate of the cost must be given early in the deliberations in order to determine if local resources can support the program. It may be proper to plan for financial support in stages, specifying special capital outlay for facilities and equipment to carry out first-stage curriculum services, then specifying financial support in the second stage for temporary staff to speed up earlier phases of implementation, permanent staff for long-range operations, and allotments for heavy production costs as the program gets underway. The third stage might cover the expansion of central facilities to include multiple studios and additional channels for district coverage. The fourth stage could specify financial support for school-building studio facilities, equipment, and staff to bring the proposal into full operation.

Some Estimates of Cost. Although we have used the term *package of TV equipment* we do not mean to imply that there is a standard television-equipment system that we can specify for all studio or classroom situations. In offering cost estimates, we are aware that prices differ from place to place and that equipment models change over the years. Nevertheless, many readers may find use for cost estimates, for the sake of comparison and for making their own plans based on general school needs. We shall therefore use information gleaned from price lists and estimates of manufacturers, and from personal experience. The price ranges indicate range in quality and are also used to prevent readers from placing too much confidence in the preciseness of the estimates. The items are given in a variety of ways enabling readers to create their own equipment systems for special purposes. In no case should these figures be quoted or used for precise planning and proposal activities without confirmation from local dealers. We suggest the following items and cost ranges as shown in the chart on the next page.

Hazardous as it may be to use the preceding estimates, they do give a general idea of the capital outlay that may be necessary to provide comprehensive ITV services in schools. When plans for equipment use have been formulated, dealers in the systems specified, should be consulted for general or specific confirmation.

It seems quite obvious that adoption or expansion of instructional television poses some large-scale problems for the media program director. On the one hand, there are specific curriculum needs that television can help meet in significant ways, and in meeting those needs with television, some radical changes in the organization of both teachers and pupils may be in the offing. On the other hand, there is a vast and complex television technology to be identified and used to achieve instructional objectives. We have dealt with several main problems in the preceding sections, but by no means all of them. We therefore suggest that the implications in previous chapters for formulating television policy for the schools be carefully considered.

In response to the need for insightful planning for the intelligent, professional, and discriminating use of instructional television, a new field-consultant service has been established by the National Association of Educational Broadcasters. The full name of the project is National Project for the Improvement of Televised Instruction.[15] Its activities are financed by a grant from the Ford Foundation. The objectives of the Project are to relate instructional television to sound learning-based theories, improve skills and insights of existing television personnel in the schools, improve preservice training programs for television practitioners, and to provide information and assistance to schools and districts about the organization and use of instructional television. The project will pay honoraria and travel expenses of the consulting teams, and the requesting institution will be responsible for the living expenses of the team members while visiting and working in the schools. The NPITI plans to implement a program of national seminars, regional workshops, and publications, and a program of cooperative action with related organizations.

We should not move on to the next chapter before we emphasize our conviction that

[15] For additional information about the Project or its services, contact: National Project for the Improvement of Televised Instruction, NAEB, 1346 Connecticut Ave., NW, Washington, D.C.

Item or Package	Cost Range
1. One Vidicon camera chain, complete with audio controls, tripod and dolly, intercom system, video monitor.	$5,000 to $9,000
2. One Vidicon or Plumbicon camera chain, complete with stand, light bar, monitor, and accessories.	$2,000 to $5,000
3. Two Vidicon camera chains in a studio package complete with all related operational equipment.	$16,000 to $24,000
4. One videotape recorder complete with modulator.	$3,000 to $9,000
5. One videotape recorder ($\frac{1}{2}$-inch, nonbroadcast).	$750 to $1,200
6. Two videotape recorders, complete with modulators, and one electronic editor on one of the recorders.	$7,000 to $17,000
7. One film chain, complete with two projectors (one 16 mm film and one 35 mm slide).	$9,000 to $14,000
8. One classroom TV receiving-recording-playback unit (without TV camera).	$4,000 to $6,000
9. One complete lighting package for one studio with control panel and circuits (suspended system only) installed on mobile track system.	$7,000 to $15,000
10. One telecasting, recording, and tape-editing studio and operational ITV unit, as a complete unit in a school building, or as an addition to centralized ITV facilities.	$55,000 to $70,000
11. Master antenna system for a 26-room school including cable and two-way outlets into all rooms.	$2,000 to $3,000
12. One television projection system for single-receiver, large-group auditorium viewing purposes such as the Kalart Co. Tele-Beam equipment unit.	$2,000 to $4,000
13. Television receiver, audiovisual model, 24-inch, on either pedestal, mobile 5-foot stand, or ceiling-suspended cradle, installed.	$200 to $400
14. Twelve-channel cable transmission system, Bell System Lease, to each school in the district (depending on the air-line distance from program source and related equipment) per month.	$400 to $5,000
15. Four Channel low-power 2,500 mHz radiation transmission system from central transmitter (cost for ten years, not including depreciation, but including maintenance and cost of money). See next item for related per school cost.	$50,000 to $60,000
16. Cost per school to install 2,500 mHz low-power radiation reception antenna and related units, not including wiring and classroom outlets.	$1,250 to $1,500
17. One dial-retrieval system for videotape programs for both large-group and individual use per school Basic relay-control and playback center with 12-channel capacity and 100 video-equipped carrels.	$100,000 to $300,000

television is the most awesome teaching medium of our time. We must face the fact that it is very doubtful that we have yet learned to use it wisely and in ways that will fulfill its potential. But television can, if we plan it that way, keep people central, and in optimum relationship to each other. Once we have a teacher and his message on tape, we can use television to deliver that message to the people who need it over and over again. Hence we have the greatest multiplier of professional effort, energy, and communicative content of our time, but this does not mean that we have learned to make it work in the right ways. To do this we must study the teaching process more thoroughly and make perhaps some rather startling decisions. We need to take seriously, before we leave the subject, the good advice of James M. Spinning, given a decade ago:

When it comes to the essence of teaching, it must still be the teacher as person, as person to person, who is central. . . . We need to adapt television to education, and only as we get a good crack at it, can we do that. But, at the same time, we need to adapt ourselves more completely to education. With or without television, we should take some of its virtues into our thinking, give more attention in all our teaching to the kind of planning and order, the sense of structure, the eye-and-ear appeal, the precise timing, and the over-all impact which are special musts for television.[16]

We must not fail to give due consideration to the fact that it is the most natural process imaginable to apply television to education, one of the most pressing problems in our

[16] James M. Spinning, "The Teacher with the Audio-Visual Mind," *NEA Journal*, Vol. 46, No. 9, December 1957, pp. 589–590.

society. It is as natural and meaningful as it is to apply assembly-line technology to the making of automobiles. Television is so deeply involved with the communication of our time, and with the technology of our society, that it cannot help but become an extensive aspect of our education. We must not forget either that just as the learner and teacher on opposite ends of a log, and a group of learners with their teacher in a room with a scroll between them constituted educational images in their time, the environment has changed and new images of man's preparation for life must be developed. Television is almost certain to emerge as a major component in future instructional systems.

Problem-Solving Activities

1. Select any five of the ten patterns set forth in this chapter for using television that have been developed around the country, and identify the particular contributions ITV makes to the curriculum. Make an evaluative judgment about the magnitude of the value that would accrue from each contribution.

2. Using your own image of what constitutes desirable teaching processes, identify and write out the specific components of teacher activity. Then (a) mark your list of items with an asterisk in each case that you believe television could make a significant contribution, and (b) select the most significant item, in your view, and show what reorganization of pupils and teachers you would recommend if you were to inaugurate a comprehensive instructional television service program.

3. Looking at the problem from a broad curriculum viewpoint, what could television do to foster the central values of the Educational Policies Commission of the NEA, as quoted in Chapter 4? Just how is the rational power of an individual developed in his school program? Based on your answer, name one role of (a) a library book, (b) a motion picture in a class presentation, and (c) a dial-selected videotape.

4. Outline a specific and significant need in the curriculum that you believe is highly significant. Amplify your outline sufficiently to show the various aspects of the need you have identified. (Do this work as a part of a later exercise to plan for implementation of plans using television to meet the need, or make a valuable contribution toward meeting it. This outline plan should be completed before operational technology is studied, but the possibility of using television should be borne in mind.)

5. In the light of the curriculum need specified in Problem 4, formulate a proposal for providing the required ITV service facilities and equipment. Keep this plan on a broad and general scale indicating only the nature of the program capability in either or both central and decentralized studios, plus classroom program origination. (It is not necessary to deal with specific equipment units needed, or the problems of transmission and reception at this time.)

6. Assume that you are going to plan a central ITV studio large enough to provide all schools with comprehensive service—large enough and sufficiently well equipped to transmit six programs simultaneously (four videotapes, one program *live*, and one motion picture film) and still preserve for continuous use one studio for making programs on videotape. Now, study the space layout in Figure 10-7 and make a new sketch showing modifications in it to make that capability possible. Cut it down in size if you can find ways of doing it.

7. Using the conditions in Problem 6 as a basis, prepare a detailed list of the equipment necessary to carry out the proposed program of services. Use manufacturers' catalogs and price lists, and specify model numbers for each piece of major equipment and its accessories. (*Alternate problem:* State your own ITV functions and specify equipment units to carry them out at a high-quality level, or work with a task force on a specially assigned set of functions, pooling your results with others to make possible a duplicated composite list for the entire planning group.)

8. Would you be in favor of setting up a centralized videotaping studio, free of all additional transmission and scheduling activity?

9. What would be some advantages of decentralizing several studios in school buildings for production of programs for specific levels, grades, and subjects?

10. The superintendent of your school system has just turned down your proposal for a 9,200 square foot production and transmission facility, and has asked you to trim your program back for a pilot program with

a maximum of two channels for transmission. He has set a space maximum of 3,600 square feet of floor area for your central studio facility. Using Figure 10-7, and the preceding list of space needs as guides, make a new rough sketch showing space allotted for specific functions. Label fully to show potential activities.

11. How does the existence of a master antenna system affect the cost and use of a school-building program producing studio?

12. State the advantages and disadvantages of each of the major ITV transmission plans now open to schools.

13. Can you name other feasible transmission methods for school districts that own and operate their own ITV facilities to use besides leased coaxial-cable, and school-owned-and-maintained, low-power fixed-service, 2,500 mHz radiation? If you can identify them, state what obstacles would have to be surmounted before adopting them.

14. Identify any school system with which you are familiar and for the number of schools involved and their distances from each other and the studio, make a cost comparison for the two methods mentioned in Problem 12.

15. Make several diagrams of specific ITV viewing situations using 23- or 24-inch receivers, as follows: (a) image-magnification facilities and equipment at a large-group teaching station (100 pupils); (b) a 500-seat teaching auditorium; (c) a 30-seat classroom; (d) using a television-projection system in a 500-seat teaching auditorium. Label all diagrams fully.

16. Make a plan in outline form for organizing and implementing the study of ITV in the curriculum for any school district identified. Using the guidelines in Chapter 2 for implementing change, identify study committees and stages of action, from possible interest-getting activities to recommendation of the plan by the superintendent of schools and its adoption by the board of education. Deal with all essential aspects of the final plan, such as curriculum needs, required staff members and their organization, cost of initial facilities and equipment, the transmission plan and its cost, and school-building ITV equipment units and their costs. (Members of the group should break the problem down into its major parts and then write plans and prepare reports and cost tables cooperatively, arranging for subgroups

to study each phase of the plan and to report to the class with handout sheets.)

17. Identify two or more school districts presently providing district-wide ITV services, and by methods that are as easy as possible for the local ITV staffs (such as a personal visit to the site for on-the-spot study and picture-taking), prepare two visualized presentations for group analysis. (Organize two task forces, one for each visitation and report.)

References

Bretz, Rudy. *Techniques of Television Production*, 2nd ed. (New York: McGraw-Hill, 1962).

Bronson, Vernon and James A. Fellows. *Standards of Television Transmission*. (Prepared under auspices of Office of Education, U.S. Department of Health, Education and Welfare, in connection with an NDEA contract, OE-2-16-027.) (Washington, D.C.: National Association of Educational Broadcasters, 1964.)

Brown, James W. and Kenneth D. Norberg. *Administering Educational Media*. (McGraw-Hill, 1965).

Clarke, R. Walton. *1966 Schoolman's Guide to ETV Communications*. (Philadelphia: Jerrold Electronics Corporation, 401 Walnut St., 1966).

Costello, Lawrence F. and George N. Gordon. *Teach with Television*, 2nd ed. (New York: Hastings House, 1965).

Diamond, Robert M. (ed.). *A Guide to Instructional Television*. (New York: McGraw-Hill, 1964).

Educational Facilities Laboratories. *Design for ETV (Planning for Schools with Television)*, prepared by Dave Chapman, Inc., Industrial Design. (New York: Educational Facilities Laboratories, 477 Madison Ave., 1960).

Educational Policies Commission. *Education and the Spirit of Science*. (Washington, D.C.: The National Educational Association, 1966).

Erickson, Carlton W. H. *Fundamentals of Teaching with Audiovisual Technology*. (New York: Macmillan, 1965).

Griffith, Barton L. and Donald W. MacLennan. *Improvement of Teaching by Television*. (Columbia, Mo.: University of Missouri Press, 1964).

Hilliard, Robert L. *Writing for Television and Radio.* (New York: Hastings House, 1962).

Institute for Communication Research. *Educational Television, The Next Ten Years.* (Prepared and published pursuant to a contract with the Office of Education, Department of Health, Education and Welfare.) (Stanford: Institute for Communications Research, Stanford University, 1962). (Out of print.)

Jones, Peter. *Technique of Television Cameraman.* (New York: Hastings House, 1966).

Lewis, Phillip. *Educational Television Guidebook.* (New York: McGraw-Hill, 1961).

Millerson, Gerald. *Technique of Television Production.* (New York: Hastings House, 1961).

Murphy, Judith and Ronald Gross. *Learning by Television.* (New York: The Fund for Advancement of Education, 477 Madison Ave., 1966).

Nisbitt, Alec. *Technique of Sound Studio.* (New York: Hastings House, 1962).

Reid, J. Christopher and Donald W. MacLennan. *Research In Instructional Television and Film* (U.S. Office of Education, a publication of the Bureau of Research). (Washington, D.C.: Superintendent of Documents, U.S. Government Printing Office, 1967).

Roe, Yale (ed.). *Television Station Management.* (New York: Hastings House, 1964).

Russell, James E. *Change and Challenge in American Education.* (Boston: Houghton Mifflin, 1965).

Schramm, Wilbur and others. *The Impact of Educational Television.* (Urbana, Ill.: University of Illinois Press, 1960).

Smith, Mary Howard. *Using Television in the Classroom.* (New York: McGraw-Hill, 1961).

Spear, James. *Creating Visuals for TV.* (Washington, D.C.: Division of Instructional Service of the N.E.A., 1962). (Reprinted 1965.)

Stoddard, Alexander J. *Schools for Tomorrow, An Educator's Blueprint.* (New York: The Fund for the Advancement of Education, 477 Madison Ave., 1957).

Sylvania Electric Products, Inc. *Equipment Guide for Classroom Television.* (New York: Sylvania Electric Products, 730 Third Ave., 1965).

Implementation of Instructional Systems

In our discussions of the various facets of the problem-solving work of the media program director, we have emphasized the newer and more vital roles of media in the teaching process. We have examined many of the problems that have to be met and dealt with by media specialists. But it is in the use of instructional systems that media directors find a new plateau of promise. With this new application of technology to education, media specialists and their supporting technicians become indispensable—and reach a new level of fulfillment as highly valued members of the decision-making curriculum team.

In previous chapters we have stressed the importance of prescribed and scheduled media use in instructional systems, and warned that the media specialist must not become an educational gadgeteer rather than an educational engineer. We therefore point out once more that only as the media program director possesses optimum balance in teaching, administrative, and technological abilities, can he fulfill his new role as he implements the use of instructional systems. As we begin this chapter, we must emphasize that all that we have said up to this point should be considered in light of the new problems we will present here.

Naturally, this chapter cannot be used as a handbook for the design of teaching systems, nor can it predict precisely the volume of the instructional systems that will be developed, but it is certain that there will be an increase of significant commercial activity to produce and market teaching systems in many alternate formats to facilitate their use in schools. What we shall attempt to do in this chapter is to examine the problems that will have to be faced and solved and to anticipate on the basis of present observations some promising kinds of leadership and management activity that are likely to be needed. We will begin with a brief overview of instructional systems concepts with special reference to roles of media and the media program director's orientation to a new set of problems.

The Nature of Instructional Systems

The use of the term *instructional system* may sometimes elicit a reaction of surprise over the intimation that we haven't tried to be systematic

System

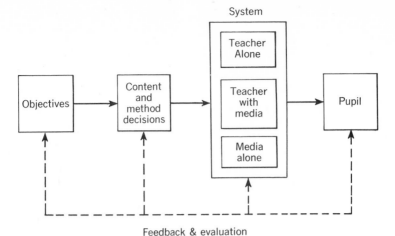

Feedback & evaluation

Figure 11-1. As shown in this schematic, the *system* involves in a total way all of the components and interrelationships. We note particularly the alternatives with regard to the teacher and media use. *Courtesy Audiovisual Instruction.*

earlier. Yet the word *systems* has new potential for meanings in our technological communications. In fact, the concept fairly explodes into a multitude of parts: teachers, learners, places, schedules, media, groupings, operations research, hardware, software, computers, teaching components, stimuli, responses, individualization, programing, and so on. Have we not done all this in education before? Have we not used a system for all our teaching in the past? Have we not made up a system when we have put media to work in our classrooms singly or in combination? We must admit that generally we haven't. What is the difference then between what so many of us have done and still do as conventional teachers and what has and is being done in some branches of the military and in the special training programs in business, and in some schools, we might add, under the name of instructional systems? We shall answer that question by implication as we explore the central concept of systems operations.

The Central Concept

Definition of "Systems" by DAVI Task Force Studying Functions of Media. In Chapter 4 we discussed some of the major roles that media play in the teaching process, and at that time we referred to the position paper, prepared by a special Task Force for the purpose in 1962, entitled *The Function of Media in the Public Schools.* In the paper edited by Barry Morris and

published in 1963 there appeared the following statement:

Instructional Systems

The newer media have led us to a new approach to instruction. This is a scientifically developed combination of instructors, materials, and technological media for providing optimum learning with a minimum of routine personal involvement by the teacher. The result is a carefully planned "system" consisting of subject matter, procedures, and media coordinated in a program-unit design which is directed toward specific behavioral objectives. A variety of learning channels are combined in such a system. Decisions as to where and how to use teacher presentation, discussion, media presentation, programmed learning sequences, or other channels will be made in terms of what and who is to be taught.[1]

Readers should check the schematic of the above quotation shown in the same position paper, and included here as Figure 11-1.

Definition of "Systems Approach" by DAVI Commission on Terminology 1963. The Commission in its official definition of the Systems Approach, published the following statement:

An integrated programed complex of instructional media, machinery, and personnel whose components

[1] Barry Morris (ed.), "The Function of Media in the Public Schools" (Prepared by a DAVI Task Force in 1962 as a position paper), *Audiovisual Instruction,* Vol. 8, No. 1, January 1963, pp. 9–14.

SUBSYSTEM DEVELOPMENT

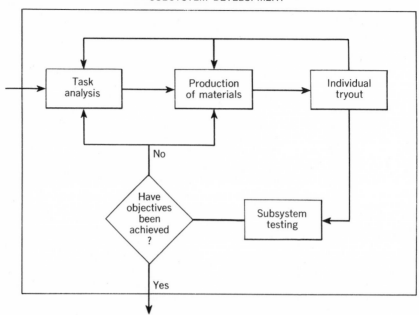

Figure 11-2. In this diagram, proper stress is given to task analysis, to the materials (including media), to their use in specific situations, and to accomplishment. *Courtesy Michael Eraut, and the Audiovisual Communication Review.*

are structured as a single unit with a schedule of time and sequential phasing. Its purpose is to insure that the components of the organic whole will be available with the proper characteristics at the proper time to contribute to the total system, and in so doing to fulfill the goals which have been established.[2]

With these two definitions to set the tone for our presentation of this overview, we cannot help but recognize the new role of media which is now rising in significance, since when they are used by the programing method they take over and carry out teaching functions for the teacher or the group of teaching personnel. But we also recognize problems of timing and sequencing, and the essential requirement of formulating and accomplishing valid instructional goals under optimum conditions. Thus it becomes obvious that everything we know about learning and teaching goes into the design and subsequent management of the required conditions to produce the desired end results.

[2] Donald P. Ely (ed.) (Prepared by the Commission), "Alphabetical Listing of Terminology," *Audiovisual Communication Review*, Vol. 11, No. 1, Supp. 6, January 1963, p. 76.

Actually an instructional system grows out of insightful deliberations about what kinds of activities will best produce a desired learning increment. We do not even consider the possibility at this point that there is anything like a standard system that will work in all situations. The preceding definitions indicate that this is as it ought to be.

For example, let us consider the nature of a particular teaching system that was worked out by a group of botanists at Purdue University with the cooperation of the audiovisual center staff there. This system had four basic aspects: (1) independent study session, (2) small assembly session, (3) general assembly session, and (4) home study session. In the book which describes this system operationally, Postlethwait, Novak, and Murray have this to say about the ingredients in their teaching approach:

First, it must include a great variety of teaching techniques, and take advantage of all the modern communication media. Each medium must be selected for use on the basis of its effectiveness and efficiency in evoking the appropriate responses. Secondly, these media must be made available in such a way that the students can pace themselves,

Figure 11-3. One of the early booths used in the Purdue Botany Program is shown at the top of this illustration. Two of the later models are shown in the bottom picture. How must a student be prepared for entry into such a booth for serious study? Besides realia, what additional media are visible or implied? *Courtesy Professor S. N. Postlethwaite, Purdue University, Lafayette, Indiana.*

omitting those things with which they are already familiar and spending extra time where necessary to bring their education up to the level of their colleagues. And, thirdly, personal contact with teaching personnel must be made available to provide motivation and interest. Each activity required of the student must be analyzed in terms of the objective and all busy work which does not really contribute to the student's progress must be eliminated.[3]

Readers may study this system as depicted in a motion picture,[4] also available from Purdue

[3] S. N. Postlethwait, J. Novak, and H. Murray. *An Integrated Experience Approach to Learning with Emphasis on Independent Study* (Minneapolis: Burgess Publishing Company, 1964), pp. 2–3.

[4] The title of the film is *Multifaceted Approach to the Teaching of Botany.*

University's Audiovisual Center. See Figure 11-3. Strange as it may seem, one of the most impressive features of this particular system is the organized and required work by students on three levels of problem-solving activity, the last level being a research problem where the student works out his own scientific method, procures the needed data and draws his conclusions. For our purposes we need not go into additional detail. It will be sufficient to show that several common elements of regular teaching procedure are involved, and so are several uncommon ones where for instance the teacher, on taped audio programs, programs a student through special workbook exercises based on observations of real objects and his reactions to other media presentations as well. The student works in an independent study carrel, surrounded by media equipment, manipulative materials and realia, at his own pace.

We must not oversimplify the process of design and preparation of teaching systems; in fact, we should emphasize continually the intricacies involved. There will be the continual need to design and produce instructional systems locally, and to select and make proper use of many teaching systems that are mass produced commercially to accomplish given sets of objectives. However, to provide some insight into the processes of analysis that are generally required, we quote a passage from a discussion of Robert M. Gagne's principles by Glaser, as follows:

To these principles he attaches such names as: task analysis, intro-task transfer, component task achievement, and the sequencing of tasks. . . . These principles imply the following activities with respect to the management of learning: (1) A task to be learned should be analyzed into component tasks which may be learned in different ways and which require different instructional practices. (2) The successful achievement of the component tasks is required for performance of a final task. (3) The component tasks may have a hierarchical relationship to each other so that successful achievement of one component task is required for successful achievement of the subsequent component task. (4) This suggests that, in designing a training program, the following steps must be taken: "(a) identifying the component tasks of final performance; (b) insuring that each of these component tasks is fully achieved; and (c) arranging the total learning situation in a sequence which will insure optimal mediational effects from one component to another."[5]

The reader is urged to consider in the light of his own experiences the principles that have been identified in the above quotation. What teacher has not discovered that a given ability depends on the prior existence of another ability? When *learning a task* is mentioned, does this not refer to an instructional objective that has been properly identified? Certainly such analyses as are indicated are essential elements of systems planning.

Using the central concept stated or implied in the foregoing excerpts, but with variations in terminology, Barson, Gordon, and Hornbaker define an instructional system as follows:

An instructional system is a complex consisting of the following components: Learner(s) and a combination of instructor(s), material(s), machine(s), and technician(s), given certain inputs and designed to carry out a prescribed set of operations. This set of operations is devised and ordered according to the most recent and pertinent evidence from research and expert opinion such that the probability of attaining the output, specified behavioral changes in the components, is maximal.[6]

We need to emphasize that in any system developed, we focus not only on teachers, but on a given learner or group of learners, media, methods, nonteaching personnel, machines, and a set of prescribed operations. Lectures may be delivered in face-to-face situations or by audio and videotape. Demonstrations may be given live or in television programs, and discussion sessions may be held regularly with small groups. Learners may do their independent study work in carrels, or at home, or in the library by means of programed texts, or by responses to programed pictorial media, or by reading library books. Media may play a large number of roles, even to taking over a large group of learners without the teacher being there at all. The flow of learners through a set of operations may have to proceed according to a rigid schedule, or freedom and individual pacing may be possible and desirable. Every single response of any given individual, or a group of learners, regardless of the number, may have to be recorded, evaluated, summarized, and reported in a matter of seconds, and here is where computers enter to make their contributions to effective progress. In developing and implementing instructional systems, great stress is placed on stratification of talent and the multiplication of personal efforts of the teacher, that is, certain kinds of effort, on the part of those best qualified to carry out a specific task. Thus technicians and laboratory assistants carry out roles, some of which are similar to what they do under conventional systems, but integrated in far different ways in the total framework of an instructional system.

---

[5] Robert Glaser, "Implications of Training Research for Education," Chapter VII, *Theories of Learning and Instruction*, The Sixty-Third Yearbook of the National Society for the Study of Education, Part I, p. 173 (Chicago: University of Chicago Press, 1964).

[6] John Barson, John M. Gordon, Jr., and W. Russell Hornbaker, "Standard Operating Procedures for a Learning Resources Center: A System for Producing Systems," *Audiovisual Instruction*, Vol. 10, No. 5, May 1965, pp. 378–379.

Media in Systems Teaching

In the technological process of using instructional systems we should realize that all media, both print and nonprint, support each other as each makes its assigned contribution to teaching objectives. We have already referred to the importance of media in a general way in the teaching process, but now we should identify both the array of media available and the roles that such media play when applied to instructional systems.

The Array of Media. We identified instructional media and described them briefly in Chapter 3, and we must explain now that any one of the media may be used singly or in optimum combination as components in an instructional system. A motion picture may be threaded and projected by a teacher who is readying a large group for an independent study phase of a given system in which an 8mm cartridge film is to be inserted into a magnetic-track sound projector by a student in a carrel. Such films may be used to present the next stimulus step to depict, for example, the proper speed for proficiency in a given act. Still pictures, in the form of illustrations in programed or regular texts and workbooks, as color slides or filmstrip frames may be then used in programed sequences for guiding learner discrimination. What we will point out soon is that it is how media are used that makes the difference between conventional and systems utilization. We then point out that because of technological advances, we not only have an array of all available media to use singly or in combination to meet identified needs, but we have teaching machines and automatically controlled media content presentation devices for making certain that media are used at the appropriate times for specified purposes so that the learner may work independently even without his teacher. We need to emphasize that the array of media includes the following: Television and videotapes, motion pictures in all formats, realia, models and apparatus, still pictures in all formats, audio program tapes, graphic symbols in all formats, and printed materials. We have tended to list only those media that lend themselves to mechanization and automation, but we quickly point out that in those aspects of an instructional system where teachers are personally involved in face-to-face presentations, and in extra-class activities, any of the conventional media and methods such as opaque projector material, field trip, dramatic participation, and bulletin boards may be put to work.

Roles Played by Media in Instructional Systems

The Growing Vitality of Media. Earlier we emphasized the shift toward *basal* instead of supplementary materials. (See Chapter 3.) We have long deplored the repeated reference to audiovisual media as enrichment materials. It must be obvious to many prospective media program directors that in the past in many situations it made little difference to school principals, department heads, or to school superintendents, whether teachers used the motion pictures, filmstrips and audio-program tapes that were purchased for their use. Even a great many language laboratories were not put to work in truly productive ways. Weak and ineffective uses of media by classroom teachers are numerous; but teachers cannot be blamed for all of them. The real reason for deficiency, however, was not necessarily due to the lack of projectors and available services. The real reason is implicit in the statement by Heinich:[7]

Television, languages laboratories, and programed instruction, unlike traditional audiovisual materials, must function in the instructional system at the curriculum planning phase.... The recent shift from classroom instruction to the curriculum planning function has been reponsible for finally alerting instructional technology to the importance of the systems approach.

As long as curriculum authorities and supervisors did not insist on bringing in and establishing media as a firm part of the teaching process, that is, as a part of the agreed-to teaching plans, media were handled on a take-them-or-leave-them basis. The reasons for using media to enhance communication, to provide vicarious experience, to provide meaningful examples of difficult principles, were valid, but if the film arrival were delayed, or if the bell rang too early,

[7] Robert Heinich, *The Systems Engineering of Education II: Application of Systems Thinking to Instruction*, p. 15. (A Monograph prepared for the Instructional Technology and Media Project.) (Los Angeles: Department of Technology, School of Education, University of Southern California, 1965.)

not much harm was done, or so it was felt by too many. Thus when conditions for providing classroom or projection-room showings were difficult or impossible to arrange, it was the teacher not the curriculum planners who could decide not to persist against the odds.

In continuing his discussion, Heinrich stated his definition as follows:

... it is necessary to distinguish between teaching activities which are incorporated in media and teaching activities conducted in the classroom environment.... A teacher whose instructional efforts are presented to students in mediated form will be referred to as a *mediated* teacher. A teacher who is physically present in the classroom will be referred to as the *classroom* teacher.

. . .

From a *system* viewpoint, *mediated* teaching and classroom teaching are simply different tactics used in the strategy of instruction.[8]

In a given instructional system, prescribed plans may call for a set of slides to be used in a classroom presentation by a teacher under his direct control as a component of a larger action pattern. But for other purposes, a set of color slides with taped instructions and a response device, or an object upon or with which to make performance responses, would guide students without the teachers being physically present. Teaching is nevertheless being expertly and effectively carried out. This latter case would be a mediated teacher in action. The teacher may be physically elsewhere, but his presence would be implied, his critical and talented work, or the work of another team member, having been completed on a programed basis at an earlier date. We may say that when media do teaching jobs alone, the teacher works in and through the medium or media. Media are therefore so arranged and presented that learners are given instruction and their responses are then guided to desired completion levels. We must see that programing and self-instruction (independent study) are essential methods by which media function within the broader spectrum of teaching activity.

Programed Instruction in Systems Teaching. All of the media we have discussed in connection

with instructional systems may be used singly or in combination. When as we have said, media are used alone, either with large groups or with individuals, various methods of programing must be used according to programing principles. A medium such as audio-program tape may present a series of programed questions calling for written or computer-recorded responses, or a television teacher may be directing a large group of learners to observe film clips of real-life examples, a diagram, and a slide depicting a pertinent situation for critical analysis, all of which meet the characteristics of programed instruction. Print and nonprint media are often programed in combination. Control of content and desired response may be easy when media and devices are appropriately arranged. We therefore see in the programing method the capability of using the full impact of any given medium or media combination, not only to show the image of the teacher as needed and carry his voice to the learner, but to present his substantive messages. We see in this programed media process, as a part of an instructional system, the route to successful teaching. We assume, of course, that all of the wisdom developed out of teaching experience and formal research in learning theory is employed in carrying out the process. We may even ask now a question that may prove to be important as specific instructional systems are produced and marketed by publishers, teachers, and programers totally unknown to the learner. The question is: Will the instructional effect be impaired if personalities other than the teacher are involved in any given system? The question should be borne in mind in the preparation of utilization plans for motivation (readiness) and for the action and/or reaction by the learners. We postulate the answer that in such cases as we have envisaged, it will be the strength of the learner's motives, the strength of the local teacher's influence in the system's operation, the nature of interpersonal relationships with teacher and pupils and between pupils themselves outside of a large group or independent study carrel, and the quality of the media in question, that taken together will make up the total impact of the purchased media packages.

The Indispensability of Media in Instructional Systems. When we consider the roles played by media in the use of instructional systems, referring to both media material and hardware,

[8] *Ibid.*, pp. 19, 20.

we assert what is obvious—that media are indispensable components of such systems. Without them a total breakdown of systems operations ensues. Hence school administrators, curriculum leaders, and the teachers themselves have a new responsibility to support recommendations for required facilities and operational staff.

A New Orientation for the Media Program Director

Increased Responsibility and New Problems. With the indispensability of media in the use of instructional systems, the program director finds not only new prestige and a new image of his work by his colleagues, but a cluster of new problems. These new problems cut across his entire gamut of activity from curriculum planning and administration to media distribution and in-service education. Now more than ever does the media specialist need penetrating insights into curriculum problems, and more than ever does he need to be well versed in technological matters. There is little doubt that with the use of systems he will have critical decisions to make regarding technical installations and operations, and will have to make new plans to safeguard against interruptions in scheduled use of media. As we shall point out, several of his conventional programs, such as film distribution and media design and preparation work, generally operating at low levels, will erupt into district-wide, large-scale, high-priority services.

Design and Implementation of Instructional Systems. The media program director will inevitably be faced with problems of meeting local needs for media materials and equipment. Many of these will be available in the years ahead from commercial producers. They will therefore have to be examined, tried out, evaluated, and purchased for use in specific situations throughout the school district. Instructional systems of the future may not only encompass an entire course but several courses in the curriculum. It is also probable that teams of teachers who have had unusually extensive experiences in planning schedules and preparing presentations with strong media support, and who have become accustomed to sharing teaching responsibilities with each other will be the first to

make rapid strides in expanding the use of teaching systems. Such teachers will also be quick to make specific instructional-systems packages of limited scope, as for example teaching arithmetic computation and problem-solving skills, and specific language skills. Many teachers in self-contained classrooms will also be quick to plan small-scope instructional systems as a natural outgrowth of incidental use of media and programing methods used with workbooks. See Figures 11-5 through 11-8. There will be a heavy demand for classroom equipment to be installed permanently in many classrooms to take care of such individual needs; however, the major problem will have to do with installations for the scheduled use of media on a district-wide basis, for all the groups of a given grade and subject. On the one hand we see the problem of expanding the facilities and staff to help teachers design and make their own systems, much as teachers would make up creative independent study materials such as worksheets and the like in the past. On the other hand, we see a greatly increased need for new purchases of media in the form of media packages. Therefore design and preparation activity will have to be facilitated and so will the purchase of ready-made media materials for use with permanent equipment installations in the participating schools.

The implementation of instructional systems, whether designed and produced locally or not, poses new problems that will have to be met in a new orientation of significance as far as media use in the curriculum goes. We should be mindful of the fact that not all teaching will take place in the context of self-instruction and systems, and moreover, some components of instructional systems will demand that media be used with teachers in direct control to play a number of roles such as motivating the learners and providing vicarious experiences with people, places, and processes. Hence the supply of many kinds of conventional media will have to be upgraded to meet the pressure of teachers who have developed new interest and concern for their proper use. We shall, therefore, discuss a number of these large-scale problems and point the way to their analysis for promising action. We turn first to some critical relationships of instructional systems to teachers and teaching, then to problems of acquisition, instrumentation, and logistics. Each of these topics will be treated in a separate section.

Relationship of Instructional Systems to Teachers and Teaching

Prospective and practicing media program directors should seek to understand the conspicuous as well as the subtle relationships of instructional systems operations to teachers and teaching. To identify and explore these relationships in depth is beyond the scope of this book. However, for the purposes of our treatment we ought to do no less than identify a few of the major curriculum and technological aspects of such relationships as guidelines for future study and planning.

New Roles for Teachers

It is believed by some that when the systems approach to teaching is employed, teachers will be able to stratify their energies and efforts at higher levels of activity in the total process. In this case they will be the programers, planners of action, and the observers and analyzers of student behavior. It is believed by others that the teacher's work will be downgraded to that of a professional assistant, managing prearranged conditions under which media will do the lion's share of the work.

Teachers As True Professionals. We see many teachers as teacher leaders in the planning process, as large-group presentors, as guiding creative work of individual students, or organizing the work of other teachers in the group to do this work with learners. These high-level teachers may also be the television teachers and the motivators. Inevitably, more work will have to be done of a creative and productive nature, and more interaction of pupils with teachers. Students under direct teaching by media will have to be observed for signs of maladjustment, and print-out reports from computers will have to be analyzed for accomplishment. These are not jobs for clerks and aides.

The Teacher As a Manager. Critical judgments are necessary in any teaching situation, and in order for the teacher to spend more time on design of activities, and on the job of making vital observations of students at work, he will need to have the support of both media service personnel and teacher aides. What we can and ought to do is to create the situation in which we can use the best teachers we have on creative activities, use teachers of lesser talent as managers of those classroom conditions that are of a professional nature, and then give adequate support to that team by using the services of teacher aides. Such jobs as surveillance of student work in teaching auditoriums and electronic learning laboratories need not be paid for at the highest professional rates. New concepts of qualifications for teacher aides and support staff may have a bearing on the total cost of systems-instruction operations.

Teacher Aides and Media-Service Technicians. Teacher aides would be associated with an instructional systems staff group, and because, as we have discussed, media become indispensable in the process, we must maintain technicians in sufficient numbers in the school's media-service center. Such technicians would possibly serve more than one school in a circuit. The most important part of their job would be preventive maintenance. We must remind ourselves that instructional systems are designed and operated because they do the instructional job better than any other plan, and the maintenance of the systems at a peak of operational efficiency is therefore essential.

Reorganization of Learner Groups and Teaching Staffs

We must not fail to identify the necessity for reorganization of both learners and staffs, but we have already appropriately emphasized this procedure in earlier references to team teaching and the use of instructional television. But we must emphasize that reorganization will have to be carried out in the light of staff functions and assignments. Students must similarly be regrouped according to existing facilities and their varied programs of learning activity. As we have said before, the emphasis on the development of rational powers (see Chapter 4) may require a hierarchy of tutors, for we must envision the need for creative problem-solving work on the part of individuals and groups.

Provision for Building Facilities

Looking back over the points of emphasis in Chapters 6 and 7, we note that great stress was placed on the highly probable need for increased space in each school building for special facilities, such as electronic learning laboratories, to which groups of learners may be routed on schedule for media-controlled activity. We must note that a few carrels in each classroom may not be sufficient. In fact, the listening centers in libraries and the teaching auditoriums and multimedia presentation centers now common will serve admirably in meeting the needs for systems-approach teaching. It will be necessary also to plan classroom installations for group-response techniques and equip them on a permanent basis with automatic filmstrip and 2×2 inch slide projectors, and television receivers in order to meet the demands made by instructional systems for a variety of presentation methods. However, we must emphasize the need for additional laboratories in a number of subject areas, greatly increased school library facilities, and many teaching and working stations for both small and large groups. Moreover, we must point out that when we use the expression *large-group*, we may be referring to a large group of individuals, each member of which is working in a carrel on self-pacing, media activities. We shall refer to such problems and their solutions in a later section under instrumentation.

The Predicted Need for In-Service Education

In Chapter 4, the problem of in-service education was opened up in the light of good leadership and supervisory practice. Programs for the use of media in the unique patterns found in instructional systems are certain to require in-service growth activities from bulletin preparation to the organization of workshops. The need for and pacing of in-service education programs led by the media program director, his school-building coordinators, and other school leaders, will be determined by the rate of system-approach development both nationally and locally. If a few teams of teachers undertake pilot programs, the pace can be slow, but if whole courses on an instructional-systems basis are introduced, then teachers will have to be taught new skills after preparatory study activities. Moreover, continuing assistance will have to be given to guide groups of teachers through their new and understandably strange procedures. Where pacing needs to be slower, a valuable inauguration procedure would be to install required equipment in a few classrooms

on a pilot basis, thus facilitating experimental trial by innovative teachers. In such try-out experiences, teaching systems of the small-scope, limited-objective variety should be employed in order to facilitate the viewing of demonstrations by local teachers. Needless to say, new schools that already have large-group, multimedia installations, electronic learning laboratories, and closed-circuit television facilities will be in a favorable position to speed up the process of applying systems thinking to teaching. Another major factor will be the speed with which commercial companies can produce high-quality media packages in widely usable formats for quick adoption and adaptation to local equipment patterns. For the present we can at best estimate that in the next five to seven years the sales of media packages for use in instructional systems will rise rapidly.

Criticalness of the Time Factor in Systems Teaching

On one occasion using a dozen carrels for a group of a dozen students in a media-preparation course, the writer at first thought to have his students work through the one carrel in which the automated slide program taught the skill of using the LeRoy lettering pen. Knowing, however, that other lettering work involving the new skill was scheduled in two hours, it was decided to not take the four required hours to route pupils through it. The substitute procedure was to set up four identical laboratory work stations and provide two technicians as instructors, thus routing three groups of four students through the learning and practice session in approximately one hour. In view of the time limitation that existed, the one-hour plan suited the instructor's purposes better.

This case illustrates the timing and scheduling needed in connection with instructional systems where media are used to present stimuli and call for responses leading to desirable levels of accomplishment via programed methods. The critical factor is the hierarchy of skills and how much time may elapse before the skill is to be used in direct application to other tasks. If students have a week or a semester to work through a battery of skills, then no problem of a critical-time nature will be encountered. The main factor is whether or not the instructional need must be met immediately. We then have a problem of logistics and must see to it that sufficient equipment is available. For example, in the preceding case, four identically equipped carrels should be available—or twelve if only twenty minutes of time can be allotted to the instruction.

The critical question just raised applies as well to a group of a hundred or more learners. Rotation of groups may not be a feasible method, or if it has to be used, the time factor may have to be altered, or the objective may have to be met by a method that involves quick conversion of a sufficient number of self-instruction carrels to the desired program capability. This requirement poses a storage problem and this aspect of logistics will be discussed in a later section.

Acquisition of Media-Supported Instructional Systems

The reader will recall that Chapter 3 dealt with the topic of selecting and acquiring media for instructional purposes. Although we need not repeat that discussion here, we should bear it in mind. The application of curriculum values to all judgments relating to acquisition is obvious, but we must add a new emphasis to the fact that there has been added a dimension of greater control over media, teaching, personnel, and learners, a control which is agreed to by all concerned. In earlier discussions we have referred to the need for use of media by all teachers concerned, and we have suggested that the so-called process of *enrichment* is not the proper way to describe the basic reason for using technological media.

Basal Nature of Media in Instructional Systems

Because curriculum groups and their leaders are inevitably involved in the decisions to use teaching systems, their choices must be made on firmly scheduled commitments to put the systems to work. We can therefore say that, instructional systems being what they are, their use will in all probability be considered to be *basal*, not supplementary. That is, teachers for whom they are purchased will have already committed themselves to their use in all groups. Acquisition of the media packages and providing facilities and media equipment to make possible

such universal use by a group of teachers automatically invokes a new dimension in acquisition policies. Thus a new and optimum balance must be found between the number of sets of media and the number of schools and the groups that will use them.

Availability of Media for Instructional Systems

Media materials are available in great quantity as individual titles and sets of titles. For the most part, these media are not very often found arranged for immediate use in an instructional system. For traditional teaching methods, a particular film or set of filmstrips may have been chosen by teachers for valuable specific uses. Under systems procedures, a filmstrip or an audio tape may have to be programed for specifically identified presentation and response-control purposes, or used in precise relationship to other media and to learner-and-teacher activities. Some instructional systems are already available, others will be on the market, and schools may make their own and exchange them. Instructional systems for the various subjects, in the form of whole courses or parts of courses, will probably be very costly, mainly because of the professional work that will be required to fabricate them out of media already available, or out of brand new productions. Media program directors and other curriculum personnel must recognize on the one hand how difficult it will be to produce high-quality instructional systems, and on the other hand they must recognize that a new dimension has been added to selection processes, a dimension of sophistication in understanding the roles of media.

Selection Processes for Instructional Systems

If we consider that instructional systems are chains of activities taking place in a close and unique relationship to each other, we can see that the decision to select and use them is a drastically different process than that which is usually carried out in selecting a particular motion picture or a set of filmstrips for earlier and traditional modes of utilization. It would be helpful to discuss a few of the ways in which this process is different and why.

Figure 11-4. We use the media packages shown in these pictures as examples of the many kinds of program content commercially available in many subject-matter fields. (See Figure 11-3 and subsequent illustrations in this chapter.) Such packages of media are for specific application and have to be immediately and continuously available. (*Top view*, courtesy Craig Corporation, Los Angeles, California. *Bottom view*, courtesy Encyclopaedia Britannica Educational Corporation, Chicago.)

The Aspect of Evaluation. No one has ever questioned the need to evaluate media for selection, but evaluating a package of media in combination, and programed for a whole course, is an infinitely more weighty problem than exists when evaluating a filmstrip for elementary school science, grade 3. Even if we have no media-equipment capability to be concerned about, essential elements in making evaluative decisions such as checking on content, established objectives, results when tried out with given groups of pupils, required time for execution, grade level applicability, present teaching staff capability, the need for reorganization of pupils, the need for reorganizing members of teams of teachers, the execution of the entire system under existing conditions, constitute a major decision-making operation. The implication is that evaluation processes must be carried out by a higher level of curriculum-planning personnel.

We must take particular note of the fact that media that are programed require specified instrumentation. Without such instruments, the media may not be usable, even though highly desirable. Obviously the levels of gravity in evaluation would vary because some teaching systems would be evaluated in light of limited use. Some teachers may be given the choice of whether or not to use a given limited-process system. In this case a teacher's own decision may be all that is necessary and a set of programed tapes, programed booklets, and a set of color slides for use in automated carrels which the teacher has permanently set up in his room would be purchased for that one situation alone. In the event that a number of teachers were contemplating the process of rotated use of one or more limited-objective systems on an exchange basis, the judgments of the teachers involved would—after clearance through a selection panel, and with the approval of the media program director or coordinator for budgetary purposes—suffice for purchase. Limited use, therefore, would not require the same level of decision making as would the application of the system to an entire course.

There is considerable content in the literature relative to the evaluation of programed learning sequences, and we can broaden the base of such content to include reference to all programed media thus providing a basis for judging value and applicability. For example, Jacobs, Maier and Stolurow[9] submitted and discussed the following check list:

9 Paul I. Jacobs, Milton H. Maier, and Lawrence M. Stolurow, *A Guide to Evaluating Self-Instructional Programs* (New York: Holt, Rinehart and Winston, 1966), p. 28.

CHECKLIST FOR EVALUATING A SELF-INSTRUCTIONAL PROGRAM

	Yes	No
Is it really programed instructional material?	____	____
How does the program fit into the curriculum?	____	____
A. Does it cover the appropriate topics?	____	____
B. Does it develop the appropriate skills and knowledge?	____	____
C. Is it at the appropriate difficulty level?	____	____
How well would the program teach in your situation?		
A. Are the conditions under which the validation data were collected relevant to your situation?	____	____
B. How well does the program meet your objectives?	____	____
Can you afford it?		

Manuals that accompany programed media should provide detailed reports about actual try-out results with learners. In regard to programed media within the broader framework of the instructional system, evaluation panels should consider what media instrumentation is required for the system being studied, and whether the school possess it or can acquire it in order to offer the required facilities. The entire change process and staff capability for implementing the prescribed system must be considered in decisions regarding the selection of new material. Who then should make the evaluation?

The Hierarchy of Evaluation Personnel. We must emphasize the point that the nature of the evaluation process and the make-up of selection panels as discussed in Chapter 3 must undergo drastic changes when instructional systems are the subject of consideration for adoption. The somewhat informal and loosely organized process of collecting information about films, filmstrips, tapes, and even sets of textbooks, from individuals or panels of teachers may no longer suffice. Although the cooperation of teachers in giving advice and counsel will be of inestimable value, other leadership personnel must inevitably be brought into the process of analysis. Thus it is likely that teachers will be called on to participate in supplying data based on observation and trial to their department heads, school principals, or a curriculum system selection panel chairman, for consideration, recommendation, and final approval by, for example, a curriculum director. Personnel in these various categories may hold varying ranks in their school district, but it can be seen that the curriculum director may be an assistant superintendent or perhaps the chief instructional authority for the elementary or secondary schools in the district. The media program director would be associated with the selection process in a number of different capacities at several levels of activity: (a) as the media specialist closest to the actual try-out situations; (b) through curriculum personnel systems selection panels of which he would be a member; and (c) as a coordinate decision maker at the curriculum director level. Since the use of instructional systems would require extensive changes in normal operating procedure, the decision to initiate would come from top levels, but the decision to explore and organize for evaluation may be the action that leads to change, and this may come from the media program director himself working with and through top-level curriculum personnel. Since the change process requires the application of various forces, some internal and others external to the school district, the school superintendent and the board of education may have vital roles to play in the process of initiating

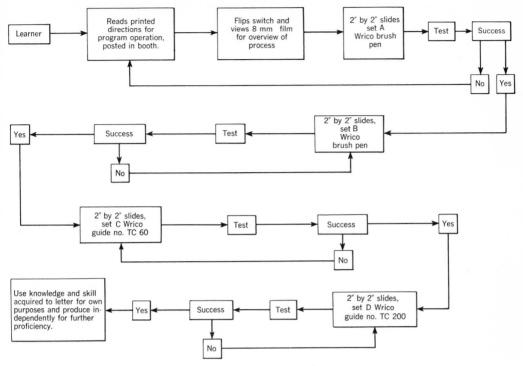

Figure 11-5. As an example of the kind of planning and implementation activity needed for systems work, we show a flow chart of a process designed to be carried out on an individualization basis. We cannot go into all the details having to do with orientation, time scheduling, and special directions in the carrel. The limited task system was designed by one of the author's students as a course learning activity, and the system has been in actual use ever since its preparation, but is in need of revision. The reader should follow the loops of this flow chart to analyze the process of design, and to ferret out possible blockages in the flow of learning activity. *Courtesy Robert A. Fischer, Jr.*

the decision to explore and evaluate instructional systems. The prospective or practicing media directors cannot help but realize in this newer orientation for evaluation and selection that they must now organize groups of evaluators that report to higher authorities, must involve higher curriculum authorities in final decisions, and must themselves be ready to make recommendations for decisions based on a number of aspects of media technology and their application to significant curriculum problems.

Design and Preparation of Instructional Systems by Teachers

Not all of the instruction systems needed in schools can be purchased from the commercial companies presently engaged in the knowledge industry. Those systems that are available have been designed by curriculum experts on the basis of carefully identified instructional needs, and without doubt have had the benefit of counsel by many teachers. Many systems, either highly specific or small in scope, and those that comprise whole courses or are integral parts of courses and units of work, may have to be produced locally. Such local systems will have to be designed and produced with the direct participation of the teachers who are going to use them. However, the media director ought to be aware of the need to supply technical services of a routine nature, so that talented teachers may expend their energies on design and planning efforts. In situations where extensive local media production is called for, cooperative effort among several task forces, or other groups in the various schools, on an exchange basis, becomes essential. It is quite clear that when teachers plan and prepare visualized presentations of any sort, whether they involve multimedia, or a single medium, hours of painstaking planning effort are required. It is therefore a necessity for media directors to provide the assistance teachers must have including consultation in the planning stage and hours of technical service in actual preparation. Chapter 9 points out the kinds of facilities and some necessary arrangements if such capabilities are to be developed and utilized.

The media program director needs to develop with staffs in schools with which he is connected high standards for productions that may be considered as components of systems. He needs to work with teachers who are interested in such activities, either in meetings or by bulletins or other contacts, to develop criteria that will enable teachers to cooperate with each other more effectively in producing programed media that may be duplicated and distributed to all teachers of a given grade and subject. Such instructional systems as are produced locally, even under the best guidance available, should be tried out with specified groups by teachers, and reports should be written and sent to a formally appointed curriculum panel for studying and approving the quality of such media-package productions. Such committees and panels would be in a favorable position to make judgments as to the need for revision of the work done by widely separated teachers or groups for specific purposes. The media program director would do well to make effective use of such steering and editorial committees in making unpleasant decisions, for the sake of his own

Figure 11-6. Along the same lines of procedure as in Figure 11-5 a first grade teacher has developed several systems. We reprint here the first half of the flow chart she developed for a limited instructional system for the use of small coins. The system proceeds on a self-instruction basis, using programed 2×2 inch slides, tape, and manipulative materials. Youngsters work in groups of four because of the lack of carrels and equipment supply. (See also Figures 11-7 and 11-8). *Courtesy Dorothy Getchell and the Public Schools, Manchester, Conn.*

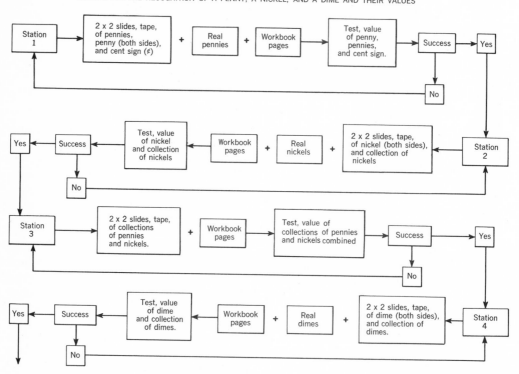

SYSTEM FOR THE RECOGNITION OF A PENNY, A NICKEL, AND A DIME AND THEIR VALUES

Figure 11-7. These two pictures show two groups of first-graders at work on familiar content. One of the youngsters activates the Carousel projector, and another starts and stops the tape player. The teacher received a grant to continue and improve her practices. If anything goes wrong, teacher is within reach, even if she is working with other children. *Courtesy Public Schools, Manchester, Connecticut.*

general welfare and the good of all concerned. What he ought to do is help organize task forces to do this work and to help such groups to set up their own standards, giving such assistance as will expedite the activities of many.

Required Volume of Deployment of Purchases

One of the major things that a media program director must determine is the number of sets of media packages or complete instructional systems that will be required to meet the needs of his school or school district. To what degree can a media package for an instructional system be circulated among individual schools in a cluster? To what degree is a particular system needed for repetitive use in one school building? Which media-service centers can be designated as repositories for the various media packages? What delivery systems can be developed to see to

it that media packages can be moved out on the proper schedule to the school or schools? We must face up to the need for "built-in" systems, where media are stored in each school for specific and repeated uses. But this is another problem, a major problem of logistics, and we shall deal with it in a separate section. For the moment we must reconsider the sense of urgency in using media as indispensable components of the teaching process, and once an instructional system has been inaugurated, breakdowns and delays cannot be tolerated. The quantity as well as the quality of instructional systems become a part of the high-level decision making process. Hence, now more than ever before, the service plan has to be formulated before the purchase, not after, as has been the case so often in the past. This is why we have said that there is a new orientation for media in the curriculum. This orientation applies to hardware as well as to software, although as we have always known, the content and the inter-

action of learners to it go straight to the heart of teaching and learning.

Software and Hardware Relationships in Instructional Systems

Throughout this book we have referred to the newer roles of media, and we have talked about media in combination and the deployment of media equipment at each teaching station, as well as other means for putting required equipment into the right places at the optimum time. We have considered the relationship between the media materials such as film cartridges, filmstrips, programed illustrated booklets, general references, audio-program tapes, videotapes, slide sets in automated trays and magazines, workbooks, and guidesheets, but we must recognize that all the films in existence would be of no consequence to a teacher without a film projector. Furthermore, all the films and all the projectors would be sadly lacking in impact—regardless of their potential—if teachers were not available to lead students to react to the content in them in desirable ways. Hence, in the same way we see that programed sequences, slide sequences, films, and tapes—that is, the software—simply must have the instruments, or hardware, by means of which they may be activated to affect viewers, listeners, and responders. The most sophisticated instructional hardware chain imaginable would not be capable of affecting a single pupil until it had been programed and activated appropriately.

Feeding monstrous dial-retrieval video and audio installations is a process that requires system-production talents and capabilities of the highest order. Yet, even when these hardware chains are programed with tape and picture, so that they are ready to guide learners along certain routes of observation and action, they are but one component of the total system by means of which pupils are educated. How are pupils to be motivated and oriented, what challenging and creative activities will pupils engage in as an aftermath of guidance by a machine? We must realize that without optimum balance among the programed content, the hardware to control it, and what teachers and pupils do with it, the whole process may well have gone on as before. Thus we must make sure that we perceive the requirement to equip our schools with hardware and software in sufficient quantity to make their utilization possible under optimum conditions, in its true perspective as means to vital ends.

Up to this point we have left to the reader's imagination and to his study of the illustrations, the job of making specific what has been discussed in general terms. Now we come to the problem of depicting the kinds of hardware that media program directors should consider for installation and in what quantities. This is a problem in instrumentation and as we analyze it we shall indicate explicitly or implicitly the nature of the media packages that may be chosen, the limitations that any given equipment installation places on the probable arrangements for grouping learners, and the ways in which teachers may have to perform in order to accomplish their objectives.

Instrumentation for Media-Supported Instructional Systems

The truly significant aspect of instrumentation is the function to be implemented. When a function is to explain by word of mouth in a face-to-face situation, the only technologies needed are those of acoustics, to minimize the distraction of noise, and of voice amplification if the group is large. In the early days of foreign language laboratories, media specialists were often called upon to give advice as to the kinds of instrumentation to specify. Their real problem was to obtain from the instructors an itemization of functions that were desired. Instructors thus had to reveal at that point a knowledge of instructional design that would presumably be employed after the facility was installed. Function, then, is an aspect of design, and design is created and implemented in light of identified objectives and insights into the desired learning processes. Design involves a set of unerring predictions of the means to achieve the ends within and in accordance with optimum conditions. The conditions established may grow out of and be oriented to processes of innovation, all of which are motivated by the professional desire to discover more effective routes to accomplishment. One of the keys to optimum pacing in such processes of change is the degree to which technological information is available and known by media program directors. Without adequate technical information at hand or knowledge of its sources on the part of school leaders, implementation of technical processes is likely to be slowed down or prevented entirely.

Technology has made it possible to create new environments for learning, using in many different forms the voice, personality, and guiding potential of the teacher. It has immeasurably speeded up some of the laborious personal processes of analyzing pupil action and has improved the means for getting at and presenting needed content. It has also provided a dependable means of control of both the presentation of content and the individual responses of the learner. In order to make effective use of these technological benefits, painstaking thought needs always to be given to the learner and his motives and to the conditions under which he will work.

It is at this point that we introduce various kinds of instrumentation. In discussing instrumentation plans we open up numerous possibilities for designing instructional systems, always relying on the reader and the people he works with to make specific applications. The truth is that at this time we can do little more than indicate possibilities available through instrumentation, because at present, although we have what we can call the hardware, we have neither the software nor the schools, beyond a few scattered examples, to implement widespread use. When media packages for instructional

Figure 11-9. These photographs indicate the variety in electronic classroom or electronic learning laboratory installations, some of which are arranged for many uses, incorporating various forms of active responding by individuals. Some of the installations utilize manual control at the console, others operate by dial-access and remote-control methods. See also Figure 7-5. (*Top picture*, courtesy Raytheon Learning Systems Co., Englewood, New Jersey. *Bottom photograph*, courtesy Switchcraft Inc., Chicago.)

systems are procured by one means or another, it is likely that they will make use of a number of instrumentation installations, and we shall now turn to a brief treatment of each of the major examples of such installations.

Electronic Learning Laboratories

It took about five years of experience with the listen-respond-record techniques of the foreign language laboratory and a vastly improved technology to popularize the use of the same practices in other instructional areas. Business education, music, typewriting, physical and natural science, social science, and elementary, secondary, and college courses seemed to open up new opportunities for student listening and responding. The electronic learning laboratories as they are often called—or aural listening, phonetics, or electronic classrooms—are so broadly applied now, and equipment is so sophisticated, that we also employ the name to refer to a group of carrels interconnected with audio and video program-resource banks. We think of electronic learning laboratories as being basic to the use of audio program tapes and of videotapes that are operated by remote control, and also operated from a master console presided over and controlled by the teacher or his assistants. The so-called electronic learning laboratory idea may be implemented with minimum equipment facilities for small groups of pupils using only headphones for listening, or with specially equipped fixed installations for large groups, or with specially equipped independent study carrels placed according to intended use in libraries, teaching stations, and laboratories. It is time now to point out the nature of a number of problems that the prospective media director will have to solve in connection with this very nearly indispensable instrumentation plan.

The Electronic Learning Laboratory As a Fixed Instrument Installation in a School Building. Because of the complexity of wires and control cables and because of the desirable reorganization of conventional plans into systems operations, carrels should be grouped in special teaching-learning stations where students can be rotated to and from other large-group and small-group teaching stations. Under such scheduling arrangements some students may be operating carrel equipment by dial- or push-button-

retrieval techniques. We must decide where to locate these special learning areas, and determine the number of carrels that should be provided for a particular instructional system or set of functions. At this point the media program leader must work with other curriculum planners to ascertain the nature of the total need in light of the objectives to be reached and the arrangements to be implemented. Each school building may need several widely separated installations, related to clusters of classrooms dealing with a given subject field, or related to centrally located libraries and instructional material centers. The number of carrels needed depends also upon the nature and scope of the specific system being employed.

Electronic Classroom Carrel Equipment. The reader may ascertain the range of equipment units generally available for carrels by studying the illustrations throughout this book. However, to mention a few kinds of equipment, we can identify:

1. Audio tape recorder with playback through headset, or playback from remote player.
2. Videotape receiver with automatic push-button or dial-access control of programs.
3. Cartridge-type, sound motion picture projector, with sound and headset.
4. Cartridge-type, sound motion picture projector, without sound.
5. Automatic student-controlled sequenced color-slide projector.
6. Automatic student-controlled sequenced color-slide projector programed with tape-cartridge sound.
7. Automatic, student-controlled filmstrip projector.
8. Small, rear-projection or front-projection surfaces.
9. Related realia, manipulative materials, microscope, typewriter, computer input keyboard, reference materials such as textbooks, workbooks, programed booklets, panels of pictures.
10. A teaching machine incorporating a combination of capabilities.
11. A computer input-output link.
12. A student-responder device for teacher and/or computer analysis.

Carrels that are associated with specific laboratories in a special field may have special

Figure 11-10. The effort to apply technology to the problem of individualization and to instructional systems implementation has resulted in a variety of carrel installations for both general and specific purposes. In the top photograph is a conventional study carrel in which a small television receiver has been connected to supply cables. In the middle view, a young man who is deaf is receiving special instruction, and in the bottom picture we note a more sophisticated arrangement to meet a number of learner needs. See also Figures 3-1 and 11-3. (*Top view*, courtesy Northern Highlands Regional High School and Sylvania Electric Products Inc., New York, New York. *Middle view*, courtesy Midwest Regional Media Center for the Deaf, University of Nebraska, Lincoln. *Bottom view*, courtesy Instructional Electronics, Radio Corporation of America, Camden, New Jersey.)

equipment, permanently fixed for prescribed operations. Other carrels in electronic learning laboratories may be so arranged and constructed that equipment may be exchanged, and new sets of realia and equipment substituted. The problems of logistics encountered under time and learning-order limitations have already been discussed briefly in an earlier section. As has been indicated in the carrel equipment repertoire, the learner may use a remote videotape player and a remote bank of audio programs on tape to which he can be connected on schedule or at will. Other items of equipment may be directly controlled by the student in the carrel according to special assignments. Thus programed slide and filmstrip sequences activated by push button, programed paper, or magnetic tape may need to be added to standard electronic classroom carrel installations. In such applications the carrel in an electronic learning laboratory installation becomes also an independent-study station, even in a large-group arrangement with fifty or more in continuous operation. Within a large-group installation, for example, twenty of the total number may be equipped one way, and thirty another. Such changeovers, however, would require technicians much as would any large science laboratory facility.

Equipment Operation in Electronic Carrels. It will generally be up to media program directors and media coordinators in school buildings to determine and recommend to school authorities such as department heads and curriculum leaders feasible methods for using technology to accomplish instructional goals. Teachers and their leaders are the content and learning activity specialists. They must be held responsible for the activities that will produce the desired instructional effects. Therefore we need to consider some of the possibilities for operating the equipment units that have been placed in the carrels that make up the electronic learning laboratory. If we consider the electronic classroom installation as a specific instrumentation plan to make possible a given teaching system, or if we try to so equip all carrels in a given location for general applicability, we then must strive to install those instruments that will be useful to a maximum degree, or only those that will suffice for specific learning activities. In any case, the media director must decide the degree of flexibility he will recommend to those

who are planning the system. He may recommend the following possibilities or some combination of them.

1. Install a dial-retrieval system for all audio-program tapes with remote control of tape playback by the student.
2. Arrange for a separate student-controlled tape recorder and a stock of standardized audio programs, as standard equipment for a given unit of work, or for a course.
3. Arrange to equip the carrels in a given location with dial-retrieval videotape programs on a scheduled or individual-selection basis.
4. Plan to have carrel equipment operated (if simplified controls are provided) by each student, in accordance with programed books and other learning guides. Trays of slides, film cartridges, and tapes would have to be signed out, or would be stored in the carrel.
5. Plan to have students operate one or more kinds of equipment such as trays of slides and cartridge-type films with pictorial sequences fully programed. The student would select from centralized banks of programs according to plan, and then carry out specialized activities of a stimulus-response nature by means of special equipment and supplies that are within reach.

Designers of such learning processes must be sensitive to the need of the learner for operational instructions that are known in advance, adequate orientation to the process, and other learning conditions that will facilitate the student in carrying out instructions without undue distraction and interfering negative reactions. We must emphasize that the design of the equipment units placed in carrels must be such as to be troublefree in operation and extremely simple to control. Standardization of carrel equipment units so that there will be transfer from one carrel to another, from year to year in a given school, is another planning essential.

The Teaching Auditorium As an Application of the Electronic Learning Laboratory Idea. The desire to put the costly space in a school auditorium to more frequent and effective use, coupled with the urgent need for areas in which to accommodate large groups for purposes of direct instruction, has led planners to incorporate operable dividing walls and instructional instrumentation in new school construction. See Figures 1-10 and 10-20. Hence we have an

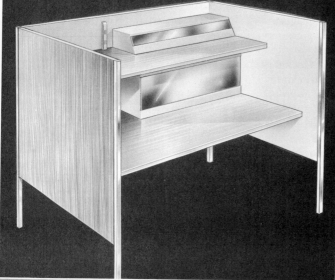

Figure 11-11. We have made many references to the need for building facilities in connection with the use of instructional technology. These views indicate the nature of the problem to provide individual study stations in sufficient number to meet special instructional needs. Some of the installations are designed and fabricated locally. Others are procured as standard models from manufacturers. All of the stations shown are ready for instrumentation, all having been designed for varying degrees of media capability. The middle-view study station was designed with the assistance of a Michigan State University group. The unit will accept a wide variety of media equipment. In the bottom picture we note the honeycomb design of the carrels at Grand Valley College. (*Top view*, courtesy The Advance Products Company, Wichita, Kansas. *Middle view*, courtesy The Worden Company, Holland, Michigan. *Bottom view*, courtesy Grand Valley College, College Landing, Allendale, Michigan.)

extension of the electronic classroom idea when we install a student push-button responder at each seat and link it to a computer for storage, analysis, and reporting purposes; install multiple television receivers, or projection-type television; install headsets and a dial-retrieval system for the use of audio-program tapes in a compartment at each seat; and install multimedia projection systems under automatic control. One or more such spaces may be arranged within the larger school auditorium, and in such cases, the planning and placement of instrumentation is a critical and exacting problem in preconstruction planning. Special seats need to be installed in the areas for automated instruction purposes that provide a writing surface, a storage cubicle for headsets, and space for attaching the student responder, and the selector switch or dial-access device for retrieving audio programs.

The Need for Identification of Instructional Functions. It is essential that when planning instrumentation for instructional systems, we proceed on the basis of required functions that the given instructional system demands. Naturally such functions will be tied irrevocably to and can only be stated in terms of specific teaching objectives—the kinds of action that need to be taken by both learner and teacher. It will be helpful to quote as an example the following listing by Brubaker, when describing architecture and equipment for the language laboratory, categorized first for the learner, then for the teacher:

The Student Can

Listen to master lessons.
Respond and hear his own voice.
Communicate with the teacher and other students.
Record both the master and his own voice.
Compare his own voice with the master model voice.
Study individually, working with a special master-tape appropriate to his own needs and at his own rate.

The Teacher Can

Direct different lesson programs to selected students.
Divide class into groups.
Monitor (listen to) each individual student's responses.
Communicate with any student, to correct and instruct.

Record any student's responses on a tape at the console.
Talk to an individual, a row, a group, or to the entire class.
Broadcast one or two students' conversation to a group or the class.
Duplicate master tapes and record master lessons on tape.[10]

When we consider the many operational requirements of specific instructional systems, we may wish to emphasize independent study; we may wish to utilize large-group response systems thus keeping large groups of learners moving together on identical content (but checking immediately on accomplishment through known and immediately analyzed interaction; and we may need recording capability, not only in foreign languages, but also in order to record responses in language arts, business study, music, science, or mathematics, to mention just a few fields. In electronic classroom facilities, we need to provide capability, as we have emphasized before, to make various kinds of responses—written, spoken, figured, drawn, or checked—as stimuli are presented from a number of sources, such stimuli may be presented by means of audio and videotapes, from realia, from sequenced illustrations, both in motion and still format, and directly or indirectly from personalities known to the student. The media program director, in his leadership and design work with teachers and curriculum workers, must be quick to discern operational differences in the working patterns of learners. Even in a large group of students, each learner is reacting and learning as an individual, but he is receiving the same communications that everyone else in the group is getting, and in general is being expected to respond actively along the same lines within a controlled time period. In other instances, according to the component of the instructional system being employed, an individual in a large-group, each in his own carrel, may be receiving unique content, from remote sources, or he may be operating his own special

[10] Charles William Brubaker, "Architecture and Equipment for the Language Laboratory." (This Sketchbook was prepared by Mr. Brubaker of Perkins and Will, Architects, for the conference at Purdue University, jointly sponsored by Indiana University and Purdue University, and made possible by a grant from the Educational Facilities Laboratories.) *Audiovisual Instruction*, Vol. 6, No. 5, May 1961, pp. 201–216.

media instruments with content he himself selects on the spot. Thus we see differences between true individualization of instruction and group reception and response plans. Media program personnel will quite probably have to work with all concerned in solving problems of narrowing down or establishing a priority for placing limits on the instructional functions that can be carried out. These problems will be dealt with later under logistics, but we must emphasize one final aspect of electronic classroom instrumentation, to which we turn our attention next.

Using Electronic Learning Laboratories in Instructional Systems. The carrels of the electronic learning laboratory and their media instruments must be made to serve the goals of the instructional system, not the other way around. So we want to know in what way an electronically equipped carrel serves instructional systems. This is a critical question that only the designers of a specific system can answer. However, we may helpfully look into some of the general probabilities.

1. Carrels may supply the working area and instrumentation for receiving direct instruction from the teacher via media, as an independent study component, thus fitted into the trunkline of course content, on a programed, self-paced basis.

2. Carrels may be equipped so as to guide students in the acquisition of basic skills in a course—skills that are later applied to critical thought processes. Learning to operate a chemical balance, a microscope, pronounce words, write equations, interpret problems, carry out specific kinds of computation, are a few examples. Some skill-development processes may take twenty minutes or less, others three hours or more. The carrel component may actually be made to take the place of some of the former functions of face-to-face instruction. It may also take the place of some of the laboratory research, writing, and library work, and it may also take over part of the burden of large-group visualized presentations.

3. Carrels with proper instrumentation may be arranged and scheduled to take the place of homework, remedial work, and make-up work. Reference sources, including programed books, may be needed for this purpose.

On the basis of the few examples cited, it seems obvious that electronic carrels may serve the use of instructional systems in major, minor, and in incidental ways. It falls to systems designers to determine which of the functions that we have indicated in general will be assigned in particular. In some respects the use of electronically instrumented carrels can be considered to be indispensable when instructional systems demand optional use of media-in-control processes.

Multimedia and Multi-Image Projection for Systems Purposes

We have discussed in earlier chapters the multimedia presentation centers that are being incorporated in new schools. Such large-group spaces are often associated with clusters of teaching stations or classrooms and thus offer unique opportunities for reorganizing learners and teachers into new working relationships. By way of differentiation we ought to point out that using a combination of media in any given situation each contributing to teaching needs, operated manually or automatically, is an example of multimedia techniques that may result in multi-image projection. However, using the same medium, such as 2×2 inch slides under automatic control with multiple projectors, thus presenting a number of images on the projection surface at the same time, is an example of multi-image technique.

Multimedia Teaching Stations. We should consider the fact that there are several variations in multimedia presentation techniques in the schools. Remote-control switches may be operated by teachers at the front of a classroom to activate projectors placed at the rear of teaching stations, or the equipment may be located in back of rear-projection screens. By means of control panels in a podium for the teacher, film, slides, and other media may be sequenced and presented in desired order in multiple-image fashion. The teacher may be in direct control at the podium, pushing the buttons at will to pace the presentation, or the entire presentation may be taped, programed, and thus automated. The same capability applies to multi-image presentations using, for example, programed 2×2 inch color slides shown from multiple projectors controlled automatically. For example, when one button is pushed, one or more projectors are activated simultaneously, thus projecting perhaps six images, or two projectors are blanked out and two activated to project called-for images for comparison at the desired time.

Use of Multimedia Teaching Stations in Instructional Systems. How will multimedia instrumentation installations serve the purposes of an instructional system? Obviously it serves as a large-group direct instruction component, in a face-to-face teacher presentation as for motivation, definition of problems, explanation, defining issues, and laying out future problem-solving work. It also serves when fully automated as an extension of the teacher's personality, giving direct instruction when the teacher is elsewhere. If we add group-response techniques and a computer link, or if we provide learners in the large viewing and listening group with interaction guidesheets for following the presentation, we can introduce self-instructional, media-in-control practices that make the multimedia teaching station a vital part of any given instructional system, be it a whole or a part of a course. Apart, however, from their service in implementing instructional systems, such teaching stations offer to team teaching and to all forms of large-group presentations the convenient control of combined media equipment including a linkage with live or videotape television unknown except by electronic combinations achieved in the television studio itself.

Teaching Machines for Instructional Systems

Teaching machines connote not only hardware but also the software or the programed content. In the present case we are discussing the instrumentation and its service to the implementation of instructional systems. We must now indicate also that we refer to a type of instrumentation that pertains solely to a unit that is operated by the student himself, and a unit that accepts packaged or cartridged content, verbal and pictorial. We have repeatedly emphasized the need for the programing method and the need for media to present content (even using the teacher's own voice) and call for and control the learners' responses. Teaching machines provide systems planners with another display and control mechanism. To be sure, these machines may be very expensive, but they also may incorporate tape playback, pictorial as well as verbal-frame programing capability, and response indicator controls. Teaching machines may be connected to computer and response-

analysis devices, and thus provide immediate information on the accomplishments of individual students or large groups.

Teaching-Machine Stations. We should point out that teaching machines can be used in conjunction with other media in any teaching-machine station, and thus a given teaching-station unit may possess a combination of operational devices. It may be necessary to provide for any given teaching-system plan, additional teaching-machine rooms through which students may be rotated or scheduled as needed. Depending on the nature of the system and the volume of instruction to be given, machines may have to be set up in permanent locations to accommodate fifty or more students at a time. See Figure 11-13 on page 482. It is of course feasible if the machines are small to use them in conventional classroom locations. We are not saying that separate stations for teaching machines and other media instruments are mandatory, but it may be far more effective in light of conditions to be implemented to arrange such facilities.

Application of Teaching Machines in Instructional Systems. We can easily understand that teaching machines may first and foremost be used as instruments to facilitate independent action on a self-pacing, self-instruction basis. Teaching machines may lend themselves conveniently for use with additional media as, for example, presentations via television or automated multimedia programs. The teaching machine component requires strong motivation and insightful scheduling, timing, and optimum balance in the diet of activity. Teaching machines in their variety of form and function are likely to become indispensable components in the instructional systems process.

Television Instrumentation for Instructional Systems

There is little doubt that videotape program capability will make important contributions to the implementation of instructional systems. Instrumentation may be extremely costly, but advancing technology holds out hope for the alleviation of this problem. We have already discussed aspects of television technology in the preceding chapter. Now we shall discuss its applications to instrumentation for instructional systems.

Figure 11-12. In addition to the rear-projection screen it can be seen that the presentor, in this case, Professor Richard Byrne, also makes use of the overhead projector. The next picture, left, reveals the nature of the media-preparation and programing effort. We see the communicator, Professor Byrne, in the center with programer R. Brooks, left, and Gerald F. McVey, program designer and manager of the facility, at work in a planning session. An assistant programer is also shown in the bottom view checking the program for correct sequence. In the next two pictures the technology of the center is depicted. Rack-mounted control equipment makes it possible to automate the program completely. Hence whenever needed the instructor may present his program via tape, and the display functions will be carried out by control mechanisms. The projection room is behind the screen in the bottom picture on the right. Note the various equipment units, including the large-screen projection television system. *Courtesy Multimedia Instruction Laboratory, School of Education, University of Wisconsin, Madison. Photographs by Jerry Capps, Staff Photographer.*

Roles of Closed-Circuit Television in a Teaching System. Referring to curriculum problems as discussed in Chapters 4 and 10, we can readily see important uses for television in instructional systems. As examples, we may mention motivation, explanation, definitions of issues and problems, demonstrations, and electronic combination of media, all of which are direct-instruction procedures applicable to large groups. We have mentioned previously a number of unique ways in which television could be employed in the curriculum and many of these may be applied directly to instructional systems. We have identified a number of media installations that contribute greatly to the potential use of carefully planned systems of teaching to achieve objectives, and television may be the means of bringing the teacher, even though vicariously, into direct contact with learners at strategic points along their routes to progress.

Videotape Storage for Repetitive Use. One of the reasons for suggesting the use of television in instructional systems is that the programs can easily be constructed, produced, and stored on

Figure 11-13. These students at Sullivan High School are working through English, mathematics, and business education programs using the AutoTutor teaching machines. One of the teacher participants in the learning laboratory, as it is called, is reloading the machines for another session. In the bottom picture carrels have been equipped with Craig reader units, and groups of students work through the available programs on a rotation basis. Incidental, or intermittent use of such equipment may not constitute instruction systems use in the true sense. What kinds of uses of equipment as we identify in these pictures would be characteristic of instructional systems? (*Top views*, courtesy Southwest School Corporation, Sullivan, Indiana. *Bottom photograph*, Craig Corporation, Los Angeles.)

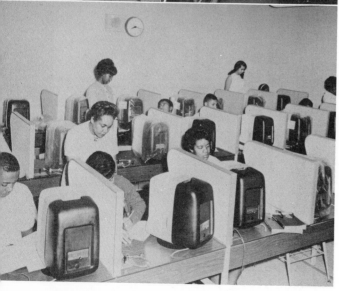

videotape. Videotaped television programs in series that direct students in their problem-solving activity, homework, or laboratory and library work, can be used at will, thereby freeing teachers for other leadership and planning activity, for face-to-face work with small groups, and for guiding the creative and productive work of their learners. The videotape is then a major source of teacher-pupil contacts—a multiplication of the teacher's efforts according to the unique needs of the system in a given field. In addition to this general potential for contribution to instructional-systems implementation, videotapes make possible new arrangements for the automatic control of repetitive playback. Electronic carrels and classrooms, both large and small, may have access to the programs they need by the simple process of dialing, or some other signal-and-call devices, using telephone relay mechanisms. Technological developments along these lines show great promise of improved simplicity and lower cost. Timing and scheduling of specified programs whether on videotape or not, may pose some vexing problems for the media program director and his staff. This is because, as we have said, instructional systems may not possess the inherent looseness of control that has often characterized the projection of motion pictures, for example, by a teacher in his class, who has his pupils under direct control at all times.

Programing the Television Program. Great stress has been given to the need for the use of programed sequences with any given medium, whether cartridge film, color slide, teaching machine, or television. Thus we need to examine the possible contributions of television not in a general way as in the preceding paragraphs, but specifically as a means of presenting programed content. Television certainly seems to offer unique capabilities along these lines. If we realize the nature of what teachers can do in a personal way using the medium of television, then we can see that teachers can call for pupil interaction and call for the same kind of active responding, that is, choosing, writing, talking, and perceiving vital relationships. The capability of such programs on videotape makes the television medium and its application to self-instruction activity all the more convenient and desirable. In one of his discussions of television as a teaching machine, Carpenter[11] described the

generalized learning cycle for programing methods and then explained television's potential contributions to this process as follows:

A generalized learning cycle, in the context of programing methods, can be thought of as consisting of four operational phases or sequential sets of functions:

Presentation of patterns or "frames" of stimulus materials, a problem, or a specific learning task.

The controlled responses of the learners.

Evaluation of the specific responses in ways to provide reinforcement and rewards.

The recording of the learning cycle events and student responses.

Television has potentials which can be adapted for mediating two of these four phases of the general learning cycle:

First, television has capabilities for presenting a wide range of patterns of stimulus materials or "frames." For example, print materials, photography (both still and motion), animation, or graphics can be used to compose programed "frames." Combinations of these frames can be organized into ordered sequences of stimulus materials. In addition, the audio or sound channels can be used for informative speech, commentaries, verbal descriptions, sounds, and learning cues.

· · ·

Second, the reinforcement functions can also be mediated through television. A wide range of response evaluations and cues can be incorporated for communicating to students the values of their responses. Furthermore, students can be guided to make their own evaluations.

The other two sets of functions can be carried out by using paper and printed materials. In experiments at Penn State, we used response forms on which students constructed or selected responses. The completed response forms provided a permanent record of each student's performance, which could be analyzed and evaluated.

Thus, by combining the capabilities of television with printed forms, we found that we could satisfy all four of the essential sets of requirements for the generalized programed learning cycle.[11]

Relationship of Television to Instructional Systems. We have identified the need to put programed materials to work as a component of systems methodology and it would appear that

[11] C. R. Carpenter, "Can TV Replace the Teaching Machine?" *Audiovisual Instruction*, Vol. 9, No. 5, May 1964, pp. 280–282.

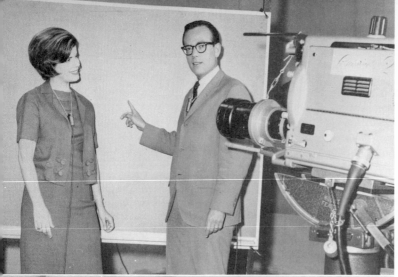

television offers high potential in this regard, and as is very important, television could "work alone." However, television as we have portrayed it in the preceding chapter may also operate as a component of a given instructional system in a way that gives it both a large-group and small-group handling capability. Hence, large groups of learners may be treated by means of the television presentations as though they were in a face-to-face situation, experiencing the work of a talented specialist carrying out expository and guidance of activity aspects of the teaching process. Television may also play an important role in making possible independent study by both programed and nonprogramed methods of presentation through automation. In order to

implement such processes, the instrumentation we discussed in Chapter 10 for comprehensive program production capability and transmission and reception facilities will have to be provided.

Group-Response Techniques in Instructional Systems

Imagine for a moment an instructor who has planned a highly communicative presentation. He has arranged to ask a series of insightful questions in reference to his visualized case studies. He has decided to offer to his 300 students several choices of answers to his questions. This instructor, having planned so painstakingly what he wants to say and do because of some specific conclusions he wants his pupils to derive, desires very much to know whether his pupils have followed his development of the crucial concepts involved. Therefore, he projects his question and the possible answers, then calls for students to raise their hands to show whether or not they know the right choice to make in the situation he has presented. But this may be only one aspect of a typical situation. Suppose the teacher plays an audio-program clip, or projects a set of color slides, or that he appears on a television receiver or a projection surface in a teaching auditorium, and as an integral part of the communication process asks questions and calls for student reactions. How can the knowledge of how 500 students react be known? How can the instructor know immediately the nature of the group's responses, or how can he know the total of the choices that any given pupil has made throughout the class period?

Modern technology through electronics makes possible what is called a group-response system. Questions and choices may be presented to students by any one of a number of means—tape, television, face-to-face by the teacher, programed frames in booklets, projected slides or transparencies, or by any combination of media. The student makes his thinking known by pressing, for example, one of four buttons, or turning a selector dial. Immediately, the teacher has a reading on a percentage meter, and other data as well, even to a computer print-out. When such meters are large and mounted in the front of a room, all students may immediately ascertain the correctness of their own reactions. Several types of operational consoles are available. Some consoles show percentage meters only, others make use of both meters and a panel of lights that indicates the response of each individual (where the instructor may check on students' answers by noting lights that correspond to the positions of the seats in the classroom or auditorium). Still others incorporate three data features—meters, indicator lights for the individual, and student-response counters. By means of the counters, the responses made by each individual are totaled and stored for the teacher's use. When groups become large, sixty or more, computers are needed to analyze fully the information from the

responders. Study Figures 11-15, 11-16, 7-7, 7-8, and 10-20, carefully.

Group-Response Instrumentation. We should emphasize the fact that learning is an individual matter, and when a student response is made as evidence of interaction with learning situations and formally recorded and reported, the results may be of value not only to the student and the teacher, but to the designer of teaching systems also. In group-response systems the student reacts, and his thinking is recorded and used for his own benefit. However, the fact remains that each individual as an individual is pinned down, so to speak, to an arbitrary, though adroit and insightful, pacing of all learners in a given group. It is obvious that whatever media an instructor wishes to use, the responder unit is the instrument for giving the instructor up-to-the-minute data about the effects of his message on his group of learners. Therefore, we can itemize several items of equipment as follows: (a) the responder; (b) a network of connecting wires to a console that doesn't record a voice, but does indicate data about the kinds of choices a pupil is making at any given instant; (c) a computer when large-group analysis demands it; and (d) one or more programing devices such as a tape player that controls the sequential use of other media. Student responders may be the plug-in type at the student's desk, or they may be built in, or set into a student's desk as a permanent fixture. We should also point out that the group-response system can be used in combination with many other arrangements involving a teacher in a person-to-person role, or a teacher in a tape or in a film, or as an observer of pupils when an entire presentation is automatically controlled.

Fitness of Group-Response Techniques for Systems Teaching. As we consider the general use of group-response techniques by a given instructor who is face to face with a group of 200 students, we may simply say that this is a large-group presentation, and as such, not necessarily a component of a teaching system at all. Now we must ask, where and how can the group-response plan be used in an instructional system? We must first recognize that a face-to-face presentation may be a vital part of a teaching system. However, we need to identify additional components of the system. Are programed media used to present stimulus materials and call for responses? In what ways

Figure 11-15. In these two photographs we observe the crucial elements, the teacher (stimuli) and the pupil (responses). The eliciting of response may of course be built into the projected images, or the teacher's spoken query. If we consider the impact on teaching processes in general we say, "Is this the best we can do?" The answer may be "No." Incorporating such processes in instructional systems may be the route to improvement. Members of this audience are future teachers in preservice programs at Illinois Teachers College, Chicago-North. This fact in itself has a bearing on the future of media use in the schools. *Courtesy ITC, Chicago-North, Chicago.*

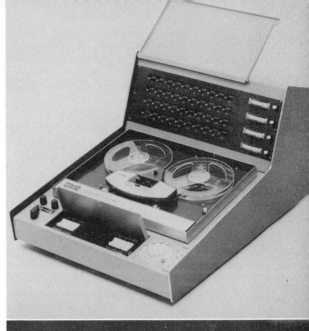

Figure 11-16. If we identify the basic components in Figure 11-15, and then add more technology, we see how we can make immediate use of student response data. In a small group of 40 to 60, the EDEX unit shown will indicate the tabulated data for any given response. The teacher can scan the percentage meters and quickly ascertain the roots of misunderstanding, or estimate how many students are not responding at all. In larger groups, for a detailed and almost instantaneous interpretation and analysis, computer technology becomes a necessity. The IBM 1403 printer shown in the bottom picture, or a specially produced model for the purpose can, of course, if it has been properly connected to the responders as inputs, provide the instructor with critical summaries in a matter of minutes. In cases where 10,000 individual responses are called for in a class session, a show of hands can be next to meaningless. (*Top picture*, courtesy Raytheon Learning System Co., Englewood, New Jersey. *Middle photograph*, courtesy Illinois Teachers College, Chicago-North, Chicago. *Bottom picture*, courtesy IBM, Data Processing Division, Hartford, Connecticut.)

do instruments and media used with them take over teaching activities? Where do printed media fit into the study activities of the learners? What jobs do teachers perform because they are freed from hours of presenting repetitive teaching tasks? We can see in group-response techniques a new vitality in teacher presentations, new ways to link electronic learning laboratories where both audio and videotape presentations may be involved, and to add a new dimension to the collection of data about student reactions. In some situations the teacher may not be there except in audio or videotape format. Thus we see that the application of group-response techniques to instructional systems in our schools may offer a rich potential, but we must be careful to assign to this component specific and identifiable roles in the network of systems activity.

Computers in Instructional Systems

We have referred to the use of computers in storing, analyzing, and reporting student responses to stimulus material. Computers have been used for several years by the military, government, industry, and the administrative staffs in schools for information-processing tasks, but for instructional purposes their use has only rarely, up to this time, moved outside

the realm of experiment. However, there are a few exceptions. According to the North Electric Company's Electronetics Division, there is a special-purpose digital computer that processes more than 40,000 dialed calls for audio-tape programs each week from students at Ohio State University. This *Datagram* system is a dial-access audio-program service that serves not only foreign languages, but other subject areas as well, and may be expanded to include video programing in the future. So although we feel free to indicate present-day needs for computer-assisted instructional processes, we do so in the sense of pointing to a much larger volume of practical usage in future applications of techniques now being employed in experimental classrooms.

It will be helpful for the reader to consider the stages in the application of computer technology to education as identified by Bushnell as follows:

Since 1955, three major stages in the application of computer technology to education have been evident. The installation of the university computing center for the solution of mathematical and scientific problems came first. The second stage was the use of EDP systems in accounting, record keeping, and logistical control activities, i.e., the automation of information and data processing systems. The third stage, in which we are now barely underway, is the use of time shared computers with on line teletypes and CRT display equipment for supporting educators and those being educated in a wide range of intellectual processes. It is this third generation application that spells a revolution in American education primarily because the development of time shared systems holds promise for the improvement of instructional processes.[12]

Developments such as those just mentioned are being tried out in a number of experimental situations. See Figure 11-17. The use of computer-controlled economics games in elementary schools is another example of application to social studies.

As reported by Richard L. Wing,[13] of the Board of Cooperative Educational Services in

Northern Westchester County, New York, one of the problems of the several being developed is called the *Sumerian Game*, designed to teach sixth graders some basic principles of economics in operation at the time of the neolithic revolutions in Mesopotamia. Another game is called the *Sierra Leone Development Project*, designed to simulate the economic problems of a newly emerging nation. Programed tape and slide presentations orient the learner to the conditions and to his new identity in time and place. The computer activates a typewriter terminal to provide special conditions that exist in the environment. Learners then proceed to make decisions, entering their answers at the computer terminal. The computer will immediately return a progress report and introduce new steps in the game calling for more complicated solutions, along with whatever adjustments need to be made in the process. Mr. Wing stated that:

The idea for the economics game as an instructional technique at the elementary school level originated with Bruse Moncreiff of IBM, who was searching for ways to individualize instruction using the power of electronic data processing equipment. . . .

The educational planning for these games is being done by Mabel Addis, a fourth-grade teacher at Katonah Elementary School, and Walter Goodman, chairman of the social studies department at Briarcliff High School. The programing is done by IBM personnel.

Equipment used in these projects includes stock 1050 typewriter terminals, an experimental random access slide projector, and an IBM 7090 computer using a time-sharing system, so that several pupils can be taught at the same time.[14]

We turn next to the following excerpts from a statement by Patrick Suppes of Stanford University who has been conducting comprehensive experimental computer-based instruction in elementary schools:

One of the most exciting aspects of computer-based education is the opportunity it offers for tailoring instruction to the individual child's needs. An individualized approach is possible at various levels of instruction. There are at least three levels of interaction between student and computer program, though the third and deepest level is still mostly beyond us from a technical standpoint. Each of these levels is called a system.

---

12 Donald D. Bushnell, "Computer Based Instructional Systems," Section IV A 1–2, in *Automated Education Handbook*, Edith H. Goodman (ed.) (Detroit: Automated Education Center, 560 Cook Road, 1965).

13 Richard L. Wing, "Computer-Controlled Economics Games for the Elementary School," *Audiovisual Instruction*, Vol. 9, No. 10, December 1964, pp. 681–682.

14 *Ibid.*, p. 682.

Figure 11-17. In this experimental computer-based learning laboratory, there are twenty computer terminals by means of which students are linked to a large digital computer. Students receive individualized program content based on their answers to stimuli in the various lessons. We may note that the terminals are of several different types. Control consoles permit the student stations to be monitored at will. In the middle picture children are shown responding to content displayed on the screen at left. Responses are then processed by the computer and appropriate information is sent back to the responder. *Courtesy Dr. John E. Coulson, System Development Corporation, Santa Monica, California.*

Drill and Practice Systems

In the drill and practice system, instruction is strictly supplementary to the regular curriculum as taught by a teacher. . . .

Tutorial Systems

In systems of this type, the aim is to provide, not a supplementary, but a nearly complete instructional sequence in a given subject. The skill subjects such as reading, mathematics, and elementary foreign languages are most easily handled in this kind of environment. . . .

Dialogue Systems

The dialogue system is envisaged as a system in which a dialogue is possible between the student and the program. Successful development in any depth, however, requires the solution of some relatively difficult technical problems. . . .[15]

Main components in the particular computerization processes identified by Patrick Suppes in connection with the work with pupils are the following:

[15] Patrick Suppes, "Tomorrow's Education? Computer-Based Instruction in the Elementary School," *Education Age*, January–February, 1966, pp. 4–11.

1. A central computer, the PDP-1 designed by the Digital Equipment Corporation.

2. Two visual display devices, one by IBM, a random-access projection device by means of which a 512 page book may be encoded on microfilm with any one-eighth of a page being reachable under random access within one second. The pupil responds to the display by using a light pen. The second display device developed by the Philco Corporation using a cathode ray tube and a typewriter for the learner to use to send information to the computer.

3. An audio system designed by Westinghouse can play prerecorded messages to the pupil in each booth by means of tape six inches wide. Each of the two tape transports has a capacity of 17 minutes, divisible into one message of 17 minutes in length, or 1,024 messages of one second each, all under random-access control. Any one of the taped messages is reachable in about one second.

4. Teletype keyboards, also connected to the computer, for receiving messages and sending

Figure 11-18. In the quoted article by Dr. Suppes in *Education Age*, January-February, 1966, several important terminal devices were shown. These devices are the communicative links between person and computer. In this group the top picture is the teletype keyboard, in the middle picture is the IBM 9405 Display Terminal, and the bottom picture shows the Philco-Ford Student Audio-Visual Interface (SAVI) unit. (*Top two photographs*, reprinted from *Education Age* with permission of 3M Education Press, Visual Products Division, 3M Company, St. Paul, Minnesota. *Bottom picture*, courtesy Communications and Electronics Division, Philco-Ford Corporation, Philadelphia.)

problem solutions from the pupil back to the computer. See Figure 11-18.

We have noted again and again the reference to the four- to five-year period ahead as being the spawning period for the burgeoning development of the use of computers in schools throughout the land. We ourselves are a little less optimistic, but nonetheless certain that the trends are clearly marked. Some of us who have been impatient over the 20- to 50-year lag in the adoption of innovations by education believe that the many possibilities for automation and for individualization and large-group instruction practices are yet so far behind that the widespread adoption of computerized processes for day-to-day instruction is somewhat farther out on the horizon than its technical proponents realize. Yet we should take note of the 1962 statement of Licklider of Bolt, Beranek and Newman, Inc., as follows:

The main conclusions we derive from our experience thus far with computer-aided teaching are the following:

1. It seems possible, by exploiting the computer's constant capability for quick response and reinforcement, to develop techniques of instruction and intellectual exploration that will 'trap' the attention of students and divert their energies from amusements and other less constructive pastimes to education. Deliberate exploitation of both reinforcement and human engineering techniques is essential to this accomplishment.

2. Computers are useful now, or will be in the very near future, in research on teaching and learning and in development of instructional programs.

3. The economic feasibility of widespread exploitation of computer-aided teaching in large schools, school systems, government, and industry depends upon the development of time-sharing computer

systems and rugged, flexible, inexpensive input-output equipment for student stations.[16]

Priority for Computer Uses in Systems Teaching. In systems teaching it is likely that student groups will be reorganized along both large-group and individualization modes. Since we have already discussed and emphasized the need for large-group instruction sessions and the importance of group-response techniques in such groups, it can be readily seen that one of the first roles for computers to play is the immediate recording, analysis, and reporting of learner response data. In fact, this also appears to be one of the simplest processes to implement at the present time.

Another equally high priority would be the use of computers to control access to banks of audio and videotapes as in North Electric's *Datagram* system. Such control devices may often be imperative as the size of the operation increases. Other needs are recognized, and even though computerized teaching machines offer many opportunities for effective learning activities and the technology for such practices is known, the costs appear to be prohibitive for widespread use. Donald D. Bushnell, writing in 1963, expressed the situation as follows:

If computer-aided instructional systems are to be applied on any vast scale, they must be economically competitive with other systems performing similar functions. Some increase in equipment costs can be justified by proved teaching efficiency and subsequent reduction in training time and operational waste. It seems clear that computer-based systems must approach the over-all cost of more conventional equipment if they are to be used for more than specialized military or industrial training applications. This development seems to be the trend, however, in miniaturized, large-capacity systems.[17]

As we ponder the software-hardware problems and the apparently prohibitive costs, we tend not to admit that there are many other deterrents as well, most of which apply to the implementation of systems instruction generally. Stolurow

and Davis[18] emphasize the point that, "The problems in achieving widespread use [of computer assisted instruction] are not those of economics; they are psychological and educational."

Computer Instrumentation for Systems Teaching. Media program directors who are faced with the need to carry out instrumentation problems in their school systems should familiarize themselves with available resources for guidance. Engineering firms specializing in electronic installations will be regionally available to discuss design problems. Installations that are to be used with group-response systems will not necessarily be complicated, since signals from the individual responders may be fed rather simply into computers in much the same fashion as teletype instruments. Print-outs are then immediately available to instructors for their critical use, or for triggering other elements of programed media. Teaching-machine computerization, as we have indicated, is destined for delay in general application until simple and rugged student stations involving computer terminals are produced at much lower cost than at present. Impetus for such development will also come from a much needed increase in knowledge about and insight into the whole process of instructional systems. Technology has already outrun our images of what the instructional process ought to be like. So we fall back on our urge to identify the function, identify the components of an action process, and then bring technological know-how to bear on instrumentation. See Figure 11-19. The leap into technology may yet have to pass through a number of developmental and preparatory phases using many of the old tools, with which unfortunately many are not yet sufficiently familiar, before the day of instructional automation dawns.

In concluding this section we feel compelled to quote the advice given by Estrin on the role of keyboard operation skills and information-processing systems.

We are rushing headlong into an age in which control of nature and of our society will be largely dependent on our ability to interact with information-processing machines. Recognition of this fact

[16] J. C. R. Licklider, "Preliminary Experiments in Computer-Aided Teaching," pp. 238–239, in *Programmed Learning and Computer-Based Instruction*, John E. Coulson (ed.) (New York: John Wiley and Sons, 1962), pp. 238–239.

[17] Donald D. Bushnell, "The Role of the Computer in Future Instructional Systems," *Audiovisual Communication Review*, Vol. 11, No. 2, Supp. 7, March–April, 1963, p. 69.

[18] Lawrence M. Stolurow and Daniel Davis, "Teaching Machines and Computer-Based Systems," in Robert Glaser (ed.), *Teaching Machines and Programed Learning, II* (*Data and Directions*) (Washington, D.C.: National Education Association, 1965), p. 207.

Figure 11-19. This "talking typewriter" can be programed to project images on a screen, pronounce words, and guide the pupil in making desired responses, such as typing out answers as a route to reading skill development. Such a machine is envisaged as having many additional computerized instructional applications. *Courtesy Responsive Environments Corporation, Englewood Cliffs, New Jersey.*

should make us consider the introduction of training for effective interaction with machines at the earliest levels of education. Our society has grown enormously through development of speech, reading, writing, art, music, and a technology permitting mass distribution of information. In general, manipulative skills such as keyboard manipulation have served a "middleman" function, independent of feedback. If the development of these manipulative skills can be made an added educational objective of the 12 to 20 years of education devoted to an individual in our society, we may be able to establish a far greater guarantee of success in reaping benefits from information-processing systems. This is not to say that we should diminish the development of the obviously powerful human skills in a machine environment containing time lags and displays characteristic of our information-processing systems and that these methods be incorporated in the set of educational objectives. If such an educational objective is achieved, while concurrently the purely human values are raised, it will be possible to develop and implement automated teaching procedures and

more powerful use of information-processing systems.[19]

Conventional Media Equipment in Instructional Systems

We must not allow ourselves to believe that everything we do when we teach is or has to be a part of an instructional system. However, when we seek more effective planning, better use of media in performing significant acts for the teacher, and when learners and teachers, and the materials and machines they both use, have been brought under optimum control for the objectives being accomplished, we will be moving closer to instructional systems implementation. We do need to perceive that conventional media equipment and materials have many roles to play in teaching in general and in instructional systems in particular. Therefore the reader should refer to Chapter 6 where we looked broadly at the implementation of media utilization in all teaching stations. Without the deployment of equipment at teaching stations, especially for large-group teaching presentations, it will be next to impossible to implement the teaching-systems idea. For it is when teachers seek to face large groups that they must rely heavily on communications media. Hence all we have said in the preceding chapters has implications for the use of media in instructional systems. Whenever teachers face groups of learners, large or small, they will need media services. They may have need of an array of equipment and media from a microphone to a transparency and a remote-controlled color slide projector; or from a motion picture in a teaching auditorium followed by a programed worksheet, the responses to which are sent to a computer, to the use of a short-exposure exercise in a language-arts group under the direct supervision of the teacher. The possibilities are limitless.

We see in motion pictures, filmstrips, slides, and other types of media for use with conventional equipment, the means of explaining, exploring, and experiencing vicariously, the cueing and reinforcing performance, informa-

[19] G. Estrin, "Interactions Between Future Computer Developments and Automated Teaching Methods," in *Programmed Learning and Computer-Based Instruction, op. cit.*, p. 288.

Figure 11-20. When we note the size of this film-text-tape media package, we ought to consider also the dimensions of the teaching objectives it is designed to accomplish. We must also consider the instrumentation capabilities of the schools and the educational points of view of the staffs that will put it to work in true instructional systems fashion. (Courtesy French Program, *Je Parle Français*, Encyclopaedia Britannica Educational Corporation, Chicago.)

tion-giving, motivation, presentation of case studies, and examples of past, present, and future situations with which students must come into contact. We must therefore reiterate our position that schools must be equipped for media action along a wide spectrum of instructional activity in the implementation of systems. The difference is a new sense of necessity, for the conventional media activities now have a better relationship to what has preceded and what must follow.

Instrumentation Capability for Instructional Systems

Looking back over the various aspects of instrumentation that we have discussed in this section, we note the following basic needs that are of interest to media program leaders.

1. Electronic learning laboratories and the teaching auditorium.
2. Multimedia and multi-image projection.
3. Teaching machines.
4. Television and videotape storage.
5. Group-response techniques.
6. Computers.
7. Conventional media equipment.

It is the degree to which a school or school system possesses these media-use potentials, or can move to acquire them, that will determine the capability to employ instructional systems effectively. Can we truthfully claim that the modern school system should have all of the identified instrumentation installations? And if so, what student capacity for any given unit is desirable? How many electronic learning laboratories should a school have? Should they

be specialized by subject area, or should they be designed to serve all subjects in any given school? Moreover, we ask, should they be interconnected, school to school, or should they be decentralized for maximum service, or expanded at central stations to meet the needs of all pupils in a given school district? These are knotty problems that are not solved easily. We can draw one inescapable conclusion, namely, that when instructional systems are employed, instrumentation in large part must be fixed, that is, available on the spot to meet the demand for scheduled services for pupils and teacher teams. Such services demand an optimum degree of instrumentation capability, but the true capability can only be determined when the components of the system are known. We shall explore several facets of this problem of instrumentation. First, we turn to the problem of meeting equipment needs for commercially produced systems.

Capability of Instrumentation for Ready-Made Teaching Systems. It cannot be denied that existing instrumentation ought to be complete enough, or flexible enough, to meet general trends in commercial production. If we point to conventional equipment such as tape recorders, filmstrip projectors, automatic slide projectors, electronic learning laboratories, and plug-in boxes, we can see a basic power to reorganize groups and to develop techniques that make possible local storage, supply, and scheduled utilization. But we must recognize that with one or more electronic learning laboratories, supplemented by large-group presentation spaces, we are likely to direct our choices of available systems, either commercially available or those that are to be made locally, along the lines of school-building instrumentation. The school district that has the added capability of television, group-response and multimedia installations will expand its capability—will, in other words, open up its field of choice. At this point we need to stress painstaking planning activity, hence we refer to earlier chapters that had to do with in-service education and the acquisition of media and the physical environment for media in each school building. We also need to express in no uncertain terms to producers of instructional systems the need for alternate forms of media in the systems packages offered for sale. In short, companies need to offer their media in various formats such as will suit the general instrumentation patterns in the schools. But this raises the question of what can be considered to be standard instrumentation.

Standardization of Components. We have long emphasized the need for standardization of media equipment in any given school district to facilitate in-service education of teaching staffs, the training of technicians, and the stocking of repair parts. This same problem now takes on even greater proportions when we consider the need for scheduled use of equipment in all buildings for a given grade and subject, for example, as when we seek to develop the use of computers with a particular kind of student teletype keyboard. The need for standardizing a set of manipulative skills with respect to operating instruments in carrels and in group-response situations becomes an urgent, district-wide matter of great economy in instructional effort and efficiency. If this is true for students, we can readily see that a variety of different makes of equipment can decrease the operational efficiency of teachers, teacher aides, and technicians who have to maintain the installations. The importance of this problem, present and future, is difficult to overestimate, hence we shall bring up the related problem of preparing specifications for procurement as one means of keeping standardization under control.

Specifications for Procuring Systems Instrumentation

The need to prepare adequate specifications when media equipment units are purchased was stressed in Chapter 3. However, it is when electronic installations of a fixed nature such as television, multimedia, learning laboratory, and group-response facilities are being purchased, that major difficulty is encountered. In any case,

whether conventional media equipment or fixed installations for the use of instructional systems are being purchased, the media program director's best friend is a reputable and knowledgeable audiovisual media dealer, or a specialist in one of the systems being installed. Reputable dealers and installation firms have on their staffs qualified engineering and technically proficient personnel to assist with the work of planning and design. It is too much to expect that a media program director will be able to operate a bureau of standards, yet he must be a master at delineating curriculum and technical functions. The requirement that he understand the intricacies of the operation of instruments by both teachers and pupils, always anticipating the difficulties that may be encountered, now becomes more important than ever. This standard of operational simplicity will guide him throughout his work with suppliers in guaranteeing that a given installation will fulfill its specified functions. Throughout the arduous job of making decisions as to what technical arrangements will meet a set of special needs, the media program director should elicit the assistance of curriculum personnel at various levels of authority.

Some Suggested Planning Procedures for Instrumentation Purchase. Much to their later chagrin, some purchasers of fixed installations have in effect said, "Let's put in an automated multimedia presentation center. We can find a way to use it later." We cannot overemphasize the importance of the advice to consider first the curriculum need, the reorganization of students, the need for developing innovative teaching patterns, and the capability to carry out specific functions that ought to be achievable. This kind of prepurchase consideration involves insightful planning activity. We suggest the following, assuming that the decision to inaugurate the innovative practices involved has been made and approved.

1. Meet and work with curriculum groups to define teaching problems.
2. Identify specific functions that have to be performed by instruments in the installation for teachers and learners.
3. Prepare in written form for group discussion, revision, and finalization, the significant curriculum aspects of the instrumentation.
4. Analyze space requirements in light of

operational functions and obtain space allotments, carrying on necessary remodeling if old buildings are involved. Provide the necessary electric supply.

5. Make plans for the demonstration of processes at an appropriate time.

6. Organize a technical advisory committee to meet and work with the media director and instrumentation installation suppliers.

7. Obtain up-to-date cost estimates for the given installations.

8. Work through school-district purchasing channels on the problems of standardizing instrumentation components for similar installations in other school buildings.

9. Consult instrumentation sourcebooks and operational case studies in the literature.

10. Visit schools with similar facilities being operated for local purposes, or arrange to invite representatives of those schools to speak to local planning groups about their facilities.

11. Obtain written reports, giving details about business relationships and the technical competence exhibited in connection with similar fixed installations elsewhere, on any electronic contractor being considered.

12. Determine levels of quality of the instrumentation output in light of teaching needs.

13. Prepare the specifications in detail, including the required contractual agreement between both parties. Employ a consultant to supervise the preparation of specifications and subsequent installation, if warranted, otherwise arrange to provide personal supervision using the local technical advisory committee.

14. Provide in written form, as a part of the construction contract, for final testing, demonstrations of specified functions, training of staff in operation of the system, for warrantee period, and the duration of free maintenance and repair service periods.

15. Issue the purchase order and execute the formulated plans.

Some Critical Factors in Preparing Specifications for Equipment Packages. It is not likely that school districts will generally have technical staffs that can take the time to install a complete electronic learning laboratory. Hence in preparing specifications it is essential to deal with both aspects of an instrumentation problem, namely, selecting and identifying the precise kinds and makes of media equipment, and their proper installation in the proper places, using appropriate furniture, mounting arrangements, and appropriate operational controls. In dealing with the problem of preparing specifications the media program director should be extremely critical of his own writing and also of the specifications prepared by others. He should seek help from colleagues and from the literature and obtain from dealers, and from other school-district media directors, copies of their previous efforts along similar lines. In studying such examples he should seek possible pitfalls that he must avoid in his own situation. What we are urging the media director to do is to avoid the uncritical acceptance of specifications prepared by others and to avoid the mistake of hoping that suppliers will read between the lines and "give" what isn't specified in the contract. Although we cannot at this time provide extensive examples of specifications for instructional systems instrumentation, we urge that the following kinds of action be carefully considered.

1. Identify the teaching functions to be carried out on the instruments, and incorporate them in the contract. There is no safer way for media specialists to work than to ascertain in advance just what the equipment is to be able to do, and to have it understood with the vendor.

2. Ascertain the known and desired standards of quality in the output of a set of instruments and get whatever help is needed to write these standards out accurately.

3. Analyze painstakingly the cost estimates supplied and find ways to pin these specified costs down to known levels under specified conditions.

4. Analyze the available space in which instruments will be installed and describe the limitations that are to be placed on the vendor with respect to positioning of components. Supply appropriate sketches.

5. Where expenditures are extensive, where standardization is contemplated for future multiple installations, and where designs and plans are technically intricate, it is essential that a consultant be employed to check accuracy and feasibility of the operation and to look for unanticipated difficulties.

6. Insist that one vendor be held responsible for the supply, installation, and servicing of all operational components in a given system, or

that complete compatibility of related instruments be fully ascertained if more than one manufacturer is involved.

7. Identify and use reliable sources of assistance.

Media program directors should be able to detect weaknesses in operational plans from a number of standpoints, namely, the learner, the teacher, the technician, the instructional objectives, the principal, and the lay citizen. Some may call this a rich store of common sense. We assert that it is the wisdom that results from skill and insight in leadership and administrative competence, competence as a teacher, and competence as a media expert and technologist, one who by virtue of his own openness to experience, alertness, and drive can manage to sense the impending technological developments in the areas of his concern. This wisdom may not come easily.

Media program directors and their advisory and planning groups must not fail to recognize the fact that a vendor is not essentially a philanthropist, nor will he often be found to be perfidious. Therefore, specifications must be looked upon as a set of communications designed to specify clear lines of responsibility and intention on the part of all concerned. This attitude, rather than one of mistrust and suspicion, must prevail. It will therefore be a mutual endeavor in most cases to work out details of agreement, and it will be to the advantage of the dealer to make sure that the limits of his commitments are fully recognized by the buyer.

Logistics: Storage, Availability, Distribution, Personnel

All we have said about instructional systems brings us now to the point of their final implementation on a day-by-day basis. It is then that we must face the final and pressing solution to the problem of logistics. Media program directors may have to alter drastically their old methods of media distribution. Loose and uncertain scheduling and delivery may no longer be workable, for too often in the past the hub of activity has been at the storehouse and not at the teaching station. The concentrated hours of staff effort are likely to be found at the film packaging desk, and in many cases it has mattered too little that only a small fraction of the teachers

utilize the media that were purchased for their use. The focus of effort must be shifted to the teaching stations. Where instructional systems are concerned, there is no choice but to reach the saturation point of media use for any given group of participating teachers. All the pupils must now move through the planned sequences of experiences, and when media are assigned specific teaching roles, it will make a vital difference when media are not at or in the appointed carrels or are not ready for large-group, group-response presentations at the right time. We thus see new patterns developing to make possible the guaranteed distribution of media packages for systems teaching. We must recognize, however, that media will not only be used in instructional systems, and that media directors will therefore have to arrange to both select and distribute media for all of the uses in the curriculum. We shall turn our attention to these problems next.

Centralized and Decentralized Storage Centers

Film libraries as we have known them in the past have not been able, generally, to engineer saturation-usage levels. The limited number of film prints for any given subject simply would not permit their use by all teachers for whom they were intended, and in general, leadership staffs were quite satisfied when their holdings were booked to capacity. When instructional systems are put to work, the multimedia packages involving sequential-use schedules will offer an entirely new problem in logistics. The way to solve it will be to move not toward regional and statewide distribution centers, but toward subcenters within school districts, in school buildings, and at teaching stations. It is doubtful that a reversion to what was once called *block booking* (or you get it when you are next in line) will suffice, because of the necessary close and sequential relationship between the components of a given system. Because of the importance of precise timing in using the components, all the required media for an entire course may have to be placed with a teaching team, be stored in an electronic learning laboratory, or duplicated for every similar course in the school district. This means that procurement and processing plans will have to undergo drastic changes. In modern media-use plans, it

Figure 11-21. What kinds and amounts of storage facilities will be required in school-building media centers to provide for essential accessibility? Is it likely that the storage problem may be as difficult to solve as the problems of capability and in-service education? *Courtesy Fremont Union High School District, Sunnyvale, California.*

may be necessary to provide not only a set of books for each pupil, but we may also have to call for a complement of audio and videotapes, filmstrips, computer inputs, and film cartridges for each group of students. Obviously we shall have to carefully consider the logistics problem in a media-oriented program and take great care in making recommendations. Under these conditions, we can hardly afford to send multimedia packages to schools across the city hoping that there will be time to get them back some day, inspect and clean them, and possibly start a new group through the course next term. The kind of scheduling that we shall have to engineer is to arrange class groups so that rotation is possible, and that a new group can begin a course when the required media are free on the next scheduled date.

In cases where instructional systems are limited in objective and scope, such as sets of automated filmstrips, sets of slides, and video-tapes and audio-program tapes dealing with specific skills, they may be stored in both central and decentralized distribution areas in sufficient quantities to meet the needs of teachers for whom they are intended. Such media will nevertheless be basal in character, but because of their self-contained content and potential, they may lend themselves to some flexibility in usage patterns. That is, teachers may choose the optimum time or cooperatively arrrange the dates for using them.

Expansion of Storage and Distribution Procedures. It is customary for media centers to distribute media on a short-term loan basis. They also procure and assign media subjects to school-building centers on a long-term custody basis. This latter function will have to undergo drastic and creative expansion in the future with particular reference to the use of instructional systems. In carrying out this function, media packages will have to undergo periodic inspection and rejuvenation processes, and will have to be checked in and redistributed to storage areas. Because many of the former functions will have to be maintained in order to serve the various needs of the school district, central media offices will be forced to seek a new and optimum balance between centralized short-term loan and long-term assignment distribution plans, with the volume of the latter being greatly expanded in significance and scope.

Some Unique Storage and Distribution Requirements. When we consider the implications of the preceding discussions of instructional systems, we see how inadequate the old book-closet idea is in our modern schools. We must now recommend not only radical increases in storage spaces in school-district and school-building media-service centers, but assert that provisions must be made for convenient storage areas for each teaching station—whether it be considered a self-contained classroom or not. We shall describe several unique requirements as follows:

1. *Need to Prevent Deterioration of Media.* Film-base media materials may become seriously embrittled unless they are stored under proper atmospheric conditions. Polyester-base magnetic tape for audio and video programs are not as seriously affected by adverse conditions. Therefore, special storage areas under temperature and humidity controls should be provided unless proper conditions are maintained throughout the building during unusually dry winter months.

2. *Media Packages Should Be Kept Intact for Maximum Accessibility.* It is likely that media of several varieties such as film cartridges, automated slides and filmstrips, programed booklets, and audio-program tapes will be purchased in packaged format for convenience in usage by both students and teachers or their aides. The disassembly of these packages may be extremely undesirable except during periods of inspection. Thus flexible storage space for the available packages may be an essential at any one or all of the following: specific teaching stations, special laboratories, school-building and possibly school-district media-service centers.

3. *Student Usage of Media.* Media items, or media packages, will have to be made accessible to students, for example, in electronic learning laboratories where all carrels are identically equipped, or made available to special independent-study carrels arranged in groups in special spaces, or at other teaching laboratory stations. Such logistics problems if not solved could result in disastrous time losses. Thus we see the inevitable need for storage cabinets and shelving units in large-group and independent-study service areas, and also for limited media-package storage in a study carrel itself. When several different subject-matter groups make use of the same large-group or independent-study spaces, media packages may have to be exchanged by aides and technicians. It is at this point that we see the need for specialized storage arrangements where, for example, carrel inserts containing required media items and related supplies could be quickly exchanged and thus prepared for a new group of students. Such carrel inserts would presumably not interfere, because of appropriate design, with permanently mounted media equipment units such as cartridge film projectors, automatic slide units, and video receivers, but they would include intact series of the media materials and supplies ready for consumption or manipulation by the learner. Solutions to these problems may require the redesigning of carrels presently on the market.

4. *Handling and Distribution at Teaching Stations.* Handling by students and teachers of media items poses a real problem of possible mixups caused by errors in returning items to storage. Such media-package handling demands that items be recognizable at a glance not only in order to return them to their proper storage places, but in order to discern whether or not a given set of media items is in a state of readiness for the next users. Hopefully, commercial or local teacher producers will discover foolproof packaging arrangements to eliminate such operational difficulties. However, easy identification and packaging in indestructible storage boxes are only parts of the problem of readiness. Difficulty of getting teachers and pupils to *put things back* may necessitate automatically controlled cartridge-type sequencing that will prevent getting materials out of order to begin with.

5. *Media-resource banks.* Automatic retrieval of media stored on magnetic tape demands extensive storage areas for fixed installations. In

such cases we need space for racks of automatically controlled tape-transport units for
playback and/or recording purposes, relay
switching equipment, and computer units. In
addition, these areas must provide on-the-spot
storage shelves for collections of audio and
videotapes that can be used to program the
playback units according to instructional needs.
The programs must either be changed for new
groups, or additional playback units to hold all
available programs must be installed. Since the
technology is vastly different, separate spaces for
audio-program tape and videotape programs
need to be provided or such services may be
combined. Despite low-heat, transistorized
modern equipment and the trend toward
miniaturization, the spaces that have to be
allotted for modern-day retrieval technology are
considerable, and generally they should be
properly air conditioned.

We have shown in this section, as a complement to the discussion of space needs in Chapters
7 through 10, the need for school-building
buyers and planners to change their ideas of
storage-space requirements in the modern
school. It will be up to the media program
director to study this problem and provide the
leadership for guiding growth toward the effective use of instructional systems.

Methods of Media Delivery to Teaching Stations

In our chapters dealing with school-building
and school-district services, we discussed the
importance of effective plans for the delivery of
media. With the increasing urgency for the timely
use of media components in instructional
systems, we must take a new look at the
efficiency of the delivery aspect of the distribution problem. This is of course in direct relation
to the plans developed for setting up sources of
supply that are close to the teacher, either in his
school building or at his teaching station, or
both.

Conventional Delivery Systems. Conventional
delivery services by truck or other vehicle are
certain to continue as in the past from central
distribution areas, but we must insist that subcenters may have to be organized, as for
example in a school building that will serve
similar schools of a district. Thus additional

delivery plans may have to be developed to
guarantee that media will be delivered on
schedule. Therefore it appears that an increase
in delivery capability will be essential. However,
in some cases, it will be possible only to locate
teaching-systems components within the school
or at the teaching station. This will become
necessary in situations where media will be in
continual use by teachers in a variety of teaching
stations. The school-building media-service
center will therefore have to serve as a clearing
house for assignments, control, and inventory
processes in a way never before envisaged.

Electronic Delivery Possibilities. Other writers
have suggested that television should deliver
other kinds of media, either by radiation or
coaxial cable, to teaching stations, the idea being
that it is more convenient to use television film
and slide chains, videotape playback units,
transmitters, MATV cable distribution networks, and television receivers than it is to use
the conventional projection arrangements in
schools. We take the view that under existing
transmission arrangements and technological
limitations, this may prove to be an unwise
suggestion. We believe that it would be better to
use television during the time that channels are
available for the transmission of a *live* or taped
television program that has its own unique
instructional objectives to accomplish than to
use the cable as a delivery mechanism. Yet, it is
recognized that in instructional-systems teaching, television, as we have already pointed out,
may play some unique roles. The film or slide
set may thus be delivered by cable or radiation,
but as we see it, not as an incidental, enrichment-
type, Friday-afternoon caprice, but as a
significant presentation in the context of an
instructional system. Advancing television technology may greatly increase the possibility of
delivering conventional media for use in conventional contexts in the future. For the present,
however, the four-channel 2,500 mHz capability
and the twelve-channel coaxial cable seem not to
be able to handle this massive distribution to
schools from district Media centers. Neither
does it seem likely that the channels of the cable
network in a school building can be saturated by
a battery of film-chain or videotape playback
transmitters delivering media for conventional
uses. Under school-building delivery-by-cable
practices, the district studio programing could
not be used because presumably the existing

channels would be taken up by transmission from the school-building studio. Any priority that is assigned to the delivery of media by television would therefore seem to be preempted by the demands of a given instructional system reaching out to all students in a given grade and subject under a special set of circumstances. It would, however, be well to pursue this particular aspect of logistics a little further. We should examine the problem of delivering media such as audio-program and videotapes, which are the kinds of media that are usually stored in automatic-access resource banks. Because we are concerned specifically with the problem of delivery—or retrieval—we should consider the related problem of interconnecting schools within a district to receive audio-program and video program tapes by dial or push-button methods.

Interconnecting Schools for Audio-Program Retrieval. The capability to send programs over wire within a single classroom space, or even within a building, is a relatively simple matter. All that we need to provide is a pair of wires from each student to some fairly standard telephone relay equipment units, a bank of automatically controllable tape playback units, the proper instruments and headsets at the pupil station, and a schedule of program numbers. The student can then make contact with a desired program by dialing the call number. Of course he may get a busy signal, or he may tune in a little late, but even these problems may be only temporary in nature, pending some techno-

logical refinements. Now we ask, if it is so easy to string wires inside a room, why not string them between buildings or run them underground? How complex is the job of interconnecting schools, and what are the major problems? The first question we have already discussed rather fully in Chapter 10 in connection with the cable transmission of television programs. The reader will remember that poles are generally unavailable, as are the underground conduits owned and operated by public utilities such as the Bell System Companies. The solution then is to rent telephone wire services that are maintenance free. In a school building, an installation may be permanent and owned by the school district, but in order to interconnect buildings, in the usual situation, media program directors must turn to the local Bell System Company for help and specific cost estimates. See Figures 11-22 and 11-23. Since media program directors will be likely at some time or other to consider the use of wire services for retrieval, the following major aspects of the problems involved may be helpful.

1. *Duplicate Installation of a Resource Bank in Each School.* If the school system wishes to avoid the cost of renting Bell System wire services a retrieval installation may be duplicated and programed for local service to the pupils. This has the advantage of concentrating the availability of the audio programs in one school situation for a particular number of student stations. Students may also be able to spend

Figure 11-22. In this illustration we provide the opportunity to observe components of dial-access systems involving audio-program tapes as installed on the Ohio State University Campus. The operational technology is called the Datagram system by the North Electric Company of Galion, Ohio. We show the electronically equipped carrels first then the audio-program tape bank connected by wire. *Courtesy, North Electric Company, Galion, Ohio.*

Figure 11-23. A dial-access service for audio-program and videotape content, similar to the one described in Figure 11-22, is in operation at other colleges. We show in these pictures, the computer arrangement for processing dial calls from students in their carrels, and also the switching equipment shown in the bottom photograph. This installation is in operation at Oral Roberts University as well as at Ohio State University. See also Figures 7-5, 7-18, and 10-2. *Courtesy Oral Roberts University, Tulsa, Oklahoma.*

more time in a given carrel, presumably using it for a wider array of media activities tying in the retrieved tapes with projected media such as slides and film cartridges. The duplicating of installations may, of course, call for costly capital expenditures. On the other hand, central resource banks of media may have to be greatly enlarged and some of the programing will have to be carried out by the scheduled playback method. That is, any number of students, depending on the individual stations available, can listen to any program, but in order to start listening at the start of a program, they must be ready at the announced time. The central audio-program resource bank must then be reprogramed from time to time according to instructional needs.

2. *Bell System Company Wire Service.* Schools may be interconnected by renting wire services, as we have discussed previously. Rates for the service are figured by the mile and vary according to a specific area rate. If conventional dial-access techniques are satisfactory, one pair of wires must run from each student station to a crossbar switching mechanism normally used by telephone companies for their own dial circuits. The switching mechanism would of course be a part of the school-owned installation. Wire frequencies may run as high as 4,000 cycles per second, although the Bell System Company

guarantees 3,000. This frequency level is satisfactory for some purposes, but not for all. Although some linguistic experts claim that a level of 7,000 to 7,500 cycles per second is desirable, in tests conducted by the Bell System Company, language students and a group of language specialists were not able to distinguish between frequency levels of 5,000, 7,000 and 15,000 cycles per second. These same people however, were able to distinguish between the 3,000 cycles per second level and the other levels. By a process known as loading, the Bell System Companies are able to reach a consistent 5,000 cycles level, and this process can be arranged for by a one-time installation charge. When a wire service that permits a 15,000-cycles-per-second response is demanded, the telephone company must use amplifiers and other control devices that eliminate the possibility of dialing on the same wire connections. This means that a separate pair of wires is required at each carrel or teaching station for the purpose of dialing the resource-bank switching equipment, thus increasing greatly the cost for implementing the interconnection project. In Abington Township, Montgomery County, Pennsylvania, six high schools are linked by a Bell System Company wire network to a central audio-program tape bank. The system operates by regular dialing procedures.

501

3. *Audio-Program Availability from Resource Banks.* The number of programs available is determined by the number of tape-playback units and the number of tracks that will play simultaneously on each machine. It would be helpful to consider a few specific cases and processes as follows:

(a) *One tape deck, full-track playback.* This means that all student stations wired to it could dial into that one program and listen to it, but if they didn't all dial in at a predetermined time, only those who did would be able to listen from the beginning. Thus, thirty decks will provide thirty simultaneous programs.

(b) *One tape deck, four-track playback.* Four programs can be dialed at once by any combination of students. As soon as the tape transport starts to play one of the four programs, the other three are also transported. Therefore they are either being played or may be retrieved at any time during the program, but the listener will retrieve only the remaining portion. If students want all four of the programs on the one tape on that tape deck, they must dial before the tape deck is activated. Thus, thirty four-track tape decks will provide a capacity of 120 programs available to the student stations wherever they are located.

4. *Independent Study Activities Through Dialing.* Independent study activities may be carried on using available tapes, but the dialing process does not guarantee that the line to any one of the programs will be free. Scheduling may be arranged on a system-wide basis through announcements. Also the use of a given set of programs may be arranged for by attendants at the resource bank who will control access to a given set of tape playback decks. Announced schedules will have to by cooperatively enforced by teachers or their aides who need to ensure the availability of programs for their own use.

5. *Sources of Programs.* Audio-program tapes may be made by teachers and local production staffs, or they may be commercially produced to achieve specific purposes. Thus, special purpose, incidental, or instructional system applications of resource-banks may by made possible. Teacher productions may by cooperative action be exchanged with school districts throughout the area, thus greatly increasing the potential value of local school-system productions.

Interconnecting Schools for Videotape Retrieval. With the advancing technology of videotape recording and automated playback techniques, we have opened up new vistas of effective media use in schools, again with special reference to instructional systems. It is not enough, as we discussed it in Chapter 10, to deal with television as a medium for unique teaching roles, but we must now refer to the automated use of television as the solution to a logistics problem encountered in systems teaching. We have already discussed the possible roles of television as a major component in instructional systems, and we have referred to the transmission problems in school districts. We have therefore established a firm basis for adding the element of dial retrieval of video programs stored in a videotape resource bank. We shall discuss some of the main aspects of this procedure as follows:

1. *Videotape As a Storage Medium.* Videotape may be used as the means for standardizing pictorial and audio portrayal through the medium of television. At the present time, schools are able to telecast only in black and white because of the prohibitive cost of color television. However, this situation may give way before new technological developments. At any rate, short of general color capability, we have the opportunity to reproduce electronically motion picture film, slides, filmstrips, study prints, and to arrange these reproductions for automatic retrieval with proper equipment. We are by no means suggesting that this is a wise course of action to follow. An hour of videotape costs something like $68, and the film to go on it may cost up to $500 if the subject is in color, or $360 if it is in black and white. Furthermore, the copyright law does not permit electronic reproduction without formal permission and attendant financial arrangements. Hence special action must be taken to make and use material transformed from one medium to another despite its value in instructional system purposes. However, in spite of the fact that the pictorial detail may not be of equal quality, tape may hold some attractive possibilities.

2. *Transmission Problems.* All we have said about linking audio-program resource banks also applies to videotape banks, except for the comparable simplicity of the cable linkages. Except for some very special video arrangements

now being experimented with, coaxial cable is the standard means by which videotape programs are retrieved automatically. We have discussed the problem of leasing cables in Chapter 10, and therefore do not need to repeat it here. However, we must point out that a cable has only twelve channels for transmission of sound and picture (RF) at the present time. Current experimental work appears to offer the promise of being able to transmit multiple video programs simultaneously on the same cable. If the promise materializes, and the audio portion of such programs can be handled by telephone-line arrangements, we may be able to simplify and expand the dial retrieval of videotape programs from remote points. Technological developments are almost certain to make possible increased program capability, as for example developing multiple-track video playback units. At present, however, by leasing a twelve-channel coaxial cable from the Bell System Companies, twelve separate programs can be dialed at once by as many students as can find their way to a dialing system in an electronic carrel. The relay system and the dialing are similar to the audio-program retrieval just discussed, but the transmission is an entirely different matter and the cost is greater by far. Again we are confronted

with a transmission problem that we have discussed before, namely, whether to transmit a video signal to each carrel, or an RF signal that combines picture and sound elements. When video signals alone are transmitted by the switching equipment, the audio must travel on a separate pair of wires to each carrel, and so must the coaxial cable. This may be feasible within a separate building, but several new problems arise when using that system to interconnect buildings. When an RF signal is sent by cable throughout a building, each carrel is tapped off from the trunk line and then each program may be dialed directly on the all-channel tuner on the television receiver. This is fine for an announced program schedule, as on TV networks, but not good for dial-access techniques. Thus we have the need for extra pairs of wires to make the dial system work, and it is the dial-access capability that makes the independent-study aspect of television retrieval so attractive in the modern school program. Hence, we see that the entire process needs to undergo a desirable simplification.

3. *Independent-Study Carrel and Large-Group Access to Available Programs.* In some installations, technical arrangements have been developed that permit dialing into video programs from independent-study carrels and from large-

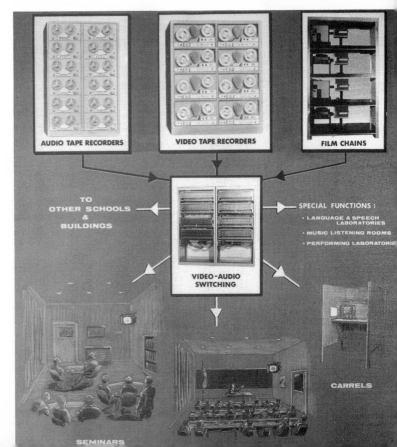

Figure 11-24. The schematic shown in this illustration indicates the various components normally required and some probable outlets for program content. Bearing in mind some of the earlier illustrations, the diagram is self-explanatory. Although they are costly, such technological systems are developing rapidly, and the increasing availability of program content, together with increased know-how of application to instructional problems and needs, will greatly increase the rate of installation. (See also Figure 7-5.) *Courtesy Continuous Progress Education, Inc., Norwalk, Connecticut.*

AUDIO TAPE RECORDERS   VIDEO TAPE RECORDERS   FILM CHAINS

TO OTHER SCHOOLS & BUILDINGS

SPECIAL FUNCTIONS :
· LANGUAGE & SPEECH LABORATORIES
· MUSIC LISTENING ROOMS
· PERFORMING LABORATORIE

VIDEO-AUDIO SWITCHING

CARRELS

SEMINARS

groups as well. (See Figures 11-10, 11-23, 11-24, 6-7, and 7-18.) Large-group use of the programs with the teacher dialing the program for the whole class, is the way to make a videotape resource bank available to the great mass of learners in any given grade or subject. Under independent-study arrangements, it is conceivable that all twelve channels could be activated by 12 students, and the rest of the learners tuning in would have to join the program in progress. The alternative is to dial according to an announced time schedule. When we consider such uses in instructional systems, we may conclude that superior teachers working on large-scale programs involving television may well preempt the available channels during certain hours of the day, thus forcing the dialing system off the cable for the hours in question. A choice would be to install separate additional coaxial-cable networks.

4. *Duplication of Videotape Resource Banks.* Videotape resource banks may be duplicated in selected schools and then interconnected with one or more nearby schools when independent study programing is stressed, but when large-group use of videotape programs is contemplated, this is not necessary, since by scheduling, all teachers in the area can contact the program for their pupils.

5. *The Nature of Programing for Identified Uses.* Preparing programs for videotape storage becomes a major hurdle to surmount in using the system for any purpose. However, we assert that the kind of program necessary for independent study may have to be vastly different from the kind of program prepared for large-group use. We perceive that when using instructional systems, videotape may have to be utilized mainly for large-group, carefully timed programing, where learners are programed through stimulus content and then guided in making controlled responses. Scheduling may have to be strictly enforced because of transmission limitations. But what we are saying is also applicable to the use of videotape programs outside of the automatic-retrieval system.

6. *Television Capability Limits.* We ought to point out a few inescapable considerations regarding television usage in any and all contexts, as follows:

(a) When a school building is telecasting from its own studio over its classroom network of coaxial cable, the school building can use only incoming programs from central studio sources, or from sources external to the school, on channels that are unused at the moment. This demands multiple-channel capability at all times with some channels being kept free for automatic retrieval.

(b) A school building may install and use a private-cable distribution system for its own automatic videotape-retrieval installation. It may also rent an additional multiple-channel cable from the Bell System Company to interconnect with nearby schools. Private additional coaxial-cables within a school will then be separate from and will not interfere with other reception systems using a separate cable system, for example, as connected to the central studio for the school district. Both cable systems may by special selector switches be combined at a given television receiver, thereby permitting the use of transmitted content on one cable or the other.

A number of critical technical difficulties have yet to be met in connection with various uses of instructional television, but with the present strides being made in this aspect of technology, it is expected that many of these problems will not exist for long.

The Indispensability of Supporting Staff

One of the main requirements for meeting the logistics problem is the availability of supporting staff, both professional and technical. We have already mentioned this need in earlier chapters, but we must emphasize it again in view of the new context of instructional systems. If, as demanded by the nature of instructional systems, we have to be concerned with the stratification of personnel talents, we must not be complacent about the continuing misuse of the energy of teachers on clerical labor. The fact that we are striving for optimum balance between personnel, media, learners, and machines to improve the products of instruction calls for critical examination of each link in the chain of activities. The implementation of instructional systems demands that the machine rooms be kept operative, that the flow of materials of all required varieties be uninterrupted, that professional, semiprofessional and nonprofessional work be completed on time, and that the learner be allowed to proceed with his work unimpeded by the inefficiency of those around him.

With our stress on instrumentation, with the need for the operation of fixed facilities, and the entirely new orientation for the use of media, we know that the modern-day teacher requires vital and indispensable support. When we consider the services and functions of the school-district and school-building media-service centers in carrying forward developmental work on systems design, in addition to the possible widespread use of commercial productions, we can safely and unhesitatingly recommend the addition of new staff members. Media program leaders will inevitably have to add electronic and projection technicians at several levels of competence, together with an additional number of media specialists. Such specialists as programers, production designers working in film and television, and graphic technicians appear to be essential. As far as the curriculum planning needs are concerned, we see considerable expansion also because there will be an indispensable need for additional content specialists and research personnel as well, generally operating at the school-district level.

Problem-Solving Activities

1. Study the motion picture *Multifaceted Approach to the Teaching of Botany* (see source list of films at the end of Chapter 4) to get answers to the following questions (a task force could preview this film, present it, and lead a discussion of the questions raised): (a) What roles do the media play? (Identify the media used and define the main role played by each.) (b) Is there a hierarchy in the skills to be developed in the instructional system portrayed? What are the main kinds of objectives in the course? How can you tell? (c) What important sources of help did the designers and producers of the system utilize? (d) Do the professors involved appear to really believe in the system they have produced? Do you believe that the problem-solving assignments for the students in three levels are important? Why? (e) What different kinds and levels of staff members are required to make this system work? (f) How can the professors tell if the system is working effectively? What can they do about it when weaknesses show up? Could

this process be called a kind of operational research as applied to instructional needs? (g) What suggestions would you make for improving the system? Why?

2. Study the motion picture *The Application of the Principles of Programing to Visual Presentations* (see source list of films at the end of Chapter 4) to answer the following questions (a task force could preview this film, present it, and lead a discussion of the questions raised): (a) What roles for media are identified in the film? How are the five utilization principles set forth in Chapter 4 of this book related to the specific roles exemplified in the film? Are teachers who use media as shown in the examples called upon to be creative? (b) Does it appear that in instructional systems, visual presentations have to be planned with creative decisions in mind? Do systems designers and programers have to be able to formulate objectives precisely? Where does the conventional lecture method fit into the visualization and instructional system process? How modified? (c) How can television programing be made a significant part of a given instructional system? (d) When media are used in instructional systems why should they be able to "work alone?" What basic processes have to be used when media are arranged to work without the teacher in control? In what way may the teacher be present and in control?

3. Explain the concept of *stratification of talent and energy* as it is applied by professional people outside of education. For example, in the medical profession involving the work of doctors, medical technicians, nurses, and receptionists. By means of a specific example, write out in outline-plan format how such a system would work for teachers using instructional systems.

4. How may presently available commercially produced and packaged media for instructional systems be evaluated and selected? Why should the selection process differ for an instructional-system media package from that set up for single films, tape, or filmstrip?

5. What kind of prepurchase planning must be done by media directors and curriculum personnel with regard to the volume and deployment of media-package acquisition for implementing the use of an instructional system?

6. What are the implications for in-service education when teachers are to embark on programs of making their own teaching-systems

productions for use in school facilities that are already available? Describe a workable plan for teacher preparation of small-scope, specific-objective systems, employing the coordination of cooperative efforts by a group of teachers.

7. In addition to extraordinary instructional needs that may require highly specialized instrumentation, what basic kinds of fixed and flexible media equipment installations would be likely to provide a school building, either elementary or secondary, with what we have referred to as *instrumentation capability*? Based on your study of this chapter, assume that you have a given instrumentation capability based on your choice of any two of the seven specific categories of media equipment installations presented in this text. With these two instrumentation categories in mind, write up in outline form a plan for implementing an instructional system in any field of your choice, with specific reference to: (a) The topic of the instructional system, expressed as a performance objective (assume that the media packages are available). (b) The ways in which media would function in stimulus-response control (that is, perform teaching roles without the teacher). (c) The size of the groups being taught in relation to the number in the class or course (all components being included), and how groups are deployed and scheduled. (d) Make labeled sketches of the kinds of installations and/or teaching stations in which pupils will be taught. (e) Make a list of the specific functions that teachers have to carry out personally to make the system operate.

(Task forces may be organized to split up the work on this project, or small groups could be assigned different combinations of principal groupings of media instrumentation. For example, one group could work out the flow diagram for student activity when using a multimedia presentation center with group-response equipment linked to a computer; another group could prepare a report for capability based on available electronic learning laboratory and a multimedia presentation center; another group could base its work on the assumption that television and teaching machines were available; all of which could assume the availability of conventional media equipment.)

8. Identify and discuss the critical aspects of the following problems likely to be encountered in the purchase of ready-made instructional systems: Decision to adopt. Financial support. Local school-district instrumentation capability. Format of media package to suit local conditions. In-service education. Continuing assistance to teachers.

9. Choose any content area and grade level with which you are familiar and make a set of sketches showing a desirable independent-study carrel complete with equipment likely to be required for instructional-system learning activities that you envisage in that area. Indicate storage provisions in or at the carrel for the media instruments you suggest, and indicate also typical kinds of manipulative materials or realia likely to be desired. (Make whatever assumptions necessary to facilitate action, but state what they are.)

10. List several topics for small-scope, specific-objective instructional systems that are obviously desirable in your choice of any content area and grade level you name. Now using standard diagraming procedures for systems, indicate for one of the titles in your list the following (Organize small working groups, each with a chairman, to complete the diagram for a given objective. Use a presentation mode, a flat or master, that will permit copying in overhead transparency or color-slide form for projection and reporting in class. An alternate problem would be to visualize several existing diagrams of known operational systems and point out the specified features in a class report): (a) How learners are prepared to enter the self-instruction component. (b) The specific media and the circumstances under which they are used (large group, independent study). (c) The separate aspects or phases of the system through which the learner moves, showing the predetermined order in which processes are carried out. (d) The nature of the criterion test for each operational phase of the system and the loop by which a learner repeats a given process to reach the criterion-accomplishment level. (e) The required activities of the teacher or his assistant.

11. Define the limits and formulate a plan for providing a given level of instrumentation capability in a school-building situation of your choice, and submit a series of sketches showing the following: (a) The plans for providing the required space. (Remodeling? Addition to the building?) (b) The relationships to the media-service center and its leadership personnel for operation and maintenance, if any. (c) The equipment units required and the estimated cost

(including both equipment and its installation). (d) Label fully, and plan to present a visualized report of the project, as for example to a group of school principals.

12. Prepare a set of labeled sketches to scale showing the various stages in the planning of a 60-position electronic learning laboratory in connection with the construction of a new building. Include the following: (a) Floor conduits and power supply outlets. (b) Location of master control rooms and/or media resource banks. (c) Media equipment units planned for installation in each carrel and their location or storage in the carrel. (d) The list of operational teaching functions by the teacher and by the student. (e) If video receivers are to be included, specify the kinds of coaxial-cable connections required. (f) If other schools are to be connected to the resource bank, make an additional labeled diagram showing the kinds of cable and their linkages.

13. Select any problem in the preceding list and prepare in outline form (but include center and side headings) a proposal for an operational pilot program in any one school-building situation, content and grade level of your choice, for instructional-system utilization. Assume that you are addressing your proposal to your superintendent of schools for transmittal to the Department of Education in your state. Assume further that capital expenditures and staff positions may be covered by the grant you expect to be awarded. (Assume that an official state plan is in effect by which your special proposal may be funded.)

14. Specify a hypothetical listing of several different kinds of typical media packages for use in instructional systems in school buildings. Formulate a plan for storage and distribution of such packages, specifying how central and decentralized storage spaces will be utilized.

15. Prepare a list of problems with their recommended solutions that are likely to attend the interconnection of schools for dial retrieval of audio program tapes. Define each problem in brief form as a difficulty that has to be overcome, then state a feasible and economical solution. Repeat this process for the dial retrieval of videotapes or other automatic ITV storage and retrieval media. (If task forces are organized to analyze these situations, their reports should be duplicated and distributed to all participants. Solutions to problems may need to be accompanied by the corroboration of competent engineering personnel.)

References

Barson, John, John M. Gordon, Jr., and W. Russell Hornbaker. "Standard Operating Procedures for a Learning Resources Center: A System for Producing Systems." *Audiovisual Instruction*, Vol. 10, No. 5, May 1965, pp. 378–379.

Beynon, John. *Study Carrels: Designs for Independent Study Space*. Stanford: Western Regional Center of Educational Facilities Laboratories, School of Education, Stanford University, 1964.

Brown, James W. and Kenneth Norberg. *Administering Educational Media.* (New York: McGraw-Hill, 1965).

Brubaker, Charles W. "Architecture and Equipment for the Language Laboratory: A Sketchbook." (Prepared under sponsorship of Indiana and Purdue Universities, and under a grant by the Educational Facilities Laboratories.) *Audiovisual Instruction*, Vol. 6, No. 5, May 1961, pp. 201–216.

Bruner, Jerome S. "The Act of Discovery." *Harvard Educational Review.* Vol. 31, Winter 1961, pp. 22–32.

———— (ed.). *Learning About Learning: A Conference Report.* (Prepared under the auspices of the U.S. Office of Education in connection with the Cooperative Research Program as Cooperative Research Monograph No. 15.) (Washington, D.C.: The Superintendent of Documents, U.S. Government Printing Office, 1966).

————. *The Process of Education.* (Cambridge, Mass.: Harvard University Press, 1960).

————. "Some Theorems on Instruction Illustrated with Reference to Mathematics," Chapter XIII. In *Theories of Learning and Instruction*, The Sixty-Third Yearbook of the National Society for the Study of Education, Part I, Ernest R. Hilgard (ed.). (Chicago: University of Chicago Press, 1964).

————, J. S. Goodnow, and G. A. Austin. *A Study of Thinking.* (New York: John Wiley, 1956).

Bundy, Robert F. "Computer-Assisted Instruction: Now and in the Future." *Audiovisual*

Instruction, Vol. 12, No. 4, April 1967, pp. 344–348.

Bushnell, Donald D. "The Role of the Computer in Future Instructional Systems." (Technological Development Project, Monograph No. 2, prepared under contract with the U.S. Office of Education, authorized under Title VII, Part B, of the NDEA, 1958.) *Audiovisual Communication Review*, Vol. 11, No. 2, Supp. 7, March–April 1963, pp. 1–70.

——— and Dwight W. Allen (eds.). *The Computer in American Education*. (New York: John Wiley, 1967).

Carpenter, C. R. "Can TV Replace the Teaching Machine?" *Audiovisual Instruction*, Vol. 9, No. 5, May 1964, pp. 280–282.

Coulson, John E. (ed.). *Programmed Learning and Computer-Based Instruction*. (Proceedings of the Conference on Application of Digital Computers to Automated Instruction, October 1961.) (New York: John Wiley, 1962).

Crossman, David M. "The Acquisition of a Language Laboratory: Circa 1966." *Audiovisual Instruction*, Vol. 11, No. 8, October 1966, pp. 632–636.

———. *The Electronic Classroom: A Guide for Planning*. (Albany, N.Y.: The University of the State of New York, The State Education Department, 1964).

Ely, Donald P. "The Changing Role of the Audiovisual Process in Education: A Definition and a Glossary of Related Terms." (Technological Development Project Monograph No. 1, prepared under contract with the U.S. Office of Education, authorized under Title VII, Part B, of the NDEA, 1958.) *Audiovisual Communication Review*, Vol. 11, No. 1, Supp. 6, January–February 1963, pp. 1–148.

Eraut, Michael R. "An Instructional Systems Approach to Course Development." *Audiovisual Communication Review*, Vol. 15, No. 1, Spring 1967, pp. 92–101.

Finn, James D. and Donald G. Perrin. *Teaching Machines and Programed Learning*. (A Survey of the Industry—1962). Prepared for the Technological Development Project of the NEA, under contract with the U.S. Office of Education, Title VII, Part B, NDEA, 1958. (Washington, D.C.: Superintendent of Documents, U.S. Government Printing Office, 1962).

Gagné, Robert M. (ed.). *Psychological Principles in System Development*. (New York: Holt, Rinehart, and Winston, 1962).

Glaser, Robert. "Implications of Training Research for Education," Chapter VII. In *Theories of Learning and Instruction*, The Sixty-Third Yearbook of the National Society for the Study of Education, Part I, Ernest R. Hilgard (ed.). (Chicago: University of Chicago Press, 1964).

——— (ed.). *Teaching Machines and Programed Learning: Data and Directions*. (Washington, D.C.: National Education Association, 1965).

Goodman, Edith H. (ed.). *Automated Education Handbook*. (Detroit: Automated Education Center, 1965).

Gropper, George L. "Learning from Visuals: Some Behavioral Considerations." *Audiovisual Communication Review*, Vol. 14, No. 1, Spring 1966, pp. 37–69.

Gross, Ronald and Judith Murphy (eds.). *The Revolution in the Schools*. (New York: Harcourt, Brace, and World, 1964).

Gryde, Stanley K. "The Feasibility of 'Programed' Television Instruction." *Audiovisual Communication Review*, Vol. 14, No. 1, Spring 1966, pp. 71–89.

Harnack, Robert S. "Teacher Decision-Making and Computer-Based Resource Units." *Audiovisual Instruction*, Vol. 12, No. 1, January 1967, pp. 32–35.

Hayes, Alfred S. *Language Laboratory Facilities* (Technical Guide for the Selection, Purchase, Use and Maintenance). Prepared under a contract with the U.S. Office of Education, authorized under Title VII, Part B, NDEA, 1958. (Washington, D.C.: Superintendent of Documents, U.S. Government Printing Office, 1963).

Heinich, Robert. *The Systems Engineering of Education II: Application of Systems Thinking to Instruction*. (A Monograph prepared for Instructional Technology and Media Project, School of Education) Los Angeles: School of Education, University of Southern California, 1965.

Hendershot, Carl H. *Programmed Learning: A Bibliography of Programs and Presentation Devices*. (Catalog, Supplements, and Revisions.) (Bay City, Michigan: Carl H. Hendershot, Publisher, 4114 Ridgewood Drive, Annual).

Jacobs, Paul I, Milton H. Maier, and Lawrence Stolurow. *A Guide to Evaluating Self-Instructional Programs*. (New York: Holt, Rinehart, and Winston, 1966).

Lindvall, C. M. (ed.). *Defining Educational*

Objectives. (A report of the Regional Commission on Educational Coordination and the Learning Research and Development Center). (Pittsburgh: University of Pittsburgh Press, 1964).

Loughary, John W., and Contributors. *Man-Machine Systems in Education.* (New York: Harper and Row, 1966).

McVey, Gerald F. "Multimedia Instructional Laboratory." *Audiovisual Instruction,* Vol. 11, No. 2, February 1966, pp. 80–85.

Postlethwait, Samuel N., Joseph D. Novak, and Hal Murray. *An Integrated Experience Approach to Learning* (With Emphasis on Independent Study). (Minneapolis: Burgess Publishing Company, 1964).

Rodgers, William A. "A Computer-Based Demonstration School." *Educational Technology,* Vol. 7, No. 1, January 1967, pp. 4–6.

Silvern, Leonard D. *Studies in the Systems Engineering of Education, I: The Evolution of Systems Thinking in Education.* (A monograph prepared for Instructional Technology and Media Project, School of Education.) (Los Angeles: School of Education, University of Southern California, 1965).

Smith, Karl U. and Margaret Foltz Smith. *Cybernetic Principles of Learning and Educational Design.* (New York: Holt, Rhinehart, and Winston, 1966).

Stewart, Donald K. "The Articulated Instructional Media Program at the University of Wisconsin." *Audiovisual Instruction,* Vol. 10, No. 5, May 1965, pp. 380–382.

———. "The Cost Analysis of Dial Access Information Retrieval Systems." *Audiovisual Instruction,* Vol. 12, No. 5, May 1967, pp. 430–434.

Stowe, Richard A. "Design of Instructional Messages: The Role of the Audiovisual Programer." *Audiovisual Instruction,* Vol. 12, No. 3, March 1967, pp. 230–232.

Weisgerber, Robert A. and Warren Rasmussen. "A Teaching System for Teaching Music." *Audiovisual Instruction,* Vol. 11, No. 2, February 1966, pp. 106–109.

12

Implementation of
Print-Medium Services

It is indeed difficult to understand that in our affluent society millions of pupils—perhaps a third of the nation's total—attend schools that do not have a library. It is indeed time for all schools to have such facilities. Thanks to the educational legislation of the mid-sixties, more schools are getting libraries. Because of the changes now being implemented, our instructional programs in the decades ahead will be richer and our intellectual future brighter. Secondary schools that have long had what they called libraries, some of them meagre and old fashioned, are remodeling and expanding them, and elementary schools that have long been without anything that resembled a library are getting them as additions, or as spacious learning centers in their creatively designed new schools. The acquisition of new materials and additional staff under the Knapp Project has had marked impact on desirable changes in the improvement of the programs involved, and as was expected, teams of interested elementary personnel have been inspired to inaugurate changes in their own libraries. This emphasis on the expansion of library facilities is long overdue, and it is good that such expansion is taking place in the elementary school where, as was pointed out earlier, vast and universal improvement is likely to set off a true revolution in education.

We have deliberately chosen to have this chapter follow the discussions of the most sophisticated of all technological media-use arrangements, television and instructional systems. Both of these media-use processes may demand entirely new configurations in the combined use of all media including print. These newer developments are likely to demand also self-instruction and independent study in many forms. Conventional media uses coupled with the media applications discussed in the last two chapters call for an instrumentation capability practically unheard of in the elementary schools of our time. We intend, therefore, to deal separately in the present chapter with the print medium to focus attention upon its unique problems, and to give this significant instructional medium the attention it deserves. Such attention is sorely needed, because there are many who, for one reason or another, believe that all school administrators have to do to solve their media-use problems is to merge the school's film, tape, and book resources.

Many times what happens is that school administrators burden an already overworked school librarian with more problems and services than he can handle. We have already dealt in considerable depth with that problem in Chapters 7 and 8, namely organizing centers for media services, and we shall mention certain aspects of it again a little later in this particular discussion.

The expansion in school library facilities and services is taking place in many other technological areas also. The facilities are often of such consequence and sophistication that to introduce such expanded programs is to face new dilemmas in providing staff and financial support not previously dealt with in the schools. We therefore must beware of and urge against administrative expediencies. Instead we recommend the formulation of well-laid plans to expand the whole new range of technological media services in the schools in a phase-by-phase accomplishment. In this process we must not lose sight of the urgent need to expand concurrently the existing print-medium resources as an indispensable adjunct of the teaching-learning process.

The Modern School Library Program

Images of the School Library

No one can possibly say that the school library and the print-medium services that it has been organized to provide are not an indispensable part of the educational system. Yet, as impoverished as their programs are, many school districts have not been willing to pay for the school libraries they so desperately need. They have, however, almost universally been willing to pay for a minimum number of textbooks. In the absence of school libraries, for example at the elementary level, some city school districts and county school-administrative units have organized large citywide and county-wide print-medium services for teachers. Under these arrangements, a teacher may order reference books for a given unit of work, in effect a small classroom library, that will be delivered to the school for a specified loan period.

With the increased recognition of the great impact of print-medium services on the educational growth of learners in general, and the

Figure 12-1. This magnificent Resource Center in the new Munster Senior High School indicates the existing and growing concern for adequate print-medium services in the schools. It also indicates the changing concepts of the need for learning resources. This Resource Center has 172 individual study stations, storage room for 11,000 volumes, carpeted floor, acoustical ceiling, and an expanded staff. See also Figures 3-2, 6-7, 6-26, 6-28, and 7-13. *Courtesy Public Schools, Munster, Indiana.*

Figure 12-2. These signs of action in elementary school libraries indicate the drive toward improvement. In the Homer Davis School, top view, a good little worker is giving the librarian some help, and in the bottom photograph the librarian in this Plainview, New York Central Park Road School (a participating school in the Knapp School Libraries Project) seems to be having a landslide of business. (*Top view*, courtesy Flowing Well Schools, Tucson, Arizona. *Bottom view*, courtesy Knapp School Libraries Project, American Library Association, Chicago.

instructional services to teachers and pupils in particular, we have developed a changed image of the school library. It may be helpful to portray several of the aspects of these images as they are emerging today.

New Concepts of the School Library. Great variety is to be found in the methods, organization, and scope of activity in specific library programs throughout the country. There is considerable agreement among school library specialists, however, that the library ought to become an all-media center. Under this policy its services to both teachers and pupils would embrace not only what may be referred to as

print-medium service, not only listening and viewing of new so-called content carriers, but a complete audiovisual media teaching-station service, including leadership activities for the utilization of television and instructional systems. It would be helpful to quote excerpts from the official policy statement of the American Association of School Librarians in 1956 as follows:

The American Association of School Librarians believes that the school library, in addition to doing its vital work of individual reading guidance and development of the school curriculum, should serve the school as a center for instructional materials.

Instructional materials include books—the literature of children, young people and adults—other printed materials, films recordings, and newer media developed to aid learning. . . . The interest a modern school now has in finding and using good motion pictures, sound recordings, filmstrips and other newer materials simply challenges and gives increased dimension to established library roles. . . . It may provide these materials and the equipment needed for their use for both individual and classroom study and teaching. . . . Primary responsibility for administering such a center, producing new instructional materials, and supervising regular programs of in-service training for use of materials may be the province of librarians, or, it may be shared. In any case, trained school librarians must be ready to cooperate with others and themselves serve as coordinators, consultants, and supervisors of instructional materials service on each level of school administration—in the individual school building, for the city or county unit, for the state. . . . School librarians are normally educated as teachers and meet state requirements for regular teaching certificates. They must also receive special training in analysis, educational evaluation, selection, organization, systematic distribution and use of instructional materials. The professional education of school librarians should contribute this basic knowledge as well as provide understanding of fundamental learning processes, teaching methods, and the psychology of children and adolescents. Also, school librarians must be familiar with the history and current trends in development of school curricula.[1]

It is apparent that the American Association of School Librarians has increased its commitment to an expansion of its print-medium services to include audiovisual-media services as well, and

[1] American Library Association, *Standards for School Library Programs* (Chicago: The Association, 50 East Huron St., 1960), pp. 11–12.

It is expected that the revision of this widely used book will have been completed late in 1968, work having been begun in March 1967 by a joint study and writing group composed of members of AASL and DAVI. The book will appear, if proposed plans materialize, under a new title, *Standards for School Media Programs* that implies working toward the unification of all media services under qualified leadership. In those cases where organizations such as print and audiovisual media are co-ordinately organized, their respective leaders would be integrated at the next higher level of administrative authority. If proposed revision plans materialize, the standards that have been quoted in the pages that follow will appear in drastically upgraded format, since it was firmly believed by participating members of the task force that media services would in the years immediately ahead undergo unprecedented expansion. See also Chapter 7, Footnote 8 and Footnote 6 in this chapter.

that it has also committed itself to recommending a vastly increased professional preparation program. The foregoing image ought to be studied in its practical application. The reader has already presumably studied the discussion of patterns of organization together with the illustrations, particularly in Chapter 7. It would be helpful to note an example of specifications for an instructional material center to be incorporated in each of three middle-school buildings in Hartford, Connecticut, each constructed to house 1,600 students.

The Instructional Materials Center Image in Hartford, Connecticut. We quote from the book of specifications prepared by Secondary Education Director Lloyd Calvert[2] with the help of his coordinators and supervisors.

The Instructional Materials Center

The instructional materials center (IMC) will be an extension of all other instructional centers in the middle school. Students will move from the other instructional centers to the IMC as large groups, small groups and as individuals. In the IMC they will do research and reference study and receive formal instruction in these skills. Here they will receive developmental reading instruction and remedial reading instruction, and through the use of various media and electronic equipment do review, make-up, remedial and enrichment assignments.

The IMC will also be an instructional research and development area for the faculty as well as a production, repair, storage and distribution area for instructional equipment and materials.

The IMC will include a general resource area, a classroom, four conference rooms, an IMC staff office, an instructional planning area, a media production area, a technical processing area, a library storage area, an audio-visual equipment storage and electronic control area and a textbook storage area.

The IMC should be located central to and adjacent to the four houses, near the science center and reasonably accessible from the creative arts center. It should also be easily accessible from the central receiving and storage room. Access to the general resource area for after-school use should be available without exposing the other components of the Center. . . .

It would be desirable to have the general resource area, classroom, conference rooms and IMC staff office on the same level to facilitate supervision. It would also be desirable to have non-load bearing

[2] Lloyd Calvert, *Educational Specifications for the Middle Schools, Grades 7 and 8.* (Hartford, Connecticut: Hartford Public Schools, 1966).

interior walls to allow flexibility for rearrangement of component spaces if necessary. L-shaped or long narrow quarters should be avoided. Special attention should be given to acoustical treatment in the Center. For this reason, the use of carpeting is recommended in the general resource area, classroom, conference rooms, IMC staff offices and instructional planning area. Special attention should be given also to climate control and glare control. Cable for closed circuit television and cable for future electronic expansion should be provided in the general resource area, classroom, conference rooms, instructional planning area and media production area. It is imperative that the Center be designed so that new developments in technology and media can be incorporated with a minimum of change and expense. Traffic patterns to distinct areas within the Center should be structured to avoid disturbing individuals engaged in learning activities.

The total square footage allotted to the instructional materials center amounts to 9,800 with the following space allotments made to areas indicated in the opposite chart and Figure 12-3.

Since we have taken note of the total space as allotted to the Hartford middle-school instructional materials center, and in view of present-day developments, we urge the reader to make comparisons with the recommended space-need areas in Chapter 7, and also with recommended library standards to be included later in this chapter. We note the effort to incorporate extended print-medium services, but when many other pupil listening and viewing services are envisaged, we see the need for taking over additional areas presumably allotted to the various houses within the school.

The Instructional Materials Center Image at Clarksville, Tennessee. The image of the library as an instructional materials center that was developed for the Clarksville-Montgomery County High School, merits our consideration before moving to other aspects of the present discussion. This school employs the latest technological materials and designs such as stainless steel wire fibre woven in the carpet to reduce static electricity shocks and electronic noise; coaxial-cable and audio-line circuits, also in the carpeting; and, delivery of audio and video by television to the student and classroom from a communication center in the main IMC. This school also has three additional IMC sub-

Function	Square Footage
One General Resource-Library Area (For 150 students, some regular and electronic carrels, reading, viewing, listening, 16,000 volumes, keys, 70% regular seating, carpeted floors, ITV cable equipped.)	4,500
One Classroom Area (For 60 students, instruction in reference skills, teacher in-service programs, ITV cable, projection screen.)	1,000
Four Conference Rooms (100 square foot each, ITV cable, small group instruction, movable walls, projection screen in one room.)	400
One IMC Staff Office (Seven people.)	400
Instructional Planning Area (Four offices, and one resource room for preview and as professional library, offices are for English, mathematics, social studies, and foreign languages, ITV cable, projection screen.)	1,200
Media-Production Area (Sink and equipment for slides, transparencies, tapes, two small tape recording booths, some duplicating.)	600
Technical Processing Area (Checking new orders, cataloging, mechanical processing, and distribution.)	300
Library Storage (Periodicals.)	300
Audiovisual Equipment and Electronic Control (For equipment to be loaned to classrooms, remote operation for classroom audio distribution, television distribution panel and outlet for conduit to roof for MATV or Coaxial-Cable.)	300

units, one in each of the three classroom clusters. Some of the classrooms have no walls, but utilize movable bulletin boards and cabinets as visual separators for complete flexibility. Specifically, however, what is the concept of the instructional materials center in this school? To answer this question, we turn to the following quotation from the descriptive booklet,

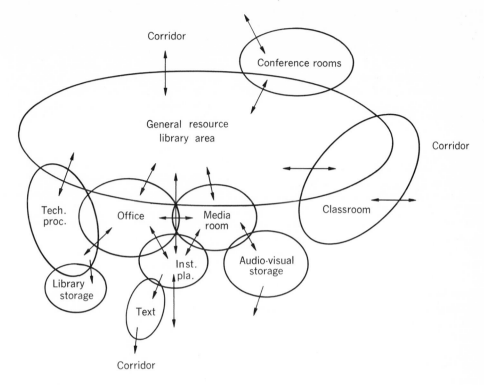

Corridor

Conference rooms

General resource
library area

Corridor

Tech.
proc.

Office

Media
room

Classroom

Inst.
pla.

Audio-visual
storage

Library
storage

Text

Corridor

Figure 12-3. The total area included in the proposed Hartford middle-school instructional materials centers, amounts to 9,800 square feet. *Courtesy Public Schools, Hartford, Connecticut.*

Profile of a Significant School,[3] published by the School Planning Laboratory of the University of Tennessee at Knoxville:

Instructional Materials Center

To provide the best possible environment for effective education materials are placed within easy access of students. The IMC and sub-IMCs are conveniently located. Each sub-IMC houses books and other materials appropriate to the subjects being taught in the adjacent classroom areas.

The IMC is an expanded concept of the school library. It is the central core of the school program and offers other opportunities for learning besides books. Slides, films, microfilms, filmstrips, video tapes, audio tapes, recordings, and microcards are stored in the IMC. A student in a sub-IMC may push a control button to request information stored in cartridges in the central IMC and the

[3] School Planning Laboratory, *Profile of a Significant School: Clarksville-Montgomery County High School.* (Prepared at the Southeastern Regional Center for Educational Facilities Laboratories, Inc.) (Knoxville, Tenn.: University of Tennessee).

information will be immediately transmitted to him via closed-circuit television.

Central Communications System

Clarksville-Montgomery County High School is modern in every concept of the word. A significant highlight of the school is the communication system.

Projection and sound equipment will be located in the nerve center. Central control equipment will permit the operator to transmit visual and audio materials via closed-circuit television directly to classrooms. The teacher will make a request to the technician for these instructional aids which she wishes to use. At the appropriate time the teacher merely dials the technician and the picture appears on the screen.

The employment of a full-time technician and use of audio-visual aids via a central communications system frees the teacher for other important educational activities. An adequate supply of equipment is available for several different programs to be transmitted at the same time. The system also provides for transmission of the same program to any

Figure 12-4. This is a view of the architect's model of the Clarksville Senior High School. The three clusters of teaching stations are largely academic ; and under the large dome, two levels of vocational areas surround the gymnasium and theater. *Courtesy Shaver and Company, Architects, Salina, Kansas.*

number of classrooms. Plans include use of a TV mobile unit so that programs may originate within classrooms.

Provision has been made for possible use of special audio-video student desks. These desks contain a viewing screen and listening device. The student may electronically request specific programmed material from the nerve center and he will immediately be able to see and/or hear the requested information. Connection of the audio-video student desks with the central communications system is accomplished via a wiring system woven in the carpeting.

As the reader can readily see, the Clarksville-Montgomery County High School is unique in many ways, but the lack of know-how on the part of teachers, generally, and the lack of professional and technical media staff members, both for the audiovisual and print media, plus lack of appropriations for producing the software for the electronic retrieval delivery system will be the weak links in the chain of implementation. We can hope for a speedier solution to all those implementation problems at Clarksville than has been observed in a number of earlier innovative schools. The reader should recheck the problems of dial retrieval and the discussion of delivery of media by TV in Chapters 11 and 10.

Having now explored the new image of the school library as an all-media service unit in the school, and having already in several preceding chapters in this book treated in depth the problems of organizing what we refer to as the audiovisual aspects of the media-service

program, we are in a better position to perceive the possibilities for combining the newer media services with those of the print medium. We can also see more clearly the problems that arise, and we can if we wish to do so concentrate our attention on the requirements and standards to be met in organizing vastly improved print-medium services for pupils and teachers. The way in which a school library is organized is an administrative problem. The level of services to be given, the breadth and scope of the media services to be offered, the financial support for staff and materials, and the amount of space to be provided, are all local problems that every community must face up to, and the sooner the better. For the purpose of this book, namely, to delineate the nature and need for increased print services in a school district so that prospective and practicing professional media personnel can more clearly perceive their roles in the total scheme of teaching and learning, we have chosen to deal specifically and solely with the print-medium services.

It has been the policy in this book to emphasize the implementation of media services in and at teaching stations in individual school buildings. To emphasize such improved teaching activity with media as a result of centralized media agencies, we dealt with the development of media-service centers in individual school buildings first, then proceeded to the treatment of the organization of school-district centers. We shall follow the same plan in connection with this topic. Since the volume and scope of school-library print services to teachers and pupils will largely determine the nature of and the necessity for centralized print services, we therefore turn next to the implementation of print-medium services in school buildings.

Implementation of Print-Medium Services in School Buildings

In the introduction to this chapter, we alluded to the indispensability of print-medium services in every school in the land. Let us examine this need for expansion in somewhat greater detail.

Need for Print-Medium Expansion

According to recommendations by the American Library Association,[4] "All schools having two hundred or more students need well-organized school libraries with functional programs of service directed by qualified personnel. Other provisions must be made for those smaller schools that cannot afford a library . . ." Since the same organization has estimated that upwards of three fourths of all elementary schools are currently without libraries, there is little doubt that the expansion of print-medium services on a national scale is in the offing.

Services to Pupils and Teachers. To clarify and substantiate this position it would be helpful to identify the kinds of activities that pupils engage in in the library. We quote the list presented by Ellsworth and Wagener[5] as follows:

Find the answers to specific questions that arise either from the teaching process or from ordinary curiosity.

Go alone or as a member of a committee sent to get information.

Carry out study hall assignments: that is, spend a specific amount of time studying in the library.

Find material for projects such as a written report, a book review, a debate brief, or a research paper.

Learn how to use the keys of a library—card

catalogs, bibliographies, reference books, periodical indexes, etc.

Look at motion-picture films, filmstrips, or other audiovisual materials. Study with a teaching machine, listen to phonograph records or tapes, listen and record voice for language study.

Locate quotations, excerpts, or data for speeches or projects.

Read just for the fun of reading—one book or a hundred.

Browse through current magazines and newspapers or look at the new book shelf.

Talk with other students.

Obviously the list was not intended to be more than representative. We would like to embellish this list by adding a few emphatic items or comments of our own as follows:

1. Carry out the research aspects of serious and creative problem-solving work organized in every course.

2. Practice solving personal, social, home, and school problems of an informal nature.

3. Learn to love to learn through successful use of print-medium services (find books for his classmates, books for class projects, for classroom-loan purposes, work toward accomplishment of personal goals).

4. Retrieve data from other than book sources, especially from microfilm devices and automatically controlled sources.

5. Get help to tap resources in other libraries on a systematic basis.

6. Work on information retrieval activity and reporting as a team member.

7. Make plans for selection of series of books for home and class use.

With the onset of media-supported instructional systems in which teachers will be freer to give guidance in special, creative, and productive problem-solving work by pupils, the library will have to assume an increased and staggering burden of guidance service for individuals and groups. Libraries everywhere will have to be bigger by far than ever planned before, and the library's staff members will likely have to appear on tape or television as a part of automated programs to provide instruction in print-medium skills. Such programs will have to be more effective and efficient than ever before. The teaching of such skills will probably be among the first to be taught in schools by

---

[4] American Library Association, *op. cit.*, p. 4.

[5] Ralph E. Ellsworth and Hobart D. Wagener, *The School Library: Facilities for Independent Study in the Secondary School* (New York: The Educational Facilities Laboratories, Inc., 1963), p. 25.

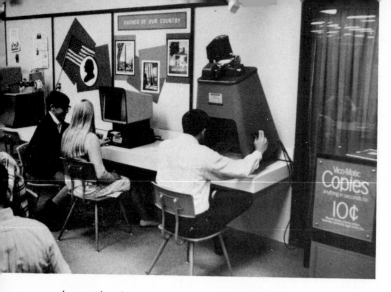

Figure 12-5. In this photograph we see the micro-form reading and study shelf at one of the Resource Centers (Language Arts, 1966-67 arrangement) at the Nova Junior-Senior High School. *Courtesy Nova Dissemination Project, Nova Schools, Fort Lauderdale, Florida.*

instructional system methods as described in Chapter 11. Teachers will be using the services of the library more frequently than ever before, and will have to work closely in planning ways to economize on the learner's time as he struggles to solve his formal problems. Writing, sketching, using calculators, dictating into small tape recorders, note taking, typing, and teletyping (as for computer inputs and outputs) may have to be heavily used for formal problem-solving work. Classrooms and laboratories, however, will have to carry the bulk of problem-defining and problem-planning activity. The time has come to reassess the roles of reading programs and to find ways to call for creative work on the part of pupils beyond anything we have had in the past. Such project work will have to be carried on everywhere in the school, and it will have to be facilitated by quantities of library services never before generally available. This means that the print-medium staff will have to work with both teachers and pupils in planning and in expediting library-use patterns. We are referring of course to a school library as it should operate in every school of the land.

Teaching stations will in all probability be permanently equipped with audiovisual media equipment for day-by-day usage, and teaching machine rooms and electronic learning laboratories will have to be used on a firmly scheduled basis for many subjects as dictated by teaching-learning arrangements. One of the main problems of the library will be to increase the ratio of total school enrollment to pupil hours of activity in the library during any given day or week. It need not be, and perhaps should not be, the center for formal electronic learning

laboratory work in a massive sense. It will have to provide print-service resources in an unprecedented way.

Standards for Library Collections. We need to understand that the formal teaching arm of the school is its staff of teachers. How these people teach will be largely determined by their skill and knowledge, their total resources and facilities. The school library must supply the print-medium resources above and beyond basic textbook materials for each student, that is, the classroom libraries. We must therefore consider this problem carefully. Just what is the nature of the standards for library collections? Before we turn to published standards and advice on the problem, it may be helpful to examine briefly the situation in one small school district having two elementary schools and one high school, all three of which claim to have reasonably good library services. These three schools have a plan to conduct a continuous, formalized instructional library-skills program from grades four through twelve. Involved in this program specifically are the main card catalogs and 55 encyclopedias, bibliographies, major reference volumes, and dictionaries. The high school (800 students) as long ago as 1962 had 8,800 books, 17 encyclopedias, 58 periodicals. The largest of the two elementary schools (500 students) owned 5,800 books, 7 sets of encyclopedias, and 20 periodicals.

Many factors influence the interpretation and application of the American Library Association standards. The Association's *Standards* were published in 1960, and the reader should use them to make his own comparisons in connection with school libraries with which he is familiar. We quote excerpts from the

American Library Association standards[6] as follows:

Books

Books are the most important of all library resources. No well-selected book collection is ever too large for children and young people. . . . Since the interests of children and young people, in the aggregate, are almost limitless and since their purposes in reading are innumerable, the book collection in their library must be rich and extensive in imaginative writings, in non-fiction, and in reference resources to meet their many wants. . . .

1. Recommendations for the minimum size of the book collections in libaries in very good schools follow:
   In schools having 200–999 students . . . 6,000–10,000 books.
   (This range for the size of the book collection is of qualitative nature and is not to be interpreted as being proportionate in relation to size of enrollment. For example, schools having 200 pupils can make effective use of collections containing 10,000 books.)
   In schools having 1,000 or more students . . . 10 books per student.
2. With collections that are large enough, books can be made easily accessible for students and teachers. At all times there is a sufficient number of books available for use in the school library, for classroom collections, and for withdrawals for home use. . . . Libraries in excellent schools, particularly those having 200–2,000 students, will far exceed the minimum recommendations for size of book collections.
3. The standards for the size of the school library book collection allow for the acquisition of duplicate copies of titles to meet the needs of students and teachers. . . . Duplicate purchases are essential to meet reasonable requests for books that are used intensively by many students in connection with their class projects or assignments. Some titles are duplicated so that they can be made available for use in classroom collections as well as in the school library. . . .
4. Library collections in schools having specialized curriculums in agriculture, in vocational or technical subjects, or in similar areas meet the needs of teachers and students for materials in these special fields. These parts of the collection are larger and more highly developed than in libraries in schools not having the specialized curriculums. The special materials are provided in addition to the basic, well-rounded collection.

Magazines

Magazines form an important part of the school library collections. . . . Students read magazines for many purposes, school related and otherwise, and it is important for students to become familiar with a wide range of good magazines. . . .

The school library collection of magazines also includes professional journals in the fields of librarianship and instructional materials.

1. Recommendations follow for the minimum number of current magazine subscriptions for the collection in the school library:
   In elementary schools (Grades K-6)   25 titles
   In elementary schools (Grades K-8)   50 titles

[6] American Library Association, *op. cit.*, pp. 77–78. (As indicated in a previous footnote, drastic revisions of standards for print medium collections are in the offing before this book went to press. We can indicate here on a tentative basis the nature of such revisions as follows: *Books*, a basic collection of 6,000–10,000 titles representing 10,000 volumes or 20 volumes per student whichever is greater; *Magazines*, for elementary schools, 50–75 titles, and for secondary schools, 125–175 titles; *Microform items*, vastly expanded; *Newspapers*, for elementary schools, 3–6, and for secondary schools, 6–10 with a minimum of 2 nationally known newspapers. And regarding *budget*: No School should spend less per pupil for *print* materials than 3 per cent of the national average per pupil cost. Using the national statistic of $619, this expenditure would amount to $18.60 per pupil. The new standard for unified, all-media service programs recommends the same minimum expenditure on the same basis for *audiovisual* media. Thus for both print and audiovisual media the total annual expenditure per pupil should amount to a minimum of 6 per cent of the national average per pupil operating cost for the programs envisioned. Innovative and expanded service programs may require far greater expenditures. Such expenditures are not to include cost of textbooks, equipment, salaries, fixed installations, and initial media purchases for new programs. See also Footnotes 1, 6, 8, and 12. For new standards relative to kinds and amounts of audiovisual media, refer to Chapter 13, Footnote 3, page 571.)

Figure 12-6. This is a view of a part of the Sedgefield School Library in Charlotte, North Carolina. Shown in the picture are the biography and fiction books. *Courtesy Knapp School Libraries Project, and the American Library Association, Chicago.*

Figure 12-7. Should reference book services be decentralized? This is a debatable question with many pros and cons. In this picture we see a teacher selecting reference books from one of the many supplementary libraries since they are located in the learning center of each of the clusters of classrooms. See Figure 6-4 showing one of the learning centers in use for multi-group activity, mainly with media. Identify one main advantage and one disadvantage of decentralization. *Courtesy Fountain Valley School District, Huntington Beach, California.*

In junior high schools	70 titles
In senior high schools	120 titles

. . .

4. Back issues of periodicals needed for reference work and for other purposes are retained in the school library for a time span covering at least five years. In an increasing number of school libraries these magazine files are kept on microfilm.
5. The school library collections include a general periodical index. Large schools need more than one copy. . . . special schools require a periodical index covering the contents of magazines in special fields.

Ellsworth and Wagener[7] after making a plea for book collections of 30,000 volumes or over, at least in secondary schools, offer the following advice:

[7] *Op. cit.,* pp. 76–77.

If the school's role is to indoctrinate, few books are needed. If its role is to teach, that is, to help students make up their own minds about the basic assumptions of their culture after having examined and analyzed the relevant facts, an extensive library is required. It is not enough to offer students books that are programed to give the answers. They need to learn questions as well as answers. They need to gain experience in working from source material. They need, too, to learn how to draw sound conclusions from raw evidence. And they also need to learn that there are some questions to which there are no answers.

A school library that can supply these needs will receive one or more local, one regional, and at least four national papers, including *The New York Times, The Christian Science Monitor,* the *St. Louis Post-Dispatch,* and *The Washington Post.* It should receive at least one foreign paper such as *The Times* (London) and one foreign language paper in French, German, Russian, and Spanish. Back files of these papers need not be kept beyond six months, though libraries should keep microfilm copies of *The New York Times.*

There should be at least 10 to 15 important general magazines such as *The Atlantic Monthly, Harper's, The Reporter, Foreign Affairs, The Economist* (London), the *Saturday Review,* and a selection of current publications of the United States Government, United Nations, and UNESCO, with selected publications from other countries where the future of mankind is being decided—China, Germany, Britain, France, Russia, the African States, the Far East, and all of the Latin American countries. Similarly, the library should subscribe to as many specialized magazines as are needed to provide material for student reports and papers. Most of these will be indexed in the *Readers Guide to Periodical Literature.*

Such a library is not easy to develop. It will require the skill of a well-educated and well-trained library staff and a corps of teachers whose knowledge of subject matter is extensive.

We turn next to another important aspect of print-medium services in school buildings, namely, the aspect of organization and control.

Organization and Control of Print-Medium Services in Each School Building

A large number of elementary and secondary schools are small schools, although decades ago a movement got underway to consolidate small school units in order to make possible a more effective instructional program at lower cost. We therefore recognize the fact that large school libraries and large audiovisual media centers may now be organized as separate operating units within each school or, as conditions favor such action, combined for administrative reasons. Under the strategem of combination, all necessary print and audiovisual media services would be provided under a unifying leadership, and each phase of the service would operate under optimum spatial, staff, and financial arrangements. Separation of print and technological media may prove to be advantageous when professional and technical services in the school are supporting an advanced program as will be the case when television, instructional systems, and electronic learning laboratories are making their full contributions to teaching and learning. This is precisely the time when we assert that print-medium services will also have to be expanded to optimum levels because it is then that teachers and pupils will make maximum use of library facilities and staff. School administrators should not assume that to push both print and nonprint technologies into minimum size quarters in a school-building unit will make their problem of financing any easier, or services to teachers and pupils any better. Actually the action to combine facilities and services of this sort may, because of the differences in functions and strategies, cause both to suffer.

Juxtapositioning of service areas may be an advantage, but not in the sense that an electronic technician could repair the torn pages of a book. He could, however, maintain the library's retrieval systems, microfilm readers, and similar devices. For this discussion it is being assumed that learning laboratories and other teaching laboratories will be under the control of teaching staffs and their aides, not under the control of the school library. The library of course will have its own media installations for its own instructional services and purposes, and as such, these units will be maintained in a technical sense by the audiovisual media technicians. Thus for the purposes of this discussion of print-medium services, we see the library receiving services of a media-design nature, for example, in preparing videotapes and visualized presentations, as would any other department, teacher, or teaching team.

In this chapter we view print-medium services as a basic service to teachers and pupils that concentrates on facilitation of formal and informal problem-solving work defined, assigned, and elicited by teachers. This facilitation demands special skills and insights of library science.

In view of the pressure for increased print-medium services in every school a discussion of several additional aspects of organization and control of school libraries is essential. What provisions should be made for leadership and operational staff in each school library? We shall answer this question first, in light of the nature of print services already discussed.

Leadership and Operational Staff for the School Library. Time and time again we have noted the use of lay personnel in the book-closet type libraries of school buildings, and it is not uncommon for such a librarian to be serving on a part-time basis. We suggest that to find ingenious ways to use part-time certifiable teachers for work in schools with enrollments below 200 pupils with a part-time clerk would be the preferred stop-gap measure until these small schools are consolidated. At the 200-pupil level, each school should have its own library and certifiable librarian. The position taken by the American Library Association[8] on this situation is that, "A truly dynamic library program of service to teachers could easily occupy the time of an imaginative, resourceful, and helpful school librarian in a school having 200 pupils . . ." The formal standards of the Association regarding leadership and operational personnel for each school library in schools of desirable size are as follows:

Librarians
For the first 900 students* or fraction thereof: 1 librarian for each 300 students or major fraction thereof.
For each additional 400 students or major fraction thereof: 1 librarian.

[8] American Library Association, *op. cit.*, pp. 51–55. We need to once again report that new personnel standards for media programs in schools are in the making. On a tentative basis, we can point out that new standards for unified, all-media services will be as follows: for each 250 pupils in a school there should be employed one professional media specialist supported by one media-aide or clerk type person and one technician-specialist assistant. See also Footnote 8, Chapter 7, and Footnote 1, this chapter.

Clerks
1 clerk for each 600 students* or major fraction thereof.

* The school having 200 students has a full-time librarian and a half-time clerk.

In larger libraries where a number of certified librarians are employed, the leadership responsibility would be held by the head librarian. The head librarian would normally be directly responsible to the school principal as shown in Figure 8-11 of Chapter 8. In large schools with expanded media services under separate print and nonprint organizations, the head librarian may be responsible to a school-building curriculum leader with the position of vice principal. As we perceive it, in a logical setting based on functions, experience and professional preparation, the vice principal may be a media generalist to whom both the audiovisual media coordinator and the head librarian would be responsible on a coordinate basis. Just to make a few other possibilities clear, a qualified head librarian may become such a vice principal and so may a qualified audiovisual media specialist.

Combining Print-Medium and Audiovisual Media Services. The reader should check carefully the discussions provided in Chapter 7 regarding organizational plans for school-building media-service centers, and make sure that the nature of space and staff needs are recognized. Then and only then should plans be made for carrying on the required services on a basis of a combined facility. As we have said, such combinations should not be implemented as expedients, as substandard and stop gap phases of developing programs. The individual with the broadest capability, training, and experience should be the one chosen for the leadership role in all cases of combination. We see the need, then, and the American Library Association also recognizes this need, as revealed in its policy statement previously quoted, for librarians aspiring to over-all media leadership positions to prepare themselves for such action. We see on the other hand the audiovisual media coordinator who aspires to serve in leadership posts as the vice principal we discussed, or the director of an all-media center, preparing himself to use new insights and abilities in print services, especially with reference to standard school library operating procedures, effective layout and space needs and arrangements, use and arrangement of library keys, organization of materials, and giving instruction in library skills.

Providing Space for Print-Medium Services

Continuing our discussion of some of the problems of implementing desirable print-medium services in school buildings, we should consider the vital need for operational spaces. As we discuss this topic, even though the treatment will have to be brief, we shall refer to the nature of the various print services in the specification of the areas for operational purposes. Since we have already made recommendations for audiovisual media space needs in school buildings in Chapter 7, the present suggestions ought to create the impression we seek to give, namely that to provide basic print and nonprint media services as vital instructional resources, we have to formulate new images of required operational areas.

Before presenting some published standards relative to space needs for print-medium services in school libraries, it would be helpful to describe briefly the space-arrangement plans for two elementary school libraries. The first is the Curriculum Materials Center for the Hillspoint Elementary School in Westport, Connecticut.[9] The full-time librarian and her part-time clerk provide a storage and retrieval service for the school's teaching staff for filmstrips, slides, transparencies, tapes, and records. Also, some supplies for making transparencies are stored in the workroom and a few units of audiovisual media equipment are stored in the two storage rooms.

In this instance, the audiovisual media coordinator is on a coordinate basis with the librarian, with released time for assigned duties. The school's enrollment in 1966 was 530 pupils in grades K-6. The approximate areas in the operational spaces, totaling 2,070 square feet, are as follows:

[9] Based on information supplied by Dr. George E. Ingham, formerly Administrative Assistant for Curriculum and Research, Westport Public Schools.

Function	Space
	square feet
Reading Room for 45 pupils	1,250
(Containing charge-out desk and card catalog.)	
Office	160
Workroom	160
(Book processing, some media preparation.)	
Two Storage Rooms: 50 square foot each	100
(Housing the school's assigned media collections and some media equipment.)	
Alcove	400
(For 12 independent study carrels and book shelves.)	

The second example is for the Learning Resource Center based on detailed specifications prepared for incorporation in two new 1,000-pupil elementary schools for grades PK-6, to be constructed immediately in Hartford, Connecticut. The learning-resource center space allotment in each of the schools is a minimum of 3,360 square feet. To describe the general plans, we shall present excerpts from the book of specifications prepared by Robert C. Miles,[10] Director of Elementary Education, as follows:

Learning Resource Center

The learning resource center is an information and instructional center which will house and distribute books, periodicals, pamphlets, recordings, slides, tapes, filmstrips, prints, models, graphic materials, and equipment.

Areas within the learning resource center and their approximate sizes are:

	Square Feet
Reading Room	1,350
(For 45 pupils, 10,000 volumes, 25 periodicals, audiovisual media storage, 4-position carrels for multimedia for 16 pupils, also 6 listening stations, perimeter raceway for future electronics.)	

[10] Robert C. Miles, *Educational Specifications for New Elementary Schools* (Hartford, Connecticut: Hartford Public Schools, 1966).

Library Classroom	700
(For 25 pupils, listening, viewing, instruction, story telling, dramatization, electronic conduits.)	
Office-Workroom	250
(Cataloging and processing, office for library specialist and clerical assistant.)	
Library Storage	120
(Periodical storage, special collections for classrooms, collections for display materials.)	
Conference Rooms, 2, 120 square feet each	240
(Folding wall for increasing size, as for viewing, electronic conduit.)	
Professional Resource Area	325
(Preview of media, planning work, staff browsing, electronic conduit, full-closure Venetian blinds.)	
Media Production Office	375
(Design and produce media by school staff, typing, duplicating, slides, tape recordings, photocopying, with single recording booth, sink, with access to corridor.)	
Total	3,360

We now ask the reader to compare space-need recommendations made in Chapter 7 in connection with the planning of audiovisual media-service centers. To facilitate comparison, we repeat them briefly here. With a 1,000-pupil school in mind, we felt compelled to call for the following space allotments to care for basic needs:

Function	Space Need
	Square Feet
Storage	460
Workroom for Handling Media Orders	200
Cart Garage for Mobile Classroom Equipment	100
Inspection and Servicing Equipment	50
Preview of Media	140
Media Preparation by Teachers, Aides, and Pupils	700
Administrative Activities	200
Total	1,850

In that same analysis we felt compelled to state the need for 6,000 square feet of space for the school library, specifically earmarked for print medium services. Rechecking the previously quoted Hartford Learning Resource Center specifications, we note that either by oversight, or failure to take into account existing needs, or by unstated plans to re-allocate spaces for the purpose, the audiovisual media-service functions, except for media preparation, were not included in the space-allotment plans. If we assume that the present Hartford spaces for previewing audiovisual media are adequate from the standpoint of our own recommendations, and further assume that our suggested media storage needs be met by using space in a part of the reading room, workroom, or reading-room storage, the specifications for two of Hartford's new elementary schools will still be shy of our recommendations for audiovisual media services alone by approximately 675 square feet. If we compare total square footage for print-medium services recommended in the Hartford elementary school specifications with our own recommendation they are less by approximately 2,640 square feet. The reader may further note that in the opening quotation, it was and is the firm intention to engage in a full media service, distributing media materials and equipment to teaching stations. On the basis of this intention, we perceive that adjustments will have to be made in final space allotments for the services envisaged. We should therefore suggest an upward revision of the entire space allotment program, even for print-medium purposes alone. Although far greater than many existing schools can claim for the purpose of a learning resources center, the specifications are inadequate, and under present circumstances, one or the other or both print-medium and technological-media services will suffer, because of the lack of adequate space, from the school's dedication day.

We should not fail to point out another essential weakness in the entire plan of this and many other new structures, namely, the lack of special-purpose rooms as would be used for electronic learning laboratory spaces, such special teaching-learning stations that serve vital, large-group, automated, independent study, and individualized instruction purposes. Teaching-learning facilities should be built into the school for a good many reasons which have already been discussed in earlier chapters. We should compliment the planners, however, in connection with program and staff planning, especially for the fact that they recommended one librarian, one media specialist, and one media clerk, as full-time personnel to carry out print and audiovisual media services. We hardly need to point out, though, that in the framework of the discussions in this book, the number of staff members, according to previously quoted standards for a 1,000-pupil school, is and will prove to be, woefully inadequate. This inadequacy, especially with regard to audiovisual media technicians and library assistants, will be keenly felt. See Figure 12-8.

The reader should not lose sight of the foregoing comparisons, for we now present some of the published guidelines relative to school libraries. It should also be remembered, however, that for our purposes we are mainly concerned with print-medium services. We shall emphasize the guidelines formulated by the American Library Association which tend to be oriented toward both elementary and secondary schools, but we shall also incorporate additional statements from the report by the Educational Facilities Laboratories. School leaders and space planners must continually bear in mind that present and future operations are based on program and specific functions that have to be carried out by and for people. Any given instructional organization has specific goals that it must attain within the context of major teaching objectives. Unless these functions are identified and unless the decision can be made as to the feasible level for executing those functions, it will be mere guesswork as to what the true space needs are. We shall deal individually with the basic operational areas, but before we do so, the following summary statement by the ALA[11] will be helpful:

A library program that stimulates learning, encourages creative teaching, and provides for individual and group guidance requires a physical environment that is functional in design and arrangement. Ample space, harmonious arrangements, good lighting, blendings and contrasts in colors, functional furnishings, and proper control of sound create an atmosphere in which students and faculty enjoy working and in which learning takes

[11] American Library Association, *op. cit.*, p. 91.

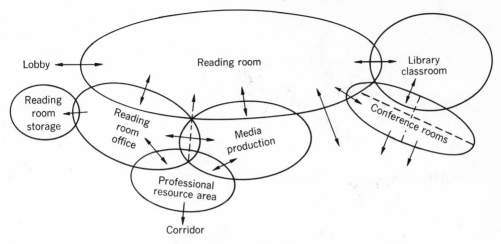

Figure 12-8. In the specifications for new elementary schools to be constructed in Hartford, Connecticut, a Learning Resources Center has been planned that will encompass approximately 3,360 square feet of floor space. The spatial relationship of these spaces were set forth in a diagram which is reprinted here for careful analysis. In terms of the size of some of the existing media centers such a suite seems enormous. The fact is that programs now envisaged will make it necessary to take over eventually several classroom spaces or to build on an addition. When constructing centers of this sort, should they be so located and planned that adding space will be facilitated? See also Figure 12-4. *Courtesy Public Schools, Hartford, Connecticut.*

place. The liking that children and young people have for the library, their feelings of ease and pleasure in its surroundings, and their satisfactions in using its materials derive from many sources. Among these influences are the attractive appearance and the convenient arrangement of the school library.

Reading Room Areas. Once more we quote the ALA[12] using excerpts from *Standards for School Library Programs*, as follows:

1. The reading room accommodates at least 10 per cent of the enrollment in schools having 551 or more students, and 45–55 students in schools having 200–550 students. No more than 100 students, and preferably no more than 80, are seated in one reading room. . . .
2. The reading room has dimensions based on an allowance of 30–35 square feet per reader (including requirements for table and chair space, space for

[12] *Op. cit.*, p. 119. In line with information presented in Footnotes 1, 6, and 8, we report the likely adoption of additional new standards that bear upon the discussions in this section, as follows: *Reading Room Space*, to accommodate 15 per cent of the school enrollment, 40 square feet for each student; *Carrels*, 30–40 per cent of seating capacity; *Entrance, Circulation and Distribution Space*, 800–1000 square feet; and the *Library Teaching Station*, 900–1000 square feet. Many additional spaces may be required. See Chapters 7, 9, 10 and 11.

heavy traffic areas, three-fourths of the book collection, shelving units, and sufficient space for the circulation desk, card catalog case, vertical-files and free-standing or mobile equipment away from the walls.

Ellsworth and Wagener[13] indicate that the card catalog, reference collection, and circulation desk need not take up more than 520 square feet of space. They insist, however, that school libraries ought to be able to accommodate up to 30 per cent of the school's enrollment, with great increases in the amount of emphasis on independent study facilities. They point out:

. . . since one reader requires a minimum of 25 square feet of floor space, a school with 2,000 students would require 15,000 square feet for readers.

Total reader space should be apportioned as follows: study carrels—60 per cent; group study rooms that may also serve as rooms for the use of audio-visual equipment—15 per cent; flat top tables—8 per cent; lounge furniture—17 per cent. . . .

Independent Study and Individualized Instruction Arrangements. Many library planners, in

[13] *Op. cit.*, pp. 45 and 51.

Figure 12-9. These pictures show spaces, arrangements, and conditions in three different schools. *Top*, a part of the Instructional Materials Center, Valley Winds Elementary School, Riverview Gardens District, St. Louis. Teachers' planning and work area is at upper level left; *middle*, a view of part of the Oak Park and River Forest High School (grades 9-12) library with 42,000 books, 229 periodicals, 1,000 filmstrips, 500 motion pictures, 400 disk recordings, 200 audio-program tapes, 600 transparencies and 2,940 slides. Personnel include 6 full-time librarians (including the director of the audiovisual media program), one part-time librarian and English teacher, 3 secretaries, 6 half-time library aides and 2 half-time secretaries; *bottom*, the pensive elementary school student in his library is a symbol of the true reason for all of our concern, namely that young people acquire the love for learning; the drive that will last a lifetime, to read, study, think, and adapt to change. Note the shelving units, book ends, and the plastic covers that may have accompanied the books at the time of purchase. (*Top view*, courtesy Shaver and Company, Architects, Salina, Kansas. *Middle photograph*, courtesy Knapp School Libraries Project, American Association of School Librarians, Chicago. *Bottom picture*, courtesy Montgomery County Public Schools, Rockville, Maryland.)

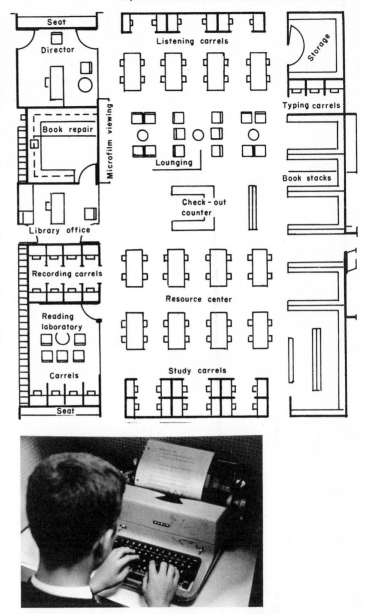

Figure 12-10. The Nova Junior-Senior High School has a number of Resource Centers. We show first in this illustration the architect's floor plan of the Resource Center for English and Social Studies. Present arrangement of furniture and equipment probably varies considerably from the original sketches. We note in this diagram the Administration space, technical work on books, recording carrels, reading laboratory, storage, typing carrels, and book stacks. The carrels, shown in Figure 6-7 are operated on a dial-access basis for both audio and video programs. A 50-position electronic learning laboratory is not shown in this illustration; however, it is located adjacent to the Resource Center off to the right. A few of the carrels, as indicated in the upper right-hand corner of the diagram, are typing carrels. *Courtesy Nova Dissemination Project, Nova Schools, Fort Lauderdale, Florida.*

their efforts to provide independent study facilities for students, recommend installing not only regular carrels for print-medium use, but several electronically equipped carrels with video and audio-program tape capability, usually a very small number of the latter. We ought to stress the fact that *independent study* may not generally be used in its broadest and most inclusive sense. Therefore we ought to make sure that when recommending space allotments for print-medium services we clearly recognize the differences in function between

independent study and individualized instruction. A place where a pupil at any age level may study alone with whatever facilities he needs to pursue his own interests, may not prove to be individualized instruction at all. Individualization implies a more formal organization of instructional activity, as a component of a larger pattern of instructional activity, as we have pointed out many times earlier. Thus, carrels that are designed for individualization programs may have to be especially equipped and may have to be made available in larger numbers than generally is the case. The reader has but to refer to the discussions in Chapter 11 on instructional systems to discover the possibilities for such formal individualization activity.

We wish, then, to raise a serious question with regard to the number of such carrels that constitutes a worthwhile contribution to the objectives of the school's formal and basic instructional program. We believe that teaching-learning activity of a teaching-systems nature does not pay off unless pupils in an entire course are deeply involved, or unless a significant and specific objective in a course can be attained by such means. Thus the number of carrels to be made available ought to be ascertained in light of the instructional need for informal and formal independent study, and also the formal individualization of instruction function which actually may neither be a print-medium service, nor one that is housed in a school library or media center. We often use the terms *listening* and *viewing* too loosely. The library or media center can hardly become a group of scientific laboratories and a complete service center for all of the teaching systems of an electronic nature for the school. We should study the need for and potential contribution of such facilities to decide whether we ought to install complex technological systems for organized use in special learning laboratories located close to associated teaching stations. Teacher guidance and control of the implied learning activities will thus be greatly facilitated.

This is not to say that print-medium services should be limited in any way, and thus we do not intend to imply that there should be no electronically equipped carrels in the school library or media center. We insist instead that there are many ways that independent study as both an informal and formal process can and ought to be provided for, and such needs ought to be fully met. It is therefore necessary that we emphasize and delineate the roles that library research by students are to play in the teaching-learning process. We believe, in view of our present emphasis on print-medium services and in view of our discussions about curriculum trends, especially those in Chapters 4, 10, and 11, that greater numbers of students need to be cared for on a reading, study, and information-retrieval basis. See Figures 12-1, 12-5, 6-7, and 6-26. The suggestions made as to the high

percentage of carrels seem to be in order for serious library work by students. The library is hardly an entertainment and gossip center for anybody. Looking toward a future of intensive media-service demands, we must not be carried away by incidental uses of the library, but rather must concentrate on the kinds of activity that will pay the greatest instructional dividends. There are many kinds of carrels, and illustrations, including Figure 12-1, show a few of the varieties in common use in libraries today. Normally, carrel study units call for a desk area of approximately 6 square feet. Ellsworth and Wagener[14] say, "Thus, most of the study space—60 per cent in fact—should be in the form of study carrels in groups of not more than 15 or 20 infused among the collections. Each carrel should allow $2 \, \text{ft} \times 3 \, \text{ft}$ of work space per reader, and more if learning machines are to be used."

Listening and Viewing. Listening and viewing activities may be carried on in a great variety of situations. Carrels may be equipped for audio-program retrieval, and for microfilm-reading activities, and some equipment units may be used in small-group or conference rooms. When listening activities are organized in carrels with proper facilities, they may be conducted in the regular reading room area. Some of these activities may also be organized to take place in the library's classroom where ample equipment should be installed on a permanent basis. The seats or desks in the classroom may well be equipped with dial-retrieval listening stations, thus providing an electronic learning laboratory station. In fact, such a classroom may also be equipped with a group-response system that would serve well in the use of automated instructional systems for the teaching of library skills and insights.

Classroom Areas. There can be little doubt that libraries need classrooms specially equipped for carrying on their instructional programs. Libraries, however, may also incorporate in their instructional plans extensive use of audio-program tape in their own listening carrels, and videotapes on a teaching-systems basis as components of instructional programs. To facilitate such media use, the library classroom should be equipped as an originating and recording studio as described in Chapter 10. Using

[14] *Op. cit.*, p. 53.

previously prepared videotapes, librarians could arrange to be free of actual repetitive presentations to devote time to other planning and leadership activities. Nevertheless, library classrooms need to be equipped with flexibility in mind and for carrying on the many kinds of teaching processes that are required by library-skill objectives. Such a teaching station may, in fact, be the ideal location for a multimedia installation. See Footnote 12.

Administrative Space. We should plan for a reasonable amount of space in which to conduct administrative activities. Generally we think of office space as being expendable. We ought to make sure that we have administrative areas set aside for personnel that need them. Their arrangement and location should facilitate surveillance and yet offer a measure of privacy for staff work and other consultations. Ellsworth and Wagener[15] indicate that reference librarians should have offices of approximately 100 square feet in size. Whenever all-media services are organized on a unified basis, additional office areas will be required. Nor should we forget that clerks and technicians need desk space also. Chapter 7 provides some estimates of such spaces with regard to audiovisual media administrative spaces, that apply generally to print-medium services as well.

Workroom Spaces. When we consider workroom spaces, we tend to be content with spaces that will barely suffice for the intended operations. Certainly we ought not to say that the space in an almost microscopic living room in a small five-room home would suffice for the workroom of a school library. In the modern print-medium service library, to say nothing of those libraries that have to carry on equipment-inspection operations, we will require a minimum of 400 square feet. Many times workroom spaces are combined with office areas as another expedient. Office functions are so different, and the people who work in workrooms are more often technical than clerical. Freed of combinations with workroom operations, office areas may then be located near reading and other action spaces where they will make administrative work easier. Book repairs are not similar to film repair, and again we need to consider the kinds of operations that take place in library workrooms that emphasize print-medium services. If we must deal with a wide range of media and media services, an entirely different standard should be used, and these are set forth in Chapter 7.

Conference and Stack Areas. In a modern print-medium program there will be an urgent need for flexible conference-room space. The library classroom may serve a number of conference purposes, but the basic need is for several small conference rooms, preferably with movable walls. At least six such rooms of 150 square feet each ought to be provided. Space for stacks and magazine storage should exceed a minimum of 400 square feet. With regard to stack spaces, the American Library Association[16] specifies the following:

1. The space for stack areas is determined by the number of books in the regular library collection that cannot be shelved in the main reading room area, the extent of the collection of back issues of periodicals . . . and the extent of other collections.

2. Stack space (which is usually needed only for large collections and, frequently, stores only little-used materials or duplicate copies) is an extension of the library, and the materials contained therein should be quickly available for students and teachers. . . .

Obviously stack areas and the means of access to them become critical matters as the size of the library increases and its services become more complex. In the examples we have used, stack-area problems may well be cared for if and when adequate storage areas as we have emphasized them are provided.

Storage Areas. We have emphasized repeatedly in this book the deplorable condition that exists throughout the media-service center world in particular and school buildings in general because of the lack of storage space. This also applies to the principal's office, the athletic department, and the academic and vocational divisions. Somehow, the image has developed that all we need is a classroom, a chalkboard, a briefcase, and an answer book. We assert that in planning any audiovisual media-service center we need to include something like 15 per cent of the total space as a minimum for storage area in any given service areas where the operational is 10,000 square feet or less. Such

---

[15] *Op. cit.*, pp. 45–46. (According to proposed new standards, a minimum of 200 square feet ought to be allocated for each professional staff member.)

[16] *Op. cit.*, p. 122.

storage areas as we refer to are not to be confused with media-access or order-filling areas. Perhaps we ought to call them *dead* storage areas with ready accessibility. Unless we provide these spaces the efficiency of our work is decreased significantly. Usually libraries need to store textbooks, periodicals (at least for a number of years), infrequently used reference works, and multiple copies of special-purpose books, to say nothing of stocks of supplies often purchased a year in advance. Storage areas should be carefully related to needs in media preparation, workrooms, classrooms, extensive listening and viewing collections, microfilm collections, maps and globes, and other display materials. For strictly print-medium services, in addition to all of the other spaces we have mentioned, we claim that a conveniently available storage facility quite apart from any specific operational area, ought to be as large as 10 per cent of the total area of the school library.

Professional Library. It is common knowledge that school-district and school-building leadership personnel in the main buy professional books sparingly. This fact can be confirmed by almost any writer of professional works and any publisher, the present effort being probably no exception. There can be little doubt that professional libraries, for whatever volume of service they are called upon to render, ought to be decentralized at least in part. We know that many school districts organize centralized professional libraries, but then there is the problem of distributing copies needed for supervisory activities. (See Figure 8-4). Regardless of these problems, the emphasis on the decentralization of professional books in the school libraries, attended by their subsequent employment in district-wide reading and study programs, seems to hold the greatest promise for significant use. The American Library Association gives emphasis to this point in the following list[17]

1. A basic book collection consists of 200–1,000 titles, the number depending on the needs and size of the faculty and the availability of other collections of professional materials for teachers in the community. . . .

[17] *Op. cit.,* p. 86. (Proposed new standards call for an allocation of 800 square feet as a minimum space for a professional library, and increased financial support.)

2. The collection includes at least 25–50 professional magazine titles.
This core collection of magazines consists of general periodicals in the education field and a selection of other titles to represent the subject areas covered in the curriculum of the school. Many schools will want more professional magazines, and if there is no district collection of professional materials for administrators and teachers, a larger number of titles is imperative. . . .

3. The professional collection includes pamphlets, filmstrips, curriculum guides, resource units, and other special instructional materials as needed by the faculty members.

4. Minimum annual expenditures for the professional collection range from $200.00 to $800.00, depending upon the needs and size of the faculty and the availability of other professional materials in the community. . . .

5. The professional collection is administered by the head school librarian.

6. Administrators, teachers, and librarians participate in the selection of the materials.

7. All materials in the collection meet standard criteria for evaluation and selection in the special fields represented. The collection is kept up-to-date and functional.

8. The collection is housed best in a special room for teachers in the school library suite, or in some part of the school easily accessible to teachers, if separate space is not available in the library. The materials can be withdrawn for home use.

Having emphasized at some length the problems that face school leaders and librarians who seek to plan for adequate print services throughout a school district, we now can point out that the route to better print-medium services must inevitably lead toward the development of the library program in each school. However, we need to ask, what kinds of organization and activities at school-district headquarters do the many libraries in the schools demand for their success? We shall seek to answer that question next.

Implementation of Print-Medium Services at School-District Headquarters

The Nature of Central Print-Medium Services

Print-medium services at school-district headquarters have developed along several basic lines in meeting instructional needs. If we look at centralized print medium services broadly we discern the following aspects or phases of the action being taken. First, there is a centralized effort, often massive in scope, to supply book services to schools without their own libraries, that is, a service to teachers in the sense of providing them with classroom libraries on loan. Such action is of course a transitional program, pending a gradual growth toward school library sufficiency. Second, there is a centralized leadership and management service designed to facilitate and expedite the action of existing school-library staffs and school-building administrative staffs. The character of the various operations at school-district headquarters therefore shifts toward an optimum balance between these two fundamental aspects of print-medium services. We ought to recognize and emphasize the fact that many school districts, particularly the small districts, provide extremely limited central services, placing total responsibility for textbook and reference book services in the hands of the school principal. In other instances, school-district supervisory personnel, and other curriculum leaders, work with principals and their librarians in guiding an evolving program. Many other stopgap methods for *taking charge* of print-medium services are to be found in city, county, and special school districts, but as programs increase in complexity, more effective and permanent arrangements have to be worked out to meet instructional objectives on a district-wide basis.

District-Wide Print-Medium Functions

As an introduction to the need for district-wide print-medium administrative control, it may be helpful to identify and discuss some of the major functions that every school district is sure to face in carrying out this aspect of its program. Certainly we shall not deal with them all, but prospective and practicing media program directors should recognize the major problems that are common and basic to school districts everywhere.

The Textbook Function. Textbook procurement and distribution throughout a school district is a print-medium service to teachers that is fundamental to teaching patterns every-

where. It must be dealt with by a well-established set of policies, covering all operational phases. It is a problem of such magnitude and urgency that it is almost always separated from other print-medium services. In the Newark, New Jersey, organization chart shown in Chapter 8 in connection with the discussion of organizational patterns, we observe that there are three separate categories of functions under Library Services—Textbook Division, Board of Education Library, and School Libraries. Although we have already presented the nature of the Newark all-media service organization, we should emphasize that officially the name of the organization is Department of Libraries and Audiovisual Education. In the Los Angeles city-school districts, we note also two separate sections, Textbook and Library, each with its coordinate supervisor, both of which are coordinate with the supervisor of the Audio-Visual Section. The Los Angeles organization chart is also shown in Chapter 8. Textbook purchases involve enormous budgetary support, selection panels that must do painstaking analysis work, formal adoption procedures, and then finally procurement, storage, and distribution. Such plans call for professional leadership and management activities that cut across the entire school-district operational structure, involving participation by curriculum leaders, school principals, and teachers. Centralization procedures of optimum scope in light of volume of service required is apparently inescapable. Plans will vary greatly, as will the levels of involvement of the school library in each school. A carefully worked out plan of procedure for handling the selection and adoption of textbooks is that of the Newark, New Jersey, public schools. Since the plan is shown in relation to the Textbook Division of the Department of Libraries and Audiovisual Education,[18] we quote it in its entirety as follows:

Textbook Division
1. Reference collection of listed textbooks located in Textbook Library
2. Textbooks, maps and educational supplies submitted for evaluation by the committee

---

[18] *Handbook of the Department of Libraries and Audiovisual Education,* pp. 6–8. Newark, New Jersey: Board of Education. Dr. Edward T. Schofield, Director of the Department.

a. Secured and organized for evaluation by text-book staff

b. Copies available for reference; additional copies secured for Chairmen of Textbook Committees

3. Textbook evaluation committees appointed by the Superintendent of Schools

    a. Members—Elementary

      (1) Basic areas

        (a) Three principals—one to act as chairman for one year

        (b) One vice-principal—three-year term

        (c) Nine teachers—one from Special Education—three-year term

      (2) Special areas

        (a) Director or Supervisor to act as permanent chairman

        (b) Nine teachers—three-year term

    b. Members—Junior High

      (1) Basic areas (English, Mathematics, Science, Social Studies)

        (a) Chairman—a teacher—one year term

        (b) One or two teachers from each junior high school—three-year term

    c. Members—Secondary

      (1) Basic areas

        (a) Chairman—A department chairman—one-year term

        (b) One representative from each high school

        (c) Department chairmen permanently assigned

      (2) Special areas

        (a) Director or supervisor to act as permanent chairman

        (b) Two representatives from each high school

    d. Duties

      (1) Evaluate new or revised material submitted for approval

      (2) Check current listing for possible eliminations

      (3) Prepare report for Textbook Council

4. Textbook Council appointed by the Superintendent of Schools

    a. Members

      (1) Chairman designated by Superintendent of Schools

      (2) Deputy Superintendent

      (3) Assistant Superintendents (Secondary, Elementary and Special Services)

      (4) Director of Elementary Education

      (5) Director of Libraries and Audiovisual Education

      (6) Three principals, one each representing the elementary schools, the junior high schools, and the senior high schools

    b. Duties

      (1) Direct and integrate the work of the textbook evaluation committees

      (2) Receive and appraise the reports of the committees

      (3) Determine the number of additions and eliminations to be made

      (4) Present the final recommended list to the Superintendent of Schools for Board of Education approval.

Reference Books. Another aspect that is more closely tied in with organization of the various school-building library programs is the need to select, procure, catalog, store, and distribute reference books. Reference libraries are needed by every teacher—but, as we have pointed out—not every school has a good library. In these cases the supply of reference books to teachers for stipulated periods of use by their classes becomes a necessity, and many of these programs of supply are extensive. When school libraries are organized and their own collections are purchased, the central reference-book supply function may be decreased in scope, but may continue to carry on specialized loans to libraries and to teachers, or through school libraries to teachers. A major aspect of centralized print services in connection with reference books has to do with the purchasing process, thus serving as a clearing

Figure 12-11. This is one of San Diego's citywide reference-book processing areas. See also Figures 1-1 and 1-2. *Courtesy San Diego City Schools.*

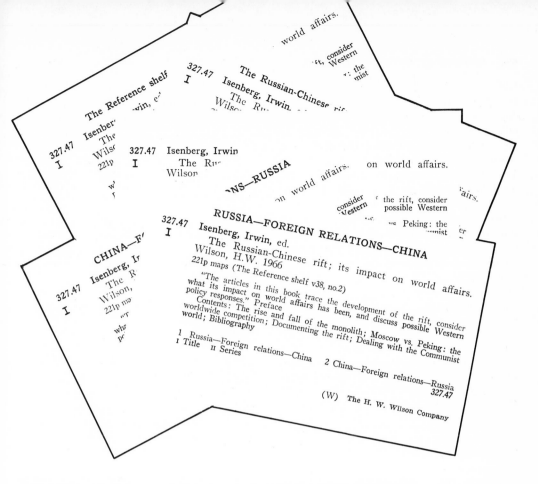

Figure 12-12. Every library book that is purchased has to be cataloged. Prior to its delivery to the purchaser, many important and time-consuming order processing tasks have to be performed. We show first a set of catalog cards that have been purchased from the H. W. Wilson Company. The next illustration shows the items available when a book is purchased that has already been cataloged. Note the following: 5 catalog cards, book card pocket, and borrower's card. The book then is delivered in its plastic binder, even with the spine tab with shelf number on it in place. (*Top illustration*, High School Library, North Haven, Connecticut. *Bottom illustration*, American Library and Educational Service Co., Glen Rock, New Jersey.)

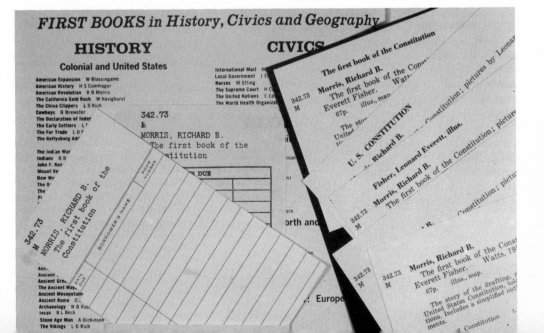

house for approved books. Such centralized operations are essential to eliminate costly duplication of effort in implementing approved business systems. Another major time-consuming process that must either be carried on centrally or in each school library is processing and cataloging. This function deserves special mention as one of the inescapable operations that ought to be solved at the district level.

Book Processing and Cataloging. The various standard processes that have to be carried on when a book is prepared for use in any given library is so time-consuming, yet vital, that creative steps should be taken to provide this print-medium service for school libraries. The American Library Association[19] gives the following explanation and recommendation:

In established libraries, the technical processing of one book, from the time when the invoice is checked to the time when the book is ready for the library shelf, takes as a minimum, 10 minutes of the librarian's time and 20 minutes of the time of a library clerk. . . .

When school systems have three or more schools, centralized processing should be introduced. . . .

Centralization of one or more of the processes of organization (ordering, receiving, equipping for circulation, classifying, and cataloging) insures economy of time and effort and also provides uniformity within the school system. It permits the librarian in the school to devote most of his time and professional skills to pupils and teachers. . . .

By the introduction of automation many of the laborious and repetitive tasks in the processing of library books may be speedily and accurately completed. For example, in the Los Angeles Library Section, the Catalog Department uses the IBM 870 Document Writing System for automatic production of typed sets of catalog cards. A key punched card, based on a cataloger's original, is fed automatically from a stack into the 836 control unit, a punched-card reader. This machine sends pulses to the three 866 typewriters which respond accordingly. Despite the fact that the Los Angeles school system with its K-14 school enrollment of approximately 800,000 students is somewhat larger than the situations in which a great many of us find ourselves, readers will be interested

in excerpts from a descriptive paper written by Mary S. Dodendorf, Librarian-in-charge of the centralized catalog department. (Refer also to Figure 12-13.) Excerpts are as follows:

The Catalog Department of the Los Angeles City Schools has the responsibility of providing cataloging services for the school libraries so that the librarians may have more time for their major responsibility which is working with students and teachers. . . . The catalog format must be that best suited for our students. It must be such that they may develop a skill in using the catalog which will give them confidence in using various types of public, college and university libraries everywhere. . . . Our librarians are free to order any titles which are needed in their individual schools and equally free to withdraw a title which is no longer useful in the collection. They are helped in their selection of books by lists of current titles which have been reviewed and evaluated by committees of librarians and teachers within our school system. . . .

Prior to the installation of our 870 System we had a number of production problems. The production of single sets of cards by manual typing, even on an electric typewriter, was slow and subject to error so that it was necessary to proof-read each card. The same conditions were true for manually typed offset masters. We were, and still are, using an A. B. Dick 350 Offset Duplicator to reproduce cards which we need in quantities of six or more. . . . We are unusually fortunate to have a cataloger who had had key punch training before she had joined our staff. She recognized what the IBM programmers confirmed which is that efficiency lies in giving one of our library clerks key punch training rather than in attempting to provide library background to a key punch operator. . . .

The greatest advantage of our 870 Document Writing System is that it is now possible for us to provide better service to our libraries on a more current basis. . . . No longer do we have a backlog of cards to be sent later after the books and the shelf lists have been received in the schools. We can now send the book with complete sets of cards, including the extensive analytics we need for collected biographies and some literary works. . . . We should not move too rapidly for we have the responsibility of providing catalog services in a format which the students will meet in public, university and special libraries as well as in their school libraries. Neither must we lag behind developments being made in other libraries. It is quite possible that as these developments occur we may change mightily. Computerized methods may better serve our needs in the future. We do not know in which direction we may swing, but at present we are moving books with appropriate catalog records more rapidly than

[19] *Op. cit.*, p. 52 footnote, and p. 112 footnote.

we used to be able to do. This is a service of greatest importance to our students. . . .

It is now widely known that reference books for library use may be purchased that have been processed with bookcard pocket, accurately numbered for shelf location, and accompanied at time of delivery by a set of catalog cards. See Figure 12-12. What must be realized is that some suppliers give this service on their books, and other suppliers do not. Thus, certain elementary school reference books may be sold with an additional processing charge, but some high school books may not be available with the same services. Hence, some books may have to be cataloged locally while others may come with one or more shelf-ready processes carried out. However, many books have been cataloged by publishers and by such agencies as the H. W. Wilson Company and the Library of Congress, so that sets of catalog cards may be purchased direct. These time-consuming processing activities may thus be minimized, but the fact still remains that in cases where a large volume of books is purchased annually for a specified number of school media centers, it will generally be more economical to set up centralized processing services.

The Supervision and In-Service Education Functions. We refer the reader once again to one of the earlier treatments of this important subject in Chapter 4. The particular orientation was of course that of audiovisual media; however, the general needs and processes are similar. We assert that such creative work with librarians, and the work done by librarians to work with their own staffs, will have great overall effects on the development of good print-medium services for pupils and teachers. Supervisory functions are inescapable, and very frequently the only promising route to success in this system-wide work is to centralize responsibility and leadership. We have already emphasized the fact that school librarians are generally responsible directly to the school principal, but these relationships do not preclude the kind of supervisory leadership that is desirable. One of the five major purposes of the Newark Department of Libraries and Audiovisual Education is as follows: *To assist in the development and supervision of libraries as centers of instructional materials in the individual*

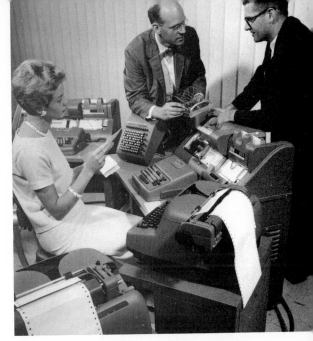

Figure 12-13. The Los Angeles cataloging department uses an IBM 870 Document Writing System similar to the one that is shown in this illustration. The Los Angeles unit uses three Typewriter Units. Results with this process are described in the text. *Courtesy Data Processing Division, IBM Corporation, Hartford Branch, Hartford, Connecticut.*

schools. The American Library Association[20] has formulated detailed statements regarding supervisory and in-service education work on a system-wide basis, and the following excerpts from its statement will be helpful:

In city school systems, in counties with a unified school system, and in co-operative arrangements involving two or more districts. . . . a functional program of school library supervision co-ordinates school library services, facilitates organizational procedures, and helps schools to reach optimum standards for their school libraries. The school library supervisor works with administrators, teaching staff, and other supervisors to provide better educational experiences for children and young people. The focus is always on the student: to help the teacher and the librarian to help the student, and to help the librarian to assist the classroom teacher. No matter what form supervisory services may take, whether they be curriculum committees, workshops, observation, or other activities, the focus remains the same. . . .

1. The school library supervisor serves as a consultant for and works with the chief administrator in such matters as:

[20] *Op. cit.*, pp. 42, 43, 44.

a. The use of school library instruction, services, and resources in implementing and enriching the total education program.

b. Methods for acquainting teachers with resource materials.

c. Planning and evaluating school library programs.

d. Staffing school libraries.

e. Planning library budgets.

f. Planning for basic collections of materials in the schools.

g. Planning library quarters.

h. Developing central purchasing, processing, and organizational procedures for library materials.

2. The school library supervisor has responsibility for:

a. Exerting leadership in creating an understanding of the role of the school library in curriculum development.

b. Interpreting the functions and needs of the school libraries in the school system.

c. Administering the school library budget as provided by the board of education and superintendent of schools.

d. Co-ordinating the program of library service and library instruction among the several schools.

e. Providing for the co-operative evaluation and selection of materials by school librarians, teachers, and curriculum specialists.

f. Directing the materials center. . . .

g. Directing the central acquisition and processing of materials. . . .

3. The school library supervisor works closely with supervisors and staff members in other departments of the central school office, and continuously provides advisory and co-operative services by means of:

a. Developing policies, procedures, and standards for the program of library services in the schools as related to all phases of the educational program.

b. Participating in curriculum study and evaluation, and recommending printed and other materials for resource units.

c. Serving as a consultant whenever needed.

d. Contributing to the in-service training of teachers.

e. Evaluating and recommending printed and audio-visual materials for purchase. If the school system maintains a separate department for audio-visual materials and services, the school library supervisor works closely with the director of that department and with members of his staff.

f. Providing library statistics, records, reports, and research.

4. The school library supervisor provides guidance and leadership in professional growth for the librarians in the school system by means of:

a. Giving advisory and consultant services, and having conferences with individual librarians about their library programs.

b. Planning in-service education through meetings, workshops, and conferences.

c. Encouraging librarians to participate with teachers, counselors, and others in solving problems of mutual concern.

d. Preparing bulletins, newsletters, and other aids for transmitting suggestions for library improvements and recirculating information about library developments.

e. Encouraging individual initiative in experimentation and research.

f. Promoting continuity of practice to assure uniformity of basic library procedures throughout the system, and at the same time encouraging continuous improvements and individual enterprise.

g. Making visits to the libraries in the schools.

h. Giving stimulation, evaluation, and sympathetic understanding to the school librarians.

5. The school library supervisor maintains a continuous program of evaluation by:

a. Analyzing and evaluating techniques and services in the school library programs and in the central office.

b. Measuring growth of the school libraries by local, state, and national standards.

c. Co-operating in national and state surveys.

d. Preparing reports and recommendations.

6. The school library supervisor maintains a program of good public relations by:

a. Co-operating with other libraries in the community in encouraging library use by pupils and adults.

b. Participating in civic projects relating to libraries, books, audio-visual materials, and reading, listening, and viewing.

c. Participating in professional education and library organizations at local, state, and national levels.

d. Contributing to professional journals and publications.

e. Providing professional and consultative service to individuals and community groups.

f. Interpreting school library service through all communication media.

This last excellent statement of duties of a supervisor of librarians and their staffs is indicative of the wide range of activities and the leadership responsibilities of the chief of library services, whoever he may be, at the school-district level. We can see that to be head of the print-medium services for a school district demands broad knowledge and insight into curriculum matters, and a full knowledge of the potential to make creative use of the rapidly developing field of information processing procedures.

The Professional Library Function. We have discussed earlier under the possible functions of the school library the development of professional library facilities. We see this important activity of school libraries as a branch of a main professional library organized and administered from the centralized school district organization. Of course in the absence of centralized facilitation, many school principals and other supervisory personnel help to inaugurate and maintain a professional library section of the library in each of the schools with which they are concerned. In fact, in well-developed and organized school-district library service sections, professional library facilities are set up as the only service center for teachers. Oftentimes, in these cases, curriculum centers are also organized and combined with professional books, local publications, and national publications. Thus, the patterns for implementing professional library services vary considerably from community to community. Since leadership is a prime prerequisite for effective in-service education, and since the professional library is a part of the atmosphere in a climate for staff growth, we see that the professional library will serve most effectively when there is an optimum balance in central and local school leadership concern for teacher growth, and an optimum balance in the availability of and accessibility to central and local professional collections.

The Printing and Publications Function. Administrators try to find someone, and sometimes in desperation, anyone, who will take on the job of printing and publication. Because of the essential character of this problem, administrators cannot avoid setting up an organization for the production of publications for the school system. One has to work quite hard at a rationale for organizing a publication production leadership. Many times, the Curriculum Center takes charge of printing curriculum guides, and in this case the various supervisors play an important part in their production for their unique purposes. In other instances, there is a formal publication section operating under an associate superintendent, with several additional departments cooperating, as for example, the audiovisual media organization providing artistic and graphic services. Hence, there are several ways, including the organization of publications under centralized library services sections, for meeting the needs of the school system. Whether this is organized under the library section or not, it is essential that appropriate editorial, graphic, and leadership services be provided to produce high-quality productions. As can be seen this publications problem is not necessarily an inescapable function in so far as the centralized print-medium services are concerned, but unique solutions to the problem will be sought continually.

Leadership for District Print-Medium Services

Having worked through the preceding identification and description of the necessary print-medium services, the conclusion can be drawn that leadership forces are essential to cope with the problems presented. Assignment of responsibility is an essential action on the part of the chief school administrator. As we have said earlier, some one person or group of people will have to accept in some measure at a specified level of service, a district-wide commitment. We can identify several of these methods and levels as follows:

Assign the district-wide print-medium service leadership task to

1. The elementary school supervisor for spearheading the development of all facilities in the elementary school libraries. In this case each school principal will be held responsible for development within his own school.

2. The secondary school supervisor for spearheading the development of all facilities in the secondary school libraries. Each principal in middle schools, junior high schools, and/or high schools will be held responsible for developments within their own schools.

3. The associate school superintendent, or to the administrative assistant for curriculum development, who will be in charge of the library development program and textbook selection with the cooperation of school

principals, preferably with centralized service facilities.

4. A director or supervisor of library services who will be in charge of the citywide program, all school principals cooperating, hopefully with centralized facilities and staff, for providing services.

5. A director or supervisor of instructional media who will administer the citywide program of print-medium services, all school principals cooperating, hopefully with centralized facilities and staff, for providing services.

There are several people who can assume the responsibility for development of print-medium services. All too frequently the district-wide program is handled on a stop-gap basis out of a brief case or a file cabinet and a budget folder. The more assignments the person in question has to carry out, the less the program is likely to prosper. Routes to accelerated growth and expansion of print-medium services in schools are most likely to be found in a concentration of leadership effort that is characterized by singleness of purpose and by positive action in councils where decisions on instructional strategy are being formulated.

Providing Space for District Print-Medium Services

On the basis of the foregoing discussion we can estimate that school systems will develop unique plans for providing print-medium services. If large cities or counties, they are likely to swing first toward centralized responsibility for services; if small cities, they are likely to swing first to decentralized responsibility with a minimum of central leadership and specific book services. Then, as programs in the schools gain momentum, the inauguration of centralized supervision and services are likely to arise to speed and give direction to school-library development at a new level of effectiveness. It is obvious that space, personnel, and financial support make acceleration possible in meeting library service needs. It is equally obvious that space needs will have to be estimated on the volume of service envisaged. We know from earlier discussions that automation of catalog-card typing and files of key-punched cards may take no more than 300 square feet, or a little more than an office space for a

librarian in a school library. However, space for other aspects of processing is also essential. By far the bulk of the needed space will be for book warehousing and processing, pending cataloging, and for storage pending distribution. Thus, unless adequate space is available at headquarters, the decentralization of receiving, logging in shipments, classifying, and other steps in the procedure had better be maintained in the various school-library units.

We have examined a number of basic organizational problems in connection with the development of adequate print-medium services. We have purposely concentrated attention on print-medium services rather than the broad spectrum of instructional media activity. We now are in a good position to make accurate observations about the needs of all phases of media service, both print and nonprint, thus possibly avoiding many serious errors in school-building planning. We have also indicated from time to time that some school administrators seek to combine print and audiovisual media services in all-media service centers and in so doing, spread their resources too thinly in the attempt to offer too much for too many. The result is overextension, disenchantment, and mediocrity in instructional processes. Optimum balance in assigning available financial support is not easy to attain. Moreover, the kind of wisdom needed in making such decisions is often hindered by not understanding the roles that various media can play, and by a lack of required technical information. It is time, at any rate, to ask the important question which gave rise to this chapter in the first place: What is the nature of possible participation of media specialists and program directors in providing print-medium services?

Participation of Media Generalists and Specialists in Print-Medium Programs

Because we have separately focused attention on many of the functions of audiovisual and print media programs in schools, we can answer the important question we have raised with considerable clarity. School district administrators are the ones who will have to struggle with the problem and reach the wisest and best decision. We shall deal first of all with the problem rather broadly, even at the expense of repeating ourselves, having discussed the problem in Chapters 7 and 8.

Organization and Control of District-Wide Print Services

Even in the absence of central leadership for audiovisual media service, school principals may organize and implement their own separate organizations for giving teachers the help they need with instructional technology. They may also, in the absence of central library services, organize and implement a fine school library. They may also combine both types of services, remodel buildings, take an insightful and informed view of media-use needs and provide space, staff, and support. They may call the new center by a variety of names. In any case it is only a matter of time before school-building leaders realize that to get optimum growth and balance in the programs they wish to develop, they need to call for and get central leadership, facilities, and support. We therefore face squarely the problem of recommending a pattern for organizing media services.

Recommending Patterns of Organization for Media Services. It is not likely that a school superintendent will find the problem of choosing to combine all media services or to set up *separate* service organizations an easy one to solve. His greatest problem will arise when he decides to choose the leader for a *combined* media-services program. In that case he must make certain that the person he chooses has the needed pedagogical, technological, leadership, innovative, and planning capabilities to make wise decisions for the good of all pupils. Should he combine two problems and try to reduce the result to one? This is the dilemma. How is it resolved? We must first recognize that print-medium services are indispensable and will become even more important than they are now in the years ahead. This is also true of audiovisual media. They are looked upon now in an entirely new light, playing roles in the teaching process that are of such magnitude that even teachers themselves become free for new tasks while the media they employ take control. Each of these major services requires specific skills and insights on the part of those who are to provide the leadership. If it is

desirable to combine the services for valid reasons, other than expediency, or to cut one or the other of the programs back in its progress, or to set up a control process to preserve, for example, a given predetermined level, the person with the broadest skills for the jobs that have to be done, should be chosen. The next step will then be to employ an additional staff member, a media specialist, to complement the work of the generalist on a district-wide level.

School District Participation

Should the audiovisual media leader be given the responsibility for the print-medium services program? The answer is, "Yes," if he knows more about the school library service than the head librarian knows about audiovisual media technology, other factors being equal. Should the head librarian be given charge on a district-wide basis over the audiovisual media program in addition to the print-medium services? The answer is, "Yes," if he is better qualified in the field of media than the audiovisual media person is with respect to the library program. We need not "go round the mulberry bush" again. Both aspects of the problem are based on preparation for meeting responsibilities. The audiovisual media leader, in such instances as are likely to arise, should be expected to prepare himself for print-service responsibility, with a view toward possible leadership in working with school principals and other curriculum personnel in developing libraries. If there is the chance to prepare, the print-medium services leader ought to do the same in the audiovisual media field. Unless this action can be taken to a high degree, the positions should be kept separate.

There are cases, at a given level of comprehensiveness and scope, where an associate superintendent of schools cannot, or should not, cope with the decisions of coordination of two leaders in thriving fields, namely, print-medium services and audiovisual media services. At this point there is the need for combination administratively under the directorship of a broadly insightful leader who will have at his disposal resources of specialized leadership. No one knows at what point such action should be taken. Chief school administrators working with their curriculum leaders and advisory councils will have to reach the decision as to the best qualified individual on their citywide staffs that can handle such an assignment and deserves the opportunity to try. In these instances, the audiovisual media program leader does not, nor does the library expert, have a right to a position of leadership. Participation becomes an earned opportunity. Work needs to be done on problems of preparation for such eventualities. The same holds true for the distinguished library specialist. We should not fail to note that the type of centralized organization decided upon will have inescapably an influence on the kind of school-building centers for media service that are established. Here is where media services pay off, as we have emphasized, because it is at the teaching station where the roles of media are carried out.

School Building Participation

Having said already that both print- and nonprint-media services are indispensable in the modern school, we face the need to provide them both according to local needs. Again the audiovisual media specialist may be so hard pressed by technologically oriented programs that he cannot undertake to administer additional print-medium staff members were he to be assigned the additional responsibilities for new services. Librarians feel the same way, but indicate the need for enough additional librarians who can share the work. The American Library Association[21] puts it this way when discussing full responsibility by librarians for the school's audiovisual program:

Full responsibility means the direction of the complete audio-visual program in the school, including: frequent consultation, guidance, and planning with teachers regarding the use of audio-visual materials in classroom instruction; formulating and implementing the integrated program of teaching students how to use audio-visual materials effectively; the examination, evaluation, and selection of materials; technical processing. . . . production of audio-visual materials; planning the school's use of television and radio programs; directing clerks in the maintenance of materials and equipment; and many other related activities. . . .

The recommendation that the size of the school library staff be increased by 25–50 per cent to perform this part of the library program should not be interpreted as meaning the appointment of additional staff whose work would be confined

21 *Op. cit.*, p. 54 footnote.

solely to audio-visual materials and services. The intention is that the work would be distributed among the library staff members and that they would have the competencies needed in relation to audio-visual materials, services, and program planning. . . .

The school principal or central media program leader has but to ascertain the existence of such skills as are required for the kinds of services that are needed throughout the school in advanced technological installations, before he makes his staff additions. We assert that no one class of professional workers has a right to a given professional position. It is professional preparation, experience, and a record of success on the job that are the criteria for decision. Therefore, in view of the previous quotation, we need not be forced to choose between a librarian and an audiovisual media specialist. We do need to choose an individual who is qualified. Unless the audiovisual media specialist is able to carry out print-medium services, he should not be given the position, and unless qualified persons are available, the services should be kept separate on a coordinate basis, each with adequate support in terms of the needs that have to be met, and both effectively integrated at the next higher level of administration. Refer also to footnotes 1 and 8.

Qualifications for Functions

The central audiovisual media program director should be a trained professional media specialist, and for such posts we have repeatedly stressed the indispensability of skill as an administrator, as a teacher, and as a technological expert. His insight and skill equip him to work in problem-solving situations that involve all three aspects. This person, being a specialist, may not be qualified, nor is it likely that he will have the time to become intimately involved in school library development. The same holds true for the school-building audiovisual media coordinator. Combination may in many cases be little more than an act of administrative expediency, operating satisfactorily *only until technology reaches an advanced stage.* The administrative distribution of the many and critical audiovisual media duties among five librarians or assistant librarians, for example, may not be the answer at all. A quick perusal of the problems in reaching a decision on local transmission of instructional television programs would indicate that prolonged and concentrated effort may have to be exerted. Programing multimedia presentations, and working with a group of teachers on the design and production of an instructional system for language instruction are other examples among many. Print-medium specialists who also have become experienced audiovisual experts and teachers will be the object of intensive search in the years ahead, and this will be equally true of audiovisual media specialists who have become print-medium experts. There is no easy answer to this problem in staffing media-service centers. We ought not to forget, however, that leadership is needed to design action in light of objectives, reach complicated decisions, energize the system, and make it work.

Problem-Solving Activities

1. Prepare in brief form two lists of specific *print-medium* services that ought to be given to teachers and pupils by a good school library, categorized under the following headings: *For Pupils; For Teachers.*

2. Identify several specific audiovisual media services that are likely to be given by a school library to pupils that may be considered to be along the lines of, or closely related to, print-medium services.

3. When a given school library is an instructional media center, what media services does it offer to teachers?

4. Write out in approximately a hundred words the modern concept of a school library as developed by the American Library Association. What are some basic technological skills that librarians must possess or develop in order to implement that concept, in light of the content presented in this book?

5. State succinctly in approximately a hundred words the modern concept of an audiovisual media specialist. Can such a person also be certified, in a state that requires it, as a librarian? Under what conditions?

6. Bearing in mind the answers to Questions 4 and 5 preceding, prepare a plan for providing on an in-service education basis the additional skills that an instructional technology expert ought to develop to become the coordinator of an advanced school-building instructional resources center. Prepare another plan, similar in nature, for school librarians to become the coordinators of advanced instructional materials center programs including such processes as the design of programed media for instructional system use.

7. Make a scaled sketch of the space allotments you would recommend for the construction of a comprehensive instructional materials center in a school for 1,000 pupils in grades K-6. Be sure to include in your plans space for all recommended print-medium services as well as the arrangements for instructional technology including a school-building television studio for producing and distributing videotapes, and ample storage for instructional system media packages. Label the spaces and give the area in square feet. Bear in mind functions and their relationships to staff and school services. (This project should be implemented by task forces exploring unique arrangements, such as combination uses of space and separate but ideally related spaces.)

8. Prepare succinct statements of what we can refer to as the old and new roles of media for teaching, as we have indicated them in this book, especially in Chapter 11. Now identify the specific major services that should be provided by the various specialists working in an instructional materials center to implement these roles in the school.

9. Choose any school-building instructional materials center with which you are familiar and proceed to prepare a case study featuring the critical analysis and evaluation of its services for teachers and pupils. Present your analysis in class as a visualized report. (Students or committees may split up the work, submitting duplicated copies to participants.)

10. The need for carrels has been repeatedly stressed for study purposes. What is the advantage of having three or four, or even 16 electronic carrels in the school library? How may 16 carrels serve 500 students? How can it be determined how many electronic carrels are needed? What is the advantage of locating carrels close to clusters of classrooms, or as a special teacher-controlled facility, or as a special laboratory installation? Prepare a set of scaled sketches based on a case study of a specific school situation with which you are familiar.

11. Why is it likely that the nature of the leadership position and the person himself (including the nature of the organizational pattern for both audiovisual media and print services) will have a bearing on operations in the individual schools of the district?

12. Is it likely that the invention of combining print-medium and technological-media services is successful only so long as media serve only the traditional roles? If so, as technological development advances, and as it is increasingly applied to direct teaching processes, will the combination of technological media with print services give rise to the need for separation for optimum expansion? If not likely, then what recommendations should be made in light of radically increased implementation of media looming on the horizon? (Participate in one or more task forces to identify and list possible strengths and weaknesses inherent in the one-roof combination of media services. Put committee reports through an editorial committee for checking, collation, and duplication for distribution.)

References

American Association of School Librarians. *Standards for School Libraries.* (Chicago: The American Library Association, 50 East Huron Street, 1960).

American Association of School Librarians (A Division of ALA). *Selecting Materials for School Libraries: Guidelines and Selection Sources to Insure Quality Collections.* (Washington, D.C.: The National Education Association, 1965).

Bergeson, Clarence O. "Relationship of Library Science and Audiovisual Instruction." *Audiovisual Instruction*, Vol. 12, No. 2, February 1967, pp. 100–103.

Darling, Richard L. *Survey of School Library Standards.* (Prepared in cooperation with the U.S. Office of Education.) (Washington, D.C.: The Superintendent of Documents, U.S. Government Printing Office, 1964).

DeBernardis, Amo, Victor W. Doherty, Errett Hummel, and Charles W. Brubaker. *Planning Schools for New Media.* (Prepared under a contract with the U.S. Office of Education, 1961.) (Washington, D.C.: Superintendent of Documents, U.S. Government Printing Office, 1962).

Douglas, Mary Teresa Peacock. *The Teacher-Librarian's Handbook*, 2nd ed. (Chicago: American Library Association, 1949).

Ellsworth, Ralph E. and Hobart D. Wagener. *The School Library: Facilities for Independent Study in the Secondary School.* (New York: Educational Facilities Laboratories, Inc., 477 Madison Avenue, 1963).

————. *School Library.* (New York: The Center for Applied Research in Education, 70 Fifth Ave., 1966).

Fargo, Lucile Foster. *The Library in the School*, 4th ed. (Chicago: American Library Association, 1947).

Giesy, John P. "A Working Relationship." *Audiovisual Instruction*, Vol. 10, No. 9, November 1965, pp. 706-708.

Hopkinson, Shirley L. *The Descriptive Cataloging of Library Materials.* (San Jose, California: Claremont House, 1963).

Iverson, Maurice, Loran C. Twyford, Jr., and James A. Boula. "Certification of Media Specialists: Illinois, New York, and Wisconsin." *Audiovisual Instruction*, Vol. 12, No. 2, February 1967, pp. 116-119.

Mahar, Mary Helen (ed.). *The School Library as a Materials Center.* (Proceedings of a conference under the auspices of the U.S. Department of Health, Education, and Welfare, Office of Education, Washington, D.C., May 16-18, 1962.) (Washington, D.C.: Superintendent of Documents, Government Printing Office, 1963).

Miles, Bruce and Virginia Jenkins. "IMC's: A Dialogue." *Audiovisual Instruction*, Vol. 10, No. 9, November 1965, pp. 688-691.

Standards for School Media Programs. In process by a Joint Committee. Scheduled for release late 1968. Available from the participating organizations, AASL and DAVI. (Washington, D. C.: The Associations, NEA).

Trenholme, A. K. "Diagram of Staff Relationship, Portland Public Schools." *Audiovisual Instruction*, Vol. 12, No. 2, February 1967, pp. 138-139.

Wedberg, Desmond P. "Microforms for Independent Study." *Audiovisual Instruction*, Vol. 12, No. 5, May 1967, pp. 435-438.

Wofford, Azile. *The School Library at Work;*

Acquisition, Organization, Use and Maintenance of Materials in the School Library. (New York: H. W. Wilson Co., 1959).

————. *Book Selection for School Libraries*. (New York: H. W. Wilson Co., 1962).

13

Budgeting for Media-Service Programs

The infusion of federal funds through the approved plans of state departments of education into school-district budgets for the purchase of media materials and equipment, introduced an entirely new dimension into media-program financing. Starting in 1958 under National Defense Education Act legislation, the virtual flood of federal spending for media materials and equipment, at first specifically for science, foreign languages, and mathematics, soon spread to additional subject areas at both elementary and secondary levels. A new image of what modern education meant in terms of technology and a strengthening of the feeling of responsibility to make new educational opportunities available to all our youth in our critical times, were the inevitable results.

Even so, some school districts either did not, or believed they could not, take full advantage of early NDEA grants because of the matching stipulation, and such budgets as they had set up were so pitifully small that even to double them made no great headway against the magnitude of the need. Fortunately many other school systems were ready for this development, and they moved quickly to double and triple their former media budgets. The more recent legislative acts and state plans without matching requirements, which provided a full potential for creative programing effort, offered a welcomed breadth of coverage and influence. We shall therefore be ever mindful of this new dimension in financing potential as we discuss the topic of this chapter. In a later section, we shall deal specifically with the major aspects of obtaining maximum support for the media programs that federal and state legislation provide. In discussing the financial aspects of media-service programs, we direct the attention of the media director to the problems associated with the business management of the school district. We refer to the budget and the budgeting process. The media administrator must help make up the budget, administer it, and now, must help finance the costs by submitting proposals for programs that will be in part financed by funds from sources outside of the district. Every budget request submitted by a director of media services ought to be, for any given year, the wisest possible financial plan to pay for the contributions of media to the attainment of instructional objectives. Actually, as will be made clear later, the budget for any fiscal year should be viewed as an annual segment of a long-term operational plan designed to reach goals of service which have been ascertained through painstaking cooperative study and analysis in terms of a local situation.

As he approaches his work on the budget, the director should keep in mind the obvious fundamental relationship between educational needs, costs involved in meeting needs, and financing. If, for example, it has been agreed by planning groups that a teacher-made media design and preparation program should be inaugurated, the media administrator must determine the costs of extra equipment, supplies, technical-staff services, in-service education activities, and even the cost for remodeling existing spaces that have been assigned by school principals. However, having determined the costs and having incorporated a request for a specific amount of money to make the required purchases and payments in the next year's budget, there still remains the task of obtaining the necessary funds from his administrative superiors who, in turn, must obtain revenues from tax levies. If such requests for funds are denied, and if the media director, with the advice of his colleagues deems it necessary to do so, he may proceed to meet the new needs partially or fully by spending funds originally allotted for other purposes, he may obtain money from sources outside the school system, or he may have to put off further action on the problem until another opportunity presents itself to make a new request for funds.

The main purpose of this chapter is to assist media program executives in making good decisions about budget preparation and administration. Although these decisions demand good business sense, they are first and foremost a product of the ability to identify needs and the ability to plan to meet those needs at an optimum tempo.

Discovery of Needs and Determination of Costs

In preceding chapters the media-service program has been described in terms of materials, equipment, and assistance for improving the quality of learning experiences in the classroom. The central school-system media headquarters was pointed out as a pumping station with pipelines of service to teaching stations in each school, where in turn subsidiary centers of service were operating to facilitate the work of teachers. The entire service program, insofar as budgeting procedures are concerned, may be looked upon as being temporarily arrested in its development, or locked into a position that can be altered only slightly, until a new fiscal year and a new plan of operation at a new and hoped-for higher plateau of support can be procured. This means that perceived needs can be fulfilled only when financial support makes possible the additional staff, media, and facilities. Therefore, the director must take steps to get the facts about needs, determine the cost for meeting them, decide how long it will take to reach desired operational levels of need-fulfillment, and then make his budget requests accordingly. Of course it is discouraging to make an analysis of this sort only to find that funds are not available. However, there is no other good way of relating a current budget request to the long-range service goals. The media director should be wary of playing guessing games. He needs to know how much the local service program will cost at any desired level of operation. An example of the process follows.

Operational Levels and Their Costs

As an example of the way the cost determination process needs to be carried out we have chosen to use as a unit for computation a 1,600-pupil middle school that planners have agreed should have something like ninety teaching stations, not including conference rooms, service suites, and the divisible auditorium. We ourselves have deliberately added to the basic building plans, in view of this example, two special learning laboratories. This situation is of course hypothetical, but general concepts of need and so-called minimum standards have also been taken into consideration in specifying what we have referred to as an *adequacy* level. In fact, adequacy, short of saturation, depends on the given program in a given school unit. It is the instructional need that ought to be met, and this need develops in the light of instructional processes and the particular capabilities of a particular group of teachers under the conditions of a given school district. We should emphasize the fact that for the purposes of this example we shall itemize the costs for audiovisual media equipment, materials and services only. We therefore exclude costs of the school's print-medium program, and we also exclude from this treatment the costs associated with centralized media services.

Limitations of the Example. Since there is no real standard, we must point out that only in a given set of circumstances can a true need be estimated. However, we should make a professional attempt to provide optimum conditions for the attainment of valid instructional objectives, and therefore we need to work toward adequacy, toward a general capability for action. The example used in this instance is a hypothetical one in part, and the specific recommendations are arrived at by means of estimated present as well as future needs. Readers therefore may seek to predict on their own an entirely different level for media operations. They may choose, for example, to base their estimate on any one of the specific examples shown in this text thus far, may choose a school with a known set of operational conditions, or they may actually visit a school to make a personal survey. Comparisons could be made between old schools and new schools, those operating at a minimum media-use level or at a media-use *saturation* level, schools with or without team-teaching operations, schools with or without media-preparation centers, schools making full or minimum use of instructional systems, schools using or not using instructional television, schools with or without group-response systems, multimedia presentations, and computer-assisted instruction programs. The point we are making is that cost determination is a process that is essential in the life of a media specialist, as it is for any administrator. Perhaps we should caution the reader against the use of the school cost or the per-pupil cost for the media program envisaged in the school that we have chosen, in the sense of its being directly applicable to any other school in a generalized way. We must refer to the cost figure, if we use the predicted total at all, in light of the given set of circumstances portrayed. There is

no doubt, however, that the use of a single school unit, with a given number of pupils, teachers, and teaching stations may facilitate some thinking that will have benefits for us all, especially as we look to the future. Now let us note carefully the steps in the process, with relation to the basic figures shown in Table 13-1. We have already pointed out that readers could easily establish their own levels for determining a new cost base.

Steps in the Cost-Determination Process. Steps in a process of cost determination, according to the recommended procedure, would be to

1. Make a complete survey to determine the present status of facilities, equipment, and materials.

2. Ascertain needs for new services.

3. Establish priorities for adding new services.

4. Establish operational levels based on (a) present status of staff and facilities; (b) improved status, that is, a *desirable minimum, or basic level*; or (c) a five-year-growth service level that approximates an "adequacy level," where all classrooms have been equipped with light-control systems, screens, and outlets, and teachers rarely find it impossible to obtain the equipment they need, and further where there are a number of fixed installations for television production and the facilitation of instructional systems.

5. Tabulate data and project costs into the future for the following aspects of the service program: (a) purchase of facilities and equipment; (b) rental of motion pictures; (c) purchase of materials to be distributed; (d) media or equipment replacement for both mobile and fixed installations; (e) servicing media equipment units and materials; (f) supplies for media production; (g) leadership and staff.

6. Formulate a system of installation cards for each school so that proper equipment and facilities will be scheduled for assignment to specific rooms and buildings in accordance with long-term plans.

7. Treat new construction as entirely separate, and either provide complete facilities and equipment at the time of construction or increase the regular budget sufficiently each year to provide for new buildings as well as the old.

Cost Estimates for Purchase of Media Equipment

In Table 13-1, on the following page, we show various phases of a media-service program. If we consider a basic media-equipment service for teaching stations, the total for our *adequacy* level amounts to $140,580. This would amount to $1,202 per teacher, or approximately $88 per pupil. If we consider the particular media design and preparation service represented, the cost figure will climb by $9,230, which represents a per-teacher cost of about $79, or a per-pupil cost of $6. Now, if we consider such additional features as instructional television, instructional systems, and multimedia presentations, all of which require fixed installations, we then must face a cost that has climbed by an additional $132,000. This would mean a per-teacher cost of $1,128, and a per-pupil cost of about $83. It can be seen that this latter phase adds an entirely new dimension to the cost figures, since it almost equals both of the preceding phases of equipment service combined.

But we should not forget to include media equipment for the school library and main auditorium (not including a smaller teaching auditorium that we already indicated when we included a multimedia presentation center). If we include both of these facilities in our estimates we must again face a substantial increase that amounts to a total of $38,000. Breaking down this total into per-teacher and per-pupil costs respectively, we get $325 and $24.75.

Now totaling the five phases of the example, we get the grand total of $319,810. The per-teacher cost on this basis amounts to approximately $2,733, and the per-pupil cost would be $200. The total cost as indicated may be met at once as for a new building, or it may have to be pro-rated over a developmental period from a given level of operation to a new one. We should neither be amazed nor apprehensive over the cost of modern equipment for the essential process of education. In any modern industrial plant that can be identified, it is likely that the equipment cost per worker is so great that the $2,733 per teacher we have indicated for basic media is insignificant by comparison.

Estimated Annual Cost for the School's Rental of Motion Pictures

Some Comments About the Problem. If, as has been pointed out, well-supplied schools use audiovisual media equipment in at least 50 per cent of all class periods during the day, and that much higher levels of use are in the offing we know that a steady stream of media materials will be moving in and out of supply sources to the school. Some of the collections will be located permanently in the school, others in centralized service depositories, but other items will have to be procured from short-term rental suppliers. Since most schools will not have resources comprehensive enough to meet all of their important needs for media subjects, they will have to procure them by renting, and costs for this service have been rising steadily. We cannot deny to teachers the valid use of significant and basal uses of rental items during interim periods when, for example, local resources are being built up or when desired media such as films are being electronically rerecorded on tape for repetitive use. Hence, there is a continuing need for a given level of rental-media service, and the medium that will most frequently be involved is motion pictures. Teaching plans, teacher competence levels and interest, and local resources will tend to establish a specified volume and hence a given cost. We alluded above to electronic rerecording of such media subjects as films. The cost for such action on the part of school personnel has not yet been established; however, it is certain that even though schools have stocks of the videotape needed, producers are not likely to permit the disregard of copyright laws simply because the purposes are instructional in nature. Producers may even supply their media materials in different forms, that is, either on films for regular projection, or on videotape to facilitate electronic manipulation. We shall therefore have to consider such electronic rerecording of media materials as an aspect of purchasing cost.

Summary of the Estimate. If we assume the existence of a motion picture distribution service in the district, we can estimate that each of the 117 teachers in the school we are using in our example would need to procure on the average three significant film subjects from sources outside the school system during the

Table 13-1. Cost Estimates for Media Equipment Units in a Single School Building (A Middle School Housing 1,600 Pupils in 92 Teaching Stations, with a Total Teaching Staff of 117)

Kinds of Media Equipment	Estimated Units Needed for Adequacy Level	Unit Cost	Total Cost
Media Equipment Units for School-wide Use			
1. Light-Control System in Each Teaching Station	92	$300	$27,600
2. Two Double Electrical Outlets (Four in New Construction)	184	30	5,520
3. Projection Screens (Wall-mounted, One minimum)	92	60	5,520
4. Mobile Projection Stands or Permanent Pedestals, One Minimum	92	35	3,220
5. Motion Picture Projectors, Standard Models. Some on long-term assignment	46	600	27,600
6. Motion Picture Projectors, Cartridge Type, 8mm	20	90	1,800
7. Filmstrip and 2 × 2 inch Slide Projectors (Combination Models)	60	100	6,000
8. Automatic Remote-Control 2 × 2 inch Slide Projectors	30	120	3,600
9. Tachistoscopic Projectors, 35mm	30	250	7,500
10. Slide Projectors, $3\frac{1}{4} \times 4$ inches	15	150	2,250
11. Overhead Transparency Projectors, Heavy Duty Models	50	400	20,000
12. Overhead Transparency Projectors, Lightweight Models	42	160	6,720
13. Opaque Projectors	5	350	1,750
14. Tape Recorders, Classroom, Manual-Control Model	50	200	10,000
15. Portable, 10-station Tape Listening Units with Plug-in Jacks and Headsets	15	450	6,750
16. Record Players, with Plug-in Boxes and Headsets if needed	20	200	4,000
17. Portable Public Address Systems	3	250	750
Subtotal			$140,580
Media Preparation Equipment			
18. Still Picture Cameras, Single Lens Reflex Model with Copy Stands and Attached Lights, including Exposure Meter, Close-up Lenses and Adaptor Rings and Blue Filter	3	$280	$840
19. Still Picture Cameras and Light Meter with Carrying Case for Loan to Teachers and Student Groups for Class Projects	2	150	300
20. Slide Duplicating Unit (such as Heiland Repronar, with Accessories)	1	360	360
21. Motion Picture Camera with Turret and Three Lenses, or Zoom Lens, and Carrying Case for Clip Production, plus Heavy-Duty Tripod, and Several Lights	1	850	850
22. Still Picture Cameras, Polaroid, with Copying Stand and Lights	1	250	250
23. Still Picture Camera, Polaroid, MP-3 Model, Reflex Unit with Stand and Lights, and with an Additional Special Lens for 2 × 2 inch Slides	1	800	800
24. Dry-Process Copier, Single-Sheet Model	4	400	1,600
25. Dry-Process Copier for Using Intermediate Sheets for Use with Books and Booklets	2	380	760
26. Diazo-coated Transparency-Making Equipment, Including Exposing and Developing Units	2	300	600
27. Dry Press for Mounting Pictures and Laminating Work. Commercial Model	2	300	600
28. Paper Cutters (24″ and 15″)	2	40	80
29. Primer-Size Type Typewriter	1	250	250
30. Motorized Spirit Duplicator	2	370	740
31. Tape Recorders (for High Fidelity Programs) Portable	2	600	1,200
Subtotal			$9,230

Kinds of Media Equipment	Estimated Units Needed for Adequacy Level	Unit Cost	Total Cost
Instructional Television Production and Systems Utilization			
32. Television Studio Package Including 2 Vidicon Cameras, 2 Video Tape Recorders with Electronic Editor, Lights, Console, Multiplexer, Monitors	1		$25,000
33. Mobile Television Recorder-Playback Unit for Classroom Use (Vidicon Camera, Video Tape Recorder, 23″ TV Receiver)	2	$6,000	12,000
34. Coaxial-Cable ITV Distribution System Throughout School (Two-Way Jacks)	1		4,600
35. A Television Receiver with mobile stand or cradle mount in Each of the Teaching Stations (Multiple receivers or projection television units as needed are not included)	92	200	18,400
36. Electronic Learning Laboratory, 30-position Dial-Retrieval Process for Audio Programs, and for Full Recording and Comparison Operations (Largely for Language)	1	$600 per booth	18,000
37. Electronic Learning Laboratory Equipped with Audio Tape and Programed Projection, as for Systems Instruction. Minimum of 40 Positions. (Cartridge-Type Motion Picture Projector, including Small Console to Provide Programed Master Tape Capability)	1	$650 per booth	26,000
38. Automatically Operated Multimedia System in the Teaching Auditorium, including Group-Response System Units at 300 Seats. Media Instrumentation to include Film, Slide and Programed Tape Capability. (Wired for later Installation of Computer-Recording Analysis and Reporting Unit)	1		28,000
Subtotal			$132,000
Media Equipment in School Library			
(Regular media equipment to be assigned to library classroom)			
39. Electronically Equipped Carrels in Clusters, Totaling 30 Positions for Individualization Activities, Near Reference and Study Areas.		$650 per carrel	$19,500
40. Carrels for Micro-form Reading and Study Activity, 30 Positions, Near Reference and Study Areas.		$400 per carrel	12,000
Subtotal			$31,500
Main Auditorium Media Equipment			
(Not including permanently installed public address system)			
41. Motion Picture Projector (Auditorium Model)	2	$1,500	$3,000
42. Overhead Projector (Heavy-Duty Model)	1	600	600
43. Slide Projector (Auditorium Model, Combination $3\frac{1}{4}$″ × 4″ and 2″ × 2″ Slides)	2	400	800
44. Motorized, Auditorium Projection Screen	1	600	600
45. Tape Recorder (Matched to Sound System)	1	1,500	1,500
Subtotal			$6,500
Grand Total			$319,810

school year. This would amount to a total of 351 shipments to be received, and at an average cost of $5 for each shipment, the total predicted cost would amount to $1,755. The per-teacher cost would amount to $15, and the per-pupil cost would be $1.10. A great many factors have a bearing on the reduction of this cost, yet in a school as well equipped as we have urged, the interest and commitments on the part of the staff will run at a high media-use level. There-fore, unless the local resources are unusually great, the cost figure, on average, is a reasonable one. Since increased availability of media equip-ment and building facilities would increase the demand by teachers, the need for greater outlay for media materials ought to be provided for in successive years. However, as the collection of

school-owned media increases in size, it is likely that the outlay for rented media subjects will decrease. Because the demand ought to increase steadily during a given development period, the cost for rental of media should at least be maintained at the proposed level. It would be reasonable to expect that at the end of a developmental period for acquisition of media collections the cost of media rental would decline considerably.

Cost Estimates for Purchase of Media Materials

Since it is generally accepted procedure for school districts to centralize the distribution of motion picture subjects, we shall include only

Table 13-2. Cost Estimates for Purchase of Media Materials for use in a Single Building (A Middle School Housing 1,600 Pupils in 92 Teaching Stations, with a Total Staff of 117 Teachers)

Media Subjects	Estimate of Units (Adequacy Level) Needed at the School	Estimate of Unit Cost	Estimate of Total Cost
Media Materials for General Use			
(Not including Science Apparatus and Maps for Social Science)			
Filmstrips	2,000	$5	$10,000
Audio-Program Tapes and Records (Commercial, not Teacher-Made)	550	3	1,650
Slide Sets (Commercial, not Teacher-Made)	200	5	1,000
Study Print Sets	200	4	800
Globes (Floor and Desk)	40	50	2,000
Transparencies (Commercial, not Teacher-Made)	500	4	2,000
Subtotal			$17,450
Media Packages for Specific Systems Applications, but Estimated in Terms of a Base Medium			
Videotape Sets (1″, 4 half-hour tapes each)	50	$600	$30,000
8mm Cartridge Film Sets (10 Films Each)	50	80	4,000
Audio-Program Tape Sets (20 tapes each, Manual or Cartridge, as for Electronic Learning Labs)	50	60	3,000
Slide Sets (30 Slides Each)	100	15	1,500
Filmstrip Sets, Silent (4 Filmstrips Each)	100	12	1,200
Filmstrip Sets, Sound (4 Filmstrips Each)	100	20	2,000
Subtotal			$41,700
Grand Total			$59,150

major kinds of media materials that are normally assigned to school buildings as a part of the school's own collection. The reader should not, however, lose sight of the impact that the implementation of instructional systems is likely to have on the purchase of media materials for permanent storage at the school building. Such desirable developments may introduce another new dimension into the acceleration of cost increases. We should point out again that we are now discussing the problem of cost determination as a problem in budgeting, not the problem of who should pay, or against whose budget (the media center's or the school's) the purchases should be charged. We are considering the costs of audiovisual media support in the light of a specific school building, and this in turn may help in clarifying the nature of district-wide budgeting problem. Media to be loaned to all schools are therefore not included in Table 13-2, but rather, only those media materials that are to be or have been already assigned for use by a given group of teachers.

We should emphasize the futility of attempting to set up a true example of the cost for purchase of media materials because of the many variables involved. For example, we have two sets of circumstances that may alter completely the dimensions of cost. One of these is general-use media, the other is the storage at the school of media packages that may involve special combinations of sets of media by means of which a part, or several parts, of a course may be taught. We are referring, of course, to the media components of a given instructional system. In this particular example, then, we do not hesitate to speculate somewhat in some of our predictions and estimates, but we have already indicated our reasons for setting forth the example in the first place. Thus it would be appropriate for the reader to be critical of the estimates provided in Table 13-2, but in case judgments are negative, he should relate his ideas to advanced operational programs that provide a flow of media to meet significant and basal instructional needs. We should point out that videotapes may cost $68 per hour just for the tape (2-inch width), and audio tape may be bought in large quantities for a fraction of the advertised list prices. Hence it is hazardous to estimate costs for a videotape series, but

obviously we are assuming that the producer of the videotape is charging for the content, just as he would if the content were on film, or on a filmstrip. This has been the basis for our estimates, and of course such costs are likely to vary greatly from our figures. In the example we have constructed, we can show a total media material cost of $59,150, with general use media accounting for only about 30 per cent of the total. The separate subtotals would be as follows: $17,450; and $41,700; with per-teacher costs being approximately $150 and $356 for a total of $506. Similar arithmetic produces per-pupil costs of $11 and $26 respectively, or a total per-pupil cost of $37. The nature of such expenditures must be one of the prime motives that would lead commercial organizations to merge their resources to develop markets such as we have indicated.

Estimates of Annual Cost for the Replacement of Media Equipment and Materials

In a rapidly developing technology we should not count on wearing out the equipment units we send into teaching stations to the point of obsolescence. Improvement in electronic and electro-mechanical equipment design, construction, operation, and dependability has been significant, and is continuing at a rapid rate. Therefore we believe that instead of establishing an operational life of ten years for equipment units, an eight-year span would be better for all concerned. Old equipment units break down, demand long hours of maintenance work to keep them running, and their output is generally inferior to newer types of hardware. Dependability, however, is most important to both students and teachers.

Media program administrators will be quick to testify to the fact that replacement policies the country over are inadequate, and the negative influence of such failures on the entire program of service is so severe that appropriate action ought to have a high priority. Table 13-3 gives some guidance in setting up better budgetary provisions. In some localities replacement expenditures will have to be categorized under new equipment purchases, or capital outlay. Regardless of how this is determined locally, the amounts in Table 13-3 may easily be added to the cost for equipment and facilities or kept separate, as in this example. Although we have urged an eight-year life for equipment units, some equipment may last beyond this, but others with heavy usage might have to be retired from service in five years. The quality of the maintenance work performed on equipment during its period of service has much to do with its longevity. It is obvious that failure to take good care of equipment leads to its early demise. This is also true of media materials such as films, tapes, slides, filmstrips, and records. We have already described these procedures in Chapter 8. At this point we should not confuse the problem of servicing and care, however, except in relationship to longevity. We are discussing the fact that materials and equipment units are often severely damaged and must be replaced, they simply wear out from repetitive use, or they should be traded in for newer and better models. We therefore present Table 13-3 as an example of the nature of the cost for this operational phase of an audiovisual media program in the school we are using as an example. The material in Table 13-3 is based on the equipment and media materials indicated at the adequacy level in Tables 13-1 and 13-2.

Based on experience with replacement, we suggest the following kinds of action:

1. All revisions of important media subjects should be ordered on an automatic basis as a matter of priority to keep the collections up to date.

2. All damaged subjects, such as filmstrips, tapes, and motion pictures that become mutilated should be replaced at once on an automatic basis.

3. All media subjects that have been superseded in the market by newer treatments should be substituted as a priority item.

4. Dated media subjects should be reevaluated and subjects of doubtful value should be deleted from the collection to make room for substitutions or new titles.

5. After ten years of service, media subjects should be culled and more important subjects of known and basal character procured.

6. Plan for a replacement expenditure of 2 per cent to protect collections against loss from accidental damage.

7. Plan for a material replacement expenditure of 8 per cent due to normal wear, providing that the collection has been in service a number of years.

8. Plan for a material replacement expenditure of 5 per cent to procure revisions or substitutions of owned media subjects.

9. Plan for a general-use equipment replacement expenditure of approximately 12 per cent due to normal wear.

10. Plan for a general-use equipment replacement expenditure of approximately 1 per cent due to accidental damage.

11. Plan for a fixed-installation equipment replacement expenditure of 3 per cent due to normal wear.

12. Plan to replace large equipment stocks by new makes and models only under circumstances of special needs. (Since standardization policies are usually concerned, large sums of money would be involved.) New models would therefore replace old models of similar makes due to normal wear.

Summary of Cost Estimates. In light of the hypothetical inventory value of the school in our example, we can perceive a somewhat more realistic relationship between the need for an adequate replacement policy and what is usually the case. The percentages we have estimated may vary from actual instances; however, we know from experience that losses should either be covered by insurance policies or by contingency financing. When administering such expenditures as become necessary because of the possible causes we have identified, the temptation not to replace should be resisted because of the obvious consequences. The total outlay for replacement purposes for the existing inventory, as is shown in Table 13-3, is close to $35,731 or a per-teacher annual outlay of $304. The corresponding per-pupil cost would be $22.

Estimates of Annual Cost for Supplies for Media Preparation

In connection with this cost estimate, the reader is referred to the detailed discussion of processes and facilities in Chapter 9. The cost

Table 13-3. Annual Cost Estimates for Replacement of Media Equipment and Materials in a Single Building (A Middle School Housing 1,600 Pupils in 92 Teaching Stations, with a Total Staff of 117 Teachers)

Total Value Media Items on School's Inventory	Replacement Outlay Due to Accidental Damage	Replacement Outlay Due to Normal Wear	Replacement Outlay Due to Revision or Substitution	Total %	Total Cost
Media Materials for General Use: $17,450	$349 (2%)	$1,396 (8%)	$872 (5%)	15	$2,617
Media Materials for Systems Use: $41,700	834 (2%)	3,336 (8%)	2,085 (5%)	15	6,255
Media Equipment for General Conventional Use: $140,580	1,405 (1%)	16,870 (12%)		13	18,275
Media Equipment Main Auditorium: $6,500	65 (1%)	780 (12%)		13	845
Media Equipment for School's Media Preparation Program: $9,230	92 (1%)	1,107 (12%)		13	1,199
Media Equipment for School's Television and Teaching Systems Service: $132,000	1,320 (1%)	3,960 (3%)		4	5,280
School Library Installations: $31,500	315 (1%)	945 (3%)		4	1,260
Totals $378,960	$4,380	$28,394	$2,957		$35,731

estimates presented should also be referred to Table 13-1 in light of available equipment and facilities. The total cost estimated in Table 13-4 amounts to $6,300 or a per-teacher cost of $54, and a per-pupil cost of approximately $4. The statistic we have arrived at in our analysis for the school in our example is by no means a complete one. (See Table 13-6.) At any rate, we know that in many a media institute around the country, a sum in excess of $40 per student was budgeted for media preparation supplies. How much more likely it is that at least this sum be provided for teachers in a school building for such activities to go on during the entire school year. We claim that the figure should be considered as a minimum.

Table 13-4. Estimates of Annual Cost for Media Design and Preparation Supplies in a Single School Building (A Middle School Housing 1,600 Pupils in 92 Teaching Stations, with a Total Staff of 117 Teachers)

Categories of Supplies	Annual Estimated Costs
Photographic Film and Supplies for Color Slides	$800
Polaroid Film and Supplies for Polaroid-Type Slides	400
Transparency Supplies (Dry-Process, also Photocopier Supplies)	800
Spirit Reflex Masters	200
Transparency Supplies (Diazo-Coated Acetate Sheets)	500
Motion Picture Film Stock	300
Heavy Paper Stock for Media-Preparation Uses (Not Including Spirit or Mimeo)	400
Dry-Mount Press Supplies	300
Lettering Supplies for Media Uses	700
Pressure-Sensitive Tapes	400
Magnetic Recording Tape : Audio	500
Magnetic Recording Tape : Video (Based on 20 Hours of One-Inch)	1,000
Total	$6,300

Estimated Annual Cost for Audiovisual Media Staff

School-building media-service centers are understaffed the country over. This is also true of centralized district media centers, but not quite to the same degree. If we seek the development of increased volume of media use on a firm basis, then we can no longer proceed as though the timely use of media really didn't matter. In other words, we have to solve the problems of logistics and meet the instructional needs. This is where auxiliary clerical and technical staff members walk onto the stage for action, and this calls for pay checks. As we consider the problem of service in our example, we can estimate that something like $44,800 will be needed in the staff budget to carry on the kind of program envisaged. This figure would amount to a per-teacher cost on an

annual basis of approximately $383, and a per-pupil cost of $28. This estimate for needed personnel falls far short of the new standard described in Footnote 8, Chapter 12.

Estimated Annual Cost for Certain Miscellaneous Items

We have already listed certain fixed installation costs, but we have not included office and shop furniture, and media-service equipment in storage areas; nor have we indicated the cost of automatic film-inspection machines, film splicers, and chemical applicators. We shall simply assume that such items of service equipment, metal shelving units, and bins and cabinets had been previously installed, at least for the purposes of our example. We are also assuming that the necessary repair services will be carried on by the technical staff members listed in Table 13-5, or by technicians at district headquarters. However, we ought to add to our tabulated estimates a number of recurring costs on an annual basis that must be met to carry on adequately the media services in our exemplary building. These items are presented in Table 13-6, and they tend to round out the cost estimates to make them more serviceable to

Table 13-5. Estimate of Annual Cost for Audiovisual Media Specialist Staff in a Single School Building (A Middle School Housing 1,600 Students, with 92 Teaching Stations and a Total Staff of 117 Teachers)

Position	Annual Salary
Audiovisual Media Coordinator (Full Year)	$12,600
Full-time Professional Assistant (A Teacher, for Programing and In-Service Education Work, Regular School Year)	9,000
One Graphic Technician	8,000
One Electronics Technician	7,600
One Secretary	4,800
Temporary Skilled Technical Service (Hourly Basis)	2,200
Consulting Fees for In-Service Education	600
Total	$44,800

Table 13-6. Estimated Annual Cost for Certain Audiovisual Media Service Miscellaneous Items in a Single School Building (A Middle School Housing 1,600 Pupils in 92 Teaching Stations with a Total Staff of 117 Teachers)

Needed Items	Estimated Annual Cost
Repair Supplies (Tubes, Transistors, Lamps, Belts, Connectors, Leader Film, Cleaning Fluids, Film Cement, Splicing Tape, Containers, Boxes, Reels, Wire and Cable)	$2,600
Spare Parts (Gears, Claws, Lenses, Parts)	1,000
Office Supplies	300
Mimeo and Spirit Duplication Paper Stock	3,000
Printing of Business Forms	600
Travel Funds for Media Staff	200
Total	$7,700

prospective and practicing media administrators as they seek to study and define their own costs more carefully. Chapters 7 and 8 supply additional details.

Adding up the cost estimates to meet specified needs along the lines of repair materials, spare parts, office supplies, paper for mimeo and spirit duplication for teachers who use the media center's services, printing business forms for requests for service by teachers, and also to cover travel to state meetings of associations and task forces at work on projects benefiting the school, we arrive at a total estimate of $7,700. This total cost for these items amounts to an annual per-teacher cost of approximately $66. The per-pupil cost is approximately $5.

Summarization of Cost Estimates to Indicate Predicted Program Cost

Table 13-7 summarizes the various specific cost estimates to give a general idea of what an audiovisual media services program would be likely to cost at an *adequate* level in a single school building housing 1,600 pupils with a staff of 117 teachers. It is difficult to obtain

budgetary information in detail, desirably categorized, and the work of analyzing it is even more hazardous, short of on-site visitation. The example we have presented provides a hypothetical basis that is valuable for analysis by readers because of the opportunity of comparing one inventory of high-level character with any given case known to the analyst. In addition to the opportunity for such comparison, the example we provide gives per-school, per-teacher, and per-pupil unit costs for comparison with other sets of data.

Comments About the Cost Summary. A perusal of the estimates and their totals shows that expenditures are of two basic types, *capital* and *recurring*. We should note further that capital purchases include new equipment units, fixed installations (remodeling or new construction not shown in our example), new media materials, and replacements of equipment and materials because of damage, obsolescence, and normal wear. Replacement costs are tabulated nevertheless under recurring costs in Table 13-7. In the school building we are using as our example, it would require a capital expenditure (exclusive of replacement costs) amounting to approximately $3,240 per teacher or $239 per pupil to establish what we have referred to as an *adequacy* level of operations. It is likely that many schools throughout the country are operating media-service programs far below this level, and therefore it is likely that many schools would require a number of years to reach our adequacy goal. In such an event the cost-determination process would be expressed in a lesser level with correspondingly lower annual capital expenditures. The cost for any given level or goal would thus be spread out over a preestablished period.

Turning now to an examination of recurring costs, we note that the operations in our hypothetical school, including the cost of leadership and supporting staff members, require an annual outlay of something like $96,286. This amounts to a per-teacher cost of $822 or a per-pupil cost of $60. To arrive at an optimum mix of capital expenditures and the annual recurring costs on the way to a new goal of development is the budgeting job of every media program director in the country. It becomes obvious that if the adequacy level were to be reached immediately in a new school like the one in our example, other factors being equal, the capital expenditure could run to $378,960 or more, and the annual recurring cost to $96,286 or more. With these figures in mind, we may estimate the cost for equipping and operating media-service programs at one level or another in any given number of schools. Those who make such estimates must naturally be fully cognizant of the many additional factors that have a bearing on the final costs determined for local circumstances.

Relationship of the Cost-Determination Example to School-District Budgeting. We have presented a cost-determination example that focused attention on a school-building unit rather than on the over-all school-district media-service center. We have repeatedly emphasized the need for media program directors to shift the bulk of leadership effort and energy away from headquarters units to teaching stations. The leadership and executive effort must, however, reside in personnel at headquarters, and certain essential services must be provided from those sources. Budgeting for the district will be the responsibility of the district media program administrator, but the budget he prepares is likely to be directed inwardly toward the centralized media services, or outwardly toward improved operational levels in every school-building teaching station. Building better budgets will therefore follow local procedures, but ought to seek optimum balance between school-district program financial support, as well as to budget expenditures for the school-building unit of which the principal is the key administrator. We chose to present the school-building cost-determination example to point out the need to develop a new image of operational levels and their inevitably higher costs.

Some Questions About the Example. As the reader studies the preceding examples of cost determination, he should keep a number of points in sharp focus. Getting the answers to the following questions will provide some insights for correct thinking:

1. How does the present inventory in a school system affect developmental costs?

2. How are desirable operational levels for a particular system determined? By statements of national minimum standards? By the local instructional demands of teachers? As a result of the promotional work of the media director? By the principals? By the media director himself?

3. What can be done to "hide" the costs of operating an audiovisual media services program? Could light-control costs be "hidden" in maintenance department budgets? Could the salaries of media specialists and technicians be "hidden" in school-building salary budgets?

4. Can per-pupil cost figures in one town be compared with per-pupil cost figures in another to form critical judgments? If not, why not? What does starting status have to do with this comparison? What does the pupil enrollment have to do with it? What would number and size of school plants have to do with it? What would the number of years that the program has been operating under good leadership have to do with it?

5. What advantages will accrue to the media director who puts forth the effort to plan expenditures to reach long-term service goals?

6. Insofar as Table 13-7 is concerned, is it likely that the *adequacy* level could be reached at once? If this level had to be reached over a long period of time, ten years, for example, what upward revisions should be made in the item for purchase of materials? What cut-backs in the media staff item? What would be the advantage of reaching a *desirable minimum* level as soon as possible and then proceeding to the *adequacy* level over a five-year period?

Budget Preparation and Administration

It has already been stated many times that the basis for any particular procedure is the long-term plan to meet definite instructional needs, and that the particular kind of budgeting system in operation must reflect such thinking and planning throughout its preparation. From the point of view implicit in this chapter, the media director obtains financial support on the basis of a budget request in which he states his monetary needs succinctly, supporting his requests forcefully. It is with the format for organizing and formulating the budget that this section is concerned because the way in which the budget is laid out is not only important in obtaining optimum financial support, but facilitates as well the later work of budget administration. If the quality and scope of the

Table 13-7. Summary of Cost Estimates for Audiovisual Media Services in a Single School Building (A Middle School Building Housing 1,600 Pupils in 92 Teaching Stations with a Total Staff of 117 Teachers)

Category of Media Service Needs	Capital Outlay to Reach Assumed Adequacy Level			Annual Recurring Outlay		
	Total Outlay	Per-Teacher Cost	Per-Pupil Cost	Total Costs	Per-Teacher Cost	Per-Pupil Cost
Equipment and Facilities (Table 13-1)						
General-Use (Mobile)	$140,580	$1,202	$88			
Media Preparation	9,230	79	6			
Fixed Installations (ITV, Instructional Systems, Multi-media)	132,000	1,128	83			
School Library and Auditorium Equipment	38,000	325	25			
Rental Fees for Motion Pictures				$1,755	$15	$1
Purchase of Media Materials (Table 13-2)	59,150	506	37			
Replacement of Media Equipment and Materials (Table 13-3)				35,731	304	22
Supplies for Media Design and Preparation (Table 13-4)				6,300	54	4
Operational Staff Members (Table 13-5)				44,800	383	28
Miscellaneous Media Service Items (Table 13-6)				7,700	66	5
Totals	$378,960	$3,240	$239	$96,286	$822	$60

local media-service program is to be clearly seen, all expense items from in-service education to fire insurance should be included.

Budget Categories and Format

Many variations exist in the manner in which budgets are set up, but the basic procedures are similar. A detailed budget breakdown is preferable, and the media director should seek guidance from school administrative officials as to prescribed budget categories and the degree of detail that is necessary. Essentially, every budget should show under locally standardized categories with which all involved are familiar, (1) the predicted total income from all sources, and (2) the ways in which this income is to be disbursed.

The budget maker needs to make sure that sufficient details appear in his budget system to show his organizational patterns and operational plans, and this can be guaranteed under almost any classification system. For example, the writer's own budgeting format is, of necessity, based on a statewide system, using four funds: personal services, contractual services, supplies, and capital outlay.

Major differences are almost sure to appear in media-service budgets, and these are understandable, since they are determined by local policies and in some cases by state law. These principal differences in procedure are implicit in the following questions, which should be noted and checked by the media director against the policies set up by school-system officials.

1. Should expenditures for motion pictures, filmstrips, models, and so on, be chargeable against capital outlay or operating expense funds?

2. Should expenditures for new equipment units be chargeable to a different account than materials, or should both items be charged against capital outlay?

3. Should expenditures for replacement of equipment and materials be chargeable to separate accounts? To the operating expense fund? To the capital outlay fund?

Established business, and especially budgeting, procedures may not permit the media planner to use his personal preferences in answering those questions because even though the definitions are often interpreted in slightly different ways, the leeway in most cases is very small. The term *capital outlay* in the writer's budgetary situation applies to the cost for land and nonstructural improvements to land, the cost for equipment such as tools and machinery, vehicles, and items of apparatus, media equipment, and materials, all of which have to be reported in the annual inventory. It applies also to the cost for buildings and improvements. The term *supplies* refers to all commodities and materials, including consumable items that are not carried on the inventory of fixed assets. Replacements of equipment and materials must, according to this system, be considered as new equipment and materials, and must be budgeted accordingly.

In the paperback volume, *Financial Accounting for Local and State School Systems*,[1] that every media administrator should have on his desk, there appears the following set of criteria that may help a purchaser procure a long-throw lens for a projector out of his supplies budget when his capital money is all gone:

Criteria for Supply Items

A supply item is any article or material which meets any *one* or more of the following conditions:

1. It is consumed in use.

2. It loses its original shape or appearance with use.

3. It is expendable, that is, if the article is damaged or some of its parts are lost or worn out, it is usually more feasible to replace it with an entirely new unit rather than repair it.

4. It is an inexpensive item, having characteristics of equipment, whose small unit cost makes it inadvisable to capitalize the item.

5. It loses its identity through incorporation into a different or more complex unit or substance.

Criteria for Equipment Items

An equipment item is a movable or fixed unit of furniture or furnishings, an instrument, a machine, an apparatus, or a set of articles which meets all of the following conditions:

1. It retains its original shape and appearance with use.

2. It is non-expendable, that is, if the article is damaged or some of its parts are lost or worn out,

[1] Paul L. Reason and Alpheus L. White, *Financial Accounting for Local and State School Systems, Standard Receipt and Expenditure Accounts.* (Prepared under Auspices of the U.S. Office of Education.) (Washington, D.C.: Superintendent of Documents, U.S. Government Printing Office, 1957, reprinted 1964.)

it is usually more feasible to repair it rather than replace it with an entirely new unit.

3. It represents an investment of money which makes it feasible and advisable to capitalize the item.

4. It does not lose its identity through incorporation into a different or more complex unit or substance.

In preparing and administering their budgets, media administrators would be well advised to not depart from established, standard budgeting and business procedures unless they do so with the advice and consent of all concerned.

Example 13-1 is a budget format that shows the diversified expenditures for media services. It should be noted that the preceding questions regarding variations in classifying expenditures for materials, equipment, and replacement have been answered for this example only. Many other systems of classification are in use.

Example 13–1

Example of Budget Format

BUDGET FOR AUDIOVISUAL MEDIA SERVICES

PUBLIC SCHOOLS OF _____

Fiscal Year _____

Account No. _____

Summary of Appropriation:

Personal Services Fund _____ _____

Contractual Services Fund _____ _____

Supplies Fund _____ _____

Capital Outlay Fund _____ _____

Total _____

Estimated Income, if Any, from Other Sources:

Parent Teacher Organizations _____

Community Service Clubs _____

Business Firms _____

Donations and Drives _____

Other _____

State _____

Federal _____

Total _____

Grand Total _____

PLANNED DISBURSEMENTS

Personal Services Fund: Total_____ (Account No. _____)

	Budget Previous Year	Increase or Decrease	Budget Current Year
Director	————	————	————
Media Specialists	————	————	————
Coordinator (SHS-1)	————	————	————
Assistant Coordinators (2)	————	————	————
Coordinator (JHS-4)	————	————	————
Assistant Coordinators (2)	————	————	————
Coordinators (E 1-10)	————	————	————
Assistant Coordinators (2)	————	————	————
Chief Technician	————	————	————
Assistant Technicians	————	————	————
Secretaries	————	————	————
Part-Time Workers (Hqts.)	————	————	————
Part-Time Workers (Schs.)	————	————	————
Consultants and Speakers for In-Service Education	————	————	————

Contractual Services Fund: Total_____ (Account No. _____)

		Budget Previous Year	Increase or Decrease	Budget Current Year
(a)	General Repair Jobs and Contracts (daily, weekly, or annually)	————	————	————
(b)	Rental of Media Materials alloted to:			
	10 Elem. Schs.	————	————	————
	4 JHS	————	————	————
	1 SHS	————	————	————
	Headquarters	————	————	————
(c)	Cartage	————	————	————
(d)	Printing, Binding, and Mounting	————	————	————
(e)	Magazine Subscriptions	————	————	————

(f) Memberships and Dues _____ _____ _____

(g) Mileage Reimbursement
(local school system) _____ _____ _____

(h) Travel Expenses
(out of city only) _____ _____ _____

(i) Fire and Theft Insurance on
Materials and Equipment
(also tel., light, heat, etc.,
if necessary) _____ _____ _____

(j) Photo Laboratory Service
Charges _____ _____ _____

Supplies Fund: Total_____ (Account No. _____)

(a) Office Supplies (printed forms,
mimeo, and other duplication,
stationary, envelopes, postage,
etc.) _____ _____ _____

(b) Repair and Maintenance Supplies
(spare parts of all kinds, lamps,
electronic tubes, film leader,
chemicals, etc.) _____ _____ _____

(c) Educational Supplies (expendable
production supplies of all kinds,
manuals, and laboratory sup-
plies for training purposes) _____ _____ _____

Capital Outlay Fund: Total _____ (Account No. _____)

(a) New Equipment Units _____ _____ _____

(b) New Titles of Media Material _____ _____ _____

(c) Replacement of Equipment _____ _____ _____

(d) Replacement of Materials _____ _____ _____

(e) Storage Facilities _____ _____ _____

(f) Office Equipment _____ _____ _____

(g) Delivery Equipment _____ _____ _____

(h) Maintenance Equipment _____ _____ _____

(i) Building and Remodeling _____ _____ _____

Comments About the Budgeting Example. Example 13-1 is predicated on the process of centralizing the media budget in such a manner that allotments are made for operations in the various school units. Thus the salaries for media coordinators are charged against a central media budget instead of against the school's own budget. Hence in Example 13-1 the media director would be allotted sufficient funds to cover all programs in the schools, and in effect, funds so allotted would be reassigned. Such budgeting may prove to be unwise, since it may appear that the total appropriation for district-wide supplies, equipment, and personnel, for example, is so large as to offer an inviting target for critics and tax-rate conscious budget choppers. On the other hand central purchasing and storage and personnel-sharing procedures may be facilitated by some combination of school-unit and school-district allotments. Strict control of disbursements must be facilitated and maintained, and unless budget controls can be exercised at the school-building level, then certainly all aspects of paperwork and actual control should be placed at the headquarters level. There is much to be said for setting up school-unit media budgets to point out the nature of school-unit operational costs, but such decentralization may not be feasible. Example 13-1 is a summary-type budget, showing appropriations in relation to the previous year, and once finalized, the media administrator would set up separate, detailed school budgets of his own, or for subsequent transmittal to responsible coordinators in various school units. Thus his budget plan for each school would be based on his own centralized budget, and would be in written format, showing in detail specific amounts for all operational expenses under the appropriate categories that have been authorized.

The standardization of classifications and account numbers for income and expenditure allows school districts everywhere to make comparisons and to adopt better budgeting procedures. Such a standardized classification of accounts was published in 1957. Example 13-2 is a condensed outline of that manual,[2] excerpting those accounts and their assigned numbers for the sake of brevity and clarity, that have direct application to media budgeting purposes.

[2] *Ibid.*, pp. 6–7, 27–35.

Example 13–2

RECEIPT ACCOUNTS

Revenue Receipts
10-40 Series

10. Revenue from Local Sources

    14. Other Revenue from Local Sources

        14-d. Rent from School Facilities

        14-f. Gifts and Bequests

        14-g. Miscellaneous Revenue from Local Sources (Sale of old audiovisual equipment)

30. Revenue from State Sources

    30-a. State

    30-b. Federal Money Received through the State

40. Revenue from Federal Sources

EXPENDITURE ACCOUNTS

Instruction
200 Series

210. Salaries

    212. Consultants or Supervisors

    213. Teachers

    214. Other Instructional Staff

        214-a. School Librarians
        214-b. Audiovisual Personnel
        214-e. Television Instructional Personnel

    215. Secretarial and Clerical Assistants

        215-b. Consultants or Supervisors
        215-c. Teachers
        215-d. Other Instructional Staff

    216. Other Salaries for Instruction (Teacher Aides)

220. Textbooks

230. School Libraries and Audiovisual Materials

    230-a. Library Books
    230-b. Periodicals and Newspapers
    230-c. Audiovisual Materials
    230-d. Other School Library Expenses

240. Teaching Supplies

250. Other Expenses

    250-a. Supplies
    250-b. Travel
    250-c. Miscellaneous Expenses (Rental of Equipment, Dues)

Operation of Plant
600 Series

610. Salaries

    610-b. Custodial Services
    610-d. Other Salaries for Operation of Plant (Stock Clerks)

640.   Utilities, Except Heat for Buildings

      640-d. Telephone and Telegraph

Maintenance of Plant
700 Series

710.   Salaries:

      710-c. Repair of Equipment (Technicians)

720.   Contracted Services

      720-c. Repair of Equipment

730.   Replacement of Equipment

      730-a. Replacements of Instructional Equipment

740.   Other Expenses for Maintenance of Plant

      740-c. Other Expenses for the Repair of Equipment (Spare Parts, and Repair Supplies)

Fixed Charges
800 Series

820.   Insurance and Judgments

      820-a. Property Insurance (Fire and Theft on Media)

830.   Rental of Land and Buildings

      830-a. Land and Buildings for Instructional Purposes (Operational Areas near Headquarters or Schools)

Capital Outlay
1200 Series

1220.   Buildings

      1220-a. Professional Services

      1220-b. New Buildings and Additions

      1220-c. Remodeling.

1230.   Equipment

      1230-a. Professional Services (Television Consultants)

      1230-b. Administration (Dictating Machines, Office Furniture)

1230-c   Instruction

1230-f.   Operation of Plant (Equipment for Warehouses and Storerooms, Motor Vehicles)

1230-g.   Maintenance of Plant (Audiovisual Shop Equipment)

Using Standard Accounts

Having presented the standardized classification of accounts, we are in a position to use the account numbers in a new classification of audiovisual media receipts and disbursements. We shall therefore construct a new budget format as shown in Example 13-3.

Example 13–3

Example of Standard Classification of Audiovisual Media Accounts

Budget for Audiovisual Media Services

for the Town of _____

Fiscal Year _____

TOTAL APPROPRIATION

Tax Source (Acct. 11-a) _____

Gifts, Rents, Misc. (Accts. 14-d, f, g) _____

State Source (Accts. 30-a, b) _____

Federal Source (Acct. 40) _____

Total Revenue _____

EXPENDITURES	Number of Positions	Amount

Instruction

Salaries:

	Number of Positions	Amount
Media Director (Acct. 212)	1	_____
Media Specialists, Hqts. (Acct. 212) Supervisory Assistants	3	_____
School-Unit Media Coordinators (Acct. 214-b)	10	_____
School Media Specialists (Acct. 214-b, e)	10	_____
Graphic Technician (Acct. 216)	12	_____
Secretaries, Hqts. (Acct. 215-b)	5	_____
Secretaries, Schs. (Acct. 215-d)	12	_____
Speakers for In-Service Education (Acct. 250-c)	30	_____

Amount _____

School Libraries and Audiovisual Materials:

Purchase of New Media Materials (Acct. 230-e) _____

Replacement of Media Materials (Acct. 230-c) _____

Media Design and Preparation Supplies for Hqts. and All School Units (Acct. 230-c) _____

Photographic Laboratory Services for Media Preparation (Acct. 230-c) _____

Rental of Audiovisual Media Materials for All School Units and Hqts. (Acct. 230-c) _____

Cartage (Acct. 230-c) _____

Amount
_____

Teaching Supplies:

Paper Stock and Supplies for Mimeo, Photocopy, and Spirit Duplications (Acct. 240) _____

Other Expenses:

Office Supplies, Hqts. and Schools (Acct. 250-a) _____

Media Supplies for In-Service Education (Acct. 250-a) _____

Professional Books and Journals (Acct. 250-a) _____

Professional Memberships and Dues (Acct. 250-e) _____

Professional Travel (Acct. 250-b) _____

Rental of Automatic Data Processing and Document Writing Equipment (Acct. 250-c) _____

Printing Expenses, Commercial (Acct. 250-c) _____

Operation of Plant	Number of Positions	Amount
Salaries:		_____
Stock Clerks, Hqts. (Acct. 610-d)	4	_____
Utilities, Except Heat for Buildings:		
Telephone and Telegraph (Acct. 640-d)	_____	_____
Supplies for Operation of Vehicles (Acct. 650-b)	_____	_____
Maintenance of Plant		
Salaries:		
Chief Technician, Hqts. (Acct. 710-c)	1	_____
Assistance Technicians, Hqts. (Acct. 710-c)	4	_____

Electronic Technicians (Acct. 710-c) 10 ————

Part-Time Technicians, Hqts.
(Acct. 710-c) 5 ————

Part-Time Technicians, Schs.
(Acct. 710-c) 10 ————

Contracted Services:

General Repair Jobs and Contracts,
Daily, Weekly, Annually (Acct. 720-c) ————

Replacements of Equipment:

Replacement of Outworn Audiovisual Media
Equipment Units (Acct. 730-a) ————

             Amount

Other Expenses for Maintenance of Plant:

Repair and Maintenance Supplies,
Spare Parts, Repair Materials
(Acct. 740-c) ————

Fixed Charges

Insurance and Judgments:

Fire and Theft Insurance on Media
(Acct. 820-a) ————

Rental of Land and Buildings:

Rental of Central Film Distribution Headquarters for the District (Acct. 830-a) ————

Rental of Book Storage and Distribution
Space (Acct. 830-a) ————

Capital Outlay

Buildings:

Remodel Five Existing Classrooms for Use
as School-Unit Television Studios (Acct. 1220-c) ————

Professional Consulting Services of Television Consultant (Acct. 1220-a) ————

Equipment:

Purchase of New Audiovisual Media Equipment
Units (Acct. 1230-c) ————

Purchase of Two New Delivery Trucks
(Acct. 1230-f) _____

Purchase of Office Equipment (Acct. 1230-b) _____

Purchase of Storage Cabinets (Acct. 1230-f) _____

Purchase of Audiovisual Media Shop
Equipment (Acct. 1230-g) _____

Purchase and Installation of a Multimedia
Center with a Group Response System,
Linked to Computer Analyzer (Acct. 1230-c) _____

Professional Consulting Services of a Multimedia Specialist (Acct. 1230-a) _____

Professional Consulting Services of a
Computer-Installation Expert (Acct. 1230-a) _____

Some Observations About Example 13-3. Again we have shown a centralized budget, and all of the items found in the first example have been included in the second under the new classification system for comparison. It is likely that any given media program administrator will either have his first budget handed to him, or he will be handed a specific format for use in preparing his proposals. Again as with the first example, the itemization is generalized, and hence the specific appropriations would be broken down into the various classifications, and then further broken down into school-unit allotments in written form. Thus it is obvious that the example, once finalized, would be developed in detail, so that each section or category would include all needed information about quantities, makes, salary, grades for each position, and the like. The *Number of Positions* column was filled in hypothetically as a further example of the detail that would be necessary. As the media director prepares his budget, he needs to consider many facets of the local environment in general and school policy in particular. He should know that the image of him and his work generally held by the public has much to do with his success in budget planning and implementation. We now turn to brief discussions of several decisions that he must inevitably make that may have an important bearing on that image.

Padding the Budget

It has already been pointed out that cost determination in terms of instructional needs and long-term plans to reach desirable opera-

tional levels are what a media director should consider in preparing his budget requests. Prudent management and clear thinking call for factual justification for every dollar requested and every dollar spent. The director should describe clearly for school authorities and the public what the status of his organization is, what services they can expect under this status, and what is clearly needed in terms of the facts. Once the facts are presented and the proper recommendations made, the responsibility shifts to those who have the final decision. Hence, attempts should not be made to obtain desired allotments of funds by overstating the amounts needed in anticipation of probable cuts.

Hiding the Cost

Repeatedly in the literature, cost figures and recommended standards for expenditures exclude leadership and staff, as though a media-service program consisted only of materials, equipment, and building facilities. This must mean that leadership and staff costs are being hidden from view, that is, they are either being subsumed under over-all instructional and administrative headings as a policy, or they are not being properly considered. Those who recognize the organizational aspects of a media-service program will realize that appropriations cannot be hidden for long. Regardless of how the matter is settled locally, and although this may be a matter of local or state policy, the media director must conduct his long-term, goal-reaching budgeting by putting his plans on paper as a basis for recommendations, and by identifying and justifying service needs. Adequate support for any operation needs to be on a firm basis, and the people will not be fooled for long. Hiding costs deliberately as a stratagem may prove to be a dangerous business. If it is done at all, it had better be substituted quickly by an educational program designed to let the people decide what kind of instruction they really want. The director should be guided accordingly as he finds the best local solution for this budgeting problem.

Administering the Budget

Even though extensive budget-accounting systems set up by the director are likely to duplicate similar activities in central administrative offices, he should establish a system that will provide a double-check on expenditures. A simple ledger in which expenditures can be entered, showing weekly or monthly balances, is suggested. When mistakes occur outside the media headquarters, this system will show them up.

The media director should never assume that financial reports distributed from central offices are correct. He should study them with care, setting up a pattern of habitual scrutiny against mistakes in encumbrances and payments. Naturally, if he finds that he has been awarded unwittingly an additional $10,000, he will call this to the attention of the business manager. However, the anguish over a situation of that sort is equalized by the pleasure derived by discovery, in time, of an incorrect encumbrance that, having gone unnoticed, would have caused serious fiscal trouble at the end of the year. Five other aspects of budget administration need serious attention.

Allotting Media Funds to School Units. The budgeting examples presented in this chapter have indicated a number of aspects of media-service operations where funds in a centralized budget have to be allotted to the various school-building units. Procuring media from sources external to the district, part-time secretarial and technical assistance, and media-preparation supplies are a few cases in point. The problem becomes an extremely vexing one when there isn't enough money to meet all of the needs for the whole school year in all of the schools involved. Practically, a fair allotment procedure must be sought, but the heart of the problem is to find an adequate method of control. It

takes hours of valuable time and energy to explain and argue the point with personnel in each school over the failure to allot enough money. Possibilities include dividing the appropriation equally among schools of each type, making allotments on a per-pupil basis, making allotments on a per-teacher basis, making allotments on a per-grade basis, and making allotments in terms of democratic action in light of the special needs of a particular instructional program. This suggestion, although more difficult to implement, is the recommended line of decision. Democratic action may be taken calling for suggestions from coordinators, sending out and collecting quick-response survey sheets from teachers in key programs, and by guiding a committee of coordinators and school principals to arrive at a wise decision.

Factors such as urgency of need, priority for specified subject-matter fields, priority for large-group and instructional-systems instruction, priority for materials keyed directly to problems and units, and priority for basal over supplementary materials, may have to be balanced to set up the first schedule. Factors such as these suggest that there may be little justice in uniform allotments. It is also suggested that a reserve fund be set up for the balance of a school year, to handle special needs, and further, that a stipulation be made to the effect that all funds be allotted subject to encumbrance for expenditure by a specified date, thus in effect providing for a second division and allotment of unexpended funds.

Switching Funds. In certain budget systems no leeway exists for the director in switching funds from one account to another. In other systems, as long as the appropriation in any given fund is not exceeded, the media director may switch charges from one account to another account within the coverage of the fund itself. That is, commercial printing expenses could in some cases be combined with film rental expenses under a main appropriation for the Instruction category. Such switching provides flexibility and often makes possible the complete spending of appropriations.

Following the Budget. Once a plan of expenditures has been set up and approved, the media administrator is committed to a controlled line of action. To change it, except for emergencies or unpredictable circumstances, is to admit lack of foresight. As a matter of policy and for the sake of good management, the director should see that he—and his staff—adheres to an agreed-upon plan. Stability of program and an enhanced reputation in business matters are bound to accrue from responsible and dependable administration.

Contingency Budgeting. Not to be confused with padding the budget, contingency budgeting is the device employed to take care of emergency needs arising beyond the control of the budget planner. Such provisions could, of course, exist unknown to the director of media services, and it is up to him to discover these or to take steps to protect his program. The director should, of course, protect his contracts by a 10 per cent specification in his budget to apply to such matters as printing, film rental accounts, and repair work. Also, in cases of equipment, the director may either specify a definite contingency amount under capital outlay or arrange to specify fewer equipment units than planned when an order is actually issued, or he may call for quotations in terms of several levels of quantity. Price-rise contingencies or other unpredictable events should, at any rate, be borne in mind in both budget preparation and budget administration.

Readiness for Windfalls. Directors who are unprepared for fast action are never in a position to profit by windfalls. In terms of priority needs for either equipment or materials, or both, special purchase lists should always be in readiness for immediate requisition and delivery. Unspent funds, left over from other appropriations, are often awarded suddenly and unexpectedly to a department that has already demonstrated worthy needs, can place orders immediately, and can guarantee delivery within desirable time limits. Directors should go after such funds, and should be able to demonstrate their readiness to take effective action without fail.

Obtaining Financial Support From Local Sources

Upon the media director rests the responsibility for a penetrating analysis of district-wide media needs and the vigorous pursuit of adequate financial support to meet those needs. This is a complex responsibility, however, because it involves balance and priorities.

Schools need many service agencies, higher salaries, and ample supplies, and into this web of local circumstances the director must direct his steps to request and obtain the needed support in optimum amount for the good of all concerned. To be sure, he need not stand alone in making such requests because allotments for his services are spread out over the entire instructional program. Thus school principals, teachers, and other curriculum specialists can be of real help in substantiating and formulating the requests to be submitted. Special budget-preparation and curriculum-study groups, and the director's advisory committee, if he has one, should make significant contributions to the formulation of sound recommendations.

Having Needs, Goals, and Costs in Mind

Knowing what needs have to be met, having definite operational goals in mind, and having a long-term plan formulated, as was indicated in the example of cost determination in an earlier section, are the first and foremost bases of success. Tabulated data in terms of operational needs and a cost-analysis plan are a means of enhancing the media director's authority. The long-term planning, possible when the facts are at hand, is recognized everywhere as good business, and the recognition of prudent management is sure to build up his reputation in the public view. Guessing and predicting what would be good to do with the money if it were provided is the other alternative, and everyone knows this is not indicative of good common sense.

Justify Requests. The best stratagem for obtaining the dollars needed to move a media program to a new level is to have a plan. A basic plan that is sound will carry authoritative weight in budget councils. Hence we must point out that it is not enough to simply ask for more money, but media administrators should also learn to ask at the right time, and when they ask, they must have adequate justification. Media leaders ought to express succinctly what their media can do to and for pupils, what they can do to improve action at teaching stations, what they can do to multiply the professional efforts of teachers. Media administrators should approach the problem of obtaining financial support with people in mind—and the most important person is the learner. Keeping adequate records through the school year is important if the director is to be prepared. Such information, properly organized and presented, supplies the facts for sound judgment.

Minimum Standards Information Is Useful. In preparing long-term development plans, and in presenting information to administrative officials and the public, authoritative statements representing national thinking are useful. Local considerations of equipment and curriculum needs must, of course, be the final determiners of desired status. Statements that have been endorsed by national educational and professional organizations such as those quoted will carry a great deal of weight. A number of sets of standards have been developed and publicized since 1944. Typical of these are (a) American Council on Education Recommendations,

(b) Recommendations of a National Committee of Fourteen, (c) Department of Education, State of Indiana, (d) Iowa State Conference on School Planning for Use of Instructional Materials, and (e) Audio-Visual Commission on Public Information. The last three were prepared in 1956.

DAVI Guidelines for Audiovisual Personnel and Equipment. The guidelines were formulated by Gene Faris and Mendel Sherman as part of a study conducted under the auspices of the U.S. Office of Education and later reported by the DAVI Subcommittee[3] on Professional Audiovisual Standards. The guidelines were reported at several levels. We shall quote excerpts dealing with the equipment aspect from this publication with respect to the *advanced* level, and where they exist, the differences for elementary and secondary schools will be indicated (see new standards in footnote 3):

Media Equipment	Elementary	Secondary
16 mm Projector	1 per 5 T.S.*	1 per 4 T.S.
Filmstrip and Slide Projector	1 per T.S.	1 per 3 T.S. plus Viewers
2 × 2 inch Slide Projector, Automatic	1 per 10 T.S.	Same
$3\frac{1}{4} \times 4$ inch Slide Projector	1 per 10 T.S.	1 per 20 T.S.
Overhead Projector	1 per T.S.	Same
Tape Recorder and Headsets	1 per 2 T.S.	1 per 5 T.S.
TV Receivers	1 per Classroom (Min. 30 Viewers)	1 per Classroom (Min. 24 Viewers)
Projection Screens	1 per Classroom (Perm. Mounted Plus Portable Units)	Same

* T.S. = Teaching Stations.

[3] "Guidelines for Audiovisual Personnel and Equipment," DAVI of the NEA, adopted 1965. Published first as follows: Gene Faris, "Tentative Guidelines for Audiovisual Personnel and Equipment," *Audiovisual Instruction*, Vol. 10, No. 3, March 1965, pp. 201–204, March, 1965. (New standards for school media programs are being published at approximately the same time as this book. See Footnotes 8, p. 259; 1, p. 513; and 6 on p. 519. New standards for audiovisual media equipment (*advanced* level only) and materials in each school are listed here in excerpted form. *Overhead Projectors and TV Sets:* same as above table except for 24 and 20 viewers, plus extras at media center; *16 mm Projectors:* 1 per 2 T.S. plus 2 per media center; *8 mm Projectors:* 1 per T.S. plus 15 per media center; *Filmstrip and Slide Projectors:* 1 per T.S. plus 1 per media center; *2 × 2 inch Slide Projectors* (*Remotely Controlled*): 1 per 3 T.S. plus 2 per media center; *Filmstrip Viewers:* total to equal 3.5 per T.S. (Elem. Sch.), and 3.3 per T.S. (Sec. Sch.); *2 × 2 inch Slide Viewers:* 1 per T.S.; plus 1 per media center; *Tape Recorders:* 1 per T.S. (Elem. Sch.) and 1 per 5 T.S. (Sec. Sch.) plus extras at media centers and headsets for all; *Record Players:* same as for tape recorders; *Listening Stations:* 1 set of 6–10

headsets and listening equipment per T.S. and media center; *Videotape Recorder System:* 1 per 5 T.S. (with minimum of 2 per building) plus a complete distribution system for each school; *Filmstrips:* 500–1000 titles, representing 1500 filmstrip prints or 3 prints per student whichever is greater; *8 mm Films:* 1.5 films per student with at least 500 titles supplemented by duplicates; *16 mm Films:* Access by students and teachers to a minimum of 3000 titles supplemented by duplicates and rentals; *Tape and Disk Recordings* (*Excluding Electronic Laboratory Materials:* 2000 titles in each school representing 3000 recordings or 6 per student whichever is greater; *Slides:* 2000 inclusive of all sizes and sources; *Transparencies:* 2000 items including transparency masters; *Study-Print Sets and Art Prints:* the number of sets to equal the total of 15 per T.S. plus 25 per media center, not including 1000 art prints as a separate resource; *Globes:* 1 per T.S. (Elem. Sch.) and 1 per 5 T.S. (Sec. Sch.) plus 2 in each media center with access to media center stock of special-purpose globes; and *Maps:* 1 map on each region studied plus duplicates and special maps, many of which should be in format for projection.)

As has been pointed out, only excerpts were quoted from the entire report of the Commission. The reader will find a number of differences between the *adequacy* level in our cost determination example and the quoted excerpts. Furthermore, the guidelines do not make mention of fixed installations for instructional systems, school-building instructional television facilities, multimedia installations, or group-response systems. These facilities have been discussed, as the reader knows, in earlier chapters. Naturally we can look for new sets of guidelines in the future, and media program administrators should make good use of them. Many state departments of education have presented their own guidelines for the purchase of media equipment and materials, and such recommended listings may reflect more sensitively the goals of the locality. See Footnote 3.

Although having and using such information will strengthen his hand, the director should take a penetrating look at local conditions and mobilize his own pertinent information, based on long-term costs, to reach predetermined levels of operational efficiency.

Being Clear on Who Should Pay

The media-service program, except as otherwise provided for through state and federal legislation, should be paid for out of regular school department funds. Any other "partial support" by civic groups, such as parent-teacher organizations, delays the day of meeting the issue squarely. In 1949, a study[4] by the U.S. Office of Education revealed that approximately 47 per cent of all the motion picture projectors then in public high schools were purchased with nontax funds. This is to be expected with the then low level of financial support. An entirely different climate for supporting technological methods exists today.

Directors of media services should, as a matter of policy and firm conviction, channel their major effort to win financial support through local tax funds. This means that they will at every opportunity urge interested PTA groups and other civic organizations to go on record as favoring new over-all school administration support policies, and if necessary, cast their ballots for an increase in the

tax rate. This is the way to provide the continuing financial support so necessary to a firm and desirable operating level. After all, a benefit bridge or a cake sale, despite its good spirit, is a pitifully weak gesture as it affects the program of the next decade. However, many a director has used the donation of a film, a projector, or a drape-traverse system as a publicity item to open the door to more desirable support efforts by all segments of the community. Whenever the director seeks, identifies, and succeeds in tapping other than regular tax-fund allotments, such income should go to the chief administrative officer for subsequent transfer to the media services budget.

Prior to Sputnik in 1957 and to the NDEA Legislation in 1958, in most communities, gifts and grants from sources outside the school district constituted little more than a trickle into the school district budget, especially for technological improvements. All of this seemed to change overnight, and the great motivating force for it was not just the uncomfortable sensation of having a whirling satellite overhead that wasn't our own. Instead, it was the triggering of an idea about the importance of education for personal and national goals. The idea had been developing slowly and tortuously, but now technology was looked upon as a means of attacking an important educational problem. See Figure 13-1. The flood of legislation created a new urgency for action, and communities that were already taking action benefited, as we have said, more than those that could not match the grants. The total support from many sources is having and has had such an impact on financing technology in education that we must consider ways to locate and tap every known source of money outside of the school district to accomplish valid goals.

Obtaining Financial Support from Sources Outside of the School District

The following classic and widely quoted statement on education by President Lyndon B. Johnson[5] now hopefully reflects the patterns of thinking behind the new age of education:

[4] Seerly Reid, "Movie Projectors in Public High Schools," Pamphlet No. 109, U.S. Office of Education (Washington, D.C., 1950), p. 11.

[5] Lyndon B. Johnson, January 4, 1965, State of the Union Message to Congress, as quoted in the booklet, *Nothing Matters More*, published by the National Audio-Visual Association, 3150 Spring Street, Fairfax, Virginia, 1966.

Figure 13-1. Early in the sixties, under a federal grant from the U.S. Office of Education, Jack Tanzman as principal investigator explored the concept of regional instructional materials centers as a promising means of providing rich media and curricular services to schools. In one sense, a number of the well-developed county media service programs served as a basis for expansion of the idea. Dr. John Shaver and his company served as architectural consultants. A scale model was constructed and detailed floor plans were worked out and publicized. We show in these two illustrations a view of the model and the floor-plan schematic. The completed developmental work received well-deserved praise, and without doubt has had a significant influence on the expansion of the image of what services ought to be available to schools everywhere. *Courtesy Jack Tanzman, Educational Council for School Research and Development, Mineola, New York.*

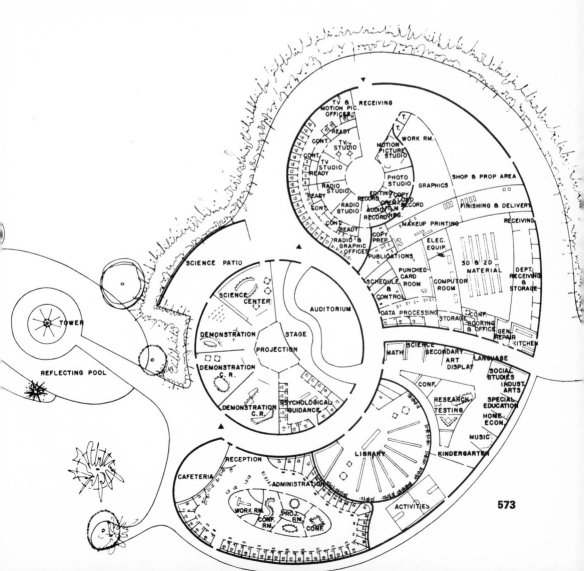

573

Nothing matters more to the future of our country: not our military preparedness—for armed might is worthless if we lack the brain power to build a world of peace; not our productive economy—for we cannot sustain growth without trained manpower; not our democratic system of government—for freedom is fragile if citizens are ignorant.

We must demand that our schools increase not only the quantity but the quality of America's education. For we recognize that nuclear age problems cannot be solved with horse and buggy learning. The three R's of our school system must be supported by the three T's: *teachers* who are superior, *techniques* of instruction that are modern, and *thinking* about education which places it first in all our plans and hopes.

In that statement we see the reflections of many legislative acts and programs that have either a direct or an indirect influence on the instructional media programs in our schools throughout the nation. Before President Johnson's statement, the National Defense Education Act of 1958 in unprecedented fashion had poured up to $90 million a year into the effort to strengthen instruction in science, mathematics, and foreign languages, and then had been broadened out to include history, civics, geography, English, and reading. The NDEA allotments to the fifty states in the three-year period from 1965 through 1967 were in excess of $230 million. And as is so well known, the expansion of the NDEA Title XI Institute Program to include media specialists within its financial support sphere had and is having salutary effects on personnel resources development. With the passage of the Elementary and Secondary Act of 1965, and its massive first-year support amounting to $1.3 billion continuing annually through a five-year period, we have the unprecedented influence on media development along a wide spectrum of services and activities. We should not fail to note the fact that the NDEA financial support for strengthening instruction was distributed through various state plans that called for matching expenditures by school districts. Also with respect to school district use of ESEA Title II allotments according to state plans and distribution requirements, school districts were eligible for funds only if they did not decrease their own unsupported expenditures for the same kinds of instructional media below amounts expended the previous year.

First Year Summary Reports on ESEA Activities

Although the U.S. Office of Education has under its administrative control the implementation of some twenty-three major legislative acts and programs, we present here information relative to the Elementary and Secondary Education Act of 1965 only. The various titles of the Act are as follows: Title I, Education of Children of Low-Income Families; Title II, School Library Resources (Instructional Media); Title III, Supplementary Educational Centers and Services; Title IV, Educational Research and Training (Amendments to Cooperative Research Act of 1954); and, Title V, Strengthening State Departments of Education. We can see in these titles the bold implications for media support and development throughout the fifty states and outlying areas. The following brief evaluational reports are quoted from the *American School & University*:[6]

Activity under Title I. During its first year of operation, with 90 per cent of all school districts eligible for assistance, Title I made $965 million available to approximately 17,000 school districts for programs reaching 7 million children. About $680 million or 71% went for salaries, and $285 million was spent for equipment, books and instructional aids. . . .

Activity under Title II. Title II provided $100 million in fiscal year 1966 and made possible the purchase of books, periodicals, . . . maps, charts, globes, recordings, films and similar materials in amounts to serve 49 million students and 1.9 million teachers in public and private elementary and secondary schools. . . . State educational agencies used administrative funds to conduct workshops, provide consultative services, and prepare publications for in-service education. . . .

Activity under Title III. Reporting on 294 operational projects approved as part of Title III, the Office of Education reports that 93,289 pre-school children participated in projects, plus 131,520 adults. Taking part in public and non-public school projects were 6,306,784 elementary school children and 3,619,075 secondary school children together with 314,571 public school teachers and 40,136 non-public school teachers. (The appropriation for this work in fiscal 1966 was $98 million for the fifty states.)

Activity under Title IV. The most recent effort of

[6] *American School & University*, Vol. 39, No. 4, December 1966, pp. 28–29.

the Office of Education's bureau of research has been the launching of regional educational laboratories as part of ESEA's Title IV. Twenty regional laboratories have been established and are under development. In fiscal year 1966 the bureau had a budget of $103 million. . . .

Activity under Title V. Eighty-five per cent of the $14,450,000 provided for Title V in fiscal year 1966 was available to the fifty states. . . . A $100,000 minimum was first allocated to each state, with applications then filed for specific grants. Fifteen per cent of the total allocation was reserved for the Section 505 projects—experimental and innovative and involving several or all of the states cooperatively. . . . Using Title V funds, more than a third of the state departments of education are helping local school districts to make constructive organizational changes including the consolidation of numerous small, ineffectual schools and school districts. Evidence indicates that such consolidations will increase at an accelerated rate. . . .

According to Nolan Estes,[7] some $53 million covered the 839 Title III projects that were finally approved, but over 2,700 proposals were submitted originally calling for an outlay of $250 million. Over 10 million schoolchildren have been involved in the projects that were approved and implemented. His concluding statement is highly significant, "The PACE (Projects to Advance Creativity in Education) design for innovation puts an end to the excuses of our school districts that they lack the capacity to change. We live in an age where we cannot afford a continued lag in the implementation of new ideas in education." See Figure 13-2. Even though we may have less direct support of media materials in PACE, we have the opportunity for vast development in ideas that may facilitate change in the future. Many of these changes will without doubt call for audiovisual and print media services.

Even though it may serve as a minor deterrent to our enthusiasms, we must point out that in the allotments of Title II funds, which amounted to $98 million, no more than $25 million went for purchases of audiovisual media materials. In perusing the terse statements describing plans for allotting funds to the various states, the published figures[8] indicated that, during

the first year at least, it is extremely rare for a state to recommend a 50 per cent expenditure for audiovisual media as compared with *print* resources. The tendency seemed to be to allot 25 per cent for this purpose with the balance going for reference books, some textbooks, and limited processing costs. However, on a recurring annual basis, such expenditures will add up to significant inventories. Moreover, these allotments may serve to indicate impoverishment in the print-medium holdings in school libraries. (See Chapter Twelve.)

Short-Range Impact

We can add up the dollars spent and realize that in many legislative acts, and the programs generated by them, we have added immense proportions to the stature of media development nationally. We readily see in the flow of financial support, both on a matching and a 100 per cent grant basis, a greatly increased inventory of media. We see new services for teachers and pupils growing out of the organized and reorganized media distribution centers in schools, and because of these services we know that teachers have moved toward more skillful and insightful use of media along a broader front of learning activities. Such broader use of media is certain to be attended by the growth of new images of the teaching process. See Figure 13-3. We see many innovative procedures being implemented in school districts, far and wide, each with its new media equipment and materials, with new groupings of pupils and teachers and new points of emphasis. These media materials as resources, and the day-by-day implementation of the new ideas in education constitute the short-range impact of the dollars from federal sources.

Long-Range Impact

The short-range impact, important as the fulcrum for change and development, is only part, perhaps a small part, of the long-range impact. It is the cumulative impact of growing inventories, the sum of programs, centers, and experiments for the disadvantaged and the privileged alike, that add up to the long-range impact on media-use development in schools. The millions of youngsters, the hundreds of thousands of teachers, and their changed

[7] Nolan Estes, "ESEA: Dimensions '67 of Title III," *Audiovisual Instruction*, Vol. 11, No. 10, December 1966, pp. 795–797, 864.

[8] Dorothy H. Currie, "ESEA: Fifty States Implement Title II," *Audiovisual Instruction*, Vol. 11, No. 10, December 1966, pp. 787–790.

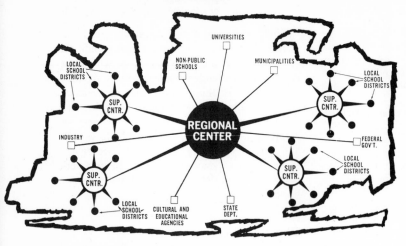

A SUPPLEMENTAL CENTER SCHEMATIC PLAN

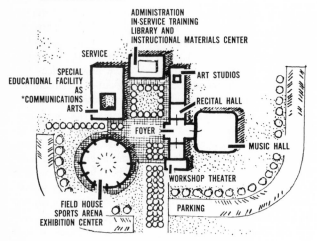

*at this center only . . .
— other supplemental centers have their own special facility

THE REGIONAL CENTER

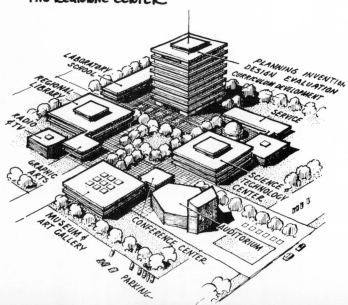

Figure 13-2. The regional media-service plan has been implemented under federal grants. Following up the work reported in Figure 13-1, Jack Tanzman became the principal investigator for a Title III Planning Project under Elementary and Secondary Education legislation to develop an expansion of the regional center concept for Nassau County in New York. The project is called SCORE, which stands for Supplemental Centers for Organizing Regional Education. Thus 56 school districts would be served by one regional center and a number of supplementary centers, each offering in-depth services along specialized lines such as data automation, instructional media, in-service education, library services, and others. The three diagrams shown here provide opportunity to study the plans that have been developed thus far by The Educational Council for Research and Development for Nassau County. The first diagram is labeled SCORE and indicates the relationships between school districts and cooperating agencies and the regional and supplemental centers. The second diagram indicates operations at the regional center, and the third offers a conceptualization of services at a supplemental center. *Courtesy Jack Tanzman, The Educational Council for Research and Development, Nassau County, Mineola, New York.*

Figure 13-3. An example of innovative efforts to broaden the base of media use is the Resource Travelab project that was planned by the Audio-Visual Department of the Pawtucket, Rhode Island Public Schools and made possible by a federal grant. The Travelab unit includes storage for films, filmstrips, overhead transparencies, tapes, study prints, records, books, teaching supplies, and media-preparation materials and equipment. The two interior views show film inspection, tape duplication, projection, and the array of media, with opportunity to look toward the front or the rear. Financial support from sources outside the schools has, since 1958, moved school programs ahead in great leaps. Many are still far behind. *Courtesy Public Schools, Pawtucket, Rhode Island.*

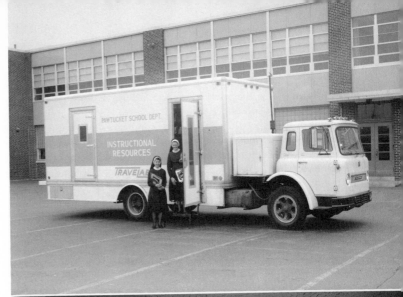

images of the value and process of education will have by far the greater impact during the years ahead. It will be the changed image in the minds of townspeople who vote the bond issues for new schools and their equipment inventories, who vote to authorize the expansion of media center services, vote to authorize new positions for the extra personnel that will be needed to carry on the new work required for many of the modern systems inaugurated that will reflect the true impact of the new support for education. The long-range effect will result in an accelerating escalation to a new plateau of media use and development, a new plateau of educational effectiveness, one that will be carried on tomorrow by the new generation for having had the significant personal experiences with modern-day methodology today. Thus a new commitment to the employment of and provision for the use of technology on a regularized and indispensable basis will be the final result and will lead to a more responsive and sensitive capability for future educational change.

Taking Appropriate Action to Obtain Grants for Media-Use Purposes

Practicing media directors need to be alert to opportunities for financing media-development programs, and doubling their presently planned capital expenditures through matching grants under NDEA state-plan reimbursements. Some of these grants may come easy, others may demand solid hours of creative effort in writing proposals. We do not advocate that the prospective media director prepare to go out and bring in all the media equipment and materials he needs, plus his own salary and the wages for his auxiliary staff, by means of fund raising activities. We do, however, urge that every reasonable effort be expended to enhance the usual efforts of a school district to improve its media holdings. Such financing opportunities are so significant today, and may continue to be so important in the years ahead, that a number of discussions on desirable media-director action are offered for consideration.

Familiarization with Sources of Financial Assistance. Media directors should make a study of all the sources of financial assistance. They should therefore take steps to locate sourcebooks or sourcelists of not only governmental agencies that administer legislative acts and programs, state plans, and the like, but also listings of foundations and business concerns, both local and remote. The director needs help in this search, and can rightly expect other school leaders to participate in the process. By virtue of his contacts, receptivity in outlook, technological search, work with committees and study groups involving his colleagues and associates in other towns and cities, the director may be in a favorable position to get information. For example the volume published by the 3M Company[9] titled *Guide to Support Programs for Education* provides vital information on such topics as the following:

Principal Laws Aiding Education
Aid to Education: Plant and Equipment
Aid to Education: Research, Development and Demonstrations
Aid to Education: Staff Training
Elementary and Secondary Schools (Public and Private), U.S. Government Aid
Elementary and Secondary Schools (Public and Private), Aid from Foundations
Elementary and Secondary Schools (Public and Private), Aid from Business
How to Write a Proposal.

State plans are widely disseminated, but other sources of assistance may have to be sought in other listings. Although it is safe to say that the bulk of federal aid to elementary and secondary schools—for example, grants under NDEA and ESEA—will come through the state as authorized under state plans, there are other government and private sources of financial aid. These sources have to be located and the nature of their contributions ascertained.

Millions of dollars in aid to education lie fallow each year because educators do not know where they are or how to apply for them. . . . foundations and government agencies stand ready to aid you and your institution. However, you must also know how to prepare a successful application for these funds.

Your first step is reconnaisance. You should obtain as much current information as possible about the donor you plan to approach. . . All foundations, including those associated with business firms, must file Form 990-A with the Internal Revenue Service each year. To learn how you may inspect these

[9] *Guide to Support Programs for Education.* (St. Paul, Minn.: Educational Services Press, Visual Products Dept., 3M Company, 1966.)

reports, inquire at the nearest office of the Internal Revenue Service. You should know also that the bi-monthly issues of "Foundation News" list every grant of $10,000 or more that comes to the attention of the Foundation Library Center, 444 Madison Avenue, N.Y., N.Y.[10]

Study the Requirements in State Plans. One of the ways of assuring success in obtaining financial aid for media-development programs is to study the specific requirements of all state plans that have been published and distributed. Using Connecticut as an example, we note that in addition to the allotment of ESEA Title 1 funds amounting to approximately $7.2 million for the fiscal year 1966, the Connecticut General Assembly passed Public Act 523, entitled An Act Concerning State Aid for Disadvantaged Children, that provided the sum of $10 million for the biennium. Thus there were two state plans for two separate legislative acts, one providing money from federal sources through the state, the other providing money from state sources only. In addition there were a number of other state plans, one concerning NDEA Title III, one with reference to $1,000 grants for establishing small demonstration centers for trying out promising ideas and educational practices, and insofar as elementary and secondary schools are concerned, one for ESEA Title II applications. Usually state plans are very specific in their requirements, and the application and proposal forms, together with specific allotments to various school districts are explicit to the degree that prompt and effective action may be facilitated. In many states unusually good consultative staffs have been established for the implementation of state plans. Under such conditions, media program administrators need to provide leadership through every available means to facilitate needed action. As an example of the simplicity of suggested application forms, we quote items 6, 7, and 8 (the preceding items deal with selection and cost estimates) from the Public Law 89-10 (Title II, Project Application form for School Library Resources[11]) as follows:

6. Please write below a brief statement describing the instructional needs to be served by the

10 *Ibid.*, p. 11.
11 Connecticut State Department of Education, Hartford, 1966.

library books and periodicals and AV materials requested in this project, e.g. elementary school reading program; revised courses in social studies in grades 10, 11, 12; improvement in the teaching of art, music, etc.

_____

_____

_____

7. Please write below a statement indicating, in general, strengths and needs for library books, periodicals and AV materials. Describe briefly your present and long-range plan for improving services with materials to the instructional program. If you do not have a centralized school library and a professional school librarian, or Audio-Visual Center and AV Personnel, state your plan for adding these.

_____

_____

_____

8. I certify that materials requested are:
   1. Suitable for the instructional programs for which they are being acquired.
   2. Not intended for religious worship or instruction.
   3. Not consumable in use.
   4. Approved for use or are in use in local public elementary or secondary schools in Connecticut.
   5. Are in addition to those materials that will be purchased by funds from state and local, or private school sources in an amount not less than such funds provided during the base year.

_____
Principal

The allotments from the state of Connecticut for the 169 villages, towns, and cities, varied according to distribution formulas from $16 to $69,500. The total of the allotments under this ESEA Title amounted to $1.1 million. Although state and other grants and reimbursements may be for purposes other than media development, we need to point out that the media director must study the *fine print* as he plans proposals and applications himself, or as he endeavors to facilitate this work by media-service coordinators, school principals, and curriculum personnel. It is almost certain that some of the individuals who write proposals of their own will desire to incorporate audiovisual and print media in them for their own purposes, and the media specialist will surely be called upon for assistance in these cases.

Get Help in Planning Action. Getting a new idea and implementing it in light of available financial support, especially along the lines of instructional technology, takes time, energy, and painstaking care. Can the media program director actually be expected to write every proposal and application for the use and purchase of media materials and equipment in a school district? The obvious answer is that if he must as an individual wield the pen that writes out every application and control every media-use plan thought up by others, then he will be the greatest obstacle that could exist. Hence we assert that the media director should locate and tap good sources of help for planning his own acts, and should find ways to facilitate the work of other groups in the district at large and in every school-building unit. With these broad aspects of action in mind, we suggest that a media program director

1. Organize study groups of media directors in nearby cities to discuss typical problems and financial-support procedures.

2. Attend statewide meetings to study state and federal, and other sources.

3. Organize, or get others to organize, local school-district study committees to evaluate existing programs with a view to discovering needs for possible innovative action.

4. Establish contacts with state department of education consultants and specialists.

5. Hold special meetings with school-building media coordinators to plan media-development programs, and elicit their help in consulting with other teachers and curriculum personnel.

6. Elicit cooperation from department heads and curriculum study committees in fields and areas covered by legislation or state and federal programs, in preparing their own proposals and recommendations for specific projects to be undertaken.

In taking such action locally, we must relate pertinent aspects of knowledge about good leadership practices and the *change process*. Actually the media services leader will become the change agent for some of the innovations being proposed, and we should be mindful of the inter-relationships between curriculum personnel, administrative staff members, and boards

of education in the matter of arriving at decisions for change. The fact remains that proposals will have to be prepared by a number of different individuals and duly constituted groups in any given district, and it is natural that media utilization in varying degrees of sophistication may have significant roles to play in them. The media administrator, and school-building coordinators as well, may therefore need to play change-agent roles, with and for other groups, and they may need to be the writers of many of their own proposals as we have emphasized previously in other chapters. Help for writing proposals, even those in which media utilization is a major part, may have to come by means of additionally employed staff on a full- or part-time basis. Thus if an assistant were to be employed to carry on specified duties at media-service headquarters, such as for example conducting the in-service education program, the media director could then devote a specified number of hours or days each week to preparing, or guiding the preparation of, a series of proposals for the district. It is not likely that an overextended media specialist putting in overtime doing professional work for a school district, can jettison one work load in favor of another, planning to catch up at a later date.

Techniques for Writing Proposals. We have already pointed out some valuable clues for the preparation of good proposals, but we need to stress a number of critical procedures. Each of the suggestions should be dealt with in depth, but we shall leave the details to imaginative media specialists.

1. Ascertain the true intent of the legislative act or program. Keep requests in line with that intention.

2. Obtain accurate information about the size of allotments that are available, and be reasonable in the amount of financial support requested in the proposed budget. This is another way of saying that the scope of coverage should be limited to a few critically important elements to facilitate funding and successful operation.

3. Follow the guidelines that have been identified and described. Include all pertinent information desired as a minimum. When proposals are lengthy, make sure that information is pertinent and essential.

4. The central idea in the proposal should be

clearly focused on the learner and the curriculum. The basic need must be stated clearly and then justified along lines of instructional effects and impact. It is important to emphasize goals rather than processes, software rather than hardware, instructional significance rather than instructional trivia.

5. Be indelibly clear about *ends* and *means* relationships. That is, state objectives in the terminology of instructional results and changes in the capabilities of people, not as processes, steps in installation, kinds of media equipment, tests to be constructed, and programs to be produced.

6. Make optimum use of visualization processes.

7. Obtain copies of proposals submitted by others, especially successful ones, but beware of uncritical acceptance of the designs presented.

8. Tap good sources of help. Join forces with colleagues.

9. Obtain all necessary clearances and get advice on local procedure.

10. Submit your proposals early enough to avoid embarrassing superiors who need time to study and approve your work.

The *Guide to Support Programs for Education*[12] also provides a list of procedural hints that includes a number of other points for the consideration of proposal writers:

A grant, however, is rarely awarded on the basis of personalities. Hence, you should devote great care to the development of your proposal. It would be well to establish an advisory group or task force within your organization specifically to draft your application. You should be prepared to explain:

The need for your project, in detail, with appropriate documentation.

Objectives of your proposal, with considerable specificity.

Precisely how the project would be conducted: its management, duration, auspices, etc. The professional background of the principals should be described.

Budget for the program; including overhead; administrative costs; staff salaries; equipment; transportation; construction; operation and maintenance of facilities and equipment; etc.

The plans for follow-up, publication of findings, use of new facilities or equipment, etc.

Optimum Balance in Using Financial Support Sources. As we pointed out in the budget

12 *Op. cit.*, pp. 11–12.

format sections, we have a total cost for a given set of instructional needs and these costs have to be financed. Thus we face the day in which we either obtain increased revenues or we are denied them. Any combination of available financial support programs may need critical attention to accomplish a desirable balance in the applications and proposals being submitted. For example, NDEA Title III may be used for purchasing media equipment and materials for use only in specified critical areas. Thus, local funds should be earmarked for other areas in good balance, or according to need and priority. ESEA Title II funds are of course for media materials, not equipment, hence such funds must be balanced against use of local funds for meeting other needs. The level of local financing must also be balanced against matching grants, even though those grants are *for restricted use*. We see then a basic pattern in the ways local funds are used to meet school-district and specific school-building media costs. Also, as we have said, state plans often require that no reduction be made in school-district expenditures for specified materials in order to be eligible for grants or reimbursements. The media director will normally have an opportunity to obtain advice on these matters from business managers and other administrative personnel and, of course, he can consult other media directors whose problems are similar to his own. His budget plans will have to take into account, in important ways, estimates of income from all sources, and he will have to make his long-term plans accordingly. Financial support from multiple sources may introduce a few new problems, such as having to set up one or more additional systems of accounting or record keeping, but no media director could possibly abhor minor irritants of that nature in view of the major results that accrue.

Problem-Solving Activities

1. Just how much participation by other people should be sought in budget preparation? Describe a plan for such participation that you believe would be effective.

2. Following the example of cost determination presented in this chapter, make a survey of the present inventory of audiovisual media materials and equipment in any school building

you wish to identify. Establish a desirable operational level to be reached in the future and write out your requirements for financial support to accomplish your objective in five years. (This means that you are to construct a new table showing existing inventory plus a desirable level of inventory plus costs.) On the basis of your figures, estimate costs for an entire school district.

3. How does long-term planning, based on accurate data that pertain to specific needs, affect budgeting procedures? Do you believe that "padding" the budget is a desirable tactic to gain your ends? What better basis can you suggest for requesting funds?

4. Make an extensive list of audiovisual media-service items for which money would likely have to be spent during a fiscal or school year, classifying them under the following fund headings: (a) Salaries and Wages, (b) Operating Expenses, and (c) Capital Outlay. Select items in terms of personnel, supplies, equipment, services, and operational spaces that you believe are desirable for a specific community with which you are familiar.

5. Study budget categories as used in your local school system (or a district of your choice) and code the items of your expenditure list (from Problem 4) to conform with this new classification. (As an alternate plan, use the standard classifications presented in the text.)

6. In the over-all school budget, as presented to local finance committees, should the media service budget be "hidden" or set forth openly as a separate budget? How do local conditions affect your recommendation on a decision in this matter?

7. How may limited funds be fairly allotted among several school units for vital media services? How can you employ the "democracy" principle here?

8. According to your own budget system, state how you can make provisions for contingencies. How would dependence upon special sources of income affect your long-term planning?

9. What plan would you propose to maintain control of expenditures in your own actual or hypothetical budget situation? That is, if other local accounting agencies maintain a check-up on budget standing, what additional check-ups would you carry out on your own to obtain up-to-date information on expenditures and balances?

10. Study the cost-determination example for a middle school of 1,600 pupils, as presented in the text, and prepare a critical evaluation of the portrayed status of technological media use in the school. Where is the system weak? Where is it strong? What additional recommendations would you make with regard to recommended expenditures especially in view of Chapters 9, 10, and 11?

11. Using the cost-determination tables presented in this text, identify and establish your own reasonable and justifiable level of operational effectiveness, changing the inventory figures accordingly. Now figure the cost per year for media equipment and materials for a five-year period to reach the level of adequacy you have specified.

12. Participate as a member of one of several task forces in the preparation of a proposal for a state grant in support of a media program for a school district with which you are familiar. Do the same for a direct federal grant. (Each task force should therefore produce two proposals for media utilization, submitting them plus a 50-word summary of each proposal together with a brief title to an editorial committee that would screen all material submitted and duplicate the best summaries for distribution to the group. State and federal guidelines and plans should be collected and studied before the proposals are prepared by the various task forces. All proposals should be prepared in direct relation to a published state or federal announcement.)

13. Making good use of latest print-medium program standards, prepare a set of cost-determination tables for the same school used in the text. Include print-medium program costs only, and use the *adequacy* level, as applied previously for audiovisual media.

References

Currie, Dorothy H. "ESEA: Fifty States Implement Title II," *Audiovisual Instruction*, Vol. 11, No. 10, December 1966, pp. 787–790.

Estes, Nolan. "ESEA: Dimensions '67 of Title III," *Audiovisual Instruction*, Vol. 11, No. 10, December 1966, pp. 795–797.

Eynon, Emily F. "Title IV: Elementary and Secondary Education Act of 1965," *Audiovisual Instruction*, Vol. 10, No. 9, November 1965, pp. 719–721.

Gauerke, Warren E. and Jack R. Childress (eds.). *Theory and Practice of School Finance.* (Chicago: Rand McNally, 1966).

Guide to Support Programs for Education. (St. Paul, Minn.: Education Services Press, Visual Products Department, 3M Company, 1966).

Harris, Chester W. (ed.). *Encyclopedia of Educational Research*, rev. ed. (New York: Macmillan, 1960).

Hughes, John F. "Title I: Elementary and Secondary Education Act of 1965," *Audiovisual Instruction*, Vol. 10, No. 8, October 1965, pp. 620–625.

Lewis, Philip, "Elementary and Secondary Education Act of 1965, Title I: Designing Projects," *Audiovisual Instruction*, Vol. 10, No. 9, November 1965, pp. 722–723.

Morse, Wayne E. "The Role of Government in Educational Change," *Audiovisual Instruction*, Vol. 10, No. 8, October 1965, pp. 616–617.

"New Legislation of Importance to the Audiovisual Field," *Audiovisual Instruction*, Vol. 10, No. 8, October 1965, pp. 618–619.

Nothing Matters More (A Summary of the Titles of the Elementary and Secondary Education Act of 1965). (Fairfax, Va.: National Audio-Visual Association, 3150 Spring Street, 1966).

Ovsiew, Leon and William B. Castetter. *Budgeting for Better Schools.* (Englewood Cliffs, N.J.: Prentice-Hall, 1960).

Phillips, Harry L., and John Lorenz. "Title II: Elementary and Secondary Education Act of 1965," *Audiovisual Instruction*, Vol. 10, No. 8, October 1965, pp. 626–629.

Reason, Paul L. and Alpheus L. White. *Financial Accounting for Local and State School Systems.* (Prepared under the auspices of the U.S. Department of Health, Education, and Welfare, Office of Education.) (Washington, D.C.: Superintendent of Documents, U.S. Government Printing Office, 1957, Reprinted in 1964).

Rugg, K. C. *Improving Instruction: Budgeting Your Audiovisual Program.* (Prepared pursuant to a contract with the U.S. Office of Education.) (Bloomington, Indiana: Audiovisual Center, Indiana University, 1960).

Stanley, Raymond J. "Title III: Elementary and Secondary Education Act of 1965," *Audiovisual Instruction*, Vol. 10, No. 8, October 1965, pp. 630–632.

Tanzman, Jack. "Three Ways to Make your AV Know-How Count," *Audiovisual Instruction*, Vol. 11, No. 10, December 1966, pp. 797–799.

14

Public Understanding and Support

Senator Wayne E. Morse was one of the two sponsors of the Morse–Perkins Act, otherwise known as the Elementary and Secondary Education Act of 1965. When he addressed the concluding session of the DAVI Convention in Milwaukee he had many words of wisdom to share with the assembled throng. It would be wise for us all, in the light of the topic for this chapter, to review his advice and his hopes for the future as expressed in the following excerpt from that address:

All that has been done and all that it is supposed to do under P.L. 89–10 can blow away as sparks upon the wind if, in the understandable exuberance of this moment, the sentiment begins to grow that the battles are won and that the apples and pears of learning will fall into the outstretched hands of the media specialists by virtue of the law of gravity. Nothing could be more mistaken.

Enactment of P.L. 89–10 has won for you the right to compete, and that is all. The claimants for the right to serve youngsters through their special approaches are legion. You are convinced that your techniques and abilities to perform effectively and efficiently the great job of educating the young are superior to many of the standard and traditional methods. Yet these views and values are not, as I am sure you recognize, shared as universally by your professional colleagues as you would wish. . . .

. . . P.L. 89–10 is threshold legislation. It is not the general federal financial aid to schools in coverage, scope, extent, or amount which many of us feel is needed. It is a most useful additional category of school assistance, but it is not even a partial answer to the major problem. . . . we still lack the master key of a general federal aid bill. We are working on it. We hope to have it fashioned and in use within a very few years. When the day comes to take that great bill through the Congress, I know we can count upon you to play the part of citizen-statesmanship and to support that great effort as effectively as you have the predecessor statutes.

We are of one mind increasingly in this country, and that is that we are determined to see to it that each and every child, no matter what his race, religion, physical disability, or economic status is, shall have the opportunity to share in the birthright franchise this country offers. In its educational aspect, that birthright is the opportunity to gain through education the development of the God-given potentialities of talent and ability.[1]

[1] Wayne E. Morse, "The Role of Government in Educational Change," *Audiovisual Instruction*, Vol. 10, No. 8, October 1965, p. 617.

It is indeed true that we must meet the challenge of our new opportunities and work for the fulfillment of the vision we have of future educational development. We must therefore recognize the major importance of our activities in the field of public understanding and support. Our work needs not only to be done along the lines of good communications with our professional colleagues, but with the lay public, and as we look ahead to the various aspects of that work, we urge prospective and practicing media specialists to assume this responsibility with all seriousness.

Perhaps it would be wise to recall that it was just about ten years before the passage of the Elementary and Secondary Education Act that the executive committee of the Department of Audiovisual Instruction of the NEA in a letter dated December 19, 1955, felt compelled to issue a strong protest to the White House Conference Committee of the Department of Health, Education and Welfare, over statements in its formal report that classed *visual aid facilities* for both elementary and secondary schools as *desirable* but not *mandatory*. That shocking pronouncement focused attention upon the apparent low level of public understanding that existed then as to the nature and significance of media for improving learning. The financial support climate is vastly more favorable now than in 1955, yet the advice that Senator Morse gave his audience that evening in Milwaukee should not be forgotten. If we take his words to heart, we will add an organized effort to develop public understanding and support for our media development programs, to the many other problem-solving activities made possible by our repertoire of skills.

The Public Relations Climate

The media director in a new position may discover that his efforts to promote good public relations will be greatly facilitated because of the existence of a well-organized and coordinated program established by his chief school administrator. He may find that high levels of good will, understanding, and support have already been reached, and in such fortunate cases he ought to keep the channels to public opinion active and supplied through continuing efforts. On the other hand, he may find that his school colleagues, through local failures of their own or because of local factors beyond their control, have failed to establish a favorable public relations environment. So, if the director finds his program has understanding and support, he needs to maintain and increase it; and if he doesn't have it, he must take steps to obtain it.

He cannot, of course, carry on alone this complex business, but by whatever pattern or method his efforts are coordinated and related to those of others, he will have a dual role to play, namely, that of helping others use good communicative techniques for their own public relations programs, and making sure that his own service program in media methods is adequately understood and supported. He needs to recognize the over-all problem of school-system public relations, and he must take necessary precautions to fit into a public relations organization as already established, striking a good balance between his own specific interests and the interests of others. If he is to be successful, he must analyze this local situation accurately before proceeding with his plans for action.

Preparations for Action

In preceding chapters, detailed plans have been recommended for adequate facilities by means of which teachers could put audiovisual and print media to work effectively. Some of the facilities, especially for expanded programs at ideal operational levels, are costly indeed, and probably no superintendent, director, or organization can singlehandedly bring about the understanding and support for the growth in services that have been set forth as desirable. If the media director is to be successful, he must undertake to identify and utilize those forces that collectively, and in good balance with other aspects of the educational program, can lead to the accomplishment of established goals. This chapter will provide guidance for the director in reaching sound decisions as to what can be done locally to achieve his goals. Such decisions should be based on sound theory.

Theoretical Basis for Promoting Public Understanding and Support

Throughout this book emphasis has been given to participation by those who are affected in the making of policy. This emphasis provides the theoretical basis of good public relations programs. Stated in simple terms, it is as follows: *Financial support and cooperation are likely to be greater when many people, laymen as well as professional, have a knowledge of, and are given a voice in, media-use affairs and have respect for the director both as a person and as a professional worker.* Olsen[2] asserts that the first principle of successful public relations may be stated thus, "If you want somebody to support a program, be sure that he understands its values and has shared with personal satisfaction in the planning and development of that program."

These statements imply that the layman has acquired knowledge and understanding and has personally shared in making plans and decisions. These implications must be recognized as constituting the two aspects of the director's effort in his public relations program. Moreover, he ought to recognize the possibility that sharing in decision may well be one of the best routes to knowledge and understanding, and as such, it is a promising method for initiating the *change* process. Once again, looking broadly at the entire public relations program, the American Association of School Administrators[3] states in its Yearbook the following all-inclusive guiding principle, "Sound school public relations must be *honest* in intent and execution, *intrinsic* in the school program, *continuous* in application, *positive* in approach, *comprehensive* in character, *sensitive* to the publics concerned, and *simple* in meaning and conception." The director who develops maximum understanding of such principles will make few mistakes as he proceeds to organize and implement a planned program of public relations activity.

Enlisting the Assistance of Colleagues

One of the surest routes to good will of colleagues is to earn their respect by establishing a record of friendly, capable, industrious, and efficient professional service. If the director has followed suggestions made in earlier chapters,

he has worked closely with school principals in solving some of their supervisory problems, and he has won the support of the superintendent through his able reports based on accurate records, through his businesslike plans, and through his general professional workmanship. Of course it is likely that if the director has laid the groundwork for support by his superintendent, he doubtlessly has also developed understanding and support among the Board of Education members, but no opportunity should be missed to demonstrate the value of technological developments to the Board members as representatives of the community. In this connection the director should be alert to the opportunity to assist the superintendent and Board members in preparing audiovisual media for their own contacts with groups within the community, thus promoting in the larger sense an understanding of and support for the total educational program. Such direct services to top administrators and Board members are often the most powerful means of gaining internal support for the specific program of media services.

The director should seek to know his colleagues, from Board members to custodians, and to become known, without being judged as currying favor in any form. Actually the director has a natural opportunity to become widely known among school staff members, and this may be an important professional asset for him. As a result of these activities internal to the school system, his status should be such that his understanding and talent for sound professional action are recognized. This is the foundation without which only limited success for the media director's program is possible. He should also recognize the essential need to enlist the cooperation of his colleagues for actual contributions of work in telling and showing the media story. For example, they will write accounts for him about their unique teaching activities; they will inform him when they sense that an activity has public relations value; they will take pictures, prepare television scripts, give demonstrations, prepare exhibits and other media for special presentations, prepare leaflets, serve on committees to plan action. In a host of other ways, both directly, and indirectly through their pupils, they can help to implement an effective public relations program.

---

[2] Edward G. Olsen (ed.), *School and Community*, 2nd ed. (Englewood Cliffs, N.J.: Prentice-Hall, 1954), p. 429.

[3] By permission. From *Public Relations for America's Schools*, 28th Yearbook of the American Association of School Administrators of the NEA, 1201 Sixteenth St., N.W., Washington, D.C., 1950, p. 17.

Public relations programs, in meeting the *comprehensive principle* mentioned earlier, should involve all the staff and all the curriculum. The media director, then, needs good will and cooperative endeavor from his school-building coordinators, and from teachers and their pupils. From his superintendent and Board members, from his supervisory colleagues, and from school principals, he needs understanding and general approval to proceed creatively with public relations contacts, unhampered except for the usual clearance and approval formalities. Such freedom of action, once bestowed, must never be unwisely used, and here the media director as a public relations man needs to be cautioned against failure to give appropriate credit where credit belongs. He needs to take care that he becomes the press agent not for himself but for the program whose growth is so vital for all instructional activity.

Planning the Public Relations Program

A good teacher will not only be a good planner of goals but will also plan the activities to accomplish those goals. It has been repeatedly emphasized also that any director of media services will be more successful if he defines his objectives and plans activities to reach them. The application of this procedure is just as valid for public relations programs. The director needs to define the objective to be reached and then to plan with the appropriate people, his own helpers or those in a formal public relations organization, the means for reaching it. Some programs may call for intensive activity brought about by some crisis that, despite carefully planned, long-term, continuous programs for understanding and support, may occasionally arise. Other programs need to be specific in appeal to highly selected segments of the community, and still other program efforts need to be very general in nature, including not only every parent but every resident, voter and nonvoter. Sometimes it is essential that activities be planned for such specific segments of the public as the school board, the finance board, town meeting participants, and sometimes for the residents who work in other cities, instead of residents who think and feel differently about the community because they have never lived

anywhere else. Sometimes programs have to be planned solely for transmission by mass communication media. The director ought to make decisions about planning in terms of his sensitivity to various groups within the community; to fail to identify such groups and their characteristic attitudes, beliefs, and value patterns is to continue to operate ineffectively. The AASA Yearbook[4] puts it this way:

In a limited sense to be aware of or sensitive to any public is to be aware of its basic drives or needs. It is not implied that the most primitive wants of man must be exploited in any vile sense to achieve success in public relations. In a more kindly interpretation, to be sensitive to and solicitous of these needs is an initial kind of respect to pay to an individual or to a public.

In achieving understanding of and support from various publics, both specific and general programs may have to be carried on simultaneously. That is, a steady flow of general-interest information may have to be directed to all publics at the same time that a specific program of activity involving talks and demonstrations, personal conferences with individuals, study-group activity, news releases, charts for town reports, and a graphically illustrated leaflet is directed toward special target groups. For example, school board members, town officials, and town meeting representatives may need to be given exclusive information for the purpose of obtaining an increase in the school's budget for

1. Replacement of outmoded media equipment.

2. A closed-circuit television studio and transmission system to all schools.

3. Raising the motion picture library to a higher level of adequacy.

4. Including adequate media facilities in construction costs of new schools.

Specific programs of action such as these need to be integrated with continuous program plans in order to avoid an excessive momentary concentration that few people understand or want and that a few individuals may have strong reasons for opposing. Media directors who have developed the desire and skill to plan their action far ahead in terms of well-defined goals will put such individuals at a

4 *Ibid.*, p. 29.

disadvantage because they will have mobilized the facts and have devised methods of using forces to offset their predicted reaction. However, this points up the need for another important aspect of preparation for action.

Identification of Positive and Negative Forces

The director of media services may, whether he likes it or not, and despite all he has done to work effectively, sincerely, and intelligently, discover that he has a fight on his hands over the attainment of *bona fide* service objectives. He may, of course, have come to the conclusion that such community conflict was inevitable, and his superiors may have even been willing to go for the showdown decision in his behalf. Now if the winning of such a decision is really important, then all favorable forces need to be mobilized calmly and effectively. But which forces are favorable? This question should not go unanswered, and it need not if the director sets out deliberately to identify these forces by thorough search. He may conduct a survey of the staff personally or by questionnaire, he may seek help from his colleagues in surveying the community, and he may have to seek the help of capable individuals in formulating his strategy. One thing is certain, a conflict in reaching an important decision should not be allowed to become anything other than a professional matter. The director must keep his facts straight and maintain a calm composure, and if the decision goes against him, he should be in a position to accept it without personal injury, since he has presented the facts, explained them, and has earnestly sought to get people to decide on what he believes they really needed. The director ought to recognize too that the identification of positive and negative forces is actually an application of the principle of sensitivity to a community's various publics. The anticipation of the beliefs and reactions of negative forces will not only be a valuable procedure in case of community-wide conflict but it will also have its values within a staff organization.

One main route to understanding and support of the media program is through citizen participation in study and decision-reaching processes. The other route is through an adequate comprehensive information-giving program for the community. The subsequent sections of this chapter deal with these topics.

Understanding and Support Through Public Study and Action

The participation of all concerned in arriving at the wisest possible media-service policy has been emphasized in this volume as one of the major aspects of the director's leadership, and in Chapter 2 a commitment to the principle of democratic action was recognized as an essential asset for administrative performance. In this section the director is challenged to undertake an even broader participation, namely, with citizen groups, in helping to study and find sound solutions for the major problems in connection with the media-service program.

The Concept of Study and Action by Citizens

Historically, there was a time when school people believed that lay citizens should accept the decisions of school officials without question, an extreme authoritarian view. The next stage of development was an emphasis by school people on explanation or interpretation. The present evolution of the concept has reached the level now recognized as one of mutual planning and cooperative decision. The concept of citizen participation as good public relations is stated by the American Association of School Administrators[5] as follows:

Cooperative educational planning removes public relations from the realm of "telling" or "selling." In its stead there is created a genuine partnership, in which, through effective teamwork and a two-way flow of information and ideas, professional educators and representative laymen plan and replan for the education of children in terms of currently recognized needs. . . . Properly conceived and practiced, it becomes another of the foundation stones on which a sound structure of public relations is erected.

This concept should be applied by the media director as well as by the school-system's chief administrator and other curriculum personnel.

[5] By permission. From *Public Relations for America's Schools*, 28th Yearbook of the American Association of School Administrators of the NEA, 1201 Sixteenth St., N.W., Washington, D.C., 1950, p. 100.

Level	Media Example	Level	Media Example
1. Studying (Assembling Data)	(a) Comparing the cost of assigning media collections to each school with the cost of expanding centralized media services. (b) Finding out the cost of an expanded instructional television program connecting all schools in the district.		gram in each elementary and secondary school building. (b) Whether or not to recommend that each school unit be provided with media specialist personnel for leadership duties together with needed clerical and technical personnel.
2. Planning	(a) How to reach a new *adequacy* level of media equipment and materials in each school building in five years. (b) Planning the development of electronic learning laboratory facilities in each school building, as a step toward the use of instructional systems.	5. Executing	(a) A part-time, donated, secretarial and media-preparation service by parents for the media center in each school, as a stopgap measure pending budgetary approval for the next school year. See Figure 14-1. (b) An agreed-to plan for donating the use of private cars and personal services for delivery of museum realia and dioramas to the schools daily from the city's museum.
3. Interpreting	(a) The present use of systems teaching in foreign languages. (b) The present field-trip program of the schools. (c) The need for an improved media equipment installation program in all new schools.	6. Evaluating	(a) The status of the media program. (b) The status of school-community relationships and specifically the school's use of community resources.
4. Deciding	(a) Whether or not to recommend that schools embark upon a closed-circuit instructional television production pro-		

We should not fail to emphasize the study and action process in its true relationship to the process of change.

Levels of Participation

The director should realize that citizens may participate at different levels. Many so-called advisory committees listen to reports of progress, ask questions, discuss problems, and approve policy recommendations made by the media director. However, even though the advisory group often lends itself well as a harmless excuse for better, more active types of participation, the trend is toward *study* groups. (See the above table.) In the preceding paragraph it was mentioned that the top level of participation was decision. Oberholtzer[6] in his discussion of problems presented by citizen cooperation, pointed out that, "In general, there are six principal levels of activity which are open to citizen cooperation in education. They are: studying (including assembling data), planning, interpreting, deciding, executing, and

[6] By permission. Kenneth E. Oberholtzer. "Cooperation Presents Some Problems," Chapter IV, *Citizen Cooperation for Better Public Schools*, 53rd Yearbook of the National Society for the Study of Education, Part I (Chicago: University of Chicago Press, 1954), p. 63.

Figure 14-1. These parents are willing to devote a specified number of scheduled hours each week to assist with school work such as helping with children's routine health checks, playground duty, and making instructional materials for the teachers. They are shown at work in the curriculum center of one of the Fountain Valley School District schools. These parents, called parent aides, execute the plans that they have made in cooperation with the school principals. Is such action common? Could it be organized more easily in a small neighborhood type of environment? Could it be planned for city school groups as well? If this work is done to help the teachers, what work of a more professional character ought the teachers to be doing? How would such unpaid workers feel about their school's instructional program? *Courtesy Fountain Valley School District, Huntington Beach, California.*

evaluating. Cooperation may be typical of any one of these levels of activity, or of a combination of some of them, or of all." Perhaps some media examples of each of the levels of participation just quoted would provide the would-be media director with helpful insights.

Limitations on Citizen Action. In this connection, special attention must be given to levels four and five because, according to law, final decision (legislation) is a prerogative of the officially elected board of education, which is an arm of the state's legal system. The director must recognize that he cannot expect decision and legislation except from the board of education itself. However, as a result of study, planning, and evaluating, any citizen group may make recommendations, which if supported by serious effort, evidence, and wide public acceptance, ought to be approved by the Board and, if possible, legislated into action or incorporated into its own formal recommendations for local law-making processes.

Guidelines for Procedure

No rule of thumb can be given to the media director who aspires to seek this plateau of school public relations, but general principles are not lacking. Morphet[7] has formulated a

[7] By permission. Edgar L. Morphet, "Co-operative Procedures Should Be Based on Sound Principles," Chapter XI, *Citizen Co-operation for Better Schools,* 53rd Yearbook of the National Society for the Study of Education, Part I (Chicago: University of Chicago Press, 1954), pp. 257–262.

set of guides for carrying out a cooperative program that points the way to good decisions. A condensed version of these guides follows:

Participating groups and committees should understand their functions and limitations . . . should have latitude to explore all possibilities included in assigned problems . . . should organize properly for effective work . . . should select individuals who believe in cooperative endeavor for leadership roles . . . should adopt a written statement of purposes, policies, and working relations . . . should utilize all appropriate resources . . . should select as consultants capable persons who can work best in a cooperative program . . . should proceed logically and scientifically . . . should open meetings to the public . . . should adopt a working plan with definite termination dates for aspects of their programs . . . should meet as often as necessary to insure continuous progress . . . should develop constructive proposals to effect improvements in the educational program . . . should center their attention on principles and issues not personalities . . . should assemble evidence concerning desirable objectives or the characteristics of a desirable program should be used in evaluating the present situation . . . should recognize the need to facilitate cooperative action in general . . . should prepare an explanatory report giving findings and conclusions . . . should assist in interpreting the report to the board of education and possibly to the public . . . when such a cooperating group is undertaking a comprehensive study, it should serve principally as a policy committee.

The important implications for procedure for the media director are quite obvious in this set of guiding principles, but a word of caution is in order. The inexperienced director must make sure that he carries on such broader participatory activities in a context of action that the board of education and superintendent have initiated or advised him to initiate. If the local climate for such action is not favourable, any premature and unilateral action on the director's part may conceivably produce some unexpected and negative results.

In cases where cooperative planning is desirable, and the media director believes that he is ready to take the lead in organizing for such action, he needs to ask the following questions: (1) What should be the ideal composition of the group that should participate? (2) Who should activate the group? Some guidance in answering these questions is provided in the following paragraphs.

The Composition of Participating Groups. Many believe that group composition above all should be representative of the agencies existing in the community. Actually, membership on a lay-participation committee should be decided in terms of interest and recognized competence in cooperative action. The nature of the problem to be faced will largely determine the size and composition of the group, and it is the problem in relation to community needs that should be the focus of consideration instead of what a particular agency or party believes is appropriate. Another aspect of composition is the desirable balance between lay and professional personnel. There are no well-defined rules for such determination. The nature and scope of the problem will have to be analyzed for guidance on this point. Certainly both lay and professional people will be needed in studying the types of problems likely to be proposed by the director of media services, and very probably these two groups should be represented in equal numbers. If the director is to make a sincere effort to promote understanding, he should encourage the selection of personnel who need to be included for their own education as well as for their potential contribution to group endeavor. In this connection it is desirable for one or more members of the board of education to be included, if they can be persuaded to accept and serve in addition to their regular school board commitments. It is obvious that unless respected lay citizens are brought into the study program in optimum numbers, the underlying purpose of the activity will never be achieved. The best group for the inexperienced director to start with would be one composed largely of representatives of parent-teacher organizations. Working with and as a part of such a group, the director will find a cohesive organization already in existence and one that is generally well-informed, interested, and willing to make recommendations.

Initiating Lay-Group Activity. As a general rule, invitations to membership should be extended by the school superintendent or through the central planning council, if there is one, and it is desirable for the director to serve as an executive secretary, if not as chairman or moderator. However, the initiative for getting a study project under way may come from the citizens themselves, and such a group may call a meeting, extending invitations to professional personnel to participate. Also, in the case of specific problems at the school-unit level, principals and teachers may initiate action. Internal suggestions for action, as made by the media director should be made through principals and other curriculum personnel or through the school superintendent for proper orientation with over-all public relations plans. The director should not confuse this discussion with action taken quite regularly by a permanently organized group often known and referred to as the Media Program Advisory Committee. Such a committee may, of course, be called into session by the director in accordance with established procedure. Initiation of other study and planning groups internal to the professional staff organization has already been discussed in Chapter 4.

The next section of this chapter deals with the media director and his comprehensive program for developing understanding and support through good communications. Communication channels open to today's director of media services are many, and their use is included in the following discussion.

Understanding and Support Through Good Communication

People need to get the facts for intelligent thinking. When the facts are given honestly, simply, and accurately, people will be less likely to misrepresent actual conditions, invent and spread rumors, or be suspicious of what is going on. These are worthwhile benefits, but many media directors still do not find ways to reap them. In improving skill in communication, the director needs to consider himself as a writer, an advertiser, a speaker, a reporter, a photographer, a visualizer, and a broadcaster; and to be effective in all these processes, the director needs to identify, understand, and bridge the barriers to communication that will face him. This is a formidable plan of action for self-teaching, and a decade of serious personal effort may be required to achieve it to any great degree of competency. The discussion and suggestions in this chapter open up the wide range of possibilities for action and are given as guides in making good decisions. The suggestions in connection with the various communication channels are more specific than general, as many basic principles and general suggestions have been stated previously.

Talking and Demonstrating

This unique channel for understanding and support ought to be utilized effectively. The most personal and direct of the several communications channels and possessing great potential for a telling impact and for the control of audience reactions, this method of communication should be employed on a planned, system-wide basis, principally for parent-teacher and civic organizations. The following suggestions are offered:

1. Formulate a series of three or four topics for each year, involving speeches, panels, and teacher demonstrations.
2. Make the programs available to PTA groups, but be cautious about flooding other civic groups with offers of free programs. Make up a schedule as near the beginning of the year as possible, and split up the work with volunteers from the teaching and coordinator staffs.
3. Help interested groups organize their own panel reports based on their own study of problems, and steer such studies into media-methods areas. Use interested principals and board members on such panels wherever feasible and appropriate.

4. Make sure that teachers and others who are scheduled to speak or demonstrate, either with or without groups of pupils, are cooperatively selected and carefully chosen for their qualifications, and are given assistance in making adequate preparation.
5. In all personal performances the director should be thoroughly prepared and should make a top-notch presentation.
6. Illustrate talks by practicing what is preached. Use color slides, transparencies, charts, motion pictures, audio programs and videotape recordings of school procedures and operations.
7. Whenever possible use a projectionist or an operator so that the media director's full attention can be given to audience participation and reaction.
8. Think up catchy titles for talks.
9. Plan the exact time schedule with program chairmen, and make all projection arrangements ahead of the scheduled time for the meeting.
10. Know what concepts need to be put over and what abilities, if any, the audience should begin to develop; then plan activities, speech content, and audience reactions accordingly.
11. If necessary, work hard at developing speaking skills. Try to be unique in style, but be concise, natural, sincere, pleasant, and interested.
12. Use interesting content from everyday activities in the schools, and use everyday activities and instructional efficiency as the basis for any new recommendations or proposal offered.

Press and Publications

In using this channel, the director of media services becomes a journalist. He has to write stories for newspapers, prepare reports, prepare and edit copy for leaflets, take and select pictures, and he has to set up a system-wide plan for learning about interesting activities. Suggestions and directions for the use of this channel follow:

1. Stimulate interest in school principals for better press and publication projects, thus expanding the scope and opportunity for greater coverage of instructional media services.
2. Call a group together to discuss publica-

tions and news reporting for the press for the school year.

3. Stimulate teachers to undertake innovative projects with media that may offer opportunity for picture-story reporting.

4. Arrange for a flow of items to the press, with two or more picture stories on instructional-media methods each year. Conduct a systematic search for potentially useful press-story content.

5. Produce a series of short leaflets carrying one or more illustrations to coincide with marking periods.

6. Use offset and letterpress processes for leaflets some of the time to break the monotony of routine duplication processes, thus making possible a higher quality of impact.

7. Clear all printed publications through the chief administrator, and develop the skill to do responsible editing and proofreading.

8. Get help from volunteer staff members, but always screen material critically, edit it, reject it, or rewrite it, if necessary. Get help from journalism teachers, or involve them directly in planning press releases and preparing publications.

9. Get help from art teachers and advanced art students for illustrations in leaflets and for cover designs.

10. Propose changes and report needs far in advance to avoid shocks and crises.

11. Introduce research findings, make comparisons with processes and procedures in preceding decades, and use visual presentations, both pictorial and graphic.

12. Take and use good pictures. That is, (a) concentrate attention on the result, process, and feeling by eliminating crowds of people; (b) keep relevant items in and distracting elements out; (c) look for the right youngsters, and if the teacher has picked several already, take the shot, then compose another substituting more appropriate subjects; (d) take several pictures, trying for facial expressions that reveal depth of reaction; (e) seek good backgrounds, or shoot downward or upward to eliminate them; (f) make sure clothes fit the action; (g) arrange subjects for optimum contrast; (h) crop pictures for maximum impact; and (i) determine and arrange for appropriate size to be used.

13. Supply appropriate captions with pictures.

14. Contact local newspaper editor and report meetings, conferences, and ideas for feature stories. Have facts ready with correctly spelled names, or when a reporter calls for an interview, have all pertinent materials, pictures, and illustrations at hand.

15. Try to develop a style of writing for newspapers and leaflets that gets away from professional terminology.

16. Keep a record of all news items and feature stories reported, and of all leaflets and other publications prepared, in order to plan for a variety of points of emphasis in successive years according to need.

17. Purchase and distribute, whenever feasible, specially designed and prepared publicity leaflets for public relations programs.

School Exhibits

Exhibits constitute a powerful means of informing a community about media services. See Figure 14-2. This is especially true today in view of the many possibilities of using colored slides with synchronized tape commentary. Well within reach of any school system are the devices to project graphic stories about the school via automatic slides or continuous motion picture projection and to play continuous tape-recorded messages in connection with displays in store windows or buildings downtown. Too often it is taken for granted that the townspeople and parents know what modern media materials and equipment units are like. Attractive displays of modern devices such as unusual maps and globes, large attention-getting pictures laminated in clear plastic, Polaroid Land camera transparency process, overhead projectors and overlays in color, electronic carrels, videotape players and computer-link display units, may provide new insights for many citizens who think they know what modern-day education is all about but who actually have inaccurate concepts of processes and materials.

Probably most important of all are exhibits of those instructional methods whereby youngsters have produced and put into practical use various communication media. A few suggestions follow:

1. Construct easy-to-set-up exhibit frames for displaying photo enlargements and objects.

Figure 14-2. Media program directors should make the most of opportunities to organize displays for public viewing. This display of publications by the Los Angeles Schools was very effective. *Courtesy Los Angeles City Schools.*

Standardize construction and simplify the changing of materials to be displayed.

2. Use professional display principles and techniques.

3. Make use of pegboard techniques.

4. Plan a wide range of exhibits for various school-public meetings in advance.

5. Use colorful posters and charts in displays.

6. Make use of tape-recorded repetitive commentaries with displays, automatic picture-changers, and videotape programs.

7. Get help from art teachers or from the sign painter downtown in solving display problems.

8. Plan for a variety of exhibit locations to reach citizens other than parents.

Radio and Television

Local radio and FM music stations are plentiful throughout the country, and if directors have access to one of these stations, they should use it to the fullest extent. See Figure 14-3. If a television channel, either commercial or educational, exists in the area, the media director should of course develop programs that will attract attention. Teachers and principals may prove to be experts in certain areas of subject matter or hobbies, and student groups may reach high levels of excellence in music, athletics, and dramatics; hence good program potentials may exist locally.

One of the recent developments in those communities and states where Community Antenna Television Service Companies have been organized is *public service cablecasting.* Such companies, often with minimum facilities, plan and implement local programing from sports to news including a wide variety of features. Where such programing is permitted, and when conditions are conducive, the media director should make a real effort to organize effective public understanding and support programs for use on such channels. The possibilities of television programs about the schools are many, and it can be readily seen that television includes the entire range of demonstrations and visualized presentations. Furthermore, the convenience with which programs may be produced by means of videotape technology, facilitates wide participation of teachers, pupils, and school leaders.

Naturally, those schools and school districts that are located in areas already having regular television stations, have CATV Companies locally organized, and have well-developed television program production facilities already in use for their own instructional purposes are in the most favorable position to use the broadcast channel. However, on the other hand, school districts located in cities and towns without daily or weekly newspapers are at a disadvantage with regard to use of the press. It is obvious then that media directors will be faced with the problem of adjusting to and making optimum use of those communication channels that are available.

One final opportunity for establishing desirable school-community public relations as it applies to the director of media services must not be overlooked in this discussion, and this opportunity is not without its problems.

Audiovisual Media Services to the Community

Media directors miss opportunities for action and service when they withdraw from community contacts by, for instance, living in another city, particularly when this prevents convenient participation in community affairs. This does not mean that the director needs to maintain office hours around the clock. It does mean, however, that many services to school people, community agencies, and citizens, of the direct consultant variety, as well as the indirect, person-to-person, after-work contacts, are bypassed.

Community Use of School Equipment. Many media center directors say firmly, though sympathetically, "No," to agencies seeking to borrow the school's projectors and tape recorders. Some directors have no problem in this area because they find themselves in community-oriented school systems where it is not strange for the school plants to be in use daily (after school and nights, that is) for adult education purposes. School equipment is thus in convenient position for use, and with a night-school supervisor assisted by one or two trained, paid student projectionists, there is little cause for worry. In some cities, in accordance with wise school-system policy, a motion

Figure 14-3. The pensive mood shown in this picture developed when these businessmen and educators listened to a tape recording made for a local community radio broadcast. The program at which occasion this picture was taken was planned and implemented by the former director of instructional materials, Franklin T. Mathewson. Panel discussions and presentations, supported by demonstrations and well-designed and prepared illustrative materials, are particularly effective on television, but unless prime time is available and the desired target can be reached by this medium, it would be better to direct efforts along other lines of communication. *Courtesy Instructional Materials Center, White Plains, New York.*

picture projector, a projection screen, and a slide projector are purchased out of school funds and set aside for loans to nonschool community agencies. However, there is little justification for a school's media center that does not have enough equipment to handle its own service commitments to loan a projector and screen to the local Boys' Club, for example, if it jeopardizes the showing of a scheduled instructional film in the first-period science class the next day.

Actually, therefore, the loan of media equipment to other community agencies may, while contributing to good public relations, work against the accomplishment of basic instructional services, and this should not be permitted to happen. The director should, if separate equipment for the purpose has not been purchased, consider recommending to the superintendent for approval a policy including at least the following basic elements (adjusted, of course, for local conditions). It is recommended that

1. Only specified equipment units such as a motion picture projector and a slide projector and two portable screens are to be loaned to community agencies holding meetings outside the school.

595

2. No equipment is to be loaned outside the school system unless an unscheduled, similar kind of unit is available and in good operating condition.

3. Loans are to be made only to community government agencies and to nonschool, youth-serving organizations, specifically for educational programs where admissions are not charged.

4. Loans of equipment are to be made at any time to school staff for professional service meetings outside the school, provided that they are returned the day following the scheduled meeting in time for school use.

5. All loans are to be processed through the director of the school system media center rather than through principals and media coordinators at individual school buildings.

Media directors may in good judgment recommend a firm, no-equipment-loan policy for groups meeting outside of the various school buildings that have media-service centers, on the grounds that the extra time for processing requests and subsequent follow-up procedures interferes with the other services of prime importance. Time and staff are the critical factors in this decision. Moreover, in this technologically advanced age, it seems reasonable to expect that media equipment needed by various community organizations can be purchased at favorable discounts or procured through charitable gift and bequest arrangements, and loans from the schools ought to be considered as a stopgap service.

We have already discussed the wide variety of channels for conducting public relations programs, and have emphasized the value of informal contacts by media personnel, other school personnel in general being no exception, with community residents and groups. We should now finally mention some possibilities for extremely valuable media communication services as another route to understanding and support. Because of the very nature of many groups in the community, we perceive real needs for instructional visualization procedures. We see in this need significant opportunity for media-specialist personnel to conduct workshop sessions along lines of media design and preparation. Such groups as local service clubs, the library, women's clubs, Y.M.C.A., boards of education, health, and finance, PTA

council, teachers' associations, School Principals' Association, and the like, are all likely candidates for such special communication services.

Problem-Solving Activities

1. The emphasis on school interpretation programs has moved from autocratic pronouncements about what has been decided, through the explanation stage (one-way selling), to participation in decision. Make in outline form a comparison of the action to be taken under each of these operational levels as you would direct it as part of a public relations plan to develop understanding and support for the inauguration of the plan to use and remunerate a full-time school-building media coordinator and a full-time technician in each secondary school and in each elementary school of 20 classrooms and over.

2. In what ways is the effective director of media services likely to become involved with public relations problems other than his own? Are such activities likely to enhance or impede support for his own program?

3. Study several references dealing with the barriers to communication. Make a list of the barriers that you can identify, and then explain how you would proceed to prepare public relations programs that would surmount any one or several of them in any single example of effort. Employ several of the communication channels in this plan.

4. Identify several hypothetical local conditions that may cause serious trouble for the media director who attempts to engage unilaterally in community participation programs.

5. Why would local PTA groups and the PTA council constitute a more propitious level than a broader community committee at which the inexperienced media director could begin his use of the cooperative planning, study, and decision technique for public relations?

6. Set up an appropriate hypothetical study problem; then (a) state the desirable size and composition of the participating group, (b) show how you would apply each of Morphet's principles as quoted in the chapter.

7. Prepare topics and ideas for at least two talks to be given before PTA groups in your

town to build understanding of and support for effective use of media. The outline must be complete with *interesting* titles.

8. Plan a picture story for reporting an interesting, significant, and newsworthy school activity centered around media methods in the classroom.

9. List three appropriate paragraph headings dealing with media that are indicative of a section that may well be included in an annual town report by a superintendent of schools.

10. Work as a member of a class committee planning a series of talks and demonstrations for a period of three years for a hypothetical community. Indicate how the plan would be operated and how many people would be involved for the desired coverage of PTA and local civic clubs.

11. List five topics for each of the following audiovisual production projects for use in public relations programs, specifically for your own department: (a) sound motion pictures with either optical or magnetic sound; (b) slide sets in color; (c) slide sets in color with tape-recorded script; (d) spot radio announcements; (e) educational television programs of 15 minutes each; (f) flip charts in sets; (g) tape recordings to be used as short illustrations only, not as radio programs; (h) exhibits for store windows downtown; (i) exhibits for school PTA meetings.

12. Select any school picture of your choice, preferably no smaller than 5 inches by 7 inches, and prepare it for a publisher by indicating on an overlay sheet the following: (a) exact limits for cropping the picture, (b) the size of picture desired for publication, and (c) the caption that is to accompany the picture.

13. Use the criteria listed in this chapter in criticizing school-activity pictures brought in by class members for analysis.

14. Take whatever steps are deemed necessary to give yourself an objective rating on the factors that lead to an acceptable appearance for contacts with lay and professional publics. If you are employing an assistant for public relations work, would you pay any attention to the good-grooming habits of the applicants?

15. Study examples of outstanding, graphic, public relations leaflets, annual reports, and promotional flyers; then design a pictorial leaflet on media methods for distribution to every home in your own community, or if a hypothetical city has to be chosen, one of known characteristics.

16. Make a survey of the public relations programs being conducted in any two cities of your choice where centrally organized media-service programs are known to exist.

17. Work as a member of one of several task force groups in the class to study and report on an assigned or chosen community with regard to the identifiable power structure in general and the key decision makers in particular. As a follow-up to the several reports, discuss the implications for the prospective media director's activity along the lines of effective public relations.

References

Baughman, Dale. "Yardsticks for Measuring School-Community Relations," *Educational Administration and Supervision*, Vol. 43, 1957, pp. 19-22.

Baus, Herbert M. *Publicity in Action*. (New York: Harper & Row, 1954).

Bernays, Edward L. (ed.). *The Engineering of Consent*. (Norman, Oklahoma: University of Oklahoma Press, 1955).

Bortner, Doyle M. *Public Relations for Teachers*. (New York: Simmons-Boardman Publishing Corp., 1959).

Brown, M. Ruth. "Ring the Bells and Let the People Know," *Audiovisual Instruction*, Vol. 2, No. 1, January 1957, pp. 10-11.

Brownell, Clifford Lee, Leo Gans, and Tufie Z. Maroon. *Public Relations in Education*. (New York: McGraw-Hill, 1955).

Citizen Co-operation for Better Schools. 53rd Yearbook of the National Society for the Study of Education, Part I. (Chicago: University of Chicago Press, 1954).

Dapper, Gloria. *Public Relations for Education*. (New York: Macmillan, 1964):

Foskett, John M. "New Facts About Lay Participation," *Nations Schools*, Vol. 54, August 1954, pp. 63-66.

Hovland, Carl Iver, Irving L. Janis, and Harold H. Kelly. *Communication and Persuasion*. (New Haven, Conn.: Yale University Press, 1952).

Kindred, Leslie W. *How to Tell the School Story*. (Englewood Cliffs, N.J.: Prentice-Hall, 1960).

MacDonald, Dora May. "Make Every Picture Tell a Story," *Audiovisual Instruction*, Vol. 2, No. 1, January 1957, pp. 12-13.

McCloskey, Gordon. *Education and Public Understanding*. (New York: Harper and Row, 1959).

Miller, William C. "Winning Staff Support," *Audiovisual Instruction*, Vol. 2, No. 1, October 1957, pp. 206-207.

Moehlman, Arthur B. and James A. van Zwoll, *School Public Relations*. (New York: Appleton-Century-Crofts, 1957).

National Citizens Commission for the Public Schools, Henry Toy, Jr., Director, 2 West 45th Street, New York, N.Y. (Several booklets as follows: *How Can We Conduct a Winning Campaign? How Can We Work With the Press? How Can We Discuss School Problems? How Can We Advertise School Needs? How Good Are Our Teaching Materials?*)

National School Public Relations Association. *Let's Go to Press*. (Washington, D.C.: The Association, 1954).

Olsen, Edward G. (ed.). *School and Community*, 2nd ed. (Englewood Cliffs, N.J.: Prentice-Hall, 1954).

Public Relations for American Schools. (Washington, D.C.: American Association of School Administrators of the NEA, 1201 Sixteenth St., N.W., 1950).

Rast, G. E. and George E. Ingham. "The Community Discovers AV," *Audiovisual Instruction*, Vol. 2, No. 1, January 1957, pp. 5, 7.

Robinson, Edward J. *Communication and Public Relations*. (Columbus, Ohio: Charles E. Merrill Books, 1966).

Robinson, Thomas E. "Ten Best Public Relations Devices," *School Executive*, Vol. 68, August 1949, pp. 36-38.

Rushton, E. W. "Telling the Community about Its Schools," *School Executive*, Vol. 68, May 1949, pp. 60-62.

Unargo, Daniel. *How to Create a Better Understanding of Our Schools*. (Minneapolis: Denison Publishing Co., 1959).

In preceding chapters the would-be media director has been urged at the turn of every page to become a superman in terms of what is considered to be desirable practice. He has been urged in fact to be a fund raiser in the sense of seeking financial support from every known benevolent agency from the federal government to business and private foundations in order to bolster the frequently all too low media budget in his own city. And in some cases after building a staff organization to do a world of work, he may have to ask that some of the work be done without pay, or to use the free services of students whose interests, even though sometimes fleeting, are similar to his own.

But this is not all. In this chapter, the media director will be urged to evaluate systematically the media program, and the many aspects of its service throughout the school district. Because then, and only then, will he perceive the need for and be likely to take action to effect desirable changes in his own administrative performance, in teachers and in pupils, and in the scope and quality of services being rendered.

The Nature of the Evaluation Process

Systematic evaluation is important because of the tendency to lose sight of important long-range goals in the pressure of day-to-day problems. When a plan for making appraisals is formulated and carried out by the director and his colleagues, a number of significant benefits are likely to result that are worth the time and effort involved.

Reasons for Evaluation

The underlying reasons for evaluation determine the nature of the benefits derived, and the main reason for appraisal is to discover pathways to the improvement of media services in general. A secondary reason, but also an important one, is the use of an evaluation process as an experience for personal growth of those individuals who do the painstaking work of measuring and evaluating, the media director included. The director should realize, therefore, that unless he involves others in the process, he may be unable to realize the full potential

15

Evaluation

599

value of his efforts. Teachers who are asked to evaluate the director's personal administrative and supervisory performance may be also led to look a little deeper and more critically at their own techniques and performance with audiovisual and print media. And because teacher competence is such an important aspect of the director's supervisory role, he cannot afford to miss this important route to professional growth. In addition to this, the director needs the help of teachers to complete the actual work involved.

The Basic Process of Evaluation

Evaluation is basically a process of making value judgments based on observed evidence in relation to desired changes. As a part of this process certain tests (even of the paper-and-pencil variety), self-analysis check lists, anecdotal records, opinion forms for teachers and pupils, and rating scales may be put to work in the sense of *measuring* present status. However, it is the emphasis on growth toward valid goals in qualitative as well as quantitative characteristics that makes the process one of evaluation and appraisal rather than measuring and testing. Implicit in the entire process is a set of standards clearly understood by all who participate. While the process of evaluation is being discussed here in its application to the media program, its relationship to comprehensive appraisal should be noted. J. Wayne Wrightstone[1] explains the outcome of comprehensive evaluation as follows: "Truly comprehensive evaluation provides evidence of the degree to which important curricular purposes are being realized." In a very real sense, evaluation of the media service program has the same reference point, curricular purpose, because it either fails or succeeds in terms of its contribution to improvement of learning where it counts most, in the learner himself. Obtaining evidence and making good judgments, however, are not easy human tasks.

Writing about evaluation of change in in-service education programs, Virgil Herrick[2]

explains clearly what the evaluator's task is, and this task is applicable as well to media program analysis. He writes:

In general the changes that are desired in programs of in-service education have to do with adequacy. We desire those changes that enable people to become more adequate as persons, as teachers and administrators, and as members of the school staff. We desire those changes that contribute to more adequate educational programs for children and youth in individual classrooms, in specific school programs. . . . The determination of the presence of change is essentially the problems of determining differences over time in the phenomena being observed. These differences can only be determined when it is possible to determine clearly either a beginning point or a goal toward which behavior is directed. Change under these conditions can either be determined by the difference that exists between the starting point (first observation) and the present position (second or last observation) on a behavior continuum or the difference that exists between successive operations of behavior and the goal to be achieved.

Herrick also pointed out significantly that "As one moves from the questions of perceiving the presence of change to the ones of determining amount, rate, and direction of change, the problem of valuing these aspects of change becomes more important."[3] Little wonder that in the past, save for a few heroic efforts such as, for example, the *National Study of Secondary School Evaluation* (formerly the *Cooperative Study of Secondary School Standards*), efforts of school personnel in general and directors of media services in particular have dealt largely with quantitative instead of qualitative evaluation criteria. It is a relatively simple matter to discover that the school system has 60 motion picture projectors, a gain of ten over the preceding year, and that according to a five-year goal of 100 projectors, the rate of change was satisfactory. It is not so simple to find out how many teachers had improved in what ways, at what speed, and to ascertain if such changes were satisfactory.

This problem points up the possibility of the evaluation process operating at various levels of concentration and efficiency. The media director needs to identify and understand these various levels of operation because he must

[1] J. Wayne Wrightstone, "Evaluation," *Monroe's Encyclopedia of Educational Research*, rev. ed., W. J. Monroe (ed.) (New York: Macmillan, 1950), p. 404.

[2] By permission. Virgil E. Herrick, *In-Service Education*, "The Evaluation of Change in Programs of In-Service Education," Chapter XIII, 56th Yearbook of the National Society for the Study of Education, Part I (Chicago: University of Chicago Press, 1957), pp. 312–313.

[3] *Ibid.*, p. 314.

judge and recommend the use of presently available evaluational instruments or take steps to construct new ones, more appropriate for the local situation.

Levels of Action in the Evaluation of Media Services

Evaluation of the media program may function at a number of identifiable levels of action. In each of these levels the involvement of the director, the role played by colleagues, the degree of refinement of the measuring instruments, the criticalness of the observation, the nature of the judgments of value, and the quantity and quality of benefits may be expected to vary. A description of such operational levels follows in order of least to greatest involvement of people.

Level 1. The media director evaluates services annually by scrutinizing, summarizing, and generalizing the data collected for his record-keeping system. He writes a report based on his findings, emphasizing comparisons, changes, and needs. He finds out what each individual school is doing as regards ordering materials. He also summarizes his own activities and totals the number of in-service education contacts made. He collects reports from his staff of school-building instructional media coordinators in accordance with previously agreed-upon plans that reveal the number of teachers using audiovisual and print media professionally.

Level 2. The director operates usually on Level 1, but he also decides to obtain and make use of, on a personal basis, one or more of the available evaluation check lists, as comprehensive in nature as possible, such as the Schwartz,[4] Durr,[5] Audio-Visual Instruction,[6] William R.

Fulton,[7] National Study of Secondary School Evaluation,[8] *Standards for School Media Programs*[9] or the modification and use of the criteria listed in this chapter. Such self-evaluation takes place from the standpoint of his own personal performance, and the director seeks to make a judgment about the adequacy of the present status of facilities and the nature and extent of the services being rendered. It is expected that at least the Fulton Evaluative Checklist will be checked off and the shortcomings and strengths noted for building an improvement plan.

Level 3. The director performs according to Level 1 annually, has also completed a Level 2 operation, and in addition he solicits the aid of a system-wide representative committee or other group to assist him in preparing a measuring instrument for evaluation in the form of a teacher questionnaire. The questionnaire will be distributed annually at the close of the school year to call in reactions and judgments of the teaching staff regarding vital aspects of the center's service, plus their judgments about the quantity and quality of their own personal selection and professional use of materials. This instrument should be bold enough to call in reactions to the director's personal performance, taking the precaution of calling for criticisms on a constructive basis.

Level 4. The director cooperates with and participates in the evaluation of a school or group of schools as carried on by a visiting team of evaluators. Such evaluation takes place on a comprehensive basis, including the entire instructional program of which the audiovisual and print media services as utilized by teachers are a part. Emphasis is placed upon instructional outcomes and the degree to which desirable standards are reached in the school's program. In addition to published criteria by Fulton and the NSSSE, a questionnaire, especially

---

[4] John Charles Schwartz, Jr., *Evaluative Criteria for an Audio-Visual Instruction Program* (Dubuque, Iowa: William C. Brown Co., 1950).

[5] William H. Durr, "What Is Your School's I.M. Quotient?" *Planning Schools for Use of Audio-Visual Materials*, No. 3, *A V Instructional Materials Center*, Department of Audio-Visual Instruction of the NEA, 1201 Sixteenth St., N.W., Washington, D.C., 1954, pp. 77–79.

[6] "Profile Your A-V Program," *Audio-Visual Instruction*, Vol. 2, Issue 7, October 1957, pp. 208–209. Also, *Evaluate Criteria for Audio-Visual Instructional Materials Services* (a project of the Committee on Accreditation of Secondary Schools), Department of Audio-Visual Instruction of the NEA, Washington, D.C.

[7] William R. Fulton, *Criteria Relating to Educational Media Programs in School Systems*, and the accompanying check list, *Evaluative Checklist An Instrument for Self-Evaluating an Educational Media Program in School Systems*. (Prepared under a contract with the U.S. Office of Education.) Copies available from W. R. Fulton, University of Oklahoma, Norman, Oklahoma.

[8] National Study of Secondary School Evaluation, *Instructional Materials Services—Library and Audio-Visual*, Section F, Washington, D.C.: NSSSE, 1960.

[9] Joint Standards by AASL and DAVI of the NEA. See Footnote 1, Chapter 12.

prepared and approved by visiting teams and the teachers themselves, is made use of in collecting evidence for judgments.

Level 5. The director performs according to Level 1, has completed Level 2 and Level 3, and in addition he sets up, with the help and advice of the superintendent, principals, and other supervisors, a team of evaluators for the elementary schools and a team of evaluators for the secondary schools. These teams study the peculiar problems of evaluating media-service programs and have the advice of several consultants from other media-service centers, both city and university. Such teams study comprehensive available evaluation check lists (see Fulton and NSSSE check lists) and statements of general criteria, developing a basic check list for services and two specific check lists for the appraisal of the way in which the program is functioning in the lives of learners in elementary and secondary schools. Meetings are scheduled for respective staffs, with the evaluating teams and the media director participating, to report, explain, and call for suggestions regarding the two check lists prepared for the classroom, one for individual teachers and the other for the students. Individual teachers distribute and collect pupil replies to the questionnaires, but teachers are free to choose whether or not they will participate in the survey of their pupils. Also, teachers are free to study pupil replies before turning them over to evaluation teams. Pupil replies are not to be signed.

As can be seen, the preceding levels offer a wide range of evaluational activity for the media director. Levels 4 and 5 may well take place once in every five or ten years, Levels 1 and 3 annually, and Level 2 possibly every time a new check list is developed or possibly every three years as a minimum. In all the levels there is a need for analysis according to a system of standards or to a system of objectives, and the refinement in the observation called for depends on the established criteria. The director needs to be able to judge the appropriateness of available check lists and to construct, whenever they are needed, evaluational instruments that will be applicable in the local situation. The important topic of criteria for appraisal purposes is discussed in the next section.

Criteria for Judging Conditions and Changes

The National Study of Secondary School Evaluation has had a marked influence on the development of educational evaluation, media-service programs included, since its organization in 1933. The development by Schwartz[10] of criteria for evaluating an audiovisual media instructional program according to its plan and format is just one example. The latest revision of the NSSSE evaluational materials is 1960, with the next one scheduled for 1970. The advantage of this format is that many school people have become familiar with this evaluational procedure, which has been applied to all subject-matter fields and services.

Since it is likely that the local director may have to devise his own measuring devices, he needs to know the sources of criteria. He can then formulate a comprehensive system for obtaining needed evidence, or he may with his colleagues decide to concentrate his efforts on a few vital aspects of his services and their impact on learning—for example, in-service education and school-building personnel services. The identification of criteria in this section is followed by a discussion of their employment in the next main topic, which deals with local evaluation instruments and procedures.

Sources of Criteria

There are many easily identifiable sources of criteria by means of which a media-services program can be evaluated, and several of these have already been presented in preceding chapters. Basically, these sources are (1) leadership principles (the way the director works with people); (2) service principles (beliefs about what the media program should try to do for each school and each teacher); (3) principles of learning and teaching and curriculum development (the framework of beliefs for all teachers' decisions); (4) principles for the

[10] John Charles Schwartz, Jr., *op. cit.*

utilization of media (the guideposts for relating media to all learning activity); (5) the roles that media play (different ways they can help teachers teach); (6) principles of in-service education (desirable ways of building teacher competence locally); (7) minimum standards for school-building service centers and the central headquarters as well as for facilities and equipment for facilitating teacher use (basic physical environment for operating the service program); (8) minimum standards for personnel services in each school building (basic professional, technical, and clerical help for teachers); (9) desirable expansion and growth of services (the rate of growth for meeting instructional needs); (10) principles of budgeting (the financial support basis for operating a service program); and (11) principles of public understanding and support (the ways in which professional and lay citizens plan and make recommendations).

To make a full statement of the criteria for an evaluation, the director has but to examine each chapter of this book for service program standards and then, in addition, expand as needed the statement of utilization principles that appeared in Chapter 4. This is a big order and this kind of exhaustive summary and restatement of items already discussed is not called for as a part of this chapter. However, it will be of service to the creative evaluator if some of the basic questions together with a number of related subsidiary questions of a more specific nature are stated as focal points for observation and analysis. Such questions are intended to represent general criteria and standards in terms of the over-all program of service, and of course, as local evaluation programs are undertaken, they may be further broken down into additional questions specific enough to facilitate penetrating observations.

Focal Points for Observation and Analysis

Using the sources of criteria identified in the preceding paragraph, several broad questions have been formulated to represent the general criteria for a comprehensive appraisal of the media-service program. Each of the major questions is then analyzed further to show how specific criteria are defined for more specific observation. The reader should note that the content of preceding chapters is the source of these criteria.

I. *Is the leadership performance of the media program director adequate for obtaining competent effort of the staff in achieving the purposes of the service organization?*

1. Does the director obtain teacher participation in the making of decisions that affect their activities and responsibilities?
2. Does the director get the facts before making plans and decisions?
3. Does the director help the group to define purposes for action?
4. Does the director act vigorously?
5. Does the director possess personal and professional integrity?
6. Does the director develop new skills?
7. Does the director welcome and consider suggestions made by colleagues?
8. Does the director seek the personal development of colleagues and his own staff members?
9. Does the director make sound decisions?
10. Does the director like to work as a member of a team?
11. Does the director mobilize information and enlist the services of people effectively?
12. Does the director possess executive ability?
13. Does the director understand and apply the principles of good teaching?
14. Does the director have adequate technical knowledge?
15. Does the director define problems and goals for his plans of action?
16. Does the director take prompt action?
17. Does the director take action in terms of a curriculum reference point?
18. Does the director analyze a situation correctly?
19. Does the director make recommendations in terms of long-range plans?
20. Does the director lead groups in the study of vital problems likely to affect the future of the service program?
21. Does the director ever have new ideas?
22. Does the director appear to have an innovating personality?
23. Is the director successful in accomplishing desirable change processes?

II. *Are materials and equipment made available to teachers, in adequate variety and quantity when needed, with a minimum of distraction and inconvenience?*

1. Do teachers use media in their classrooms?

2. Where classrooms are not yet equipped for projection, is the environment of the projection room conducive to learning?

3. When classrooms are not yet equipped for projection, can the teacher move the class without serious disruption?

4. Is the classroom light-control system adequate for each teacher?

5. Are other classroom media facilities adequate: Outlets? Bulletin boards? Modern chalkboards? Projection screen? Mobile equipment stands?

6. Can each teacher obtain media materials and equipment on time with confidence? Are there equipment supply subcenters?

7. Is it easy to order materials and equipment?

8. Does the teacher have access to a well-trained projectionist crew for delivery and operation of equipment on schedule?

9. Is it easy for each teacher to find out what media are available?

10. Does each teacher select his media?

11. May the teacher obtain professional help at both central and at the school-building level?

12. Can each teacher find out quickly which media items are basic and which are supplementary in nature for the existing curriculum plans?

13. Does each teacher have access to a sufficient variety of materials in planning needed educational experiences: Realia? Exhibits? Models? Mock-ups? Motion pictures? Television programs? Transparencies? Slide sets? Filmstrips? Study-print sets? Opaque projector material? Audio programs on tape or disk? Videotapes? Maps? Globes? Charts? Production supplies: motion picture film stock, film for color slides, prepaid processing mailers for slides, film, Polaroid-Land transparency film stock, cover glass, binding tape, slide mask, magnetic tape, flannel board, bulletin board and display supplies? Print-medium resources?

14. Is it easy for teachers to examine media before regular classroom use?

15. Is the school-building service-center space large enough to facilitate giving assistance to teachers?

16. Are the fixed installations adequate: for instructional television, for instructional systems, for electronic learning laboratory activity, for multimedia presentations, for group-response systems, and for computer-assisted instructional activities?

III. *Is the growth and expansion of the service program proceeding in accord with well-thought-out, long-term plans?*

1. Have teachers participated in detailing needs for media materials, equipment, and classroom facilities?

2. Have the facts concerning the needed specific items of equipment, based on a valid, comprehensive survey, been summarized and incorporated in annual purchase plans?

3. Have adequate priorities for media materials and equipment been established?

4. Have annual purchase plans for all needed items been incorporated in written, five-to-ten-year growth plans: materials, equipment, classroom light-control systems, classroom electrical outlets, classroom bulletin boards, classroom chalkboards, fixed media installations?

5. Have plans been made for new services in terms of teacher study and participation in decision? Television? Media design and preparation facilities? Instructional systems? Expanded library facilities?

6. Is the rate of growth geared to a specific, desirable level of program operation?

7. Is the rate of progress toward the desired operational level satisfactory?

8. Have available sources of financial support external to the school district been successfully tapped?

IV. *Do the in-service education activities reflect the best concepts of teacher growth and an adequate understanding of the learning process?*[11]

[11] Questions 4 and 5 in the statement of criteria included in this list deal with the important area of in-service education. The arrangement of criteria within these two focal points for observation and analysis follows the categories appearing in the author's check list in "A Yardstick for Your Inservice Program," *Audiovisual Instruction,* Vol. 8, No. 9, November 1963, pp. 678–680. That article was in turn based on the original statement of criteria in the first edition of this book, 1959.

Process: Channels for Organizing Activity

1. Is the in-service education program activity viewed as a teaching and learning program for teachers? Are valid teaching objectives being identified? Are technological and print materials being selected and used and are facilities being properly organized? Are challenging learning activities being set up and worked on by in-service groups? Are in-service groups being taught effectively as an example of excellent teaching procedures?

2. Are several channels for organizing teacher learning activity being utilized in good balance? Teachers' meetings? Extension classes? Short courses? Workshops? Institutes? Reading programs (special bulletins)? Service projects by individuals? Service projects by committees?

3. Are mass-communication media being utilized in the teaching activity? Bulletins? Tapes? Television? Large-group methods?

4. Is the in-service program being carried on in accord with long-term plans?

5. Have priorities for in-service education been established?

6. Is the use of the various channels organized for maximum impact?

7. Do the channels utilized result in a rate of progress satisfactory to the school system in accordance with advancing technology?

Leadership

8. Does the media program director work effectively through and with other supervisors and principals in conducting the in-service education program?

9. Does the central office staff obtain teacher participation in the making of decisions that affect their activities and responsibilities?

10. Is the on-going program of in-service education an outgrowth of recognized needs, interests of teachers, and their purposes?

11. Does the media director operate so as to mobilize fully the available resources for the program?

12. Does the central office staff use its energies effectively at the appropriate levels for maximum impact? Make and check plans? Execute? Maintain continuity? Prevent deterioration of operations? Motivate? Expedite? Give credit? Take charge of team operations?

Prepare materials including special kits for action at meetings?

Operational Basis

13. Do teachers participate in defining goals and problems and in formulating in-service education plans?

14. Are in-service programs based on adequate information about teachers' status and qualifications?

15. Are in-service programs based on surveys of needs identified by the teaching staff?

16. Are speedy communication and voting procedures utilized among staff? Bulletins for stating interests and preferences? Summaries and reports on decisions? Scheduling procedures?

17. Do teachers receive full credit for participation and are adequate records maintained of such credits?

18. Do teachers receive formal recognition for personal contributions to the program?

19. Do the available operational channels give the teachers a choice of in-service education experiences?

20. Is participation voluntary?

21. Are opportunities available through special plans for the rapid upgrading in ability of new teachers?

22. Are in-service group activities so organized as to be repeated in other schools and at other times with a minimum of preparation?

Operational Staff.

23. Have talented and skilled teachers been properly identified and their assistance enlisted for the in-service education program? Principals? Curriculum workers? Teachers? Building coordinators? Hobbyists? Writers of how-to-do-it bulletins? Committee members appointed for service projects (Instructional designs and plans, guidebooks, kits)?

24. Are teams of workers organized and taught how to repeat a specific meeting or demonstration or a series of such meetings and demonstrations for other groups in other schools on follow-up schedules?

25. Has the central office staff been given additional budgetary support for supplementary personnel (full-time, part-time guest demonstrators) and materials for the in-service education activity?

V. *Is teacher performance with instructional media creative and significant as far as pupil activities and responses are concerned?*

Performance: Selection of Material Phase

Do teachers possess the ability to:

1. Identify and write out in clear and consistent form, valid teaching purposes—the understandings, abilities, attitudes, and appreciations that they hope to develop in their students?

2. Select specific media to make optimum contributions to these valid teaching purposes?

3. Use media sourcebooks and catalogs?

4. Predict that an identified learning experience, among many, will influence students in desirable, specific ways?

5. Relate various kinds of selected media to specific problems as individuals and groups work on them?

6. Select media for use in new and efficient ways to involve students in self-instruction processes and large-group methods?

7. Select media to play a variety of instructional roles? (To provide experience, introduce a unit, present information, and call for responses in programed situations.)

8. Judge the quality and suitability of specific media on the basis of the interests, experience, maturity, and comprehension powers of an individual or a group of learners?

9. Plan and prepare the more simple, specialized media such as slides, transparencies, instructional tapes, and displays?

10. Design and produce such complex, specialized media as magnetic sound motion pictures, television programs, and instructional media packages for use in the classroom or school system?

Readiness for Material Phase

Do teachers possess the ability to:

11. Make valid, specific plans of what to do and say before presenting media?

12. Employ a variety of methods to build *readiness* in pupils, including the problem base procedure of building readiness by setting up a class problem or problems before the materials are presented, and including readiness plans in written form for each student to use with specific media or combinations of media in self-instructional processes.

13. Use a number of sources of information in making decisions about readiness, such as teaching purposes and knowledge of pupil characteristics?

Control of Physical Arrangements Phase

Do teachers possess the ability to:

14. Operate the kinds of media equipment that are made available by school authorities?

15. Detect improper functioning of equipment in use?

16. Judge degree of light control needed for proper viewing of projected images?

17. Arrange proper placement of screen, seats, loudspeakers, and other equipment for optimum pupil attention and participation?

18. Make proper arrangements for viewing and handling models, charts, maps, demonstration materials, and related devices?

19. Plan proper timing for presenting material in accordance with objectives and existing schedules, and especially in connection with use of media as components of instructional systems.

Pupil Action Phase

Do teachers possess ability to:

20. Identify and call for pupil action in direct relationship to specific teaching purposes?

21. Formulate and use valid, provocative, and illuminating thought questions?

22. Employ good discussion techniques based on known and accepted problems, topics, and issues?

23. Organize pupil action around imaginative, challenging, and unique problem-solving projects?

24. Prepare worksheets calling for specific programed responses in the light of (a) objectives, (b) a given visualized presentation, and (c) a given instructional environment; or employ the commercially prepared programed sequences that are available?

25. Employ media for unique teaching roles?

26. Organize significant learning activities around the production of media? (Producing a sound film, set of slides, writing a booklet, or making a mural.)

Evaluation Phase

Do teachers possess the ability to:

27. Evaluate their own techniques with specific media in the light of valid objectives and valid principles of teaching?

28. Judge whether or not the responses of learners indicate desired insights and abilities in accord with their teaching objectives?

29. Judge the worth of a given medium in the light of teaching objectives?

VI. *Are the relationships between curriculum planning and the instructional media-service program fruitful, cooperative, and geared to community needs?*

1. Does the work on curriculum problems involve the people who are responsible for the media-service program?

2. Do subject-matter specialists in the schools make use of media services in preparing their bulletins and curriculum guides?

3. Do curriculum specialists and the director of media services team up to provide the best learning experiences possible?

4. Do media and curriculum staffs assist each other as opportunities permit?

5. Do curriculum guides and other publications contain notations of all *basic* and *supplementary* media available?

6. Does the teacher make use of a variety of media as made available to him?

VII. *Are instructional media-center physical facilities in both school-district and school-building units adequate?*

1. Have space needs been correctly analyzed for needed services?

2. Has space allotted been correctly utilized?

3. Have limitations in space been stated in writing, stressed, and repeated in annual reports to school authorities?

4. Is space allotment at the centers sufficient to carry on service demands efficiently?

5. Have space needs been planned and sketched to scale for new services?

VIII. *Are adequate records kept and reports made to appropriate authorities?*

1. Does the media director know the total distribution figures? By schools? Per teacher average?

2. Does the director know what the distribution figures would be if all teachers used technological media every scheduled instructional period each day?

3. Does the director know which teachers have had pre-service and post-graduate courses in the media field?

4. Does the director know which teachers use media creatively?

5. Does the director know which teachers have made and which teachers can make significant contributions to in-service education?

6. Does the director report regularly what the continuing needs are from year to year?

7. Does the director know and report what the special needs are and when they have to be met?

8. Does the director know what expenditures ought to be made each year in each category of the budget in order to reach specified goals or operational levels?

9. Does the director know when media materials and equipment were purchased? repaired? replaced?

10. Does the director keep a system of records for comparison year by year to reveal growth and trends?

IX. *Has a strong and effective system-wide organization been established to meet the media needs of teachers?*

1. Have qualified individuals been selected and organized into a working force?

2. Are persons who contribute substantial amounts of time and energy adequately remunerated?

3. Have personnel services been organized in each school building to give the help needed by teachers?

4. Is the work of individuals recognized by top-level school authorities?

5. Are lines of communication firmly established between individuals who do the organization's work?

6. Are the individuals in the organization held together cohesively?

7. Is each working group made to feel that it is an indispensable part of the organization?

8. Have responsibilities been properly assigned to individuals and groups?

9. Is the performance of individuals checked and evaluated regularly?

X. *Are effective efforts being put forth to ascertain strengths and weaknesses in the instructional media-service program?*

1. Have surveys been conducted to collect data?

2. Have principals and teachers been consulted to collect opinions and suggestions for improving services?

3. Have collected data been sufficiently analyzed, summarized, and interpreted?

4. Are programs being planned to correct any weaknesses detected?

5. Have ways been found to utilize reactions of learners?

XI. *Are effective efforts being made to promote community understanding of the power of instructional media in the teaching-learning process?*

1. Have groups of laymen and professional colleagues been selected to study and plan wise courses of action?

2. Have study groups been properly recognized by the superintendent and board of education?

3. Is the media director making use of a variety of information channels?

4. Does the director seek to give communication services to his colleagues and to school officials in important communication projects?

5. Has the director balanced his use of communication media in terms of available facilities and adequacy of coverage?

6. Has the director succeeded in reporting and publicizing the school's activities comprehensively?

7. Do public relations programs for media services show signs of careful planning?

8. Are appropriate talents among the staff being utilized for public relations work?

9. Does the director recognize communication barriers in his community?

10. Does the director go about the process of surmounting communication barriers correctly?

11. Do school system authorities, particularly the school superintendent, school board members, curriculum specialists, and principals encourage the use of all instructional media by what they say and do?

XII. *Are effective efforts being made to assess the significant values accruing to learners through the media-service program?*

1. Are students learning to communicate more effectively through graphic expression?

2. Have students been asked for their opinions and value judgments?

3. Are research studies being conducted to determine unique values of media methodology?

The preceding questions, extensive as they seem to be, in no sense constitute an inclusive list, but they are nevertheless important. It should be noted that all the preceding questions have been so phrased that, with reference to the implied standards, positive answers always indicate strength, and negative answers indicate weakness. However, many of the questions should be answered according to a scale of responses. This pattern of response is shown in connection with the discussion of a later topic, "Choice of Measurement Symbols."

These basic questions point the way for the courageous director of media services to gather estimates of desirable change. He needs, of course, to choose with his colleagues the particular operational level at which proposed evaluation projects need to be conducted, and he needs to consider also the selection of appropriate local evaluation instruments and procedures.

Local Evaluation Instruments and Procedures

The job of local evaluation presents a number of knotty problems such as deciding on the appropriate operational level, the preparation of instruments for measurement, the establishment of standards or goals as reference points, the choice of measurement symbols for the desired degree of judgment, and taking action on the results. Because the director can hardly escape the task of formulating wise local policies and making sound decisions in solving these problems, suggestions will be made concerning them.

Suggestions Regarding Choice of Operational Levels

In connection with an earlier section dealing with the process of evaluation, five levels of evaluative action were described. These should be reviewed by the reader in connection with the suggestions that follow. *Level 1* is the absolute minimum, and this is the kind of continuous evaluative that every media director should arrange to carry on. Throughout this book he has been urged to collect facts, to know what is going on, to discover weaknesses, and to undertake programs to correct them. But other levels of evaluative action are also highly desirable. *Level 2* is helpful, and the director is urged to employ it, but this level may be made even more helpful, objective, and accurate by expanding the self-evaluation aspect of it to include school coordinators and a few other school colleagues. *Level 3* is another level of evaluation action that every director could and should organize and execute. This and *Level 1* constitute the desirable minimum of action. *Level 4* is, of course, only an occasional process, and *Level 5*, although desirable, can also be carried out at widely spaced intervals. This level of action requires great organizational ability and a considerable amount of time and effort. When the media director undertakes to operate at this level, he should make sure that the program is anchored to in-service education and curriculum planning so that outcomes may be more directly related to continuing activity for improving over-all teacher competence. This relationship also brings to the enterprise a reservoir of curriculum contributors. In making a final decision to operate at higher than Levels 1 and 2, people who are to be affected by the decisions should be consulted and invited to participate.

Selection and Preparation of Evaluation Instruments

This problem could be more easily solved if a variety of short, thoroughly tested, valid instruments were available that could be selected according to need. The fact is that the available evaluation scales and check lists are not always directly applicable to the local situation. Thus, the media director is urged to start with the major and subsidiary criteria listed earlier in the chapter and to prepare instruments for the occasion, getting help from representative groups as needed. Suggestions for preparing instruments are:

1. Study available criteria and the format of various examples of practical evaluation procedures, getting permission to duplicate acceptable material or purchasing copies as needed.

2. Use representative teacher committees to study problems involved, and help prepare instruments for their own and pupils' execution.

3. Decide on what aspects of the program need most to be evaluated.

4. Choose sections of the criteria presented in this chapter and expand them, taking care

that additional questions call for quick, though penetrating, responses.

5. Prepare, if teachers are willing, the kind of instruments that can be validated, and whose reliability can be computed.

6. Prepare instruments that are brief and specific rather than time-consuming and comprehensive.

7. Prepare instruments for pupils as well as teachers, for media directors, principals, and media coordinators also.

8. Make sure that instruments are based on accepted principles.

9. Decide first on what needs to be done with the data collected; then make sure that the responses called for will facilitate the desired judgments and action plans.

10. Choose instruments that will work best at the chosen operational level.

11. Decide before making the instruments if responses are to indicate status, change, direction of change, and rate of change; then strive for usable units, symbols, and indices.

12. Make sure that adequate instruction is given to teachers by bulletins, in teachers' meetings, or incorporated in the instrument, to obtain the best possible observations and responses to each item in the instrument.

Several examples of evaluative instruments, either in complete or excerpted form, are now presented for quick reference as suggestions of activities, format, and areas that can be explored for constructing local evaluative devices. The media director should, of course, keep abreast of developments in this field through study of periodical literature and by means of contacts with national committees and organizations.

Example 1. The following example is a brief excerpt from a check list prepared by the Connecticut State Department of Education for use in connection with its secondary-school evaluation program. The title of the instrument is *Teacher Self-Evaluation Check-List, How Do You Evaluate Your Audio-Visual Activities?*[12] The sections of criteria for checking by the

---

[12] Connecticut State Department of Education, Hartford, Connecticut. The entire check list appears in Appendix A of *The School Administrator and His Audio-Visual Program*, Charles F. Schuller (ed.), Yearbook, Department of Audio-Visual Instruction of the NEA, 1201 Sixteenth Street, N.W., Washington, D.C., 1954, pp. 301–304.

teacher are arranged in the following four categories: Equipment, Organization, Utilization, and Teacher Education. In the utilization section, there are twenty-two short groups of questions. Groups 8, 11, and 21 follow as excerpts:

8. Do you make use of field trips as a learning device? Are you making the most of your community resources? Do students engage in the planning for field trips?

11. When a motion picture is used in your classroom or shop, do you adhere to a plan of *preparing* the group before showing the film, and following the showing with adequate *discussion* and *follow-up* activities? Do you select motion pictures which provide a challenge to the best judgments of the students? Do your students have a clearly defined purpose in the use you make of the motion pictures?

21. Do students work cooperatively with you in the planning and execution of an audio-visual learning situation?

Example 2. The type of pupil instrument included by Schwartz[13] in his comprehensive set of criteria is shown in the example that follows. He lists ten questions to be asked students, with teachers taking notes on replies.

[13] John Charles Schwartz, Jr., *op. cit.*, pp. 24–25.

Questions 1, 4, and 9 are quoted as follows:

1. Have audiovisual media which have been used in your classes helped clarify ideas or problems for you? Can you give definite examples?

4. What instances of the use of audiovisual materials do you remember most? Why?

9. What are some of the strengths or weaknesses of the use of audiovisual materials as you have seen them presented in your classes?

Example 3. In this example we present two system-wide evaluative instruments devised locally and used in the Westport, Connecticut, Public Schools.[14] The first survey form to be presented is the more comprehensive of the two, and it refers to audiovisual media only. The second part of the example is an evaluative survey that as can be seen refers to media programs in general, and is composed of thirty-one items calling for personal reactions to conditions and services. The first form is shown in its 1961 format, and the second which was devised shortly thereafter and used is shown in its 1966 form.

[14] Division of Curriculum and Research, George E. Ingham, Administrative Assistant, Town School Office, Westport, Connecticut.

First Survey Form

WESTPORT, CONNECTICUT, PUBLIC SCHOOLS
Audiovisual Program Survey

As usual, your faculty Audiovisual Advisory Committee is interested in your reactions to this year's program and your suggestions for its improvement. We would appreciate, therefore, your taking a few minutes of your time to complete the following short questionnaire. Since we appreciate your candid and impartial opinions, we have provided space for your comments. In order that we may begin our planning before the end of this school year, we ask that you return this completed form to your Audiovisual Building Coordinator no later than Thursday, May 9.

* * * *

My evaluation and suggestions regarding our Westport AV program are as follows:

Signed _____ School _____

1. How effective in the teaching process do you consider your use to be of the following types of AV media and techniques? Please check in the proper column only those which you utilize:

	Great Deal	Some	Very Little
Sound Films	_____	_____	_____
Filmstrips	_____	_____	_____

Flat Pictures	_____	_____	_____
Slides	_____	_____	_____
Bulleting Boards	_____	_____	_____
Flannel Boards	_____	_____	_____
Dioramas	_____	_____	_____
Table Tops	_____	_____	_____
Objects	_____	_____	_____
Models	_____	_____	_____
Specimens	_____	_____	_____
Maps	_____	_____	_____
Charts	_____	_____	_____
Globes	_____	_____	_____
Chalkboards	_____	_____	_____
Field Trips	_____	_____	_____
Demonstrations	_____	_____	_____
Resource Persons	_____	_____	_____
Disk Recordings	_____	_____	_____
Tape Recordings	_____	_____	_____
Radio Programs	_____	_____	_____
TV Programs	_____	_____	_____

Your comment: _____

Sometimes teachers state that they cannot take advantage of AV media. Some of the reasons often given are listed below and coded by letter. If any apply to you, please indicate by writing the proper letter or letters in the space immediately following the material or practice.

Reasons for non-use by letter

A.   Lack of locally owned materials in my field.
B.   Need help in finding suitable materials in my field.
C.   Need help in preparation of materials.
D.   Need more training in proper utilization.
E.   Need help in operation of equipment.

Materials and Practices

Sound Films____Filmstrips____ Flat Pictures____Bulletin Boards ____Slides ____
Objects ____ Models ____ Specimens ____ Maps ____Charts ____ Globes ____Flannel ____
Boards ____ Dioramas____Table Tops____ Chalkboard ____ Field Trips ____ Demonstrations ____ Resource Persons____ Disk Recordings____ Tape Recordings____
Radio Programs____ TV Programs ____
Comments: _____

Some of you have indicated that our central school library of AV media is weak in the areas in which you are interested. Please check those areas in which you feel we are lacking. Add those which may have been overlooked here.

Mathematics _____ Language Arts _____

Social Studies _____ General Science _____

Biology _____ Chemistry _____

Physics _____ Industrial Arts _____

Homemaking _____ Arts and Crafts _____

Music _____ Modern Language _____

Health _____ Safety _____

Guidance _____ Other _____

Comments: _____

4. Westport is a community rich in resource persons who should, when properly selected and oriented, be very valuable in our classrooms. Please indicate your reactions to resource persons in the proper spaces below.

a) The resource persons I use in my classroom during the school year number approximately _____

b) I do not use resource persons because (1) they can't come when needed ____; they talk over the heads of my class ____; they talk down to my class ____ ; they seem to be afraid of juvenile audiences ____; there is no information about who is available ____ ;

c) I would be interested in having a guide prepared as to what resource persons are available and their specific interests.
Yes ____ No ____
Comment _____

5. Please indicate whether you have had one or more AV media courses on the undergraduate level, ____, graduate level, ____, extension course ____, or in a local in-service workshop ____.

6. Please write below any general suggestions you may have for improvement of our Westport AV media program. Try to be as practical as you can.

WESTPORT, CONNECTICUT, PUBLIC SCHOOLS

Survey
May 1966

MEDIA AND LIBRARY PROGRAMS

Directions: Please indicate by an "X" in the proper column your objective response to each of the following items. If you have any specific comments about any of these or about some aspect of these programs which you feel has been omitted, add your comments at the end of this survey. It is not necessary to sign your name unless you so wish.

	Item	Yes	No	No Opinion
1.	Commitment on the part of administration to the improvement and expansion of the media (AV materials) program is obvious.			
2.	Suggestions made by me for improvement of the media (AV materials) program have apparently received careful consideration.			
3.	A variety of materials for use in the instructional program has been provided me.			
4.	Encouragement has been given me for designing and creating materials applicable for specific instruction uses.			
5.	I have received recognition from administrative and/or supervisory staff for my efforts to create new materials and/or instructional techniques.			
6.	Selection of locally-owned materials has been facilitated through use of Westport and of Fairfield listings.			
7.	Requests made by me for materials from the central library in the Town School Office have received prompt attention.			
8.	Personnel in the Town School Office have, upon request, assisted me in various aspects of the media program.			
9.	My AV Building Coordinator has given assistance in the media program.			
10.	There are adequate facilities - electric outlets, projection screen, room darkening materials, etc. - in my room for the proper use of audiovisual materials.			

Item	Yes	No	No Opinion
11. Generally, AV equipment has been available when needed.			
12. Opportunities to participate in the evaluation of new materials have been offered me.			
13. Assistance in the planning of and preparation for field trips has been easy to obtain from personnel in the Town School Office.			
14. Encouragement has been given me to create and to produce a variety of instructional materials.			
15. In-service training for competency in the various aspects of the media (AV materials) program has been planned and conducted in terms of my needs.			
16. Generally, the Westport teachers' guides of recent years - The Field Trip, The Mid-Fairfield County Youth Museum, Programed Learning and Self-Instruction, and Tape Recording - have been of value to me.			
17. Useful information for staff has been contained in the Curriculum Bulletins originating from the Town School Office.			
18. It would be helpful to me if there were a central media center at which I might familiarize myself with a variety of materials, both commercially- and locally-produced.			
19. It would be helpful to me if there were a central media center at which I might be able to produce, with the assistance of technical staff, a variety of materials.			
20. At the invitation of my school librarian, I have assisted in the selection of materials for my school library.			
21. My school librarian has assisted me in selecting library materials for enrichment purposes.			
22. My school librarian has set up reserve collections at my request.			
23. I have been alerted by my librarian to new materials added to the library collection.			

Item	Yes	No	No Opinion
24. Upon my request, the librarian has prepared bibliographies and specialized booklists for me.			
25. Collections of professional materials useful in curriculum development and for instructional purposes have been available in the library.			
26. The librarian has kept me aware of new materials added to the Public Library collection.			
27. The expansion of the library from the traditional role of being only a depository of books to a resource center, housing a variety of instructional materials has been of benefit to me in the instructional program.			
28. The new color-coded cataloguing system for all materials housed in the library has been of value to me in selecting a variety of materials to use in my instructional program.			
29. There should be more non-book teaching materials - filmstrips, transparencies, slides, records, tapes, etc. - deposited in my school library.			
30. The librarian works well with and cheerfully assists students in making effective use of library resources.			
31. Our school library is attractive, relaxing, and conducive to study.			

Example 4. With the permission of William R. Fulton of the College of Education, Oklahoma University, we are quoting his skillfully developed *Evaluative Checklist* in its entirety, with the exception of some introductory material. It is offered as a model of a plan for rating scales that may be made locally to emphasize specific aspects of a school-district or school-building program. It is also quoted to encourage its use as a periodic evaluational instrument to indicate progress in the implementation of long-range, developmental plans. The *Evaluative Checklist*[15] follows:

[15] William R. Fulton, *op. cit.* (see Footnote 7).

EVALUATIVE CHECKLIST

DIRECTIONS:
      Mark <u>one</u> of the spaces at the left of the statement that most nearly represents the situation in your school system. If a statement accurately describes your school, mark the <u>middle space</u> to the left of that statement. If you feel that the situation at your school is below what is described, mark the <u>lower numbered space</u>; if above, mark the <u>higher numbered space</u>. In any case mark only <u>one</u> space.

EXAMPLE:

1   2   3   There is no full-time director of the media program.

4   5   6   There is a full-time director in charge of the media program.

7   8   9   There are a full-time director and a sufficient number of clerical and technical personnel.

I. SCHOOL SYSTEM EDUCATIONAL MEDIA SERVICES

CRITERIA

- A school system should have a program of educational media services administered through a school media center, and building centers if such are needed, which provides teachers with an adequate supply of appropriate instructional materials.

- The educational media center should be a separate service unit that operates at the same level as other major school services.

- A school system should have clearly defined policies, procedures, and plans for its educational media program, including short-range, and long-range goals.

- There should be a sufficient number of professional media staff members to administer the educational media program and to provide consultative services to teachers throughout the school system.

A. Commitment to the Media Program

1   2   3   The school's educational media program consists of services from a media center managed by clerical and technical staff numbers. The services are not well coordinated and no person has been given administrative responsibility for system-wide media activities.

4   5   6   The school's educational media program consists of a media center with clerical and technical staff. The program is directed by a staff person who has some educational media training but not enough to qualify him as an educational media specialist. He reports to the administrative officer in charge of instruction.

[7] [8] [9] The school has an educational media program including an educational media center and necessary building media centers directed by an educational media specialist who reports directly to the administrative officer in charge of instruction. He is provided with facilities, finances, and staff essential in meeting the media needs of the instructional program.

B. Commitment to Educational Media as an Integral Part of Instruction

[1] [2] [3] The School provides some educational media and services for teachers who request them, but teachers are not particularly encouraged to use the services.

[4] [5] [6] A variety of educational media and services are generally available and some attempts are made to acquaint teachers with the services, and to encourage their use.

[7] [8] [9] The school provides the quantity and variety of educational media and services needed by all buildings and encourages teachers to use media as integral parts of instruction.

C. Commitment to Providing Educational Media Facilities

[1] [2] [3] Although some new and remodeled facilities provide for the use of some types of educational media, the school gives little attention to media utilization at the time buildings are planned.

[4] [5] [6] The school provides most new and remodeled buildings with light control and other facilities necessary for the use of some types of educational media. Old buildings are being modified as fast as possible to provide for effective use of media.

[7] [8] [9] All new buildings are equipped for the greatest possible use of educational media and are designed to permit adaptation for new developments in media. Old buildings are being modified as fast as possible to provide for effective use of media.

D. Commitment to Financing the Educational Media Program

[1] [2] [3] Finances for the educational media program are inadequate to provide the services that teachers need and are prepared to use. There are no written policies relative to allocations, income sources and charges against the budget.

[4] [5] [6] Finances for the educational media program are sufficient to maintain the status quo, but the current media services are not sufficient to meet the instructional needs. Long-range curriculum plans do not include provisions for financing needed educational media services.

7 8 9   The educational media program is financed entirely from regularly appropriated school funds. The budget reflects to some degree long-range educational media plans and includes provisions for special media for unusual curriculum problems. The budget is prepared, presented, and defended by the director of the media services in the same manner as that of any other budget unit.

E. Commitment to Staffing the Educational Media Program

1 2 3   The responsibility for educational media services is assigned to various staff members whose primary commitments are in other school jobs.

4 5 6   The responsibility for educational media services is delegated to a person who has had some training in educational media. He is provided with some clerical and technical assistance.

7 8 9   Leadership and consultative services are provided by an educational media specialist and a qualified professional staff. An adequate clerical and technical staff is also provided.

II. EDUCATIONAL MEDIA SERVICES - CURRICULUM AND INSTRUCTION

CRITERIA

- A school system should engage in a continuous evaluation of its educational media program as it relates to the instructional program.

- Continuous inservice education in the use of educational media should be carried on as a means of improving instruction.

- The faculty and the professional media staff should cooperate in planning and developing the parts of the instructional program that make provisions for the use of educational media.

- Professional education media personnel should be readily available for consultation on all instructional problems where media are concerned.

A. Consultative Services in Educational Media Utilization

1 2 3   Educational media personnel render consultative assistance in the instructional application of educational media when they are asked to do so and are free from other duties.

4 5 6   Educational media personnel are usually available and are called on for consultative assistance in the use of educational media.

7 8 9   Educational media professional personnel work, as a part of their regular assignments, with teachers in analyzing teaching needs and in designing, selecting, and using educational media to meet these needs.

B. Inservice Education in Educational Media Utilization

1 2 3

Inservice education is left entirely to building instructional units and is limited to their own capabilities and such other resources as they can find.

4 5 6

Professional educational media staff members are available on request to assist teachers and supervisors in inservice education activities relative to the use of educational media.

7 8 9

Professional educational media staff members are involved in planning and conducting continuous inservice education activities concerned with the selection, development, production, and use of all types of educational media.

C. Faculty-Student Use of Educational Media

1 2 3

Only a few teachers make any use of educational media in their classrooms. Students rarely use media in class presentations.

4 5 6

Quite a few teachers make occasional use of educational media in their classrooms. Students occasionally use media in class presentations.

7 8 9

Most teachers use appropriate educational media in their classrooms. Students use appropriate media for individual and group study, as well as for class presentations.

D. Involvement of the Media Staff in Planning

1 2 3

The professional educational media staff is seldom involved with teachers in planning for the use of educational media.

4 5 6

The professional educational media staff is occasionally involved with teachers and supervisors in planning and producing materials for use in the instructional program.

7 8 9

The educational media specialist and his professional staff are usually involved with teachers, supervisors and other curriculum workers in planning for the use of and in experimenting with educational media in the instructional program. He is also regularly involved in decision making activities relating to the integration of educational media with the curriculum and instruction.

III. THE EDUCATIONAL MEDIA CENTER

CRITERIA

• Educational media centers should be organized around the concept of offering a wide variety of services and media to all instructional and administrative units of a school system, with leadership, consultative help, and other services provided by professional media specialists and other media center personnel.

- The instructional program should be supported by an adequate supply of educational media and a system of making them accessible to the faculty and students.

- The educational media center should provide such media services as procurement, maintenance, and production of appropriate educational media to support the instructional program.

A. Location and Accessibility of Educational Medial

1 2 3   The location of the school's educational media center is such that media are not accessible to most teachers. The school's educational media center is not supplemented by building centers where media are placed on long-term loan.

4 5 6   The location of the school's educational media center is such that media are not very accessible to teachers. The school's educational media center is supplemented by a few building centers that provide some media and services not available from the school media center, but merely duplicate others.

7 8 9   The location of the school's educational media center and the presence of necessary building centers make media highly accessible to all instructional units. Both the school's and the buildings' educational media centers are adequately equipped to support a quality instructional program.

B. Dissemination of Media Information

1 2 3   Information concerning educational media is seldom disseminated to prospective users, but there are no definite plans or channels for such dissemination.

4 5 6   Information concerning educational media is disseminated to teachers and staff members on an occasional basis or when requested.

7 8 9   Information concerning all educational media and programs is frequently disseminated to teachers and staff members as a matter of policy.

C. Availability of Educational Media

1 2 3   The quantity of educational media is so limited that significant delays occur between requests for materials and their availability. Reservations must be made on a "first come, first served" basis, and the media must be picked up by the user.

4 5 6   The quantity of educational media and the distribution system makes it possible for media to be delivered to teachers on relatively short notice.

7 8 9   There is a sufficient quantity of educational media and an adequate distribution system to insure the delivery of all

media to teachers on any day during the week in which they are requested.

D. Storage and Retrieval of Media

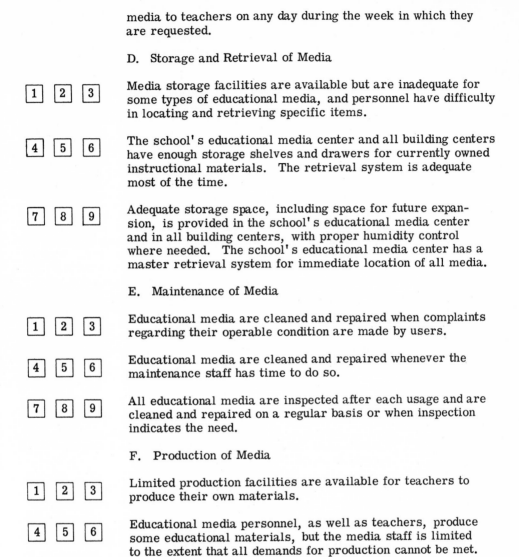

| 1 | 2 | 3 |

Media storage facilities are available but are inadequate for some types of educational media, and personnel have difficulty in locating and retrieving specific items.

| 4 | 5 | 6 |

The school's educational media center and all building centers have enough storage shelves and drawers for currently owned instructional materials. The retrieval system is adequate most of the time.

| 7 | 8 | 9 |

Adequate storage space, including space for future expansion, is provided in the school's educational media center and in all building centers, with proper humidity control where needed. The school's educational media center has a master retrieval system for immediate location of all media.

E. Maintenance of Media

| 1 | 2 | 3 |

Educational media are cleaned and repaired when complaints regarding their operable condition are made by users.

| 4 | 5 | 6 |

Educational media are cleaned and repaired whenever the maintenance staff has time to do so.

| 7 | 8 | 9 |

All educational media are inspected after each usage and are cleaned and repaired on a regular basis or when inspection indicates the need.

F. Production of Media

| 1 | 2 | 3 |

Limited production facilities are available for teachers to produce their own materials.

| 4 | 5 | 6 |

Educational media personnel, as well as teachers, produce some educational materials, but the media staff is limited to the extent that all demands for production cannot be met.

| 7 | 8 | 9 |

Educational media personnel, as well as teachers, produce a variety of educational media not otherwise available, and meet most production demands for such media as films, filmstrips, slides, graphics, and recordings.

IV. PHYSICAL FACILITIES FOR EDUCATIONAL MEDIA

CRITERIA

- Each classroom should be designed for and provided with essential facilities for effective use of appropriate educational media of all kinds.

- Each classroom should be equipped with full light control, electrical outlets, forced ventilation, and educational media storage space.

- Classrooms should be equipped with permanently installed bulletin boards, chalkboards, projection screens, map rails, and storage facilities needed for the particular type of instruction conducted in each classroom.

A. Physical Facilities in Existing Classrooms

1 2 3   A few classrooms have been modified for use of educational media. However, no systematic plans have been made to adapt all classrooms for the use of educational media, except that some departments have made such plans for their own classrooms.

4 5 6   Some classrooms have been modified and equipped with such physical facilities as light control and electrical outlets and others are partially equipped. A plan for systematically equipping all classrooms is in operation.

7 8 9   All classrooms have been modified and equipped for optimum use of all types of educational media.

B. Physical Facilities in New Classrooms

1 2 3   Some new classrooms are provided with physical facilities such as light control and electrical outlets, but only in special cases are provisions made for the use of a wide variety of media

4 5 6   Most new classrooms are provided with physical facilities that make possible optimum use of educational media.

7 8 9   All new classrooms are designed for and equipped with physical facilities that make possible optimum use of all types of educational media by faculty and students.

V. BUDGET AND FINANCE OF THE EDUCATIONAL MEDIA PROGRAM

CRITERION

Financing the educational media program should be based on both the school system's long-range goals and immediate educational needs. The budget should reflect a recognition of a long-range goals, and be sufficient to support an adequate media program for optimum instructional improvement.

A. Reporting Financial Needs

1 2 3   The financial needs of the educational media program are reported to the administrative officer in charge of instruction only when immediate expenditures are urgently needed.

[4] [5] [6] The financial needs of the educational media program are regularly reported to the administrative officer in charge of instruction.

[7] [8] [9] Regular reports reflecting the status and needs of the educational media program, including facts about inventory, facilities, level of utilization, and effectiveness of the media program, are made to the administrative officer in charge of instruction.

B. Basis for Budget Allocations

[1] [2] [3] The educational media budget is based on an arbitrary allotment of funds irrespective of need.

[4] [5] [6] The educational media budget is based almost entirely on immediate needs, though some consideration is given to long-range goals.

[7] [8] [9] The educational media budget is based on both the immediate needs and the long-range goals of the school and reflect clear-cut policies concerning allocations, income sources, and budget practices.

C. Development of Media Budget

[1] [2] [3] Each building instructional unit develops its own educational media budget without consulting an educational media specialist.

[4] [5] [6] The budget of the educational media program reflects the media needs of most building instructional units. However, some buildings have their own media budget which has no relationship to the educational media program.

[7] [8] [9] The budget of the educational media program reflects the media needs of the entire school system and is developed by the professional media staff in consultation with financial officers, principals and other school administrators.

VI. EDUCATIONAL MEDIA STAFF

CRITERION

The educational media program should be directed by a well qualified full-time media specialist who is provided with sufficient professional, clerical, and technical staff to provide adequate media services to the entire school system.

A. School System Media Staff

[1] [2] [3] A staff person has been assigned to look after the media program. He performs more as a clerk and a technician than as a professional media person.

4 5 6
A professional media person with some special training is in charge of the educational media program and has some professional, clerical, and technical assistance. He and his assistants are primarily oriented toward the mechanical and technical aspects of the program.

7 8 9
The educational media program is directed by a well qualified media specialist who is provided with sufficient professional, clerical, and technical staff to provide adequate media services from the school media center. Professional media staff members are oriented toward curriculum and instruction.

B. Building Media Staff

1 2 3
Some buildings have a teacher, a clerk, or someone else assigned to help obtain materials and care for equipment, but no released time is granted from other jobs to coordinate media activities in the building.

4 5 6
Most buildings have a teacher, or a member of the professional staff assigned to coordinate media activities, but he has not been given sufficient released time from other school tasks, or enough clerical and technical assistance to permit him to render media services needed in the instructional program.

7 8 9
A full-time professional educational media coordinator serves each building. Buildings that do not have sufficient teachers and media utilization to warrant a full-time coordinator share his services. He is provided sufficient clerical and technical assistance to supply all media services needed in the building. He reports to the school's educational media director and works closely with the media staff, supervisors, and other curriculum workers.

PROFILE SHEET

To develop a Profile image of your program, transfer your mark from each item of the Evaluative Checklist to this sheet. Connect the marked squares by straight lines. Then turn the sheet to a horizontal position. This will pictorially demonstrate the "peaks" and "valleys" of attainment for your program.

WEAK ———————————————→ STRONG

Section I Item A	1	2	3	4	5	6	7	8	9
B	1	2	3	4	5	6	7	8	9
C	1	2	3	4	5	6	7	8	9
D	1	2	3	4	5	6	7	8	9
E	1	2	3	4	5	6	7	8	9

Section II
Item A   [1] [2] [3]   [4] [5] [6]   [7] [8] [9]

B   [1] [2] [3]   [4] [5] [6]   [7] [8] [9]

C   [1] [2] [3]   [4] [5] [6]   [7] [8] [9]

D   [1] [2] [3]   [4] [5] [6]   [7] [8] [9]

Section III
Item A   [1] [2] [3]   [4] [5] [6]   [7] [8] [9]

B   [1] [2] [3]   [4] [5] [6]   [7] [8] [9]

C   [1] [2] [3]   [4] [5] [6]   [7] [8] [9]

D   [1] [2] [3]   [4] [5] [6]   [7] [8] [9]

E   [1] [2] [3]   [4] [5] [6]   [7] [8] [9]

F   [1] [2] [3]   [4] [5] [6]   [7] [8] [9]

Section IV
Item A   [1] [2] [3]   [4] [5] [6]   [7] [8] [9]

B   [1] [2] [3]   [4] [5] [6]   [7] [8] [9]

Section V
Item A   [1] [2] [3]   [4] [5] [6]   [7] [8] [9]

B   [1] [2] [3]   [4] [5] [6]   [7] [8] [9]

C   [1] [2] [3]   [4] [5] [6]   [7] [8] [9]

Section VI
Item A   [1] [2] [3]   [4] [5] [6]   [7] [8] [9]

B   [1] [2] [3]   [4] [5] [6]   [7] [8] [9]

The scaled judgments available from the evaluation responses make it possible to get a profile of the media program by adding the specific subjective scores to the profile sheet. An increase in the number of judges making the evaluation would presumably increase the accuracy, but this would of course depend upon the qualifications of the evaluators, and on the time devoted to collecting and interpreting evidence. The reader has without doubt already noted Fulton's technique of stating three levels of condition within each category, and facilitating judgment by three scale scores for each level, thus the total range is from a rating of 1 for poorest to a high of 9 for best.

Establishing Standards of Reference

In this discussion the sources of criteria have already been enumerated, and these criteria are the ultimate standards to which all judgments of change are referred. The following basic questions need to be asked and answered: When is a school or classroom adequately equipped? When is a director superior? What is a good in-service education program? What is a good public relations program? When are teachers competent in using instructional media? When is the information program adequate? When is a service system in each school adequate? What makes a good media center? When is a personnel organization adequate? The chapters in this book provide, or point the way to, satisfactory answers. Standards for reference should be stated in definite and succinct language. If higher local goals than seem to be implicit in published documents are desirable in a given situation, they should be formulated and utilized when preparing written plans and proposals. Standards of teacher competence, above all, must be defined in terms of valid curriculum planning and recognized professional excellence.

Choice of Measurement Symbols

Careful consideration should be given to the problem of symbols of judgment when measuring instruments are constructed. In general, evaluation forms should be arranged for quick reponses; however, in some cases evaluators believe that teachers will reveal deeper insight into meaningful relationships if they write out answers to penetrating questions that have been explicitly phrased. This is a moot question. The examples and references already presented reveal that the following symbols of status and change have been commonly used:

1. Yes and no.
2. Satisfactory and unsatisfactory.
3. Condition 1 (missing), condition 2 (poor), condition 3 (fair), condition 4 (good), condition 5 (excellent).
4. 5—very superior, 4—superior, 3—average, 2—inferior, 1—very inferior.
5. Great Deal, Some, and Very Little.
6. 1—constantly, 2—periodically, 3—seldom, 4—never.
7. + (Condition is present or satisfactory), − (Condition fairly or poorly met), 0 (Condition not met, or unsatisfactory), N (Not applicable to the situation).
8. Slightly, Moderately, Excellent.
9. Poor, Fair, Good, Very Good, Excellent.

Such symbols lend themselves to processes of summary, tabulation, generalization, and to certain forms of graphic potrayal. Also, when such symbols are accompanied in reports by adequate descriptions, they will be quite serviceable for local use. However, the media director and his study committee should attempt to identify objective units to represent behavior as well as physical conditions.

Among earlier suggestions it was emphasized that the director and his committee should decide whether the responses to a particular instrument will suffice for the purpose originally intended. For example, a questionnaire filled out by teachers may reveal that 50 per cent of all respondents tied their usage of motion pictures to problem-solving activities developed with the students. Will such an index of utilization be satisfactory? Will it lend itself to a year-by-year comparison of teacher growth? Suppose further that a five-point rating scale dealing with bulletin board usage is made up by a teacher committee for all the elementary schools, and the teachers then rate themselves from (*1*) *poor* to (*5*) *excellent* on each item. Suppose also that scores show an average of (*4*) *very good*, with 25 per cent of the teachers scoring themselves at (*3*) *good*, or below. Should principals, a committee of teachers, or the media coordinator for the building also rate the teachers, using the same forms? Directors and their committees will not only have to decide in all cases what measuring units will be suitable and of maximum usefulness, but they will have to decide also who should do the rating, writing, or testing. Such matters, of course, cannot be decided apart from knowledge of the nature and purpose of the evaluative device itself and apart from what will be acceptable in a given local situation. In the case of rating scales, as for comprehensive check lists or even for shorter lists of items that call for subjective judgments, it is desirable to arrange at least three terse descriptions along a multiple-point scale for each item as was done in the Fulton *Evaluative Checklist*. When clusters of such observations and judgments appear, it is likely that dependable indications of strength, weakness, or average status will be shown. In the matter of equipment and facilities growth, observations of changes may, as has already been pointed out, be easily objectified in terms of specified goals, based on desired local services or nationally recognized standards and recommendations.

Caution and critical appraisal are called for because such symbols of measurement as percentages and total class periods where one or more kinds of media were used, even though helpful in general, may not after all lead to accurate evaluation of desirable growth. A few possibilities for the director to explore in seeking more objective methods of scoring and rating than "yes" or "no" are as follows:

1. Construct evaluational instruments in the form of teacher tests of the objective-type, and score them with keys, using point scores that may be treated statistically.

2. In grading essay-type answers, make up scoring rules and use point scores that may be interpreted statistically.

3. Assign arbitrary point scores in accordance with degree of adequacy, provided that appropriate scales have been constructed.

4. Express the change in equipment and facilities status as the percentage of net increase in units above the basic inventory in any given category. That is, if the number of motion picture projectors increased from fifty to sixty, the percentage increase or change would be 20 per cent.

5. Express rate of change as a percentage of the distance covered enroute to a recognized goal. That is, to reach a long-term, five-year goal of 100 motion picture projectors from a base of 50 projectors, the rate of change would have to be 20 per cent per year on the average.

6. Establish numerical units for behavior, such as (a) number of times films were used by a teacher, for instance, in direct relation to problems; (b) number of teachers who used all films designated as *basic* in terms of specific teaching units and problems; (c) number of times films were used to introduce units of work; and (d) number of times materials were produced as learning activities.

7. Make repeated similar observations to obtain comparison of scale readings and other judgments.

8. Set up a system of marking symbols, using the same letter grade as currently in effect in the regular school department marking system, and define each symbol verbally or quantitatively as the case demands.

Taking Action on Evaluation Findings

The time of an evaluation, with its system-wide participation of the teaching staff, provides a unique climate for action. Media directors

and their general-study and school-building committees ought never to allow an opportunity for follow-up activity to slip through their fingers. Evaluation programs that are oriented toward curriculum improvement and in-service education lead naturally into the following recommended processes: (1) summarization and generalization of the evidence; (2) reporting results interestingly to staff in written and graphic form by bulletins; (3) suggesting study of results prior to sectional, school, or committee meetings; (4) holding a series of analysis and planning meetings where some significant problems may be listed in priority for consideration; and (5) ascertaining in those meetings the underlying causes for weak conditions, and formulating a set of recommendations for action and improvement.

When inaction follows a period of critical appraisal, something is wrong; something is weak about the media director's leadership. Of course, to plunge in, disregarding what is known about the effects of improper pacing, and attempt to correct all the ills at once would be professional suicide, but of course there is little danger of this if those who are to be involved in the decisions help make them. Furthermore, it is certain that not all the ills will be eliminated by work on the part of teachers. Desirable follow-up action may well provide the opportunity for the entire teaching staff as well as for lay representatives to exert pressure on top school administrators, supervisors, school board members, and city officials to share the burden of responsibility for bringing about recommended modifications. Opportunities like these may come all too seldom. They need not be missed.

Problem-Solving Activities

1. Prepare in skeletal form a comprehensive evaluation instrument, using the six basic principles introduced in Chapter 1 for organizing an audiovisual media-service program as the major division of criteria.

2. What would the media director be likely to gain if he added to his own personal evaluation activities those described briefly in the *third* level of action discussed in this chapter?

3. Examine several of the presently available

appraisal scales and selected examples of city-program evaluation check lists, scales, or survey forms, and answer the following questions: (a) What units of measurement were called for? (b) What standards were stated or implied? (c) What modifications in the *one* check list or form you liked best would you suggest if it were to be applied to a local situation with which you are familiar?

4. Using declarative sentences for each item, state what in your best judgment is the most definite and reliable standard that you and members of your working group know about: (a) in numerical units for the number of films for a school system film library, and the number of films to be used by grades in elementary schools and by subject in secondary schools; (b) in numerical units for school equipment and classroom facilities; (c) in verbal descriptions of levels of action on a three-point scale for teacher use of materials in terms of their relationship to problem solving only; (d) the same as (c) for the relationship to teaching units; (e) the same for organizing and handling physical arrangements for their use; (f) the same for their relationship to the introduction of new work; (g) the same for their relationship to teacher purposes (educational objectives at the usable classroom level).

5. In some selection procedures, materials are designated as "basic" and "supplementary" and are so described in official publications of source units and curriculum guides. How could summaries of such recommendations, if at all, be used in setting up tentative and quantitative standards of frequency-of-use levels?

6. Study the recommendations made regarding long-term planning for budgeting purposes, and explain how having numerical figures of total needs helps in stating the evaluational judgments of status, amount of change, and rate of change?

7. How would you obtain and quantify specific knowledge of teacher media-competence status?

8. In any appraisal plans that you formulated, would you be able to collect and utilize evidence of improved learning? If so, how would you go about it? Would standardized tests help you in this regard?

9. In what specific ways could you enlist the assistance of teachers in an evaluation program?

10. Construct, in accordance with plans agreed on in class, a system of evaluation instruments in the form of objective test questions involving raw scores for interpretation purposes. Which of the general criteria (that is, the twelve focal points for observation and analysis) identified in this chapter would lend themselves for the written objective examination type of analysis? Under what conditions do you believe teachers would approve of such evaluation proceedings?

11. Is a comprehensive school-system survey of physical facilities an important foundation for any contemplated evaluation program? Explain.

12. Throughout this book the director has been urged to "get the facts." Make a list of the kinds of facts that a director ought to obtain (a) just once; (b) every five years; (c) every year; (d) every month.

References

Evaluative Criteria, 1960 Edition. (Washington, D.C.: National Study of Secondary School Evaluation, 1960).

Fulton, William R. *Criteria Relating to Educational Media Programs in School Systems.* (Prepared under auspices of the U.S. Office of Education.) (Norman, Oklahoma: University of Oklahoma, 1966).

————. *Evaluative Checklist: An Instrument for Self-Evaluating An Educational Media Program in School Systems.* (Prepared under auspices of the U.S. Office of Education.) (Norman, Oklahoma: University of Oklahoma, 1966).

Goodman, Samuel M. *The Assessment of School Quality.* (Albany, N.Y.: State Department of Education, 1959).

Harris, Chester W. (ed.). *Encyclopedia of Educational Research,* rev. ed. (New York: Macmillan, 1960).

"Profile of Your AV Program," *Audiovisual Instruction,* Vol. 2, No. 7, October 1957, pp. 208–209.

Index